South Africa
pushed to the limit

The political ecomony
of change

Hein Marais

Zed Books

LONDON | NEW YORK

South Africa pushed to the limit: The political economy of change was first published outside of South Africa in 2011 by Zed Books Ltd, 7 Cynthia Street, London N1 9JF, UK and Room 400, 175 Fifth Avenue, New York, NY 10010, USA

www.zedbooks.co.uk

Published in South Africa by UCT Press, an imprint of Juta and Company Ltd, First floor, Sunclare Building, 21 Dreyer Street, Claremont, 7708 South Africa

www.uctpress.co.za

Typeset in Cambria 10.5 on 13 by Lebone Publishing Services
Editor: Glenda Younge
Cover design: Rogue Four Design
Printed and bound in Great Britain by the MPG Books Group, Bodmin and King's Lynn

Mixed Sources
Product group from well-managed forests and other controlled sources
www.fsc.org Cert no. SA-COC-1565
© 1996 Forest Stewardship Council
FSC

Distributed in the USA exclusively by Palgrave Macmillan, a division of St Martin's Press, LLC, 175 Fifth Avenue, New York, NY 10010, USA

A catalogue record for this book is available from the British Library
Library of Congress Cataloging in Publication Data available

ISBN 978 1 84813 860 5 hb
ISBN 978 1 84813 859 9 pb

Contents

Acknowledgements

Grateful thanks go to Asghar Adelzadeh, Samir Amin, Pierre Beaudet, Franco Barchiesi, Patrick Bond, Jaclyn Cock, Mary Crewe, Jeremy Cronin, Sandile Dikeni, Andries du Toit, David Everatt, Ben Fine, Bernard Founou, Bill Freund, Gillian Hart, Mark Hunter, Dennis Lewycky, Dawie Malan, Charles Meth, Thandika Mkwandawire, Seeraj Mohamed, Robert Molteno, Mike Morris, Monty Narsoo, Joan-Anne Nolan, Vishnu Padayachee, Corina Pelser, Devan Pillay, Vishwas Satgar, John Sender, Michelle Williams and Langa Zita. Special thanks to Sandy Shepherd, for presiding, Glenda Younge for editing, and most of all to Susan O'Leary, for persevering. Any errors are my doing.

The book is dedicated to Susan, to Annelie and to Sandile Dikeni.

Introduction

Someone awoken from a 20-year coma would surely find twenty-first century South Africa unrecognisable. The apartheid era has been consigned to history books, several successful democratic elections have been staged and political violence has disappeared. Black millionaires are no longer a curiosity. Once shunned, South African businesses are now ubiquitous in Africa and jostle for custom across the globe. A liberal constitution anchors this new South Africa and laws protecting the rights of citizens—not least the workers among them—pepper the statute books.

The economy has recovered some zest. Vital social improvements are being made. Access to schooling and healthcare, and provision of water, sanitation and electricity have broadened, especially in urban areas. Infrastructure development sped up in the 2000s and institutional changes have been made to boost these advances.

But the efforts to change the lives of South Africans for the better are running up against formidable hindrances. Some are legacies of history, some stem from specific policy choices, others emanate from malfunctioning systems or spring from misjudgements, shoddy management or sheer bad luck.

South Africa pushed to the limit tries to gauge where South Africa's journey beyond apartheid is headed and why this is happening. And it proposes some modest interventions that could bring the prospect of wellbeing and genuine emancipation within the grasp of millions more citizens. To this end, it analyses the dynamics that have shaped the country's history, its main social forces and the choices they have made or spurned. The book therefore takes as its starting point the analysis presented in *South Africa: Limits to Change* (Marais, 1998 & 2001), but substantially extends it and other analyses offered in the hefty body of critical literature on South Africa published since the late 1990s.

The book is structured into chapters that can be read separately, but that are most rewarding when approached as a whole. Readers will encounter several themes of analysis that link the book's parts.

The first section appreciably condenses and updates the first six chapters of *South Africa: Limits to Change* (2001), scanning a familiar history, but from unfamiliar angles. It examines South Africa's political economic undercarriage, the structure of its economy, the developments that led to the political settlement in late 1993, the terms on which the transition would play out, and the relative weights of the main forces contesting its outcome.

Chapter one focuses on the economic, political and social patterns of capital accumulation from the late nineteenth century. It chronicles the initial phases of industrialisation and the moulding of the economy; the early stirrings of organised resistance; the apartheid system's origins, heyday and gradual disintegration; and the popular movement's evolution and tactics up to the late 1970s.

Chapters two and three zero in on the apartheid system's demise, the upsurge of resistance in the 1980s, the contours of the eventual political settlement, and the undertow of economic changes that were occurring. This provides the backdrop for Chapter four, which examines the 1996 imposition of a structural adjustment policy, the controversies that erupted around it and its key outcomes. This section shows that the end of apartheid is best understood not as a miraculous historical rupture, but as a dramatic phase in an ongoing struggle to resolve a set of political, economic and social contradictions that became uncontainable in the 1970s. The salience of 1994 was therefore also the collapse of the alliance of social, economic and political forces that had presided over that unstable order. The ANC's ascent to political power did not immediately fill the vacuum. Rather, it recast a struggle to determine which alliance of social forces would prevail, and to establish the decisive terms of such an alliance. The tales, cherished on the left, of an essentially progressive (even nominally 'socialist') ANC tricked and cajoled by external forces into adopting a neoliberal development path are unsatisfactory. Nor were the choices smuggled in through mere stealth and deceit. The prevailing balance of forces has shaped the trajectory of change.

While Chapter four chronicles the drama of economic adjustment in the 1990s, Chapter five assesses the economy's performance in the first decade of the twenty-first century. It pinpoints the underlying biases of the economy (particularly the enduring weight of the minerals and energy sectors) and discusses the unnerving continuities that link key post-apartheid economic policies with the fitful neoliberal adjustments with which the apartheid regime flirted in the 1980s. The effects are profound. South Africa's largest corporations have been able to restructure, consolidate and globalise their operations. This has entrenched their dominance in the local economy, helped fuel the turbocharged surge of the financial sector and wedged open the economy for speculative international capital.

While the rewards of South Africa's modest economic growth are being cornered in small sections of society, punishing costs are being imposed on the poor. Close to half the population could reasonably be said to be living 'in poverty' and income inequality is now wider than ever before. Tempering the ordeals of the poor are the government's attempts to expand social protection and public-works programmes — schemes that became crucial *political* imperatives in the 2000s, as unemployment rates worsened and community protests multiplied. But, as Chapters five to eight show, these 'safety nets' operate in a framework that expresses basic neoliberal 'rationalities'. This is especially obvious in the stigmatisation of social protection as 'handouts', the attempts to productivise what are essentially forms of indigent support, the privatisation of personal security and the firm rationing of citizens' claims on the state.

Chapter six details the many-faceted ways in which the world of work is being reshaped, the trade-union movement's efforts to regain the initiative and the outlook for attempts to reverse South Africa's extraordinarily high unemployment levels. It shows that the traditional narrative of economic modernisation seems to be running in reverse, generating greater informality and fewer decent jobs. Despite the labour-law victories of the mid-1990s, workers (including those with jobs) are embattled. The hunt for profits has applied a tight squeeze to the use of labour, wages and terms of employment. Measured as a share of national income, company profits rose from 26% in 1993 to 31% in 2004, while workers' wages fell from 57% to 52% (Makgetla, 2005).

For a large proportion of society, job creation along the current development path does not offer a viable basis for social inclusion and wellbeing; wages and salaries are the main source of income for only about 5.9 million (57%) of the 10.3 million African households (Statistics SA, 2008c). Neither is having a job a solid hedge against oblivion (Barchiesi, 2008). Four million people living below the poverty line survive in households where at least one person works for a wage that is too meagre to lift them out of poverty (Meth, 2006 & 2008). The quest for more jobs is crucial, but it has to occur as part of the wider realisation of social rights.

Nevertheless, impressive and life-changing achievements have been made since 1994. Chapter seven surveys the accomplishments, closely examining trends in poverty, inequality and hunger, and in the distribution of the 'social wage'. Several developments temper these gains, including the steady increase in the scale of need, faltering local-government systems and stringent cost-pruning and -recovery policies. By the mid-2000s the pace, scope and quality of change was clearly lagging. The share of households connected to the electricity grid, with access to potable water and refuse-removal services changed relatively little in the 2000s (Statistics SA, 2009). A focus on targets rather than outcomes has seen quantity trump quality, and has caused the vital matters of maintenance and sustainability of services to slip down the rung of priorities (Roberts, 2005).

Ironically, the strongest inroads against poverty have been made with interventions that were not designed for that purpose. Chapter eight reviews the origins, merits and achievements of South Africa's social grant system, which ranks among the most impressive in the so-called 'developing' world. Social grants have turned out to be the single most effective anti-poverty tool deployed after 1994 (Meth, 2007). Yet they are allocated begrudgingly. A flinty aversion to alleged 'handouts' and 'dependency' prevails and the social protection system 'remains constrained by narrow conceptions of the state and by distrust of rights-based demands on state resources' (Hassim, 2005b:3–4). This chapter deciphers this paradox, questions the binary logic that pits 'welfare' against 'development', 'job creation' against 'dependency' and lays out the emancipating potential of an overhauled and expanded grant system.

There have been some disastrous setbacks in South Africa, mostly affecting the health prospects of its citizens. Health outcomes have deteriorated since the mid-1990s and are now worse than in many low-income countries (Coovadia *et al*, 2009). Much of this represents the overhang of history. But regarding the present merely as an instance of the past tells only part of the story, as Chapters nine and ten reveal. Life expectancy in 2008 was 12 years lower than in 1996 and both child and maternal mortality rates have worsened since the early 1990s. This is due largely to the AIDS and tuberculosis epidemics and the bungled manner in which these were handled. Chapter nine presents a close analysis of the political economy of AIDS, an epidemic that is changing South Africa. Some of this impact is vivid, but a great deal of it is cumulative, subterranean and channelled into the lives and communities of the poor.

Pushed to the limit

The ANC and the government have announced their determination to tackle the many outstanding challenges. In 2010, government finally launched an AIDS campaign that did more than go through the motions. The disastrous outcomes-based education experiment was abandoned and a national health-insurance scheme was being crafted (discussed in Chapter ten). A new industrial strategy was unveiled and more plans to revive job creation were in the works (Chapters five and six). These and other potential breakthroughs are hugely important and can be augmented with many other feasible initiatives.

But the formative compass points of the transition have stayed largely unadjusted, despite the efforts of the ANC's allies on the left. The post-apartheid development path manifestly favours domestic (and international) corporate capital. Economic policies have shifted the balance of power further in their favour, particularly those sections that have managed to insert themselves deeper into the global system. Parts of the state (and, more so, the ANC) are now also entangled in that circuitry. Simply turning back the clock is not an option.

Meanwhile, the inequities that decide the fate of millions continue to be reproduced underfoot. As long as this persists, the biggest challenge for the ANC, the state and capital is how to maintain legitimacy, reproduce consent and achieve social and political stability. Above all, this has to be achieved in an economy that seems structurally incapable of providing jobs on the scale and terms required and where large parts of the public service are oxymoronic, inequality has widened, precariousness is routine and a palpable sense of unfairness is rampant. The problem is not simply one of 'poverty'—a lack of means—but of the glaring disparities that assault people day in and out. A seething sense of injustice exists, generating rancour and insubordination.

Quicker and more extensive material improvements are possible, but within stubborn limits. Many of the changes that lit and powered the struggle for liberation do not seem possible within the current political economy. The underlying structure of the economy, and the stunted and skewed character of its industrialisation, for instance, limit the extent to which waged work can serve as a reasonable basis for wellbeing. Many of the liberalising adjustments of the past 20 years have had a similar effect—by weakening the state's leverage for safeguarding the wellbeing of citizens. The leverage is far from exhausted, but it is not boundless.

There are other limits to be vaulted. The ANC now hosts such a disparate assortment of interests, ideologies and ideals that its progressive impulses are mitigated by a mishmash of coarse tendencies. It can no longer credibly claim to be the custodian and manager of a coherent 'liberation project'—yet it will continue to dominate electoral politics and the state. The entanglement of the party (via its investment ventures) and the fact that a substantial proportion of its office bearers are in profit-grabbing gambits favour the imperatives of the market. Almost one third of the party's National Executive Committee also serves as directors of black economic empowerment companies. Powerful sections of the ANC have acquired a reflexive sympathy for policies that put the market ahead of society, and that push the pursuit of social justice deeper into the shadows.

Partly as a result, the ANC is polluted with intrigues and feuding. A central problem is that both political and acquisitive ambitions are being channelled through the machinery of a party that monopolises the political system, yet is dissonant and unruly. The days when the ANC's knack for maintaining internal discipline drew a mixture of awe and trepidation are gone. Vendettas are now waged in full public glare, with the offices of the state often the arena. This is aggravating the strategic and functional incoherence that plagues the ANC and parts of the state, particularly at local levels. The overall effect is disruptive and debilitating, and powerfully contradicts the pretences of a 'developmental state' (as discussed in Chapter eleven).

The old left errs in clinging to the myth that this calls for a struggle for the 'soul of the ANC'. There is no 'soul' to be captured or 'essence' to be reclaimed. The ANC has grown incapable of mustering the ideological and strategic coherence it needs to manage and sustain a *progressive* project of change—even when the balance of power inside the organisation seems to shift in that direction. Consequently, gains are embattled and prone to reverse. This means that the ANC is now one of several fields on which the struggle to shape, achieve and defend change must be waged. Vital change can and must be achieved from inside the organisation—but this will occur within cramped limits. Because of these dynamics, victories for the left will be temporary, unsteady and tentative; and they will flounder unless linked to other advances in ways that begin to shift the underlying balance of forces. For now, both the old and the new variants of the left seem befuddled, as Chapter fourteen shows. Outgunned and outsmarted, they have little to show for their exertions of the past decade.

In such circumstances, there emerges an ever-greater need to retain power and replenish authority — not for any single goal, but precisely to facilitate the pursuit of disparate objectives. This formlessness forces the ANC to advertise its 'radical' credentials with bluster and selective deeds. The organisation still commands enough attributes and means to continue patching together its dominance; no other political or social force rivals it on that front. But its political *authority* — and its ability to govern effectively and manage change, any change — hangs in the balance. As long as the current central terms of change — the pre-eminence of capital accumulation over the wellbeing of citizens — stay unaltered, hegemony is unlikely to be achieved. Power and consent can then only nominally depend on material betterment, forcing greater recourse to ideology, the grammar of the liberation struggle, and rousing affirmations about entitlement and belonging.

Chapters twelve and thirteen show that, along with more profane impulses and calculations, President Jacob Zuma's rise to power was made possible by an elemental yearning for consolidation, for mooring society to values that seem to reflect more faithfully a dominant sense of 'who we are' (which is always another way of asserting 'who we should be'). The assertion of conservative values speaks to the visceral unease and insecurity, the sense of 'things falling apart', which formed the basis of Zuma's triumph. His campaign tapped strong currents of disorientation and restiveness in and around the ANC, which the new social movements had failed to mobilise or channel. Zuma, it was hoped, would reset the controls and steer the transition back to the future. These illusions quickly dissolved, but the underlying disquiet has not. With the economic and social crises unresolved, increasing instability is likely. The tried and trusted way of responding to such uproar is by affirming and valorising bonds that can muffle discord or channel it in more manageable directions. There is a serious risk that exclusionary interpretations of belonging, citizenship and rights will prove politically rewarding.

During the 'Rainbow Nation' interlude of the mid-1990s, the terms of belonging were undemanding and structured around the embracing principle of 'live and let live'. In the abstract this seems appealing. But it is unsatisfactory in a society with a history as brutalising as South Africa's, a history that in many ways still constitutes the present and decides the future.

More normative notions of belonging become attractive. They might be inflected with racial and ethnic chauvinism and with narrow, exacting interpretations of culture and tradition; of who constitutes a 'true South African' and on what terms they do so. Antipathy toward the 'alien luxuries' of liberal constitutionalism might gain support; heartfelt misgivings about 'hollow rights' and a 'paper Constitution' already circulate. This adds up to a likelihood of experiments with populist nationalism, where social conservatism (invested with pinched interpretations of culture, tradition and identity) can be combined with licence for acquisitiveness and immoderation, and with targeted, conditional largesse. These shifts will be hotly contested. But it would be foolish to take for granted a progressive outcome.

Amid all this there remains enormous need and ample opportunity for changes that boost the wellbeing and liberty of citizens. The same effervescent intrigue that undermines the ANC's authority also opens spaces for other tactical forays and inroads. It offers the left—both old and new—opportunities to build focused alliances in and around the ANC and the state, zeroing in on specific objectives. These alliances will tend to be fickle and unreliable; gains will need to be defended scrupulously and imaginatively. But there is great scope for pushing past the limits to change, toward the ideals of emancipation, solidarity and equality.

CHAPTER ONE

The making of a polarised society

A wealthy country by continental standards, South Africa is also one of the most unequal societies on Earth. It has more luxury-car dealers than any country outside the industrialised north, yet almost half of its population lives in poverty and more than one third cannot find waged work. An average assistant manager punching the clock in the service sector would need to work more than 102 years to earn the average annual salary of a corporate CEO and 520 years to match the take-home salary and bonuses that the top-paid banking-industry executive earned in 2009.[1] In 2005, the country 'produced' 5 580 new US dollar millionaires; at the time, one in nine families admitted that their children went hungry at least 'some of the time'.[2] The country boasts shopping malls selling beds that cost up to USD 67 000, while the domestic workers who change the linen on those beds command a minimum wage of USD 44 a week.[3] Health tourists flock to South Africa for sophisticated cosmetic and dental surgery and other high-end medical procedures, but its public health system is shambolic and overburdened.

One does not expect such descriptions to apply 15 years after the official end of the apartheid system. In the political realm, that system was vaporised. But efforts to improve the wellbeing of black South Africans have fared less well. Millions of houses have been built, but at a pace that lags behind population trends. Water pipes and electricity grids are now within the reach of millions more residents, but very many of them cannot afford the user fees. The doors of learning have been opened to all, but the quality of teaching is shockingly poor. That apartheid entrenched these features with grotesque fastidiousness and inhuman severity is a matter of historical record. However, attributing these outrages solely to the apartheid system hides the political-economic contours of inequity that still define South African society. It also confounds efforts to forge a society that not only extols but also realises the dignity, desires and rights of its citizens.

In many respects South Africans' visions of the future rest on foreshortened perspectives of the past. This applies centrally to the millions who engineered, administrated and savoured the complex of exploitative practices that penetrated every aspect of lived reality—few of whom will admit today to their authorship of, or moral culpability for, the devastation they achieved. Nor are they under much pressure to do so; their indifference is indulged, even encouraged, in the quest for reconciliation.

At the same time, an abbreviated and elliptical sense of the past is also evident, though in very different respects, within the former liberation movement. The history of successful liberation projects tends to be rendered in terms that portray an unequivocal and linear advance towards triumph. History is cleansed of failure, ambivalence and blemish. And yet, when history is reflexively celebrated and left uninterrogated, the past ferments in the present.

The mould is cast

The origins of South Africa's systematic polarisation lie in the late nineteenth century, when the development of capitalism accelerated rapidly with the onset of diamond mining in 1867 and gold mining in 1886.[4] Pockets of commercial and agricultural capitalism had been established in the coastal regions colonised by Britain. But the hinterland remained pre-capitalist, with Boer trekkers engaged in rentier exploitation, living off rents in labour and in kind, which they extracted from indigenous peoples whose land they had seized or whom they had enslaved. Racial prejudice was already rampant, though it was flanked with class division and religious bigotry as a basis for systematic social polarisation.[5] In large parts of the country, an economically independent African peasantry survived.[6] In many cases these societies remained organised within their own social and political systems; in some cases they were militarily powerful enough to inflict bloody defeats on British colonial armies.

The discovery of gold and diamonds, however, upped the ante, transforming the territory, at least in the eyes of British colonialists, from a geopolitical asset (hence the focus on controlling coastal strips) into a potentially huge capital asset. Mining set in motion processes that would definitively shape South African history. A huge influx of foreign, mainly British, capital put the mining industry on the world map and spearheaded the highly centralised character of an industry that would remain at the core of the South African economy for the following century. There was a rush of European immigrant labour, which supplied the semi-skilled and skilled labour required by the industry and boosted the numbers of white settlers beyond the levels typical in other African colonies.[7] Also generated was the need for a steady supply of cheap, unskilled labour. The dismantled African peasantry would become the chief source of this labour, while a range of coercive measures would be applied to guarantee and regulate the supply of labour. Administrative systems were used to establish and police a racial division of labour separating skilled white (mainly European) labour from gangs of unskilled African labour. Organised white labour would lobby strongly (and act militantly) to entrench those measures. This established the basis for a political alliance between the capitalist class and white labour, which was to survive until the 1970s.

For the next 50 years, the accumulation strategy centred on mining and, to a lesser extent, agriculture, with manufacturing an incipient feature of the economy. As the huge gold fields yielded low-grade ore, the mining industry was faced with three central needs: a hefty flow of capital to establish and run mines; a reliable, cheap labour supply to keep the profit margin attractive; and reliable supplies of cheap energy. The first requirement saw the integration of the 'South African'[8] economy into the world economy as a source of primary commodities (the value of which was set in the European metropoles) and a destination for investment capital. The second requirement sketched the pattern of labour and social relations that would become a defining feature of the society, while the third helped thread powerful links between the mining industry and the state. The most penetrating analysis of this remains that of Fine and Rustomjee (1996), along with Fine's recent updates

(2007, 2008).[9] They show that the economy became dominated by a minerals-energy complex (MEC), which incorporated a core set of industries associated with large-scale mineral extraction, energy provision and associated downstream sectors. This MEC sat 'at the core of the South African economy, not only by virtue of its weight in economic activity but also through its determining role throughout the rest of the economy' (Fine & Rustomjee, 1996:91).[10]

Capital accumulation would be based on the exploitation of a low-wage, highly controlled, expendable African work-force that was to be reproduced in a system of 'native reserves' at minimal cost to capital. Importantly, this work-force would be recruited from the entire subcontinent: until the 1970s, the mining industry employed more non-South African than South African workers.[11] This accumulation path seemed to correspond to those in other African colonies, with the important distinction here being that a large settler population, itself segmented culturally and socio-economically, soon became ascendant in the political, administrative and, later, economic realms. The resemblance would later lead the South African Communist Party (SACP) to develop its theory of 'Colonialism of a Special Type'.[12]

The economic independence of the African peasantry was gradually dismantled through a barrage of administrative and punitive measures, which transformed this surplus-producing peasantry into a pool of labour for the mines and emergent capitalist agriculture. The effects were crushing. The African peasantry dwindled from 2.5 million in 1936 to 832 000 people in 1946. A trio of factors drove this process: increased mechanisation of agriculture, the crushing effects of the Depression and, centrally, state expropriation of land. A legislative climax was the mammoth expropriation effected by the 1913 Land Act, which barred Africans from acquiring land outside 'native reserves' (7.3% of the South African land area). That process was augmented by the 1936 Natives Land and Trust Act, which doubled the land area 'set aside' for 'native reserves' in a bid to reverse the 'incapacity of the Native Reserves to provide even the minimum subsistence requirements', as one government report later put it.[13]

Mining became the centrepiece of the South African economy, and determined its incorporation into the world economy on terms that would remain relatively consistent over the next half-century. In addition, definitive and systematic divisions were imposed on society:

- A racial division of labour was imposed in urban centres, separating skilled white labour (both immigrant and domestic) from unskilled African labour (essentially 'economic refugees' fleeing the remnants of wrecked pre-capitalist zones). White workers imported the trade union tradition, and organised artisans and craftsmen. They vehemently defended their privileged status against 'encroachment' by African workers when, for instance, mining bosses tried to loosen the colour bar in a bid to lower wage costs by allowing black workers some upward mobility.[14]

- African societies were fiercely marginalised. Not only were they transformed into reserve armies of labour, but they were burdened with the principal costs of reproducing that labour supply. Often deprived of their means of production (land), they were barricaded into 'native reserves' outside the mining and industrial zones, where they were denied access to the types of health, education, welfare and recreational networks introduced in the urban centres. Measures such as the pass law system regulated the flow of labour into the cities and deflected the cost of reproducing labour to the periphery. This laid the basis for a highly profitable cycle of capital accumulation. In essence, the 'native reserves' (and later the homelands) would subsidise capitalist growth in South Africa.

■ Large numbers of Africans were forcibly proletarianised, a trend 'which distinguished the class structure of South Africa from the peasant economies of African colonies to the north' (Fine & Davis, 1990:14). By 1946, the number of urbanised African people had increased by 36% over the previous decade. One third of them were women, suggesting long-term urbanisation. But the urban/rural dichotomy was not rigid: hundreds of thousands of people traversed those zones. With the rise of an urban working class would come new forms of resistance: trade union organising, strikes, boycotts and other mass protests.

■ Within white society, divisions materialised. Marked by the consolidation of large farms and their mechanisation (a process accelerated by the 1929–32 recession), the advance of capitalist agriculture drove thousands of Afrikaner settlers off the land and into cities, which they entered at a disadvantage to European immigrant workers. A category of newly proletarianised 'poor whites', mainly Afrikaners, arose. Until the 1930s what passed for 'Afrikaner capital' was restricted mainly to the agricultural sector, which represented a tiny fraction of gross domestic product (GDP). These material realities combined with a history of enmity towards British imperialism (expressed explosively in the two Anglo-Boer wars) and a hermetic cultural framework derived from apocalyptic readings of the Old Testament of the Bible. All this aided the elaboration of a distinct Afrikaner identity, a process that would be developed into the political-ideological project of Afrikaner nationalism.

■ Significant tensions developed between mining capital, and agricultural and industrial capital. Internationalised in terms of markets and capital input, mining capital preferred 'free trade' policies. Agricultural and industrial capital was localised and demanded state intervention in the form of subsidies and protection, financed largely through taxes drawn from mining capital. The rudiments of different approaches to state-capital relations were taking shape.

A skewed regional economy was also fashioned around migrant labour for the mines, but extended also to trade, water supply, transport and capital-investment patterns. As Davies *et al* (1993:14) noted,

> the principal poles of accumulation came to be located in South Africa (and to a lesser extent in Zimbabwe) while the other territories were incorporated in subsidiary roles as labour reserves, markets for South African commodities, suppliers of certain services (such as transport) or providers of cheap and convenient resources (like water, electricity and some raw materials).

The rise of the working classes

The manufacturing industry grew in earnest in the early decades of the twentieth century, thanks to lavish state support in the form of protective measures and tariffs, subsidies and major infrastructure projects that underpinned its development. The shift from artisanal to mechanised production was rapid and the African proletariat swelled to number some 800 000 by 1939. Workers had become increasingly combative, with African and white workers (usually separately) staging strike actions.

In 1913, shortly before the First World War, about 19 000 white miners and 10 000 African miners went on strike. A year later the state mobilised thousands of troops to crush a railway strike. In 1918 African miners won a wage increase after striking. Two years later 70 000 African miners went on strike for better pay, while in 1922 a white miners' strike was put down by 20 000 troops, killing 214 people. Five years later the black Industrial and Commercial Workers' Union claimed a membership of 100 000.

The rise of an urban African working class raised the prospect of multiracial industrial action that could evolve into a more forthright challenge against the system. This precipitated a political realignment that brought to power, in 1924, the Pact government, which strove to give white workers a bigger stake in the system. Wider (racial) wage disparities, job reservation for whites and expanded social benefits all deepened white racism and encouraged white workers to throw in their lot with a system constructed around a racist class alliance. The trappings of a social-welfare state were extended gradually to a tiny, racially defined minority, while the majority was expelled to the physical and socioeconomic margins of the system, subsidising the privilege of the 'insiders'. By the mid-1930s several related developments were afoot that would leave deep imprints on the future of the country.

Strong economic growth after 1933 boosted industrialisation, though the manufacturing sector remained relatively small (until the 1940s, when it grew considerably during mobilisation of production for the war effort). This in turn increased demand for African labour, some of it skilled. The reserves into which Africans had been driven were becoming increasingly unsustainable, with overcrowding and resultant poor environmental management of marginal land rendering huge parts of the periphery economically unviable. Urbanisation accelerated. In the urban areas, meanwhile, at least one generation of African workers had sunk roots. These trends, the intense poverty and the violent manner in which labour relations were controlled spurred trade union organisation—from which sprang the first sustained cycle of modern, militant resistance in South Africa's history.[15]

These trends should not be exaggerated. Despite the rise of an African proletariat, the vast majority of Africans still lived in rural areas. Although in decline, the peasantry remained a social and economic force in parts of rural South Africa. In addition, African urban workers retained strong links with rural communities due to the migratory character of African labour. The greatest concentration of African labour was to be found on the mines where, separated from wider society, they were subjected to fierce disciplinary regimes. This limited their role in the 'wave of resistance' which, some historians have claimed, would generate a crisis in the ruling bloc in the mid-1940s. In the estimation of Robert Fine and Dennis Davis, the social weight of the African working classes in the 1930s and 1940s (and the threat they posed) was actually less formidable than claimed in some historical accounts:[16]

> We have to abandon the simplified image of the organisation and combativity of black workers ever escalating in the 1940s and of the defeats inflicted on labour struggles [...] serving only as a stimulus for yet more militancy from below (1990:99).

The 1946 miners' strike is often portrayed as a landmark event that announced a crisis in South African capitalism. In the conventional reading, worker militancy in support of higher wages and better working conditions challenged the basis of a system that pivoted on an abundant supply of very cheap, controlled labour. 'The violence of the state's response not only indicated the degree to which it felt threatened, but foreshadowed the extreme repression after 1948,' according to Dan O'Meara (in Saul & Gelb, 1981:14). Typically, the National Party's (NP's) victory at the polls in 1948 was interpreted as a consequence of that trepidation and as a mandate for a hard-line solution to the 'crisis'.

Illusions of strength

There is no discounting the impressive scale of the 1946 strike, which saw 70 000 miners and 6 000 iron and steel workers down tools. But an appraisal must account for the ease with which the state crushed the strike. In fact, the drama was something of an anomaly. In the run-up to the strike, the number of black workers organised in trade unions had been declining, as had the number of strike actions. An alternative reading, therefore, could regard the 1946 strike as 'the last gasp rather than the high point of the wartime strike wave' (Fine & Davis, 1990:12). In the following year, a mere 2 000 workers went on strike and in 1948 only 1 500 took similar action. By 1950, the African Mineworkers' Union (which had organised the 1946 miners' strike) was a shadow of its former self and could claim barely 700 members. According to government calculations, 66 trade unions became defunct between 1945 and 1951.[17] It seems more plausible, then, to link the rise of apartheid not to an alleged surge of African working-class militancy, but (at least partially) to the defeats that class had suffered. Those defeats arose from several factors.

Firstly, both the liberal wing of the ruling elite and its reform programme had been marginalised.[18] As John Saul and Stephen Gelb (1981:14) noted, several commissions had seen virtue in fostering a stable, semi-skilled labour force and accepting the permanent urban residence of African workers. The proposals were spurned. Secondly, state repression had a withering effect on workers. And thirdly, 'the lack of numbers, concentration and bargaining power of the black industrial proletariat' prevented it from sustaining the threats it seemed to pose (Fine & Davis, 1990:18). A fourth, subjective, factor also deserves consideration. After the Nazi invasion of the Soviet Union in 1941, the Communist Party of South Africa (CPSA)[19] had abandoned its support for intensified class struggle and switched to a people's front policy. This demanded support for the Allied war effort and opposition to industrial action and put both CPSA and African National Congress (ANC) policy on an accommodationist track[20], which

> presupposed that the rulers of South Africa were ready to reach an accommodation with the black working class and that the black working class had the social weight to force an accommodation on the rulers. On both counts the policy was mistaken. The state turned against consensual politics, directing its fire instead to extinguish the threat posed by black workers, while black workers themselves lacked the power to resist the attacks mounted on them (Fine & Davis, 1990:56).

So, after an impressive rise, black working-class organisations had suffered telling setbacks, which the sectarianism that plagued the Left compounded. The late 1940s saw a drift away from class politics—leaving space for the dramatic rise of African nationalism as the dominant current of resistance. Although periodically challenged, African nationalism would decisively shape resistance strategies and, eventually, help establish the parameters of accommodation with the ruling elites in the 1990s.

The rise of African nationalism

The setbacks experienced in the workplace did not mean that resistance had been quelled. Urban workers endured extreme hardships and these constantly sparked community-based struggles. Several decades old, the ANC was still lodged on an accommodationist track, however, and was unable to augment and transform those struggles into more than sporadic expressions of discontent.[21]

Formed on 8 January 1912 as the South African Native National Congress, the ANC initially functioned as a vehicle for the aspirations of the African middle classes. It remained largely in that mode until the 1940s. Assembled around a relatively privileged layer of independent African peasants, the organisation followed a liberal trajectory, petitioning for the extension of voting and other rights to 'civilised' Africans. Its jaundiced view of so-called 'blanket' or 'uncivilised' Africans was unabashedly conveyed in leaders' statements and writings. As late as 1942, ANC president general Dr A B Xuma wrote to General Jan Smuts, assuring him that

> we are anxious not to embarrass the government [...] We humbly and respectfully request the Prime Minister to receive a deputation from the ANC and CNETU [Council of Non-European Trade Unions] [...] to assist you toward settlement of recent strikes and prevention of future strikes.[22]

The ANC's early decades were not auspicious. By 1935, the CPSA's J B Marks would pronounce the organisation 'literally dead'. Causing its decline was the failure to register gains for its constituency and the rapid erosion of its peasant social base, whose ranks had been denuded during the Depression years. The ANC could not point to a single concession it had wrested from the state. Furthermore, the decline of the liberal wing of the ruling bloc removed any prospect of belated success for its policy of appeasement. In the early 1940s, the CPSA lamented the fact that the 'African people have been frustrated by a Congress leadership which does not organise mass support nor carry on mass action to improve their living standards'.[23] That assessment was hardly controversial, as ANC veteran Govan Mbeki would later confirm:

> [The ANC] was not in a position to go to the people with any plan of action, being top-heavy with very little support amongst the masses of people [...] As a result, not only were the masses not provided with an effective leadership, but those who were at the head of the ANC felt helpless to do anything (1992:37).

It was into this vacuum that a new generation of more militant urban African intellectuals stepped in the mid-1940s, organised within the newly formed ANC Youth League (ANCYL). They were dismayed by the moribund state of the ANC, which the president of the ANCYL, A P Mda, labelled 'an organisation of gentlemen with clean hands'.[24] The Youth League favoured a passionate brand of African nationalism, which drew on the 'Africa for Africans' philosophy popularised by the followers of Marcus Garvey. These militants (mostly doctors, lawyers, teachers and clerks) scorned both liberal ideology and class politics in equal measure. They idealised an imagined past of unity and harmony among Africans, and envisaged a liberation struggle that would be led by the 'African nation' and a new society that would be ruled by it. This would be achieved by reviving mass struggle under the aegis of a reconstituted national movement in which the politics of African nationalism would eclipse class politics as the driving dynamic.

By 1949, the African nationalists had established their authority inside the ANC, which adopted key parts of the Youth League's manifesto in its 'Programme of Action'. The focus would be on organising mass struggles in urban areas, along the lines of the subsequent 1952 Defiance Campaign. But the African nationalist upsurge was already diverging into two currents. Eventually dominant within the ANC was a more moderate stream that viewed South Africa as comprising four nations (African, Indian, coloured and white), of which three were oppressed (Everatt, 2009). Meanwhile, an ultranationalist stream insisted that South Africa belonged to Africans only. In 1959, this stream split from the ANC and formed the Pan-Africanist Congress (PAC).

Blame for the decline of the working-class movement cannot fairly be laid at the feet of the ascendant African nationalists. In fact, causality seemed to run in the opposite direction: it was the defeat of a nascent working-class project in the mid-1940s that enabled the rise of African nationalism as the hegemonic force within a broad, evolving resistance movement. And it was this historic turn that laid a basis for the class compromise that was eventually achieved in the 1990s. Class contradictions would become submerged in the discourse of African nationalism, which would prove ill equipped for the task of breaking South Africa's mould of inequality. Viewed against the backdrop of history, the abbreviated nature of social progress after 1994 becomes less surprising.

Afrikaner nationalism's triumph

The pattern of South Africa's 'development' hardened radically when the white supremacist NP achieved a surprise victory in the 1948 election under the banner of Afrikaner nationalism.[25] The margin of victory was a slim, five-seat parliamentary majority (won with a minority of votes cast). But the NP immediately set about implementing a rigorously codified racist project. Henceforth, race would become the definitive criterion for South Africans' access to privilege and opportunity, further restricting the social and economic mobility of black South Africans through a battery of legislative, administrative and other coercive measures. Hardest hit was the African population. Deprived of political rights and full citizenship, they would eventually be decreed to belong to specific 'nations' in assigned homelands on the 13% of land assigned to Africans.

But the NP's policies did not represent a rupture in the country's historical narrative. While they intensified levels of oppression and dispossession, they proceeded along paths staked out over the preceding half-century. The broad patterns of inclusion and exclusion from the productive and consumptive centres of a growing economy rested on existing trends. Mainstream historical accounts tended to overlook this continuity and preferred to view the NP's apartheid policies as a unique programme designed to fulfil the perceived needs of Afrikanerdom. Many of those accounts approached the 'apartheid era' from an ethnographic angle and regarded Afrikaners as a curious, undifferentiated group. Consequently, as Dan O'Meara has shown, the NP would become viewed through the prism of ideology and cod psycho-politics. Its election victory was 'taken to represent the triumph of the frontier over the forces of economic rationality—of ideology over economics'.

Hard-line policies would be ascribed to Afrikaner 'intransigence', a 'laager mentality' or a 'frontier sensibility'. More moderate approaches would be attributed to the rise of 'modernising' currents in the party. The NP was reduced to a mere instrument of Afrikaner nationalist ideology, a perspective that obscured the evolving class character of the apartheid state and that led to a fixation on the secretive, highly ideological Broederbond as the orchestrating hand behind apartheid policies. The approach abstracted Afrikaner nationalist ideology from 'the material conditions, contradictions and struggles in the development of capitalism in South Africa' (O'Meara, 1983:3). In fact, Afrikaner nationalism, as elaborated and pursued from the 1930s onward, had at its core the ambitions of aspirant bourgeois Afrikaners, who assiduously promoted an 'ideology through which Afrikaner capital developed' via an 'extensive network of cross-cutting organisations' (op cit, p. 149).

The NP rose to power on the back of a nationalist class alliance, the rudiments of which had been established 30 years earlier. It included agricultural capitalists, white workers (especially newly proletarianised Afrikaners), layers of the growing Afrikaner middle classes and fledgling manufacturing capital. The party pledged to advance and guard the interests of those constituencies by restructuring the economy in their favour. Consequently, its 1948 election rhetoric reflected the ambiguous and often contradictory demands of their various interests.[26] This occurred in a wider context, where contradictions were emerging within the system of economic production—contradictions that affected the various sectors differently and which the state seemed unable to resolve.

Key to the development of South African capitalism was the dependency of the mining, agriculture and industries on a guaranteed supply of cheap, controlled African migrant labour. The reserve system was used to suppress labour costs, but along with white farmers' intense exploitation of labour tenants and the increased mechanisation of agriculture, it forced increasing numbers of African men and women to seek work in urban areas. A growing, semi-permanent African proletariat settled in 'shantytowns' in the country's cities and major towns. New waves of urban resistance were launched, black trade union organisations gathered strength, and strike action became more common. But O'Meara's claim that 'the problem of political control over Africans became acute' seems overwrought (1983:229). As noted, trade union organising and action was declining in the mid-1940s, the ANC was ailing as a political force, and the boycotts and other protests were sporadic and localised, and lacked a political centre of gravity. The analysis of Robert Fine and Dennis Davis seems more plausible; in their view, 'it was through the defeat of [black] resistance that apartheid was able to resolve the crisis of segregationism in its own racist and dictatorial fashion' (Fine & Davis, 1990:7).

Also vitally important were the contradictions that had emerged among industrial capitalists and the state, and the different solutions they sought for their respective dilemmas. Manufacturing production had risen sharply during the Second World War (when the sector's share of GDP actually exceeded that of mining). Manufacturers, however, favoured reforms that could ensure a large, permanent, urban labour supply, which could be regulated through recognised trade unions and restrictive bargaining structures. In their view, influx control, pass laws and rules preventing Africans from taking certain jobs had to be relaxed. They sought a more liberal labour regime. Mining capital, on the other hand, reasoned that the collapse of the reserve system threatened its supply of cheap migrant labour. Reliance on a stabilised (though more expensive) urban work-force was an option, but it was rejected. Instead, the mining moguls chose to try to shore up the rural reservoirs of migrant workers. Meanwhile, agricultural capital favoured tighter influx control and pass laws as a way to halt the exodus of African workers into cities and towns. O'Meara captured this fission well:

> As the 1940s progressed, the differing forms of state policy demanded by various capitals came into increasing contradiction with each other, opening deep divisions within the capitalist class [...] The ruling United Party [UP] was no longer able to organise together the increasingly contradictory demands of the various capitals and act as the political representative of the entire capitalist class ... [this] gave rise to a gradual realignment in the party political organisation of class forces (1983:232).

The previous UP government had been unable to resolve these various demands and needs within a new regulatory framework. After 1948, that task would shift to the NP. Some of its anti-capitalist rhetoric invited concern, but the bluster was geared mainly towards marshalling a class alliance that could bring it to power. History would confirm that 'apartheid was designed to secure labour for all capitals, not to deprive any employer of it' (O'Meara, 1983:237).

This is not to say that there existed a seamless 'fit' between the imperatives of capital and apartheid state policy, nor that the racist ideology of Afrikaner nationalism was a mere shadow play.[27] But it is to caution against the Poulantzasian insistence on the 'autonomy of politics', a line of analysis that overdramatises the 'relative autonomy' the state and the political system achieve in capitalist society.[28] The sweep, vehemence and details of the apartheid system certainly disclosed the power of Afrikaner nationalist ideology. It was around this cultural, historical and political mythos that Afrikaners were organised into a political and economic force. After 1948, it was this ideology (and its translation into practice) that preserved the core political base of the NP. Spawned within it were numerous idiosyncratic laws (for example, prohibiting sexual union between whites and blacks or excluding blacks from 'white' buses and park benches) that were enforced at considerable cost. But these so-called 'petty apartheid' interventions were hardly central elements of South Africa's development path. The fact is that, for almost 40 years, the apartheid system remained functional to the needs of the capitalist class; had it not, the state would have been plunged into genuine crisis early on.[29]

The NP won subsequent 'white' elections by broadening the class alliance that constituted its core base. The material and ideological interests of Afrikaners were advanced, but not at the expense of other key economic interests. It did so within a restructuring programme that resolved many of the contradictions of the 1940s with comparative ease. Exploitation intensified and rates of profit increased; the apartheid state ensured that benefits were distributed intensively among whites. In fact, a distorted and hyper-exploitative developmental state was created. Formidable hegemony was achieved among white South Africans, but it would never be extended further; beyond them, coercion and brute force (whether held in reserve or unleashed) would constitute the basis for the exercise of power (see Chapter thirteen).

Iron fist 'development'

The NP regime quickly applied two key sets of interventions. Influx control of African workers and the pass-law system were expanded and tightened, intensifying efforts to reduce the African population to a labour army serving industry and agriculture.[30] Organisations representing the interests of the African majority (especially trade unions and the CPSA) came under sustained attack. African wages were thrust downward and continued to decline in real terms until 1958/9. Alongside those interventions was a gallery of racist regulatory measures that reorganised numerous aspects of social and economic life along racial lines. The notion of an 'activist' or 'interventionist' state featured prominently, with the state acting forcibly in social and economic affairs, especially around the allocation and control of labour. Webs of administrative structures were spun, including the notorious Bantu Administration Boards, which managed the influx control system.

Rising profits lured foreign investment. In spite of the NP's earlier threats, the new government refrained from introducing anti-monopoly legislation. On the contrary, 'tariff protection policies [...] and fiscal and taxation policies favourable to efficient firms, all encouraged the trend towards monopoly capitalism' (Davies *et al*, 1985:23).[31] The state also intervened to aid the survival of marginal enterprises (especially in agriculture) and to assist in the birth of new, mostly Afrikaner-owned, ones. Through a concerted affirmative action programme it augmented the Afrikaner capitalist class and advanced Afrikaners in all spheres of public life. Government bank accounts were moved to an Afrikaner-controlled bank, government contracts were handed to Afrikaner-owned firms and Afrikaners were appointed to top positions in state departments, the military, official boards and commissions. Cultural production by Afrikaners was supported and widely promoted through a range of cultural bodies, festivals and publishers. History books were rewritten to reflect the myths of Afrikaner nationalism and school curricula were altered accordingly. The contracts for new textbooks went to Afrikaner-owned publishers. The state bureaucracy was expanded and made to absorb huge numbers of Afrikaner workers who thereby gained access to soft loans, housing bonds and other benefits[32]—'a parasitic layer' subsidised by the state. From that platform an increasingly affluent Afrikaner middle class quickly emerged. The NP's victory and defence of state power boosted the status, sway and wealth of Afrikaners to unprecedented levels.

The post-war growth path

Within 20 years, Afrikaner capitalists were propelled into the upper reaches of the economy, where they became steadily integrated into an evolving web of conglomerates. 'English' monopolies launched significant joint ventures with 'Afrikaner' corporations. In one instance the Anglo American Corporation virtually handed over its General Mining and Finance Corporation to a subsidiary of the Afrikaner-owned insurance giant Sanlam. The graduation of Afrikaner capital as a junior partner in the (still English-dominated) economy was in full swing. But the fundamental structure of the economy did not change dramatically.

Hulking at the core of South Africa's economy was a network of corporations active in the mining and energy sectors, with branches extending into manufacturing and other industrial activities. The emphasis was on industries that supported or linked into the core sectors. Flanking this were efforts to boost the domestic manufacturing sector, using state intervention to protect it against imports. Mass production of consumer commodities was linked to the growing consumptive power of whites, including white workers (whose wages were rising). This aspect of the accumulation strategy was therefore 'racially structured'. Stephen Gelb would later project that feature onto the post-war economy as a whole and describe the growth model as 'racial Fordism'. Importantly, however, he recognised that the foundation of the model 'was the expansion of exports of gold and other precious metals, and their stable prices on world markets' (1991:2). Despite the efforts to boost and expand industrialisation, the economy remained anchored in the production and export of minerals. The manufacturing industry grew, but a capital goods and intermediate sector of note did not emerge. To understand this pattern of economic development, it is useful to revisit Ben Fine and Zavareh Rustomjee's classic 1996 analysis of the minerals-energy complex (MEC).

The minerals-energy complex

Fine and Rustomjee (1996) trace the origins of the MEC to the early twentieth century.[33] From early on, as Renfrew Christie (1984) showed, the mining industry was highly dependent on stable and 'affordable' energy supplies, and it both backed and relied on state-driven energy development.[34] Linkages between state and private corporations played a vital role in the evolution and consolidation of the MEC— not least through key industrial strategies such as the development of large-scale electricity-generating capacity and of an indigenous fuel-chemical industry.[35]

The MEC's outlines became especially vivid during the consolidation of the apartheid system in the 1950s and 1960s. The apartheid state funded and managed large parastatal corporations (notably the steel manufacturer Iscor, the electricity supplier Eskom and the petroleum-from-coal supplier Sasol), expanded and upgraded transport and telecommunications infrastructure, and erected high tariff and non-tariff protective walls around certain industries. By the late 1950s, Afrikaner-controlled finance institutions had become powerful enough to begin inserting themselves into productive corporate sectors, including large industrial operations.[36] Over the next decade, the earlier ironclad distinction between Afrikaner and English capital withered[37] and economic collaboration became more commonplace, with the state increasingly acting as interlocutor and facilitator of new linkages (O'Meara, 1996). Some divisions remained and would handicap the development of intermediate and capital goods capacity (Fine, 2008b), but the cartoonish picture of an apartheid state exclusively obsessing with promoting Afrikaner interests had become a manifest distortion.

The economy became characterised by corporate conglomeration that focused especially on minerals production (and some processing), energy provision, chemicals and finance—all of it capital-intensive. Cheap coal and a deeply skewed minerals policy 'resulted in limited diversification of the economy and high levels of inefficiency' (Swilling, 2010:11). The role of linkages between state enterprises (involved in electricity, steel and transport, especially), the financial sector and key industries in South Africa's economic development became more evident. In Bill Freund's (2008:14) summary:

> [T]he links that tie the MEC together are not just metaphoric or even forged by the state; critical to this is the financial sector and the interconnection between the parastatals such as Eskom, the government and the private sector.

The largest corporations focused their expansion strategies on the minerals and energy sectors, which remained the hub for most large-scale industrial diversification. Alongside this an array of other industrial ventures emerged (focused chiefly on consumer goods and buffered by strong state protection). Ostensibly, the prospects seemed good for a vigorous industrialisation drive, a grand phase of 'catching up' (which received wisdom views through the lens of import substituting industrialisation, or ISI).[38] These two 'streams' of industrialising activity were scarcely integrated, however. South Africa's industrial development stayed biased towards activities with tight linkages to the core MEC sectors. Tensions between core MEC and non-MEC manufacturing were reflected in government policy, access to investment, and in levels of output and employment. This had decisive effects on the character and path of the country's industrialisation efforts. Tariff protection, typically associated with import-substitution, did not form part of a coherent strategy, for example. This slowed export growth and handicapped efforts to transform and develop industrial production (Bell *et al*, 1999).

The state refrained from the concerted interventions in investment and pro-duction decisions, research and development and so on that characterised the East Asian newly industrialised countries. In Taiwan and South Korea, for example, the emphasis was on producing labour-intensive goods and developing markets for them—a strategy aimed partly at absorbing an influx of workers from ailing rural areas. South Africa, by contrast, chose to persist with an exclusionary industrialisation strategy and regime of accumulation. Instead of absorbing an increasingly precarious labour surplus it barricaded it along a periphery that took economic, social, political and geographic forms.[39] The strategy favoured capital-intensive production, which meant limited absorption of the labour surplus and an (increasingly mechanised) agricultural sector marked by very low wages and dismal working conditions. State and capital were sowing the seeds of crisis.

The homeland system made it possible to deflect the social and economic costs of rising unemployment and the reproduction of African labour into the hinterlands of the 'reserves'. Massive forced removals saw the labour tenant system replaced by a contract labour system. Between 1960 and 1982, 3.5 million people were forcibly removed by the state—one of the largest ever peacetime movements of populations. The majority of those evicted from their home and land were Africans who had lived on white-owned farms or on their own land in African districts. About 700 000 more people were removed from urban areas that had been declared 'white' (Surplus People Project, 1983). Most were removed to patchworks of land the state had grandly categorised as 'homelands'. Influx control was tightened, pre-venting Africans from being physically present in urban ('white') areas without the permission of state authorities.

The prime function of the homeland system was, to paraphrase Alain Lipietz, the production of an immense reserve army of people available for wage-labour as and when required (1987:149). As late as 1980 an apartheid think tank would still propose that 'the problem of race relations' could be solved through 'a system of separate political sovereignties' joined in 'economic cooperation' with 'white' South

Africa.[40] The economic logic of the homelands was obvious. But political calculations would also become prominent, as apartheid planners sought to corral the post-war surge of nationalist militancy into barricaded political entities.

Fight-back

The imposition of apartheid revived popular resistance in the form of sporadic strikes and consumer boycotts in towns and cities and more militant (occasionally violent) action in rural areas.[41] Goaded by its newly formed youth wing, the ANC emerged from its slumber. Its 1949 Programme of Action had incorporated several elements of the ANCYL's manifesto and signalled a turn to 'mass struggle' under the ambit of African nationalism. Although the organisation's core base had shifted to the urban African working class, the organisation was by no means under working-class leadership: its top ranks (including rising stars of the ANCYL such as Nelson Mandela, Oliver Tambo, Walter Sisulu and Joe Matthews) were drawn from the African middle class.

The sway of African nationalism was not yet assured, however. Following a leftward turn, the CPSA produced a scathing critique of African nationalism and the ANC. Its 1950 Central Committee report warned that 'the class conscious proletariat cannot rally under the "national" flag of the bourgeoisie' and lambasted the black middle class for failing to provide effective leadership to the masses.[42] Fine and Davis (1990) have argued, however, that the main thrust of the report was actually to radicalise the nationalist struggle. The CPSA would continue to fight for socialism, but the immediate task was the struggle for national liberation under the leadership of a revolutionary nationalist organisation. In essence, the framework for an alliance between the CPSA and ANC had been sketched. Relations between the two organisations were not tranquil, as shown by the angry reaction of ANC conservatives to the joint May Day stay-away, which the CPSA and Transvaal ANC called in 1950.[43] A month later, the CPSA dissolved, in anticipation of the promulgation of the Suppression of Communism Act by the NP government. Three years later it reconstituted itself as an underground organisation, the South African Communist Party (SACP).

The first major resistance action organised by the ANC was the Defiance Campaign of 1952. African women, led by figures such as Dorothy Nyembe, Lilian Ngoyi and Annie Silinga, played central roles. The ANC Women's League, hitherto an ineffective group dominated by the wives of ANC leaders, was 'transformed into a fighting arm of the ANC' (Mbeki, 1992:73). The campaign spawned joint actions with other political groups, a move that would lead to the formation of the multi-racial Congress Alliance in 1955, and the drafting of the Freedom Charter.[44] At the height of the campaign, ANC membership rocketed from 4 000 to 100 000 (Mbeki, 1992:64).

The Defiance Campaign was a landmark attempt to mount a coordinated challenge against the apartheid state. Again, though, official history tends to exaggerate its accomplishments. The campaign intended to force the apartheid regime to repeal six sets of legislation introduced or reinforced since 1948[45]—but failed to do so. By early 1953, the flow of volunteers for civil disobedience actions had slowed to a trickle and the government had responded with new repressive legislation that outlawed political protest. By the end of the year, the ANC's membership had shrunk to 28 000, prompting an anonymous ANC writer to complain that 'the building of the organisation did not correspond to the enthusiasm the campaign had aroused [...] we did not consolidate our gains'.[46]

Attempts to assemble the fragmented elements of popular resistance around the banner of African nationalism continued. The most dramatic of these was the creation of the Congress Alliance, its historic adoption of the Freedom Charter and the launch of the ANC-aligned South African Congress of Trade Unions (SACTU). The Freedom Charter for the first time presented South Africans with the outline of a democratic alternative to apartheid. Its pronouncements were sweeping, but they pointed to a new order where liberal democratic rights could be combined with a welfarist socioeconomic order. The Charter and its drafting process would, in decades to follow, become intensely mythologised: the Charter became the touchstone of ANC policy and assumed sacrosanct status as the product of the 'will of the people'. That status is perhaps controversial (Everatt, 2009). Nevertheless, the Charter gained immense political value and was put to powerful use in the ANC's efforts to establish its hegemony among the anti-apartheid opposition. For its part, the state would use the Freedom Charter as the basis for laying charges of treason against 156 leaders of the Congress Alliance. All the accused were eventually acquitted, but the five-year 'Treason Trial' effectively removed them from political activity.

Formed in 1955, SACTU represented the trade-union wing of the ANC. With 19 affiliate unions, its membership would more than double by 1961, reaching some 55 000. It was tasked with furthering 'political unionism', a conception that linked (or, said critics, 'subordinated') workers' struggles for better wages and working conditions to the broader struggle for national liberation. SACTU played a significant role in the rise of industrial militancy between 1955 and 1958. The number of strikes rose markedly between 1954 and 1958, leading some historians to suggest that the militancy contributed to halting the decline in African wages.[47] But organised African workers constituted a tiny proportion of the 300 000 Africans working in factories, the 150 000 working in transport, the 800 000 in services, and the million who were toiling on farms at the end of the 1950s.[48]

SACTU, meanwhile, was experiencing the suffocating weight of 'political unionism'. In 1958 it had pushed for a national strike in support of demands for a minimum wage, shorter working hours and recognition as a trade union.[49] ANC leaders were intent, however, on launching a mass campaign to coincide with the whites-only election in April. In the end, a three-day stay-away was called, nominally including the union demands but actually focusing on the election (as the slogan 'Defeat the Nats' made clear). The stay-away was called off after the first day, to the dismay of some union leaders.[50] Leftists blamed the ANC leadership for undermining the militancy of the masses. Great controversy still surrounds the election stay-away and the decisions taken around the earlier 1957 bus boycotts, when ANC leaders were also accused of restraining the apparent militancy of workers. Whatever the verdict, by the end of the decade, the working-class movement was decidedly weak—partly, in the view of Fine and Davis, because of the 'internal fragmentation of the working class', its 'structural position' in production and the lack of 'distinction of the working class as a party in its own right from other class forces' (1990:153). More than ever, its demands and aspirations were being refracted through the prisms of race and nation.

Meanwhile, tensions between the ANC mainstream and its Africanist elements had led to a split when a breakaway group led by Robert Sobukwe formed the PAC in April 1959. It was the PAC that organised the anti-pass-law campaign during which police shot dead 69 protestors in Sharpeville and 17 in Langa, outside Cape Town. The regime declared a state of emergency and banned both the ANC and PAC on 8 April 1960.

The turn to armed struggle

The ANC's banning forced the organisation underground and gave rise to a dramatic shift away from its strategy of non-violent resistance. There remains some dispute about the manner in which the decision to launch an armed struggle was taken. Govan Mbeki acknowledged that there was strong disagreement on the matter as late as June 1961 (1992:90), while other writers claimed that the decision came about fitfully.[51] Nevertheless, an armed wing, Umkhonto we Sizwe ('Spear of the Nation') or MK, was set up under a National High Command, comprising ANC and SACP leaders. It carried out its first bombings on 16 December. In its manifesto, MK declared:

> The time comes in the life of any nation when there remain only two choices: submit or fight. That time has now come to South Africa. We shall not submit and we have no choice but to hit back by all means within our power in defence of our people, our future and our freedom [...] Refusal to resort to force has been interpreted by the Government as an invitation to use armed force against the people without fear of reprisals. The methods of Umkhonto we Sizwe mark a break with that past.[52]

The focus was to be on rural areas, where recent peasant uprisings (in Pondoland, Witzieshoek and Zeerust) suggested to some an untapped potential for a guerrilla war—an improbable enterprise in a countryside dominated by white-owned farms and white-run towns, and which lacked impenetrable natural features usually associated with such warfare.[53] Even more surprising was the fact that this strategic turn was taken by an organisation whose major organised support base lay in the urban working class. Not all ANC and SACP leaders were convinced. Figures such as Walter Sisulu and Bram Fischer slammed the decision as the 'unrealistic brainchild of some youthful and adventurous imagination'.

Left analysts (notably Harold Wolpe)[54] would, in varying ways, segment the resistance strategies into distinct phases during which largely objective conditions purportedly prescribed certain forms of struggle. Thus 1948–60 saw legal, non-violent mass resistance, 1961–73 was a period of illegality and armed struggle in the form of guerrilla war and post-1973 allowed for a synthesis of the two forms. The posture of the apartheid state was seen as the central determinant in each phase. So, for instance, the state's decision after 1961 'to rule by force alone', thereby shutting out 'all lawful modes of opposition'[55], would be presented as the clinching rationale for resorting to armed struggle. But, in the view of Fine and Davis, that line of analysis ignores

> the conscious, rational side of social movements; their capacity to make programmatic and operational choices, to learn from the past and from theory, to combine their own experience with the experience of other movements abroad, to question themselves through debate and criticism and to rebuild afresh (1985:25).

Armed struggle might have been the most attractive option, but it was not the only viable one, despite the severity of the state's crackdown. In the aftermath of the Sharpeville and Langa massacres, protests erupted in the country's industrial heartland and in Cape Town, along with strike actions. The state's repressive capacities were strained as police reinforcements were shuttled frantically from flashpoint to flashpoint—it had not yet achieved a blanketing, systematic and co-ordinated repressive presence. In addition, domestic and foreign capital had grown markedly nervous. Large outflows of capital had started even before the Sharpeville massacre and accelerated afterwards. Gold and foreign reserves dropped by 55% as the stock market and gold price plummeted. This amplified tensions in the ruling bloc: neither in the state nor in the capitalist class was there unanimity about the appropriate response. Indeed, acting Prime Minister PO Sauer openly supported reforms in key areas (pass laws, some political rights for Africans, improved wage levels), while five major business associations petitioned government for policy reforms (Fine & Davis, 1985:41).

One should not exaggerate those developments, but all other strategic options had not, it seems, been sealed off. Although very difficult under prevailing conditions,[56] a 'war of position' approach was perhaps available—by marshalling the militancy of African workers, women and other sectors of the urban African population. The fundamental question was whether such an option was feasible. An answer required an assessment of the comparative strengths and weaknesses of the popular sector and the extent of disorientation and strategic wavering in the ruling bloc. Instead, the movement's historians and strategists have bequeathed a version of history that denies the existence of any other strategic path.

Into the doldrums

The turn to armed struggle marked not only a major strategic but also a crucial paradigmatic shift.[57] Henceforth, reforming the system would be considered impossible and practically treasonous.

The ANC and SACP adopted, in Howard Barrel's opinion,

> *an assumption that revolutionary armed struggle was not merely the means by which ultimately to contend for state power but also the principal means by which to progress in each phase of escalation towards that goal* (1991:69).[58]

This conviction would become dominant in the liberation movement, launching resistance struggles on a path of outright conflict with the apartheid state. SACP leader Joe Slovo's formulation of the strategy at a December 1960 SACP conference captured this thinking well. The liberation struggle would entail

> *a long-term, multi-staged campaign of: disciplined violence in which a hard core of trained militants, supported by mass-based political activity and crucial external aid, confront state power with the ultimate goal of seizing it.*[59]

As Mike Morris later noted, 'a tendency was born which threatened to equate armed struggle with revolution and legal struggle with reformism'. Removed from the range of options was any

> *conception for political activity [that] centred on open internal struggle, on taking advantage of fissures within the state, of incremental change, of operating within the system, of using existing institutions for organisational activity or policy work* (Morris, 1993b:6).

Rhetorically deemed an element of the new strategy, mass struggle was actually moved on the backburner. Armed struggle dominated the strategic stage, thereby fortifying the vanguardist and militaristic tendencies in the movement. Although demonstrably still capable of mounting telling resistance initiatives, the urban African masses were reduced to passivity. Their return to the stage of history depended on a *deus ex machina*, a guerrilla war that would founder for the next two decades. If anything, it would validate philosopher Paul Virilio's warning:

> *The principle aim of any truly popular resistance is thus to oppose the establishment of a social situation based solely on the illegality of armed forces which reduces a population to the status of a movable slave, a commodity* (1978:55).

These observations were hardly heterodox. By Slovo's own later admission, the armed struggle entrenched

> *an attitude both within the organisation and amongst the people that the fate of the struggle depended on the sophisticated actions of a professional elite. The importance of the masses was theoretically appreciated, but in practice mass political work was minimal.*[60]

Something of a refinement occurred at the ANC's 1969 Morogoro consultative conference, which endorsed the guerrilla warfare strategy but emphasised that it could not occur in a political vacuum. A decision was taken to build the ANC's underground structures inside South Africa, but progress was fitful and faint. Champions of guerrilla war held their ground until 1978, when a study tour to Vietnam persuaded many of them (Slovo included) that an armed struggle had to be based on, and arise out of, mass political support—'all military activities at all times had to be guided and determined by the need to generate political mobilisation, organisation and resistance' (Bundy, 1989:7). But nesting in the shift to armed struggle was a binary outlook, which condemned compromise and anything resembling it. The all-or-nothing approach would yield the tenets of 'ungovernability' and 'non-collaboration', and generate the calls for 'insurrection' and a 'people's war' in the 1980s. The strategic disorientation of the liberation movement in the late 1980s cannot be understood without taking into account the uncompromising certitude that had seized hold of it.

Meanwhie, the 'dark decade' of the 1960s ensued. In the early 1960s, most of the ANC leadership who had not been imprisoned moved into exile and guerrilla training camps were set up in Tanzania. Conditions hardly favoured guerrilla warfare. South Africa was surrounded by a *cordon sanitaire* in the form of the Portuguese colonies of Mozambique and Angola, white-ruled Rhodesia and South African-occupied South-West Africa. Internally, the country offered few of the geographic features associated with rural guerrilla warfare: large, secluded mountain ranges and forests. 'By the end of 1962,' Govan Mbeki recalled, 'most [MK] units could no longer operate since they did not have the materials to carry out their sabotage activities (1992:94).' The ANC was cut off from its support base inside South Africa and turned its attention to mustering international support for its struggle. It was not until 1967 that a major effort would be made to launch a guerrilla war when MK fighters tried to infiltrate into South Africa through the Wankie Game Reserve in Rhodesia—apparently in response to growing disaffection among cadres in the training camps. The attempt failed when Rhodesian security forces intercepted the 80-man force, killing 30 guerrillas and capturing 20.[61] For the next decade, the armed struggle remained little more than a strategy on the drawing board.

The state, meanwhile, reorganised its repressive capacities. It viciously crushed remnants of internal resistance and set about resolving some of the main sources of tension in the ruling bloc. Buckled by state repression, after 1964 SACTU shifted its focus to international solidarity work. Only 13 black trade unions existed in 1969, compared with 63 in 1961.

Apartheid's harvest

The post-war development strategy established an affluent welfare state for whites. White workers were guaranteed access to jobs, enjoyed rising wages and were cushioned by a wide-ranging social-security system, along with easy access to credit and loans. This increased their consumptive power, making them (and the ballooning middle class) the consumptive core of a growing economy. White trade unions won collective bargaining agreements for white workers and successively defended their privileges against some employers' attempts to cut wage costs by shifting the job colour bar upwards and elevating low-paid African labour into semi-skilled jobs. Vast resources were invested in education, health, cultural, recreational and sports infrastructure and services for whites. In short, the class alliance that had returned the NP to government in successive whites-only elections was diligently shored up. As long as black South Africans' claims to full political rights could be held in check, the political survival of the system could be ensured— or so it seemed.

In African communities, the effects were the reverse, with the great majority of Africans ruled out of these circuits of production, distribution and consumption. Access to skilled jobs was severely restricted, through discrimination in the workplace and an education system that, until the early 1970s, was explicitly designed to equip Africans with only the rudiments required for entry into the lower ranks of the labour market.

Class formation in African communities was curbed. Some segmentation did occur within the African working classes, as a semi-skilled urban layer emerged, but an African middle class remained a distant prospect. The state had closed off access to most accumulatory activities and continued to drive black entrepreneurs from central business districts. Even the informal sector was closed down through a barrage of regulations, forcing African consumers to spend their money at white-owned businesses. Wages rose but, in the absence of a social security net and with destitution increasing in the homelands, they had to be distributed widely throughout extended family networks. The rate of savings was negligible and disposable income was much too small to afford most items deemed 'essential' by whites.

At the same time, the weight of the apartheid system was distributed unevenly among Africans, coloureds and Indians, as state budget allocations to housing, education and health departments showed. Along with white workers, Indians and coloureds predominated in the expanding sectors of the economy and were accorded some mobility within and between jobs (Hindson, 1991). By the 1970s there had emerged in both 'groups' a significant middle class, comprising mostly professionals and merchants. Although politically disenfranchised, these small minorities were deemed to be citizens of 'white' South Africa.[62]

Cracks in the system

Apartheid's 'golden age' lasted from the early 1960s to early 1970s. For state and business leaders, that period seemed like halcyon days. Capital accumulation sped along, with the economy growing at an average 6%.[63] As restiveness about the Sharpeville massacre waned, foreign capital flooded back, lured by investment returns reputed to be among the highest in the world. Dan O'Meara (1996:174) cites an estimate that US corporations were netting 18% returns on their South African investments, compared with 8% in the United Kingdom. The economy seemed to be relatively mature and diversified—at least in relation to much of the rest of Africa. Living standards of whites kept rising and concerted anti-apartheid resistance seemed a thing of the past. Beyond South Africa's borders armed struggles continued, but to little manifest effect. In Rhodesia, the Ian Smith regime seemed to have matters in hand, while the Portuguese colonialists in Angola and Mozambique claimed to be unperturbed by the efforts of the *Movimento Popular de Libertação de Angola* (MPLA) and the *Frente de Libertação de Moçambique* (Frelimo).

For government planners and business leaders alike, the dream of an industrial powerhouse emerging at the tip of Africa seemed within grasp. The manufacturing sector was performing well, driven by a boom in the production of consumer goods. Overblown expectations reigned. The liberal economist D Hobart Houghton (1967), for example, asserted confidently that South Africa's secondary industry would become 'fully self-supporting' and predicted that the economy would achieve full 'maturity' (in other words, achieve consumer-driven affluence) by 1993.[64] On the contrary, the development of a capital goods sector was stymied by the 'concentrated conglomerate ownership of the engineering and other sectors' which 'confine[d] engineering's linkages to dependence upon mining, mineral processing, chemicals and energy industries' (Fine & Rustomjee, 1996:215–16). Consequently, industrialisation extended fitfully and very partially into the intermediate and capital goods sectors. What seemed to be an unfolding, linear process of industrial development turned out to be much less auspicious.

Within a few years, the complacency was shattered. Although performing impressively at first glance, the economy stood on shallow, rickety foundations. By the mid-1960s, the manufacturing sector was growing at almost 12% annually, but the economy was becoming more capital-intensive as new machinery and technologies were introduced. This meant a drop in the number of workers employed per unit of capital. The need for semi-skilled, skilled and technical labour grew, while unskilled migrant labour became increasingly superfluous to industry. A significant shift was underway in the labour market. Structured for decades around access to cheap, unskilled migrant labour that could be contracted in, it was now developing a bias towards a relatively stable, semi-skilled urban work-force (O'Meara, 1996).

The manufacturing sector did not become export-oriented, nor did it diversify sufficiently into capital and intermediate goods production. This meant that the bulk of the technologies, machines and equipment had to be imported. Industrial development was therefore dependent on the ability to pay for capital and intermediate goods imports. Even though manufacturing's contribution to GDP in 1960 was almost double that of the mining and agricultural sectors combined, it comprised a small part of foreign earnings, which depended overwhelmingly on the export of minerals (with gold the biggest earner). This reinforced the terms of South Africa's participation in the global system:

- It exported strategic minerals and imported capital and intermediate goods, and oil; and
- The foreign exchange needed to pay for those imports came mainly from two sources: minerals (principally gold) and foreign capital inflows. On average it depended on mineral products for 70–85% of its export earnings.

By 1975, agriculture and mining accounted for three-quarters of merchandise exports, while manufacturing relied heavily on an almost saturated domestic market (Davies *et al*, 1985).[65] The capital-intensive growth in manufacturing therefore depended on a high rate of capital goods imports (destined both for the private manufacturing industry and the massive parastatal industries set up by the

NP government), which strained foreign reserves. Overall, the fortunes of the South African economy still hinged on two *external* factors: the gold price and access to foreign exchange. In that respect, it resembled most 'developing' economies.

Despite its industrialising pretences, South Africa was actually an unusually well developed exporter of mineral products. The economy operated with clear handicaps. As long as foreign capital could be attracted, the gold price remained high and a strong exchange rate could be maintained, the structural vulnerability could be managed. But the terms of South Africa's insertion into the international economy rendered it highly exposed to shocks at the global level—which is what transpired in the mid-1970s. By the end of the decade, a combination of local and international developments had battered the economy into recession and forced the apartheid regime onto the defensive:

■ Internationally, the 1973 oil crisis had precipitated a global recession and hastened the emergence of a crisis of capital accumulation globally;

■ A modern, industrial labour movement was emerging, starting with the 1973 strikes in and around Durban;

■ Black Consciousness had become a powerful mobilising ideology;

■ Unemployment soared among African workers (the numbers almost doubled from 582 000 in 1962 to one million in 1970; O'Meara, 1996);

■ The 1976 Soweto Uprising drew a line under the heydays of apartheid; and

■ Foreign capital inflows virtually dried up overnight. Long-term foreign investment shrank from R 1.6 billion in 1975/76 to R 452 million in 1976/77, while short-term capital gushed out. As foreign exchange dried up, industrial expansion slowed.

These were jarring shocks. The economy was bogged down in a deep crisis that exposed the limits of the apartheid accumulation strategy (O'Meara, 1996). The annual growth rate slowed considerably. By the early 1980s growth was running at under 2%, a sign that the post-war accumulation strategy was in trouble. Mainstream economic analysis blamed the travails on 'inappropriate' government policies and disruptions in the global economy.[66] In fact, the problems ran considerably deeper; South Africa was experiencing more than a 'cyclical downturn'. Against the background of a global recession and a revival of working-class organisation and action, several chronic handicaps had emerged:

■ Capital-intensive growth prevented the economy from absorbing surplus labour;

■ The manufacturing sector's dependency on imports and its failure to become a significant exporter deepened the economy's vulnerability to external factors (such as world market prices for precious metals and currency fluctuations) and heightened balance-of-payment difficulties;

■ Manufacturing investment had become tardy, betraying a tendency towards over-accumulation;

■ The domestic market was too small to sustain manufacturing centred on luxury import-substitution;

- Productivity growth had slowed, partly because of a shortage of skilled black labour and the deliberate depreciation of social capital under the apartheid system; and
- South Africa's industrial development was more or less arrested around the MEC and its basic status as a primary commodity exporter stood unchanged.

Arrested development

An import-substituting logic was certainly evident in industrial development up to the 1960s, but the standard explanation for its demise does not convince. Import-substituting industrialisation is commonly said to have faltered due to constrained demand from a small, mainly white consumer market. Drawing on French regulation theory, Gelb (1991) described South African capitalism as a form of 'racial Fordism'. Secondary industry had emerged on the back of gold mining and had flourished, even though it was largely uncompetitive and unable to penetrate foreign markets. This form of accumulation then fell into crisis, not least because of its reliance on the form of social and political regulation provided by the apartheid system. In other words, South Africa undertook but failed to complete a strategy of import-substituting industrialisation. This analysis would have a decisive effect on post-apartheid industrial policy.

But lacking in that analysis, said critics, was a convincing account of the structure of the economy and of the interplay of economic and political interests that shaped key policy choices. The analysis neglected the major sectors of the economy, laid undue emphasis on the consumptive sectors and failed to explain why the capital and intermediate goods sector did not develop (Fine, 2007 & 2008).[67] South Africa's stunted industrialisation, they argued, was a symptom of the distorting weight of the MEC; demand constraints (a numerically limited white market and impoverished black market) were not the main culprit. Industrial development ended up falling between several stools. Privileged consideration went to ventures and institutions supporting the MEC, alongside which non-durable consumer-goods manufacturing developed and some piecemeal promotion of some intermediate and capital goods manufacturing occurred. But import-substitution never matured into a coherent strategy. The reasons for South Africa's misshapen industrial profile lay on the *supply* (and not the demand) side (Fine & Rustomjee, 1996).

In the standard sequence, import-substituting industrialisation commences with the production of consumer goods, which triggers knock-on effects to the production of intermediate and, eventually, capital goods. South Africa did not follow that path. Early industrial production focused mainly on non-consumption goods and was especially geared to service the core mining sector. Eventually, consumer-goods production did take off, but the forward linkages from the MEC core sectors were weakly promoted and disorderly.[68] What looked like import-substituting industrialisation were actually poorly co-ordinated and erratically supported entrepreneurial forays that lacked solid linkages into the core sectors of the economy. The favoured policies were those that supported the core MEC sectors, at the expense 'of other industrial policies of diversification away from economic dependence on South Africa's resource base' (Fine & Rustomjee, 1996:14). That trend persisted in the 1980s (when the crisis of apartheid prevented a coherent alternative strategy from emerging) and the 1990s, when monetarist liberalisation reigned.

This contention has often been misunderstood as a claim that industrial output did not diversify,[69] when the focus is actually on the *weak linkages* between sectors, and the lack of integration across them. The import-substituting industrial efforts that peaked in the 1960s seemed to follow a logic independent of the MEC, which accounts for its haphazard and halting development. Measured by investment levels, state support and eventual scale, the import-substituting industrialisation ventures were dwarfed by industrial activities linked to the MEC. Thus, robust industrial expansion mainly involved activities closely linked to the mineral and energy sectors, and the production of (mostly non-durable) consumer goods.

These distinct understandings of industrialisation in South Africa are not trifling matters. Blaming import-substituting industrialisation, behind protective barriers, for stunted industrialisation and economic frailties (as Terrence Moll, 1990, and others did) would lead post-apartheid policymakers toward a particular package of remedies. The MEC analysis pointed to different exit routes.

On the ropes

The economic boom of the 1960s and early 1970s had been financed with large foreign-capital inflows. But even before the Soweto uprising, capital was flowing out at prodigious rates. The economy lost a quarter of its foreign-exchange reserves in the first three months of 1976, forcing resort to an emergency loan from the International Monetary Fund (IMF). Total investment dropped by 13% between 1975 and 1977 (Saul & Gelb, 1981). In industry, productivity remained low, with manufacturing outputs dropping and production costs rising. The economy had entered a period of stagflation. Rising rates of inflation fuelled a revival in worker resistance in the early 1970s, signalling the breakdown of the disciplinary regime in the workplace.

The rigid racial structuring of production and consumption patterns made whites (and, to a much smaller extent, the coloured and Indian minorities) the core market for the manufacturing sector.[70] That market was now too small to sustain production growth. A demand-driven recovery was not on the cards. The lack of infrastructure in African areas compounded the problem: consumers without electricity, for instance, were not going to buy electrical goods. Simply increasing wages would not solve the problem either: the soaring unemployment rate and rising inflation meant that wage-earners' pay packets had to stretch further, since more people in their extended families depended on them as breadwinners. Thus, even when wages increased (as they did in the 1980s), disposable income did not expand at the same pace.

Destitution in the homelands, increased mechanisation in agriculture and the expulsion of labour tenants from 'white' farms forced more of the huge labour surplus to seek salvation in the urban centres. The state continued to fiercely apply influx-control measures and introduced a variety of grandiose schemes (including very costly efforts to redirect these economic refugees into new 'economic growth zones' set up inside or on the borders of homelands). The idea of blockading Africans in literal peripheries was in crisis. The reality of an exponentially growing, permanent, urbanised African population had become irreversible.

Meanwhile, it was not salvation that awaited Africans in the cities and towns. Work was scarce, wages remained low and the state continually harassed residents. Unemployment kept rising among black workers. In the lived experience of Africans (and many coloureds and Indians) the struggle to survive became couched increasingly in political terms.

The tumult in the global economic system had sent both the gold price and mining profits soaring. With capital controls stifling the (legal) export of capital, this seemed to favour substantial investment in downstream manufacturing.[71] But that did not transpire. Anxiety about the upsurge in anti-apartheid resistance acted as a deterrent, as did the advances made by liberation movements in neighbouring countries. For corporate South Africa, new long-term investments were positively unattractive options.

This combination of political and economic instability thrust policymaking into a reactive and capricious mode. Tensions grew between the apartheid regime and some of its business allies,[72] squabbling intensified between sections of the state and infighting eventually split the ruling National Party in 1982. Damage control was the order of the day. The regime sought to steady the ship with a haphazard sequence of privatisation and deregulation. The prospect of a refurbished industrial strategy was pushed even further to the margins, which suited the dominant corporate players. In Sampie Terreblanche's (2002:74) summary, they were 'given an institutionalised role in the reorganised state sector, of formulating and implementing "free market" economic policies'.

Another major complication was the debt crisis of 1985 and the financial sanctions that were applied soon afterwards. Forced to source funds on the domestic market (and at high interest rates), corporations curbed their investments (Cassim *et al*, 2003) and instead recycled their profits in an orgy of mergers and acquisitions that also targeted the operations of divesting foreign corporations. Scores of companies were absorbed into massive conglomerates through mergers and takeovers.

Mining monopolies marauded into the financial, industrial, property and agricultural sectors; insurance giants launched raids into the mining and industrial sectors. Four corporations in particular had controlling interests in major mining, manufacturing and financial ventures: Anglo American Corporation, Rembrandt Group, Sanlam and Old Mutual (Lewis, 1991:33). Among the winners was finance capital, which expanded feverishly and developed new institutions (such as merchant banks) and services (especially credit). By 1981 a mere eight conglomerates controlled more than 60% of assets in the private sector (Davies *et al*, 1985:61–64). They then turned on one another; by 1985, four conglomerates (Anglo American, Sanlam, Old Mutual and Rembrandt) controlled more than 80% of the listed shares on the Johannesburg Stock Exchange (McGreggor, 1985). Unwieldy conglomerates straddling numerous sectors were assembled, but in the absence of any industrial strategy capable of providing strategic direction and synergy. There was no co-ordinating economic framework linking state and private enterprise, and the potential advantages of economies of scale were never realised. 'Muddling' is perhaps the best description for this period, which is incisively described in O'Meara's *Forty Lost Years* (1996).

In this strategic vacuum, the MEC—as a system of accumulation—was consolidated further. It continued to benefit immensely from mammoth new capital-intensive energy projects (including expansion of the oil-from-coal Sasol ventures, the Mossgas natural gas development project, and the expansion of electricity-generating capacity). The state also exploited MEC linkages to create a formidable domestic armaments industry, as well as a nuclear industry (Freund, 2008). In the context of intensifying political and social upheaval, a strategy of industrial diversification scarcely entered the frame. The financial sector, however, grew voraciously (see Chapter five). In essence, two decisive trends prevailed in the 1980s:

■ The corporate sector became increasingly concentrated, with conglomerates extending themselves far beyond their core operations; and
■ There emerged a powerful and sophisticated financial sector that was tied in with those conglomerates.

Therefore considerable economic power and political weight continued to be concentrated in and around the MEC, key elements of which were now strategically focused on globalising their operations. Within a decade, that goal would be realised.

The MEC left the economy with strengths and weaknesses. The strengths, according to Fine and Rustomjee (1996:252), lay in 'the productive and infrastructural capacities that have been built up around its core sectors'. The weaknesses involved the failure to vertically integrate those capacities 'forward into the rest of the economy'. All this had other

> *considerable implications for the formation and impact of macroeconomic policy, as well as for industrial policy, where the development of economies of scale and scope in manufacturing continues to be constrained by limited domestic commitment on the part of conglomerate capital* (Fine & Rustomjee, 1998:698).

These features would have profound effects on the scope and kinds of adjustments that were attempted over the next two decades. But by the early 1980s it had become clear to some that South Africa had arrived at a major turning point. The accumulation strategy was running up against contradictions that could not be solved within the frame of political and social management imposed over the hundred years prior. Inside the apartheid regime, the young head of National Intelligence, Neil Barnard, understood this when, in early 1980, he urged President P W Botha to 'make peace now while we're masters of our destiny' (Gevisser, 2007:491). Profound restructuring was needed and this could, and would, occur within the capitalist framework. Initially, the repairs would be focused on the social and political structures that underpinned economic growth path, and which had become increasingly dysfunctional to it (Gelb, 1991). Next in line would be revisions to the accumulation strategy.

Endnotes

1 'Average CEO earns R 5.3 million a year', *Business Report,* 8 October 2009. The figures were drawn from a report by Mabili human capital management company. The same 2007 survey found the average CEO earned R 6.1 million (USD 850 000) annually. See 'Corporate fact cats are skimming all the cream', *The Times* [Johannesburg], 7 November 2007.

2 According to the Merril Lynch *World Wealth Report 2006.* The hunger data are from Statistics SA (2008d) and are discussed in detail in Chapter seven.

3 The statutory minimum wage for domestic workers in Johannesburg in 2010. The USD 67 000 beds were being sold by Hastens at a shopping mall in Fourways, Johannesburg. Nearby is the largest Porsche dealer outside Germany. For a full list of minimum wages in South Africa, see www.mywage.co.za.

4 For a terse account, see Colin Bundy's 'Development and inequality in historical perspective' in Schrire (1992:24–38).

5 According to Davies *et al*, in the British-held Cape Colony, for instance, class position 'rather than outright racial discrimination determined the patterns of economic and political power' (1985:6).

6 An independent African peasantry survived in significant numbers until the early 1930s, when its dissolution was intensified by the Depression; see Bundy (1979). Until then, this peasantry served as the main social base of the ANC. Its decline coincided with the ANC's slump during the 1930s and early 1940s.

7 The exception was Algeria, where a similar pattern of settler domination occurred.

8 South Africa, of course, would only emerge as a geopolitical entity in 1910 with the establishment of the Union of South Africa.

9 For a summary, see Bell, T. Note also Bill Freund's suggestion that Merle Lipton, particularly her work *Capital and Apartheid* (1986), was also something of 'an intellectual forerunner to the Fine & Rustomjee thesis' (2008:5).

10 Some critics of the model have neglected this *relational* aspect and focused on the literal weight of ostensible MEC sectors in the economy. Thus Bell and Farrell (1998), for instance, challenged the MEC model by claiming that the MEC's share of GDP peaked at 29% in the mid-1960s and declined to 24% in the early 1990s. Fine and Rustomjee (1998:692) replied that 'the MEC as a system of accumulation cannot be satisfactorily defined by the weight in the economy of a fixed set of sectors [...] What we would include within the MEC because of its close linkages with mining and energy, would be excluded by standard industrial classifications'.

11 For more, see Legassick and De Clerq (1978).

12 See *The Road of South African Freedom: Programme of the South African Communist Party* (adopted in 1962). The SACP's theory distinguishes between a 'White South Africa' with 'all the features of an advanced capitalist state in its final stage of imperialism' and a 'Non-white South Africa' with 'all the features of a colony': hence the notion of 'internal colonialism'. In the late 1990s, the ANC would use this dualistic framework as a basis for its notion that South Africa contained two distinct and structurally divorced economies (see Chapter five).

13 *Economic Planning Council Report* No 9, 1946, cited in Fine & Davis (1990:15). The intervention failed. Seven years later the Lansdown Commission would conclude that 'reserve production [is] but a myth' (cited in O'Meara, 1983:230).

14 In one of many incongruities, white workers combined this racist chauvinism with militant action, under the banner of socialism, against capital. In 1922, a miners' strike mushroomed

into the Rand Revolt—a bid to overthrow the state and replace it with a 'White Workers' Republic'.

15 The famous Bambata revolt of 1906 belonged to the pre-capitalist epoch. As noted, the 1922 white miners' strike ostensibly fitted the tradition of trade-union militancy but was geared mainly at shoring up racial privileges. By 1945, however, about 40% of African industrial workers were unionised, with some 119 trade unions fighting often-fierce wage struggles (Davies *et al*, 1985:12–16).

16 As argued, for instance, by Saul & Gelb (1981) and Davies *et al* (1985).

17 Botha Commission, cited in Fine & Davis (1990:11).

18 Marginalised, but not entirely forgotten. In fact, several of the apartheid regime's reforms in the late 1970s harked back to proposals that had been rejected in the 1940s.

19 The CPSA was formed in 1921 out of the International Socialist League, which had been founded in 1915, following a breakaway from the South African Labour Party.

20 From 1935, CPSA policy had vacillated, largely in response to directives from Moscow. Between 1936 and 1939, CPSA policy focused on mustering a popular front based of opposition to 'imperialism, fascism and war'. The 1939 Hitler-Stalin pact triggered an abrupt shift (following the Soviet Communist Party's decision to portray the Second World War as an 'imperialist war') towards advocating heightened class struggle. After that, the Nazi invasion of the USSR in 1941 led to another sharp turn, this time toward building a people's front. For more on these twists and turns see Fine & Davis (1990:36–57).

21 In addition, the African peasantry continued to resist the restructuring of the countryside, actions that were largely unconnected to the wellsprings of resistance politics in urban areas.

22 Cited in Fine & Davis (1990:47).

23 *Inkululeku*, 18 September 1943, cited in Fine & Davis (1990:95).

24 Cited in Fine and Davis (1990:74).

25 Dan O'Meara's 1983 book *Volkskapitalisme: Class, Capital and Ideology in the Development of Afrikaner Nationalism, 1934–1948* remains the benchmark study of Afrikaner nationalism's rise to power.

26 Its anti-capitalist, anti-monopoly and anti-imperialist postures, for instance, were designed to win over white farmers and workers and were abandoned soon after the election victory. Surprisingly, serious efforts to organise Afrikaner workers did not occur until the Second World War, when the *Arbeidsfront* (Labour Front) and *Blankewerkers se Beskermingsbond* (White Workers' Defence League) were formed in 1942 and 1943, respectively.

27 ANC intellectual Harold Wolpe would later critique the notion of a tight fit between apartheid and capitalism; the relationship, he argued, was 'historically contingent' and 'Janus-faced, being simultaneously functional and contradictory' (1988:8).

28 The work of the Marxist Nicos Poulantzas exerted a strong pull on the thinking of left intellectuals inside South Africa during the 1970s and 1980s, particularly his *State, Power, Socialism* (1978).

29 Recall that white South Africans lived in a (racially exclusive) parliamentary democracy and that political authority in that rarefied realm required the constant marshalling of consent. Failing that, a drastic reconfiguration of (white) political society would have ensued. Instead, the NP consolidated itself as an integral element of a reconstituted ruling bloc that would survive until the late 1970s. After its precarious 1948 victory, the NP expanded its base. It won subsequent elections by ever-widening margins, an unlikely feat had its exercise of state power proved dysfunctional to the needs of powerful sections of 'white' society.

30 The earliest influx control measures actually date back to 1760 and were applied against slaves in the Cape Colony (Davies *et al*, 1984:171). The pass laws were applied with astonishing zeal. In the 1940s, on average 158 000 black South Africans were convicted each year for contravening the pass laws. In the 1950s, that number doubled to 319 000— and it kept rising, to 469 000 in the 1960s and 542 000 in the first half of the 1970s (Wilson, 2001).

31 Davies *et al* (1985:23). Contrary to its title, the 1955 Regulation of Monopolistic Conditions Act did not curb monopolies.

32 This also served as a stimulus for housing, vehicle and other durable goods markets.

33 Bill Freund (2008) provides an incisive review of the MEC analysis and its links with other economic historiography. Surprisingly perhaps, he highlights Merle Lipton (1985) as an 'intellectual forerunner', thanks to her grasp of the important differences and tensions that existed between various sectors in the economy and their complicated relations with the state. More obscure—yet to the point—is his excavation of Nancy Clark's work (1994), in which she demonstrated 'how the interests of mining capital, the security needs of the state and a developing concept of the importance of industrialisation focused on heavy industry came together to mutual benefit, particularly in the pre-apartheid Smuts era' (Freund, 2008:8).

34 See Christie, R (1984) *Electricity, Industry and Class in South Africa*, Macmillan, London. Thanks to Bill Freund for again underlining the seminal importance of Christie's work.

35 For a critique of the thesis, see Bell & Farrell (1998), who seem to have misunderstood important aspects of it, as Fine & Rustomjee (1998) insisted in their response.

36 In 1954–55, Afrikaners owned about 1% of mining operations in South Africa. This increased to 10% in 1963–64 and 18% in 1975. In manufacturing, Afrikaner ownership increased from 6% to 10% to 15% over the same periods, while in finance it increased from 10% to 21% to 25%. See O'Meara (1996:139, Table 3).

37 This gradual process was also marked by some prominent catalysing collaborations, among them the co-operation between the apartheid state and (English) mining capital around infrastructure investment to develop the Orange Free State gold fields, as Mohamed (2009) reminds.

38 Fine & Rustomjee (1996) contend that the foundations of ISI were in place *before* the apartheid regime took power in 1948.

39 This is not to imply that South Africa could easily have aped South Korea, a country in which social polarisation was much less severe and which lay closer to expansive markets (see Chapter eleven).

40 Bureau of Economic Research, Organisation and Development report cited by Saul and Gelb (1981:52).

41 Such as the 1950 Witzieshoek rebellion, when at least 15 people were killed (including two policemen) and more than a hundred injured.

42 See Fine and Davis (1990:111) where they also accused the CPSA of being disingenuous: '[T]he Central Committee failed to mention that it was the Communist Party itself which for most of the 1940s had allied itself with the old guard of the ANC on a patriotic programme of constitutional reform and the curtailment of illegal forms of direct action, so that one function of the report was to displace all responsibility for this strategy from the shoulders of the Communist Party onto those of African nationalism.'

43 Nineteen workers died and twice as many were injured in the action.

44 See Everatt (2009) for a fascinating account of politics in and around the ANC and SACP during this period.

45 The Group Areas Act, the Suppression of Communism Act, the pass laws, the Voters' Representation Act, the Bantu Authorities Act and the Stock Limitation Policy.

46 See Lodge (1983:44). It was in response to the defeat of the campaign and growing state repression that Nelson Mandela devised the 'M-Plan', designed to enable the ANC to operate under conditions of illegality.

47 The overall number of participants was low, though—a mere 6 158 workers participated in the 113 strikes launched in 1957, for instance; see Fine and Davis (1990:159).

48 Part of the problem lay in the many divisions that fissured the working classes: racial, ideological and administrative (with or without legal recognition).

49 See Fine and Davis (1990:168–75) for a critical overview.

50 The NP won the election handsomely, while the opposition UP was virtually wiped out at the polls.

51 Stephen Ellis and the pseudonymous Tsepo Sechaba contended that 'the ANC's National Executive Committee in June 1961 debated the issue but took no position on it' (Ellis & Sechaba, 1992:32).

52 For the entire text, see Karis and Gerhardt (1977:716).

53 Govan Mbeki recalled that 'the most important books on guerrilla warfare that were available at the time in South Africa were the writings of Mao Tse-Tung on the Chinese experience and of Che Guevara on the Latin American experience [which] emphasised the importance of enlisting the support of the peasantry if a revolutionary war is to succeed' (1992:89).

54 See Wolpe (1980 & 1984).

55 Nelson Mandela, 1978, *The Struggle is My Life* speech at the Rivonia Trial, IDAF, London, p. 156.

56 It is worth noting that the state's crackdown, while severe, was not instantaneous: the new security legislation only took effect in 1963, although detention without trial had been introduced in 1961.

57 For a lucid overview, see Barrel (1991).

58 A great deal of the theoretical impetus towards armed struggle stemmed from the SACP's *Colonialism of a Special Type* thesis, according to Bundy: 'An analysis which viewed class as subordinate to the national question looked to guerrilla action not only for its military gains but also for its contribution towards politicising and mobilising the masses (1989:5).'

59 J Slovo, in Davidson *et al* (1977:186).

60 J Slovo in Davidson *et al* (1977:193).

61 Leading the force was Chris Hani, later secretary-general of the SACP. According to Ellis and Sechaba, 'the security forces noted with consternation that the guerrillas' performance and training was far superior to anything yet seen in Rhodesia' (1992:49).

62 In the Cape province, coloureds lost their qualified vote only in the 1950s, a move that sparked heated disputes even within Afrikaner ranks, where their mutual linguistic and cultural bonds were recognised and even celebrated. In South Africa's first democratic election in 1994, coloured voters would provide one-third of all votes cast for the NP.

63 Figures cited by Anthony Black, 'Manufacturing Development and the Economic Crisis' in Gelb (1991:157). Other, higher figures are also cited. Merle Holden, in Schrire (1992:315), pegged average growth for the same period at 7.4%. Some economists (Terence Moll among them) have argued that the 'golden' years of the apartheid era were little of the sort and that the economic growth rates of the 1960s were in step with international trends at the time (Moll, 1992). But that misses, as Bill Freund (2008:9) reminds, 'the one element where South African capitalists did succeed so well, that is to say, profits'.

64 See Freund, B (2008) *The significance of the Mineral-Energy Complex in the light of South African economic historiography*. Seminar paper, 28 August, University of KwaZulu-Natal, Durban.

65 This pattern persisted. In the mid-1980s, mining represented only 11% of GDP, but contributed 70% of foreign exchange earnings.

66 They would often point to the 1980–81 rise in economic growth rate as proof that the economy was undergoing short-term cyclical swings. That brief upswing, however, was sparked by a gold-price rise in response to the 1979 oil-price shock after the Iranian revolution (when gold topped USD 600 per fine ounce). By 1985, the gold price had almost halved (to USD 317) (Wilson, 2001).

67 This was more than an academic spat. Economists associated with the racial Fordism analysis would go on to shape post-apartheid economic policy, including a makeshift industrial strategy that would operate in the shadow of liberalised trade policies and relaxed capital controls. An especially keen supporter was the National Union of Metalworkers of South Africa's (NUMSA's) Alec Erwin, who became Ministry of Trade and Industry.

68 It was that sequencing that led Fine and Rustomjee (1996:14) to state that the ISI trajectory in the South African economy actually 'ran in the opposite direction' to the standard trajectory. In their view, 'import substitution had largely taken place before 1945' (1996:221), after which imports ran at about 40% of manufacturing output.

69 See, for example, Bell and Farrell (1998).

70 Hence Stephen Gelb's description 'racial Fordism'. In Western Europe, Fordism had rested on boosted mass consumption (through wage increases, greater social spending) and stabilised

labour relations (through corporatist arrangements). Similar measures were attempted in South Africa, but only within the white society.

71 The soaring oil price no doubt persuaded even doubters to back decisions to construct the Sasol II and III plants in 1974 and 1979, respectively.

72 In the 1980s, the Sanlam chair was chastising the regime for being too timid in its political reforms and urged acceptance of 'the inevitability of total racial equality' (O'Meara, 1996:308).

CHAPTER TWO

Saving the system

Gathering around the apartheid state were ranks of formidable challenges that spanned the political, economic and social dimensions. The state responded with a series of fitful adjustments in the social and economic spheres, but chose to defer decisive political change far into the future.

Deep contradictions had emerged in an accumulation strategy that depended on cheap, expendable African labour. The vast majority of the population remained banished to the political margins and material penury, which generated many forms of resistance, ranging from low productivity and absenteeism to outright rebellion that rejected the legitimacy and potentially threatened the authority of the state. A multidimensional crisis was developing. It did not (yet) augur the collapse of the system, but it stoked tensions in the ruling bloc, rendering it less coherent and presenting anti-apartheid forces with new possibilities for advance. Indeed, Harry Oppenheimer, chair of the country's largest corporation, Anglo American, had observed in 1971 that

> *we are approaching the stage where the full potential of the economy, as it is at present organised, will have been realised, so that if structural changes are not made, we will have to content ourselves with a much lower rate of growth [...] Prospects for economic growth will not be attained so long as a large majority of the population is prevented by lack of education and technical training or by positive prohibition from playing the full part of which it is capable in the national development* (cited in Gelb, 1991:19–20).

A new wave of resistance

In 1972 the first signs emerged that a crucial pillar of the post-war development path was disintegrating. The disciplinary regime in the workplace, combined with the coercive regulation imposed by the pass-law system, had helped maintain a stable, low-wage labour force. African workers were prevented from organising independently.[1] But in late 1971, industrial workers again began challenging the labour-relations system. In October, 4 000 dockworkers in Durban and Cape Town went on strike for higher wages. The militancy spread to textile factories and transport companies. Soon workers were striking in other industrial areas, including East London and Johannesburg.

Low wages and rising prices of basic consumer items provided the initial trigger for the strikes, but workers' demands grew to include the legal right to organise. A clutch of new black unions was formed and training and other support structures were created. Some of the organisers included former SACTU and ANC activists who had been in hiatus for most of the 1960s, but many also came from a new generation of radical white and Indian students and intellectuals. Mindful of SACTU's experience of state repression, most of the new unions eschewed the 'political unionism' approach and concentrated on shop-floor issues.

The strike wave peaked in 1973–74, although strike actions continued until 1976.[2] In most cases management, supported by the police, reacted with fearsome force. Many of the workers' demands went unmet and membership of the new unions fell quickly. Organisers turned to the painstaking process of building worker organisations sturdy enough to weather setbacks and defeats. Crucially, though, working-class resistance had re-emerged in its own right more than two decades after the defeats of the late 1940s and the subsequent rise of African nationalism. The strike wave announced the end of apartheid's 'golden age': for the first time in almost 25 years, a class struggle was re-emerging in ways that could unsettle the rhythms of capital accumulation. Soon the Soweto uprising would rock the country. Unexpectedly, and within a few years, the entire system was tumbled into damage-control mode. The odds were still stacked dramatically in its favour, but the easy ride of the 1960s was over.

Four developments drove the resurgence of popular resistance in the 1970s. The first related directly to the economy. Unemployment kept growing and inflation was rising, imposing severe hardships even on employed African workers, who reacted with militancy last seen in the 1950s. The second development was the advance of national liberation struggles in southern Africa, with both Mozambique and Angola winning independence from Portugal in 1975. Those triumphs reverberated in South Africa, and compounded a deepening sense of siege among whites, while immeasurably boosting the resolve of black South Africans. Logistically, the makeshift armed struggle also benefited as the infiltration of guerrillas and the exodus of new recruits into exile became easier and communication channels could be revived with underground cells operating inside South Africa. For the first time since its banning, the ANC was able to narrow somewhat the distance between itself and the realities unfolding inside South Africa.

Thirdly, drawing on the writings of African radicals and American black nationalists, an ideological rejuvenation occurred in the form of Black Consciousness. A new emphasis on self-reliance and non-violent militancy emerged from the Black Consciousness Movement's propagation of 'psychologism' (the conviction that the key to black liberation lay in psychological liberation). This would be expressed explosively in 1976, when the Soweto uprising erupted, as school students protested a foolhardy decree that half the subjects in African schools be taught in the *Afrikaans* language.[3]

Black Consciousness was perhaps the last independent ideological current to filter into the discourse of the national liberation movement. By the late 1970s, though, state crackdowns had deprived the Black Consciousness Movement of its leadership (through murder, as in the case of Steve Biko, or imprisonment). Thousands of younger adherents fled the country, determined to return with guns in hand. In exile, however, they discovered they could survive only by joining either the ANC or the PAC—and were thus absorbed into the mainstream liberation traditions.[4] Black Consciousness turned out to be a godsend for the ANC, which drew into its ranks a new generation of committed and astute young activists.

The fourth development was the growing tendency within the broad opposition to attribute all forms of deprivation, oppression and discrimination to the apartheid system, thereby enabling a heightened and more widespread politicisation of the oppressed. A fresh resolve became evident in popular organisations, which multiplied in numbers, drawing ever-younger activists into resistance activities. The desolate 1960s were over. From now on, the state and capital would have to contend with successive waves of resistance as they sought answers to frailties that had emerged underfoot.

The party's over

In the economic sphere, the apartheid growth model was decaying. In the political, ideological and social spheres, the 'conditions which had sustained a form of capital accumulation based predominantly on cheap, unskilled black (African) labour' was beginning to undermine that accumulation strategy (Davies *et al*, 1985:37). Citing the Italian Marxist, Antonio Gramsci, Saul and Gelb (1981:3), in an influential intervention, declared the crisis to be 'organic':

> *A crisis occurs, sometimes lasting for decades. This exceptional duration means that incurable structural contradictions have revealed themselves [...] and that, despite this, the political forces which are struggling to conserve and defend the existing structure itself are making efforts to cure them within certain limits, and to overcome them. These incessant and persistent efforts [...] form the terrain of the conjunctural and it is upon this terrain that the forces of opposition organise* (1971:178).

The authors tried to avoid a shallow distinction between 'reform' and 'revolution', reminding that 'while "reform" is not genuine transformation [...] it is not meaningless or irrelevant either, for it can affect the shape of the field of battle' (Saul & Gelb, 1981). Discourse within the resistance movement, however, was orbiting around a schema that rigidly contrasted reform and revolution. Centred on the dictum that 'apartheid cannot be reformed', reforms were disparaged as attempts to undermine the revolutionary momentum. This posture was closely related to the paradigm shifts that accompanied the turn to armed struggle and was later reinforced by the victories of armed liberation movements in Angola and Mozambique. Gramsci's counsel that 'wars of position' had to supplant militaristic 'wars of manoeuvre' scarcely featured in the ANC and SACP's strategic debates, although it earned greater favour among intellectuals linked to the new trade unions. The exiled organisations' strategies were geared towards mobilising resistance forces for an outright conflict aimed at a cataclysmic outcome: the overthrow of the apartheid state. As well as imposing strategic limitations, this thinking would consolidate within the liberation movement a culture based on a mix of coercion and loyalty, a matter explored in more detail below. Generalising, Mike Morris would later characterise the approach as follows:

Radical participation in state structures to take advantage of spaces and gaps created by the regime, to create cracks and exacerbate crises, is mostly dismissed as collaborationist, granting legitimacy, confusing the masses, and reactionary. Often those advocating such courses are regarded as more dangerous than the regime. The discourse of opposition becomes concerned with a fear of cooptation, preservation of the real principles of the struggle, and the correct strategies to create islands of alternative power to that of the regime (1993a:99).

From the mid-1970s onwards, the ruling bloc's efforts to establish a new configuration of social, economic and political relations would open numerous spaces and opportunities through processes of 'reform from above'. With the eventual (though partial) exception of the trade-union movement, popular forces would not take an effective hand in shaping these reforms.

There was no pristine strategy guiding the state reforms, but nor were they the mere products of panic (even though they became increasingly improvised). The complex of difficulties arising in the 1970s had amplified tensions within, as well as between, the state and capital. Simultaneously, popular organisations exerted fresh pressures, while changes in the regional and international contexts also influenced the search for solutions. Each set of reforms was shaped as much by 'objective need' as by a shifting balance of forces within and between the state, capital and popular forces.

Resolving the accumulating difficulties required innovations on two fronts. The political and ideological basis for apartheid rule had to be adjusted and 'modernised'. And the post-war accumulation strategy had to be restructured (Morris & Padayachee, 1989). The latter required adjustments not only in economic policies but also in the extra-economic underpinnings of that strategy: social relations, state structures, political formations and the circuits of interaction between the state, capital and civil society.

From the mid-1970s onwards, an array of reform initiatives touched on some of those elements, sometimes sparking and sometimes retreating before revived bouts of resistance. At their most basic level, they were aimed at shoring up the two fundamental foundations of state power in capitalist society—coercion and consent—and at reshaping the spheres of production, distribution and consumption in order to resuscitate faltering economic growth. As summarised by Stadler (1987:160), this involved attempts 'to remodel political institutions, increase economic and educational opportunities for blacks, and institutionalise relations between capital and labour, in order to generate some legitimacy for the social order'.

The reforms crystallised out of intense differences and debate within and between the state and capital about appropriate courses of action. Intensifying popular pressures and shifting political relations would shape their content and implementation. Hindsight allows us to compartmentalise these reforms into three phases (Morris & Padayachee, 1989), without suggesting they were conceived or pursued with such coherence (O'Meara, 1996).

Recasting the divide

First came bids to restructure two important aspects of the social relations underpinning the accumulation strategy: the labour regime and urbanisation policy. The political crisis continued to be couched as a *security* problem. The response involved the large-scale militarisation of white society, closer co-operation between the state and capital, and new initiatives geared at taking 'into account the aspirations of our different population groups' in order to 'gain and keep their trust'.[5]

The apartheid regime appointed the Riekert Commission to explore changes to urbanisation policy and the Wiehahn Commission to propose changes in industrial relations that could answer corporate capital's demands for a larger, more stable supply of African semi-skilled and skilled labour. Nervous about the regime's flustered reaction to the Soweto uprising, corporate capital meanwhile had created its own urban policy research body, the Urban Foundation. Set up in 1977 and funded mainly by the Anglo American Corporation and the Rembrandt Group, it focused on urbanisation strategies and housing policies. The underlying aim of all these ventures was to 'ensure that as many people as possible share in prosperity and find their interests best served by an alliance with capitalism'[6]—they had to pre-empt attempts to overthrow the system.

The 1979 Riekert Report proposed that Africans be divided into two categories: 'qualified' urban dwellers and the 'disqualified' rest, who would be confined to the homelands. The division of South Africa between capitalist and pre-capitalist sectors persisted, but with a small layer of urban Africans admitted into the enclave of 'insiders'. In Saul and Gelb's view the effect was 'to tighten, not relax, the mechanisms of influx control' (1981:49). After forcefully compressing classes within African townships, the apartheid state was now relaxing some of that pressure. Industry, it was hoped, would gain access to a more settled and skilled African labour force and a layer of comparatively privileged urban Africans would emerge to douse the ardour of the masses, as an article in the *Financial Mail* made clear:

> [T]he small group of privileged urban blacks whose quality of life will undoubtedly improve may well become less urgent in their demands for political power and serve as the lid on the kettle of revolution for some years to come.[7]

This notion of a buffer of African moderates was evident in the Commission's proposal that control and revenue generation in townships be decentralised. Local township councils would be elected and tasked with duties hitherto performed by white apartheid officials. A kind of privatisation within an authoritarian framework was attempted, with the central state appearing to retreat from the day-to-day management of Africans' lived realities.[8] In part this was aimed at defusing township discontent. But the attempts to 'depoliticise collective consumption in the townships produced its direct opposite—the massive politicisation of struggles', as Morris observed (1991:46). Residents rebelled against huge increases in rent and service fees, and targeted the new councils as 'puppets of apartheid'. But other changes were also set in motion. Competition for jobs and resources intensified between settled or permanent African workers and their migrant counterparts.

This would fuel animosities and lead to open, violent conflict in the years ahead, as well as provide bridgeheads for the Zulu Inkatha movement in the industrial heartland around Johannesburg.[9]

The Wiehahn Commission, meanwhile, was tasked with restructuring labour relations along two broad lines. It had to revise the disciplinary regime imposed on black workers and design measures to increase the productivity and spending power of a better-trained, skilled African urban work-force. The Commission was explicit about its aims: 'The unions' potential strength meant that they must be controlled—their present weakness—meant that this should be done soon'.[10] It warned that reliance on outright repression 'would undoubtedly have the effect of driving black trade unionism underground and uniting black workers—against the system of free enterprise' (Saul & Gelb; 1981:72). Repression was to be replaced with mechanisms that could lock black trade unions into the disciplinary workings of the labour-relations system. This bid yielded the 1981 Labour Relations Amendment Act—a fateful development. The Act granted black trade unions the right to register and negotiate, as well as participate in the Industrial Council system, a mediating apparatus designed to deflect worker issues from the shop-floor into a highly legalistic and bureaucratic process. Statutory job reservation for whites was abolished. A select layer of urban workers would benefit, as Morris and Padayachee (1989:74) recognised:

> The purpose of this new 'reform policy' was to ensure maximum division and differentiation of the popular classes: divide the black petty bourgeoisie from the working class by satisfying some of the former's socio-economic aspirations; pacify the working class by granting trade union reform; divide the general black population by driving a wedge between 'insiders' (with access to urban residential rights) and 'outsiders' (with no urban residential right).

Unions were divided over whether to participate in the new system. Some worried that registration subjected them to a debilitating set of controls, while others argued that registration offered opportunities that could be creatively exploited. Contentiously, the Federation of South African Trade Unions (FOSATU) opted for participation if non-racial unions were allowed to register. FOSATU was controversial in other respects, too: it departed from the tradition of 'political unionism', which SACTU had spearheaded in the 1950s, by deciding to not prioritise community and political issues that did not bear directly on workers.

Seizing opportunities

The reforms played out in the context of a global economic recession. In South Africa, economic policy took a sharp turn to the right in the late 1970s, leading to a host of neoliberal adjustments (exchange controls for non-residents were lifted, key surcharges were dropped and monetary policy was tightened). As a result, 'the liberalisation of South Africa's economic links allowed for the easy transmission of the worsening international economic situation into [the] South African economy' (Morris & Padayachee, 1989:76). This led to rising inflation, more job losses and the removal of state subsidies on basic consumer items. Black workers responded by seizing the new spaces in the restructured labour-relations system; they rebuilt their organisations and launched a fresh wave of strikes. In the process, the unions also became vehicles for political protest.

The central state's attempts to reduce its fiscal burden by offloading the provision of township services also failed. In order to fulfil their financing and regulatory role, the new township councils were forced to pass on the costs to residents (higher rents, rates and service charges), sparking convulsive protests. Instead of consolidating control over African urban workers, the reforms became the basis for renewed protests. The 'beneficiaries' pushed the reforms far beyond the limits imposed by the state. Something of a 'war of position' seemed to be unfolding.

Several other developments meanwhile had ignited fresh tensions in the ruling NP and undermined the quest for stronger strategic coherence in the ruling bloc. These included the upsurge in organised resistance, a large outflow of capital and the onset of a recession. Intense power struggles erupted in the NP (O'Meara, 1996). A band of reformist challengers (grouped around Defence Minister P W Botha) eventually won out. 'Modernising' sections of Afrikaner capital became dominant in the party, confirming a dramatic shift in the class alliance on which the NP had been built. The traditional core of the NP (white workers, Afrikaner middle classes and small farmers) was marginalised and broke ranks to form the far-right Conservative Party.[11] Both the ideology and class basis of Afrikaner nationalism were being transformed, a shift that laid a basis for more far-reaching adjustments.

'Total strategy'

The next phase of reforms was both bolder and more haphazard. The NP had shed its most extremist constituencies, black worker organisations were growing in scope and sophistication, organised community protests were reviving and international hostility was reaching a pitch. The apartheid state was, to a significant extent, caught in the slipstream of dynamic developments beyond its control. The interplay between burgeoning popular demands and the reactions of the state and its corporate allies fuelled other social dynamics. Class differentiation in African townships was sharpening. Worker struggles had won increased social benefits, covert entrepreneurship (including organised crime) had increased, informal trading boomed and the influx of vulnerable homeland refugees became a source of accumulation for shack lords and homeowners (who rented or sold living spaces and other services to the newcomers).

The reforms were a hodgepodge of tactical adjustments. The state was becoming increasingly perturbed and incoherent in its actions as different government departments vied to shape and control reforms. The tensions were both ideological and pragmatic: as resistance intensified security departments demanded (and won) greater authority and access to resources. The usual bureaucratic procedures were often bypassed and rule books seemed to count for little. In addition, the 'political distance' between the state and capital undermined the achievement of a strategic programme of change, despite efforts in the 1970s to involve business organisations in consultative committees. Capital customarily engaged the state not through corporatist channels but in fragmented, often informal ways. Afrikaner capitalists, for example, found that social networking with government planners and ministers paid handsome dividends. Different business organisations often represented the same industries, adding to the confusion. The various corporate sectors also desired different types of policy adjustments.

Perhaps most importantly, the state's reforms ran up against the political limits of the apartheid paradigm. As long as the state tried to 'solve' the national question by trying to retain the literal division of South Africa along racial and ethnic lines, its reforms would suffer built-in obsolescence, as the anti-apartheid opposition capitalised on the failure to address the central political crisis.

Despite these constraints, the reforms ventured much further than the earlier adjustments. Most dramatic was the official end to influx control in 1986. Pass laws were abolished, allowing Africans to enter and work in urban areas without state permission. This was a major shift: it announced nothing less than the acceptance of the 'interdependent and interconnected nature of the South African political economy', as Mike Morris noted (1991:51). Labour would henceforth be reproduced 'wholly within the confines of capitalist society' through a revised process of regulated urbanisation (Morris & Padayachee, 1989:80), with access to housing the main rationing device. Other initiatives were geared towards redistributing resources and accelerating class differentiation among urban Africans (particularly the 99-year leasehold of homes offered to some residents). These schemes were not plucked from thin air. The Urban Foundation's thinking exerted a strong pull on government housing and urbanisation policies:[12]

> [O]nly by having this most responsible section of the urban black population on our side can the whites of South Africa be assured of containing on a long term basis the irresponsible economic and political ambitions of those blacks who are influenced against their own real interests from within and without our borders.[13]

The state channelled more resources into black education and supported improvements in township infrastructure (such as electrification schemes in Soweto). The upgrading was selective and targeted those townships deemed to pose potential security problems—so-called 'oil spot' development. The intention was to undermine political mobilisation by removing some material sources of discontent. Again, one of the consequences was to redefine and deepen the divisions between 'insiders' and 'outsiders', which would explode tumultuously in ways the main anti-apartheid forces failed to anticipate.[14]

All this occurred in the context of worsening economic troubles. After a brief economic upswing in 1980–81, the imports bill ballooned. Then the gold price fell steeply. The result was a balance-of-payments crisis. In 1982, the apartheid regime sought an IMF standby loan.[15] The conditions demanded stern adjustments, at punishing cost to black workers. Subsidies on essential consumer items were withdrawn and sales tax was raised (pushing the inflation rate to almost 17% in

1985), while rents, rates and service payments were hiked in black townships.[16] Job losses increased. In the metal industry alone, 84 000 jobs were cut between 1982 and 1984. In agriculture, rising production costs and a sustained drought led to massive retrenchments, which accelerated the influx of African workers into cities and towns. Shortly afterwards, exchange controls were lifted for non-residents, triggering a large outflow of capital. Fiscal spending soared and the budget deficit increased as the state sought to meet its external 'defence' and internal 'law and order' needs, finance the homeland system and bankroll its reform initiatives.

As the recession deepened, the state was forced to scale back its fiscal commitments. At the same time, attempts to integrate new sections of the African urban population into 'modern South Africa' added new spending burdens. One way around this was to opt for private-public partnerships and to delegate housing provision in townships to private developers. This deepened class differentiation in townships. Meanwhile, the transport system was deregulated (creating space for the emergence of communal taxi entrepreneurs) and informal trading was legalised. Towards the end of the 1980s, the state also privatised several state assets. Fitfully, and under severe duress, it was trying to 'modernise' its rule and align itself to the emerging neoliberal global order.

Aspects of social life were deracialised. Non-racial trade unions were allowed to register, which opened space for the emergence of the trade union federation COSATU (Congress of South African Trade Unions) in 1985. 'Petty apartheid' measures were dropped, although the class undertones of this relaxation were obvious since access to deracialised consumptive and recreational activities would now be determined by income. Laws prohibiting interracial sexual intercourse and marriage were also abolished. The most telling effect of these reforms lay in their ideological impact: the relaxation of apartheid clashed with the stern dogmatism of the apartheid project and further alienated the former hardcore social base of the NP. The far right had become a headache, but it carried no weight inside the NP or government. Ranged alongside this, however, were other attempts to *re-racialise* political life, including the creation of a 'tricameral' parliament (with racially exclusive white, coloured and Indian chambers) and racially segregated government departments. The latter ploys involved extending limited voting rights to coloureds and Indians, who could cast ballots in racial elections for their 'own' representatives. The state was still unable to address—even nominally—the national question by, for instance, incorporating Africans into such a manoeuvre. Thus, the long-mooted 'fourth' (African) chamber in parliament never materialised. Once again, limited liberalisation became the basis for a new wave of protest.

Old popular organisations were revived, new ones were built and fresh alliances were struck around an increasingly implacable opposition against the apartheid system. This intersectoral, cross-class mobilisation converged on the United Democratic Front (UDF), which was set up in 1983. Its first major campaign targeted the tricameral system.

As resistance activities multiplied, reforms became more inchoate. Partial relaxations in the political and ideological spheres were reversed in 1986, as protests and resistance reached fever pitch and the government imposed a state of emergency. But this did not signal a sheer regression back to the 'old days'. The 'democratising' reforms were withdrawn and a series of repressive measures were introduced to restore the stability required for the other, redistributive reforms to proceed. Indeed, 'the slogan of the early 1980s—"there can be no security without reform"— [was] turned on its head', as Swilling and Phillips noted (1989b:147). The state stayed its course in other respects, particularly the restructured urbanisation process and the selective redistribution of resources. It had crossed at least a tributary of the proverbial Rubicon. Behind the scenes, it had opened channels for political talks with the main liberation movement.

Panic attack: from resistance to 'revolution'

The first two phases of reforms coincided with the emergence of widespread organising and mobilising of black workers after 1979. The revival of union organising was of a scale that exceeded all previous recoveries and marked a dramatic advance for the black working classes. Among several factors fuelling the resurgence, three stood out: the manufacturing sector had become dominated by black workers (many of them occupying skilled and semi-skilled jobs); the effects of the economic recession were disproportionately deflected onto black workers; and the legalisation of black trade unions opened up new organising opportunities.

Black trade unions boasted 1.4 million members in 1984 (SAIRR, 1985). Rather than embark on 'do-or-die' actions, most of the new unions focused on the painstaking process of building their organisations and seeking recognition from employers. But militancy also saw strikes multiply from 101 in 1979 to 342 in 1981. Civic and other popular groupings often drew their leadership from union ranks, a trend that introduced a greater degree of leadership accountability, democratic participation and organisational solidity.

Two distinct patterns were discernible in the union revival. The 12 unions that had formed FOSATU in 1979 were reluctant to become embroiled in wider political struggles. Their focus was on 'strong factory organisation as the expression of a truly independent working-class consciousness' (Lodge & Nasson, 1991:28). Contesting that approach was a variety of 'community unions', which deemed 'it impossible to separate workers' factory demands from their township problems' and which openly identified with the liberation movement. In essence, this was a continuation of the 'political unionism' practised in the 1950s by the ANC's union wing, SACTU (Baskin, 1991; Lodge & Nasson, 1991).[17] Inscribed into the revitalised workers' struggles of the 1980s, therefore, was the enduring tension between nationalist and class consciousness. This sparked fervent conflict between so-called 'workerists' and 'populists'.

'Workerists' and 'populists'

'Workerists' concentrated on building robust shop-floor organisations. They were accused of neglecting the broader struggle against apartheid (Friedman, 1987a), treating 'other issues beyond the point of production [...] as secondary matters' and downplaying 'the very important struggle for state power'.[18] Consequently, 'attempts to revive socialism in the South African struggle', as Dave Lewis (1986) pointed out, were equated with 'a narrow workerism'. Grouped largely in and around the UDF, the 'populists' insisted on 'uniting the spheres of "economic" struggle with the "political" struggle, in a common assault on the apartheid system' (Pillay, 2008:8). They, in turn, were accused of playing down the class dynamics of oppression and even of 'hijacking' working-class struggles.[19] These were caricatures, but they acquired currency on the factory floors and streets of South Africa. The tensions would persist after the 1985 formation of COSATU, which sought to draw together these two currents of trade-union activity. The Charterist[20] tradition's emphasis on national oppression would win the day.

Devan Pillay's (2008:8–12) handy dissection of the 'workerist' tradition distinguishes between four currents. The 'economistic' current focused on workplace issues and expressed what Lenin had termed 'trade union consciousness'. Its radicalism tended to be shallow and often yielded to 'sweetheart' relations with employers. The 'syndicalist' current encouraged participation in political struggle, but insisted that this should involve the democratic processes honed on the shop floor. The upshot was that participation in community struggles was often spotty and weak. The third current harboured larger political ambitions and favoured the creation of a union-based political formation with a socialist programme to rival the Charterist movement dominated by the ANC (externally) and UDF (internally). A fourth, 'independent socialist' current recognised the importance of the national liberation movement, but sought to maintain the independence of working-class organisations and held out the possibility of forming an alternative workers' party.[21] The latter probably came closest to articulating race and class into a potentially radical political project. But each of these currents ran up against the same reality: the fact that nationalist consciousness struck stronger chords than class consciousness among workers. 'Capitalism,' Pillay (2008:10) later reflected, 'may have been the primary contradiction, but racism was the dominant contradiction.'

Various understandings of the interplay of race and class did the rounds in the national liberation tradition. One saw apartheid and capitalism as inextricably enmeshed; the struggle against the one automatically also targeted the other. Until well into the 1980s, this was the dominant position in the ANC and SACP. A more sophisticated view recognised that capitalism could be delinked from apartheid (Wolpe, 1988). Working-class formations needed to operate as part of a broad alliance against apartheid, but had to retain their independence. A tenable and effective articulation of nationalist and socialist struggles would prove elusive—even if the SACP's 'two stage theory' provided the illusion of reconciling these different conceptions within the Charterist tradition.

'Everything is political'

Intensifying material hardships were an important spur for the surge in resistance activities. Thousands of local township organisations and civic groupings were formed. While their organisational forms differed, they all focused on so-called 'bread and butter issues', such as housing, services, transportation, rents and township infrastructure. Increasingly, though, their struggles would become couched in political terms. A ferment of more overt political activism was underway. The women's movement was revived, black professionals joined in progressive groupings, while activist religious organisations were formed or revived (including the talismanic Young Christian Students). National schools and campus boycotts underlined the generational tensions between youth and parents that had exploded to prominence with the Soweto uprising. Student organisations tried to close that gap through greater involvement in other community issues, but the schisms persisted. As Tom Lodge noted, the members of the youth congresses and other bodies that sprang up

> were the children of the strongest and most sophisticated urban working class in Africa. Their instincts were shaped by a community that had undergone one of the most rapid industrial revolutions in recent history. A large proportion of them were considerably better educated than their elders. Of all generations, the 'children of Soweto' were the least inclined to accept the limits and restrictions of the apartheid system (Lodge & Nasson, 1991:38).

It was this multiplicity of organisations that the UDF sought to unite. Launched in August 1983, it targeted the elections for new black local authorities and the introduction of a tricameral parliament intended to draw coloureds and Indians into the political system. Misnamed, the UDF was in fact a broad popular front boasting 565 affiliates when it was officially launched. Its links with the workers' movement were weak: trade unions comprised only 18 of its affiliates in 1984. Youth, student and civic organisations were preponderant; among them the symbols, traditions and rhetoric of the ANC proved especially resonant. The UDF successfully projected itself as the standard bearer of the nationalist movement, but it struggled to become an organised national movement. Its influence was spread unevenly across the country and was formidable in the eastern parts of the Cape and parts of the Transvaal but relatively weak in Natal and western parts of the Cape (Seekings, 2000). Depending on the township, its affiliates were either a handful of activists or well-organised, 'representative' grassroots groups (Friedman, 1987).

Lodge and Nasson (1991) divided the UDF's development into five phases. The first lasted until mid-1984 and was marked by blustering national campaigning akin to the ANC's populist campaigns of the 1950s 'in which large and excited gatherings, powerful oratory and strong, attractive leaders substituted for systematically structured organisations, carefully elaborated ideologies and well-coordinated programs' (1991:62–3). A dramatic shift then occurred. After the Vaal uprising of September 1984, the UDF lost the initiative to militant, local resistance activities dominated by township youth and schoolchildren. In a bid to catch up with local dynamics, it adopted a controversial line that held grave implications for the democratic movement: it endorsed the ANC's January 1985 call for South Africa to be 'rendered ungovernable' and was caught up in the insurrectionary reveries that swept through the movement. By the UDF's own account, it was forced to react to the 'spontaneity of actions in the townships' and was 'trail[ing] behind the masses, thus making it more difficult for a disciplined mass action to take place'.[22]

The declaration of a state of emergency in July 1985 led to further shifts as the UDF reacted, often creatively, to fierce state repression. But it had lost the strategic initiative. The second state of emergency in 1986 proved withering and pushed the UDF into retreat. Resistance activities became much less coherent and disciplined, culminating in the UDF being banned in early 1988. Later that year, the internal anti-apartheid forces regrouped as the Mass Democratic Movement (MDM), led by church and union figures and launched a campaign of mass disobedience.

The UDF resembled the kind of broad popular front outlined by the ANC's Politico-Military Strategy Commission in 1979, a front that 'should express the broadest possible working together of all organisations, groups and individuals genuinely opposed to racist autocracy' (Barrel, 1991:85–6). The Commission had been set up as part of the ANC's 1978–79 strategic review conference where unusually strong criticism of the ANC's performance was vented. Its report accused the organisation of having 'for too long acted as if the repressive conditions made mass legal and semi-legal work impossible', and warned that its 'efforts would reach a dead-end unless they had a broader political base'.[23] Some of the campaigns of the early 1980s took after recommendations by the Commission. The Freedom Charter was to be reinserted into resistance discourse (utilising its thirtieth anniversary). Significantly, the Commission urged campaigns against township authorities aimed at their 'permanent destruction' in order to thwart 'their effective functioning and [reduce] the capacity of the enemy to govern our people' (Barrel, 1991:88). Political and military struggle became hitched together in a perspective which held that:

> *Preparation for the people's armed struggle and its victorious conclusion is not solely a military question. This means that the armed struggle must be based on, and grow out of, mass political support and it must eventually involve our whole people. All military activities must, at every stage, be guided and determined by the need to generate political mobilisation, organisation and resistance, with the aim of progressively weakening the grip on the reins of political, economic, social and military action.*[24]

It was a tactical shift. Political mobilisation and organisation were to be elements of an overall strategy that still pivoted on an armed seizure of power, as Howard Barrel noted:

> *The perspective developed by the 1978–79 strategic review still turned on the popular armed struggle for the seizure of state power [...] The strategic vision remained one in which political organisation was ultimately seen as subject to military imperatives* (1991:89).

In the early 1980s, the still-exiled ANC had moved to occupy the symbolic centre of resistance and narrow the distance between itself and the militancy inside South Africa. Covertly, it set up activist cells and underground networks. Its statements and propaganda, issued from Lusaka, reached local activists and came to function as increasingly authoritative reference points. ANC figures such as Govan Mbeki contended that the internal organisations 'were not random developments but the result of a deliberate strategy to form all kinds of mass-based organisations', claiming further that 'there is no doubt that a majority of them were led by people who belonged to the ANC underground or were sympathetic to the ANC' (1996:46). But political affinities did not mean the ANC furnished the organisational impetus of those structures, nor did it warrant the claim that the organisations arose as internal expressions of ANC strategy (Barrel, 1991:91). A much more complex process had occurred. The flowering of organisations inside South Africa and the radicalising impact of the influx of Soweto uprising activists into the ANC had confirmed to the organisation's leaders not only the need but also revealed the conditions for reasserting its hegemony over internal resistance activities.

The formation of the UDF had occurred largely on the basis of internal dynamics that were organisationally independent of the ANC. The ANC was not able to direct resistance tactics. But its growing authority at the ideological and symbolic levels did enable it to strongly influence the overall terms in which resistance actions were couched—hence the formidable resonance of its calls for 'ungovernability' and a 'people's war'. By the late 1980s, the ANC was clearly the main political beneficiary of the UDF's campaigns. They were not unmitigated gains. In some cases, activists used the symbols and rhetoric of the ANC to discourage or prevent independent organising initiatives and suppress ideological heterogeneity, prompting Steven Friedman to observe that 'the symbolic strength of the exile movement has often weakened attempts to build grassroots power within the country' (1991:61). The ANC's ideological predominance among the internal anti-apartheid movement seemed increasingly indisputable.

The state shifts course

In 1987, the state changed tack in a bid to restore stability. The overall thrust of the reform process would be maintained, but within the framework of the National Security Management System (NSMS). The NSMS had been set up in 1979, as part of the 'total strategy', but in the early 1980s NSMS officials were doing little more than 'keeping the seats warm' (Swilling & Phillips, 1989a:76). As resistance intensified, it was fully activated and became 'a parallel system of state power' that vested massive repressive and administrative powers in the hands of the military and police. The NSMS spanned a national network of several hundred committees, each of which comprised local security officials, administrators and business people—forming a 'shadow bureaucracy running alongside the official government bureaucracy' (Morris & Padayachee, 1989:88). These committees monitored and recommended appropriate actions in 'trouble spots'. Implementation agencies were then dispatched to perform the upgrading of services and infrastructure, bypassing the sluggish procedures of the state bureaucracy.

The full-scale activation of the NSMS shifted the balance of forces within the state. Already, the president had acquired executive powers; now even more power was concentrated in his domain, and in that of the security forces (especially its intelligence arms) and the Law and Order Ministry. Some analysts likened these developments to a 'palace coup' that transferred power to the security establishment. In fact, the NSMS functioned parallel to the political apparatus. But it did gain 'golden boy' stature. The commandist apparatus of the NSMS now directed the selective upgrading to ensure speedy and efficient 'delivery'. Thirty-four of the most volatile townships (the so-called 'oil-spots') were targeted for rapid improvement, while a further 1 800 urban renewal projects were launched in 200 other townships (Swilling & Phillips, 1989a). The thinking was that

> [t]he lack of a classroom is not a security matter, but a lack of proper facil-
> ities or sufficient facilities can become a security problem [...] Nobody can tell a
> (government) department they must build a new school. But from the security point
> of view you can tell them that if they don't there is going to be a problem. It is now
> your problem to build the school; if you don't it will become my problem and the
> [security] system's problem. And prevention is better than cure.[25]

This was the most sophisticated attempt yet to combine reforms and repression in ways that might alter the balance of forces. But still eluding the state was a strategy for capitalising on the temporary containment of resistance. Feelers were being delicately extended toward the ANC, but to unclear ends.

Costs of insurrectionism

Two signal developments had left their mark on the democratic movement, each highlighting the other: the ANC's success at achieving hegemony (though not organisational control) within the movement and its push for a 'people's war'. An all-or-nothing paradigm prevailed in resistance discourse, which increasingly looked to a headlong onslaught against the apartheid state.

Between 1981 and 1985 debates had raged in the SACP's *African Communist* journal between activists advocating the 'arming of the people'[26] and critics who argued against 'too narrow and military-technical a view of arming the people' (Trevor, 1984). Officially, the SACP and ANC leaderships had misgivings about the insurrectionist strategies. Soon, this changed. At the ANC's Kabwe Consultative Conference in 1985, the national executive spoke of preparing for a 'people's war'. In July 1986, the SACP's Joe Slovo came out supporting the insurrectionist line.[27] Soon, Mzala (1987), one of the chief theorists in the ANC, was writing confidently that an insurrection was on the cards. A year later, SACP analyst Harold Wolpe declared that 'the mass insurrectionary political movement is the principal agent of the struggle for national liberation'.[28]

The insurrectionary approach presumed that a revolutionary situation was developing, but this was a corrupt reading of reality. No doubt, the political and ideological dominance of the ruling bloc was at its lowest ebb and it faced unprecedented opposition. But its complete collapse was not on the cards. Severe tensions had surfaced, as shown by the 1982 split in the NP, struggles between state departments (especially after the activation of the NSMS) and the defection of some ruling-class intellectuals. But other developments mitigated them—notably the centralisation of power in the NP and government and the success of the latter in marshalling support from corporate capital for its repressive interventions. In Colin Bundy's judgement, 'the cohesion and capacities of the state remained largely intact' (1989:16). The prevarications of liberal sections of capital had grown faint and the state was entrusted with the restoration of 'order'.

Moreover, the security apparatuses remained relatively cohesive. They were unthreatened militarily and insulated ideologically against the tumult of resistance. They were able to contain and invert militant energies within townships by isolating certain townships and concentrating repressive force on them and by introducing or supporting vigilante groups. This turned the 'revolutionary' violence inward, catalysing a frenzy of internecine bloodletting that assisted state control. In addition, the core elements of these apparatuses were white and, despite the efforts of the End Conscription Campaign, remained mostly unmoved by calls on their consciences.[29] There was not the slightest prospect of meeting a central precondition for revolution: the breakdown of the armed forces.[30] Inside South Africa, the state's security capacities were at no point stretched to the full.

Whether or not 'dual power' situations arose is moot. In some townships, certain state functions were arrogated. These instances, though, were sporadic and localised, with little if any spillover effect on the broader functioning of state administration. Thus, the state could seal these challenges within particular communities and attack them through a combination of repressive force and development interventions—often successfully. Generally, the popular initiatives were ephemeral and quickly escaped the bounds of disciplined co-ordination; only in exceptional, short-lived cases were they 'controlled by, and accountable to, the masses of people in each area'.[31] As Friedman noted at the time:

> [W]hile some street committees appear to have enjoyed the support of residents, others seemed to have been imposed on them. While some 'people's courts' seemed to enjoy a high degree of legitimacy, others were allegedly used to impose the will of small groups of unelected activists (1987:62).

What looked like 'dual power' to the insurrectionists were usually situations of 'ungovernability'—where power had not been usurped but rather destabilised and dispersed. These situations were marked by the absence of effective control by either the state or its challengers. As long as the police and army isolated those zones, they posed no wider threat to the functioning of the state. At no point were 'liberated zones', in any meaningful sense of the term, established where popular forces could organise and defend elements of a 'proto-state'. Neither was resistance in the townships simultaneously building to a crescendo. The geographical focus shifted constantly as the state concentrated its repression on the 'hot spots'. In fact, the 1986 state of emergency was remarkably successful at narrowing the options for mass mobilisation:

> Short-term mobilisation is likely to pose an enduring threat to white rule only if it creates a space in which long-term organisation can emerge. Boycotts, stayaways and similar actions are often the products of organisation, but many

have been imposed by small groups of activists without thoroughly consulting their constituents (Friedman, 1987:61).

The spectacle of mass campaigns and the seemingly inexorable succession of militant actions obscured the UDF's failure to build and consolidate an organised national power base. Despite valiant efforts, the Front failed to overcome poor communication with its grassroots components and a weak capacity to direct and discipline their activities. In Friedman's assessment,

> *its national leadership is often not in control of events on the ground. Despite gains over the past three years, it is a long way from becoming a disciplined and organised national movement which could pose a direct threat to white rule* (1987:63).

Throughout, the UDF tried to overcome these problems.[32] The formation of the South African Youth Congress in April 1987, for instance, was intended to try to draw militant youth back into line. But caught up in insurrectionary fervour, its fierce rhetoric seemed to have the opposite effect. Many real or potential supporters were alienated by a situation where 'the children called the tune and our only role was to sit and listen, in angry silence'.[33] State repression induced and compounded many of these weaknesses by 'decapitating' popular organisations, fomenting internecine violence, banning organisations and (especially from late 1986 onwards) severely narrowing the political space. By late 1987, most of the UDF leadership was either in prison, in hiding, or dead: almost 30 000 activists (70% of them members of UDF affiliates) had been arrested or detained and more than 3 000 people had been killed. More vigilante groups (usually comprising older African men) sprung into action, supported by the security forces; victims of so-called 'black-on-black violence' appeared to outnumber those killed directly by the security forces.

No compromise

The strategy of insurrectionism and the ferocious impact of state repression together pushed the resistance campaigns of the 1980s off the rails. Coercive tactics and 'revolutionary violence' had, by 1986, become acceptable methods of struggle among many of the youth on the frontlines. While it is true that the UDF never openly endorsed these practices, its leaders were slow to denounce them. It was only after Winnie Mandela's infamous statement in April 1986 ('With necklaces and our little boxes of matches we shall liberate this country') that the UDF unequivocally condemned the methods. The UDF and its key affiliates tried to regain the initiative by mounting new, co-ordinated campaigns, but the driving impetus of resistance at the local level lay with youths, whose millenarian determination placed many of them beyond the discipline of coherent, strategised initiatives that could consolidate and extend gains. There had emerged a struggle ideology that mirrored the very exclusionism of the system that was being opposed: any engagement with the enemy other than outright confrontation was deemed to carry the risk of contamination and betrayal. Instead of separating 'those elements of reform, such as "democratisation" and "deracialisation", that were integral to their own struggles and required defending, all reforms were denounced as mere window-dressing' (Morris & Padayachee (1989:84).[34] This tunnel vision was by no means unique to South Africa, as Morris reminded:

> *Ideologically exclusionary regimes of a totalitarian nature, when viewed from the perspective of those who are excluded, create conditions which often make it extremely difficult for the excluded to comprehend the possibilities, and hence take advantage of, incremental reformist measures in order to stretch these to the maximum and create internal regime crises ... Principles and strategies are conflated and [...] slogans such as boycottism, non-collaboration, non-participation predominate* (1993a:98-9).

The success at resisting and scuttling reforms was confused with the ability to selectively reject some reforms and extend the limits of others within an alternative strategic programme. This absolutism took hold during a period when, for the first time since 1948, the state's fitful restructuring efforts were creating highly favourable conditions for a 'war of position'. The democratic movement used those spaces, but mainly to try to build a critical mass of resistance which, it hoped, would soon topple the regime.

Rejectionism had not been an intrinsic feature of the Congress tradition. Why then did it take hold? Firstly, the turn to armed struggle was an important shift, which introduced a confrontationist/militarist paradigm. Secondly, the ANC had since the late 1970s taken on board the rejectionist approaches of the Black Consciousness Movement when large numbers of Black Consciousness activists joined the organisation. But the prospect of a cataclysmic confrontation with the apartheid state resonated loudly with young township militants: the ANC was also slipstreaming behind their militancy. The alternative (to advise a cautious and incremental strategy) would likely have diminished its stature. Having finally arrived on the brink of achieving hegemony over the internal resistance forces, the ANC was disinclined to squander the moment.

Taking stock

The insurrectionary challenge was defeated, but the same could not be said of the democratic movement in general. Although bruised by the recession (which reached its deepest ebb in 1988–89) and by hard-fought strikes, the trade-union movement had emerged as the most powerful, organised component of the anti-apartheid forces inside South Africa. With the UDF battered onto the sidelines, popular organisations regrouped around the union movement and progressive church bodies, which together assumed the mantle of political leadership of the MDM in 1989. But its defiance campaigns did not belong in a linear narrative of cumulative advance; they were the beginnings of an arduous process of rebuilding.

Popular forces had multiplied and matured. But they were less an irrepressible juggernaut than an aggregation of widespread but uneven activism and initiatives that occasionally pushed the system onto its heels, but never really threatened its overthrow. At rare points, the variety and sweep of initiatives, broadly gathered under the canopy of the anti-apartheid struggle, offered hints of Gilles Deleuzes's concept of rhizomatic phenomena: a flowering of autonomous activities, linked laterally and not subjugated to hierarchical ideological and strategic conformity. But these periods of ostensible flux and experimentation were short-lived. Robert Fine would describe them as a search for a 'third way'. By the mid-1980s, the codes of post-Bandung era liberation movements had been reimposed, principally by the ANC and SACP. Although it was not in control of events, the ANC's ideological presence was more imposing than ever. It had manoeuvred itself to pre-eminence as the ideological and political custodian of the struggle.

The fortitude, determination and sacrifice of millions of South Africans carried traumatic costs. Thousands had died and countless more bore the physical and psychological scars of conflict and repression. Fighting escalated between rival factions as resistance became increasingly violent, disorganised and alienating. The 'comtsotsi' phenomenon (lumpen township elements who combined politics with crime), the use of young gangsters as political shock troops and the remorseless, and sometimes violent, intolerance shown towards dissent and heterodoxy within the popular movement combined with the brutal methods of the apartheid security apparatus to sap resistance of direction and discipline.[35] A culture had developed in which any means were justified in the struggle against the apartheid state. These tendencies existed alongside and sometimes eclipsed the publicly hallowed traditions of pluralism, debate and tolerance. They were displayed across the country, perhaps most horrifyingly in the 'Natal war' between supporters of the UDF and the conservative Zulu Inkatha movement led by homeland leader Mangosuthu Buthelezi.

The imminent defeat of the system was not on the horizon. But neither had the interventions fashioned by technocrats and security strategists resolved any of the underlying contradictions; they merely bought time. Corporate capital had temporarily grouped around the state's turn to outright repression. But severe differences had surfaced within its ranks, and in those of the state and the NP government, over how to defend the capitalist system in the medium to long term. The economic crisis dragged on, exacerbated by increased international isolation. All this registered in grim terms: formal-sector unemployment hovered around 30%; services in most townships had collapsed; violent crime boomed; balance-of-payment problems worsened; the far right (exploiting the economic and physical insecurities of rural and working class whites) was maturing into a potential political threat; and the anti-apartheid opposition was slowly regrouping around the MDM. A new terrain of imperatives and possibilities had emerged. The single achievement of the challenges mounted during the 1980s was to have deepened and extended the complex of difficulties faced by the ruling bloc, forcing it to consider new responses that could resolve the central political contradictions. By the late 1980s, it was clear that this had to involve a radical shift toward political democracy.

The end of the decade brought some respite. Popular organisations were slowly regrouping around tactics reminiscent of the 1950s. The armed struggle had been eliminated from the ANC's arsenal by the Soviet Union's decision to push for a settlement and the shutting down of ANC bases in the region. On the security front, the state held the upper hand but was riven with internal conflict (Shubin, 2008). In the background, a proto-negotiations process was gathering steam. A point had been reached where all sides could, indeed had to, raise their heads above the parapets, scan the terrain and weigh their options.

More than a decade of chopping and changing had profoundly restructured the social and ideological undercarriage of the post-war accumulation strategy and fitfully began adjusting the economic realm. But because the reforms had steered a wide berth around fundamental political change, South Africa did not turn away from what seemed a slide towards chronic instability, tempered only by crisis management. No matter the alarmist rhetoric of the state, it was not so much the prospect of a revolution that had jolted the apartheid managers: it was the likelihood that the state and opposition would become entangled in a death embrace that could destroy South Africa's integrity as a nation-state and a viable zone for doing profitable business—and with it white privilege.

Stalemate

A stalemate had been reached. One option for the apartheid state was to resort to an indefinite period of unmitigated totalitarian management of society—basically a tactical response awaiting the emergence of an alternative strategy. Another was to extend political reforms, but this was likely to accelerate the recovery of popular organisations and generate another security crisis. The other option was to dramatically restructure the political basis of the system, on the basis of the adjustments made since the 1970s in the social and economic spheres.

State analysts had viewed the political crisis in two complementary ways: as a security issue and, at a deeper level, as a symptom of socioeconomic 'dysfunction'. The political was seen as contingent on more elemental material contradictions (mimicking Marxist accounts of societal crisis). Each of the three reform phases had circumvented the political dimensions of the crisis. But the final phase had the hallmarks of a 'preparatory' intervention aimed at undercutting the organisational capabilities and momentum of the anti-apartheid movement, in order to tilt the balance of forces more in the state's favour (O'Meara, 1996). The influence of US and French counter-revolutionary theory was discernible in the groundwork laid during the 1980s for a strategic shift to moderate and tightly managed transition, which the SACP's Jeremy Cronin would describe as 'low-intensity democracy' (1994a).

What the regime's strategists underestimated was the extent to which the anti-apartheid movement had politicised poverty, dispossession, landlessness and social disintegration. Every conceivable ill had been made attributable to apartheid,[36] to such an extent that a reform project based mainly on adjustments in the socioeconomic realm would falter. Early in the 1980s, former president P W Botha had warned whites they had to 'adapt or die'; by the late 1980s it was clear that adaptation within the paradigm of apartheid offered no escape. The political and social stability needed to restore and consolidate a new cycle of accumulation required a new political model that had to incorporate the basic demands of the political opposition: a non-racial democracy based on universal suffrage in a unified nation-state. As early as March 1986, NP ministers had grasped this point; flummoxing them was how to proceed. This excerpt from notes of a special cabinet meeting on 1 March 1986 conveys the rudderless mood of the time:

> Internal violence and foreign pressure was on the increase, and (President P W Botha) wanted to know whether the NP should implement more dramatic things in the country, in place of the programme of gradual adaptations which apparently was not taken to heart by anybody. Mr Heunis [Minister of Constitutional Planning and Development] responded by saying (a) the NP did not know where it was going, and (b) the government was not in a position to deal with the circumstances in the country. Mr De Klerk was of the opinion that (a) negotiations with people who counted were on the rocks, (b) he was almost powerless because qualifications which accompanied change were often allowed to lapse, (c) there were fundamental differences between ministers over the question of where the NP and the country was heading, and (d) measures of the present did not meet the demands of the time.[37]

A leap was needed. But the required strategic coherence was absent. Compounding this was the 'political incoherence' of South African capital (Morris & Padayachee, 1989), a common feature of capitalist societies, which tends to be overcome only in extraordinary periods. Corporate capital's input in political and social policy therefore tended to be hidebound and parochial; concentrated pressure and coherent macroreform proposals seldom materialised (the Urban Foundation was a notable exception). The norm was to slipstream behind state policies, intervening when specific interests were at stake. Sections of capital had also sponsored a succession of gadfly opposition political parties opposed to the naked racism of the apartheid system. In 1986, corporate capital fell in line behind state repression—but without offering a congruous strategy for how to proceed once the uprising had been quelled. By the mid-1980s, however, a cluster of 'visionary' corporate and political figures in the ruling bloc (including top security officials) understood that a political exit had to be carved open and that it would have to involve the ANC.

Meanwhile, two developments had combined to create a favourable balance of forces within the NP and the government. The NP had jettisoned its far-right supporters and power had been centralised within the party and government. Reformists took heart from the crushing of the 1980s uprisings: by 1990, a five-member committee headed by the Minister of Justice, Kobie Coetzee, and National Intelligence Service chief, Neil Barnard, had met with Nelson Mandela 47 times (O'Malley, 2007; Sparks, 1994). The 'facilitation' provided by social-democratic entities like the Institute for Democracy in South Africa (IDASA)[38] (funded by Western governments and development agencies) was instrumental in establishing the climate and forging the trust that would lead to formal political negotiations. In February 1990, the ANC, PAC and other anti-apartheid organisations were unbanned, and Nelson Mandela and other political leaders released from prison. A new pack of cards had been dealt.

At the crossroads

The factors that combined to create this conjuncture have been discussed in detail elsewhere (Shubin, 2008; O'Malley, 2007; Gevisser, 2007; Sparks, 1994) but they bear brief repetition. Many of them resonated simultaneously (though distinctively) in the ANC, the NP and government, and corporate camps. Together, they tilted the balance of power towards the proponents of political negotiations. Other factors helped to establish a broader context that seemed to favour that route. Yet official accounts and even the personal memoirs that have emerged still offer little insight into the debates and struggles that raged in the top echelons of ANC, NP and government. Still, it is fairly certain that the following factors weighed on the minds of the NP and the government:

- International sanctions handicapped efforts to slow the slide of the economy, although how severely remains a point of debate. Certainly, government's options for dealing with internal resistance were influenced by the prospect of harsher sanctions. At the same time, South African exports experienced an upturn from 1987 onwards, despite sanctions. The main impact of sanctions seemed be their negative effect on foreign investment flows and on government's ability to secure financial assistance to offset balance of payments difficulties. Those pressures would not relax substantially until a political settlement was reached. The alternative was a constricting cycle of economic decline and political instability. In other words, the economic sphere could only be rescued if the political framework could be restructured.

- The absurd duplication of state institutions (three chambers of parliament, dozens of government departments performing the same tasks for racially defined sections of the population, expensive homeland administrations), as well as the cost of the Namibian occupation and the war in Angola, all increased fiscal strains at a point when the economy was slumping into its worst recession since the 1930s.

- The NP had weaned itself from its old multiclass social base, enabling it to free its policies from the ideological straitjacket of apartheid and transform itself into a party championing the interests of the white middle classes and bourgeoisie. A power struggle in the ruling NP ended in the election of F W de Klerk as leader, with the party's 'young turks' grouping around him.

- The internal anti-apartheid forces had regrouped within the MDM and were capable of mounting resistance campaigns which, while not posing immediate threats to the state, could further raise the costs of avoiding a political settlement.

- Negotiations required the existence of a coherent political force with sufficient legitimacy and authority among the excluded majority to make a deal stick. The ANC had clearly emerged as that force.

- A profound process of class restructuring was underway in urban African communities. A small but distinct black elite had emerged, especially in the homelands where this layer was also invested with political and administrative power. The rise of the Inkatha Freedom Party (IFP) in particular (and with it organised, politicised ethnicity) raised hopes that the hegemony of the ANC could be reduced during and after a negotiations process. These developments fed exaggerated expectations within the NP that a 'non-racial' centre-right political alliance could be mustered to challenge or hold the ANC in check.

- The military defeat suffered by the South African Defence Force (SADF) at Cuito Cuanavale in Angola pushed militarist hardliners onto the defensive, as did Namibia's almost anti-climactic achievement of independence and the progress towards a peaceful settlement of Angola's civil war.
- Pressure from Western governments, principally the US, and their touting of the reassuring examples of 'managed transitions' to democracy in the Philippines and Namibia softened reluctance to opt for negotiations.

The options appearing before the ANC, in particular, and the anti-apartheid movement, in general, were influenced by the following factors:

- Withering state repression, along with organisational and strategic dysfunction in the democratic movement, had dashed the dream of overthrowing the apartheid state by force. A long period of rebuilding the internal popular forces lay ahead. This weakened those ANC elements that favoured an unremitting confrontation with the apartheid state.
- The armed struggle never reached a point where it posed a military threat to white rule. By the late 1980s its potency had faded to the point where the ANC would later admit that 'there was no visible intensification' (ANC National Executive Committee, 1992). After the Namibian settlement, the ANC lost its military bases in Angola and was forced to transplant them as far afield as East Africa. There was no foreseeable prospect of re-establishing them in the region (Shubin, 2008).
- The collapse of Eastern Europe and the Soviet Union's shift towards demilitarising its relations with the West (and dramatically reducing its support for revolutionary projects in the south) deprived the ANC of its main backers and effectively curtailed its armed struggle, and accelerated an endemic retreat by radical forces worldwide.[39] The radical social transformation projects attempted in Mozambique and Angola had been destroyed, in large part through a massive destabilisation campaign by the apartheid state, reinforcing South African hegemony throughout the subcontinent.
- During the 1980s, the ANC had achieved substantial ideological hegemony among the popular masses and their main forces, bolstering its claim to be the 'government-in-waiting'.
- The balance of power within the ANC tilted towards a well-organised pro-negotiations faction that got the upper hand over hardliners embarrassed by the collapse of their insurrectionary strategy and alarmed by the disappearance of long-term support traditionally drawn from the Soviet bloc (Gevisser, 2007).

Internationally, the main Western powers had since the early 1980s successfully pushed for and facilitated a series of transitions to democracy on terms that prevented or stymied efforts to achieve deep social transformation. Similar pressure was exerted on the apartheid government. It was warned that shirking this historic opportunity would end their policies of 'constructive engagement'. At the same time, the ANC was notified that it, too, was best served by seizing the opportunity. The collapse of the Soviet bloc meant that post-apartheid South Africa would be knotted into a world economic system dominated by the US, Western Europe and Japan.

Neither side could claim to have triumphed, but the balance of forces still favoured the incumbents, who remained in control of the economy, the state (particularly its repressive apparatus) and the media. South Africa's political and economic elites retained substantial space for manoeuvre. The apartheid state had weathered turbulent uncertainties and retained the (provisional) support of powerful Western governments. The retreat of radical projects internationally favoured the consolidation of centrist political alternatives. Growing class differentiation and the emergence of other contradictions in African communities emboldened those who believed they could save the system by sacrificing it.

Leap into the unknown

Formal 'talks about talks' began in 1990. NP politicians understood the need to incorporate the democratic opposition into a restructured political system, but the terms on which incorporation could occur were unclear. They also understood the need to constrain the ANC's ability to wield political power in the service of a radical agenda of socioeconomic transformation, but not how this could be achieved. So the NP would experiment with a bewildering assortment of proposals, frustrating ANC negotiators by 'constantly cutting and changing their positions'.[40] This was not tactics, it was muddling. Doubtless, there were nervous recollections of the insurrectionary course taken by popular forces when much narrower political openings had appeared during the early 1980s. The floodgates of possibility had not suddenly been opened, but the outcome of forthright political restructuring was by no means certain.

Understandably, the ANC and its allies claimed a historic victory. Alongside the insurrectionary headiness of the mid-1980s stood pronouncements by the ANC leadership that seemed to light a path toward negotiations. In 1985, at the height of insurrectionary fervour, the Lusaka leadership had issued preconditions for negotiations—the same year in which its annual '8 January' statement had called on supporters to prepare for a 'people's war'. Throughout the subsequent period, the organisation issued starkly contradictory statements, some conciliatory, others patently martial. In part these were directed at specific audiences: moderate postures were designed to shore up the ANC's impressive knack at winning support on the international front, while the injunctions issued to its supporters glossed over any talk of compromise and negotiations with 'the enemy'.

By the end of 1987 (after Mandela had commenced his talks with the government and with the internal movement on the retreat), the ANC had seemed more inclined towards a negotiations route. It had refined its preconditions and two years later formalised them in the Harare Declaration, which made it public knowledge that the door was open for negotiations. Inside the ANC, the pro-negotiation moderates had been gaining the upper hand. Yet the speed with which De Klerk seized the initiative and began meeting the preconditions caught the ANC and the internal anti-apartheid movement by surprise. Mere weeks before Mandela's release in February 1990, Mzala was still declaring that

> there is no prospect of the apartheid regime under De Klerk agreeing to the most elementary demands of the ANC such as the establishment of a one-person, one-vote political system (1990:571).

What surprised the ANC and its allies most was that the apartheid government opted to approach the negotiations table in circumstances that were far from 'insurrectionary'. Unlike the NP and its allies (which had tried to avoid far-reaching adjustments in the political sphere), the anti-apartheid movement (and the ANC in particular) was guilty of over-privileging the political. It reduced the circumstances of the black majority, and indeed the entire system of exploitation, to the political and ideological form of the apartheid state. Crudely put, the ordering of economic and social relations pivoted on the state; once it changed, everything else would follow. In such logic, the apartheid regime could not initiate the reforms demanded by the ANC, since this would trigger the collapse of the entire system of white privilege. Such thinking stated that South African capitalism could not exist without apartheid. This political reductionism did not prepare the movement for the ruling bloc's gamble that the defence and recuperation of capitalism required abandoning the exclusionary political and ideological framework of the post-war growth path—and that a point had arrived when, perhaps for the last time, the balance of forces still favoured that bloc strongly enough for it to decisively shape a politically inclusive restructuring.

The confusion gripping the internal popular movement had important ramifications for the negotiations process and the settlement it produced. A mere five years earlier, the ANC had been labouring to catch up with dynamic internal developments; now the woozy state of the internal movement rendered it more prone to the organisational and strategic discipline of the ANC. The UDF was disbanded in March 1991, with UDF leader Patrick Lekota justifying the decision with the claim that 'the purpose for which we were set up has been achieved'. Endorsed was the mistaken view that the UDF (and, by implication, the bulk of the internal movement) was a mere stand-in for the ANC-in-exile. The move evoked impotent grumbling at rank-and-file level. Within a short space of time the South African Youth Congress (SAYCO) and several women's organisations also opted to be absorbed into their counterpart structures in the ANC. Jeremy Cronin termed this the 'B-team mentality':

> People abandoned their organisations and joined the main political organisation. The real experience and worth of the popular movements was not understood; they were seen as a kind of 'B-team', a substitute until the 'A-team' [the ANC] could enter the playing field.[41]

The ANC's ideological pre-eminence was now supplemented by organisational supremacy, with the partial exception of COSATU. Despite its political allegiance to the ANC, the trade union federation retained an independent base and massed organisational strength. But in slightly more than a decade, the ANC had returned from the wilderness and assumed the now incontestable mantle of a government-in-waiting.

Government-in-waiting

One might expect an organisation that opts for negotiations during a period that seems to bristle with radical fervour to invite internal turmoil. Yet there is little to suggest this happened inside the ANC. As an assembly of different classes, political traditions and cultures, the ANC's ideological character and strategic direction had been contested since the 1940s. One of its several achievements was to have prevented this heterogeneity from generating the sorts of internal turmoil that plagued other liberation movements (including the ANC's offshoot, the PAC). Strategic and tactical positions were debated and contested but became inviolable once they had been decided. The discourse angled toward the overthrow of the apartheid state had been shadowed by a more moderate one that seemed inclined towards a negotiated settlement. It was the failure of a strategy centred on an insurrectionary variant of armed struggle that tilted the ANC onto the negotiations path reconnoitred by Nelson Mandela since 1986 (Gevisser, 2007).

The ANC was careful to present its basically social-democratic constitutional principles in mid-1989 as a distillation of its historical vision of change. That vision orbited around the Freedom Charter, which had served as an ideological bedrock and key hegemonic instrument. Idealistic and emotively phrased, it bore close resemblance to the French Declaration of the Rights of Man or the Declaration of Independence of the North American colonies. It was not a policy document, but a statement of broad principles that would be used as a mobilising instrument.[42] Thus the Charter was hoisted above debate and dispute; it came to hover in a sacred zone of popular consciousness in the ANC. Like all liturgical texts, it contained accommodating ambiguities. In order to marshal a broad and large a constituency beneath the banner of African nationalism, the ANC had refrained from elaborating and imposing precise interpretation of the Charter. Thus sanctified, its vision of a post-apartheid order remained stirring but inexplicit. The Free Nelson Mandela campaign (started in the early 1980s) marked a similar feat. The ANC in particular and the liberation struggle in general was personalised, condensed within the persona of Mandela. A powerful link was forged between Mandela, the legality of the ANC and the legitimacy of the struggle for national liberation.

Even the armed struggle's most telling impact lay in its symbolic and affective power. Though armed attacks had multiplied in the 1980s,[43] they were in military terms a mere irritant. Their significance lay in their symbolism and in the cathartic, vicarious thrill they conveyed by suggesting that the system could be struck at its 'heart'. Armed action was later also linked to community and union resistance, but there, too, the prime effect was to stiffen the activists' resolve (as opposed to effectively defend activists against repression) and confirm the pre-eminence of the ANC in the liberation struggle. In Lodge's view, 'Umkhonto's most significant contribution to the liberation struggle was helping the ANC exercise political leadership over constituencies it was unable to organise directly' (Lodge & Nasson, 1991:183).

In the diplomatic field, the ANC achieved dazzling victories. By stressing the non-racial and moderate aspects of its programme, it built a huge network of international representatives (outnumbering the emissaries of the apartheid state) and a powerful network of backstage and public solidarity groups and sympathisers. The ANC's inclusive rhetoric (counterpoised against the horrifying evidence of apartheid violence in international media) drew waves of international solidarity that vexed other liberation organisations. In continental (the Organisation of African Unity) and international forums (the United Nations, sports and cultural bodies) the ANC established for itself the status of a 'government-in-waiting'. This enabled it to spearhead an array of international boycotts and sanctions against the apartheid system. By the mid-1980s South Africa had become a domestic issue in most Western countries and the ANC was able to position itself at centre stage in these solidarity initiatives as the 'authentic voice' of the oppressed majority.

Indeed, the ANC's pre-eminence stemmed less from its officially exulted 'successes'—mass mobilisation and the armed struggle—than from its mastery in the arenas of diplomacy and symbolic struggle. Those achievements also reflected the absence of viable alternative political forces.[44] The only possible challenger, the PAC, was racked by chronic organisational dysfunction, internal rivalries and corruption scandals; it was not until the late 1980s that it recovered a semblance of international respect, thanks mainly to pressure from the governments of Nigeria and Zimbabwe.

For all these successes, the ANC's conceptions of a post-apartheid society remained impressionistic—a shortcoming that would prove telling during the negotiations and beyond. Roughly hewn, they had, until the mid-1980s, drawn heavily on the Soviet model and 'Third World' visions of the Bandung era. Shortly before 1990, the ANC hurriedly set up embryonic policy structures to explore economic and land policies. The failure of the SACP (prominent in so many other aspects of the organisation) to assume a talismanic role in policy formulation was remarkable. ANC policies, according to Tito Mboweni (deputy chief of the organisation's economic planning department at the time), would eventually emerge out of inputs from the ANC's

organisational structures; the policy departments; the positions of allies of the ANC (in particular Cosatu); the experiences of developing countries; the lobbying efforts of capital, the media, western governments, and independent commentators; and the policy research work of the IMF and World Bank (1994:69).

Deadlock

Less than five years had passed since a writer in the ANC's journal, *Sechaba,* had exhorted supporters to stand firm against the temptation of negotiations:

> [T]he enemy has no role in the solution of our problems ... There can be no going back to the practice of frittering away our energy in activities calculated to prise the case-hardened conscience of white oppressors to invite us to negotiations to bring about a dispensation acceptable to them and us.[45]

The political basis of the South African system had to be revised and it had to include (and, most likely, pivot on) the ANC. The gamble taken by the state (and supported in rough outline by the economic elite) was to suspend its desultory attempts to achieve stability via socioeconomic reform packages and to try to resolve the political dimension of the crises rocking the country. This, it hoped, could provide a relatively stable basis for recuperating the economic sphere. The eventual settlement would constitute the most sophisticated and successful attempt yet to achieve this. But it could only survive if the consensus could be extended across the political and social terrains. The next few years would determine whether a sturdy enough envelope of restraint could be fashioned to ensure that the ANC and its popular allies did not transgress the boundaries of permissible change desired by the ruling bloc.

Endnotes

1   These included outright repressive measures (banning unionists, crushing strikes) and a system of parallel unions whereby African workers' interests had to be presented to management and the state via white-controlled union bodies.

2   In 1972, black workers staged 71 strikes. The following year that figure rocketed to 370 strikes, then to 384 in 1974, before decreasing again to 275 in 1975 and 245 in 1976. Severe repression saw only 90 strikes staged in 1977 (Davies *et al*, 1985:34).

3   The South African Students' Movement (SASM) was a prominent force in the uprising. Equally important was the fact that in the early 1970s a new generation of African students had begun teaching in township schools. Influenced by the Black Consciousness Movement, some conveyed Black Consciousness thinking to their students. The ANC's role in the uprising is unclear. There is little evidence of an active hand, although some researchers have claimed that the ANC managed to establish underground cells in Soweto via SASM; see Marks and Trapido (1991:4–5).

4   Politically, Black Consciousness underwent traumatic detours, with the Azanian People's Organisation eventually emerging as the standard bearer of the tradition. It soon drifted to the far left and entangled itself in rejectionist postures that even saw it boycott the April 1994 democratic election.

5   Army Chief of Staff (later Defence Minister) General Magnus Malan, cited in O'Meara (1983:253).

6   The editorial view of the *Financial Mail*, the country's flagship business weekly, cited in Davies *et al* (1984:39).

7   *Financial Mail*, 25 January 1980, quoting liberal critic Sheena Duncan; cited in Saul and Gelb (1981:49).

8   In the Riekert Commission's phrasing, 'black communities [should] bear to an increasing extent a greater part of the total burden in connection with the provision of services in their own community'.

9   These antagonisms were not new. In the 1950s, violent riots rocked Soweto when migrant hostel dwellers attacked 'permanent' township residents (Stadler, 1987:175). By the early 1970s, however, those tensions appeared to have abated. Migrant workers strongly supported the new trade unions that had emerged earlier in the decade. Indeed, sociologist Ari Sitas found that, until the late 1970s, 'the distinction between urban and migrant workers was apparently dissolving, as was the relationship between migrant trade unions and the community' (cited in Marks and Trapido, 1991:14).

10 Paraphrased in Baskin (1991:26).

11 In 1982 the NP split and the far-right Conservative Party adopted these former core constituencies, equating their interests with the defence of 'classic' apartheid ideology. Violent racism and bigotry and the promotion of hermetic and nostalgic versions of Afrikaner culture became the preserve of the far right. This freed the NP, as a party, to spearhead further reforms that departed from 'classic' apartheid. But it also raised the spectre of a challenge to its authority within the white electorate emerging from the far right.

12 See, for instance, Josette Cole's account of its role in squatter conflicts around Cape Town (1987).

13 Urban Foundation statement, cited in Davies *et al* (1984:122).

14 These upgrading schemes bypassed migrant-worker hostels whose residents were also becoming marginalised and alienated from wider society. Inkatha later capitalised on such material and social tensions, establishing footholds in hostels, while tensions between residents living in formal townships and those living precariously in squatter camps or hostels would later explode violently. See Cole (1987), Segal (1991), Everatt (1992), Marais (1992a), Hindson and Morris (1992).

15 For more, see Vishnu Padayachee's 'The politics of South Africa's international financial relations, 1970-1990', in Gelb (1991).

16 The new councillors exemplified the process of class differentiation in African townships: 'Councillors were often members of a growing commercial and entrepreneurial middle class [who] had benefited from the government reforms.' Their duties of fiscal administration in the townships 'greatly expanded the opportunities for venality [...] and made them the target of widespread discontent generated by the economic recession' (Lodge & Nasson, 1991:31).

17 Borrowing another tactic of the 1950s, the unions buttressed their factory actions by enlisting community support for consumer boycotts against employers.

18 'Izizwe', 1987, 'Errors of Workerism' in *South African Labour Bulletin*, Vol. 12, No. 3, cited in Fine and Davis (1990:278).

19 See, for example, Foster, J (1982) 'The Workers' Struggle—Where Does FOSATU Stand?' *South African Labour Bulletin*, Vol. 7 No. 8, pp. 67–86.

20 A perspective that became codified in the Freedom Charter, and which underpinned the ANC's thinking.

21 This tradition was especially powerful in the National Union of Metalworkers of South Africa (NUMSA), the Commercial, Catering and Allied Workers' Industrial Union (CCAWUSA), and the Chemical Workers' Industrial Union (CWIU).

22 Report to UDF national congress, 5 April 1985.

23 Paraphrasing of the report by ANC officials, interviewed by Barrel, *op cit*.

24 'Green Book', ANC Files, p. 5, cited by Mbeki (1996:43).

25 Senior NSMS official, quoted in *Weekly Mail*, 3 October 1986, cited in Morris and Padayachee (1989:89).

26 See, for instance, Mzala (1981) and (1987).

27 Slovo, 1986, 'SACP: One of the Great Pillars of our Revolution', *African Communist*, No. 107 (Second Quarter); paraphrased by Bundy (1989:8). Supporters wrote enthusiastically of the factors required for a transfer of power: '[T]he South African state and its military power must be destroyed; the country must he conquered; the will of the enemy must be subdued'; see Cabesa (1986).

28 Wolpe (1988), cited in Bundy (1989:9).

29 For a survey of attempts to undermine the military system from within, see Cawthra *et al* (1994).

30 'No government has ever fallen before revolutionists until it has lost control over its armed forces or lost the ability to use them effectively'; C Brinton, *The Anatomy of Revolution*, cited in Bundy (1989:1).

31 As claimed, for instance, by Zwelakhe Sisulu in his keynote address to a National Education Crisis Committee (NECC) conference in Durban, 29 March 1986. Only in the small, compact towns of the Eastern Cape (especially the Karoo) did such claims contain even a measure of accuracy and then only for short periods.

32 Among them the 'Black Christmas' campaign of 1986; the 'People's Education' campaign of the NECC which, however, made only marginal inroads against the 'No Education Until Liberation' rhetoric popular among many students; and worker stayaways.

33 Journalist Nomavenda Mathiane's account of a 1986 meeting called by students (cited in Lodge & Nasson, 1991:97). Her description applied also generally to adult township residents' reactions to the careening militancy of activist youth.

34 There were exceptions to this trend, notably in small Eastern Cape towns such as Port Alfred. In 1985, through boycotts and other campaigns, telling divisions were fomented within the business community and local state structures. Rather than press ahead blindly, local activists exploited the disarray of their opponents by negotiating—and winning—specific local reforms.

35 Intolerance and authoritarianism had been apparent also in exile, where it had led to tragic episodes in the ANC's Angolan camps (Marais, 1992b). Even a prominent intellectual like Pallo Jordan did not escape the Stalinist culture imposed in exile; the ANC's security apparatus, Mbokodo, detained him for criticising the security system. According to the Motsuenyane Commission, later appointed by Nelson Mandela to investigate abuses committed in the camps, detention centres such as the notorious Quadro 'developed a widespread reputation as a hell-hole where persons were sent to rot'; see *Motsuenyane Commission Report*, 1993, 'Executive Summary', Johannesburg, p. iii. In many cases, the distinctions between seditious activity, the expression of genuine grievances and sincere dissent, or sheer ill-discipline was erased.

36 An eminently practical basis for mobilisation, enabling activists to 'make visible' the underpinnings of oppression and suffering and to focus protests more acutely. But it also fed the notion that the removal of apartheid would unlock a cornucopia of opportunity and power.

37 Excerpts from an expurgated political biography of former President P W Botha, *Sunday Times*, 28 August 1994.

38 Known at the time as the Institute for a Democratic Alternative in South Africa.

39 Particularly in Latin America, where radical forces had failed to seize state power (El Salvador), were besieged (Nicaragua) or were repositioning themselves to enter existing political systems on highly compromised terms (Brazil, Chile, Colombia).

40 Author's interview with ANC negotiator Mohammed Valli Moosa, November 1992.

41 Presentation to the 'Prospects and Constraints for Transformation' workshop, December 1994, Johannesburg.

42 See, for instance, Suttner and Cronin (1986).

43 Up from about 23 in 1977 to 228 in 1986, by Tom Lodge's count (Lodge & Nasson, 1991:178). See also Lodge (1987).

44 This, of course, is not a rare phenomenon in oppositional struggles. The socialist parties in Portugal and Spain, for instance, shrewdly capitalised on the organisational deficiencies of their respective communist parties and popular forces on the eve of transitions to democracy in the mid-1970s. For a detailed account see Poulantzas (1976:134–62).

45 Cassius Mandla, 1985, 'Let us move to all-out war', *Sechaba* (November), p. 25, cited by Lodge (1989:46).

CHAPTER THREE

Contours of the transition

[T]his was a war without absolute winners ... the two major political forces in South Africa had fought to a draw. And so it happened that the oppressor and the oppressed came together to chart the road to a democratic South Africa.
— *Govan Mbeki (1996:119)*

There began in February 1990 a fitful, convoluted and often impenetrable process of 'talks about talks', 'protocol meetings' and, finally, negotiations. In the background, convulsive violence raged, signalling a possible 'centrifugal pull towards anarchy' (Saul, 1993:104). To a considerable extent, the violence was facilitated, if not outright promoted, by the apartheid state, as subsequent revelations would confirm (Greenstein *et al*, 2003). The effect was to embolden attempts by the leadership of the democratic movement to reach a negotiated settlement. As an SACP analyst put it:

> South Africa is on fire from end to end. The horrifying catalogue of assaults and killings must be brought to an end if we are not to sink into a state of self-perpetuating violence in which all our hopes of reform and social progress will be destroyed.[1]

The intrigues and manoeuvres of the public meetings, secret consultations, consultative seminars and talk-shops, the two main multiparty negotiating forums, breakdowns and worse are documented in reams of reporting, analysis and punditry.[2] Fascinating as some of those chronicles are, we are not concerned here with the minutiae of negotiations, but with the underlying agendas, dynamics and trends that laid the basis for the settlement and that established the parameters of the transition.

Big stakes, high risks

In broad outline, this phase stemmed from the apartheid state's failure to resolve the political dimensions of a multifold crisis and the liberation movement's inability to dislodge that state. The liberation movement had long distilled its struggle to a non-negotiable political essence: nothing short of drastic political change would suffice. The state and capital had assiduously sought to avoid such an outcome. But by the late 1980s, powerful sections were scanning the future through the prism of politics. Corporate South Africa, as Morris noted, was recognising that

> economic growth will not occur without a political settlement, and long-term peace and stability demands policies that can restore political and social conditions for economic growth (1993c:9).

A resolution had to rest on two pillars. It required, firstly, a political settlement that could allow the ruling bloc to reconfigure itself around a political axis that was capable of building and managing a genuinely national consensus. Secondly, a new accumulation strategy capable of guiding South Africa out of its economic crisis had to be devised and implemented. Both between *and* within the democratic forces and capitalist organisations there was considerable disagreement about the details of such a strategy (Morris & Padayachee, 1989; Morris, 1993c).

Meanwhile, corporate moguls themselves disagreed on the policies that were most likely to restore profit-making to the levels last savoured in the early 1970s and produced desiderata that contained a mix of neoliberal and crypto-Keynesian features. But their central concerns were transparent and aggressively promoted: the need for a market economy, for social and political stability, for broad continuity in state institutions and for restraint from radical redistributive programmes. Unanimity was also absent among the democratic forces. Officially, the ANC supported a mixed economy. Its constitutional proposals, Tom Lodge noted, 'fell well short of a socialist reconstruction of South Africa'. Indeed, 'the political provisions of the guidelines suggest[ed] a more radical degree of restructuring than [did] the prescriptions for the economy' (1989:49). But within the ANC, and among its allies, debates raged on how strong a role should be reserved for the state. In some quarters, the Jacobin call for 'a dispensation that excludes the enemy as a factor in its making' retained some currency.[3] Though befuddled by the collapse of 'existing socialism' in the Soviet bloc, many SACP members clung to the idea of a commandist state. Others rejected that approach and, like former unionist (and later Trade and Industry Minister) Alec Erwin, argued for a 'planned socialist alternative' based on a 'democratically controlled economy which goes beyond simplistic notions of nationalisation' (1989:47). Overshadowing such differences, though, was the shared desire to fashion a development path that could overcome the worst legacies of apartheid.

So, in Gramscian terms, hegemony had to be built along dramatically new and inclusive lines.[4] For leftists, this involved a major risk: the dominant political force in the anti-apartheid movement (the ANC) might be saddled with the task of salvaging South African capitalism. The ANC's history had not equipped it with an intrinsic aversion to such a role. As a liberation movement, it was angled largely towards the ideals of democracy, sovereignty and civil rights. Its remarkable political unity had been built partially by consigning the class dimension to the margins of its analyses, which identified the apartheid state as the core engine of poverty and oppression. The ANC, the apartheid state and corporate capital now shared an understanding of the need to recast the *political* and *ideological* bases of state power. The major differences centred on the extent to which the terms of that process would violate or maintain continuities with the past. The ANC's historical privileging of the political over the economic invited a settlement that would allow for significant restructuring of the political sphere, and broad continuity in the economic sphere.

The NP understood that it had to yield ground, but it also retained crucial advantages. It still controlled the state apparatuses (not least its repressive machinery, which had been augmented by an assortment of covert and allied forces euphemistically referred to as the 'Third Force') and it retained the overall support of the capitalist class. Nevertheless, negotiations thrust the country onto treacherous terrain. The NP government could (be forced to) abandon the process and retreat into the defensive laager of the repressive state if the terms of the likely settlement seemed unacceptable. Likewise, sections within the anti-apartheid movement might exploit the new space, reignite the insurrectionist blazes of the mid-1980s and try to topple the regime. As full-blown negotiations creaked into motion, neither alternative could be ruled out with confidence. Active on the fringes, meanwhile, were increasingly militant ultra-right white groupings, skittish homeland administrations and an ambitious IFP that was institutionally ensconced in the KwaZulu homeland and militarily supported by elements in the security apparatuses.

Taking the plunge

At hand was not the replacement of the old by the new, but their integration, on terms that had yet to be established. In Morris' view:

> The negotiations process is not about a government negotiating its surrender because it was defeated by a superior force. It is not about an already cemented nation poised on the brink of decolonisation or the seizure of power. It is about a political struggle to forge a new nation and new alliances that can ensure the broadest basis of social consent. The opposition is not sweeping aside the old institutions of state power. It has to try and shape the terms on which it is incorporated into the state as a new ruling group (1993c:8).

Staking the boundaries of possible change were factors that the ANC's National Executive Committee (NEC) candidly itemised in a November 1992 paper (ANC National Executive Committee, 1992:48–53). It noted that the regime appeared highly divided but still commanded 'vast state and other military resources' and 'enjoyed the support of powerful economic forces'. The liberation movement had attained 'a very high level of mass mobilisation and mass defiance', but was hamstrung by 'many organisational weaknesses' and a paucity of financial and military resources. These rendered it 'unable to militarily defeat the counter-revolutionary movement or adequately defend the people'. Meanwhile, the radically recast international context had increased pressures for a peaceful settlement that fell 'in line with the emerging international "culture" of multi-party democracy'. The NEC's conclusion was that this stalemate could best be surmounted through

> a negotiations process combined with mass action and international pressure which takes into account the need to combat counter-revolutionary forces and at the same time uses phases in the transition to qualitatively change the balance of forces in order to secure a thorough-going democratic transition (op cit, 1992:48–53).

The sobriety of the analysis was noteworthy. The ANC was especially troubled by the prospect that South Africa might implode and fragment, as Yugoslavia was doing. Shadowing its negotiating positions therefore was the need to preserve the South African nation-state. The organisation's moral and political weight would be mitigated by the perceived need to bring its main antagonists 'on board' with compromises that might rile supporters. According to SACP deputy general secretary (and ANC NEC member) Jeremy Cronin, the perceived counter-revolutionary threat alarmed the ANC to such an extent that

> most of its energy went into trying to engage those forces [...] We may have exaggerated the threat (our sources were often the government intelligence forces), but we shouldn't be complacent about the threat we were facing.[5]

Breaking the rules

By late 1992, the ANC was trying to forge a political consensus through 'certain retreats from previously held positions which would create the possibility of a major positive breakthrough in the negotiating process without permanently hampering real democratic advance' (Slovo (1992:37).[6] Prominent among them was a 'sunset clause' providing for a period of compulsory power-sharing in the form of the Government of National Unity, an offer not to purge the security forces and civil service of 'counter-revolutionary' elements and the willingness to establish (during negotiations) a set of Constitutional Principles that had to be honoured in the final Constitution.

This caused considerable consternation in the democratic movement. NEC member, Pallo Jordan, accused his colleagues of elevating negotiations to the level of strategy and warned that they risked giving 'away what we have won on [other] fronts' (1992a:15). SACP Central Committee member, Blade Nzimande, accused SACP chief Joe Slovo of developing a scenario in which 'the masses are absent and, instead, the issue becomes primarily that of tradeoffs between negotiators, constrained by the logic of the negotiations process' (1992:20). Troubling them were signs that the negotiations would produce an elite compromise. Many activists shared their consternation. But, as writer Anthony Marx observed, the ANC's arsenal had been depleted:

> The ANC's suspension of its armed struggle and reorganisation of underground structures into legal entities, together with international pressure to end sanctions, had by early 1991 weakened three of the congress's 'four pillars of struggle', leaving mass mobilisation as its only remaining form of pressure on the state (1992:264).

Intense violence provided the backdrop to these debates. On average, 86 people were killed each month during the uprisings of the mid-1980s; in the early 1990s, as negotiators haggled behind closed doors, 250 people were dying each month in political violence. Between Nelson Mandela's release in February 1990 and the democratic elections in April 1994, 14 800 people were killed, compared with 5 400 from 1985–89 (Hamber, 1998).[7] The message rang loud: moderation, stability and compromise might avert a cataclysm.

Apartheid police units and death squads, state-supported vigilante gangs and warring IFP and ANC activists had transformed communities into war zones. Fighting raged in KwaZulu-Natal, ostensibly between ANC and IFP supporters. Transformed from a moribund cultural organisation in 1975, and led by the politically nimble Mangosuthu Buthelezi (a former ANC member), Inkatha had resorted to the 'political mobilisation of ethnicity to compete for power and privilege' (Mare, 1992:3).[8] By manipulating Zulu history and identity, Buthelezi positioned Inkatha as a vehicle for rescuing what he portrayed as a proud but denigrated people and culture. Controlling access to resources in the KwaZulu homeland (via a system of patronage deployed through the homeland administration and networks of appointed chiefs), Inkatha expanded its support in rural areas and extended it into some urban areas. In addition, Inkatha controlled the KwaZulu police and benefited from the support of the apartheid security forces.[9] When the UDF had tried to unseat Inkatha-supporting chiefs in rural areas in the mid-1980s, a de facto civil war erupted, pitting the pan-ethnic, nationalist traditions of the ANC against the Zulu chauvinism advanced by Inkatha (Aitchison, 2003).

Horrific bloodshed accompanied the IFP's attempts to expand its base into townships around Johannesburg and nearby industrial towns. Massacres (such as the attacks on funeral vigils in Sebokeng, Alexandra and Soweto) were commonplace, along with terror attacks on train commuters. Many of the incidents betrayed evidence of state complicity in the violence, prompting international human rights organisations to accuse the security forces of going about 'business as usual'.[10] Subsequent evidence (emerging during the Truth and Reconciliation Commission hearings) indicated that a strategy of low-intensity conflict was being applied. The units engaged in those operations included the cynically titled Civil Co-operation Bureau (CCB) and sections of Military Intelligence, among others (Dugard, 2003; Everatt, 2003; Pigou, 2003).[11] Those efforts exploited and exacerbated the multifold lines of tension coursing through many African townships. Inkatha shock troops were trained at SADF bases and provided with arms, intelligence and logistical support. Reports abounded of police allowing marauding Inkatha gangs access to township areas, not intervening in the attacks or arresting the attackers. Attempts by residents and the ANC structures to marshal community defence units turned many townships on the East Rand and in KwaZulu-Natal into virtual war zones. Overlapping were other dynamics, including competition for scarce resources, feuding between warlords and criminal gangs, disputes over the control of taxi routes, tensions between settled residents, squatters and hostel dwellers, political conflicts and more (Greenstein, 2003b). For millions of South Africans the threat and reality of violence was chronic. A pervasive air of insecurity, demoralisation and disorganisation was fomented.

The view that the NP government was following a 'twin-track strategy' (negotiating with the opposition while simultaneously trying to destabilise it) became axiomatic within the ANC. The June 1992 Boipatong massacre, in which 48 residents were slaughtered, saw the ANC walk out of the negotiations. It launched a campaign of 'rolling mass action' which, unofficially, culminated in early September with Ciskei homeland troops mowing down ANC protestors outside Bisho in the Eastern Cape. A mood of panic was palpable in ruling circles. The patchwork of political allies the NP government had tried to assemble around the negotiating table was disintegrating. In addition, there was deep concern as to whether the ANC could 'control' its supporters and resume negotiations. On the latter score, the fears were unfounded. The mass action campaign was halted when the NP signed a Record of Understanding with the ANC in late September 1992. This both salvaged and repositioned the multiparty negotiations process; henceforth it would orbit mainly around the NP and ANC. Consensus-building became the name of the game, directly giving rise to the strategic debates outlined here. Meanwhile, Mandela had made his views of rank-and-file anger known:

> We are sitting on a time bomb. The youths in the townships have had over the decades a visible enemy, the government. Now that enemy is no longer visible, because of the transformation taking place. Their enemy now is you and me, people who drive a car and have a house. It's order, anything that relates to order, and it is a very grave situation.[12]

The upshot was a strategic outlook that saddled the ANC with the responsibility of establishing a new national consensus, a mission that would become elaborated in its nation-building endeavours. But this involved political compromises that could restrict the scope for change. In addition, a kind of short-term 'two-stage theory' emerged. Guiding the ANC's negotiating strategy was the need to devise compromises that could yield a lasting settlement. This meant that the ANC—only temporarily, it hoped—retreated from certain positions necessary for establishing and safeguarding a bedrock for decisive socioeconomic change. The political-ideological project of nation-building became paramount and overshadowed the socioeconomic dimensions of the crisis. 'The tendencies propelling us towards a new 50% solution', Morris warned, rest 'in the downplaying of the social and economic fault lines in our society'—a tendency he detected in much of the anti-apartheid movement's history (1993c:8). Societal crisis tended to be cast in *political* terms, spawning an assumption that once the political and constitutional issues were resolved, 'the dozing South African "economic giant" would lumber to its feet and cart us off to the land of promise' (Morris, 1993c:9). The SACP's Blade Nzimande was among the few alliance figures to draw public attention to this legacy. Quoting Mexican sociologist Carlos Vilas, he reminded that

> most important about 'transitions' [initiated by previously repressive regimes] is that 'they do not project into the economic sphere, nor do they provide a framework for any substantial changes in the level of access of subordinate groups to socio-economic resources—by income redistribution, creating employment, improving living conditions, etc.' (Nzimande, 1992:17)

Terms of the deal

Interrupted periodically by deadlocks and brinkmanship, three years of formal negotiations ended in late 1993 with a political settlement that detoured significantly from the positions held initially by the NP and ANC. Post-apartheid South Africa would be a constitutional democracy, as defined in an interim Constitution agreed to in late 1993. Eventually adopted in 1996, the final Constitution would replicate much of the 1993 version—with the exception of refinements introduced in some areas, notably on property rights, access to information, minority rights and the delegation of powers to provincial governments. The new system would be based on universal suffrage in a unitary state; the separation of legislative, executive and judicial powers; multiparty elections every five years; gradual (and circumscribed) delegation of power from central to local levels of government; and the enshrinement of individual and collective rights in a Bill of Rights that ranked among the most liberal in the world.

The Bill of Rights outlawed discrimination on the grounds of 'race, gender, sex, pregnancy, marital status, ethnic or social origin, colour, sexual orientation, age, disability, religion, conscience, belief, culture, language or birth'. It also allowed for the declaration of states of emergency under certain circumstances. A Constitutional Court would adjudicate disputes arising from the Constitution. Parliament comprised two houses: a National Assembly (400 members) and a National Council of Provinces (10 members from each of the nine new provinces). Several parastatal bodies would monitor and promote implementation of the Constitution, including a Public Protector's Office (to ensure democratic and ethical practices in the public service), a Human Rights Commission, a Commission on Gender Equality, an Electoral Commission (to organise democratic elections), an Independent Broadcasting Authority (to regulate the electronic media), an Auditor-General and a Cultural Commission (to protect minority cultural rights).

The final Constitution had to comply with a set of 33 binding constitutional principles, which crystallised key compromises reached in the final stages of negotiations.[13] Altering those principles required a two-thirds majority in parliament. They demanded, for instance, that

- The 'diversity of language and culture' be protected;
- 'Collective rights of self-determination in forming, joining and maintaining organs of civil society' be recognised and protected;
- 'The institution, status and role of traditional leadership' be recognised;
- Exclusive and concurrent powers and functions be delegated to provincial governments;
- National government be prevented from exercising its powers in ways that 'encroach upon the geographical, functional or institutional integrity of the provinces';
- Minority parties be enabled to participate in the legislative process; and
- The 'independence and impartiality' of the Reserve Bank be protected.[14]

Most dramatic was the postponement of genuine majority rule to 1999. Until then, a Government of National Unity would govern the country, with executive power shared between political parties that win more than 5% of the popular vote (the ANC, NP and IFP, as it turned out). Consensus-making was temporarily formalised in the executive in order to bolster political stability.

The terms of the settlement also reflected the influence of forces outside the final negotiations, including the white far right. The NP welcomed those destabilising pressures and deflected them onto the ANC, which made some surprising concessions in the final stages of negotiations. For example, it agreed to a provision that reserved 30% of the seats in some local government structures for minorities. Fearful of disloyalty in the security forces, the party also agreed to an amnesty that allowed human-rights violators to evade criminal and civil-action court cases—on condition that amnesty seekers fully disclosed their crimes. Drawing on Latin American experiments (Marais & Narsoo, 1992), a Truth and Reconciliation Commission (TRC) was chosen as a potentially less destabilising method to pursue human-rights abuses. The TRC began functioning in April 1996. The powers of the Zulu monarchy and, less publicly, other traditional leaders were protected, lending politicised ethnicity a menacing lease of life, while also threatening to diminish and delay democratisation in rural areas (see Chapter thirteen).[15] The NP had demanded an 'education clause', allowing parents and students to choose the language of instruction in state or state-assisted schools; eventually, the ANC agreed to a compromise clause guaranteeing that right where it could 'reasonably be provided' (see Chapter ten).

Corporate capital succeeded in fashioning a crucial detail of the settlement: the Bill of Rights sports a clause protecting property rights. Although diluted in the final Constitution, this limits the circumstances in which the state can expropriate private property and narrows the scope of a land-reform programme (Marais, 1994b). The settlement favoured capital in another, less obvious respects. The Bill of Rights provides a basis for constitutional litigation as a pathway towards sabotaging or holding up attempts to push ahead with socioeconomic reforms that breach the comfort zones of capital. Furthermore, the 'independence' of the Reserve Bank (an institution excessively alert to the needs of capital) now enjoyed constitutional protection.[16]

Despite such limitations, the settlement was a massive political breakthrough and earned the admiration and envy of citizens and governments internationally. A seemingly intractable and potentially catastrophic conflict had been resolved. The new Constitution guaranteed collective bargaining and the right to strike, as well as the right to freedom of expression, speech and assembly, privacy, equality before the law, access to information and freedom of sexual orientation, opening new pathways towards freedom and equality. The settlement paved the way for the historic 1994 elections, a spectacle watched with awe and admiration around the world.

At the polls, the ANC won a resounding victory. Its 62.7% of the vote earned it 252 of the 400 National Assembly seats, putting it well clear of the NP (20.4% of the vote) and the IFP (10.5%).[17] In some provinces, the ANC's share of votes ran as high as 90%. Less joyful results awaited the ANC in KwaZulu-Natal and the Western Cape, however. In the latter, white and coloured voters ensured the NP won control of the provincial government. The outcome in KwaZulu-Natal was more controversial. Chaotic logistics and allegations of widespread fraud saw the Independent Electoral Commission adjust the results to reflect an allegedly projected outcome, handing victory to the IFP (whose 50% of votes outstripped the ANC's 32%). In a bid to prevent widespread violence in the province, the ANC's national leadership prevailed on its provincial counterpart to accept the result.

Overall, the results confirmed the ANC's status as by far the most popular and the only truly national party in South Africa. Even where vanquished, it won a third of the votes, a feat no other party could match. Politically and symbolically, South Africa had crossed into a new realm. Centuries of colonialism and half a century of apartheid were over.

Hidden hazards

The ANC assumed the task of constructing and administering a hegemonic project that would be based on a radical break with the exclusionary paradigms enforced under apartheid. The principles of conciliation and concession replaced conflict and triumph as the mooring points for the transition. Abandoned were visions of change that centred on momentary historical ruptures, the seizure of power, the destruction of the old and the construction, as if on a blank slate, of the new. The exclusionary basis of South African society was replaced with an inclusionary one and political franchise was restored to the African majority. The dominant discourse came to orbit around postulated common interests and destinies, rather than difference, contradiction and antagonism. Commonalities (authentic or invented) would be spotlit and glorified. A century-old ideological model was heaved onto the dust heap. These were momentous changes:

> All the secure landmarks of the past, the defining features and political geography of the apartheid regime and its counterpart in the liberation movement [...] started to crumble. Instead of revolution, negotiation; instead of uncompromising transformation, compromising concession; instead of a violent struggle for the seizure of power, negotiation over the distribution of power; instead of sweeping aside the old order and all who had implemented it, dismantling the old order jointly with its old architects; instead of radical exclusion of the old to the benefit of the new, inclusion of both old and new in a newly created social framework (Morris, 1993a:11).

The settlement and the ensuing transition hinged on the recognition that friend and foe had make concessions and compromises in order to avert disaster for their respective agendas. The principle of inclusion and common destiny became the central ideological tenet of the new South Africa. Not only were all South Africans now deemed equal in one nation-state, but the reconstruction and development of society was presented as a collective endeavour, hence the intense pressure on the popular sector to 'exercise restraint' in its demands and pursuit of change. The transition would proceed on the basis of policies, initiatives and mechanisms designed to 'reconcile'—even *transform*—conflicting outlooks and interests into inclusive policies and endeavours. This constituted nothing less than an attempt to forge a new, durable basis for national consent, which was essential for any viable bid to reconstruct South Africa. The impulse of some leftists to detect in the very principles of inclusion, assimilation and conciliation the seeds of betrayal was mistaken.[18] Those principles did not themselves scuttle attempts to marshal a popular transformation project. The real issue was the terms on which inclusion and assimilation occurred, specifically, which social classes' interests would be privileged. In the South Africa of 1994, the class content of that project was still undefined—even though telling clues were available.

There was an evident conviction that the appeasement of domestic and international capital had become unavoidable. Moreover, the collapse of the former Soviet Union and its satellites, the pre-eminence of neoliberal prescriptions and the ANC's longstanding neglect of economic policy development left it exposed to the incursions of orthodoxy (see Chapter four). Days after the 1994 election, Nelson Mandela was assuring investors that 'not a single reference to things like nationalisation' remained in ANC economic policies and that these had been cleansed of anything 'that will connect us with any Marxist ideology'.[19] Months later he lambasted striking workers in the auto and service sectors for causing instability and putting their interests above those of their compatriots. These and other developments prompted the SACP's Jeremy Cronin to acknowledge that 'real inroads have been made by capital into the ANC ... [T]heir arguments are more attractive and more persuasive to a wide range of ANC leadership than the counter-arguments that are less confident, less coherent'.[20]

The ANC lacked more than sturdy counter-arguments. It had negotiated the settlement without a vivid programme for overhauling the structural foundations of a society in which injustice and inequality had been horrendously fused. It was this shortcoming that had prompted trade unionists to devise the Reconstruction and Development Programme (RDP), which the ANC adopted shortly before the 1994 election. But the transformative thrust of the RDP was soon dispersed as the ANC pruned its potentially conflictual elements and refashioned it along ostensibly consensual lines.[21] The left would cling to the RDP as the blueprint for transformation. But the version eventually endorsed by government hardly constituted a coherent, strategic programme for popular transformation (see Chapter four).

The settlement and the 1994 elections in some respects created and in others punctuated, major shifts in South African society. The salient achievement was to resolve the political dimension of South Africa's crisis—an outcome that all but a tiny minority of society desired and supported. But a solution to the underlying economic and social crisis required more than constructing a viable political basis for consent. It also demanded co-ordinated social and economic restructuring—a new development path, in other words. Left unanswered by the settlement was the fundamental question: which social and economic interests would that path privilege?

The answer would launch the country in one of two possible directions. One involved the redistribution of resources, power and security in favour of the 'excluded'. The guiding principle would be social equality and justice. Such a strategy could provide a basis for thoroughgoing, durable hegemony. The other option would adjust, but not displace the fundamental contours of society. It would engineer a small, increasingly multiracial enclave of privilege (buffered by a steadily expanding layer of black middle classes) and seek to gradually reduce the numbers of South Africans trapped in precariousness. Social and economic restructuring would differentially benefit various layers of society and the costs of that restructuring would be dispersed across society. Because such a venture is dissonant when set against the historic ideals of the liberation struggle, building and maintaining political consent becomes even more crucial. The ideological dimension therefore assumes paramount importance (see Chapter thirteen). And it faces the considerable danger that consent might wither, eventually requiring resort to combinations of overt coercion and demagoguery. The convivial ideology on which the settlement was propped neither settled nor suspended the contest to determine which of those outcomes would prevail. The contest continued on new terms and on new terrain.

In summary, the settlement constituted (and inaugurated) not a rupture but an ambivalent (though dramatic) series of reconfigurations that extended beyond the formal political agreement. In some respects they favoured the popular forces; in others they accentuated existing dilemmas and introduced new ones. Political negotiations had started because, as Govan Mbeki put it, 'this was a war without absolute winners' (1996:119). But they also ended without a clear victor. The settlement reshaped the political and ideological terrain on which ongoing struggles to shape a new development path would continue. In short, it marked a sea change—but in ways and to degrees that far exceeded conventional assumptions—and it occurred against a backdrop of profound change internationally.

Tectonic shifts

During the final years of the apartheid system, the world shifted on its foundations. The political-ideological divisions of the Cold War era had enabled developing countries to achieve various degrees of latitude (and imperial support) for the pursuit of 'alternative' development models. The first generation of newly industrialised countries in East Asia (South Korea, Taiwan and Singapore) arose in this context, as did the next generation (Malaysia, Thailand and Indonesia). In all instances, the achievements were closely linked to US largesse and support that was purposefully inserted into the most hotly contested regions during the Cold War (Anderson, 1998). In Africa, several countries won space for their developmental experiments thanks to the West's nominal indulgence and support from the Soviet Union and China (albeit uneven and inconsistent). The Cold War context basically defined those relationships. The same applied in the Middle East and North Africa.

The world system was 'tridimensional', comprising, in rough outline, the welfare capitalist West, the 'sovietism' of the Eastern bloc and the 'developmentalism' of the Third World, with each nation state acting as a basic unit in that system (Amin, 1997:6). During the 1980s, that system disappeared. The resultant geopolitical and economic fields stemmed not only from the end of the Cold War, but from the collapse or deep erosion of the three development models that had shaped societies over the prior 50 years. Deprived of their respective developmental paradigms, progressive movements everywhere were thrown into disarray as their ideological moorings dissolved and their strategic options seemed to narrow. Vexing them was 'the apparent failure of all programmes, old and new, for managing or improving the affairs of the human race' (Hobsbawm, 1995:563).

None of the traditional models seemed capable of ensuring sustained growth, full employment and universally humane living standards. Visions based on the elimination of private enterprise and the rule of the market, and their replacement by state ownership and central planning or by social ownership of production and distribution, had disintegrated. Even 'what might be called the intermediate or mixed programmes and policies which had presided over the most impressive economic miracles of the century' were on the retreat (Hobsbawm, 1995:564–5). These programmes had been demonstrably successful. They had produced rapid development, stimulated economic growth, improved living standards and dramatically reduced social inequalities. Now, they seemed dwarfed by new dilemmas.

The late twentieth century also saw increasing contestation between the major capitalist powers—a development that was closely linked to the absence of a single, global economic hegemony. Despite its military, cultural and diplomatic dominance, the US was no longer able to maintain the hegemony it had built in the economic realm during the third quarter of the century. The world economic system had become dangerously volatile, with growing and deepening economic rivalries played out between the US and the other powerful industrialised countries, mainly Western Europe, Japan and, later, China (Wallerstein, 2003; Burbach *et al*, 1997).

It was in this context that neoliberal globalisation breached the boundaries of national productive systems, reshaping and incorporating them as segments of a worldwide productive system driven by the 'laws' of the free market. The outcome was the unprecedented extension of market economies across the planet, the global dispersion of production processes (dominated by multinational and transnational corporations) and the ubiquitous and ceaseless circulation of financial capital. Profound changes occurred, with neoliberalism serving as the organising ideology for this process of restructuring. The recipe for success was said to lie in sets of adjustments that corresponded to the 'Washington Consensus' and that defined the first, hardcore phase of neoliberal adjustments in the 1980s. Countries that conformed to those dictates, it was claimed, would share in rising volumes of global trade and investment, develop more rapidly and eventually overcome their various economic and socioeconomic weaknesses (see Chapter five). The outcome, it was claimed, would be an integrated world economy in which benefits would spread more equally than ever before.

Change and continuity

By the mid-1990s, however, a strong body of critical research and analysis was in circulation, some of it disputing the allegedly unique character of globalisation.

There certainly were continuities with earlier phases of globalisation (as far back as the late nineteenth century and earlier), but qualitative changes were also underway. The ratio of trade to output had grown massively, with imports and exports constituting a bigger share of economic activity than before. On the investment front, multinational and transnational corporations accounted for much larger shares of productive investments and dominated international consumer markets on an unprecedented scale. By the late 1990s, those corporations were responsible for one third of world output and two thirds of world trade. About one quarter of world trade was occurring *within* these corporations.

Crucially, the nature, scale, speed and sway of financial transactions had changed. Since 1980 the volume of trading in currencies, bonds and equities had surged and was now five times quicker than the GDP of the industrialised economies. Foreign-exchange transactions had ballooned to stellar proportions: by 1992, they outweighed world trade sixty-fold. By 1998, some USD 1.2 trillion was changing hands daily in 'casino capitalism' deals, an amount one fifth larger than the combined foreign currency reserves of the world's central banks (Gray, 1998). Whereas the personal capital of wealthy families in Britain and Europe had financed most of the nineteenth century short-term capital investments in bond and equity markets, at the end of the twentieth century most of these global transactions were excessively leveraged. They were being financed with the anticipated (but unrealised) gains of earlier transactions, creating a rickety house of cards. Periodically, that structure would come tumbling down, only to be rebuilt in ever more exotic proportions.

Two definitive features of this latest era of globalisation, therefore, were transnational and multinational corporations' mammoth shares of investment, output and trade, and the massive expansion and acceleration of purely financial activities. Both developments were made possible by technological innovations: production, transport and logistics systems that enabled the segmentation and dispersal of production and distribution across the globe, and information and communication technologies that allowed financial transactions to occur at the speed of light, 24 hours a day, 365 days a year. The acceleration of purely financial activities did not, however, stem simply from technological progress; it reflected profound adaptations in the mode of capital accumulation. Neoliberal globalisation was not just another stage in the headlong advance and refinement of capitalism. It was, and remains, a variable set of adjustments made in response to structural weaknesses in the system.

Plaguing the world economy from the late 1960s has been a sustained and system-wide economic downturn that registered profoundly in the most advanced capitalist countries (Arrighi & Silver, 1999; Wallerstein, 1999; Amin, 1998; Brenner, 1998; Arrighi, 1997).[22] Compared to the preceding two decades of accumulation, the system had entered a long trough of relative stagnation. 'Throughout these economies,' Robert Brenner showed, 'average rates of growth of output, capital stock (investment), labour productivity, and real wages for the years 1973 to the present [1998] have been one-third to one-half of those for the years 1950–73, while the average unemployment rate has been more than double.' After growing at an average annual rate of 3.6% from 1950 to 1973, per capita GDP growth fell to 2% in the subsequent 15 years—a 45% drop. The underlying cause was massive overcapacity and overproduction in manufacturing in the industrialised countries. In Robin Blackburn's (1998:iv) summary:

> Once rival complexes of fixed capital were locked in national confrontation with each other, with no easy escape into alternative lines of production, profits fell dramatically and in tandem across the whole advanced capitalist world.

One reaction was to lower input costs by depressing wages and shifting production to low-wage zones. This was achieved through assaults on organised labour (first in the neoliberal *blitzkriegs* of the Reagan and Thatcher eras, then more systematically and pervasively). New production technologies and systems were also deployed, causing economies to shed jobs faster than they could replace them. Assisting those responses were advances in transport, production and logistics systems, which made it easier to parcel and then articulate production and distribution chains across the globe, with components manufactured and then assembled into final products at various sites across the world. The development of container shipping, for example, was a formative factor on this front.[23] Such restructuring required unfettered access to national economies and provided the impetus for the lifting of trade barriers, removal of investment conditionalities and other capital controls. Neoliberal ideology (initially codified in the Washington Consensus) would serve as a battering ram for those breakthroughs.

A simultaneous reaction was the tight rationing of productive investments, a route fraught with danger. New outlets and opportunities for profit-making constantly have to be realised in order to prevent the devalorisation of capital. Stashing capital under the proverbial mattress would suffocate the system. The trend of financialisation stemmed from that imperative. Issuing loans to 'developing' countries became an important response. The 'Third World' debt had served as a crucial source of ballast for Western capitalism, enabling surpluses to be recycled as profit-yielding 'development' loans. Africa's debt burden in 1996 stood at USD 321 billion—roughly USD 400 for each person living on the continent. The bulk of that debt (74%) was owed to bilateral and multilateral creditors. Three decades earlier, Africa had owed about USD 3 billion in debt.[24]

Bypassed

Another route was the time-honoured one of exporting capital in the form of foreign direct investment (FDI). Between 1983 and 1989, global FDI flows rose almost 29% annually—considerably faster than world GDP increases (Sweezy & Magdoff, 1992). Global FDI in 1997 topped USD 400 billion, but almost 60% of it went to industrialised countries and much of it was directed at cross-country mergers and acquisitions (UNCTAD, 1999). Of the FDI that went to 'developing' and 'transition' countries in the 1990s, more than 80% ended up in only 20 countries (UNDP, 1999). Most of that was channelled to countries of two types: those with attractive petroleum reserves and those with low wages, relatively educated labour forces, growing consumer markets and sufficiently sophisticated transport and telecommunications infrastructure.

These trends contradicted the ANC's optimism that an adjusted South African economy would attract large volumes of foreign investment. While economists were drafting South Africa's new FDI-dependent macroeconomic policy, data showed that fully one third of all FDI flows to Asia, Latin America and Africa went to one country: China. Of the FDI directed at Latin America, more than half went to Brazil, Mexico and Argentina. Meanwhile, Africa's share of 'developing' country inflows had nosedived, from 11% in 1986–90, to 5% in 1991–96, down to 4% in 1996. 'Africa has not participated in the surge of FDI flows to developing countries,' the United Nations Conference on Trade and Development lamented. By 1998, Africa's share of global FDI was slightly more than 1% (UNCTAD, 1997 & 1999). The global economy, in other words, was becoming even more polarised during this era of alleged 'global integration'. And Africa was linked into it mainly as a zone for resource extraction or through its debt relations with the advanced capitalist countries.

Crucially, the composition of FDI was also changing. In 1966, a mere 4% of US FDI had gone toward the banking, finance and insurance sector; by 1990, the figure was 24% (Sweezy & Magdoff, 1992:16). The reflex to retain capital in its financial form and to hunt profits in the financial realm had become formidably strong. Financial capital, long regarded as subordinate to production, was becoming an end in itself, despite the obvious fact that production remains the main engine of capitalist expansion. In its liquid form, capital now flashes across the globe in search of profit-taking opportunities, frequently without even momentarily settling in any one place. In David Gordon's summary:

As the rate of return on fixed investment in plant and equipment has declined and as global economic conditions have become increasingly volatile, firms and banks have moved toward paper investments. The new and increasingly efficient international banking system has helped to foster an accelerating circulation of liquid capital, bouncing from one moment of arbitrage to another. Far from stimulating productive investment, however, these financial flows are best understood as a symptom of the diminishing attractiveness and uncertainty about prospects for fixed investment (1988:59).

Huge demand was created for new forms of transactions. Advances in information technologies abetted the process. Crucially, free passage for speculative capital had to be engineered across the globe. Neoliberal ideology and its institutional guardians obliged on that front, making capital liberalisation a priority. South Africa would not escape these seismic shifts—in fact, its policymakers would encourage them.

The impetus for neoliberal globalisation, therefore, resided in the structural dynamics of the capitalist system—specifically, as Brenner (1998:8) reminded, the periodic crises spawned by 'the unplanned, uncoordinated and competitive nature of capitalist production, and in particular individual investors' unconcern for and inability to take account of the effects of their own profit-seeking on the profitability of other producers and of the economy as a whole'. Periodically, the almost instantaneous global churn of capital (much of it 'fictive', in the sense that it is premised on speculated, unrealised outcomes) would spin out of control, rocking countries, regions and, eventually in 2008–10, the entire world. Punctuating each crisis would be calls for greater regulation of financial markets and 'new international financial architecture'. Typically, though, action would be rare and faint.

Underway, in other words, was 'less the establishment of a stable and new international regime of capital accumulation than an aspect of the decay of the old social structure of accumulation' (Gordon, 1988:59). Compressed into the doctrine of neoliberalism, the adjustments associated with globalisation were aimed primarily at altering the terms of economic interaction between the dominant industrialised powers themselves, as well as between them and other national and regional economies. The emergence of China and India as economic powerhouses would complicate those rivalries considerably. The uneven or 'eclectic' application of injunctions said to define the very 'essence' of globalisation was not accidental: it disclosed its discriminatory and polarising character, and the intense rivalries shaping it. Globalisation represented a profound paradox: its homogenising and integrating thrust led to ongoing polarisation at the global level. As Burbach and his colleagues noted (1997:5), globalisation

> is both centripetal and centrifugal. It concentrates and integrates capital, commerce and trade in and between the metropoles, while at the same time casting off industries, peoples and even countries it has no use for.

This underlined a feature of neoliberal globalisation: economies are articulated to one another within an overarching frame of polarisation at the global level. The majority of 'developing' economies that become more tightly linked into the global system do so on exceedingly unequal terms, and in many cases the integration is temporary (as their 'comparative advantages' fade). These periods of intensive articulation usually exhibit frenetic bouts of domestic accumulation. Potentially, this could lay a basis for speedier economic development and some improvements in socioeconomic wellbeing. The distribution of those benefits, though, tends to be unequal, while the costs of 'progress' are steep and are usually borne by vulnerable sections of the peasantry and working classes (with women invariably bearing the brunt). Even the 'success stories' are unequal and highly contingent (internally and at the global level). Their accumulation strategies do not necessarily constitute a viable basis, or provide space for sustainable strategies of redistribution.

It was in this global context that the battle to determine the adjustment of South Africa's accumulation strategy intensified in the early 1990s.

Salvaging the economic system

While politicians haggled over the terms of a political settlement, a proverbial elephant lumbered around the room. South Africa entered its historic transition hauling along a bedraggled economy. Mainstream economists sought solace in ephemeral cyclical upswings, but the economy was bedridden. The post-war accumulation strategy had broken down.

Export earnings depended largely on mineral commodities and were vulnerable to exchange-rate variations and fluctuating commodity prices, especially shifts in the gold price.[25] Even short periods of economic growth deepened reliance on imported capital goods, aggravating balance-of-payment problems. In 1982, this forced resort to an IMF loan (see Chapter two). Partially in compliance with the loan conditions, the apartheid state had applied severe deflationary measures. It tightened monetary policy, hoisted interest rates to encourage savings (with no success), froze consumer subsidies and offloaded the fiscal burden onto the poor by increasing indirect taxation. The immediate effect was to lower living standards—a key factor in the mid 1980s uprisings.[26] No amount of fiddling could nurse the economy toward recovery:

- GDP growth was feeble, and had fallen from a 5.5% average during the 1960s to 1.8% in the 1980s, eventually plunging into the negative range (–1.1%) in the early 1990s;[27]
- Personal savings were unusually low; as a proportion of disposable income they had shrunk from 11% in 1975 to 3% in 1987;
- The economy was marked by industrial decay, reflected in ageing capital stock, limited capital-goods production and the failure to develop exports by beneficiating raw materials and expanding the scope of the manufacturing sector. Manufactured products' share of total exports declined steadily from 1960 (31%) to 1988 (12%) (MERG, 1993:241);[28]
- The state had failed to encourage productive investment by private capital, which 'led to an orgy of speculative investment and the shrinking of the manufacturing sector'.[29] Rates of gross fixed investment had fallen, leading to underutilisation of manufacturing-plant capacity (dropping from 90% in 1981 to 78% in 1993) and declining competitiveness. Corporations and individuals were spiriting their capital abroad;
- Balance-of-payment difficulties were a chronic problem, partly due to a heavy reliance on minerals exports and prices. Attracting—and keeping—capital inflows to offset those problems proved tough;
- Investment in research and development was low and most technological development was focused around the armaments, energy and tele-communications sectors;
- Unemployment levels kept rising and the economy was patently unable to create enough new jobs to absorb new entrants into the labour market. Under-investment in labour-intensive sectors was aggravating this trend;[30]
- There was a shortage of skilled and a surplus of unskilled, poorly educated and low-productivity labour—the cumulative result of business treating 'black workers as a replaceable factor of production rather than as a human resource';[31]
- Industrial relations were conflict-ridden and destabilised; and
- The distribution of social infrastructure (such as housing, education facilities, healthcare and transport) was grossly unequal, which hampered labour productivity and distorted the labour market.

Between early 1989 and late 1993, the economy sank into its longest-ever recession, registering negative real growth until an upturn in agricultural production (after a scorching 1991–92 drought) brought some respite. The mood among economic elites was morose, with Reserve Bank governor Chris Stals warning that the country would plunge into ungovernability by 1996 if the annual growth rate remained at around 1% (SAIRR, 1992:406–7).[32]

Other economic indicators confirmed the gravity of the situation. Real fixed investment growth stayed negative (improving slightly from –7.4% in 1991 to –3.1% in 1993). Private (non-housing) investment amounted to 10% of GDP, well below the 16% target. Domestic savings stood at 16.5% of GDP in mid-1994, down from the 24% mark (achieved in the 1980s) that the Reserve Bank believed was needed for annual economic growth rate 3.5%. Per capita disposable income was declining (it had shrank by 11% in real terms between 1980 and 1993).[33] The manufacturing sector was in the doldrums.

Job losses continued. The mining sector, responsible for 66% of export earnings in 1991, shed 30% of its work-force between 1987 and 1995, with employment levels tumbling from 752 000 to 513 000. Responding to low commodity prices on the world market, companies shut or scaled back mines they viewed as unprofitable. Employment levels in the two largest sectors (gold and coal) shrank by 35% and 47%, respectively.[34] Agriculture's contribution to GDP also dropped, from 9% (1965) to 6% (1988), and about one third of farm workers were sacked in the same period (SAIRR, 1992:396). In the 1990s, farmers laid off hundreds of thousands more, in anticipation of new legislation aimed at bolstering the rights of rural workers and labour tenants. The sector remained hampered by periodic droughts, low returns on investment, low levels of liquidity and a steady build-up of debt.

Various calculations pegged unemployment levels in the early 1990s at 30–33%. More than 400 000 formal sector jobs were lost (excluding agriculture) between 1989 and 1993[35] and almost eight in every 100 positions became redundant (SA Reserve Bank, 1994). The labour-absorption capacity of the economy virtually collapsed. Estimated at above 90% in the 1960s, it fell to 22% in the 1980s and reached 7% at the end of that decade (SA Reserve Bank, 1991). The negligible welfare provisions for unemployed Africans resulted in income earners supporting more jobless family members and friends, forcing them to make more stern demands for higher-than-inflation wage increases.[36] Nominal wages increased, then fell in the early 1990s (from 18% in 1989 to 11% in 1993), adding strain on cross-subsidisation as a makeshift safety net.

Meanwhile, the decline of the formal economy was accompanied by the exponential growth of an underground economy, commonly referred to as crime. A 1996 Nedcor survey claimed that crime cost the country R 31.3 billion (USD 4 billion), ignoring the fact that the bulk of this money continued to circulate in the economy in ways that ranged from basic consumption to real estate and productive investment (shopping complexes in rural towns, transport firms, small- and medium-scale enterprises, retail outlets, etc).

One positive factor was the country's relatively low external debt-to-GDP ratio. In 1990, this stood at 27%—'lower than for any Latin-American country in that year, with the exception of Chile, [and] lower than for all ASEAN countries' (ILO, 1996:31). By 1994, it had dropped to 23%. The country, therefore, had not stepped into a 'debt trap'—an ironic 'benefit' of financial sanctions, which granted the new government some latitude for devising an alternative economic strategy. Balance-of-payment problems persisted, though, as the lifting of sanctions and hopes for an economic upturn triggered an increase in imports (mainly luxury items, new machinery and technologies). There was an expectation that a rise in capital inflows would offset those difficulties, a notion rooted in the belief that the disinvestment of the 1980s had been purely politically motivated. But South Africa's reasons ran deeper: it had become an unprofitable zone for investment:

> Rand-denominated profits had been significantly reduced by the long-running recession, and, via the falling external value of the rand, there had been further serious reductions in attributable foreign currency value of these profits. In short, the fundamental problem of the relationship between political risk and financial rate of return [...] had finally reasserted itself with a vengeance (Blumenfeld in Schrire, 1992:71).

In late 1993, the caretaker government (the Transitional Executive Council, which included the ANC) had approached the IMF for a USD 850 million five-year loan to help it through balance-of-payment problems. The government signed a controversial 'letter of intent', which, as Vishnu Padayachee recorded, 'was at pains to point to the dangers of increases in real wages in the private and public sector [and] stressed the need to control inflation, promised monetary targeting, trade and industrial liberalisation, and repeatedly espoused the virtues of "market forces" over "regulatory interventions"' (1994a:26). There were 'striking' similarities between those commitments and the NP government's controversial Normative Economic Model, which the ANC had vilified a few years earlier. Some economists argued that the IMF would have accepted a less conservative letter of intent. But crystallised in that letter were the desired parameters for post-apartheid economic policy. These amounted to a resumption of the neoliberal adjustments that the apartheid government had begun implementing in the 1980s (see Chapter four).

South Africa in the global economy

South Africa's economy exhibited two key features, common to most middle-income countries. It was heavily reliant on commodity exports for foreign exchange and it had an industrial sector that was arrested in the semi-industrialised phase (with familiar tendencies, including low productivity, a limited skills base, ageing plants, large surplus capacity and a dependency on capital-goods imports).

Despite the hobbling effect of sanctions in trade and investment fields, a great deal of the South African economy remained outward looking. But its industrial sector had failed to keep pace with new technological developments. In truth, South Africa's economy had been integrated into the world economy along lines similar to most other semi-industrialised countries. In one respect, the economy had acquired an inward-looking bias: in the production of consumer commodities. But capital goods and large proportions of components were still imported from abroad. The economy had not developed capital or intermediate goods sectors of any note. A more accurate description, therefore, would speak of 'a pedestrian middle-income developing country' that 'does not add up to a great deal in global economic league tables' (Thomas Scott in Mills *et al*, 1995:200).

Attempts had been made to promote the manufacturing sector behind protectionist barriers, enabling it to grow until the late 1960s, after which it 'entered an as yet endless spiral of decline' (MERG, 1993:212). The sector depended heavily on imports, which had to be financed through commodity exports. Also hampering the sector's development was the high cost of locally produced raw materials to domestic downstream manufacturers.[37] The decisive, structuring weight of the minerals-energy complex was formidable (see Chapter one).

The economy relied on resource- and energy-based products that were of declining importance in world trade and subject to drastic price fluctuations. According to the United Nations Conference on Trade and Development (UNCTAD), most African countries rely on one or two primary commodities for 90% of their export earnings. In South Africa's case, the figure in the early 1990s was about 65% (Kahn, 1991). Meanwhile, its heavy dependence on capital-goods imports and foreign technology left it extremely vulnerable to balance-of-payment difficulties.

So, South Africa's incorporation into the world economy had remained largely unchanged for most of the twentieth century and rested on three narrow pillars: it was a primary product (mainly minerals) exporter, an importer of capital goods and technology, and a net recipient of indirect portfolio investment and direct foreign investment by multinational corporations.[38] Trend swings occurred in each of these aspects, but they reflected the essence of the country's incorporation into the world economy.

Trading trends

In this relatively extroverted economy, trade represented about 60% of GDP. But South Africa did not share in the more than 30% growth in the volume of world trade that occurred in the 1980s; in fact, its share of world exports dropped from 1.3% in 1980 to 0.7% in 1989, while Africa's share in the same period fell from 6% to 2.6%.[39]

Mining was without doubt the most outward-oriented sector (accounting for 62% of exports in 1990, down from 73% in 1980), while the agricultural sector exported grains, wines and deciduous fruits (accounting for 5% of exports in 1990). The specific character of the economy's relative openness was notable. Gold dominated exports (accounting for almost half the total value), followed by non-precious metals. Manufacturing's share of exports had shrunk dramatically after 1960. South Africa's share of global manufacturing exports had also dropped steadily from the late 1960s, as had its share of agricultural exports. The agricultural sector, as Bill Freund noted, was marked 'by a negative international trade balance in most years, heavy debts and low productivity in many spheres' (1994a:46). The sectors that performed best in more open markets were timber and steel. Secondary industry has never been competitive internationally, except in neighbouring countries, where South Africa enjoyed the advantage of lower transport costs and bilateral and regional trade deals weighted in its favour. In the import side, capital goods dominated. The sourcing of imports became more concentrated, with the four largest suppliers (the US, the UK, Germany and Japan) increasing their share of total imports by 1992.[40]

Trends in financial relations

For most of the twentieth century, South Africa had received significant amounts of portfolio investment. During the boom years of the 1960s, it attracted large inflows of FDI, mainly from the US and most of it invested productively in the manufacturing sector. In the 1970s, that changed. Syndicated bank loans and bonds raised in the international capital markets comprised the bulk of foreign investment after 1976. Subsequently, economic decline and political instability wreaked havoc on South Africa's international financial relations and eventually forced it to declare a debt standstill in 1985. After that, the country became a net exporter of capital, reversing the positive flows that had prevailed for most of its modern economic history.

Massive capital flight occurred in the 1980s, as some 40% of transnational firms disinvested,[41] with capital outflows from 1982 to 1988 exceeding USD 5.5 billion. In addition to the net outflows of FDI and portfolio investment, from 1985 to 1988 the country lacked access to long-term debt capital, failed to secure syndicated bank loans and made no private or public bond issues. Most forms of foreign capital inflows dried up altogether. There was one exception, however. Although no official development assistance was received in the period 1985–92, there were strong funding flows to anti-apartheid and humanitarian organisations.

On the positive side, the regime had repaid and discharged all its loan obligations to the World Bank in 1976 and it had repaid its 1982 IMF loan within five years. As a result, South Africa's ratio of foreign debt to GDP was low by international standards.

Portfolio (equity) capital flows to South Africa revived again in the 1990s as the recession bottomed out, the gold markets rallied and political negotiations progressed. Between 1985 and 1993, the net *outflow* of capital had averaged at 2.3% of GDP, but from 1994 to 1996 annual net *inflows* ran to 2.6% of GDP.[42] Net purchases of equities by foreigners on the Johannesburg Stock Exchange (JSE) also increased in the early 1990s. But the renewed access to foreign capital was limited mainly to equity capital and bond issues on the European capital markets, most of it short-term credit at relatively high cost. This trend in the flow of equity funds to emerging markets was in line with global developments and represented volatile, short-term investments that were swiftly and easily sold off. The same pattern would hold subsequently.

Shifting the terms of incorporation

While the world feted South Africa for its successful transition to democracy, other major conundrums stood unresolved. One was how to devise a set of policies that could reconcile the country's insertion into the global division of labour with the commitment to improve the living standards of the majority.

That far-reaching adjustments were needed was not in dispute, but that was where agreement ended. The platitudes that accompanied those debates were often mind-numbing. Proposals ranged from standard neoliberal packages of free markets, trade and financial liberalisation, to supply-side formulas, to strategies that envisioned a creative division of labour between the private sector and the state within the context of targeted policies.

The need to attract substantial amounts of foreign investment was treated as axiomatic. So narrow was the debate that Jeremy Cronin was ridiculed in the business press for suggesting that the best advert for foreign investors would be large productive investments by domestic firms. This was 'simply not happening, as millions of rands continue to be disinvested, or used speculatively on the stock exchanges and in shopping mall developments', he noted.[43] Private-sector (non-housing) fixed investment constituted a scant 10% of GDP in early 1994.[44] At the same time, capital outflows persisted, causing the economy to lose as much as 2% real GDP growth annually, according to some estimates.[45] While demanding increased liberalisation, the country's major corporations in the 1990s embarked on a spree of investments elsewhere in Africa and beyond (including in Australia, Brazil, Chile, China, Ecuador, Indonesia, New Zealand, Venezuela and Vietnam). The Trade and Industry Ministry would defend this trend, claiming that South Africa needed a corporate presence in countries with which it traded.[46]

Success, according to Paul Krugman, depended on whether South Africa 'can get any restructuring of property rights behind it; if it can demonstrate that it is more market-oriented than investors now expect; and if it can offer what appears to be a more competitive rand' (Baker *et al*, 1993:47). By mid-1996, substantial adjustments had occurred on those fronts. Property rights were ensconced in the Constitution, the government's new macroeconomic strategy heeded the standard neoliberal injunctions and the rand had devalued by more than 30% in six months (see Chapter four).

Global flows of FDI described a much more differentiated 'developing world' than that advertised by orthodoxy. Neoliberal policies offered no guarantee of large capital inflows.[47] 'Instead of flowing more and more widely around the globe', David Gordon found, 'capital is on the contrary settling down in a few carefully chosen locations', of four types mainly. The newly industrialised countries of East Asia received investment mainly for financial services and production for re-export back to the advanced countries. Latin American countries represented a second category and received foreign investment aimed chiefly at production for large domestic markets. The third comprised oil-exporting countries, whose fortunes 'vacillate with the cob-web cycles of price hikes and oil gluts'. Finally, there were between 75 and 80 developing countries that were 'shunted off to a side spur, virtually derailed in the drive for access to global resources' (Gordon, 1988:57).

Among policymakers, however, a strong sense of South African 'exceptionalism' prevailed. Somehow, South Africa would avoid the experiences of the rest of Africa—where overall FDI had grown by one third from 1980 to 1990, but the continent's share of overall global FDI shrank from 6.8% to 2% in the same period (World Bank, 1996b). Capital outflows in 1991 alone equalled 90% of Africa's GDP and were worth five times more than total investment, 11 times more than private-sector investment and 120 times more than foreign investment. 'Not only has the region lost ground to the rest of the world as an investment location', noted one assessment, 'but within Africa the pattern of flows is heavily skewed in favour of oil-producing nations which account for two thirds of the total [FDI]'.[48] Thus Nigeria attracted 45% of FDI to sub-Saharan Africa from 1990 to 1994, while South Africa experienced a net outflow.

After the 1994 elections, foreign investment in South Africa did revive, but along three lines. Direct investment increased as firms that had divested returned to the country and expanded or upgraded their operations. There was also a surge of mergers and acquisitions and a trend towards investment in stocks and bonds. New, 'greenfield' investment was rare and there was an 'almost total lack of investment in outward-oriented manufacturing', according to Alan Hirsch.[49] In his view, 'the problem is that most [FDI] is basically buying market share and going into partnership with South African companies, or buying control of South African resources for export'.[50]

The triumph of orthodoxy

Government's strategy for economic growth called for aligning the economy to neoliberal orthodoxy and invigorating an export-oriented manufacturing sector. The guiding doctrine became that of 'enhanced competitiveness', often compressed into the purported need to get the 'prices right', with trade liberalisation held out as the best device. Flanking this was an emphasis on boosted productivity, which, in business discourse, tended to be reduced to labour productivity. The importance of capital productivity and managerial productivity hardly entered the margins of official discourse.[51]

It was true that the inherited tariff system was fiendishly complex and that, in economist Sanjaya Lall's view, the system '[protected] industries without regard to their competitive potential'. Yet, as Lall cautioned, 'neither theory nor practice supports the case for completely liberal trade policies'. There was 'no instance of a developing country mastering complex industrial activities [...] without protection or subsidisation to overcome the costs of learning' (Lall in Baker *et al*, 1993:61–2). Indeed, the apartheid government had had no strategy for promoting new infant industries; now the 'strategy' was to expose them to liberalisation.

There was a strong case for restructuring (as opposed to dismantling) the protective system. South Africa took a rather more direct route and signed the 1994

Uruguay Round of the General Agreement on Trade and Tariffs (GATT), incurring weighty obligations that included deep tariff cuts. Government's reformed trade policy became explicitly geared towards fostering exports and featured a dogged move towards trade liberalisation and reliance on supply-side measures.[52] The latter included efforts to improve productivity and work organisation, nurturing small and medium-sized enterprises, helping to develop new industries (especially in biotechnology and information technology), encouraging more investment in research and development, lowering the corporate tax rate and providing more tax incentives and human-resource development.

Some ANC economists, such as Rob Davies, warned that South Africa was seeking to hop aboard the export-led bandwagon at a time 'when [a]lmost all semi-peripheral and many peripheral countries are now attempting such a strategy under global conditions that are becoming less and less favourable for all to succeed' (1995:63). The caution went unheeded.

In August 1994, the new Department of Trade and Industry announced tariff cuts in clothing and textiles and automobile components that far exceeded those demanded under GATT.[53] There was no broader strategic package to coax and support those industries into new or more competitive directions. It was 'sheer economic Darwinism', as one commentator put it. Remarkably the same department declared that 'the worst case for this economy is for us to throw our industries [...] to the vagaries of international competition rapidly and so destroy investment and jobs'.[54] Worst hit by the tariff cuts was the labour-intensive clothing industry (one of the largest industrial employers of women) and the agricultural sector, particularly maize farming.

Capital controls were also soon lifted. These had been introduced first in 1961, to stem capital outflows after the Sharpeville massacre. Regulations were modified in subsequent years, including strong liberalisation in the early 1980s following the gold-price boom. The apartheid regimes' 1985 debt standstill and the township uprisings had triggered massive capital outflows, prompting the tightening of controls.[55] Globally, however, the prevailing dogma now regarded exchange controls as a hindrance to the free flow of capital and a barrier to foreign investment. South Africa's low savings rate and declining investment levels added weight to that policy stance. As a result, the South African debate was not whether or not to discard these controls, but whether this should be done in one, fell swoop (a 'big bang') or in phases. Financial institutions pushed for the 'shock therapy' option, which the IMF also backed.[56] The government opted for a phased approach. As a first step, the financial rand was abolished in 1995. By 1999, about three quarters of the capital controls had been removed.

Referring to the experiences of the newly industrialised countries in Asia, Lall reminded that 'the experience of the most dynamic industrialisers in the developing world suggests that their [states'] selective interventions determined the nature and success of their industrial development' (Lall in Baker et al, 1993:69). South Africa's democratic government, however, refrained from such 'selective interventions'. Yet few of the advantages that had aided the newly industrialised countries were available to South Africa. Both South Korea and Taiwan had used their geostrategic significance during the Cold War to great effect, winning preferential access to US markets without having to reciprocate by opening their own markets. Moreover, as Davies (1995) noted, 'they embarked on export-led growth when most industrialising countries were still pursuing import-substitution programmes'. Instead of an authoritarian regime able to suppress labour, South Africa now had a democratic government and a comparatively powerful labour movement. It did not have the 'luxury' of a weak capitalist class, nor a homogenous population or a relatively favourable income-distribution pattern—key elements in Taiwan and South Korea's successes (see Chapter eleven). Its rural economy could not function as an employment and income safeguard. Situated in a sub-region and on a continent with barely a toehold in the world economy, it lacked dynamic markets in close proximity.

South Africa could have fashioned a development path that combined carefully selected orthodox adjustments with traditional Keynesian measures and some radical innovations. It shunned this admittedly difficult route and opted for a path that would leave it prone in a world system in which, as Samir Amin reminded, 'capital adjusts the weaker zones of the world to the requirements of global accumulation'.[57]

The anticipated pay-off would be an economy capable of gradually 'catching up' with the industrialised world—a familiar fantasy. In the post-1945 era, decolonised states without exception had concentrated great efforts on such a venture. In Latin America, Africa and the Middle East, this occurred largely via the route of inward industrialisation, behind protective barriers, often with the material support of one of the two former superpowers and without exception fuelled by highly active 'development states'.

What are the prospects of 'catching up' in a political economic world system characterised by the enforcement of 'a new hierarchy in the distribution of income' and greater, not less inequality, on the world scale (Amin, 1997:14)? Fundamentally skewed, that system is marked by an ensemble of monopolies in precincts that includes the development and deployment of weapons of mass destruction; domination in the world financial markets; monopolises access to the world's natural resources; domination of multilateral institutions tasked with managing the operation of the market at the global level; predominance in the fields of media and communication; and domination in the development and deployment of new technologies. The notion of 'catching up' loses its allure in a system organised along such lines. 'Catching up' no longer implies entry into a centre defined by levels of development and competitiveness, but by pre-eminence in those zones. A different paradigm is required to the 'catching up' frame. It has to focus attention on arrangements that could offer enough leeway and manoeuvring space for the achievement of national development priorities while realising the rights and entitlements of citizens.

Endnotes

1 Anon (1990:10).
2 See, in particular, Friedman (1993b); Sparks (1994 & 2003); Mandela (1994).
3 Cassius Mandla writing in *Sechaba* (November, 1985), cited by Lodge (1989:46).
4 A hegemonic project can be defined as 'societally projected policies aimed at concretely resolving particular conflicting (primarily class) interests by defining a socially acceptable national general interest' (Morris & Padayachee, 1989:67). See Chapter thirteen.
5 Cronin addressing the 'Prospects and Constraints for Transformation' seminar in Johannesburg, November 1994.
6 At first Joe Slovo's 'own individual contribution' to debates in the ANC alliance, this perspective soon prevailed in the ANC leadership. See, for instance, the October 1992 'Strategic Perspectives' document, which the ANC Negotiations Commission drafted.
7 There was continuity between this phase and the low-intensity conflict strategy employed from the mid-1980s onward and marked by the increased use of covert and unconventional forms of state violence. Overt violence continued, but there was a clear rise in clandestine variants carried out by apparently 'unknown' persons or groupings. State agencies provided support to forces that opposed or undermined anti-apartheid formations, principally the IFP and KwaZulu police, although the support was extended also to vigilante groups, criminal gangs and paramilitary outfits operated by local warlords and chiefs. Those 'injections' meshed with a complex of other organic contests and conflicts (Hamber, 1998). One prime effect was to discourage organised forms of resistance and to exacerbate destabilising dynamics in communities.
8 See also Mare and Hamilton (1987), and Forsythe and Mare (1992).
9 In 1985 (two years before the conflict erupted) Buthelezi had approached security-force leaders for military assistance. In response, the R 3.5 million 'Operation Marion' was launched, following a meeting of the State Security Council. A group of 200 Inkatha members received military training at Hippo Camp in the Caprivi Strip and were sent into action against UDF and COSATU supporters in KwaZulu-Natal, with ongoing support from the police and army. These events formed the basis of the trial of 13 top security officials in 1996. See Aitchison (2003).
10 The violence was extensively analysed at the time. For examples, see *Africa Watch* (1991); Human Rights Commission (1991); Everatt (1992); Morris & Hindson (1992); Marais (1992a).
11 The origins, nature and role of political violence in South Africa's transition during the early 1990s are examined in these and other essays collected in Greenstein (2003b).
12 *The Star*, 15 September 1992, cited by Bond *et al* (1996:37).
13 In fact, the Constitutional Court in September 1996 refused to uphold the final Constitution agreed to four months earlier because it violated some of those principles. Altered accordingly, the Constitution came into effect in December 1996.
14 See 'Schedule 4: Constitutional Principles' of the 1993 *Interim Constitution,* pp. 244–9.
15 See Chapter thirteen for more on the strengthening of those powers in the late 2000s.
16 For an overview of this debate, see Bowles & White (1993).
17 The PAC collapsed in the election, garnering a mere 1.3% of the vote—less than the urban and largely white DP's 1.7% and the right-wing Freedom Front's 2.2%.
18 See, for instance, Bond *et al* (1996).
19 Quoted in an interview published on 1 May 1994 in the *Sunday Times* [Johannesburg].
20 Interview with author, October 1994. Soon, as Devan Pillay reminds (2008:15), 'key union leaders, such as Cyril Ramaphosa, Marcel Golding, John Copelyn and others [would] become wealthy businessmen, using union investment companies as stepping stones to untold wealth'.
21 The RDP draft the ANC carried into office broadly sketched such a programme. But its details would be revised and its semantics adjusted, leaving it a more ambiguous (and therefore also pragmatic and agile) document.
22 The oil crisis saw massive amounts of oil profits channelled into Western financial institutions at a time when profitable productive investment opportunities were be waning. See Sweezy and Magdoff (1992); Amin (1998); Arrighi and Silver (1999); Wallerstein (1999).

23 See Witold Rybczynski, 'Shipping news', *New York Review of Books*, 10 August 2006, for a useful summary of that development.
24 See Larry Elliott, 'Why the poor are picking up the tab', *Mail & Guardian*, 15 May 1998.
25 In 1993, 64% of exports were primary or primary processed products—upending the conceit that the economy was substantially industrialised and diversified.
26 Anthony Marx was one of few analysts not guilty of this oversight: 'With no cushion for hard times, South Africa's urban poor have been highly vulnerable to economic shifts reflected most directly in higher prices for corn ("mealies") and other food on which they spend much of their income. Their anger over increased hardship has exploded during economic downturns [...] the unrest in 1976–77 and 1984–87 came in the wake of major recessions' (1992:245).
27 South African Reserve Bank figures (June 1995), calculated in 1990 constant prices.
28 For more, see Kahn, B, 'Exchange rate policy and industrial restructuring' in Moss and Obery (1991); and Black, A, 'Manufacturing development and the economic crisis: a reversion to primary production?' in Gelb (1991).
29 *Ibid.*
30 During the 1960s, with the economy at its peak, 74% of new entrants into the job market found jobs in the enumerated sectors. By the late 1980s, this had dropped to about 13%, forcing the government to admit that the unemployment crisis was structural (Gelb, 1994:3). By the early 1990s, fewer than 7% of new entrants found work in the formal sector. See Dave Lewis in Gelb (1991:244–66), and ILO (1996) for surveys of the unemployment crisis.
31 Former COSATU spokesperson, Neil Coleman, writing in *Business Times*, 3 July 1994.
32 The remark reflected poorly on Stals' political savvy, but it reflected the widespread concerns about the economic malaise.
33 Standard Bank, 1994, *Economic Review* (Third Quarter), Johannesburg.
34 Mineral Bureau figures, cited in ILO (1996:277).
35 Derek Keys, Budget Speech, June 1994, Cape Town. Keys was finance minister at the time.
36 According to the 1994 October Household Survey, only 2.4% of unemployed African men and 0.9% of African women received unemployment benefits. See ILO (1996:109).
37 'Exports rise as domestic demand cools', *Business Day,* 13 June 1997.
38 Grateful thanks to Vishnu Padayachee for sharing material and comments used in this section.
39 UN, World Economic Survey, 1992, cited in Baker *et al* (1993:24).
40 *Trade Monitor*, August 1993, p. 11.
41 Many, however, retained an indirect presence through financial and technology arrangements.
42 'Indicators point to progress on growth', *Business Day*, 11 June 1997
43 Jeremy Cronin, 'Exploding the myths of the neoliberal agenda', *Business Day*, 9 November 1994.
44 The rise in private-sector fixed investment during 1994 (by approximately 13%) was 'mainly limited to a number of major projects, spurred by tax concessions', according to the *South African Reserve Bank Quarterly Bulletin*, No. 197 (September 1995), p. 5.
45 Figures cited by Standard Bank chief economist Nico Czypionka in *The Argus* [Cape Town], 25 June 1994.
46 *Business Map Update*, 10 February 1997.
47 As even a 1995 Ernst & Young survey noted, 'the primary motivation for entering countries' was 'not low production costs' but the 'potential rate of return and local market demand'—a self-evident point.
48 According to the International Finance Corporation, cited in 'Africa left out in the cold', *Financial Times*, 15 June 1996.
49 Hirsch, A, 1995, 'Productive investment trends in South Africa' (workshop paper).
50 Cited in *Business Map Quarterly Review* (January 1996), p. 12.
51 See ISP, 'Meeting the global challenge: A framework for industrial revival in South Africa' in Baker *et al* (1993:93–7).
52 See 'Support measures for the enhancement of the international competitiveness of South Africa's industrial sector', a document the Department of Trade and Industry released in 1995.

An earlier version prompted one business journalist to ask whether its 'brand of economics' represented 'Keynesian Thatcherism, or the opposite?' (*Business Day*, 14 September 1994).

53 A bruising, five-week auto workers' strike ended hours after that announcement.

54 Trevor Manuel, quoted in *Business Day*, 1 September 1994.

55 It relied especially on the financial rand mechanism. The financial rand traded at a lower rate than the commercial rand and was the principal means for moving capital in and out of South Africa, whether in the form of direct or portfolio investments. Capital could only be removed at a discount and was thus encouraged to remain, in theory protecting foreign exchange reserves.

56 'Forex controls "need to go with a big bang"', *Sunday Times* [Johannesburg], 18 September 1994.

57 Interview with author, Johannesburg, August 1993.

CHAPTER FOUR

Sticking to the rules the evolution of post-apartheid economic policy

In our economic policies ... there is not a single reference to things like nationalisation, and this is not accidental. There is not a single slogan that will connect us with any Marxist ideology.

—*Nelson Mandela, quoted on 1 May 1994*

South African leftists and conservatives have very little in common—except for the heartfelt belief that deep down inside the ANC there is a socialist project groping toward the surface. For decades, the claim served as a siren call in anti-ANC propaganda. It is still blared about, especially in prelude to ANC policy confabs and leadership tussles; typically the left broadcasts similar claims at such times, as it renews its seasonal 'struggle for the soul' of the organisation.

Mandela's assurance was meant to calm nerves—which it did. Business figures reacted with unalloyed relief. Despite ample evidence to the contrary, they still worried that ANC economic policy might lurch in a radical direction. In their discomfort, they recalled Mandela's assurance four years earlier, upon his release from prison, that 'the nationalisation of the mines, banks and monopoly industry is the policy of the ANC and a change or modification of our views in this regard is inconceivable'.[1] Those words had triggered near-apoplexy. Within hours stock-market traders were, as one observer put it, 'unceremoniously falling out of bed' to launch a selling spree.[2] More than any other aspect of ANC policy, the party's economic thinking would careen along a roller-coaster ride, jolted by threats, ridicule and badgering from business organisations, financial institutions, Western governments, activists, trade unions, foreign lending institutions, economists and consultants.

First in the line of fire was the ANC's alleged penchant for nationalisation[3], which it soon dropped, to the alarm of many supporters. Nationalisation was a red herring, though. Its resonance in popular discourse stemmed less from its literal prescription than from its symbolic power. Encoded in that acclamation was a commitment to redistribute resources and opportunity in favour of the majority. Mandela's May Day statement signalled the extent to which the terms of the political transition had also been projected into the sphere of economic policymaking. The need to defuse potential hostility and assuage doubt—'to bring everybody along'—held the day and it befell the ANC to distil from antagonistic interests economic policies that could win wide endorsement. If the scope for triumphalist action was limited in the political arena, it was beginning to seem almost non-existent in the economic one, at least to the top echelons of the ANC. With a few important exceptions, neoliberal policies were ascendant globally and the Thatcherite assertion that 'there is no alternative' seemed convincing to many, particularly in an organisation that had paid scant attention to economic policy prior to 1990s. Its main reference point until the late 1980s had been the developmentalism that had characterised most post-colonial projects since the early 1950s—the anticipated Eastern bloc largesse being an important factor. By 1989, this had been softened into a professed commitment to a mixed economy, with the state still seen as a central economic actor. Before long, the collapse of the Eastern European variant of socialism, the end of the Cold War, the supremacy of neoliberalism and an increasingly graphic sense of the veto powers wielded by capital more or less erased those compass points.

During the 1990–93 political negotiations, the ANC scampered to make up lost ground, but it relied on weak advice. Its historical neglect of economic policy left it prone to the counsel of business and mainstream experts that set about schooling ANC lenders in the 'realities of the world'. The residue of left-Keynesian economic thinking (generated mainly from within the internal mass movement) had not entirely dissolved, but its persuasive power was waning. As South Africans celebrated the 1994 election results, there was already sturdy evidence that post-apartheid economic policy would conform to the pronouncement, made seven years earlier, by Anglo American Corporation's Clem Sunter that 'negotiation works; rhetoric is dropped, reality prevails and in the end the companies concerned go on producing the minerals, goods and services'.[4] Indeed, the penny had dropped earlier for some ANC leaders. In 1991, Mandela told an audience of investors in Pittsburgh, in the US, that

> the private sector must and will play the central and decisive role in the struggle to achieve many of [the transformation] objectives [...] let me assure you that the ANC is not an enemy of private enterprise [...] we are aware that the investor will not invest unless he or she is assured of the security of their investment [...] The rates of economic growth we seek cannot be achieved without important inflows of foreign capital. We are determined to create the necessary climate which the foreign investor will find attractive.[5]

By 1996 the ANC government's economic policy had acquired a distinctive class character. It was geared, first and foremost, to service the respective prerogatives of domestic and international capital along with the ambitions of an emerging black capitalist class. The benefits, it was hoped, would cascade into the lives of the impoverished majority, as the state sought to remove or soften the most egregious outrages endured by poor South Africans. This seemed a momentous shift from the rhetoric of an organisation with a strong working-class constituency, with sturdy links to a powerful trade union federation (COSATU) and a surprisingly resilient communist party (the SACP), and with influential cadres of avowed socialists in its leadership ranks. The South African left would spend years agonising over these apparent contradictions, preferring to view them as temporary aberrations. The 'shift' would prove to be considerably more durable.

Catching up

When the ANC was unbanned in 1990, it had no economic policy to speak of, a peculiar situation for an eight-decade-old liberation organisation, despite the efforts internationally on the left to train a cadre of ANC exile economists. Its 'constitutional guidelines' had committed the organisation to a mixed economy. But that avowal hung in a policy vacuum and invoked vague passages of the Freedom Charter that had pledged that:

> *The People shall share in the country's wealth! The national wealth of our country, the heritage of all South Africans, shall be restored to the people; The mineral wealth beneath the soil, the banks and monopoly industry shall be transferred to the ownership of the people as a whole; All other industries and trade shall be controlled to assist the well-being of the people; All people shall have equal rights to trade where they choose, to manufacture and to enter all trades, crafts and professions.*[6]

This is not to suggest that a blueprint should have been devised. But the outline of a coherent economic programme, based on sound analysis of both local and global economic realities and options, was necessary as a platform from which to bargain a new economic dispensation. In 1990, the ANC had no such platform. Economic literacy among cadres and leaders (only a sprinkling of whom had economic training of note) had not been a priority. Slogans and exhortatory (but ambiguous) pronouncements were in ample supply, though. The embrace of orthodoxy would be unnervingly swift and emphatic.

Back to school

The ANC's first serious attempt to fill this policy vacuum had taken the form of a 1990 'Discussion Document on Economic Policy', issued by its new Department of Economic Policy (DEP). In the main, the document reflected work done by COSATU's Economic Trends Group, which, until then, had been responsible for the most substantial efforts to chart a sustainable, progressive economic strategy. Central to the ANC document was the 'restructuring' of the economy.

The DEP document envisaged an active role for the state in planning industrial strategy and overcoming racial, gender and geographic inequalities. It stressed the need to restructure a financial sector which, it said, 'does not sufficiently direct savings into productive activity nor into critical areas of infrastructural development', instead encouraging 'a scramble for short-term speculative profit' (ANC Department of Economic Policy, 1990:12)—analysis that would remain apposite in the decades ahead. Foreign investment would be funnelled into targeted areas of the economy. Basic needs would not be met through 'inflationary financing', but by marshalling domestic savings and raising corporate tax rates. Also advised was the unbundling of conglomerates in order to stimulate competition and allow entry by small and medium-sized enterprises into the economy. Calls from business for a low-wage economy geared to achieve 'international competitiveness' were rejected, while a central role would be reserved for organised labour in devising and implementing policy.

The overriding theme was 'growth through redistribution', a formula 'in which redistribution acts as a spur to growth and in which the fruits of growth are redistributed to satisfy basic needs' (ANC Department of Economic Policy, 1990:8). In the later summary of economist Laurence Harris:

> *In its original formulation this strategy took a form that would have been familiar to left wing Latin American followers of Prebisch in the 1950s and 1960s, emphasising that the state should take a strong role in redistributing income and wealth toward the masses, simultaneously developing domestic industry's production to meet the demand for increased living standards and essentially growing on the basis of that domestic market while seeking simultaneously to increase the competitiveness of export industries (1993b:95).*

The 'growth through redistribution' approach, as a 1991 Development Bank paper recognised, rested on a combination of export promotion and inward industrialisation and was geared towards boosting both domestic demand and social infrastructure. The Keynesian overtones were obvious. In Kentridge's (1993:8) summary, the logic was that:

> *the poor consume goods made with a higher labour component, in which direct import content is lower, and that spending by the poor not only multiplies the GDP more than that by the rich, but that it does so primarily among the poor. In short, growth from redistribution would boost output and employment more than a similar injection among the rich.*

Mainstream economists lambasted the 'growth through redistribution' approach for its 'socialist' undertones and 'populist' leanings. Driving growth with state spending, they said, would overheat the economy and stall it in a tangle of foreign-exchange shortages, currency devaluations, rampant inflation, severe indebtedness and cuts in real wages. Chile (1970–73) and Peru (1985–89) were paraded as examples of such folly. 'The Mont Fleur Scenarios' would forecast the outcome of the 'growth through redistribution' route by likening it to the fateful flight of Icarus:

> *After a year or two, the programme runs into budgetary, monetary and balance of payments constraints. The budget deficit well exceeds 10%. Depreciations, inflation, economic uncertainty and collapse follow. The country experiences an economic crisis of hitherto unknown proportions which results in social collapse and political chaos (Le Roux et al, 1993:8).*

Economists such as Nicoli Nattrass contended that the 'growth through redistribution' route was chosen largely 'because it served the political purpose of uniting various constituencies within the ANC—implying a certain degree of expediency and an awareness that the policy was expendable. Indeed, by mid-1992, ANC leaders had already been weaned off such Keynesian 'delinquency'. Its May 1992 economic policy guidelines made no reference to 'growth through redistribution' and activists were discouraged from referring to it. Over the next two years, the party's economic thinking would increasingly take aboard central precepts of neoliberal dogma. 'Macroeconomic stability' became the watchword, and the virtues of liberalisation and privatisation were soon being sung to party members.

It is difficult to disentangle the process of conversion. Considerable pressure was applied to ANC leaders, not all of whom were convinced that orthodoxy could or should be challenged. Too many of those who did desire a more radical path were ill served by an unsteady grasp of economics. A multipronged assault that hammered home neoliberal dogma would be their undoing.

Drawing pictures

A plethora of corporate scenario-planning exercises was unleashed after 1990 and had a telling impact in staking out the terms of the debate (Bond, 1996c). The first was Nedcor/Old Mutual's *Prospects for a Successful Transition*, launched in late 1990 and completed in 1993. Next came the insurance conglomerate Sanlam's *Platform for Investment* scenario, followed by 'The Mont Fleur Scenarios'. Other counsel, such as the South African Chamber of Business' (SACOB) 'Economic Options for South Africa', was also thrust into the fray, followed by the South Africa Foundation's 1996 'Growth for All' document.

The interventions shared an overarching set of assumptions and tenets. Economic policy, they urged, had to be grounded in relationships of trust, negotiation and consensus building. This implied imposing 'a kind of "coerced harmony"', analogous to the central dynamic applied in the political negotiations (Bond, 1996c:2). In Patrick Bond's view, 'the scenario exercises reflected the desire [...] to come up with a deal—rather than with good analysis' (1996c:3). Steering that process was a set of cardinal assumptions, notably the need for macroeconomic stringency, restraint in social restructuring, an outward-oriented economy and a facilitating (as opposed to interventionist) state. They all demonised a redistributive approach as 'macroeconomic populism' and rejected the notion of grounding economic policy in a mutually reinforcing dynamic of growth and redistribution.

The key messages were promoted lavishly and ubiquitously in books, videos, multimedia presentations and newspaper supplements, and in a frenetic assortment of seminars, conferences, weekend 'get-aways', 'fact-finding' junkets abroad and high-profile visits of carefully chosen foreign experts—all financed by business, donors and multilateral agencies. The ideological barrage was incessant and the corporate-owned media ridiculed any signs of heterodoxy in ANC thinking. By 1993, Sanlam's *Platform for Investment* document could justifiably gloat about the 'close working relationship between the ANC, the World Bank, the Development Bank of Southern Africa, the Consultative Business Movement, and other organisations which are painstakingly pointing out the longer run costs of many redistributive strategies'.[7]

Broadly indicative of this counsel was SACOB's *Economic Options for South Africa* and its blithe assurance that free enterprise was 'the remedy for poverty and ensured economic growth'. Economic reforms were needed to create optimal conditions for free enterprise to flourish. The state's main business was to ensure social and political stability—without breaching the policy parameters required by capital. The document proved to be remarkably prescient. It advocated 'the promotion of small business, the reduction of corporate tax, the maintenance and upgrading of the country's infrastructure, and a reordering of government spending priorities to tackle poverty, unemployment and the skills shortage' (Kentridge, 1993:18)—an accurate précis of what was to come. Welfarist elements were seen as a 'political accessory', appended to an economic strategy—'necessary evils rather than the basis for creating a new set of social alliances, a new era for economic growth and the bedrock for social stability in post-apartheid society', in Morris's view (1993b:9). Almost two decades later, the ANC's economic strategy bore an uncanny resemblance to SACOB's counsel.

The World Bank also weighed in with advice. Soon after the 1990 thaw, it had opened channels to the ANC and trade unions, and began contracting researchers associated with the democratic movement. The soil of conciliation and consensus was diligently tilled. The Bank's 1994 *Reducing Poverty* report became the public component of an intensive process of lobbying and 'trust-building' with the ANC and other popular organisations. 'This is the only country in the world where we speak to the opposition,' its representative later boasted.[8]

In the Bank's view, growth would depend on private-sector-led expansion in labour-intensive sectors of the economy, with the state assuming a subsidising (through incentives and credit) and facilitating (through investment in health and education) role: 'South Africa's unequal legacy cannot be reversed solely by market reforms because those disenfranchised by apartheid will be unable to obtain the resources necessary to exploit market opportunities.'[9] The report was studded with contradictions, though. It criticised the capital-intensive character of industry and heavy state subsidies for large-scale capital-intensive projects, but claimed that 200 000 to 400 000 fewer jobs had been created in the 1980s as a result of the African workers' wage increases. While urging 'continuing fiscal discipline' and 'happier industrial relations', it counselled that labour should not 'bear the brunt of reduction in real wages'[10]—advice the IMF would not countenance. The latter's 'Key Issues in the South African Economy' document meanwhile paraded its customary arguments. Along with slashing the budget deficit, lowering inflation and maintaining macroeconomic stability, liberalised trade and financial relations were presented as prerequisites for increased exports, foreign investment and access to credit. It warned against 'excessive' government expenditure on education, health, training and complementary infrastructure, while declaring that the 'remedy for structural unemployment is to increase the productivity of labour, to lower the real wage or some combination of the two'. (Both trends would indeed occur over the following decade, though with scant effect on structural unemployment.) 'At least since Keynes, no serious economist would use [wages] to explain joblessness of the order of half the labour force,' economist Neva Makgetla countered (see Chapter six).[11] Some in the business press urged speedy implementation of IMF-style structural adjustment:

> The IMF will want measures such as currency liberalisation, reducing government spending, cutting subsidies to blue chip companies, privatising state assets and

busting the cartels in labour and other markets. Some will complain about a loss of sovereignty, but we would have undertaken these reforms years ago had we not been thwarted by vested interests ... we've been unable to make the reforms that will give us 6% growth. Perhaps the IMF will help.[12]

The apartheid government's Normative Economic Model (NEM) indeed drew heavily on IMF dogma. Having hopped the neoliberal bandwagon in the 1980s, the NP government had touted privatisation, trade liberalisation, spending cuts and strict monetary and fiscal discipline as the way forward. The conversion to neoliberal economics, however, proved half-hearted and its economic policy in the 1980s wavered between Thatcherite adjustments and statist reflexes. The NEM was more coherent. It bore the hallmark of a 1992 IMF 'occasional paper' that had reversed the 'growth through redistribution' formula. Its recipe for economic growth included corporate tax cuts, higher indirect taxation, wage restraint (and higher productivity), lower inflation, restricted capital outflows, budget-deficit cuts, more spending on training and on research and development, boosted manufactured exports, improvements in the social wage and subduing unions' strength via collective bargaining and corporatist arrangements. A trickle-down model, in other words, with government providing some support (through welfare measures and public-works projects) to the 'short-term' victims of adjustments. The ANC and COSATU dutifully slammed the NEM. Even mainstream business journalists concurred, predicting that 'neither the model's scenario nor that of the IMF have [sic] any hope whatever of being achieved'.[13] They spoke too soon: within three years the democratic government's macroeconomic strategy would feature elements close to the hearts of the NEM's authors.

The jostling for influence continued meanwhile. In late 1993, 'The Mont Fleur Scenarios' was unveiled. Supposedly leaning toward the social-democratic end of the spectrum, it would end up assisting the march of orthodoxy. It agonised over the dread prospect of macroeconomic populism and decried redistributive state spending. The timing was key. The Macro-Economic Research Group's (MERG's) 'Making Democracy Work: A Framework for Macroeconomic Policy in South Africa' report was still months away from completion. Eagerly awaited on the left, that report was expected to chart the ANC's thinking on economic policy. But, by the time it arrived, the race had already been run. Skittish expediency would win the day.

Converted: ANC economic policy in the early 1990s

By late 1993, 'the language and tone' of ANC and business policy documents were 'so similar that at times they appear interchangeable' (Kentridge, 1993:26). During the political negotiations, the ANC's consultation with its membership and political allies was patchy and perfunctory, and the formal relationship between the negotiations and economic policy formulation virtually non-existent. Pressure from ANC and trade union activists had kept on the agenda demands such as restructuring the financial sector and progressive taxation—but only until 1992, when they were dropped from ANC resolutions. The organisation had also begun mooting the need for property-rights guarantees and privatisation. Its rhetoric still orbited around a 'developmental state' that would 'lead, coordinate, plan and dynamise a national economic strategy' aimed at job creation and redistributing resources to the poor.[14] But evidence of such an approach was scant. ANC economic thinking had come to reflect, according to economist Viv McMenamin, 'a shift away from policies which may be morally and politically correct, but which will cause strong adverse reaction from powerful local and international interests' (Kentridge, 1993:10).

The ANC's 1992 guidelines had also endorsed an export-oriented growth strategy (see Chapter three), despite warnings from the General Agreement on Tariffs and Trade (GATT) that 'export-led growth, while beneficial to the balance of payments, is unlikely to immediately affect levels of unemployment, given the capital intensity of the export sector, unless labour-intensive downstream industries can be developed'.[15]

The left, too, was enamoured with an export-led growth path, a route promoted by the COSATU-supported Industrial Strategy Project (ISP) (Joffe et al, 1994a). It saw trade in manufactured exports as the way forward to growth and prosperity that would benefit workers, as well as relieve South Africa's current account difficulties and reduce its reliance on primary commodity exports. The growth in world exports (the ratio of exports to world GDP had doubled since the 1960s) emboldened planners, but they misread the vitality and character of South Africa's manufacturing industries, which were misshapen and stunted (see Chapters one and two).

The ISP was confident that the required restructuring could be achieved. Unlike business, it stressed that competitiveness derived not so much from lower input costs (such as cheaper wages) as from product quality and variety, speedy innovation, capital and labour productivity and 'the endowment of widely spread skills' (Joffe et al, 1994b: 17). Special emphasis was placed on high-value-added products. Rather than subject industry to attrition by randomly removing protection, the ISP proposed 'a trade policy that attempts to sharpen the flow of incentives from the international market' within an overall industrial strategy. The desired alchemy required from the state supply-side measures and a range of (dis)incentives that could make the market function better—'a kind of liberal Keynesianism', according to one team member. Elements of the ISP plan could have augmented industrial revival structured around popular domestic demand. Instead, they were deployed in a framework that pivoted South Africa's economic revival around exports, even though the ISP itself had warned that

> entry in external markets is increasingly difficult, partly because of the growth of protectionist barriers in key large economies and partly because of heightened competition. At the same time, most of the developing world (including South Africa) is being forced to open domestic markets to imports (Joffe et al, 1994a:91).

These retreats did not pass unchallenged. At the ANC's 1992 policy conference, activists had softened the wording of some placatory pledges. But the gist of the new post-1990 'realism' was endorsed, thanks partly, as Nattrass has suggested, to the personal presence of ANC leaders Nelson Mandela, Walter Sisulu and Cyril Ramaphosa in the economic policy debates at the conference. The draft policy guidelines emerged substantively intact though semantically adjusted. Thus the word 'privatisation' was replaced with an unwieldy phrase designed to soothe dissent.[16] The exception was the reappearance of a call for greater control of financial institutions.

COSATU, in particular, tried to hold a progressive line. Its calls for stronger social transformation negated attempts to portray the federation as the guardian of a narrow set of interests. In the media, though, the labour movement was ridiculed as a narrow and 'privileged' interest group, a caricature that resonated among the ANC's growing middle-class constituencies. Emphasising the need for job creation and for redistributing access to health, education and housing, COSATU pushed for a stronger institutionalised role in economic and industrial policymaking. It wished to see decision-making on key economic issues transferred into a forum where trade unions could wield influence. Key ANC figures, such as Trevor Manuel (the party's shadow finance minister), openly disapproved and insisted that economic policy was the preserve of government. The compromise was to set up a National Economic Forum (NEF) in 1992.[17] COSATU saw it as a negotiating body, but the ANC and corporate leaders preferred it to be an advisory body. These tensions would plague the NEF in its later incarnation, the National Economic Development and Labour Council (NEDLAC), which became little more than a 'consultative structure' with faint influence on policy decisions.

Potentially much more important was the development of a Reconstruction Accord, which COSATU wanted the ANC to adopt as a government programme once it assumed power. In return, COSATU would campaign for an ANC victory. The accord would eventually mature into the Reconstruction and Development Programme (RDP), which formed a central plank in the ANC's 1994 election campaign.

'No alternative'

A solid framework of accommodation was being hammered into place, though. By late 1993, the ANC had agreed to enshrine Reserve Bank independence in the Constitution, effectively removing monetary policy from democratic oversight and accountability. Explaining the decision, Mandela later said: 'We argued for the independence of the Bank [...] not only because we are committed to the sound economic management of the country, but also because we want to send out a strong signal to the international and local business and financial communities that we are serious about this commitment.'[18]

In economist Stephen Gelb's opinion, the move was less ominous than it seemed, since the constitutional clause 'was sufficiently vague that the relation between government and the Bank would continue to depend de facto on the personal styles and relationship of the Governor and the Finance Minister' (1999:12). That view, however, over-personalised the Bank's location in the economic and political system. In periods when finance capital is dominant, the structural intimacy between a country's central bank and the wider financial sector tends to deepen. As economists Paul Bowles and Gordon White have shown, the central bank then more strongly 'reflects the interests and ideology of that sector'.[19] The Reserve Bank clause had not been debated in the ANC. A precedent had been set for an approach that later would see the 1996 macroeconomic plan barged through. Meanwhile, the ANC (as part of the transitional government) had also entered into a secret USD 850 million loan agreement with the IMF to help tide the country over balance-of-payment difficulties.[20] Attached to the loan was a statement of intent, which read like a preview of the 1996 macroeconomic strategy:

> [A]n easing of monetary policy would have risked a further undermining of confidence and a resurgence of inflation [...] the thrust of SA's monetary policy during the past year will be maintained [...] despite the pressures for additional expenditure that will arise in transition, there is widespread understanding that increases in the government deficit would jeopardise the economic future of the country [...] Given the importance of maintaining a competitive tax structure, [fiscal policy] will emphasise expenditure containment rather than raising taxes.[21]

For the ANC's top leadership, the choices had become stark and binary: either yield to the injunctions of corporate capital or expose the economy to the wrath of the markets (and put the democratic transition at risk). But an explanation of this capitulation to neoliberal orthodoxy has to consider additional factors, among them the threadbare investments the organisation had made in economic policy and literacy. As Jonathan Michie and Vishnu Padayachee reminded, the ANC 'did not at the beginning of the negotiations possess a ready institutional capacity on the economic policy front to counter the power and resources available to its main opponents and other institutions' (1997:229).

In fact, there was a patent absence of technically rigorous economists at the helm of the ANC's DEP. In a rush to make up lost ground, top cadres were dispatched on training courses and corporate giants were happy to oblige. For example, Tito Mboweni (head of the ANC's DEP and later Labour Minister and Governor of the Reserve Bank), Maria Ramos (later Deputy Finance Minister) and Lesetja Kganyago (Director-general of the National Treasury) all underwent 'training' at the investment bank Goldman Sachs in the early 1990s.[22] The corporate world applied great effort to 'patiently and systematically educate blacks into the economic realities of the world', as the *Financial Mail* had urged earlier (Kentridge, 1993:4). It conducted a vigorous political and ideological struggle at a nominally technical level, deploying massive resources to great effect. Conservative figures in the ANC drew heavily on business advice (paraded as being in step with 'global standards') and jargon as they sought to convince their colleagues on the need to steer policy along more 'realistic' paths. The choice, the ANC leaders had come to believe, was to yield or be broken. Received wisdom held that there was no alternative. Yet, other viable approaches were being mapped— most notably the ill-fated MERG proposals.

The quiet death of the MERG report

The ANC had set up MERG in 1991 to develop a new macroeconomic model for South Africa.[23] There was grumbling about the strong presence of foreign economists on the research team and resistance from members of the ANC's DEP, who feared the initiative would eclipse them. MERG members, meanwhile, complained that the DEP was frustrating their work with spoiling tactics (Kentridge, 1993). By the time the group presented its neo-Keynesian final report, 'Making Democracy Work', to the ANC in late 1993, its proposals were well out of line with dominant thinking on economic policy within the ANC. The report was summarily shelved, even though economists such as Nattrass acknowledged that the recommendations were 'carefully costed and situated in what appears to be a sound macroeconomic model' (1994b:2).

Central to the document was the argument that the economy could best be restructured through the labour market (improved training, education and skills-building, and higher wages) and interventions aimed at improving the structure and operation of business. The goal was a 'strong private sector interacting with a strong public sector', the authors noted (MERG, 1993:265). The model predicted annual growth of 5% in 2004 and the creation of 300 000 new jobs a year. It centred on a two-phase growth plan (comprising a 'public-investment-led phase' and a 'sustained growth phase') that tied growth to expanded and efficiently deployed savings and investment. A robust role was reserved for the state, including

> state intervention in output and pricing decisions in the minerals sectors, regulation of the housing and building supplies market, tightening and extending controls on mergers and acquisitions, monitoring the behaviour of participants in oligopolistic markets, and creating supervisory boards (consisting of bank, trade union and other represented interests) for larger companies (Nattrass, 1994).

MERG saw state investment in social and physical infrastructure (housing, school education, health services, electrification and road development) in the first phase accounting for more than half of growth, triggering sustained, growth-inducing effects throughout the economy. In addition, it proposed that the state strategically apply a mix of incentives and regulations to restructure and improve industrial performance and recommended a national minimum wage (pegged at two-thirds the subsistence level for a household of five). It saw a need for the state to 'provide leadership and coordination for widely-based economic development' and to 'intervene directly in key areas' (MERG, 1993:281).

'Making Democracy Work' was the most coherent progressive option available. But mainstream media and economists savaged it, a reaction some ANC leaders reportedly shared.[24] Some of its key proposals would be exhumed in COSATU's 'Social Equity and Job Creation' document two years later. By then it was too late. The left had failed to defend MERG politically and advance its proposals within the ANC. By the time it arrived on the scene, it was seen to threaten the emerging consensus that was being assembled. The report was ignored. The left had been outgunned. Within three years, the ANC government's Growth, Employment and Redistribution (GEAR) strategy would apply the final nails to the coffin.

Marching with history

The ANC was hardly the first liberation movement to encounter obstacles once it assumed office; limits to change were not novel. But in South Africa's case, the idealism that had fuelled the struggle against apartheid dissipated with disarming ease. By 1994, economic policy had been emptied of heterodox content. Orthodoxy had acquired the status of self-evident 'truth'.

Yet the many variants of capitalism practised across the globe belied the notion that the neoliberal version constituted a kind of Platonic ideal. The Chinese hybrid had emerged from familial and communal networks of production and distribution. It was vastly different from the individualistically grounded Anglo-Saxon models. They, in turn, could hardly be confused with the paternalistic *chaebol* (conglomerates) of South Korea or with the bondage of corporate loyalties that underpinned the Japanese version. In each of those variants, the state had adopted a decisive set of duties and powers in relation to the economy. As for the claim that the era of globalisation had rendered the state powerless, that notion drew its authority less from empirical evidence than from sheer repetition (see Chapters one and three). Neoliberal globalisation constituted a significant constraining dynamic, but the room for manoeuvre was considerably wider than conventional wisdom allowed. The ANC ended up adopting a highly conservative and timid interpretation of globalisation, one that formed the ideological bedrock of policy packages that conformed faithfully to the dictates of conglomerate capital.

All this occurred in a wider, debilitating context. The collapse of Soviet-style socialism and the crisis of Western European social democracies had badly shaken the confidence of both radicals and left-leaning social democrats. For many, the sheer ability to think in terms of alternatives was absent (see Chapter three). Eyes were cast toward other growth models (the Asian tigers attracted considerable attention), but the examinations were shoddy. Having neglected the economic realm, the ANC's resistance levels were low, particularly in an era advertised as the 'end of history'. With the organisation's earlier makeshift reference points discarded into the proverbial dustbin, its appetite for risk was weak. The low road of submission held great appeal.

The allure was especially strong among those in the ANC who nursed strong acquisitive appetites. Their sway was unexpectedly strong, a reality conveniently overlooked by those who preferred to regard the SACP-engineered radical posturing of the 1980s as an intrinsic feature of the organisation. In reality, as Sipho Maseko would note, those strata had 'emerged more prominently and significantly from the 1960s onwards' and especially in the 1980s and 1990s as the 'decompression' of class differences within African communities gathered steam. Moreover,

> the African National Congress has since its inception sought to promote the interests of this class, as well as other classes. During the liberation struggle, particularly

before the ANC's banning in 1960, it articulated an ideology favourable to the development of the black capitalist class.[25]

Indeed, the notion of 'black economic empowerment' (a post-1994 siren call of the ANC government) was first trumpeted by the National African Federated Chambers of Commerce, founded in the 1960s. Along with the Black Management Forum, 'it popularised an idea misleadingly referred to as "black economic empowerment"—misleading because it implied socioeconomic improvement of the general black population, yet it called for the enrichment of the minority black capitalist class', in Maseko's opinion.[26] Those aspirations were hardly anathema to an organisation that staked considerable hope on the rapid growth of a black 'patriotic bourgeoisie', a notion with a strong pedigree in post-colonial Africa and Asia (see Chapter eleven).

Together, these factors fed a naïve hope for a mutually beneficial accommodation with domestic and international capital, in which drastic and conservative economic adjustments could be reconciled with the goal of quickly engineering a black capitalist class and achieving social upliftment.[27] The quest for policies acceptable to business proceeded as if they could be appended to a set of progressive (and politically palatable) social objectives.

The compromise carried a steep price: trade and financial liberalisation, a privatisation programme, a regressive tax system, ultra-low inflation targets and a battery of other business-friendly adjustments. The ANC had endorsed fiscal and monetary stringency, chosen a restricted role for the state in redistribution and supported the restructuring of trade and industrial policies in line with an export-led strategy. Capital controls were removed, and tariff and non-tariff protections were cut. Social and industrial unrest would be regulated with social accords, co-determination agreements and restructured labour relations. Commendable changes to the labour market would follow, reflecting the countervailing weight of the trade union movement. The labour market changes, however, would be easily sidestepped (see Chapter six). The adjustments inordinately benefited domestic conglomerates and international financial corporations; their impact in the lives of ordinary South Africans would be punishing.

The prevailing view made two central claims: the juggernaut of globalisation left the democratic state no choice but to march in step with neoliberal orthodoxy, and compliance would eventually bring the desired rewards. Each of the claims had graduated to received wisdom.

The myth of the weak state

Free market ideologues portrayed globalisation as a veritable force of nature that would erase the 'distortions' and 'aberrations' blocking the supposedly self-regulating and rational operation of free markets. Such deception was not new. Half a century earlier, Karl Polanyi had laid to rest this fallacy in his study *The Great Transformation*:

> *It was not realized that the gearing of markets into a self-regulating system was not the result of any inherent tendency of markets [...] but rather the effect of highly artificial stimulants administered to the body social in order to meet a situation which was created by the no less artificial phenomenon of the machine* (1944:140).

The free market economy in fact required prodigious degrees of state intervention: introducing economic and social adjustments, enforcing them, reorganising the body social and the body politic, as well as defending the adjustments against challenges by social forces. As Polanyi (1944) noted, the free market required the muscular support of the state, while the regulated market tended to emerge by its own accord as social forces resisted the destructive effects of a laissez-faire system:

> *The road to the free market was opened and kept open by an enormous increase in continuous, centrally organised and controlled interventionism. To make Adam Smith's 'simple and natural liberty' compatible with the needs of a human society was a most complicated affair. Witness the complexity of the provisions in the innumerable enclosure laws; the amount of bureaucratic control involved in the administration of the New Poor Laws [...] This paradox was topped by another. While laissez-faire economy was the product of deliberate state action, subsequent restrictions on laissez-faire started in a spontaneous way. Laissez-faire was planned: planning was not.*

The state, therefore, has become neither impotent nor disarticulated from capital. The reproduction of capital still occurs within the framework of regulations and adjustments introduced and managed by the state. It plays a 'central role in organising, sanctioning and legitimising class domination within capitalism' (Panitch, 1994:22). Neoliberalism represented an attack not on the state per se, but on the manner and interests according to which state resources would be allocated in society. A reorganised world economy was not rendering states powerless, but it was encumbering them in new ways. States would become increasingly divorced from the social roles and responsibilities assigned to them a few decades earlier—a trend that vividly expressed the class character of neoliberal globalisation. The intensity of that shift differed from place to place and over time. As the destabilising impact of the first phase of restructuring registered, certain forms of highly conditional social provisioning by the state then moved back onto the agenda (see Chapter five). As Hobsbawm noted,

> *the state, or some other form of public authority representing the public interest, [is] more indispensable than ever if the social and environmental iniquities of the market economy [are] to be countered, or even—as the reform of capitalism in the 1940s [showed]— if the economic system [is] to operate satisfactorily* (1995:577).

In fact, the hardcore phase of restructuring (associated with the Washington Consensus) had effectively dissolved by the final years of the twentieth century, at a point when the South African government was straining to comply with key precepts. By then, a second phase of neoliberal adjustment could be discerned. At the global level, transnational corporations and the governments of the industrial powerhouses redoubled their push to tighten control over intellectual property rights, soften resistance to privatisation and remove barriers to their exports and capital. Alongside this was recognition of the need for some social safety nets (largely to pre-empt mass privation, and social and political rebellion) and state intervention (especially to underwrite and enhance social reproduction via greater investments in health and education) at national level.

Many African countries could justifiably claim to have had little choice but to submit to IMF-decreed structural adjustment programmes. But the complicity of national elites in those adjustments and the benefits they sought to draw from them were a consistent and decisive factor as well. This was especially true for South Africa, where the leverage of the IMF and World Bank was minor. Idling on a neglected siding of the world economy, South Africa's large conglomerates desperately required an overhauled accumulation strategy. For them, the way forward demanded entry into the liberalised routes of accumulation that were being threaded across the globe. In short, they had to 'globalise'. A new, democratic government that had paid little attention to economic policy prior to 1990 and whose main paradigms of development had been shattered by the events of 1989 in Europe and the dissolution of Third World 'developmentalism' proved eminently understanding of their needs.

Rude awakenings

Like other national liberation movements, the ANC had anticipated a boundless vista of possibilities once it took power. Central to this (in mobilising terms, understandable) outlook was the singular objective that had driven anti-systemic movements since 1848: the seizure of state power. Most of them envisaged transformation as a two-phase project: winning state power, then using it to pursue far-reaching social and economic transformation. It was assumed that political victory equalled political power and thereby unlocked a bounteous realm of national sovereignty and autonomy. As numerous other liberation movements discovered, this assumption was at odds with the realities of the world system. In Immanuel Wallerstein's (1996) summary, such faith

> assumed that sovereign states are autonomous. But of course they are not autonomous and they never have been [...] All modern states, without exception, exist within the framework of the interstate system and are constrained by its rules and its politics. The productive activities within all modern states, without exception, occur within the framework of the capitalist world-economy and are constrained by its priorities and its economics [...] Shouting that one is autonomous is a bit like Canute commanding the tides to recede.

A decade earlier, such a reading would have seemed anathema to the ANC. But by the time it had put pen to the political settlement, its sense of constraints was well developed. Indeed, the alibi it was invoking for its preferred development path was that of denuded state sovereignty, with globalisation the main culprit.

In Philip Nel's view,

> emphasis on the loss of sovereignty makes it possible to shift some of the blame for domestically unpopular policies to faceless international forces [while convincing] doubters that what is happening is to a large extent inevitable (1999:23).

In his political report to the ANC's 1997 national conference, for example, Nelson Mandela repeatedly referred to globalisation, particularly to the integration of capital markets that 'made it impossible [to] decide national economic policy without regard for the likely response of the markets'. Rejecting the possibility of a stronger role for the state in the economy, trade and industry minister Alec Erwin, for instance, insisted that South Africa had little choice but to 'implement policy packages that are similar to those of the other developing countries'.[28] Yet the routes followed by other middle-income countries were hardly of a type. In fact, the most promising emerging economies were violating many of the rules the South African government was now straining to obey.

The GEAR plan

Adopted in June 1996, the Growth, Employment and Redistribution (GEAR) plan became the centrepiece of South Africa's growth path and, consequently, its broader development path. Drawn up in 'somewhat secretive conditions' (Gelb, 1999:16), GEAR was released after perfunctory 'briefings' of a few top-ranking ANC, SACP and COSATU figures who, according to one participant, were shown 'only the section headings' (Webster & Adler, 1999:16).[29] 'I confess even the ANC learnt of GEAR far too late—when it was almost complete,' Mandela would later admit.[30] In the later opinion of Stephen Gelb, who had participated in the plan's drafting,

> close affinity with the 'Washington Consensus' characterised not only the substantive policy recommendations of GEAR, but also the process through which it was formulated and presented publicly ... This was 'reform from above' with a vengeance, taking to extreme the arguments in favour of insulation and autonomy of policymakers from popular pressures (1999:16–17).

Former Finance Minister Trevor Manuel quickly declared the plan 'non-negotiable' in its broad outline, although the government was willing to negotiate 'the details with our social partners'. The left's disarray was palpable. Although well stocked with SACP and COSATU leaders, the ANC's national executive committee endorsed GEAR. Remarkable levels of discipline were maintained in the ANC's top ranks and among its allies. So firm was the ANC's hold over the SACP that the latter issued a woolly media release endorsing the objectives of the plan. Astonishingly, it claimed that the strategy resisted 'free market dogmatism' and 'envisage[d] a key economic role for the public sector, including in productive investment'.[31] A year would pass before the SACP would harden its stance and call for GEAR to be scrapped and replaced with a 'coherent industrial policy'.[32] It was left to COSATU to vituperate. The federation's Zwelinzima Vavi declared GEAR unworkable and unwinnable.[33] Strangely, though, it did not release the detailed critique of GEAR it had commissioned from the National

Institute for Economic Policy.[34] In both COSATU and the SACP, a pragmatic view prevailed: public opposition would be trumpeted to persuade the ANC government to revise specific features of the macroeconomic plan. Thus, COSATU's sixth national congress rejected GEAR, but did not demand that the government rescind it.

Putting the best foot forward

Devised by a coterie of mainstream economists,[35] and apparently based on a Reserve Bank model similar to that used for the apartheid government's NEM proposals a few years earlier (see Chapter three), GEAR's prescriptions lit up the faces of business leaders. The similarities between GEAR and the NEM were glaring; the new plan, charged the National Institute for Economic Policy, represented 'a recourse to the policy goals and instruments of the past apartheid regime'.[36]

Government claimed that GEAR's 'integrated approach' would create an average of 400 000 jobs annually, achieve an annual economic growth rate of 6% by the year 2000, boost exports by an average 8.4% per annum and drastically improve social infrastructure. Redistribution would emerge from 'job creation and more focused public expenditure' according to former Finance Minister Trevor Manuel:

> The higher growth path depends in part on attracting foreign direct invest-ment, but also requires a higher domestic saving effort. Greater industrial competitiveness, a tighter fiscal stance, moderation of wage increases, accelerated public investment, efficient service delivery and a major expansion of private investment are integral aspects of the strategy. An exchange rate policy consistent with improved international competitiveness, responsible monetary policies and targeted industrial incentives characterise the new policy environment. A strong export performance underpins the macroeconomic sustainability of the growth path (Department of Finance, 1996:21).

The plan had been drafted in a rush and it showed in its lack of rigour. A year later, the deputy director of finance, Andre Roux, would made the astonishing admission that more research was required into the link between economic growth and job creation.[37] Moreover, the plan hinged on an implausibly large increase in private-sector investment. At root, GEAR was an attempt to endear South Africa to private capital by:

- Reducing the deficit, limiting debt service obligations and countering inflation by restricting state expenditures;
- Liberalising financial controls and eventually removing all obstacles to the free flow of capital;
- Privatising 'non-essential' state enterprises and partially privatising other state-run utilities;
- Liberalising the trade regime by drastically reducing most tariffs and other forms of protection;
- Keeping the exchange rate stable and at a 'competitive' level;
- Adding infrastructure to address service deficiencies and backlogs;
- Adding tax incentives to stimulate new investment in competitive and labour-absorbing projects; and

- Seeking wage restraint from organised workers and introducing 'regulated flexibility' into the labour market.

Stripped to basics, GEAR sandwiched government policy between two stringent prescriptions. Fiscal austerity (reflected in a determination to drive the budget deficit down to 3% of GDP by the year 2000) would be used to reduce the total public-sector debt. Savings on interest payments would go towards social spending. Meanwhile, as a share of GDP, tax revenue would not exceed 25% (later increased to 26.5%). Increased government revenue and spending would depend on strong economic growth (and, in the short term, improved revenue collection). A surge in private investment would serve as the main engine of growth. The corporate sector praised the manner in which the plan 'responds to many of the concerns expressed by business'.[38] Business journalist Jenny Cargill noted that 'the government has met most of [business'] macroeconomic demands' and remarked that it was 'certainly difficult to identify social equity as an explicit feature of the strategy'.[39]

GEAR's growth projections (from 3.5% in 1996 to 6.1% in 2000) hinged on increases in private investment and net non-gold exports. The private sector would be the main source of investment and key partner in government's efforts to meet its infrastructural and other obligations. As economist Asghar Adelzadeh warned, 'the projected growth rate is almost completely dependent upon the rapid success of government policy in stimulating private investment' (1996:6). Yet one of the models used in GEAR'S drafting contradicted that logic, by showing that fiscal stringency would depress private-sector investment and economic growth. According to Gibson and Van Seventer's Development Bank model, 'if the goal is to reduce the public-sector borrowing requirements as a share of GDP, the result must be a fall in income, output and employment, all other things being equal' (1995:21). All that indeed transpired later (see Chapters five and six).

No specific measures were proposed to ensure the private sector met its assigned duty of productive investment. Affected instead was a crude act of seduction. GEAR's adjustments were meant to simulate an attractive posture for private investment. Most important were the commitments to remove capital controls, avoid corporate tax increases and run tight monetary and fiscal policies. GEAR offered no direct causal link, as ANC MP Rob Davies noted, 'between the measures proposed' and the achievement of its 'growth and employment targets' (1997:2):

> These results depend on assumptions that lie beyond the macroeconomic policy measures proposed, viz that the new policies generate 'confidence' among domestic and foreign private investors, who respond by significantly increasing investment [...] Whether investors really do respond to policy packages of this nature in this way, rather than to a record of growth and profitability, is clearly much more debatable (1997:2–3).

The gradual, eventually complete removal of capital controls envisaged in GEAR amounted to government-sanctioned capital flight—in a strategy that demanded greater domestic investment. Once domestic corporations and markets became entwined in global financial circuitry and the footloose passage of capital in and out of the economy was allowed, the state would find its influence over private investment decisions drastically denuded.

By buying into the argument that a fiscal deficit of 1996 proportions (under 6%) 'crowded out' private investment, the plan stigmatised state spending as an impediment to economic growth. The 'crowding out' argument claims that when the state borrows to finance a deficit, it competes for funds with the private sector, which supposedly reduces investor confidence, drives up interest rates and slows growth.[40] So the plan was to reduce the fiscal deficit (to under 4%), which would lead to lower real interest rates, boost investor confidence and trigger a dramatic rise in private investment. Yet, testifying to the plan's shoddy logic, an insistence on an ultra-low inflation effectively demanded high interest rates.[41] Reviewing other similar inconsistencies in the plan, Nattrass noted that there were

> so many 'shift parameters' in GEAR's integrated scenario projection that its 'technical' status is severely compromised. The growth and employment outcomes are in large part the product of a set of optimistic guesses about the likely effects of the economic policy package (1996:38).

Rather than see investment as a direct function of investor confidence, a more empirically solid approach would have viewed it as 'primarily determined by *profitability* of investment and the complementarity between investment by the state and the private sector' (ILO, 1996:29). Moreover, as Adelzadeh reminded, internationally greater attention was being paid to

> the role that public productive expenditures on infrastructure (such as investment on roads, transportation and housing) and social services (such as education, health care and welfare) play in promoting not only a country's economic wellbeing and growth, but also in encouraging private investment (1996:8).

In such an approach, public expenditure 'crowds in' private investment. GEAR, however, treated public spending as part of the problem and envisaged significant increases in public capital expenditure very late in the day—toward 2000, when it could be 'afforded'. The plan also bought into the monetarist obsession for managing relatively minute shifts in the inflation rate—an approach which, in Ha-Joon Chang's view, was 'misinformed' and served the interests of the financial sector to the detriment of industry.[42] South Africa's inflation rate was not unusually high. It peaked at 15% in 1991 and fell to 7% in 1996. Yet GEAR made a very low inflation rate one of the cardinal objectives of monetary policy, without demonstrating how this would affect other factors.

Cross-country evidence did not support the view that the relationship between inflation and economic growth was necessarily negative (Ghosh, 1997). But in dominant discourse, the monetarist view had become crudely contrasted with 'macroeconomic populism' (unbridled deficit-led social spending)—as if these were the only options. They were not. Macroeconomic balances could be assessed, maintained or restored over specified periods (a 10-year recon-struction cycle, say). This would have allowed for the positive results of particular policies to work their way into improved growth rates, rather than enforcing often arbitrary macroeconomic targets throughout the cycle. Within a sustained growth environment, certain macroeconomic (im)balances could temporarily be stretched if key social and economic indicators (such as employment figures, spending power and investment rates) were positive (Padayachee, 2005; Padayachee & Valodia, 2001). In the South African debate, such perspectives had become heretical.

GEAR's other key features require brief mention. It foresaw a drop in the share of foreign revenue provided by gold exports and aimed to boost manufactured exports and trigger a staggering 23% increase in the export/GDP ratio within four years. Somehow, it was to achieve this in the absence of 'a carefully formulated and precisely targeted industrial strategy geared to those sub-sectors that have potential for export growth', as Adelzadeh noted (1996:14). The plan provided no detailed linkages between its macroeconomic adjustments and industrial policy.[43]

The proposed restructuring of taxes was manifestly non-progressive. In 1996, 37% of tax revenue was derived from indirect taxation (value-added tax, which as currently structured discriminates against low-income earners) and so-called 'sin taxes' (levies on tobacco and alcohol that have a similar, discriminatory effect), with the likelihood of increases. There were several options to achieve greater progressiveness, including a capital gains tax,[44] a tax on luxury consumption and a tax on unproductive land (Adelzadeh, 1996:9). Instead, personal and corporate taxes were to be reduced and tax holidays proffered for selected investments. Overall, revenue was slated to increase by way of more effective tax collection. Analysing the tax system, Gensec Asset Management found that the contribution of personal income tax to total taxes had risen dramatically from the late 1970s to the mid-1990s— while the relative contribution of corporate taxes had shrunk.[45]

Despite the attempts to align GEAR rhetorically with the socially progressive objectives of the RDP, GEAR set no redistributive targets and demurred on the linkage between growth and income redistribution. It also failed to integrate its main elements: for instance, the impact of restructuring government spending on employment and redistribution was sidestepped, while the relationship between the plan and industrial policy was left undeveloped. Far from constituting a cogent strategy, the overriding aim, according to Stephen Gelb,

> was to signal to potential investors the government's (and specifically the ANC's) commitment to the prevailing orthodoxy. In 'marketing' the strategy, senior Department of Finance officials made explicit its close parallels with the approach of the international financial institutions, while emphasising at the same time the idea that GEAR was 'homegrown' in South Africa (1999:15–16).

The corporate world looked on approvingly. South Africa's economic policies were being managed, a *Financial Mail* journalist noted, by 'ANC politicians who have graduated from freedom fighters to the real new world'.[46] The real world, though, was looking decidedly unpleasant.

Report cards

By mid-1998, a modest and short-lived economic recovery had run out of steam. Statistics SA in 1999 applied a new accounting methodology, which conjured a marginally rosier picture. The adjusted figures showed the economy grew by 0.6% in 1998 (GEAR had predicted 3.8%), and 1.2% in 1999 (against GEAR's 4.9%). The relative output of goods-producing sectors continued to decline, while that of business and financial-service sectors was on the rise. This trend would deepen in the years ahead (see Chapter five). Yet the Finance Department's director-general, Maria Ramos (one of the Goldman Sachs trainees from the early 1990s), declared the economy buoyant and resilient. The data, she said, proved that South Africa was benefiting from globalisation.[47] Government was especially excited by news that the public debt and deficit were shrinking. By 2000, its defence of the GEAR plan had become positively Orwellian. Thus former President Thabo Mbeki told parliament that 'many major indicators point to the excellent work that has been done to place our country on a strong growth path'.[48] When he spoke, real GDP per capita was 2.6% lower than it had been in 1996.

Private domestic investment was sluggish and FDI absent. The private sector's share of total fixed investment had fallen to 68% (Adelzadeh, 1999:2), most of it in the category 'machinery and equipment'—'in all likelihood a reflection of the continuous process of substituting capital for labour', according to the Reserve Bank (1998:10). In 1999, domestic private fixed investment declined by another 5.5% against the 1998 figures. The economy was now heavily reliant on capital inflows and these were being lured mainly with privatisation ventures (notably the auctioning of a 30% stake in the telecommunications monopoly, Telkom, in 1997) and the unbundling of large local conglomerates. South Africa lagged behind Algeria, Angola, Egypt, Nigeria, Tunisia and Zimbabwe in the ranking of FDI recipients in Africa.[49] The little FDI that did land on its shores was going mostly toward mergers and acquisitions (see Chapter five). This kind of investment rose by 19% in 1995 before rocketing by 160% in 1996 and 130% the following year (when it constituted almost 60% of FDI). As Adelzadeh reminded:

> *Mergers and acquisitions bring the possible benefits of improved productivity (through processes of rationalisation, the introduction of new technologies and overhaul of management and even production systems). But they do not on the whole increase productive capacity in the economy. Neither do they typically create jobs. On the contrary, [they] tend to be marked by rationalisation of labour inputs—in other words, job cuts (1999:4).*

There was a dramatic rise in net short-term capital inflows, most of it destined for the bond and equity markets. The values of these flows increased five-fold between 1996 and the end of the decade. Their volatile nature hit home in 1998, when almost USD 1 billion gushed out in the third quarter alone, triggering exchange-rate instability and interest-rate hikes. Meanwhile, South African corporations were queuing up to make offshore investments and some of the largest conglomerates were soon be allowed to list offshore (see Chapter five). The reasoning for allowing those moves was notable. Foreign investors eyeing post-1994 opportunities, it was argued, found an economy dominated by sprawling corporations, leaving little space for bulky new entrants. By encouraging offshore investments, government hoped to create 'space' in the economy for foreign investors (and emerging black capitalists), since firms shifting abroad would sell non-core local operations in order to raise investment capital.

By 1998, Trevor Manuel was conceding that 'the results, in the short term, have not always reached the targets we set for ourselves', adding that some of the targets could become 'even more elusive'. But it was 'precisely at times like this that our resolve and commitment is tested', he urged (Manuel, 1998a:3).

Not hiring

On the job front, the plan's performance was abject. More than half a million (non-agricultural) jobs were lost between 1994 and 2000 in a trend that dated back to the 1980s. Driving it was the introduction of labour-saving technologies, increased outsourcing and a determined shift toward casual and contract labour (see Chapters two and six). Some 200 000 more jobs were lost on the country's farms, as farmers mechanised production and retrenched workers to pre-empt the effects of new labour legislation aimed at improving farmworkers' job security and working conditions. The narrow (non-agricultural) unemployment rate stood at 23% in 1999, according to Statistics SA. Once unemployed workers who had not sought work in the month prior to polling were included, unemployment topped 37% (up from 32% in 1994). Hardest hit were the sectors that contributed about 80% of total formal non-agricultural employment: manufacturing, mining and quarrying, construction, transport and electricity.[50] In those mainstay sectors, jobs were vaporising, at agonising personal and social costs. The economic effects were no less alarming. The National Institute of Economic Policy calculated that sacking a semi-skilled gold miner cost the economy R 83 000 (USD 13 400) a year; the figure rose to R 132 000 (USD 21 300) in the case of a skilled miner.[51] In wider perspective, the miners retrenched in 1997

> cost society about R 5.5 billion—or 0.8% of national GDP. Because the economy absorbs only a fraction of this unemployed labour, the social cost to the economy in the following year was roughly R 8.8 billion (using a simple multiplier of 1.6 and an inflation rate of 6%, in addition to assuming that 10% of these retrenched miners would have been absorbed into the economy). So, in 1998, the social cost associated with miners retrenched in 1997 was equal to 1.2% of national GDP (Nicolau, 2000).

Government clung to the hope that the structural adjustments ('clearing away deadwood to allow the new to grow', as Trade and Industry Minister Alec Erwin put it) eventually would solve the unemployment crisis. Trevor Manuel declared that 'the prospects for a recovery in employment in manufacturing [were] strong' (Manuel, 1998b:3), but there was no basis for the expectation. Between 1989 and 1996 the manufacturing sector had spent R 30 billion (USD 5.7 billion at 1996 exchange rates) on plant and equipment (in addition to upgrading old machinery). The sector shed some 145 000 jobs in that period.[52]

Manuel would soon revise his sunny prognosis. '[G]overnment, labour and business can pontificate and collectively lament the absence of jobs,' he said in 2000, 'but they aren't capable of creating jobs.'[53] Salvation would now be sought in the small-business sector, while the land-reform policy was revised to focus more on aiding (black) small farming enterprises (see Chapters five and seven). The informal sector had also acquired an unlikely allure. Challenging the view that 'the economy is not growing and that this stagnant economy is shedding jobs', Thabo Mbeki, then deputy president, had told unionists in 1998 that nothing was being said of the so-called 'grey economy' of informal trading and other small-scale enterprises. Those, he claimed, were creating jobs and generating growth.[54] Manuel followed suit, alleging that 'much of the employment growth that is occurring' was not being captured in conventional statistical measurements (1998b:3). Yet Statistics SA had found that 80% of the country's informal sector was survivalist and that most people active in it were living below the poverty line. The International Labour Organisation (ILO) was stating the obvious when it concluded from its cross-country surveys that 'no economy has successfully industrialised or boosted its productive employment primarily or largely through a massive expansion of informal own-account or petty activities' (ILO, 1996). It also warned against conceptually stratifying the labour market into formal and informal sectors. Such dualisms, it said,

> *tend to lead to debates about the merit of removing or exempting the 'informal' from regulations and of providing credit or subsidies to small-scale (informal) units on a preferential basis, paradoxically introducing arbitrary distortions into the market structure [...] in reality, nothing is quite so simple. Increasingly, even large-scale firms resort to 'informal' forms of employment, through sub-contracting, out-sourcing, use of casual labour and so on* (ILO, 1996:11).

Official discourse would ignore that advice. Within a few years the notion that South Africa comprised two structurally separated economies would become received wisdom, and guide economic and development policy (see Chapter six).

Defending GEAR

Government's defence of GEAR would present the plan as an elaboration of principles and perspectives contained in the RDP. It 'simply seeks to set out clearly and unambiguously the key economic requirement for achieving [the RDP] goals', as Trevor Manuel put it (1996:2). Other leaders went further, arguing that the specific measures in the GEAR plan were merely refinements of positions established in the RDP. As Mbeki (1998b:4) put it:

> *In clear and straightforward language, the RDP identified a high deficit, a high level of borrowing and the general taxation level as, to quote the RDP again, 'part of our macroeconomic problem' [...] Comrades also appear to have forgotten that, having noted the fiscal crisis, characterised in part by a large budget deficit, and having called for new macroeconomic ratios, the RDP did not then go on to say what these ratios should be. For some strange reason, when work is then done to translate the*

perspective contained in the RDP into actual figures, this is then interpreted as a
replacement of the RDP by GEAR.

The claim had some basis. As shown, a great deal of consistency was evident in the
ANC's economic thinking from 1992 onwards. As for the RDP, despite its overriding
progressive character, on macroeconomic matters it was elliptical and timid.
Gelb (1999:13) correctly detected 'consistency in the ANC's position on macro
policy between 1993 and 1996 or between the RDP and GEAR'.[55] Also, the main
structures created in 1994 to implement the RDP perforce operated within those
macroeconomic parameters. Thus, the RDP Fund was funded (as prescribed in the
RDP White Paper) not by increasing overall expenditure, but by 'reprioritising'
departmental budgets. RDP funding, in other words, was contingent on 'fiscal
discipline'. What's more, the RDP Office was allotted very little influence over
fiscal policy and none over monetary issues or other aspects of macro policy (Gelb,
1999:16). The pecking order became more explicit in early 1996, when government
shut down the RDP Office and dispersed its functions among other 'conventional'
line departments, with the RDP's 'command centre' shared between the deputy
president's office and the Finance Ministry. The left had trained its gaze on those
parts of the RDP document that highlighted the need for popular participation and
state intervention in the economy and neglected other sections that called for fiscal
restraint and endorsed privatisation.

Meanwhile, chastened by the economy's poor performance, government officials
would play up GEAR's contribution to economic stability and the achievement of
'sound fundamentals':

> *Since our own savings levels are inadequate, we have to attract foreign savings.*
> *However, we do so in a rapidly globalising world where capital moves relatively*
> *freely across borders [...] The lessons we draw from all these experiences is that*
> *what matters are sound economic policies and solid economic institutions* (Manuel,
> 1998a:2–3).

Within a few years, though, government pronouncements would shift into a full-
throated register as the economy eventually seemed to respond to the adjustments
and growth began to speed up.

Endnotes

1   *The Sowetan*, 5 March 1990.
2   Labour consultant Duncan Innes, quoted by Kentridge (1993:3).
3   Based on a disputed reading of the Freedom Charter's phrase: 'The mineral wealth beneath
    the soil, the banks and monopoly industry shall be transferred to the ownership of the people
    as a whole.'
4   The quote is drawn from Sunter's 1987 book, *The World and South Africa*, cited by Bond
    (1996c:4).
5   'Continuation lecture', University of Pittsburgh, 6 December 1991, quoted in Gelb (1998:13).
6   See Kans and Carter (1977:206).
7   Cited in Bond (1996c:7).

8   Isaac Sam, *Business Day*, 15 August 1994. The World Bank went even further; leading one of its teams was Geoff Lamb, a former SACP member.
9   Isaac Sam, *Business Day*, 15 August 1994.
10 *Ibid.*
11 *Business Day*, 10 August 1994.
12 Editorial, *Business Times* [Johannesburg], 21 August 1994.
13 *Finance Week*, quoted by Bond (1996c: 10).
14 ANC, 'Draft resolution on economic policy', p. 3, quoted by Nattrass (1994c:15).
15 As argued in a 1993 study by GATT staff, cited by Bond (1996c:8).
16 'Privatisation' became 'reducing the public sector in certain areas in ways that will enhance efficiency, advance affirmative action and empower the historically disadvantaged while ensuring the protection of both consumers and the rights of employment of workers'; ANC, 1992, Department of Economic Policy, *ANC Policy Guidelines for a Democratic South Africa*—as adopted at the National Conference (28–31 May, p. 24).
17 The key negotiations on macro policy in the NEF, according to at least one account, were led by former unionist Alec Erwin, who 'consistently adopted a conciliatory and defensive posture towards government and business'; author's interview, December 1996.
18 'Mandela on the record: What the SA business community can expect of and from the ANC', *Finance Week*, 31 March 1994; quoted by Gelb (1999:12).
19 Quoted in Marais (1999c).
20 Strictly speaking, the deal was signed by the Transitional Executive Council (the country's caretaker government at the time), of which the ANC was a member.
21 Excerpt from the 'Statement of economic policies', reprinted in *Business Day*, 24 March 1994 and cited by Gelb (1999:12–13).
22 'I have known these folks for a long time, and when it was not fashionable it opened its doors to young ANC economists and took them for training in New York,' Mboweni said in April 2010, after being appointed an adviser to Goldman Sachs. Months earlier, he had been appointed chairman of AngloGold Ashanti. See Marcia Klein, 'Mboweni to join troubled Goldman Sachs as adviser', *Sunday Times* [Johannesburg], 25 April 2010; Ethel Hazelhurst, 'Troubled Goldman Sachs appoints Mboweni', *Business Report*, 26 April 2010.
23 Its tasks included training black economists and supporting COSATU on economic issues. MERG later became the National Institute for Economic Policy (NIEP).
24 For an illuminating debate on the MERG report, see the essays by Nicoli Nattrass, Raphael Kaplinsky and John Sender in the *Journal of Southern African Studies*, Vol. 20, No. 4 (December 1994), pp. 517–45.
25 Sipho Maseko, 'The real rise of the black middle class', *Mail & Guardian*, 21 May 1999.
26 *Ibid.*
27 Years later, a SACP strategy and tactics document would note that 'we have not, as an ANC-led liberation movement, collectively thought through the implications of the new world situation for our national democratic revolution'. SACP (1995:4).
28 'Interview with Alec Erwin', *Global Dialogue*, Vol. 4, No. 1 (April 1999), Johannesburg, p. 19.
29 Trevor Manuel would later claim that 'Blade [Nzimande] and [Zwelinzima] Vavi want to wiggle out of the fact that we sat in Madiba's old house in Houghton and discussed this issue [of GEAR]'. See Ferial Haffajee, 'Not in my father's house' [interview with Trevor Manuel], *Mail & Guardian*, 13 December 2007.
30 'Business unconcerned as Mandela yields to political expediency', *SouthScan*, Vol. 12, No. 34, 1 September 1997.
31 SACP statement, reported by SA Press Association, 14 June 1996.
32 SACP media statement, 10 June 1997.
33 COSATU media statement, reported by SA Press Association, 14 June 1996.
34 The study was presented to COSATU, which apparently used it to brief top leadership; author's interview October 1996.

35 Including Iraj Abedian, Brian Kahn, Stephen Gelb, Andre Roux, Andrew Donaldson and Ian Goldin.

36 NIEP (1996:2).

37 'Govt pessimistic about job creation', *Business Day*, 13 May 1997.

38 *Business Times* [Johannesburg], 16 June 1996.

39 'Growing pains?', *Democracy in Action*, August 1996, p. 27.

40 The South African Foundation's 'Growth for All' document had belaboured this argument, but the National Institute of Economic Policy found 'no empirical evidence to suggest' that this process 'has ever occurred in South Africa' (1996:6).

41 Indeed, South Africa's vulnerable balance of payment situation soon saw the Reserve Bank hike interest rates. In 1998, as capital drained out of South Africa, interest rates exceeded 20%, depressing economic activity.

42 'Bank's monetary policy "misinformed"', *Business Day*, 15 June 1997.

43 Growth in export/GDP ratios registered by other countries invited scepticism about GEAR's 23% target; between 1970 and 1994, the average figure for the Organisation for Economic Cooperation and Development (OECD) countries was 6%, for Brazil it was 5% and in South Korea it was 4%.

44 A capital gains tax was later introduced (in early 2000) and drew little more than murmurs of protest from the business community.

45 'Revisit GEAR, review the tax system', media statement from Gensec Asset Management, 21 October 1998.

46 'Spare us from this collectivist twaddle', *Financial Mail*, 21 May 1999. The article described critics of the GEAR plan as 'naïve believers in the ability of government intervention— even worse, activism— to get an economy moving'.

47 'GDP defies expectations', *Business Day*, 22 June 1999.

48 'Mbeki bullish on economy, names top advisers', *Mail & Guardian*, 4 February 2000.

49 'Foreign direct investment plummets', *Business Day*, 28 September 1999.

50 On the gold mines, for example, jobs were vaporising. The trend dated back to the late 1980s. Total employment on gold mines operated by the Chamber of Mines fell to 424 000 in 1991, and then plunged to 222 000 by 1999, the lowest total in more than 70 years (Wilson, 2001).

51 The calculations measured the social burden created by the loss of the miner's consumption expenditure, as well as the loss of tax payments and remittances supporting dependants. Those effects extended across the country's borders. Almost half (47%) the workers on South Africa's gold mines were migrant labourers who, on average, sent about 60% of their wages home (mainly to Lesotho and Mozambique). The amounts were calculated at 1998 prices, while the dollar figures were calculated at 1998 exchange rates.

52 'No one has really thought about new bill's effects', *Business Day*, 31 October 1997.

53 'Left blamed for economic failures as Manuel woos foreign investors', *SouthScan*, Vol. 15, No. 1, 14 January 2000.

54 'Virtues of "grey economy" questioned', *SouthScan*, Vol. 13, No. 14, 10 July 1998.

55 He was wrong, however, in claiming that 'GEAR in other words did not represent the abandonment of the RDP'. GEAR eclipsed many of the RDP's progressive proposals on social policies.

CHAPTER FIVE

All dressed up: the economy in the twenty-first century

Superficially, the economy in the early 2000s bore faint resemblance to the bedraggled and wheezing version the ANC encountered when it took office in 1994. GDP growth was gaining momentum, trade relations had multiplied, financial investors seemed to be eyeing South Africa as an attractive 'emerging' economy. At street level in the major cities, unabashed buoyancy was on display. Real-estate developments mushroomed; gleaming imported sedans sped from one gridlocked intersection to another; shopping malls filled with customers even before the final brick was laid. Ratings agencies praised government for its sensible stewardship. Public debt had been trimmed, as had the budget deficit. Tariff barriers and capital controls were being dismantled.

Social realities composed a very different and much dimmer picture. But government assured all that as long as the economy kept growing, the benefits would keep spreading wider. 'Solid fundamentals' made it possible to start building a developmental state that would harness the new economic vibrancy for social progress: the pain was done; the gain would now come. These were heartfelt claims. A decade later, they remained just that: claims. A brief review of the subplots of post-apartheid economic restructuring will help explain why.

Rewind: South Africa's economic makeover

South Africa's economy was derelict and misshapen in the early 1990s, dominated by ponderous conglomerates desperate to restructure and venture into global markets but unable to do so until a political settlement unlocked new economic policy options. Although their holdings extended across many sectors, most of these conglomerates were still anchored in the minerals and energy sectors (see Chapter one). They needed, and worked tirelessly to bring about, policy arrangements that would liberate them from the fetters of the South African economy and enable them to reorganise their holdings and operations within the global system. For them the imperative was to restructure and globalise—and, according to economist Seeraj Mohamed (2010), to reduce their exposure to possible interventions by a democratic government. This hinged on their ability to export capital and assets. Appreciating this pressure to disinvest became one of the new government's early educations, as the former finance minister, Trevor Manuel, later conceded:

> *After years of isolation, the pent-up demand for foreign investment by institutional investors and companies was huge. The extent of this demand is illustrated by*

the fact that, from the introduction of the asset-swap mechanism in 1995 till its abolition in 2002, institutional investors invested R100 billion abroad.[1]

South African businesses were indeed spiriting huge volumes of capital abroad. Mohamed and Finnoff (2004) estimate that *illegal* capital flight from South Africa ran to about 5.4% of GDP between 1980 and 1993 and almost doubled to 9.2% of GDP from 1994 to 2000. The new government seemed to see only two options. It could try to stem the illicit outflows of capital (at a stage when global orthodoxy demanded the opposite) or it could formalise and regulate capital flight in return for certain concessions. The latter option won out and government embarked on a steady process of financial liberalisation, which accelerated after implementation of the GEAR plan in 1996.

The cardinal economic legacy of post-apartheid economic policies has been the facilitation of capital flight and divestment, the globalisation of South Africa's largest corporations and corporate unbundling and restructuring. The quid pro quo for the ANC was the prospect that large-scale unbundling would open opportunities for an emerging black or 'national' bourgeoisie whose wealth-making ambitions presumably would be shaped by a nationalist commitment to aid social transformation.

The adjustments posed major risks. Capital outflows had to occur without depreciating the value of the rand. The disinvesting entities demanded a strong local currency, since the domestic assets they sought to transfer abroad were denominated in rands. Since a drastic removal of capital controls (the 'big bang' approach demanded by some) very probably would have collapsed the rand, those controls were relaxed in phases.[2] Meanwhile, capital inflows had to be attracted to counterbalance the long-term outflows. That challenge required appropriate macroeconomic postures, including an aggressive monetary policy, with high interest rates serving as the bait for short-term capital. These and other adjustments were introduced under the mantle of GEAR. To a considerable extent, therefore, South Africa's macroeconomy was being 'managed to allow for such capital flight on favourable conditions to the conglomerates' and to deal with the 'overhang of disinvestment' (Fine, 2008b:4,7). By early 2010, financial controls had been relaxed on 27 occasions, most recently under the stewardship of Jacob Zuma (and a government which, allegedly, had shifted to the 'left').[3]

The official pretext was weak, yet widely accepted. Once domiciled in London or New York, those erstwhile South African corporations would be able to recapitalise and invest afresh in the South African economy (as 'foreign' investors). Unspoken was the cost of this accommodation. Corporations will have exported capital and assets away from the possibly 'intrusive' hand of the democratic government. Seven of the country's largest corporations moved their primary listings abroad. Two of them, Old Mutual and Liberty, shipped vast amounts of pension-fund capital abroad. Two others were major mining corporations (Anglo American Corporation and Billiton, formerly Gencor, now part of BHP Billiton), while South African Breweries (now part of SABMiller) and two major infotech corporations, Datatec and

PQ Holdings, followed suit. The moves also insulated them against later, sharp swings in the value of rand.

As government eased the sluice gates open, vast wealth was transferred out of the country. Much of it had been amassed with the labour of South African workers and by extracting mineral resources from the country's soil. The word 'looting' comes to mind. Yet it occurred not in a broken-down system (as in Russia in the 1990s), but as a part of a phased economic strategy, managed by a democratic government espousing an African Renaissance.

Trevor Manuel's great achievement, believes Ben Fine (2008b:7), lay in 'managing the outflow of capital by the domestic conglomerates [and] presenting it as something else in terms of macroeconomic objectives'. Wesso's (2001:64) calculations at the South African Reserve Bank showed a net *outflow* of investment running at about R 386 million per quarter between 1991 and 2000, due 'mainly to South African firms receiving exchange control approval to invest offshore'.[4] While capital gushed out of the South African economy, private investment (domestic and foreign) trickled in, despite kindly assessments of the economy from the major ratings agencies and the World Bank's approving verdict that the

> *investment climate is mostly favourable—power is cheap and relatively reliable,*[5]
> *the burden of regulation is not excessive, corruption is low, the ports function*
> *relatively well, access to finance does not seem to be a major problem for most*
> *enterprises, and most people trust the court system* (Clarke *et al*, 2007:14).[6]

Many critics of GEAR err in seeing the plan as the result of sheer ideological conversion or persuasion. The plan's progressive apologists have also fed that perception, by claiming that government had no choice but to be seen to swim with the tide of orthodoxy. Doing otherwise, it is claimed, would have deterred investors, choked access to credit and aggravated macroeconomic instability. That makes sense only insofar as one can detach economic policy from the requirements and prerogatives of powerful interests and from the balance of power between them and the state.

Post-apartheid investment patterns

Now more or less footloose, these globalising corporations succeeded in transferring abroad capital that had been accumulated in South Africa and in recasting their relationships with the democratic state. And they did so with the approval of that state. Historically, pension funds were a major source of long-term investment in many developmental states.[7] Yet in South Africa's case, government allowed Old Mutual, one of its largest pension-fund providers, to relocate and list in London.[8] The Finance Ministry claimed that the moves would ultimately aid growth and development in South Africa; offshore listings approved by the Finance Ministry would enable conglomerates to raise capital internationally for investment in South Africa. Large amounts of funds were indeed raised internationally, but little of it has been channelled productively back into the country. The preference has been to expand into other countries. According to Chabane (2006), the total stock of *outward* FDI grew from USD 8.7 billion in 1995 to USD 28.8 billion in 2004.[9] Major inward investment has been limited largely to acquisitions of stakes in state utilities (chiefly Telkom and South African Airways) and the return of firms that had disinvested during the 1980s (Roberts 2004).[10] But the divesting corporations did retain strong policy influence inside South Africa via their global standing and their remaining holdings in the country.

In the early 2000s, capital inflows increased. Overall, they surged in 2002–05, rising to 5% of GDP, compared with an average 1% in the previous decade. But the character and consequences of those inflows gave less cause for cheer, as we discuss in more detail later in this chapter. In 2005, Absa Bank's sale to Barclays generated a large share of the inflow, while most of the rest took the form of equity holdings in mining and finance. Foreign direct investment languished.[11]

The inflows did not spark an increase in domestic investment either. By one account, South African firms were involved in 2 100 foreign operations in the mid-2000s, almost two thirds of them in Africa and a fifth in Organisation for Economic Co-operation and Development (OECD) countries. Those firms included 82 of the top 100 firms listed on the Johannesburg Stock Exchange (JSE), as well as 'a substantial majority of all JSE-listed companies, together with numerous major unlisted corporations and all the major state corporations' (Gelb, 2006b:6). 'Most of this investment', Stephen Gelb added, was 'market-seeking'—that is, aimed 'at overcoming the limits and constraints of market size in South Africa' (*ibid*).

The main economic effect of the inflows was to underwrite a weakening currency and rising balance of trade deficit (which reached 4% of GDP in 2005, up from an average 0.5% for the previous decade). In essence, high interest rates served to attract short-term capital inflows, which buoyed the rand to artificially high levels. This helped finance soaring imports (thus stabilising the balance of payments), but at the cost of hobbling manufactured exports. Between 2000 and 2005 the volume of imports increased 44% (while export volume rose by 12%).[12]

The mid-2000s marked the zenith of the post-apartheid economic growth, achieved largely on the back of a global commodity boom and characterised especially by a red-hot real-estate sector and credit-financed consumption.

It is not surprising, therefore, to discover that new job creation has occurred mainly via public-works programmes, business services and the wholesale and retail trade sectors (see Chapter six). Employment growth in the latter sectors was a by-product of debt-fuelled economic growth, which was driven mainly 'by unsustainable growth in consumption, fuelled by credit extension', as Trade and Industry Minister Rob Davies would later put it. Between 1994 and 2008, South Africa's productive sectors grew by an average 2.9% annually, but the consumption-driven sectors mushroomed by 7.7% annually. Even as GDP growth peaked (at 5% between 2005 and 2007), unemployment levels dipped only marginally. The manufacturing sector remained insufficiently dynamic.[13] While it languished, the financial sector steamed along.

Nip and tuck: the conglomerates restructure

Yet several objectives were achieved. South Africa's major conglomerates were able to restructure themselves on a global scale (an economic imperative) and reduce their risks within the South African economy (a political imperative). On the latter front, they also covered their bets by inaugurating a series of black economic empowerment (BEE) deals in the early 1990s (discussed in more detail later in this chapter).

South Africa's largest corporations dismantled their bulky pyramid structures, reorganised their portfolios, offloaded cross-holdings and globalised their operations and holdings. Unbundling deals ran to about R 80 billion (USD 10 billion) in 1999 alone, according to Chabane (2006). This was accompanied by a mergers and acquisitions frenzy that topped R 300 billion (USD 38 billion) in value in 1998 (most of them local) and exceeded R 500 billion (USD 63 billion) in 2001 (almost all of them offshore).[14] Within 10 years, the value of mergers and acquisitions by South African corporations had increased 50-fold—a rate of growth that outpaced the global average. South African activities cooled subsequently until 2007, when they again totalled more than R 500 billion.[15] A great many of those deals served to dismantle bulky corporate structures that were difficult to manage and unattractive to potential investors:

> Of the 20 largest South African deals reported in 1992–1998, 75% correspond[ed] to the simplification of the corporate structure, 10% to consolidation in financial industry, 10% to foreign acquisitions, and only one deal—TransNatal's acquisition of Rand Coal to form Ingwe Coal in 1994—a 'genuine' South Africa merger (Goldstein, 2000:17).[16]

Except for the financial sector muscling onto the scene, key historic features of the economy remained in place. The core MEC sectors still constituted the economy's centre of gravity, as Mohamed (2010) observed:

> With the exception of a few sectors, such as automobiles and components, manufacturing remains dominated by sectors with strong links to the MEC. These sectors, with the exception of engineering and capital equipment, are capital- and energy-intensive process industries, such as electricity generation, minerals beneficiation (iron and steel, aluminium) and the Sasol oil-from-coal process and its chemicals by-products. Downstream, value-added manufacturing sectors have not been adequately developed and manufacturing remains relatively undiversified.

Value added by the industrial sectors of the economy did not exceed 35% of GDP since the mid-1990s. This compares poorly with a random selection of other middle-income countries, as shown in Figure 5.1. In the early 1990s in Chile, Indonesia, Iran, Malaysia and Thailand, for example, the value added by industry (as a share of GDP) was roughly the same as in South Africa (about 40%). By 2008, it had risen to at least 45% in those countries, but in South Africa it stood at under 35%.

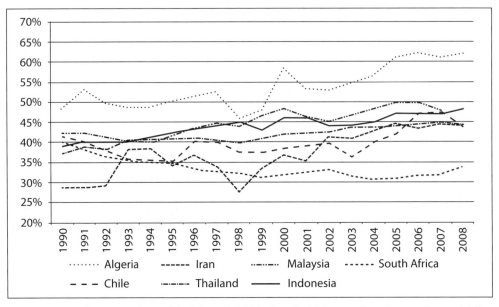

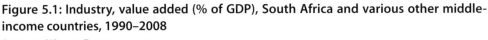

Figure 5.1: Industry, value added (% of GDP), South Africa and various other middle-income countries, 1990–2008

SOURCE: WORLD BANK DATABANK

Melting into the air: the financialisation of the economy

Perhaps the most dramatic and far-reaching structural change since the 1980s has been the financialisation of South Africa's economy, which follows global trends.

The shift of power from a non-financial sector to a gargantuan financial sector has been most glaring in the US, where financial-sector profits as a proportion of total corporate profits reached 50-year highs in the 1990s and averaged at 17% (Brenner, 2002:91). A key feature of neoliberal globalisation, the latest rise of the financial sector traces back to the early 1970s. The current process of financialisation is qualitatively different from the rise of finance capital in previous eras. As examined by Hilferding (1981), previously the primary role of finance capital was to promote industrial development through the merger of industrial and financial capital. In other words, finance capital developed and operated largely as a function of industrial growth. In the current epoch, that bond has been severed.

Finance capital no longer spurs industrial development, but is geared at extracting maximum returns, even by dismantling or destroying industrial capacity. Its metabolism is now fundamentally parasitic. Paraphrasing Epstein (2005:5), one can now define financialisation as the increasingly domineering role of financial motives, markets and institutions in the operation of economies. Even in non-financial corporations, this generates a structural pull away from nurturing productive investments and toward hunting for short-term returns. Trade-offs are forced between accumulation via financial activities and accumulation in the real economy. Long-term visions, strategies and fundamentals count for little in these frenzies (except insofar as they may spark short-term speculative gains or losses).

Corporate structures and management decision-making are adjusted and aligned to service those shifts (Crotty, 2003).[17]

Earlier allegiances of stakeholders to long-term corporate goals have frayed, and planning horizons have shrunk. Corporate salary structures embody these changes. By the turn of the century, stock options were the main component of pay for management teams in major non-financial corporations in the US and elsewhere. These devices reinforce the compression of time and bend strategic thinking toward a chase after quick returns. Shareholder value (or financial worth) dominates and eclipses longer-term economic calculations and social values. An addictive concoction is at work:

> *Institutional investors [demand] that non-financial corporations produce rapid earnings growth so they could satisfy their clients, while top non-financial corporate managers [need] to generate rapidly rising stock prices or their stock options would be worthless* (Crotty, 2003a:3).

Crotty (2003a & 2003b) pinpoints the hostile takeover movement of the 1980s in the US as a key moment in this global narrative.[18] Mergers and acquisitions multiplied in the US and beyond. Globally, the value of mergers ballooned from about USD 150 billion in 1992 to more than USD 2 000 billion in 1998 and USD 3 400 billion in 2000 (Nolan, 2002).[19] Corporate raiders were using debt to finance their takeover bids, while the managers of targeted companies loaded their books with debt-financed baggage (buy-backs and special cash dividends among them) to inflate debt levels and, hopefully, ward off the pillaging raids. High stock prices were the other deterrent and managers increasingly became obsessed with keeping those prices aloft. Increasing shares of corporate revenues and profits came to be derived from financial (rather than productive) assets. They were riskier, but the paybacks were quicker and bigger. 'Asset churning' in pursuit of short-term capital gains became a habit—so much so that turnover on the New York Stock Exchange rocketed from about 20% in the 1960s and 1970s to 100% in the 1990s. On average, stocks in the US are now held for about one year.

These processes have generated a powerful momentum for deregulation and liberalisation. As the finance sector expands, its need for new avenues and circuits of accumulation grows, as does its political and economic leverage (Fine, 2008b). After analysing the shifting relationship between non-financial corporations and the financial markets, Crotty (2003:6) arrived at an unnerving conclusion:

> *Neoliberal globalization is destroying conditions in both product and financial markets that are necessary for the successful long-term performance of large non-financial firms and the economies that depend on them. It will not be possible for non-financial corporations to lead either advanced or developing nations to long-term prosperity unless the neoliberal project is abandoned.*

South Africa's economy was predisposed to similar developments. The mining-finance nexus, combined with the presence of pyramid conglomerates and powerful mutual corporations, provided the financial sector with considerable sway over the non-financial sectors (see Chapter one). Already entwined with other conglomerates, the financial sector had expanded and became more concentrated in the 1980s, following deregulation of the banking sector in the early years of the decade and the divestment of major foreign banks (including Barclays, Standard Charter and ABN Amro). These financial institutions underwrote the spree of mergers and acquisitions in the 1980s (discussed earlier). Somewhat isolated from global trends after 1985, they grew in bulk. As sanctions were lifted and political negotiations acquired steadier footing, those institutions adapted rapidly to the new context and opportunities and became key players as South Africa's conglomerates restructured and extended their activities across a global field of opportunities. The consequences have been profound.

■ The financial sector's share of South Africa's GDP grew steeply after 1994, from about 6.5% to 12% in 2007 and almost 20% in 2009—an unusually large proportion in a country that is not a net exporter of financial services.[20]

■ Flush with liquidity once capital inflows resumed, South Africa's financial sector flooded the market with credit. Instead of financing productive investments, the bulk of the credit bankrolled financial and real-estate speculation and debt-fuelled consumption.[21] This aggravated underlying vulnerabilities in the economy, including a tendency toward trade deficits when imports grow on the back of a debt-financed growth spurt. In 2008, the trade deficit stood at 7.5% of GDP.

■ Household debt as a percentage of household disposable income rocketed from a little over 50% in 2002 to over 80% in 2007. That, in turn, underwrote increased investment in the wholesale and retail sectors (which accounted for a considerable proportion of new jobs created in that period). Office parks mushroomed on the edge of the major cities, as did gated cluster-home complexes and shopping malls. A massive housing bubble was another outcome, as banks granted more mortgages. The cumulative effect was the spurt of GDP growth experienced after the early 2000s.

■ Meanwhile, household savings as a percentage of disposable income have been stuck well below 10% since 1980 and fell precipitously after 1992, before turning negative in 2005 (Mohamed, 2010).

■ Credit extension to the private sector also increased, particularly in the 2000s, when it rose by 22% between 2000 and 2008. This trend, however, was not reflected in an increase in private business investment, which expanded by a stingy 5% between 2000 and 2008. Instead, it was the acquisition of financial assets that swelled across all sectors.

■ South Africa's non-financial corporations now also earn increasingly large shares of corporate revenues and profits from financial activities that do not directly link to their core operations. Flow of funds data from the SA Reserve Bank show that forays into financial markets and other financial investments, now outstrip these corporations' fixed investments (Mohamed, 2010). Research in industrialised countries suggests that such trends usually are associated with lower levels of real investment and lower levels of capital accumulation.[22]

■ Only about 10% of private credit extension went toward productive investment in the 2000s. Investment and capital formation was concentrated in the financial services sector and in the services sector. The top investment destinations in the private sector in 2008 were business services (14% of total investment), finance and insurance (13%), communication (10%), transport and storage (10%) and wholesale and retail trade (10%).

■ Despite increases in the capital budget since 2000, gross fixed capital formation—in other words total investment—remained far below the 25% target (16% of GDP in 2003, 17.3% in 2005, and 19.2% in 2006, down from 27% in 1982 and 20% in 1989) (Various SARB Quarterly Reports). It is generally assumed that capital formation needs to top 20% for sustained economic expansion.[23] In the mid-2000s, about one third of total investment was directly state financed.[24]

■ Having fallen precipitously since the early 1980s, gross fixed capital formation recovered in the early 2000 and rose to 21–22% in 2008 and 2009 (see Figure 5.2 below)— but on the back of a state-financed infrastructure-spending spree, significant portions of which went towards preparations for the 2010 Soccer World Cup.[25] Gross fixed-capital formation in the private sector hovered around 10% of GDP from 1996–2003, despite the GEAR plan's avowed role of boosting private investment. It then climbed to about 13% in 2005–09 (when GEAR supposedly was superseded by the Accelerated and Shared Growth Initiative for South Africa, or AsgiSA, framework). Meanwhile, gross fixed-capital formation in central government and public corporations (combined) averaged at just over 4% (of GDP) from 1996 to 2005, then more than doubled to 8.5% in 2009 (various SARB reports).

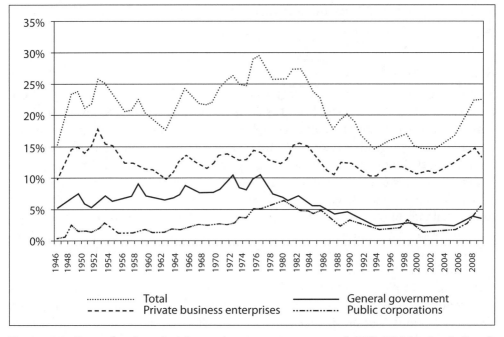

Figure 5.2: Gross fixed capital formation as percentages of GDP (2009 prices), South Africa, 1946–2008

■ Investment outside the services sector has targeted mainly the capital-intensive MEC sectors, where high levels of resource and monopoly rents can be extracted. Capital stock growth in the manufacturing sectors in 2000–06 was low, a trend that dates back to the 1990s. Automobiles and components were the only exception, thanks to generous subsidies and other support from the state (Mohamed, 2010).

Like many other countries, South Africa's economy has acquired a huge penumbral dimension. Its financial sector seems turbocharged, and has been described as 'one of the largest and most deregulated within the emerging markets' (Economist Intelligence Unit, 2007:54). The sector generates a blur of acts of exchange, yet produces little of real value. Having grown almost twice as fast as GDP since 2000, it has positioned itself in a parasitic relationship with the real economy. Consequently, it

> absorbs a quarter of what is produced and, to add insult to injury, leaves less produced as a consequence, as well as dictating much of macroeconomic policy (Fine, 2008:8).

The apparent zest in the economy came from a handful of sectors (financial and business services, construction and retail), none of which structurally sit at the core of the economy. Growth in those sectors absorbed 40% of the overall growth in investment, but with scant benefit to the real economy. Meanwhile, in 2002 to 2005, the manufacturing sector grew at half the rate of the economy as a whole, while mining and agriculture languished.[26] 'In these circumstances', as economist Neva Makgetla euphemised, 'economic growth remains exclusive and unstable'[27]—and its social benefits are scant.

Recap: a familiar story

South Africa is saddled with a stagnating industrial base in an economy where ownership is at least as concentrated as 20 years ago and which remains excessively dependent on the minerals-energy complex (MEC) for export earnings. The capital and intermediate goods sector has hardly stirred from its slumber. Consequently, technological innovation, industrial growth and infrastructure development depend on ever-increasing imports. Those have to be financed with the earnings of precious mineral (mainly gold) exports and short-term capital inflows, which add up to a balance of payments constraint on growth. Monetary policy has been used to counteract that turbulence—mainly by keeping interest rates high enough to attract speculative capital. This exposes the economy in a number of respects.

Since South Africa spends and invests more than it saves, it relies heavily on short-term inflows to pay for imports and finance its current account. This compounds the economy's vulnerability and constrains manoeuvring room for economic policy. That vulnerability is often viewed as a price worth paying, since capital inflows have enabled South Africa to reach and maintain unusually low levels of foreign debt. South Africa's debt service burden in 2007 was 6% (of export earnings), compared with the 16% average for other upper-middle-income countries (in Brazil it was 28%). The arguments against a sizeable foreign debt are well rehearsed and important. But the price for a low foreign debt (in South Africa's case) is an addiction to fickle portfolio investment and a precarious dependency on world capital markets. South Africa is effectively an onlooker as investors channel speculative capital in and out of its economy. Highly speculative capital inflows can be discouraged by imposing a nominal tax on short-term transactions (as Brazil does) and by requiring investors to place a share of their capital in long-term holdings, for example. But South Africa's policymakers are averse to using debt to steady the current account and therefore recoil from actions that could deter skittish speculators. Lower debt, they claim, has bolstered South Africa's economic sovereignty. That is a fallacy.

Capital inflows readily reverse into outflows—on terms and in volumes that the government prefers to leave in the hands of the market. Thus an abrupt and massive exodus of portfolio capital sparked the 2001 currency crisis, hoisting the inflation rate (as imports grew more expensive) and prompting the Reserve Bank to hike interest rates. Unemployment increased dramatically. Capital inflows then caused the rand to strengthen, impeding exports but encouraging imports. This pushed the current account into the red (as happened between 2004 and 2007, when the negative balance on the current account more than doubled from 3.4% to 7.3% of GDP) (Mohamed, 2010). There is nothing 'stable' about such a state of affairs.

The Finance Ministry looks to speculative capital much as farmers eye distant rainclouds. Sometimes the investments materialise in sufficient volume; mostly, they speed off again as quickly as they arrived. In 2007, for example, capital inflows with quick turnarounds totalled about R 100 billion (USD 12.5 billion); as Makgetla has shown, they are very costly. Net income payments abroad[28] came to 10% of exports in 2007. Treat them as debt payments and South Africa's debt-service ratio would have been higher than the norm for middle-income countries. In sum, 'for every dollar South Africa's exports earned abroad, the country paid about 16 cents to foreigners in the form of interest and dividends' writes Makgetla, 'and unlike debt-service figures, the payment of income on portfolio investment did not reduce the capital liability'.[29] Whereas foreign debt involves relatively transparent obligations, dependence on portfolio investment demands unfailing subservience to an almost mystical force, 'the markets'. It is a very powerful disciplinary device and current policy traps South Africa in its grasp. South Africa's reliance on short-term capital flows is at least as expensive as foreign debt would be and it further dilutes the country's economic sovereignty.[30]

The other defining feature of the economy, as shown above, is the intense financialisation that has occurred in the past two decades, alongside an enduring reliance on the mineral sector. The MEC is now symbiotically entwined with a politically domineering financial sector. Braided into that circuitry are the junior partners of corporate South Africa, the few dozen moguls who have monopolised the spoils of black economic empowerment to date.[31] This phenomenon would be a footnote in the political economy of post-apartheid South Africa, were their financial heft not so important to the ANC—in fiscal, political and ideological respects.

The ANC appears to have internalised many of the conservative prerogatives of South African capital. Some of this accommodation is grudging. There is some truth to economist Dawie Roodt's quip that 'in South Africa, the official opposition is not the [centre-right] Democratic Alliance, it is the financial markets'.[32] In September 2008, when Finance Minister Trevor Manuel hinted he might resign, the South African currency went into a tailspin, only to recover when he said he would stay on.

The meanings of neoliberalism

In the conventional telling, South Africa's development path since the early 2000s has veered from most of the neoliberal co-ordinates of the GEAR plan. Leftists disagree. This 'debate' often verges on pantomime. As a blend of ideology, policies and practices, neoliberalism seems to elude a watertight definition, even in scholarly circles. On the left, the habitual use of 'neoliberal' as a pejorative term has eroded its meaning and the word has become something of a medicalised slur, evoking a kind of pathology or blight. The word's accusatory force is considerable, but its descriptive value has faded.

The customary picture of neoliberalism depicts a retreat of the state from its social provisioning and regulatory duties in favour of the 'invisible hand' of the market. Judged against such a definition, even the GEAR plan did not inaugurate a fully fledged neoliberal adjustment phase in South Africa (Swilling *et al*, 2005). Government would add that adoption of the AsgiSA framework in 2006 dissolved most of the neoliberal elements. Those claims rest on a simplistic notion of an absent state and triumphant market, which was always a distorted description of neoliberalism—even in its early, Washington Consensus phase. In its utopian form, neoliberalism is associated with minimal, even absent, state regulation, but this is basically a 'thought experiment' since, as Antonio Gramsci (1971:60) pointed out almost a century ago, 'Laissez-faire, too, is a form of State "regulation", introduced and maintained by legislative and coercive means.'

An accurate definition has to capture the fact that neoliberalism refers to more than a particular set of policy choices: it constitutes the contemporary form of global capitalist accumulation and involves the systematic use of state power to recompose the rule of capital in economic and social life. Once this political dimension is brought into focus, in David Harvey's (2005) analysis, neoliberalism appears as a global and unified class project, aimed at restoring or shoring up the supremacy of the ruling class. He traces its origins to the mid-1970s and regards New York City and post-Allende Chile as the first, full-blooded neoliberal experiments. The weakness of that approach is that it implies homogeneity of means and unanimity of purpose. In fact, once neoliberalism is understood as a set of political economic practices, it becomes obvious that it varies over time and differs from place to place. The notion of neoliberalism as a homogenous phenomenon is then upended. Neoliberal practice is considerably more variable, adaptive and supple than the 'tired "neoliberalism versus welfare state" frame' conveys (Ferguson, 2007:84). Analysts of Latin American economic and social policy have arrived at similar conclusions.

The idea of neoliberalism as a pristine, ironclad blueprint is a fiction.

Neoliberal transitions have significantly transformed the material basis of societies as diverse as Brazil, Britain, India, Poland, South Africa, South Korea, the United States and Zambia. In each, the restructuring has occurred along distinct lines, but it shared key features that span the safeguarding and extension of private property rights (including intellectual property rights), free trade, the deregulation of business activities (especially financial transactions) and privatisation of collective assets. In broad outline, then, neoliberalism encompasses policies and practices that:

- Guarantee legal security for property rights;
- Establish and police fiscal 'discipline';[33]
- Focus public spending in areas that can boost economic growth;
- Impose tight monetary policy;
- Achieve a broad tax base with moderate marginal tax rates;
- Advance trade liberalisation;
- Liberalise capital controls; and
- Privatise public entities and, more broadly, commodify public goods.

The first, 'shock' phase of neoliberalism (usually conflated with the Washington Consensus era) seemed to heed the Nike slogan, 'Just do it.' Social and political consequences scarcely entered the picture as economies were adjusted and societies wrenched into new arrangements. One strong focus was on privatising public services and, where applicable, economic entities, typically at horrendous social cost.[34] The early guinea pigs were mainly in Latin America and Africa, though Eastern Europe (especially Russia) would later also feel the brunt of this hardcore variant. It has been estimated that male mortality rates increased by an average 13% in Eastern Europe during the privatisation sprees of the 1990s (Stuckler, King, McKee, 2009).[35] Elsewhere similar setbacks were visible. Careful analysis of the data shows that, as neoliberal adjustments became ubiquitous, the rate of improvements in health indicators slowed significantly in most regions of the world during the 1980s but especially in the 1990s (Cornia & Menchini, 2006; Deaton, 2004; Deaton & Drèze, 2002).[36]

This initial phase ended in the mid-1990s. In its wake came a wider array of dictates and practices (associated with the so-called post-Washington Consensus) that had to be flexible enough to contend with the 'collateral damage' wrought by the initial *blitzkrieg* of adjustment. It was in this phase that poverty relief moved up the agenda, the importance of health and education for economic growth and social stability were emphasised, the concepts of social and human capital became vogue and civil society was being celebrated as a wellspring of community resilience and inventiveness (see Chapters seven and nine). Public-private partnerships became the talk of the day. In short, a particular, abridged understanding of social policy was back in the frame—tasked not only with mitigating poverty and distress, but also with nurturing and shoring up regime legitimacy.

Variations on a theme

A constant and fundamental feature of neoliberalism throughout its evolution has been the process of financialisation. This has grown inexorably in both pace and scope, encompassing an ever-expanding range of activities associated with both economic and social reproduction (Fine, 2009:5). The *political* weight of finance was especially vivid in the state-funded bail-outs of banks and other financial institutions in 2008–09. By the end of 2008, it was estimated that a mere 5% of the value of the bail-outs in the US and United Kingdom alone would have been sufficient to provide basic water and sanitation for all inhabitants of the world's largest cities. According to Hall (2008), the value of the 'nationalisation' of insurance giant AIG alone was equal to reversing every privatisation exercise that had taken place in the former communist states of central and Eastern Europe. The current sway of finance capital, and the imperative of protecting it, is possibly unprecedented. In Fine's (2009:5) view, 'preserving finance takes absolute precedence over all other aspects of state economic intervention, including those associated with privatisation'.

Neoliberalism is characterised, then, by the expansion of opportunities and options for private capital accumulation. But the state is assigned key roles in engineering and facilitating such expansion, and in managing the political and social consequences of the adjustments. Thus, the state's surveillance, intelligence and policing activities tend to proliferate in the neoliberal era. Its regulatory powers might also strengthen, though they tend to be deployed to ensure stable, low-cost environments for capital, as the World Bank's World Development Reports in the 2000s have shown clearly. Alongside that, social provisioning tends to be structured along lines that may appear contradictory, yet are oriented toward a central logic. Social protection might be refurbished or expanded in certain respects and the state might assume larger responsibility in supporting the reproduction of human and social capital (to use the fashionable jargon). The provisioning, though, is highly rationed and typically conditional. Responsibility often is devolved to local-government levels, where service delivery is made to hinge on cost-recovery practices. The tactical use of these tempering and stabilising interventions by the state has been a core feature of neoliberal practice since the late-1990s. Latin America's 'new social policy' experiments can be seen as a particular elaboration of this phase, which Peck and Tickell (2002) have described as the shift from roll-back to roll-out neoliberalism.[37]

Civil society, generally, and 'the community' and 'community initiative' in particular, occupy important places in these arrangements, functioning, as Bob Jessop (2002:455) puts it, 'as a flanking, compensatory mechanism for the inadequacies of the market mechanism'. This is especially striking in the Third Way variants of neoliberalism, where 'the community' becomes tasked with 'fostering civic responsibility' (Khan & Pieterse, 2006:170). The idealisation of 'self-help' and the nurturing and deployment of existing but overlooked assets in poor communities as part of 'anti-poverty' strategies, it can be argued, are other cardinal 'compensatory mechanisms' that not only endorse but reinforce neoliberal rationality (see Chapter seven).[38]

The changes detected during the 2000s in South Africa by Padayachee and Valodia (2001), Fine (2007) and Mohammed (2009) match those patterns. Fiscal parsimony was replaced with a programme of infrastructure rehabilitation and expansion, redrawn industrial policy, a more generous social-protection package and a revamped public-works programme. Government advertised these moves as a break with the GEAR programme, which, it claimed, had done its job of pegging back government debt, establishing macroeconomic stability and restoring investor confidence. South Africa had passed through a crossroads and a shift to a developmental state was now underway. Paradoxically, in singling out and demonising GEAR as the grand moment of rupture and betrayal, the left helped government and corporate South Africa script their claims of a qualitative break. GEAR no doubt was a profound intervention, but it was a dramatic element of a longer narrative of restructuring that dates back to the halting efforts of the apartheid regime in the early 1980s and which now arcs forward beyond GEAR (see Chapters three and four). It formed part of an evolving process that has not yet runs its course.

That course is not preordained, nor is it the preserve only of policymakers and vested interests. Gillian Hart (2007) is correct to recognise the economic and social policy modulations of the 2000s as strategies of containment. Economic growth was plodding, job creation was feeble, and state statisticians were discovering that poverty had worsened during the 1990s (see Chapter seven). GEAR was delivering modestly on only one ('growth') of the promises advertised in the acronym. Globally, the 1998 Asian financial crisis had scuffed the remaining veneer off the Washington Consensus and anti-neoliberal protest movements were proliferating. In South Africa, there were similar stirrings. As in many countries, privatisation schemes sparked enough social resistance and political embarrassment to force a halt to those programmes. Community protests signalled the need for modifications.

The specific forms that neoliberal practice assumes in a given place at a given time therefore represent much more than the stamp of distant (structural) forces. They are shaped by shifting balances of forces, and by the histories of contesting social forces, as well as the societies in which they operate. Neoliberal projects and practices operate 'on terrains that always exceed them' (Hart, 2007:14). Thus, from country to country one detects common themes alongside variations in policies and practice—all resting on an underlying framework of value-laden precepts (and ethics) for the organisation of society. Neoliberalism therefore reaches its fullest expression not in any specific set of government policies, but when these anchoring precepts become generalised and axiomatic, part of the 'natural order'. In Hart's (2006:22–3) summary, drawing on the work of Graham Burchell (1993) and Nikolas Rose (1999), neoliberalism:

> represents a new modality of government predicated on interventions to create the organizational and subjective conditions for entrepreneurship—not only in terms of extending the 'enterprise model' to schools, hospitals, housing estates, and so forth, but also in inciting individuals to become entrepreneurs themselves [...] This process of 'responsibilization' often goes hand-in-hand with new or intensified

> *invocations of 'community' as a sector 'whose vectors and forces can be mobilized, enrolled, deployed in novel programmes and techniques which encourage and harness active practices of self-management and identity construction, of personal ethics and collective allegiances'.*[39]

'Muddling along'?

This approach of 'governmentality' encourages a useful focus on the internal dynamics of decision-making in a state which, as Mark Swilling and his colleagues put it (2005:15), 'is simultaneously integrating itself into the global economy and responding to popular pressures from below to address poverty and inequality'. The outcome, they suggested, was that 'policy-making communities get ripped apart'—with economic decision-makers ascending into the thin air of global economic policy while their counterparts, trying to tackle socioeconomic realities, are 'sucked into the messy local worlds' of hobbled systems, protest and disaffection. Their argument (2005:16) was that

> *instead of integrating developmental, fiscal, monetary and exchange rate policies, these policy-making arenas were subjected to sharply differentiated pressures and strains resulting in severe policy dysfunctions and policy outcomes.*

That line of analysis has superficial appeal. No doubt there are tensions and conflicts between policymaking communities within the state, but they are not as sundered and dissonant as portrayed. The picture of thwarted good intentions seems too convenient. It clears a path for claims that the post-apartheid state 'has followed neither the classic neoliberal state model, nor the developmental state model' (Swilling *et al*, 2005:16) and instead sought to dismantle a 'uniquely configured apartheid state system that was deeply rooted in South Africa's economy of racial capitalism' (*ibid*).

That portrayal ignores the demonstrable continuity between cardinal late-apartheid and post-apartheid economic policy choices. And it treats neoliberalism as an ontological phenomenon that is materialised though a fixed, unsparing blueprint of policy choices that leaves little space for improvisation. It also harks back to a misguided tradition of treating South Africa as an exceptional case. Few observers would dispute describing the shock therapies administered in the 1990s to countries of the former Soviet bloc as 'neoliberal', yet those adjustments also dismantled 'uniquely configured ... state system[s]' that were tied to a particular form of accumulation.

The value of Swilling's contention lies more in its refusal to lock analysis into the clean, angular world of structure and in highlighting the sometimes messy and contingent ways in which policies are made and applied. But those insights are mistakenly elevated to the status of first-order explanation. If policy really were that contingent and haphazard, that prone to chance, then paradoxically it would be *constantly* quirky and unpredictable, leaving a trail of zigzagging patterns. Instead, we can discern profound consistency in post-apartheid economic policies.

Neoliberalism continues to provide the organising framework and ethical compass points for South Africa's transition. This is especially stark in relation to the state's obligations towards citizens. The stigmatisation of social protection as 'handouts', private-public partnerships, prepaid water and electricity meters as devices for self-administered service 'cut-offs', the attempts to productivise what are essentially forms of indigent support (through public-works programmes and workfare), the privatisation of personal security and the tight rationing of citizens' claims on the state all express basic neoliberal 'rationalities'. The social-grant system and the public-works programme are invested with strong disciplinary overtones (see Chapters six and seven). Grants are means-tested, while the expanded public works programme is favoured over a basic income grant, partly because the latter, as Hart (2006:26) noted, 'lacks points of leverage for instilling in its recipients the "correct" attitudes and aspirations'. The underlying ethics call to mind Perry Anderson's (2000) remark that

> the winning formula to seal the victory of the market is not to attack, but to preserve the placebo of a compassionate public authority, extolling the compatibility of competition with solidarity.

It is in this sense that the tale, cherished on the left, of a nominally socialist ANC bullied by external forces into imposing neoliberal policies is so unsatisfactory. Nor were the policies smuggled in through stealth and deceit. A neoliberal development path was adopted, and has been maintained, because the balance of forces within the ANC alliance, and between it and corporate capital, favours such a course (see Chapter thirteen).

Stuck in the middle

The stated aim of the government's economic and social policies has been to assemble a development project that is capable of reducing the high levels of unemployment, poverty and inequality—in short, to resolve an ongoing social crisis. Achieving this requires overcoming structural weaknesses in the economy, shifting the bias from mining- and mineral-related activities towards more labour-intensive, value-adding activities and drastically reducing the current concentration of wealth and resources (Mohamed, 2009). How much leverage can the state marshal?

The main institutional casualty of globalisation has been the nation state, more specifically its ability to inhibit capital's scavenging for profit and to harness the dynamism of capitalism to achieve social progress. A profound feature of neoliberal globalisation is the reconfiguring of the domestic bourgeoisie into alliances with international capital. This both diffuses and thickens the presence of capital and it poses new challenges to state sovereignty and popular movements.

It also undermines one of the pillars of nationalism and national liberation—the idea of nurturing a national patriotic bourgeoisie that serves national development. That era seems to have gone, replaced by one in which the ANC's investment company, for example, owns stakes in multinational corporations that then win state tenders and contracts.[40] Powerful sections in the ANC have developed a reflexive sympathy for policies that put the market ahead of society. Many of the organisation's top officials and cadres have acquired significant business interests, much of it via the estimated R 300 billion (USD 37 billion) worth of BEE deals crafted since 1994.[41] Almost one third of the party's National Executive Committee also serves as directors of BEE companies.[42] Meanwhile, the ANC relies heavily on the largesse of these and other corporations to fund its operations and election campaigns.[43] Ahead of the 2009 national election, the ANC was staging lavish fundraisers that netted up to R 30 million (USD 3.7 million) a night from corporate moguls.[45] These are the tips of the iceberg: political parties in South Africa are not required to divulge their funding sources.

Back from repairs: black economic empowerment in the 2000s

There have been two phases of BEE. The first commenced in 1993, when Sanlam sold Metropolitan Life to New Africa Investment Ltd. South African corporations masterminded and initiated the initial deals in the absence of an overarching framework. The preferred method was the sale of subsidiaries, funded by debt, which the seller often provided. The shares constituted the security and loan repayments were tied to rising dividends and share prices. BEE therefore was bolted into a process that revolved around share values.

By engineering these early BEE ventures, corporations in effect were managing their side of a tacit political compromise. The BEE deals would help lever the rapid emergence of a black African bourgeoisie sympathetic to the ideals of national liberation. For ANC leaders who had tired of the despondency inherent in dependency theory, this was an enticing prospect. These pioneering black capitalists would constitute the thin edge of a wedge that, eventually, would challenge or even displace the incumbent white elite. The thinking sat in a well-worn tradition that reserved a starring role for a patriotic bourgeoisie. 'BEE in itself will create successful entrepreneurs, wealthy black people, a black middle class,' according to Wendy Luhabe. 'Ultimately, whatever benefits black people benefits the country.'[45] In the view of Tokyo Sexwale (2005), former premier of Gauteng province and one of the country's wealthiest individuals, BEE is about

> job opportunities, it is about rural development, it is about educating people and training them. It's about skills development. It's particularly about developing the young and women. And yes, it's about creating small business and large businesses [...] We give money to schools, we fight HIV/AIDS, we provide university fees, we build clinics, we build hospitals.[46]

BEE appealed on a more profane level, too. Members' dues were insufficient to bankroll the ANC, at least not at the levels needed to function effectively and win elections comprehensively. Having a business elite 'on tap' would be a huge boon, not only to the ANC as an organisation, but also to individuals within it. The conglomerates eyed other rewards. At an elementary level, BEE was an 'expedient strategy to appease the possible rise of nationalisation sentiments' (Goldstein,

2001:15). During the 1980s, the apartheid regime had sought to cultivate a 'moderate' black middle class. This time, corporate leaders understood that,

> *to entrench conservative interests, there is a need to promote sections of black business to serve as a buffer against more extensive assaults on the structure of ownership and modus operandi of corporate capital* (Fine & Rustomjee, 1998:699).

They harboured larger ambitions, too and hoped that their 'magnanimity' would help bring the ANC around to endorsing the kinds of corporate restructuring (and disinvestment) they desired. Here, an odd meeting of minds occurred. If large South African corporations shifted parts of their operations abroad in the context of a BEE drive, some in the ANC reasoned, a black capitalist class could be assembled more rapidly in the abandoned spaces. In addition, so glaring was the lack of confidence of these incumbent elites in the 'new' South Africa, that their departure was seen as a price worth paying if it created the space to build a new, 'patriotic' capitalist elite.[47] Local conglomerates, meanwhile, were desperate to globalise their operations, which is one of the reasons why both the ANC and corporate capital supported the liberalisation of capital controls.

The first BEE deals appropriately featured as part of corporate unbundling schemes, as firms refocused the operations around core activities. The initial spate of deals arrived rapidly. By 1997, 28 black-controlled firms listed on the JSE had a market capitalisation worth 9.3% of the JSE's total. The figure had doubled within six months. A year later, more than 230 BEE deals had appeared on the JSE, with a total value exceeding R 35 billion (USD 4.5 billion) (Gelb, 2006b). But the 1998 stock-market crash dragged many of the newcomers down with it. By the end of 1999, black control of market capitalisation on the JSE had plunged to 6.8%.

There was strong public disapproval and much moral condemnation of the narrow, elitist nature of BEE. Small cliques had cornered the first generation of deals, which had been precariously engineered and were highly leveraged to enable newcomers to buy assets, effectively without financial capital of their own. Their contribution to economic growth was negligible. Heavily loan-financed, the new companies struggled to secure additional credit. The luminaries at their helm, meanwhile, were not shy about whittling 'rent' payments out of whatever profits materialised (Freund, 2007b).

The functions of BEE

An overhaul of BEE was needed. Black business associations took the initiative and set up a Black Economic Empowerment Commission, which called on government to adopt a more interventionist strategy. Government had already begun moving in that direction. The new approach would involve official and voluntary sectoral charters that included steps to boost black ownership, but also ranged further to include black management control and skills development. Broad-based BEE would codify this approach. In this expanded form, BEE came to include the ownership and control of assets and companies, affirmative action at senior management levels, human-resource development and employment equity (Satgar, 2008).

This more thoroughgoing variant of BEE, it was hoped, would cultivate a productive black capitalist elite capable of operating in tandem with government. BEE would thereby serve the grander project of building a developmental state. Here, as Freund (2007a & 2007b) has pointed out, the ANC borrowed unabashedly from the 'Malaysian model' where, starting in the late 1960s, the 'New Economic Policy' was consciously aimed at building a Malay elite that would command economic power. State procurement, tenders and the granting of business licences were used as levers in that endeavour. Similarly, the current pretences of building a developmental state in South Africa (see Chapter eleven) depend fundamentally on the rise and influence of

> an elite that has internalized developmental goals [and that can] navigate the waters of corporate South Africa but [stay] fundamentally loyal to the ruling African National Congress and [remain] tied to its hegemonic political control of the country (Freund, 2007b:663,664).

The ANC has pursued this goal with diligence. As Roger Southall (2010) reminds, 27 ministers and deputies in Jacob Zuma's government were registered as active directors or members of companies. Many of those firms do official business with government. According to the Auditor-general's 2009 report, more than 2 000 government officials had directly or indirectly benefited from government tenders worth more than R 600 million (USD 80 million). 'It can be taken for granted,' Southall notes, 'that resignations from top civil service or cabinet positions are followed by individuals being taken up in the BEE world, but today the deed is done before and without resignation [...] The seams are hardly visible.'

Among the early corporations with close ties to the ANC was Thebe Investments, launched in the early 1990s. Others include Chancellor House, effectively an investment arm of the ANC, which former ANC Member of Parliament Andrew Feinstein (2007) describes as 'an elaborate network of companies [...] established to utilise black economic empowerment deals to raise money for the ruling party'. According to ANC's Treasurer-general, Matthews Phosa, who presides over a large business and empowerment portfolio, 'NEC members, like any South Africans, have a right to participate in business. It's their constitutional right.'[48] Many of the ANC top officials and cadres have acquired significant business interests, much of it via the estimated R 300 billion (USD 37 billion) worth of BEE deals crafted since 1994.[49] The ANC itself relies heavily on these companies for funding—as, increasingly, do individual political aspirants.

The real test of a 'patriotic bourgeoisie', though, does not lie in the amassing of wealth and dispensing of charity, but in its ability to constitute a driving, economically productive force. The performance has been unflattering. The highly leveraged financing formulas of BEE ventures have placed great emphasis on rapid profitability. Consequently, the selection of key business activities, operational practices and managerial ethics of BEE firms usually mirror those of their white-controlled counterparts. The same holds generally for firms controlled by holding companies in which trade-union investment companies are prominent stakeholders.

Whatever their pigmentation, South African business leaders incline towards similar ideological dispositions in relation to the labour market, taxes, monetary policies and the regulatory environment. Thus Cyril Ramaphosa, the former general secretary of the National Union of Mineworkers turned billionaire businessman, would castigate the 'unduly prescriptive' nature of the labour regime without doing ostensible harm to his political stature inside the ANC; at the ANC's 2007 national conference, he again was voted into the ruling party's National Executive Committee. Gauged in terms of productive investments, job creation, income growth, redistribution and working conditions, BEE firms are indistinguishable from 'white' firms.

Besides that, the actual influence of black business figures as directors and owners of corporations seems modest. Most are tethered to large, long-term loans issued by the dominant source of finance. And many, if not most, of the black directors of JSE-listed corporations are non-executive. Black business figures comprised a mere 10% of executive directors in listed firms in the mid-2000s (Hirsch, 2005). Moreover, the capacity (not to mention inclination) of this emerging but junior elite to 'shift the basis of growth away from the sale of natural resources' is highly questionable (Freund, 2007b:671). It is much more likely to be drawn into familiar, 'easier' paths of accumulation. The new elite, in Freund's (*op cit*, 674) verdict, 'remains limited in capacity, fragile and very dependent on the ANC remaining in power'.

Moeletsi Mbeki paints a picture of ties forged between 'a small class of unproductive but wealthy black crony capitalists made up of ANC politicians, some retired and others not' and the incumbent 'economic oligarchy'. A key outcome, he says, is a 'black elite' that is cast as 'junior support players to white-controlled corporations'.[50] The judgement is harsh, but not misplaced. Notwithstanding claims to the contrary, BEE remains mired in rent-seeking and is reflexively angled toward opportunities that allow enterprises to buy cheap and sell dear. The state's preferential tendering regime (which pushes black-owned firms to the top of the queue) ensures a steady abundance of such opportunities. When US and Malaysian investors sold their stake in Telkom to a trio of black South African investors (two of them reportedly closely connected to the ANC), even the business press was alarmed enough to warn that

> *as sure as the sun rises, this enrichment of the few, this constant bagging of state assets by the same rich and connected blacks and this bagging of the same rich and connected blacks by white business desperate to get its empowerment targets out of the way, will lead to trouble in SA. One day.*[51]

Some observers, though, have spotted silver linings. Gelb, for example, has suggested that the BEE charter process shows that South African business does have a tolerance for 'disciplinary planning'—and might be amenable to a more interventionist developmental state. The process reflected, says Gelb (2006b), an acceptance by business of 'collective action against individual entities on the basis of transparent, public and non-arbitrary regulations'. That optimism seems strained. After all, as Gelb (*op cit*) goes on to note, the first BEE phase was initiated by business (with the state little more than a supportive onlooker) and even in the second phase, *the state's involvement is still somewhat limited and confined to setting broad objectives, strategic capacity being limited and regulatory capacity to monitor and discipline still in their infancy.*

BEE has served two primary functions. It has provided a vehicle for elite enrichment and the brisk engineering of a black bourgeoisie that rides side-saddle behind incumbent corporate capital. In the process, new alliances are being forged with incumbent capitalist elites, both in South African and globally.[52] And it has created a powerful political lobby inside and around the ANC against radical change. It is no coincidence that corporations lodged in the MEC (see Chapter one) were the first to proclaim black empowerment targets, that some of the most powerful new moguls (Macozoma, Motsepe and Sexwale among them) are tied deeply into the MEC or that some of the wealthiest black figures now sit at the helm of key parastatal entities (Freund, 2007b & 2008). These incestuous linkages raise serious doubts about the willingness and capacity of the ANC to promote an industrial policy that diverges significantly from the co-ordinates fixed by the MEC.

There is also a real risk that policies will muddle along in service of the shifting and sometimes conflicting prerogatives of a partially deracialised corporate elite. When President Jacob Zuma took the oath in May 2009, he stood in the shadow of hefty IOUs to the BEE moguls who had bankrolled his bid and the political fixers who had worked the room. Those two groupings overlap significantly. In the wings lurked the incumbent economic elites, who command a different kind of sway. The ANC presidency is now leashed to these clusters of power and influence.

State of denial

So as the first decade of the 2000s neared its end, the structural weaknesses in the economy were well known, yet the denizens of corporate boardrooms and chambers of political power maintained their jaunty spirits. Their talk stuck to more comforting themes: an economy full of verve, 'solid fundamentals', the maturity of the banking sector and the avowed underlying strengths of the economy.

The country's overall debt in 2007 stood at a respectable 31.3% of GDP (down from close to 50% a decade earlier), and the budget deficit had been pared to 0.3% (down from 4.6% in 1996–97).[53] Reflecting on the previous decade, the presidency in 2003 declared that government's policies had turned the economy back from the brink of fiscal crisis, secured macroeconomic stability and launched South Africa on the path of investment and growth. Ignored were the chronic balance-of-payment vulnerabilities and periodic currency crashes, such as the 2001 nosedive that stripped 35% off the rand's value against the US dollar in a matter of weeks.

South Africa had spent 15 years trying to ingratiate itself with international markets and investors, and integrate deeper into the global system an economy that was still heavily reliant on commodity exports. The reward was a decade of modest economic growth that scarcely outpaced the global average and which lagged behind many other middle-income economies. The average annual rate of GDP growth was 2.8% between 1994 and 2003 (Gelb, 2005) and approached

5% between 2004 and 2007. Annual per capita income growth ran at under 2% in 1994–2003 and then increased to 3–4% (various SARB Quarterly Reports). At its most robust, GDP growth ran below the average for upper-middle-income countries and far below the average for lower-middle-income ones (see Figure 5.3). In short, the celebrated-spurt of growth in South Africa during the 2000s followed a global trend for middle-income countries, yet ran well below the average.

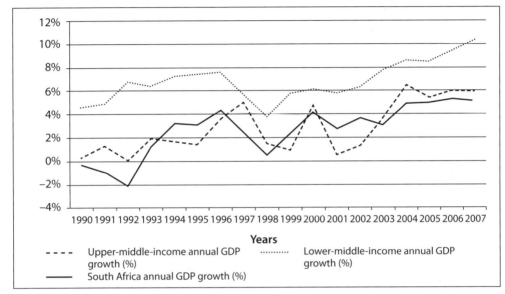

Figure 5.3: Annual GDP growth (%), South Africa, upper-middle-income and lower-income countries, 1990–2007

SOURCE: WORLD BANK DATABANK

The numbers also hid an unsightly underbelly. Cutting the budget deficit had been achieved at the cost of several years of stingy public spending that ran down institutional capacities, left vast numbers of state posts vacant and postponed a huge bill for infrastructure rehabilitation and expansion. Worse, income inequalities had widened to unprecedented levels (see Chapter seven). Although the underlying structure of the economy has changed little, trade and financial liberalisation had left the economy with paltry buffer against global instabilities.

Despite the economy's greater exposure to the dynamics of an unstable global system, policymakers and economists were confident that the 2008 global financial crisis would leave little more than a few scrape marks on South Africa's 'glimmering' economy. Even as global credit tightened, commodity prices fell and demand shrank, local economists were heralding a predicted 1.2% GDP growth rate for 2009 as 'heroic'[54] and praising (then) Finance Minister Trevor Manuel for his 'prudent' determination to maintain 'sustainable finances' despite falling tax revenues. As investors turned tail in the global economy in late 2008, Manuel was issuing assurances that 'we are not looking at a recession in South Africa'.[55] 'We were assured our financial sector was prudentially managed and well regulated,' SACP intellectual, now deputy transport minister, Jeremy Cronin, wrote ruefully a few months later. 'We were, supposedly, relatively well insulated. A growth rate of 3–4% for 2009 was still confidently predicted.'[56]

The usually bubbly *Economist* magazine did not share the bullishness of the government. Assessing the vulnerability of middle-income counties to global 'contagion' in February 2009, it stamped South Africa as the riskiest of the 17 surveyed countries. A current-account deficit of 8% or more of GDP was predicted (roughly the size of Thailand's on the eve of its 1997–98 crisis), its short-term debt was estimated at 81% of reserves, and its bank loan-to-deposit ratio at 1.09.[57]

The cycle of economic growth had, in fact, reversed in late 2008 already. The economy shrank by 0.7% in the final quarter of 2008 and by 7.8% in the next quarter.[58] Overall, GDP contracted 1.8% in 2009.[59] Such was the desperation to add a sheen to reality that Statistics SA announced it was adjusting its GDP survey to include estimates for the 'non-observed economy', including the illegal drugs trade, abalone poaching and various opaque parts of the informal sector.[60]

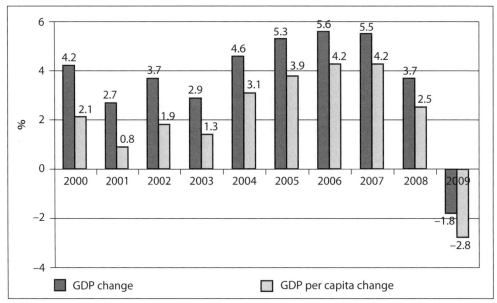

Figure 5.4: Annual percentage changes in GDP and GDP per capita, South Africa (2005 prices)
SOURCE: SA RESERVE BANK DATA

'We have entered a recession,' President Jacob Zuma finally admitted in June 2009, yet felt it necessary to add that 'South Africa has not been affected to the extent that a number of other countries have'.[61] The recession had hardly kicked in when the former governor of the Reserve Bank, Tito Mboweni, was claiming that 'the worst is probably behind us'.[62] Doleful statistics told another story.

The value of the country's exports fell by 24% in the first quarter of 2009, as demand dried up and commodity prices fell. That piled further pressure on one of the economy's chronic vulnerabilities, its current-account deficit, which swelled to an alarming 9% of GDP in early 2009.[63] Output in the mining sector shrank by 33% in the final quarter of 2008, its biggest decrease on record.[64] The manufacturing sector (which, together with retail, accounts for about one third of total output) shrank by 22% (another record)[65] and more than 21% of factory productive capacity was idle.[66] Consumer spending was on the skids (shrinking by almost 5%, its biggest contraction for 13 years);[67] there was a 47% rise in company failures in the first four months of 2009; and household debt had risen to about 80% of disposable income (from around 50% six years earlier).[68] The deficit would have been even bigger were it not for (mainly short-term) capital flows to bonds, shares and equities.

The impact of the global economic crisis was channelled into the economy along two main routes: falling commodity prices and the drying up of easy credit. There was a tiny slice of good fortune, though. As confidence in the dollar waned, gold's lustre again grew, sending its price soaring as the recession dragged on. And as the economy sagged so too fell imports, softening pressure on the balance of payments. But the social costs were punishing and they were to leave their mark far beyond the official 'end' of the recession.

Responding to the recession

Government reacted to South Africa's worst recession in 20 years in languid fashion. This was partly because the recession coincided with the transition from a caretaker government to Jacob Zuma's presidency. Fearful or unable to lead the line with bold measures, the new government chose to tread the path of its predecessor, which meant bowing to the authority of the Treasury. Not a single out-of-the-ordinary step was taken. The response had four main elements, the most substantial of which built on initiatives already underway:

- Negotiate a framework for a unified response by business, government and trade unions, with an emphasis on avoiding, where possible, retrenchments;
- Interest-rate cuts;
- Proceed with a three-year infrastructure investment programme; and
- Proceed with an expanded public-works programme.

Government, trade unions and organised business agreed to a framework plan in December 2008. Job losses would be prevented (where possible), two million new jobs would be created and households in distress would receive emergency food and other relief.[69] The agreement mainly reiterated existing commitments. It took six months to pencil in details and they stayed sketchy thereafter. By early 2010, an estimated 20 000 jobs had been 'saved'. The framework adopted a docile tone towards the private sector, which was requested 'to maintain and improve wherever possible their levels of fixed direct investment'. Meanwhile, government proved willing to bail out embattled companies; by mid-2009, several had been thrown lifelines (worth R 500 million, or USD 63 million) by the Industrial Development Corporation and another R 3 billion (USD 380 million) was set aside to help other companies in distress.[70]

The Reserve Bank cut interest rates, but kept the repo rate high enough to tempt investors to dip their toes in the local market so capital inflows could sate the ravenous current account. The Bank allowed the rand to appreciate steeply against major currencies, which reduced the value of mineral and manufactured exports in the face of rapidly shrinking global demand, but also reduced the cost of imports destined for government's overhaul of transport, energy and other infrastructure. There probably were deeper, structural imperatives at play, as well—including a desire to prop up the purchasing power of the rand to support the investment raids of South African firms and conglomerates in Africa and beyond.

A large infrastructure programme was already underway, with state-owned enterprises said to be poised to become the 'drivers of growth and development' (Mbeki, 2005:19). Trade unions and others on the left had been calling for such interventions since the early 1990s, when international evidence showed clearly that strong public spending has a 'crowding in' effect. The 'crowding out' argument, however, was a central tenet of the Washington Consensus, and a favourite among GEAR's champions, who used it to argue for the spending cuts decreed in that plan (see Chapter four). Ideological fads, though, are fickle. In the 2000s, the World Bank disavowed the injunctions of the Washington Consensus, and instead was counselling that

> public spending on infrastructure—roads, ports, airports and power—crowds private investment in. It expands investment opportunities and raises the return to private investment. By paving the way for new industries to emerge, it is also a crucial aid to structural transformation and export diversification (2008:36).

Modifications

Government policymakers had eventually caught up with that script. One outcome was the 2006 Accelerated and Shared Growth Initiative for South Africa (AsgiSA), a revamped framework for economic growth that preserved many of the precepts of the GEAR plan but laid greater emphasis on public-infrastructure investment and staked even greater hopes on small and medium enterprises.[71] AsgiSA was said to consummate the transition from GEAR to a new phase in the country's development, which would now be led by a 'developmental state'.[72] A central feature was the Keynesian infusion of public funds to rehabilitate and expand infrastructure, and extend the public-works programme. These were welcome developments, although their transformative impact should not be exaggerated (see Chapter six). Public-sector investment was scheduled to increase to about 8% of GDP, with a large share (about 40%) destined for parastatal enterprises such as Eskom and Transnet. That posture scarcely challenged neoliberal orthodoxy, which, in the 2000s, had 'rediscovered' the pro-growth virtues of public spending on education, healthcare, and infrastructure.

Government's R846 billion (USD 106 billion) infrastructure expansion pro-gramme focused on upgrading and expanding transport infrastructure (which had been poorly maintained since the early 1980s); boosting electricity production and provision; repairing a deteriorating public-health system that is buckling under the world's worst AIDS and TB epidemics; and expanding the provision of water and sanitation. As the recession began easing in 2010, much of the momentum in the economy came from public spending and from preparations for the 2010 Soccer World Cup.

In the early 1990s, the Macro-Economic Research Group had proposed similar, relatively interventionist policies—reasoning, heretically at the time, that the economy has to serve society (see Chapter four). As the star of the Washington Consensus waned in the late 1990s, Ben Fine and Zavareh Rustomjee again saw scope for such an approach. The alternative, they warned, was a 'pale and weak version of Keynesiasm/welfarism and modernisation' (1998:698). The prescience was uncanny—in that and other respects. A decade later, the gravitational pull of the MEC was still obvious in the state's investment surge. In Fine's (2008a:2) reading,

> policy is now working itself once more towards a state-led expansion of the MEC core, reminiscent of the 1970s, through renewal of public investment in state corporations, especially around energy and transport, but with as much private participation as can be engendered (domestic conglomerate, foreign direct investment and, of course, parasitic BEE).

Also earmarked in the AsgiSA framework for a revamp was the industrial policy framework. Industrial policy traditionally has favoured programmes in relatively high-tech, capital-intensive industries. The showpieces in South Africa's post-apartheid industrial strategy have been capital- and energy-intensive mega-projects, along with the Motor Industry Development Programme (MIDP), underwritten by bounteous state subsidies, credits and tax breaks, despite their poor job-creating potential. In the AsgiSA overhaul, MEC core sectors were still well represented among the priority sectors (which also included capital and transport equipment, automotives and components, chemicals, plastics, pharmaceuticals, forestry, clothing and textiles, and pulp and paper). Oddly, the framework singled out business-process outsourcing and tourism 'for special priority attention' (Presidency, 2006)—sectors that had been internationally fashionable for more than a decade.[73] State interventions were to include more industrial financing, tightening of competition laws, tariff reductions and steps to reduce labour costs.[74]

The decision to prioritise the automotive and components sector was surprising. The Automotive Production and Development Plan (APDP; formerly the MIDP) has been the flagship of industrial policy since 1994 and has absorbed profligate support from state. In 2002 and 2003 subsidies paid to the automobile industry exceeded R 15 billion (USD 1.9 billion)—50% more than the entire education budget and roughly equal to South Africa's total customs revenue collection in each of those years. By 2003, the government had sunk R 55 billion (USD 6.9 billion) into the scheme, R 21 billion (USD 2.6 billion) of which went to two German multinational, luxury-sedan manufacturers (Flatters, 2005). As late as 2009, a further R 870 million (USD 109 million) in production subsidies over three years was earmarked for the APDP[75]—despite the fact that its main impact, according to Canadian economist Frank Flatters, 'is to transfer income from South African consumers to the shareholders of the company making the investment'.[76]

Reviving South Africa's industrial drive

Those industrial policies had been fashioned on Mbeki's watch. Subsequently there was more talk of rebuilding local industrial capacity, avoiding deindustrialisation and shifting to a more diversified industrial strategy. The remodelled plan unveiled by the Zuma government in early 2010 laid emphasis on boosting labour-intensive industrial production. But the sectors targeted in the 2010–13 Industrial Policy Action Plan were the same as those in the earlier plans (including the automotive sector), except for the addition of a new cluster: 'nuclear, advanced materials and aerospace' (Davies, 2010). Its goals, though, were ambitious: it promised 2.4 million jobs within a decade as a result of a core programme of manufacturing expansion. The latter was heavily reliant on procurement funding from the Industrial Development Corporation (control of which had shifted to the Economic Development Ministry). Roger Southall (2010) was not alone in worrying that the plan would 'be hugely complicated both by demonstrable weaknesses in the state capacity and by the problems of corruption and patronage'.[77]

The concerns, though, run deeper. If an overhauled industrial strategy is to diversify the industrial sector and hoist it onto a path that generates large numbers of jobs for low-skilled workers, it will have to challenge the status quo. Capital-intensive megaprojects would need to make way for more mundane, workhorse operations. The inordinate sway of the corporations at the hub of the MEC would need to be reduced. Ben Fine is correct in stating that 'industrial policy cannot be successful' until South African conglomerates 'are co-opted [...] into supporting a domestic programme of industrial development and diversification'. BEE would have to shift towards arduous, risky but potentially productive ventures. Alongside such changes and co-optation, macroeconomic policy and the financial system would need to be adjusted accordingly.[78]

A host of factors feeds the reluctance of South African corporations to politically support and invest massively in a renewed industrialisation drive capable of creating large numbers of viable jobs. For one, it would mean vesting strong interventionist authority and power in a state that the incumbent elite still regards with distrust and anxiety, fearful that such authority might be put to radical use. That lack of trust, combined with the state's weakened leverage over South African corporations, makes it difficult to build a consensus for a genuinely new industrial strategy. Key imperatives of most of the largest conglomerates have been met already—they were allowed to move abroad and relaxed capital controls mean that they can circulate their profits virtually anywhere on the planet. Their domestic operations are now aspects of global corporate strategies and do not enjoy privileged consideration. The state therefore probably will have to 'buy' support for such a strategy by underwriting and financing very large parts of it (through subsidies, tax breaks and other incentives). In doing so, its ability to leverage other funding seems cramped. Pension funds could be a potentially potent source of financing, but government has allowed some of the country's biggest funds to move offshore. Unlike the Asian 'tigers', its sway over the banks and financial sector is slight. Moreover, a great deal of capital allocation occurs through a decentralised market, the stock exchange, which is prone to jittery, irrational reflexes.

The new Industrial Policy Action Plan (IPAP) announced in early 2010 looked to use 'concessional financing', procurement leverage, tariff policy[79] and enforcement of competition laws to drive the revamp (Davies, 2010).[80] This latest attempt to use tariff policy to engineer shifts in the industrial sectors has the benefit of South Africa's experience since the early 1990s. Mistakenly, the Finance Ministry had long regarded tariff policy as a form of industrial policy, with quicker tariff cuts triggering sharper shifts in the patterns of industrial production. Thus the average tariff on manufactured imports in the late 2000s was 8% (down from 23% in the 1990s); on imports from the European Union it was under 5%, and on imports from the South African Development Community it was almost zero.[81] The ministry believes that, while the cuts brought on some pain, the benefits were substantial: tariff policy, it claims, strengthened the export orientation of the economy, with non-commodity exports rising smartly in the 1990s. After that, trade liberalisation slowed and so did the benefits. The facts state otherwise.

South Africa's manufactured exports have remained havily dominated by resource-based sectors, with resource processing and vehicle-making the main drivers. Both those industries benefit from generous state support. This was hardly the market working its magic. Already by the the mid-2000s, the Trade and Industry Ministry was holding at bay pressure from the Treasury for deeper tariff cuts: 'Proposals for unilateral trade liberalisation, outside of a coherent industrial and trade policy, represent a fundamental misreading of the South African and international empirical evidence,' was how (then) Trade and Industry Minister Mandisi Mpahlwa put it.[82] The ministry has stuck by that position, but it remains to be seen whether it will be able to prevail over the more orthodox, neoliberal outlook of the Treasury.

The stakes are high. Job creation on the scale needed depends heavily on an overhaul of industrial strategy. The 2010 industrial plan, according to the Ministry of Trade and Industry, would create close to 2.4 million direct and indirect jobs by 2020. That target, if reached, would require an average 250 000 new jobs a year—or 1.25 million by 2014. Government's standing pledge is to create four million new jobs by 2014, which means that almost three million new jobs would need to be created outside of the main targeted industrial sectors. These are worthy but lofty goals: in the first decade of the 2000s, while the economy grew heartily, only 1.7 million new jobs were created. A large percentage of these were casual, temporary and low-paid. The recession later stripped almost 900 000 jobs out of the economy. Semantics might ride to the rescue, though.

Government now prefers to speak of 'work opportunities'. Even in the throes of the economic recession, it promised to create 500 000 such 'opportunities' in 2009—and, remarkably, it came close to delivering on this. The vast majority of those 'opportunities' were created through the Expanded Public Works Programme and each of them lasted an average of two months. There is no proof that those jobs are serving as the advertised 'bridges' toward more secure, long-term employment, but for a while at least they do help households meet some basic expenses and reduce debts (see Chapter six).

Breaking the mould

Deep restructuring is needed. In 2010, the economy was still inordinately reliant on the extraction and beneficiation of natural resources and on a buoyant but inherently unstable financial sector. Salient features of the economy have been reinforced, but additional destabilising characteristics are now also operating—notably the intense financialisation that has occurred since the early 1990s. In Seeraj Mohamed's (2010:38) downcast summary:

> The integration into global financial markets has increased the risk of financial crisis and vulnerability to contagion from financial problems elsewhere. The weak industrial structure and continued dependence on mining and minerals exports creates a balance of payments risk [...] Unless there is a huge effort to address the industrial decline in South Africa and new economic policies [are] implemented to support industrial growth and transformation, the majority of South Africans will face an increasingly bleak economic future.

Avoiding that outcome demands overhauling the overarching economic policies. The biggest challenge is whether and how the structural bias in economic decision-making can be overcome (Fine, 2008a; Freund, 2008). Inside the state, major battles were underway to determine the nature and extent of economic policy shifts. But the balance of power seemed largely unchanged. COSATU's attempts to curtail the power of the Finance Ministry (by expanding the brief of the Economic Development Ministry) brought few rewards. Meanwhile, policymakers maintained a disarming cheerfulness. No sooner had the recession shown signs of easing than Finance Minister Pravin Gordhan announced that

> the global storm has subsided, and the South African economy is on the path to recovery. Sound macroeconomic and fiscal policies ensured that we were well prepared when the storm broke, and these policies will be maintained.[83]

The first budget of the Zuma government saw little more than cosmetic alterations applied to the economic policies followed during Mbeki's second term. Inflation targeting continued despite COSATU's protests, taxes were not increased and there were hints of labour-market reforms. In late 2009, as many other countries tightened financial regulations, Zuma's government raised the limit companies could invest offshore from R 50 million (USD 6.3 million) to R 500 million (USD 63 million), and handed banks (rather than the Treasury) the authority to give the go-ahead for those transactions.[84] A few weeks later, banks were allowed to invest up to 25% of their deposit base offshore. Standard Chartered's Razia Khan called it 'a sign of faith in the South African economy that the authorities are willing to ease the way for outflows'.[85] Very few barriers remain to prevent South African and foreign corporations from shipping capital abroad.

Overall, the MEC has been consolidated and economic ownership is as concentrated as ever. Most sectors are dominated by a handful of vertically integrated corporations. The MEC model has been neither refuted nor supplanted, as Freund (2008) reminds. By exposing the structural undercarriage of South Africa's economy, and the interlocking interests that congregate there, the analysis underscores why particular strategies have prevailed and why other options have failed to survive beyond the drawing board (see Chapter one).[86] The social and political costs of South Africa's development path have revived those tussles. Many expected the economic recession to tilt the scales in favour of innovations with greater potential to serve society. Internationally, there was a brief interlude in late 2008 and early 2009 when this seemed likely—'moments of euphoria', as Joseph Stiglitz put it, 'when we were all Keynesians [...] It was not just Keynesian macroeconomic policies, it was the need for regulation and the recognition that economics had failed'.[87] That moment soon passed. In South Africa, though, it never appeared. A soft-Keynesian tilt was already underway. The recession presented government with the economic and political opportunity to go through the gears and deepen that shift; instead it opted to idle forth, tinkering around the edges of an unjust and unsustainable development strategy.

The ecological frailty of South Africa's development path

Awareness of the ecological limits and costs of South Africa's development path has increased, including in government. Since the late 1990s, it has funded scientific research into the resource and energy constraints and opportunities that may affect its developmental options. Yet the ecological dimension remains at best an afterthought in government's showcase strategies. An appreciation of ecological constraints, Swilling (2010:1) notes, 'has had limited impact on economic policy-making and virtually no impact on the underlying theories of economic growth that inform the thinking'.

The ANC's 2007 resolutions adopted at the Polokwane conference contained important and extensive statements about the environment and climate change. But these are not yet reflected in government policy. In his first State of the Nation address, Jacob Zuma (2009c), for example, spoke of the need for 'an environment for jobs and business opportunities', 'an environment conducive to sustainable economic growth and development' and 'an enabling environment for investment'. The 'other' environment, though, earned this solitary mention: 'South Africa, being a dry country, requires urgent action to mitigate adverse environmental changes and to ensure the provision of water to citizens.' Nor did he mention the environment or climate change in his inaugural address (2009d).

Even more resistant to change is the philosophical foundation in which development thinking is anchored. The equation of growth = development = progress remains axiomatic. As Environment Minister Buyelwa Sonjica put it in early 2010: 'We can't take an extreme view of environmental conservation at the expense of development.'[88] Policymakers, business leaders and much of the public, too, continue to believe that the biggest barriers blocking progress are technological and institutional—and that these ultimately and always yield to human resolve and ingenuity. Nature is implicitly regarded as boundless, inexhaustible and unfailingly resilient. It is a perspective that shaped Western modernity. And it is fundamentally flawed.

An inexorable contradiction operates at the heart of mainstream development thinking. Progress is seen to require and involve ever-expanding production for ever-growing consumption—yet this has to occur within a closed system of finite resources. The energy and materials needed for production are not limitless, nor is the environment's capacity to absorb the waste and pollution associated with such production. Worse, the image of nature as inexhaustible, and of economic growth as an unassailable virtue, has brought the planet to the verge of a global warming[89] tipping point, as the increasing volume of emitted greenhouse gasses traps heat in the atmosphere. Radical evasive action is the sensible course of action. Formidable interests, however, line up on the side of business as usual.[90] The current wave of intense financialisation acts as a further drag on progressive responses by inducing an obsessive focus on the immediate and transforming the future into something 'that happens when we get there'. 'Intergenerational environmental equity,' writes John Bellamy Foster (2002:11), 'cannot be incorporated within the short-term time horizon of non-philanthropic capital [...] A long-run point of view is completely irrelevant in the fluctuating stock market.'

Globally, growth models are angled toward a constant rise in production to meet a presumed constant rise in demand. The cycle, however, relies on materials that are finite. An estimated 55 billion tons of material were extracted in 2000, according to the International Panel for Sustainable Resource Management. A business-as-usual approach would require the extraction of a steadily increasing volume of material each year, reaching 140 billion tons in 2050. There is no scientific evidence that the required material exists on such a scale (Swilling, 2010). Vital inputs, such as fossil fuels, will very likely be in chronic short supply by that date. By several accounts, the world already has passed its 'peak oil' point, at which more than half the oil reserves in existence have been exploited (Maass, 2009).

Not only is South Africa implicated in this narrative, it seems committed to it. Its development path remains fundamentally based on ever-rising economic growth powered by abundant energy that is both cheap and dirty. Some of the excesses can, and shall, be tempered with stronger regulation and incentives. But the core principles of its development path are unsustainable and ultimately self-destructive.

Burning down the house

Official South African studies underscore the need to shift toward less energy- and pollution-intensive alternatives. The two key documents are the National Climate Change Strategy (NCCS) (2004) and the Long Term Mitigation Scenario (LTMS) (2007). The NCCS pointed to the impact of climate change on health, water supplies, maize production, biodiversity and rangelands, and noted that mitigation efforts would affect the energy and mining sectors. But the document clung to an insistence that mitigation should not occur at the expense of economic growth and development, a position to which government clings.

Cabinet in mid-2008 adopted findings from the LTMS exercise, which painted an alarming outlook if South Africa persisted along its current path. It advanced two scenarios. One envisaged 'growth without constraints', the other involved a set of interventions 'required by science'. In the 'growth without constraints' scenario, the focus is on energy-intensive industries that are powered by coal and nuclear electricity generation, with coal-to-liquids fuel production also expanded—in other words, business as usual. Total greenhouse gas emissions would quadruple by 2050,[91] with fuel consumption rising by 500%. Meeting energy needs would require building seven new coal-fired power plants, 12 nuclear pebble-bed modular reactor plants, 68 integrated gasification plants, and five new oil refineries. In his critique, David Hallowes (2008:7) exposed important flaws in the scenario's underlying assumptions, including that 'climate change does no damage' in the interim and 'that oil, water and other resources are available to meet demand'.[92] In the 'real' world, in 2010, emissions appeared to be rising in line with that scenario and Eskom's planned expansion drive was destined to hold it to that path at least until 2020.

Meanwhile, the 'required by science' scenario (which Cabinet endorsed) also made questionable assumptions. It supposed that countries of the global South would benefit from technology transfers, that peak oil would spark greater energy efficiency, that carbon capture and storage is a viable technology and that greater reliance on nuclear energy is an appropriate response (Hallowes, 2008).

Yet even the flawed scenarios have left faint to no imprint on the country's macroeconomic and industrial strategies. The National Industrial Policy Framework (2007) did not include viable eco-systems or the long-term supply of natural resources among the four preconditions for successful industrialisation. The underlying understanding is that 'natural systems [...] are intact and durable' (Swilling, 2010:21).[93] AsgiSA suffered the same blind spot and did not list environmental factors among South Africa's binding constraints.[94]

Hoodwinked

South Africa is hardly alone in privileging growth. One may add that the scale of misdoing in 'emerging' economies is negligible compared with the abuses committed by the industrialised countries over the past two centuries. It is not unreasonable to feel aggrieved by demands for radical shifts to protect the environment when those shifts involve sacrifices. But the indignation is short-sighted and both morally and ethically suspect.

The South African government played an ignominious role at the 2009 Copenhagen climate summit. The final political (and non-binding) accord, signed by 28 countries, kicked aside a more inclusive and financially generous UN-brokered deal and probably set back efforts to avoid runaway climate change by several years. Siding with Brazil, China and India, South Africa first opposed setting a goal of a global peak in emissions by 2020, halving world greenhouse gas emissions by 2050 and limiting global warming to a maximum of 2°C above pre-industrial times.[95]

'If we were to agree to targets now, we think that could hamper our economic growth,' government spokesperson Themba Maseko had explained a few months earlier. [96] After an outcry, the position underwent semantic repairs, yet still called to mind former US president George W Bush's explanation for opting out of the Kyoto protocols: '[W]e will not do anything that harms our economy [...] That's my priority. I'm worried about the economy.'[97]

Eventually, government offered a set of targets that would see South Africa's emissions peak between 2020 and 2025 and plateau for a decade before declining—on condition that the industrialised countries provided financial and technical support. Hailed as a 'bold move' by some, the proposal's wording was painstakingly—and deliberately—obtuse. South Africa would 'undertake mitigation actions which will result in a deviation below the current emissions baseline of around 34% by 2020 and of around 42% by 2025'.[98] It was not clear which baseline was being used or whether the 'deviation' involved a reduction in total emissions or in growth of emissions.

Eventually decoded, the proposal meant South Africa would reduce emissions against the 'business as usual' scenario outlined in the LTMS exercise. 'I want to allay the fear of business,' said South Africa's environment minister. 'This is not an extra burden on business.'[99] The proposal envisages South Africa's greenhouse-gas emissions rising until around 2025, at which point they would level off before beginning to decline around 2035. By that point, the planet almost certainly will have passed an irreversible climate-change tipping point. The logic behind South Africa's proposal was simple: 'We are going to develop, if it's the last thing we do.'

Shifting the blame

Industrialised countries are responsible for most of the accumulated carbon in the atmosphere—as much as three quarters of CO_2 emitted since the mid-1800s. Yet, the major industrialised countries have not honoured their commitments (under the 1997 Kyoto Protocol) to reduce greenhouse-gas emissions and several of them have resisted moves to limit the rise in global temperature to (a probably devastating) 2°C.[100] It is widely recognised that such a target would require reducing emissions to substantially less than their 1990 levels (in the major economies).

'Emerging' economies such as South Africa, meanwhile, gripe that restrictive emissions targets will prevent them from attaining the levels of prosperity and quality of life that industrialised countries take for granted. They also complain that the major industrialised countries balk at guaranteeing the levels of financial assistance and technology transfers they need to have any chance of meeting meaningful emissions targets. There is substance to those objections. The funds pledged to 'developing' countries to reduce emissions and manage the impact of global warming amounted to a pittance compared to the bail-outs of financial institutions in industrialised countries in 2008–09.

Yet this dichotomy is also misleading. 'Emerging' economies are no longer minor contributors to global warming. By 2009, they were responsible for more than half of global CO_2 emissions, according to research by the Global Carbon Project. This reflects explosive growth in the burning of coal and manufacturing of cement, both potent sources of CO_2. The world's biggest polluters are now China and the US. In 2006, the US expelled six billion metric tons of CO_2 into the Earth's atmosphere (compared with 5.9 billion tons in 2000); China 6.3 billion metric tons (versus 2.9 billion tons in 2000); Europe 4.7 billion metric tons (up from 4.5 billion tons in 2000); and India 1.4 billion metric tons (against one billion tons in 2000).[101]

In a global contest of per capita greenhouse-gas emissions, however, the rich win hands down. The average US citizen generates about 20 metric tons of CO_2 a year, with Japan and the United Kingdom emitting close to 10 tons per person per year. In China, the number is about 3.8 tons, and in India, it is 1.2 tons per person.[102] The US, Canada, Europe and Japan therefore carry a disproportionately large responsibility for rapidly reducing greenhouse-gas emissions. They blithely continue to shirk their mitigating roles, however. At the Copenhagen summit, for example, the US proposal amounted to a 3% reduction in greenhouse gas emissions off the 1990 baseline. Industrialised countries as a whole offered 19% cut below 1990s levels by 2020, even though science requires a 25 to 40% cut if there is to be any chance of avoiding runaway global heating. According to South Africa's chief climate negotiator, countries like South Africa are caught in a 'core disagreement between developed and developing countries'. But Walden Bello's analysis is more convincing. A dysfunctional climate-change regime, he believes, suits both the industrialised countries and 'catch-up' aspirants in the south:

> When the Bush administration says it will not respect the Kyoto protocol because it does not bind China and India, and the Chinese and Indian governments say they will not tolerate curbs on their greenhouse gas emissions because the US has not ratified Kyoto, they are in fact playing out an unholy alliance to allow their economic elites to continue to evade their environmental responsibilities and free-ride on the rest of the world.[103]

At climate negotiations, South Africa nowadays plays the 'Third World nationalism' card. Yet it is responsible for 39% of Africa's total annual CO_2 emissions (Boden, Marland, Andres, 2009) and releases close to 400 million metric tons of carbon into the atmosphere each year (Sengul et al, 2007).[104] In 2006, it emitted the equivalent of 8.59 metric tons of CO_2 for every person in the country, twice more than the global average. It ranks as the 44th worst CO_2 emitter on the planet (out of 212 countries)[105], with per-capita emissions that outweigh those of countries such as Argentina, Egypt, Hungary, Malaysia, Poland, Spain, Ukraine, Venezuela and that were only slight less than those of Germany (9.74 metric tons per capita) and the United Kingdom (9.39 metric tons) (UN Statistics Division, 2010). In fact, South Africa ranks among the 20% of worst emitters of CO_2 per person on the planet and it contains the world's single largest emitter of CO_2, Sasol's coal-to-liquid plant at Secunda, which spews 72 million tons of CO_2 into the atmosphere each year (Earthlife Africa, 2009).[106]

Meanwhile, fully 28 of the 55 African nations for which data are available have per-capita emission rates of less than 0.5 metric tons of carbon per person per year.[107] According to the World Bank, the average individual electricity consumption in sub-Saharan Africa is barely enough to power 100-watt light bulb for three hours a day.[108] South Africa should not be able to insinuate itself into that (blameless) company. Its economy is unusually energy- and pollution-intensive, especially for a semi-industrialised country that is not an oil producer and 'its prevailing approach to growth and development' breaches 'key ecological thresholds' (Swilling, 2010:7). Yet it chooses to couch its negotiating position on CO_2 emission targets in the discourse of 'Third World' nationalism.

Untenable growth

The fossil fuels coal and oil are the mainstay of South Africa's energy sector,[109] which is responsible for more than 90% of the CO_2 it belches into the sky each year (Swilling, 2010). The major culprits are Eskom's coal-fired power stations, Sasol's coal-to-liquid plants and other industries involved in extracting and beneficiating minerals. Eskom provides at least 95% of South Africa's electricity, 90% of which is generated in coal-fired power stations. Accordingly, the volume of coal extracted each year[110] has increased steadily since 1980 to feed a coal-based electricity-generation industry that supplies some of the cheapest electricity in the world, thus subsidising the country's industrial sector. If electricity consumption increases at a rate of 4.4% per year, the CO_2 emitted by its power stations will double within 20 years.

Indeed, South Africa consumes electricity at rates comparable to some industrialised Asian countries. On average, each citizen uses about 4.53 kilowatts of electricity per hour—double the world average, nine times more than the average for Africa and within range of the 5.90 kilowatts per hour the average South Korean uses. Of course, it is not literally the case that every South African uses electricity at this rate. Close to 30% of the population is either not linked to the power grid or uses electricity very rarely and in very small quantities.

Industry, in particular mining, is the single biggest user of electricity and, along with Eskom, the largest emitter of CO_2. The mining industry alone consumes an estimated 15% of Eskom's total output.[111] Beyond it, industrial and agricultural firms in their own right contribute 7% and 11%, respectively, of the country's annual CO_2 emissions, while transport adds a further 9%. According to Earthlife Africa, Eskom sells electricity to industries 'at below the average cost of production and, in some cases, below the actual cost of production'.[112] Eskom refuses to divulge the details—even to the National Energy Regulator, which estimates that the gap between industrial and domestic electricity tariffs is 'way over 100%'. In most emerging economies, it tends to be in the 60 to 80% range.[113]

Several dozen 'special pricing agreements', some of them dating back to the final decade of the apartheid era, are believed to be active. In early 2010, Eskom admitted it had 'secret' tariff deals with 138 corporations, some of which paid as little as 9c per kilowatt-hour. The average cut-price tariff for industry was believed to be approximately 17c per kilowatt-hour. The deals include 10 major ones that were concluded during the apartheid era and which are not subject to tariff increases.[114] The beneficiaries include industrial giants such as BHP Billiton, which operates the massive Bayside and Hillside aluminium smelters; its tariffs appear to be pegged to the market price of aluminium. The corporation imports aluminium, which it smelts at these operations before exporting it.[115] At full capacity, the two smelters consume more electricity than the city of Johannesburg.

It is believed that a significant part of Eskom's debt may be due to such cut-price tariff deals. Eskom in effect cross-subsidises part of those discount rates with the elevated tariffs it charges household and regular business users. The durability of these practices is a testament to the ongoing weight of the MEC, which for decades has relied on cheap, coal-based electricity. The MEC is still capable of generating what sociologist Karl von Holdt has termed 'policy juggernauts' that coalesce around particular sets of interests and hold sway in policy and planning, despite running against the grain of common wisdom and public interests.[116] Mitigating efforts require that 'everyone does their part', but the weight of culpability (and responsibility) is distributed unevenly. Remedial strategies have to reflect that fact.

Is it really everybody's problem?

Balk as it may, South Africa will not escape the effects of global heating. Scenarios commissioned by what was then known as the Department of Environmental Affairs and Tourism forecast:

- ▪ rainfall declining by 5 to 10% overall;
- ▪ shifting rainfall patterns (higher rainfall in the east, less in the west; shorter summer rainfalls in the north-east);
- ▪ wetter conditions in the east, which could lead to the expansion of malaria zones;
- ▪ higher daily maximum temperatures in the west of the country; and
- ▪ extended summers.

Impoverished and marginalised communities will bear the brunt of the havoc created by climate change—yet their ecological footprint is tiny and faint. Internationally and within countries, the privileged and the industries that service them, do the most damage. According to the United Nations Development Programme (UNDP) (1998), the wealthiest 20% of humanity was responsible for 86%—and the poorest 20% for a mere 1.3%—of consumption spending at the turn of the century. This pattern holds also in South Africa.

The bulk of the environmental costs of South Africa's development path over the past 120 years have been imposed on poor communities. It is their local environments and health that have been degraded the most, yet they have benefited the least from development 'progress'. The potential health effects of industrial schemes did not trouble apartheid planners. On the contrary, plants were often erected upwind or upstream from black townships and neighbourhoods or, as in the south of Durban, built right in their midst. About half the country's population lives in areas that are subjected to unsafe levels of air pollution (Gibson *et al*, 2008). The burning of fossil fuels (including the indoor use of coal and wood fires for cooking and heating) is responsible for an estimated R 4 billion (USD 500 million) in healthcare costs annually.[117] Parliament in 2005 passed tougher legislation to regulate air pollution (the Air Quality Act), but monitoring and enforcement is weak. Loose environmental justice groupings are trying to confront industrial polluters, expose the lacklustre enforcement of regulations and laws, and link environmental concerns with social-justice struggles (Cock, 2006). Some seek to push further, by focusing 'on the production of ... injustices' (Ruiters, 2001:112)[118] and linking environmental issues to the urban-development models and cost-recovery policies that frame the lives of the urban poor.

Meanwhile, wealthy South Africans consume and waste at prodigious rates. If the lifestyle of a well-off Cape Town suburb were extrapolated to all of humanity, we would need between 4.5 and 14 planets to satisfy its consumptive excesses, according to Swilling's (2006) calculations. On average each South African disposes of about two kilograms of solid waste a day, more than three times the European average. The affluent are by far the most wasteful; residents in informal neighbourhoods discard about 0.2 kilograms of waste a day. Individual consumption is only part of the story: the mining industry generates more than 80% of total waste, according to official estimates (Department of Water Affairs and Forestry, 1998).[119]

Waste recycling is increasing in some cities (in Cape Town about 60% of industrial waste is recycled) and hinges especially on the labour of independent 'waste pickers' who link into complex recycling chains, a common phenomenon in many other cities of the global south (Samson, 2008). Still, about 90% of municipal waste nationally is trucked to landfill sites. Waste recycling is a viable, cost-effective and job-creating alternative that is certain to become more commonplace in South Africa's cities, following adoption of a National Integrated Waste Management Act by Parliament in 2009. Ideally, it should be structured around community-based operations (Swilling, 2010). But it leaves untouched the central problem, which is excessive consumption.

To the last drop

The use, spoilage and waste of water resources occur on similarly unequal terms. South Africa is on the verge of serious, recurring water crises. About 98% of available water resources are already allocated or in use and its rivers and dams are so highly polluted that they have lost the ability to dilute effluents (Turton, 2008).[120]

Approximately 62% of total water resources are used for agricultural irrigation, 25% for 'urban activities', while mining, electricity generation and other industries consume the remainder (Department of Water Affairs and Forestry, 2004). There is scarcely any surplus water capacity to service anticipated economic development (Turton, 2008)[121] or match the surging needs generated by urbanisation. Domestic water consumption is set to triple between 1996 and 2030, while mining and industry's water needs will more than double in the same period (Department of Water Affairs and Forestry, 2006). Water security in cities and towns is a serious concern. According to the Department of Water Affairs (2009), 'water shortages are predicted for the majority of large towns in the short to medium term, necessitating urgent intervention'. Building more dams and intensifying the use of groundwater are options, but mainly in the south of KwaZulu-Natal and eastern parts of the Eastern Cape (CSIR, 2009).

To be sure, existing resources can be distributed more fairly (away, for example, from irrigating golf estates and lush suburban gardens and toward meeting the basic needs of low-income households). But those adjustments will still run up against the fact of a finite resource. Water-use strategies require radical change. Even if demand increases by only 1% a year, South Africa will experience severe shortages of water by 2014 (Swilling, 2010). Of the 19 water-management areas, the water security status of six was 'shortage' and that of a further nine was 'in-balance', according to the Department of Water Affairs (2009).[122] Water availability and access will soon become a central fault line, heightening institutional conflict inside the state and aggravating social instability.

The outlook is sullied further by deteriorating water quality. The economic heartland in and around Johannesburg and Pretoria relies on a watershed that has been intensively polluted by industrial development. Decades of mining for gold and other minerals have left much of the water supply heavily polluted with heavy metals and other pollutants (Turton, 2008). Nationally, the water resources are toxin-contaminated to an extent that rivals China.[123] Salinity has increased to a disturbing degree, mainly due to mining, industrial and sewage effluent, and to the leeching of agricultural fertilisers and other chemicals into water sources (Gibson *et al*, 2008).

Development—be it a new industrial venture, office park or residential expansion—occurs with barely any regard for these constraints. Water-saving methods are seldom among the criteria that guide planning approval, state tenders or subsidies. One obvious reason is a lack of awareness or concern. But the chief culprit lurks in the background: the conviction that growth and development trumps all and that natural resources can be taken for granted. Water must be placed at the heart of all development planning decisions.

Mixing it up

Some of the legislative and policy foundations for shifting to a cleaner and more sustainable energy mix exist. The Constitution contains explicit commitments to sustainable development, even though they are diluted with caveats. Official recognition of the need for greater energy efficiency and use of renewables dates back to the 1998 White Paper on Energy. The National Framework for Sustainable Development, adopted in mid-2008, also recognised the stress on natural resources and environmental systems, and adopted a relatively standard approach of 'decoupling' economic growth from unsustainable natural-resource exploitation (Gibson *et al*, 2008). Buried in laws and departmental strategies are a welter of other commitments and pronouncements that relate to air pollution, water supply, waste management, land and soil management, renewables, public transport and more.[124] But the overarching growth and development strategies reflect neither the awareness nor the remedies set out in those various documents.

So tangible progress has been unhurried. An energy efficiency strategy was only produced in 2005. Government's White Paper on Renewable Energy emerged in 2003 and foresaw around 5% of South Africa's energy mix being sourced from renewables over the following decade (Department of Minerals and Energy, 2003). Groups like Earthlife Africa (2009) contend that a feasible renewables programme built around solar and wind energy, biogas and biofuels could significantly reduce reliance on fossil fuels and create more than one million new jobs.

Most of the debate is fixated on big fixes. Eskom's R 343 billion (USD 43 billion) capital-investment plans call for an energy mix that includes clean coal, gas, nuclear and renewables. But the focus is on building new coal-fired power stations, rehabilitating decommissioned ones and constructing open-cycle gas turbines.[125] The centrepieces in its strategy are the Kusile and the 4 800-megawatt Medupi coal-fired plants. Eskom was hoping to finance the project with a R 30 billion (USD 3.75 billion) World Bank loan (R 6 billion of which would be used to develop alternative energy sources).

Eskom defends its plans saying that no feasible alternative based on renewables is available. Government's preference, according to the Department of Energy, is for 'proven technologies'. But that stance stems from an out-of-date bias toward highly centralised models of electricity provision by large power plants. A conglomeration of smaller-scale, decentralised options could dramatically alter the mix of energy sources, reduce reliance on coal-based electricity and free funding for the reduction of coal-fired plant emissions. Solar and wind farms cannot, on their own, replace entire power plants. But when combined with other initiatives (energy-saving schemes, electricity feed-ins by independent producers, etc) they conceivably can, within a decade or so, supplant the need to bring new power stations online. If one million residences were to be provided with subsidised solar panels, for example, this could cut 2 500 megawatts of demand from the grid by 2012.[126]

Ultimately such decisions rest in the hands of the state; Eskom, after all, is a state utility. A combination of regulations and subsidies can be used for the large-scale introduction of solar heaters for residences, for example. Instead, subsidies and credits have been pumped into capital-intensive and energy-guzzling megaprojects. It is a familiar story: a lucrative mix of subsidies is funnelled toward core MEC industries that also benefit from cut-price energy provision. Even as South Africa's climate-change officials were finessing their negotiating position ahead of the 2009 Copenhagen summit, the Trade and Industry Department was hoping to salvage its mammoth Coega heavy-industry scheme near Port Elizabeth—despite the ruinous environmental costs. The Rio Tinto Alcan aluminium smelter at Coega was eventually shelved in October 2009, when Eskom failed to issue the desired electricity-supply guarantees. The smelter would have used about 1 350 megawatts of electricity, equivalent to the entire output of a coal-fired power station. Eskom has not revealed the tariffs it offered Rio Tinto Alcan, but Earthlife Africa estimated them at 12 to 14 cents per kilowatt. The tariff Eskom charged for residential use of electricity in late 2009 was 50.4 cents per kilowatt.

South Africa's electricity system faces other complications, too. China consumed half the global output of coal in 2008 (2 098 million metric tons, almost three times as much as the US)[127] and its expanding electricity grid is being supplied mainly by coal-fired power stations. Demand is soaring in other emerging economies, as well. South Africa, meanwhile, commands about 5% of the global coal reserves. Its chronic balance-of-payment vulnerability will dearly tempt it to use those reserves to generate foreign revenue—potentially squeezing coal supplies available for local electricity-generating demand. The upshot seems self-evident: the less reliant South Africa is on coal for its electricity, the better.

The search for low-emission sources of electricity is tempting a partial turn to nuclear power. South Africa currently operates one nuclear power station at Koeberg, near Cape Town. Built in the 1980s, it yields 1 800 megawatts of electricity, roughly 6% of the country's electricity needs. Both the plant's units are approaching the end of their 40-year lifespan, though retrofitting can extend that by another 10 to 20 years. According to former Minerals and Energy Minister Buyelwa Sonjica, 'nuclear power is one of the least carbon-intensive generating technologies'—a claim environmental researchers dispute. They argue that, once the refinement and waste-management and-disposal processes are factored in, nuclear power is not much more emissions-friendly than new, high-tech coal-fired power stations.

Renewables in perspective

The prevailing approach favours industrial corporations (including multinationals) and remain deeply biased against 'start-ups', green or otherwise, in the energy sector, despite the Trade and Industry Ministry's avowed endorsement of energy-saving and green technologies. In this climate, Eskom has paid little more than lip service to renewables. Much less than 1% of electricity originates from renewable sources, although government in the early 2000s had committed to sourcing 5% of electricity from renewables.[128] Eskom's vaunted solar water heater programme was meant to install 900 000 water heaters over five years; in 2008, only 800 were installed. Its one wind farm (at Klipheuwel in the Western Cape) generates about 0.25% of the country's electricity (Earthlife Africa, 2009).

Wind and solar-power technologies are feasible alternatives that can have a quick impact on the energy mix and be expanded into long-term sources of renewable energy. Solar power is a very promising alternative in a country with average daily solar radiation of between 4.5 and 6.5 kilowatts per hour per square metre and where sunshine is well distributed and relatively predictable. Another simple, highly attractive venture would be a national programme to deliver residential solar water heaters, an undertaking that was being revived in 2010.

Several other countries have set out on such paths. In Germany, renewable energy accounts for 9.5% of total energy consumed and it supplies 15% of electricity (half of the 15% comes from wind power). In 2007, it added renewable capacity equivalent to two nuclear power plants. Appropriate government legislation and subsidies, especially feed-in tariffs, have been key factors (Ho *et al*, 2009). A similar approach offers huge opportunities for rebooting South Africa's transformation. Such an approach

> could be more effective in eradicating poverty than traditional strategies that depend on primary exports or exports of cheap manufactured goods underpinned in both cases by resource depletion and/or environmental degradation (Swilling, 2010:6).

Renewables are criticised for being costly, piecemeal solutions. Both claims are disingenuous. Any energy mix aimed at climate protection by definition comprises a set of simultaneous interventions—the so-called 'wedge approach', popularised by Stephen Pacala and Robert Socolow in their 2004 *Science* article. The challenge of achieving large carbon reductions is parcelled into various elements, or 'wedges', each of which is assigned to a particular strategy or technology. In a sunny country, such as South Africa, photovoltaic solar energy, for instance, is a viable and attractive wedge. As for cost, as Earthlife Africa (2009:37) reminds,

> if the full costs to the economy of power generation using highly polluting fuels such as coals were explicitly acknowledged in national accounts, then renewable energies would already be cheaper.

Moreover, renewables create more jobs (especially low- and semi-skilled jobs) than either fossil fuels or nuclear power generation. A recent scoping exercise found that in some areas renewables were already 'financially cheaper or very close to the cost of fossil fuel counterparts' and that once environmental and job-creation benefits were factored in they became 'economic in a wider range of scenarios' (Holm *et al*, 2008). Had government funded renewables research and development on the scale it invested in the ill-fated pebble-bed modular reactor, the country could have had a functioning renewables industry built around solar power (Hallowes, 2008).[129] Besides the ecological benefits, the job-creating and life-quality-enhancing effects would have been huge. A reasonable, popular alternative was shunned in favour of a secretive, capital-intensive folly.

Unfortunately, awareness, commitment and responsibility for addressing the environmental dimension is dispersed across the state and has not yet penetrated the inner bastions of decision-making and allocation. This is less a matter of ignorance than conscious choice. There are signs that the Treasury, for example, is alert to the risks of persisting along the same development path. 'Our economic growth over the next decade and beyond cannot be built on the same principles and technologies, the same energy systems and the same transport models, that we are familiar with today,' (then) Finance Minister Trevor Manuel told Parliament in February 2008.[130] Save for a tiny environmental tax, that sentiment is yet to be translated into any forthright action from the Treasury. Ministries such as Housing, Science and Technology, Environmental Affairs and Tourism seem amenable to innovative thinking, but they rank low on the rungs of voice and power inside the state. South Africa needs to create an environmental focal point or hub within the presidency, so that the motley undertakings can be shored up and harmonised more effectively. Those efforts need to be integrated into an explicit, overarching strategy that is championed and driven by the presidency, and that is clearly reflected in industrial, minerals and macroeconomic policies.

New approaches to growth

In doing so, South Africa must move beyond the 'decoupling' approach, which is usually associated with the hypothesis that capitalism is moving toward a 'weightless society' in which efficiency gains increasingly 'delink' economic growth from the environment. In this functionalist narrative, the market eventually adapts by creating incentives for innovation and disincentives for pollution and waste. Smaller amounts of energy and materials are used and less waste is produced for each incremental increase in GDP. The economy, it is claimed, gradually 'dematerialises'. These hopes are as familiar as they are mistaken.[131]

Decoupling has been most visible in relation to industrial pollution in Western Europe, where so-called 'end-of-the-pipe' innovations have reduced the intensity of pollutant outflows. But per capita waste flows actually increased—as did the absolute volume of materials dumped into the environment—in line with rising production and consumption. According to the World Resources Institute (2000:35): 'We have learned that efficiency gains brought by technology and new management practices have been offset by [increases in] the scale of economic growth'.[132] The guiding logic of endless growth offsets the impact of 'decoupling'. In Elmar Altvater's (2007b) phrasing:

> Entropy production in the economic process always makes sense so long as the other side of the double-sided production process, ie the valuation process, results in a surplus value and thus in profits and an acceptable profit rate.

Improvements in efficiency and a shift away from fossil fuels (and toward renewables) are imperative if we are to have any chance of reducing the odds of catastrophic global heating. But such techno fixes alone cannot sufficiently slow the depletion of natural resources, limit the degradation of the environment and stabilise greenhouse-gas concentrations in the atmosphere[133]—not while the ethos of endless, 'virtuous' growth reigns. The world economy quadrupled in size since 1960 and it will double again by 2025. It took all of human history to grow to the USD 7 trillion mark it reached in 1950; at the moment, the world economy grows by that amount every decade.[134] Very dramatic changes in consumption are needed if catastrophe is to be avoided—not only in the industrialised countries, but also in the privileged zones and layers of the global south. In the opinion of James Gustav Speth, former administrator of the UNDP:

> All we have to do to destroy the planet's climate and biota and leave a ruined world to our children and grandchildren is to keep doing exactly what we are doing, [even] with no growth in the human population or the world economy (ibid).

Recognition that endless growth is unsustainable is not new. John Stuart Mill foresaw economies eventually coming to rest in a 'stationary state'. 'The increase of wealth is not boundless,' he wrote in 1848, the same year in which the *Communist*

Manifesto was published. There exists, he insisted, an 'irresistible necessity that the stream of human industry should finally spread itself out into an apparently stagnant sea'.[135] Karl Marx (1973:409–10) also noted with discomfort capitalism's tendency to transform nature into 'purely an object for humankind, purely a matter of utility' that 'ceases to be recognised as a power for itself'.[136]

Such lucidity, though, was rare. Western modernity careened forth, confident that 'there never comes a time when more labourers will not produce larger harvests [and] there never comes a time when additional capital introduced into agriculture cannot secure for itself some return'.[137] The notion of zero growth seems anathema to capitalism. For Adam Smith, to single out one example, life for most people would 'be pinched and stinted in a stationary condition of wealth' and could only be enhanced and satisfactory if the economy constantly grew.[138] Smith was pinpointing both the war cry of capitalism and its core expansionist logic.

The most well known recent attempt to question such logic came in 1972, when the Club of Rome's 'Limits to Growth' report raised hackles by drawing an explicit link between environmental destruction and economic growth, and called for new strategies that could sever that link.[139] The report was a momentary hiccup in the cementing of orthodoxy, which much preferred the counsel of the 1987 Brundtland report, 'Our Common Future'. It played down the natural resource constraints and elevated the importance of institutional and technological factors.[140] That sensibility has held sway since. But a sense of impending doom is gradually dislodging it. The limits to growth used to be capital, technology, human labour and the institutional arrangements in which they are deployed. To that list we have now added an overwhelming additional factor: natural resources.

There is increasing awareness that the dominant growth models have to change, and that economies have to shift to some form of 'non-material' growth or even 'non-growth'. Can capitalism function or survive with constantly slow or even zero growth? The answer is not clear. Robert Solow, who won the 1987 Nobel Prize for his neoclassical analysis of economic growth, has suggested that 'there is nothing intrinsic in the system that says it cannot exist happily in a stationary state'.[141] Economist Herman Daly and others have sought to add rigour to that sentiment and demonstrate the feasibility of a 'steady-state' economy.[142] For 'developing' countries, the mere suggestion of a no-growth strategy, however, is heresy. It seems to appeal to those who are already affluent and comfortable, and who, as British socialist Anthony Crosland once quipped, seem to 'want to kick the ladder down behind them'.[143]

An outlook that encompasses the next two to three hundred years has to recognise the need for radical change if the planet is to remain a viable home to the human species (and countless others). The pace and intensity of such a transition would depend on the levels of wealth, development and social progress achieved in different countries. Ultimately, though, sustainable development requires that total material consumption stabilises (for ecological sustainability) and a reasonable threshold of material consumption for all people is not exceeded (for social and political sustainability) (Oberg & Gallopin, 1992).

That implies, among other things, shifting our measurement of progress and development away from exclusively material indicators (economic output, income and expenditures, asset ownership, etc). Criticisms of the GDP measure are as old as the yardstick itself, but they have gained heft in recent years. GDP, after all, measures output according to place, rather than who actually benefits from economic growth and at what cost. It does not, for example, capture the costs imposed by negative externalities (pollution, environmental degradation, resource depletion, species annihilation, disease and worse) that are associated with particular productive and consumptive practices. And the measure involves patent absurdities. To the extent that a vehicle accident, toxic spill or disease outbreak requires the provision of services (repairs, clean-up, medicine) they are deemed to *contribute* to growth. Equally absurd is the fact that the steady depletion of natural resources is tallied not as a drain on growth, but as an addition to growth. Worse, to the extent that scarcity elevates prices, stripping natural assets can boost economic growth even further. Mainstream ecology therefore needs to guard against 'capture by the ideology of vulgar economics', as Samir Amin (2010) warns.

There have been calls for adjusting the ways in which national accounts are calculated, by internalising the environment and the environmental effects of particular activities. Seemingly sensible, that route, however, is entirely compatible with neoclassical economics, since it would 'turn the environment into a commodity which can be analysed like other commodities'.[144] For orthodox economists, explains Foster (2002:27), 'ecological degradation is evidence of market failure' and the remedy involves fully commodifying the environment by incorporating it fully into the market system by way of a rational price structure—which is rather like enlisting the arsonist to put out the fire. The environment is threatened, Foster therefore warns (*op cit*, 30), not only when environmental costs are externalised, 'but also by the attempted incorporation of the environment into the economy—the commodification of nature'. Ultimately, capitalism

> *in typical fashion, sees any crisis as emanating from barriers to the expansion of capital rather than the expansion of capital itself* (*op cit*, 35).

Amartya Sen and Joseph Stiglitz have called for a shift away from the current 'excessive focus on GDP metrics' to a new system capable of capturing features such as broad access to public services, distribution of income, an eco-friendly economy, good work-life balance and more.[145] One may extend those facets to include culture, personal safety, a sense of belonging and solidarity, health and more. The Himalayan kingdom of Bhutan has devised a system for gauging 'gross national happiness', complete with 72 indicators of happiness. Practical or not, such experiments highlight the moral and ethical dimensions of the challenge. Successfully defending the environment

> *requires a break with the tyranny of the bottom line and a long revolution [...] in which other, more diverse values not connected to the bottom line of the money-driven economy have a chance of coming to the fore* (Foster, 2002:40).

Endnotes

1 Cited in Fine (2008a:7).

2 Not that the currency was unscathed. Steyn (2004:126), hardly a dissident on these matters, concluded that 'there can be no doubt that easing of exchange controls contributed to the rand's slide during the period that [Trevor] Manuel has been finance minister'.

3 As of November 2009, South African firms could open foreign bank accounts without prior approval and could invest up to R 500 million anywhere offshore without prior approval (USD 63 million), up from R 50 million (USD 6.3 billion) previously. 'This is definitely unexpected and a pleasant surprise,' remarked Standard Chartered's regional research chief. The moves were touted as an attempt to weaken the exceptionally strong currency in a bid to boost export earnings. Within a week of the announcement, the currency had strengthened even further, however. See Mariam Isa, 'Gordhan cuts forex controls to curb rand', *Business Day*, 28 October 2009.

4 Cited in Fine (2008a:7)

5 This was before the electricity crisis of early 2008, obviously.

6 Cited in Fine (2008b:6).

7 In Malaysia and Singapore, for example, very large proportions of savings have been channelled through pension funds.

8 According to analyst Moeletsi Mbeki, brother of the former South African president, the decision to allow that move was taken by the South African Cabinet (comments at an HSRC seminar on 'Transformative social policy and the developmental state: Lessons for South Africa', 1 November 2007, Pretoria).

9 Cited in Fine (2008b:5).

10 Such was the desperation for inward investment that the state sold part of its heavy steel producer ISCOR to the multinational Mittal Steel with, according to Swilling (2010), 'a back-to-back agreement that Mittal could buy South African iron ore for cost plus 3% forever'. According to Mittal, its South African operations are more profitable than any other. Government defended the deal, saying it hoped that Mittal would provide steel to the local market at 'developmental' prices (which Mittal did not do). See Lynley Donnelly, 'ANC linked company gets Sishen rights', *Mail & Guardian*, 19 March 2010.

11 Neva Makgetla, 'Worrying facts underlie the economy's patina of health', *Business Day*, 21 April 2006.

12 *Ibid.*

13 Rob Davies, appointed Trade and Industry Minister in 2009, listed among the reasons for this languid performance, 'a volatile and insufficiently competitive currency; the high cost of capital relative to our main trading partners, particularly that channelled towards value-added sectors such as manufacturing, resulting in a too limited allocation of capital to these sectors; the monopolistic provision and pricing of key inputs into manufacturing; an aged, unreliable and expensive infrastructure system; a weak skills system; and the failure to adequately leverage public capital and other large and repetitive areas of public expenditure'. He was addressing the National Assembly on 18 February 2010. See 'Rob Davies unravels SA's industrial plan', *Moneyweb*, 18 February 2010; available at http://www.moneyweb.co.za/mw/view/mw/en/page295025?oid=347867&sn=2009+Detail&pid=292520

14 At the time, companies were allowed to invest up to R 250 million within the Southern African Development Community (SADC) and up to R 50 million beyond SADC. 'It does not take a corporate genius,' writes Fine (2008b:5), 'to work out that you get more out of the country if you break up a conglomerate into separate companies and benefit from the multiple allowances.'

15 Judy Gilmour, 'Rude reality', *Financial Mail*, 3 April 2008. The data are from Ernst & Young.

16 Cited in Mohamed (2009:13).

17 Epstein (2005) and Crotty (2002), cited in Mohamed (2009).

18 This section is especially indebted to Seeraj Mohammed's recent research and analysis of these trends.

19   Cited in Mohamed (2010).

20   Thanks to Seeraj Mohamed for sharing these data and the following data (unless otherwise indicated).

21   Mohamed (2010) reminds that, in South Africa's case, long-term investment capital tends to be sourced from retained earnings or the securities markets—not from banks and other financial institutions. The latter specialise in extending short-term credit, home mortgages and vehicle-lease arrangements.

22   Mohamed cites Orhangazi, O (2005) 'Financialization and capital accumulation in the non-financial corporate sector: a theoretical and empirical investigation', Working Paper 149, Political Economy Research Institute, University of Massachusetts, Amherst; and Stockhammer, E (2004). 'Financialization and the slowdown of accumulation', *Cambridge Journal of Economics*, Vol. 28, No. 5, pp. 719–41.

23   Neva Makgetla, 'Worrying facts underlie the economy's patina of health', *Business Day*, 21 April 2006.

24   *Ibid*. Once state subsidies, tax and other incentives, and other forms of state support to private firms are factored in, the share of investment financed from state coffers rises considerably beyond this level (of one third).

25   These data, drawn from various sources, are cited in Mohamed (2010).

26   Neva Makgetla, 'Worrying facts underlie the economy's patina of health', *Business Day*, 21 April 2006.

27   *Ibid*.

28   These are basically payments of dividends on shares and interest on local bonds, after subtracting the international income earned by South African investments and individuals.

29   Neva Makgetla, 'Low levels of direct foreign debt mask a less savoury reality', *Business Day*, 10 June 2009.

30   Additionally, the reliance on short-term capital flows discourages domestic savings. Between 2003 and 2007, as Makgetla shows, domestic and company savings fell from 4.8% to 0.4% of GDP, before recovering slightly to 2% in 2008. Government savings ran at about zero in 2008. International experience indicates that economic growth tends to run out of steam unless private savings are the main source of funding for domestic investment.

31   They are not the only beneficiaries of BEE, but they are the biggest and most powerful ones.

32   Economist Dawie Roodt, quoted in 'Zuma victory could make markets edgy', *Pretoria News*,18 December 2009.

33   A weasel phrase, since it automatically tarnishes other approaches as 'ill-disciplined', 'populist' or worse.

34   Britain, during Margaret Thatcher's reign, provided the prototypical example. Mines, auto manufacturers and other nationalised producers were privatised, along with large sections of the public service. The National Health Service evaded the onslaught, most probably because the political risks were forbiddingly high.

35   Stuckler and his colleagues found that 'rapid mass privatisation as an economic transition strategy was a crucial determinant of differences in adult mortality trends in post-communist countries' (2009:399). In their commentary, Bobak & Marmot (2009) noted that mortality rates rose more sharply in countries coming off a lower economic baseline and where inequalities had widened the most. Historical trends were also pertinent. Mortality rates in the former Soviet Union had fluctuated before the collapse of communism—an indication of poor and vulnerable health status (and high risk) generally. Even slight shifts in social provisioning could therefore have severe effects on people's health.

36   The slow-down was evident even after controlling for the effects of diseases such as AIDS.

37   Cited in Hart (2007).

38   A sterling example is the contention of Peruvian economist, Hernando de Soto Polar, that granting formal legal title to squatters and 'slum dwellers' for the land they live on would release massive amounts of previously 'dead capital' into 'informal' economies and drastically reduce poverty. The research evidence for this theory is hardly edifying. Critiques

abound, including Rossini, R G and Thomas, J J (1990) 'The size of the informal sector in Peru: A critical comment on Hernando de Soto's El Otro Sendero', *World Development*, Vol. 18, No. 1, January, pp. 125–35; and Woodruff, C (2001) 'Review of de Soto's The Mystery of Capital', *Journal of Economic Literature*, Vol. 39, No. 4, December, pp. 1215–23. Practical experience suggests that individual titling often sparks speculative raiding that displaces squatters once their neighbourhoods become 'formalised'. Grassroots movements such as South Africa's *Abahlali baseMjondolo* and Brazil's Homeless Workers' Movement reject individual titling as a blanket solution and favour communal and democratic systems of collective land tenure. For a trenchant take on how the idealisation of self-help has played out in South Africa's low-cost housing sector—and how easily an ideology of mutual-help and solidarity was seized upon to legitimate and help salvage a failing state housing policy—see Khan and Pieterse (2006:170–2).

39   This Foucauldian pespective emphasises the technologies and modalities of governmentality. Its compatibility with a Gramscian perspective (which emphasises politics and ideology, and the internalising of key values and precepts) is a matter of heated dispute. Yet at a superficial level a dialogue does seem possible between the two approaches. In order to endure, the ordering principles of governmental projects of rule have to be insinuated into everyday thinking and practice, and have to become accepted generally as 'the way things are'—or, better, 'the way things ought to be'.

40   Thus Chancellor House, believed to be the ANC's investment arm, owns a 25% stake in Hitachi Power Africa, a subsidiary of the Japanese multinational Hitachi, which in 2008 won a contract to supply boilers to two massive new coal-fired power stations in South Africa. According to one report, Chancellor House stood to make R 5.7 billion (USD 700 million) from the deal. See Peroshni Govender, 'ANC defends stake in Eskom-linked energy deal', *Mail & Guardian*, 21 January 2010. Former ANC Member of Parliament Andrew Feinstein (2007:242) describes Chancellor House as 'an elaborate network of companies ... established to utilise black economic empowerment deals to raise money for the ruling party'. (Chancellor House was the name of the building that housed the law offices of Nelson Mandela and Oliver Tambo in downtown Johannesburg.)

41   'Gravy train on track: More than R 300-bn worth of BEE deals since 1994', *Business Times*, 13 July 2008. According to ANC's treasurer-general, Matthews Phosa, who presides over a large business and empowerment portfolio, 'NEC members, like any South Africans, have a right to participate in business. It's their constitutional right' (*ibid*). The NEC is the ANC's National Executive Committee, its highest decision-making body.

42   Newspaper reports indicate that at least 27 members of the NEC had interests in at least 69 companies. They included Jacob Zuma himself, Tokyo Sexwale, Enoch Godongwana (former general-secretary of NUMSA), Joe Phaahla, Hlengiwe Mhkize, Sicelo Shiceka and Siphiwe Nyanda. The Zuma camp did not start this trend. By 2006, five members of the ANC's NEC ranked among the 70 richest individuals in South Africa and had a combined wealth of R 1.5 billion in shareholdings alone. These were Saki Macozoma, Cyril Ramaphosa, Popo Molefe, Mohammed Valli Moosa and Smuts Ngonyama. See Adriaan Basson and Qudsiya Karrim, 'Zuma's Cabinet Inc.', *Mail & Guardian*, 15 May 2009; Simpiwe Piliso, 'ANC turns on fat-cat comrades', *Sunday Times* [Johannesburg], 30 January 2007; and 'Many others set to score from Zuma's term in office', *Sunday Times* [Johannesburg], 18 July 2008.

43   The oldest of which is Thebe Investments, launched in the early 1990s.

44   As did an event staged in Johannesburg's Sandton suburb in October 2008. Invitees paid up to R 250 000 (USD 31 000) a seat to attend. See Karima Brown, 'Black business still donating to the ANC', *Business Day*, 6 November 2008.

45   *Financial Mail*, 5 August 2005, cited in Seekings (2006:29).

46   Tokyo Sexwale, 'BEE is very simple—it's about fixing up the mess', *Sunday Times* [Johannesburg], 6 March 2005.

47   Freund (2007b:671) makes the point that white South African capitalists had become a 'mature capitalist class' that was drawn toward investments in financial speculation,

property, technology and leisure—hardly the 'potential industrial investors' government sought.

48 'Gravy train on track: more than R300-bn worth of BEE deals since 1994', *Business Times*, 13 July 2008.

49 *Ibid.*

50 See Moeletsi Mbeki, 'The oligarchs are still in place', *Sunday Independent*, 14 June 2009 (Available at: http://www.africafiles.org/article.asp?ID=21064); and Mbeki, M (2009) *Architects of Poverty: Why Africa's Capitalism Needs Changing*, Picador Africa.

51 *Business Day*, 10 November 2004.

52 Freund (2007b:666) provides the example of the high-speed Gautrain rail service linking Johannesburg's OR Tambo airport to the city centre, some suburbs and Pretoria. The multibillion-dollar building contract went to 'a company with the fetchingly African name of Bombela' but which in fact comprised a large established South African multinational, a British subsidiary of a Canadian corporation and 'a previously completely inexperienced black empowerment company called Loliwe'. A French multinational will manage the train service.

53 National Treasury, Medium-term Budget Policy Statement and Budget Review data, cited in Presidency (2008).

54 Konrad Reuss, Standard & Poor's (S&P's) MD for South Africa and southern Africa, quoted in Mariam Issa, 'SA's expected growth rate "looks heroic"'. *Business Day*, 12 February 2009.

55 Wendell Roelf, 'Manuel sees no recession but inflation to fall', *Mail & Guardian*, 18 November 2008. The major ratings agencies were impressed enough to maintain South Africa's mid-investment grade credit rating of BBB+ and the World Bank shared that optimism; as late as March 2009, it was still forecasting positive GDP growth of 1% for 2009 in South Africa. See Mariam Issa, 'SA's expected growth rate "looks heroic"'. *Business Day*, 12 February 2009; Edward West, 'Market recovery stalls on grim World Bank forecast', *Business Day*, 23 June 2009.

56 Jeremy Cronin, 'Endless, resource-depleting growth is no longer possible', *Business Day*, 13 March 2009.

57 The current-account forecast was not far off the mark: the deficit reached 7% of GDP in the first quarter of 2009, before narrowing to 4%. See 'Domino theory', *The Economist*, 26 February 2009.

58 Gordon Bell, 'Contracts most since 1984: GDP fell annualised 6.4%', *Reuters*, 26 May 2009.

59 'GDP growth at 3.2%', *Mail & Guardian,* 23 February 2010. The 3.2% referred to the fourth quarter annualised growth in 2009.

60 'SA to rebase GDP, revise growth data', *Mail & Guardian*, 6 November 2009.

61 Jacob Zuma, State of the Nation speech, 3 June 2009, Parliament, Cape Town.

62 Mariam Isa, 'Mboweni signals a recession as output plummets', *Business Day*, 20 May 2009.

63 Mariam Isa, 'Weak exports put pressure on current account deficit', *Business Day*, 19 June 2009; Ethel Hazelhurst, 'Current account gap widens to 7%, but rand remains firm', *Business Report*, 18 June 2009.

64 Gordon Bell, 'Contracts most since 1984: GDP fell annualised 6.4%', *Reuters*, 26 May 2009.

65 'SA trade deficit hits record in January', *Mail & Guardian*, 27 February 2009.

66 Ethel Hazelhurst, 'Household spending still in descent', *Business Report*, 18 June 2009; Mariam Isa, 'Shrinking factory output points to rates cut', *Business Day*, 13 May 2009.

67 Mariam Isa, 'Weak exports put pressure on current account deficit', *Business Day*, 19 June 2009.

68 Ethel Hazelhurst, 'Export spending still in descent', 18 June 2009, *Business Report*; Stuart Theobold, 'Banks paint a dark picture of bad debt and big write-offs', *Sunday Times* [Johannesburg], 15 March 2009.

69 'Plan to tackle crisis gathers momentum', *Business Day*, 12 June 2009.

70 Brendan Boyle, 'Global economic crisis has SA companies running for cover', *Business Times*, 13 June 2009.

71   The other main components of AsgiSA were sector investment (or industrial) strategies, skills and development initiatives, 'second economy' interventions (including the Expanded Public Works Programme), macroeconomic management and improvements in public administration.

72   Official AsgiSA documents are available at http://www.info.gov.za/asgisa/

73   Business-process outsourcing, said government, had the potential to create 100 000 new direct or indirect jobs by 2009. Nothing of the sort transpired.

74   Mathabo le Roux, 'State to target four key sectors for intervention', *Business Day*, 3 August 2007.

75   Qudsiya Karrim, 'Motor industry welcomes Manuel's R 870 m boost', *Mail & Guardian*, 11 February 2009. South Africa aims to more than double the annual vehicle output from 527 000 in 2008 to 1.2 million by 2020, the bulk of it for export. Meanwhile, two-thirds of vehicles sold in SA are *imported*. Another example of policy dissonance: among the auto components produced in South Africa are pollution-inhibiting catalytic converters, yet the law does not require these to be fixed to vehicles using South Africa's roads.

76   Nic Dawes, 'Playpen economics', *Mail & Guardian*, 13 August 2007.

77   By way of example, the auditor-general's 2009 report had found that more than 2 000 government officials had directly or indirectly benefited from government tenders worth more than USD 80 million; see Southall (2010).

78   Ben Fine, 'SA needs more equitable developmental state', *Business Report*, 30 July 2007.

79   World Bank research indicates that South Africa was among a handful of countries that did not raise tariff levels during the global economic crisis; see Lynley Donnelly, 'Zuma-ites eye higher tariff walls', *Business Day*, 19 May 2009.

80   Davies, R (2010) 'National Assembly statement on IPAP2 by Dr Rob Davies, Minister of Trade and Industry', 18 February, Parliament, Cape Town.

81   Lawrence Edwards, Frank Flatters, Matthew Stern, 'Faltering mechanism of SA trade needs bolder repairs', *Business Day*, 5 September 2007.

82   Mandisi Mpahlwa, 'Proposal to go it alone on trade misreads the evidence', *Business Day*, 7 November 2007.

83   Pravin Gordhan, Minister of Finance, 'National Budget Statement', 17 February 2010, Parliament, Cape Town.

84   Hilary Joffe, 'Behind the paradigm shift in exchange controls', *Business Day*, 3 December 2009.

85   Mariam Isa, 'Treasury takes a market-friendly line', *Business Day*, 18 February 2010.

86   Both Fine and Freund have commented on the faint imprints this line of analysis has left on policy in South Africa, despite its cardinal insights. Part of the reason, Freund (2008:16) suggests, is that political-economic analysis has proved to be 'enormously less interesting' to intellectuals in the post-apartheid era, including those ostensibly working in a critical tradition.

87   Larry Elliot, 'Credit crunch lessons "ignored"', *Guardian Weekly*, 19 February 2010.

88   'Greenhouse targets no burden business—Sonjica', *Business Day*, 15 February 2010.

89   Ecologist James Lovelock insists on the phrase '*global heating*', which emphasises the crucial role of human conduct in current climate change.

90   Once largely the preserve of the automobile and fossil-fuel industries, the outright denial of global warming has been attracting increasing support from political parties in some countries. The House of Representatives of the US state of Utah, for instance, in 2010 passed a resolution disputing the scientific basis for global warming; see Suzanne Goldberg, 'Utah scoffs at climate fears', *Guardian Weekly*, 19 February 2010. For a sharp rebuttal to such thinking, see Joseph Romm, 'The cold truth about climate change', *Salon.com*, 27 February 2008, available at http://www.salon.com/news/feature/2008/02/27/global_warming_deniers/

91   From 446 metric tons of CO_2 equivalent in 2003 to 1 640 metric tons in 2050.

92   Sasol's planned coal-to-liquid plant in Limpopo alone will consume 40 million cubic metres of water a year (Earthlife Africa, 2009).

93   The four preconditions listed were: a stable and supportive macroeconomic environment; an adequate supply of skilled labour and a supportive education infrastructure; an adequate traditional and modern infrastructure; and capability to foster domestic technologies and systems.

94   It highlights the following main 'binding constraints': currency volatility; skilled-labour shortages; state capacity; costs and efficiency of the transport-system; barriers to entry and limits to competition; and regulatory hindrances.

95   'Big developing nations oppose halving CO_2 by 2050', *Reuters*, 2 December 2009.

96   Quoted in '"Unrealistic" for SA to set emission targets', *Mail & Guardian*, 10 September 2009.

97   Quoted in Bill McKibben, 'The coming meltdown', *New York Review of Books*, 12 January 2006. Even after pulling out of the accord, the US continued to exert decisive influence on its content. In order to gain ratification by Australia, Canada and Japan, the European Union yielded on most of the major points of its negotiation position and eventually accepted the positions the US (along with those three countries) had pushed. For an incisive summary, see Foster (2002:13–22).

98   Simon Mundy, 'SA surprises with 42% emissions slow down', *Business Day*, 8 December 2009.

99   'Greenhouse targets no burden on business—Sonijca', *Business Day*, 15 February 2010.

100 A 2°C warming above preindustrial temperatures is widely regarded as dangerous, although climate scientist James Hansen told the US Congress in June 2008 that the 'goal to keep global warming less than 2°C is a recipe for global disaster, not salvation'. Hansen puts the 'safe level' of atmospheric carbon dioxide at 'no more than 350 ppm (parts per million) and it may be less'. By mid-2008, though, the CO_2 concentration was 385 ppm and was rising by about 2 ppm per year. Other research showed the rate of CO_2 emissions accelerating at a pace faster than predicted in 'the most fossil fuel intensive of the IPCC emissions scenarios developed in the late 1990s'. See Raupach M *et al* (2007) 'Global and regional drivers of accelerating CO_2 emissions', Proceedings of the National Academy of Sciences (cited in Hallowes (2008:10); James Hansen (2008) 'Global warming: twenty years later', 23 June, Worldwatch Institute. Available at http://www.worldwatch.org/node/5798

101 Andrew Revkin, 'Imagine everyone was equal, in emissions', *New York Times*, 15 February 2008. For the four major CO_2 emitters, 1990 levels were five billion metric tons (USA), 4.6 billion (Europe), 2.3 billion (China) and 0.6 billion (India).

102 Andrew Revkin, 'Imagine everyone was equal, in emissions', *New York Times*, 15 February 2008.

103 Walden Bello, 'The environmental movement in the global south: the pivotal agent in the fight against global warming', 12 October 2007, *Focus on the Global South*, cited in Hallowes (2008:14).

104 Algeria, Egypt, Libya, Morocco and Nigeria together were responsible for 47% of Africa's CO_2 emissions in 2006.

105 The three worst per capita emitters of CO_2 were Qatar (56.24 tons), Kuwait (31.17 tons) and the United Arab Emirates (32.85 tons). Of the industrialised countries, the US ranked ninth (18.99 tons), Australia 10th (18.12 tons) and Canada 11th (16.72 tons). China emitted 4.6 metric tons of CO_2 per person. These data are from the Millennium Development Goals indicator database, available at: http://mdgs.un.org/unsd/mdg/SeriesDetail.aspx? srid=751&crid

106 Sasol's planned efforts to reduce CO_2 emissions hinge on carbon dioxide capture and storage technology. In the meantime, it has announced plans to build a new 80 000 barrels per day coal-to-liquid plant in Limpopo province. Government has approved the plan, arguing that it would reduce reliance on imported petroleum.

107 The data are drawn from the Millennium Development Goals indicator database, available at: http://mdgs.un.org/unsd/mdg/SeriesDetail.aspx? srid=751&crid

108 Xan Rice, 'A torrent of cash required', *Guardian Weekly*, 9 April 2010.

109 The energy sector includes electricity generation, oil and coal refining, coal mining and gas extraction, wood burning and the burning of coal and oil to industrial purposes.

110 South Africa's share of global coal production was 4.2% in 2006, when it had about 5.4% of global coal reserves; see Sengul *et al*, 2007.

111 Siseko Njobeni, 'Recession protects SA from power shortage', *Business Day*, 26 August 2009.

112 See 'Earthlife Africa welcomes end to Rio Tinto smelter', media release, Earthlife Africa, Johannesburg, 16 October 2009.

113 Zweli Mokgata, 'Eskom's regulator defends unpopular tariff increases', *Sunday Times* [Johannesburg], 7 March 2010. The argument for these tariffs is that large industrial users purchase the electricity in bulk and directly from the electricity utility (thus avoiding the need for costly relay infrastructure).

114 The Department of Energy regards the agreements as contractual arrangements between Eskom and the corporations: 'We are not privy to this,' said the department's director-general. See Melanie Gosling, 'Eskom's secret business deals come to light', *Business Report*, 10 March 2010.

115 See Mamphela Ramphele, 'Cheap energy is SA's double loss', *Sunday Independent*, 7 March 2010.

116 Analyst Ebrahim-Khalil Hassen describes a 'policy juggernaut' as 'a dense cluster of institutional, personal and economic interests, which coalesces around particular policy decisions and has an overwhelming momentum of its own, and is relatively impervious to rational dialogue or debate over alternative policy option'. See Ebrahim-Khalil Hassen, 'Eskom's electricity pricing juggernaut', 15 October 2009. Available at http://www.sacsis.org.za/site/article/370.1

117 Department of Environmental Affairs data, cited in Kenichi Serino, 'Air pollution costs SA R4bn in healthcare', *Mail & Guardian*, 12 October 2009.

118 Cited in Cock (2006:215).

119 These are the most recent available data of total waste generation.

120 In late 2008, the (state-controlled) Council for Scientific and Industrial Research (CSIR) prevented renowned water scientist, Anthony Turton, from presenting this and other information in a keynote speech to a CSIR conference in Pretoria. He was suspended and charged with bringing the CSIR into disrepute. The Minister of Water Affairs at the time, Lindiwe Hendricks, assured Parliament a few weeks later that 'we do not have a "water crisis" resulting from poor planning; our planning systems are strong and we have looked at future water needs'. By late 2009, however, government had become worried enough to earmark R 70 billion (USD 8.7 billion) for improving water security.

121 Cited in Swilling (2010).

122 More stringent measures to reduce industrial pollution of water resources are vital. Recycling urban wastewater and harvesting rainwater are viable ways to save water. Introduced at scale, such measures could reduce domestic water consumption by up to 40%. Some of this can be achieved by attaching appropriate conditions to planning approval for new residential, commercial and industrial developments.

123 For more on the environmental devastation wrought by the Chinese 'miracle', see Wen, D and Li, M (2007) 'China: Hyper-development and environmental crisis'. In: Panitch, L and Leys, C (eds) *Coming to Terms with Nature: Socialist Register 2007*, Monthly Review Press, New York.

124 For an inventory (and critique) of national policies and strategies that relate, at least partially, to climate change, see Earthlife Africa (2009:29).

125 A 'feed-in' scheme was being considered in 2010 to allow independent electricity producers to feed power into the national grid, but it is biased towards large-scale producers and there were concerns that it may be used as a Trojan horse to partially privatise the utility.

126 'Power crunch expected in 2011', *Reuters*, 5 March 2010.

127 International Energy Agency coal statistics, cited in Victor & Morse (2009).

128 See Department of Minerals and Energy (2004), 'Capacity building in Energy Efficiency and Renewable Energy', Report No. 2, 3. 4–19, *Economic and Financial Calculations and Modelling for the Renewable Energy Strategy Formulation*, Department of Minerals and Energy, Pretoria.

129 In the 2000s, the government invested some R 7 billion (USD 880 million) in the development of a pebble-bed module reactor, based on a design that was widely deemed outmoded. In early 2010, government seemed intent on pulling the plug on that project.

130 Cited in Swilling (2010:24).

131 It is not only the hopes that are familiar: 'Raw materials-savings processes are older than the Industrial revolution, and they have been dynamic through the history of capitalism,' as the environmental sociologist Stephen Bunker has reminded. See Bunker, S (1996) 'Raw materials and the global economy: oversights and distortions in industrial ecology', *Society and Natural Resources*, No. 9, pp. 419–29; cited in Foster (2002).

132 Cited in Foster (2002:23).

133 See Michael Byers, 'On thinning ice', 6 January 2005, *London Review of Books*.

134 James Gustav Speth, 'Global warming and modern capitalism', *The Nation* [New York], 17 September 2008.

135 The quote appears in John Stuart *Mill's Principles of political economy*, Book IV, Chapter VI, in the section entitled 'Of the stationary state'.

136 Marx, K (1973) *Grundrisse*, Vintage, New York; cited in Foster (2002:31). For a dense, methodical exploration of Marx's thought in relation to the environment, see Burkett, P (2006) *Marxism and Ecological Economics: Toward a Red and Green Political Economy*, Brill Books, Boston.

137 The American economist Francis Amasa Walker, writing in 1892, cited in Steven Stoll, 'Fear of fallowing: the specter of a no-growth world', *Harper's*, March 2008.

138 The words belong to John Stuart Mill, paraphrasing Smith's thinking (*op cit*).

139 After modelling the interaction of rising populations, pollution, industrial production, resource consumption and food production, *Limits to Growth* warned that exponential growth would lead to economic and environmental collapse. Its Malthusian themes were unfortunate, but they were not the reason why most economists panned the book or why governments ignored the recommendations. It struck a chord among citizens, though, and became a best-seller. A recent study assessing the accuracy of the report credits it with uncanny prescience, and concludes that 'the observed historical data for 1970–2000 most closely matches the simulated results of the *Limits to Growth* "standard run" scenario for almost all the outputs reported; this scenario results in global collapse before the middle of this century.' See Turner, G (2008) 'A comparison of the *Limits to Growth* with 30 years of reality', *Global Environmental Change*, Vol. 18, pp. 397–411. Available at: http://www.csiro.au/files/files/plje.pdf

140 The Brundtland report also bequeathed the popular though unsatisfactory definition of sustainable development, as 'development that meets the needs of the present without compromising the ability of future generations to meet their own needs'.

141 Quoted in Stoll (2008).

142 See Daly, H (1977) *Steady-state Economics: The Economics of Biophysical Equilibrium and Moral Growth*, W H Freeman, San Francisco. For a summary, see http://dieoff.org/page88.htm

143 Anthony Crosland, 'Class hypocrisy of the conservationists', *The Times* [London], 8 January 1971, p. 10.

144 British green economist Michael Jacobs, quoted in Foster (2002:26).

145 The proposals featured in a report entitled 'The measurement of economic performance and social progress revisited', produced by a commission which Stiglitz headed. See David Jolly, 'GDP seen as inadequate measure of economic health', *New York Times*, 14 September 2009. In Stiglitz's words: 'If a foreign transnational opens a mine, takes away the minerals, pollutes the environment, damages people's health and pays no taxes, if you focus on GDP you would say the mine's a good thing.' Because GDP also measures government inputs (such as health spending) rather than outputs (such as quality of healthcare), it ignores improvements in productivity and quality. More politicians seem sensitive to these kinds of criticisms. Standard metrics, after all, paint pictures that often do not resemble the realities lived by large parts of society and that 'cognitive disjuncture' undermines citizens' trust in the state.

CHAPTER SIX

The world of work

I've worked myself up from nothing to a situation of extreme poverty.

—*Groucho Marx*

Economic growth and job creation did not turn out to be the handmaidens government had envisaged when it settled on the title for its 1996 structural adjustment plan (the Growth, Employment and Redistribution policy or GEAR). South Africa's labour force grew by almost four million people between 1970 and 1995, but only one million more employment opportunities were created (Terreblanche, 2002). That trend continued for much of the first post-apartheid decade, causing consternation in government.

The South African economy grew at an average rate of 2.9% in 1994–2000, with growth then accelerating to 4.1% in 2000–08: hardly a spectacular performance in the context of a global boom (various SARB Quarterly Reports). Services (especially financial services, which powered along at a 10% growth rate in 2007) provided a great deal of the momentum (see Chapter five). Since these sectors rely heavily on outsourcing and subcontracting, new jobs tended to be of the low-wage, unstable variety.[1] More jobs were being created after 2003, but the average wage was declining (Mohamed & Roberts, 2007). Meanwhile, the manufacturing sector, the economy's second-biggest sector (contributing about 16% of GDP), had become a net shedder of jobs.[2] Nor were significant numbers of new jobs being created in the industrial showcases, such as the capital-intensive smelting and mineral refining operations that have dominated South Africa's attempt at industrial rejuvenation. The multibillion-rand aluminium smelters, for example, created only 2 000 jobs—at huge environmental cost.[3]

Not hiring

Official unemployment rates have shilly-shallied over the past decade, as survey methodologies and definitions were altered.[4] South Africa has now settled on an official (or 'narrow') definition of unemployment. The *official* rate, though, is a fanciful barometer of reality. Since it does not count as 'unemployed' anyone who has 'not taken active steps' to find work in the four weeks prior to being surveyed, it allows statisticians to remove from their tally of the unemployed those citizens who are too demoralised, penniless or marginalised to line up at factory gates at dawn or tread the suburbs for piecemeal work. They are simply not deemed 'unemployed'. Nor, since the early 2000s, are those persons who report earning an income from 'hunting', 'begging' or growing their own food; Statistics SA counts them as 'employed'.[5] By 2008, according to the Labour Ministry, about half the work-force was in casual and temporary jobs.[6]

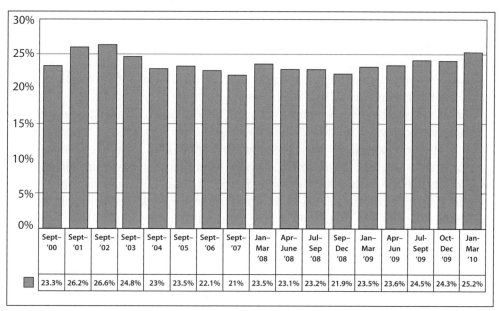

	Sept–'00	Sept–'01	Sept–'02	Sept–'03	Sept–'04	Sept–'05	Sept–'06	Sept–'07	Jan–Mar '08	Apr–June '08	Jul–Sep '08	Sep–Dec '08	Jan–Mar '09	Apr–Jun '09	Jul–Sept '09	Oct–Dec '09	Jan–Mar '10
	23.3%	26.2%	26.6%	24.8%	23%	23.5%	22.1%	21%	23.5%	23.1%	23.2%	21.9%	23.5%	23.6%	24.5%	24.3%	25.2%

Figure 6.1: Official unemployment rates, South Africa, September 2000 to March 2010
SOURCE: *STATISTICS SA, DRAWING ON THE REVISED LFS 2000–07 AND QLFS 2008–10*

As the graph shows, unemployment levels declined after 2002 before levelling off in 2008 and then rising as the recession hit. Approximately two million new jobs were created in 2002–08, as the proportion of working-age in employment rose from about 39% to 45%. The international norm is 60%. Even using the narrow definition of unemployment—and after a decade of uninterrupted economic growth—roughly one in four working-age South Africans was not employed. Internationally, the average unemployment rate for middle-income countries hovers in the five to 10% range. When workers who have given up on looking for jobs are counted, the unemployment rate ranged between 34% and 40% in the 2000s. In September 2007, the 'expanded' unemployment rate stood at 38.3%—up from 37% a year earlier.[7]

Traumatic realities are buried in those numbers. Large shares of the unemployed have either never held a waged job or are long-term unemployed: 40% of African workers and 21% of coloured, Indian and white workers unemployed in 2003 had been without a job for more than three years (Kingdon & Knight, 2005). Almost half of young Africans have never had a waged job. One in three people without a job beat the odds and completed their secondary schooling (Statistics SA, 2005a), but still struggled to find employment (see Chapter ten).[8] Such is the desperation that when the KwaZulu-Natal Education Department advertised 3 000 security guard jobs in late 2008, it received 150 000 applications.[9]

Government has felt bullish enough to question the official joblessness statistics. 'They would imply,' said an incredulous former President Mbeki in the mid-2000s, 'at least four million South Africans walking about in our villages, our towns and cities.' Earlier, Trevor Manuel, then the finance minister, had aired similar reservations: 'If you look at the surge in expenditure [on] consumer durables or the white goods sector and take that as a proxy for a series of things [...] I think the story that comes out is that this is not a country with unemployment at 32% or 40%.[10] Researchers, though, could find 'no research to sustain the Minister of Finance and Statistician-General's scepticism about the statistics produced by the agency they control' (Seekings, 2006a:18). In fact, the official data probably applied an undeserved sheen to reality.

The trend in the data rewards a closer look. Some of the early decline in unemployment levels in the 2000s stemmed from changes in measurement (Casale, Muller, Posel, 2005). By Seekings' reckoning (2006), those changes may have accounted for about one third of the two million net new jobs officials say were created in the early 2000s, with the remaining two-thirds of new jobs divided roughly equally between formal and informal[11] sector jobs. The expansion of the capital budget and the Expanded Public Works Programme, would have had an effect, as well.

Most of the new jobs were going to men. The March series of Labour Force Survey data shows unemployment rates for men fell significantly between 2001 and 2007 (23% to 19.3%) and declined even more impressively when measured from the 2003 peak of 25.5%. Women experienced a different trend. For them, unemployment rates rose between 2001 and 2007 (26.4% to 28.4%). The data reveal other disparities, as well. It was particularly among African and coloured female workers that unemployment rates rose between 2001 and 2007; among their white counterparts, the unemployment rate was halved (from 8.8% to 4.3%). It also fell among their Indian or Asian counterparts (Statistics SA, 2008e). New jobs were being created in patterns that matched the gender and racial disparities of the past.

Recession

The misleading nature of the official definition of unemployment was even more evident when the recession hit in 2009. Unemployment was still being described as 'relatively stable' at 23.6% in the second quarter of 2009, compared to 23.5% in the first quarter (Statistics SA, 2009c). Yet the number of people defined as 'not economically active' had grown by 419 000 in three months—fully three-quarters of them people described as 'discouraged work-seekers' who 'gave up hope of finding work or felt that there were no jobs in the area in which they lived that matched their skills' (Statistics SA, 2009c:i). By the end of the year, the expanded (that is, the actual) unemployment rate stood at 34.2%. The economy added 89 000 jobs in the final quarter of 2009, most of them in the informal sector, according to Statistics SA.[12]

All in all, 870 000 jobs were lost in 2009; employers had put 5.6% of the labour force on the street.[13] It is very likely that at least some firms were using the recession as an opportunity to trim and restructure their work-forces. The assumption that resumed economic growth would bring back the lost jobs was questionable.

The patterns of job losses were highly skewed, with low-paid, insecure workers hit the hardest. In the first six months of 2009, according to Labour Force Survey data, 59 000 formal jobs were lost, but almost four times as many informal and domestic-worker jobs disappeared (Statistics SA, 2009c). Workers in those sectors (in which women are over-represented) are among the worst paid in the country.[14] Public-works schemes and social grants were all that stood between many of the affected households and destitution.

Explaining the 'jobs bloodbath'

Most explanations for South Africa's high unemployment levels point to a cluster of factors: low rates of economic growth, restructuring of production in an increasingly globalised economy, skills shortages, a misshapen manufacturing sector, the increased entry of women into the labour market and population growth. These factors doubtlessly feature, but alone they neglect the subjective dimension of conscious choices that are aimed at shifting the balance of power further in favour of employers (Mohammed, 2009). This counteroffensive intensified from the mid-1990s onwards, as progressive labour laws appeared on the statute books.

Also circulating are familiar complaints about wages (too high), productivity (too low) and red tape (too much). The facts do not support those claims. The average working week increased by 1.5 hours to 49.1 hours and women were working two hours longer in 2005 compared with 2000.[15] Nor can so-called 'wage push'[16] be blamed for the unemployment levels. In little more than a decade, wages as a share of total output shrank from 57% to 51% (1990–2002), while profits grew from 43% to 49% (Gelb, 2003). The upshot is that

> the wage share of national output has been falling rapidly throughout the transition, while the profit component has been increasing ... [R]elative to capital, labour's gains have been limited in this transition (Habib & Valodia, 2006b:238).

Real individual incomes actually *declined* between 1995 and 2000 (Leibbrandt, Levinsohn, McCrary, 2005), with the drop steepest among the lower half of income earners, especially among younger workers, women and Africans. Whether that trend continued in the 2000s is not clear, due to difficulties in interpreting the official data. According to Banerjee *et al* (2006), average real wages *decreased* by some 10% in 1995–2005. Burger and Yu (2006) tried to reconcile various data sets, and concluded that the real wages of formal-sector workers rose slightly in 2000–05, while those of workers in the informal sector seemed to remain stable. Meth (2006) fixed a trend between those two bounds and concluded that average real wages either stabilised or decreased in the first decade of democracy. A closer look at those data over the 1995–2005 period reveals other important trends:

- Average real wages earned in the formal sector[17] rose marginally (by 4%) between 1995 and 2005, but those of African workers stayed at the same level (while those of white workers rose significantly);
- Women working in the formal sector were earning less in real terms in 2005 than a decade earlier. Their relative wages also fell. In 1995, wages earned by

women were roughly 78% those of men; by 1999, women were earning about 66% as much men (Statistics SA, 2002b:147);[18]

■ Workers without tertiary qualifications lost about 20% of their average real wage in 1995–2005, which means that the overall increase spotted by Burger and Yu (2006) mainly reflected wage trends for high-skilled workers (Banerjee *et al*, 2006:25);[19]

■ Among low-skilled workers, such as domestic employees, real earnings declined by 19% in 1995–2003, while those of self-employed persons fell by 62% (Kingdon & Knight, 2005);[20]

■ Wage levels are especially dismal in the agriculture, service and domestic sectors. A 2005 study of wage agreements (by the Labour Research Service) found that a substantial percentage of workers in the formal economy were being paid an average of R 253 (USD 32) for a 47-hour week;[21]

■ Within sectors, the gaps between the top- and lowest-income earners have widened. Earnings at the bottom end have been pushed down to the sectoral determination level, while those at the top have reached stratospheric heights, with multimillion-rand executive remuneration packages now the norm in large corporations and parastatal institutions.

The average real wage in South Africa, therefore, is propped up by the improved fortunes of comparatively small numbers of high-skilled, high-salary workers. Even then, the median wage in 2009 stood at a paltry R 2 500 (USD 310) per month. Between 1995 and 2005, according to Burger and Yu (2006:12), the wage trend was one of 'increasing inequality between groups [of workers], with little gains of the average wage increase accruing to women, non-white population groups or unskilled workers'. Overall, trade unions have succeeded mainly in stalling or limiting the decline in some categories of workers' wages (Banerjee *et al*, 2006; Kingdon & Knight, 2005).

Burdensome regulation is the other alleged culprit. There are perennial calls from sections of business for a more flexible labour market, in which certain categories of employment would be removed from the full ambit of labour-law protection. Thus far the trade-union movement has prevented government from relenting. But the mere fact that the proposal has been the subject of both research and debate in the top tiers of ANC speaks volumes (more later in this chapter).

There are glaring flaws in the arguments for greater labour flexibility. Webster and Bezuidenhout's (2005) research, for example, found extensive de facto flexibility in a labour market that increasingly is characterised by 'shell' wage agreements 'where labour wins high standards on paper that apply to fewer and fewer workers in reality' (2005:25). Furthermore, 'how can our labour market be rigid when half our workers do not belong to a trade union?', as an exasperated Labour Minister, Membathisi Mdladlana, asked Parliament in 2008.[22] Indeed, if labour laws were a major underlying cause of unemployment, job growth should be most vigorous in those sectors where the laws have the least impact, such as agriculture, domestic and formal work. The opposite seems true.[23]

The main reason for South Africa's extraordinarily high unemployment levels lies in the underlying structure of the economy, which remains centred on minerals, energy and large capital-intensive ventures and which in addition has acquired a powerful but parasitic financial sector. Changes in the labour regime will not shift that structure (Webster & Bezuidenhout, 2005).

Working poor

Access to paid employment is the single most important factor affecting the poverty status of households in South Africa.[24] But the converse does not necessarily hold. Vast numbers of workers earn low wages and do so on such insecure terms and so often without attendant benefits that their jobs do not shield them against poverty. Even formal-sector employment is increasingly insecure, wages and benefits poor and less easily distinguishable from informal-sector employment. Out of the entire work-force of 13 million in 2008, 5.8 million workers were not covered by unemployment insurance, 2.7 million did not have written contracts and 4.1 million did not have paid-leave entitlements, according to the Ministry of Labour.[25]

The number of working poor has increased markedly. Using a purchasing power parity USD 2 per day poverty line, Casale *et al* (2004) calculated that the number of employed workers living in poverty increased from just over 900 000 in 1995 to about two million in 2003. One quarter of them were deemed self-employed. Of the 18 million people living below the poverty line[26] in 2004, four million lived in about 700 000 households that contained at least one income earner (Meth, 2006). Most—but not all—of those workers toiled in the informal sector, with scant or no regulatory protection. Almost half (43%) of domestic workers earned less than R 500 a month (USD 62) in the mid-2000s, as did one third of other workers employed in the informal sector. A surprising proportion of workers in the formal sector did not fare dramatically better: almost one fifth (18%) of them, totalling 1.4 million workers, earned less than R 1 000 (USD 125) a month (Statistics SA, 2005a).

Driving these trends are two factors: the sustained shift towards the use of casual and subcontracted labour, and the related decline in real wages for low-skilled workers (Roberts, 2005; Banerjee *et al*, 2006). At root, the shifts in the labour market express companies' attempts to compete in a global market that imposes new paradigms of work. Companies everywhere now rely on a shrinking core of skilled full-time workers and a larger stock of less-skilled, casual or outsourced labour that is deprived of the wages, benefits and rights enjoyed (for now) by their better-off peers.

This is a far cry from the outcomes expected when South Africa's new labour laws were added to the statute books in the mid-1990s. The centrepieces of that new order were the Labour Relations Act (1995), the Basic Conditions of Employment Act (1997) and the Employment Equity Act (1998).[27] These would entrench collective bargaining and a system of mediation-centred dispute resolution (via the Commission for Conciliation, Mediation and Arbitration)[28], among others and assign legal recognition to the role of shop stewards. A decade on, it was clear that these legal and regulatory frameworks were neither the only nor the most decisive adjustments made to South Africa's labour market.

Facilitated by liberalised economic policies, the economy has been more thoroughly globalised—which has increased both the perceived need and opportunities for companies to sidestep the provisions of the new labour regime. In Webster and Omar's summary (2003:195), companies have 'adapted to this new environment by restructuring production, establishing new patterns of work organisation and/or relocating production units'. Those shifts began in the 1980s, but acquired formidable momentum subsequently (Habib & Valodia, 2006b). The mining industry, for example, began outsourcing some functions in the 1980s; by the 1990s it was subcontracting even core mining functions. Typically, contract workers are neither unionised nor covered by death and funeral benefit schemes and large portions of their wages are determined by team outputs. The route taken in the footwear sector, by contrast, was to 'transform' workers into 'independent contractors', thus evading labour legislation. Many of these 'contractors' now work in sweatshop conditions (Webster & Omar, 2003).

Paradoxically, write Webster and Buhlungu (2004:40), the labour market now 'strengthens the rights of labour, while [at the same time] it erodes them and bypasses the new institutions' tasked with enforcing those rights. Trade unions have struggled hard to put 'decent work' on the map. Yet, amid such restructuring, the phrase evokes an almost forgotten era of rights, dignity and workers labouring in the service of society. Indeed, as Castells and Portes (1989:31) pointed out more than two decades ago, the restructuring undermines organised labour in fundamental respects, and

> contribute[s] to the de-collectivization of the labour process and to the reversal
> of material conditions that historically allowed the emergence of the labour as an
> organized force.

Bereft of reliable regulatory protection, the working poor straddle the 'first' and 'second' economies (as shown in more detail later). They are deprived not because they are excluded, but because of the terms of their *inclusion* (Barchiesi, 2006). Labour conditions in the 'second' economy contribute to the erosion of wages and standards in the 'first' economy.

Gender inequality channels the effects of greater labour flexibility differently for men and women. Three-quarters (75%) of African women younger than 30 years are unemployed. Usually, those with jobs work in the worst-paid and worst-protected sectors of the labour market. Yet women also bear the bulk of responsibility for social reproduction (Hassim, 2005a) and they head more than 40% of households, the majority of them single-parent households. Little wonder that female-headed households are disproportionately likely to be poor. Outside of waged employment, social grants, remittances and various forms of gift exchange serve as their lifelines.

Migrant workers from elsewhere in Africa, particularly those lacking residence or work permits, are among the most exploited. From a certain angle, it looks like apartheid redux. Driven by desperation and hope, and stripped of rights, black workers enter the maw of capitalism. Nowadays, instead of travelling from Bantustans, they trek from elsewhere in Africa to toil in the interstices of the system. Operating in a no-man's land of illegality, lacking recourse to state protection, unable to depend on the safety nets of family and kinship networks, they are likely to work ultra-hard for long hours at very poor wages.[29] Complaints invite dismissal or being reported as 'illegals' to the police.

The availability of large numbers of relatively skilled, legally insecure and economically desperate workers enables employers to circumvent and steadily undercut 30 years' worth of gains of the trade union movement. This generates intense hostility from jobless South Africans, who tend to aim that wrath not at the employers, but at the migrant workers. To a significant extent, the 2008 pogroms (see Chapter thirteen) vented this fear and loathing.[30] The obvious antidote would be to legalise migrant workers, making them a little less prone to limitless exploitation. The political costs, however, seem too steep for government.

The myth of the magic portal

The binary perspective that equates unemployment with poverty and employment with relative wellbeing, fits reality less and less, yet it continues to define the jobs discourse.[31] Job creation in the putative 'first' economy takes pride of place in government's long-term poverty reduction plans.

Also vintage is the conceit that a state of affairs will be created in which everyone able and willing to earn a living wage shall do so. When asked in 2007 whether the economy could absorb the unemployed, (then) Finance Minister Trevor Manuel responded with the whimsy that 'it could, you know, it could'.[32] He was not stating a literal fact, but signalling distaste for the alternative, since extensive social provisioning is regarded with reserve, even disdain (see Chapter eight). Government speaks, for example, of the poor 'graduating' from dependence on social grants to employment and hails public-works participation as 'a bridge' into the blessed world of formal employment. Received wisdom therefore touts skills enhancement as an important remedy for the jobs crisis. Once workers are well educated, trained and skilled, they would be able to enter the charmed circle of full-time, relatively well-paid employment, it is claimed. But the structural trend runs in the opposite direction: toward *reducing* the size of that core of workers. Economic informality is growing in South Africa and it is irreversible: the traditional narrative of economic modernisation seems to be running in reverse (Ferguson, 2007).

From the late-1970s until the 1990s, South African companies sought to counter increases in workers' wages with high levels of fixed-capital expenses—upgrading machinery and introducing new technologies to achieve higher productivity and reduce reliance on militant, organised workers. Eventually the dividends dwindled. Sporadic currency crashes since the mid-1990s also inflated the cost of imported technology. The hunt for profit required another squeeze and it was applied to the wages of workers who are not shielded sufficiently by labour laws and shop-floor organising. '[T]he ability of employers to transfer resources from wages to profits,' writes Franco Barchiesi (2009:41), 'relies increasingly on hiring vulnerable, exploitable and contingent workers.' One outcome is that the growth in company profits has outstripped increases in workers' wages. Measured as a share of national income, company profits rose from 26% in 1993 to 31% in 2004, while workers' wages fell from 57% to 52% in the same period (Makgetla, 2005).[33]

The shifts in South Africa's labour market—trends in employment, the kinds of jobs that are being created and the terms and wages attached to them—have both global and localised dimensions. They certainly fit global trends. In Mexico, for example, the proportion of GDP going to wages plummeted from 40% to 19% between 1976 and 2000, a period of rapid globalisation, punctuated by two major economic crises (Palma, 2006). In industrialised countries, the trend is similar, though less extreme. Company profits in Britain in 2006 hit their highest point since records began in 1965. In the US, according to Goldman Sachs, the investment bank, profits reached an all-time high in the first quarter of 2006; among the most important factors driving that trend was 'a decline in labour's share of national income'.[34]

But operating alongside these impersonal, structural shifts was an acute self-awareness among corporate managers in South Africa, as they reacted to the shifting balance of power between employers and workers from the mid-1970s. The growth of casualisation and subcontracting, and the squeeze on workers' wages and terms of conditions, are closely related to the power of the trade-union movement which, by the late 1980s, was capable of shaping the regulatory realm and defending members' interests with gusto (Webster *et al*, 2008). But bound up in such 'strength', paradoxically, were significant weaknesses that pointed also to the limits of trade-union power and its significant dependence on the state. Employers have reacted to the new labour regime by exploiting gaps in the regulatory framework and expanding their use of wage-poor, insecure employment (on the back of a longer-term shift toward capital-intensive production). Consequently, the division between formal and informal employment in South Africa's labour market has become progressively fictive, with informal workers increasingly found inside formal enterprises through the rapid growth of casual and subcontracted work.[35]

A stinging irony is at work. The more rationed and precarious employment becomes, the more reliant individuals and households are on it. '[T]he combination of informalized work,' writes Barchiesi (2009:27), 'and the growing commodification of life strength[ens] households' dependence on the labour market as monetary income becomes increasingly inadequate.' So the image of waged work as a magic portal that opens unto wellbeing is reinforced in an era when work is unattainable to many millions of people (see Chapter eight). This signifying power of waged work is rarely mentioned, let alone critiqued, in contemporary labour scholarship in South Africa.[36] Dominant instead is the celebration of employment as the pathway toward 'socioeconomic emancipation, the true foundation of proletarian consciousness, and the [ideal] vehicle of workers' political demands within national liberation politics' (Barchiesi, 2009:32).[37]

Holding the line

If trade unions seem tetchy it is partly because they have been pushed into retreat. Employers are determined to shift towards decentralised bargaining, bypassing the system of fixing and regulating wages and conditions of work at national and sectoral levels and promoting agreements at company level (Mohamed, 2009b; Webster & Buhlungu, 2004). New worker-management practices that erode shop-floor unity have been introduced. COSATU remains strongly committed to centralised bargaining and some of its affiliates have mounted successful campaigns in defence of sector-wide bargaining. But powerful pressures are shoving in the opposite direction, as part of wider efforts to dilute the power of trade unions and widen the scope for profit-taking.

Compounding matters is the labour movement's failure to organise the 'new working poor' in meaningful numbers. Observers claim that this has allowed for the emergence of a 'structurally divided working class' in which workers are 'locked in a competitive battle for survival against each other' (Appolis, 2006:104). In Devan Pillay's view (2008:22), 'organised workers to a large extent form part of the "insiders" that have benefited from the post-apartheid dispensation'. Seekings and Nattrass (2005:46) make a similar point, although they seem to think that merely having a job merits entry into an exclusive inner circle. '[T]hose with jobs have come to be a relatively privileged group,' they claim, even though wage data draw a much more mixed picture.

These changes did not sneak up on the labour movement, certainly not on COSATU. Its September Commission highlighted many of these developments and warned (as early as 1997) that a failure to organise the emerging layers of 'flexible workers' could see union power dwindle to 'a shrinking section of the working class' (September Commission, 1997:140). But unions have struggled to check employers' clawback of power. Improved regulation and enforcement by the state is needed. Accidentally or not, 'temporary work', for example, is ill defined in current regulation. Webster *et al* (2008:vi) argue for a *different* approach to regulation, which might include regulating labour standards in ways that can disrupt 'the flow of goods or services from buyers who do not comply with decent work standards'. Another step would be to restrict labour-broker operations.

With friends like these ...

The labour movement does not lack foes within the ANC and government, however, where calls for greater labour flexibility still earn sympathetic hearings. There have been several forays inside the ANC to relax labour laws and introduce workfare programmes, including proposals put to the ANC's 2005 National General Council meeting.[38] These outlined a dual labour market, in which the minimum wage and other collective bargaining arrangements would be waived for certain categories of workers. Also proposed was the exemption of certain industrial development zones from labour laws (redolent of the apartheid regime's decentralised development follies of the 1970s and 1980s). The incursion was repelled, but the idea of introducing wage subsidies for low-wage workers (underscoring the assumption that 'high wages' deter hirings) has survived in policymaking circles.

The arguments for the proposals centred on the generic claims that South Africa's labour laws were unusually restrictive and imposed excessive costs on employers. The 2005 document provided no evidence for that claim, which nevertheless circulates widely in business circles. It argued, for example, that the system of bargaining councils compelled small-scale employers to pay unaffordable wages.[39] Yet bargaining councils covered well under 20% of private-sector workers at the time and those councils granted exemption from minimum wages to more than 80% of small-enterprise applicants (Makgetla, 2005). Indeed, the claims lack proof and are based mainly on the subjective opinions of surveyed business leaders.[40] Customarily invoked as evidence are the *Employing Workers Indicators*, published by the World Bank. These claimed to measure the regulatory burden in 182 countries, and South Africa usually ranked mid-table. The reports' methodologies drew damning criticism, however and the publications were eventually discontinued. By contrast, the Organisation for Economic Co-operation and Development's (OECD's) 2008 country survey concluded that South Africa's labour market was relatively flexible. Compared with the OECD's 29 members, only the US applied less restrictive laws on hiring and hours of work than South Africa and its employment-protection legislation was more flexible than that of Brazil, Chile, China and India (OECD, 2008).

The labour flexibility proposals were more than an ideological slip of the mind; geared at small and medium-sized entrepreneurs, they conformed to the interests of substantial sections of the ANC's base. Similar proposals were again aired in the ANC's 'Social transformation' discussion document in mid-2007 and Jacob Zuma mooted greater labour flexibility as a way to reduce poverty in 2008. In early 2010, government announced plans for a wage subsidy scheme for young jobseekers; employers taking on workers younger than 25 years for a two-year period would receive cash reimbursements. This would help school leavers enter the job market and gain work experience, said Finance Minister Pravin Gordhan and it would counteract 'our bargaining agreements [that] push up entry level wages, pricing out inexperienced work seekers'.[41] It is perhaps not a coincidence that, in 2009, the World Bank had advised South African policymakers to look to the Marshall Islands as an example of 'best practice'. That Micronesian archipelago, Paul Benjamin noted, 'has no legislation dealing with hours of work, occupational safety and health, child labour or forced labour'.[42]

The analytical wellsprings of the labour-flexibility proposals lie in the 'two economies' schema. Reducing the costs of labour and capital, it is argued, would help bridge the gap between the 'two economies' (discussed later in this chapter). The thinking is freighted with World Bank dogma, particularly the refurbished competitiveness approach adopted after the collapse of the Washington Consensus. In rough, this calls for the optimal operation of market mechanisms, while a strong state ensures a stable, low-cost and productive environment (by investing, for example, in infrastructure and skills development and social schemes designed to assist the indigent) (World Bank, 2005). 'Strong state intervention' is needed, in the concise phrasing of South Africa's leading business newspaper, but 'ironically, this partly involves less regulation'.[43]

The absence of regulation is especially glaring in the practice of labour broking, which enables business to evade statutory obligations, effectively denying large numbers of workers protection under post-apartheid labour legislation. About 3 000 labour-broking agencies operate in South Africa, with a combined annual turnover in the region of R 26 billion (USD 3.3 billion). A common practice is to retrench workers, only to re-employ them as subcontracted labour provided by these brokers. Other abuses of workers' rights are widespread and include illegal deductions of 'fees' and 'repayments' from subcontracted workers' wage packets. Research by the Sociology of Work Unit at the University of the Witwatersrand has uncovered cases where the 'take-home pay' of miners totalled about one tenth of their gross wage packet.[44]

Some trade unions seek an outright ban on the practice. But shutting down labour brokers, argues journalist Allister Sparks, 'will mean shutting the door on millions of part-time workers' who 'won't get full-time jobs because many of the small operations that now use them will close'. The problem, he claims, is that COSATU 'wants labour broking made illegal' on the basis that it is 'frankly hostile to the informal sector'.[45] Thus the struggle for a living wage and humane terms of employment is painted as a barrier in the path of a less poor, less unequal society. Orwell would have marvelled. Government, meanwhile, seemed torn on the issue. The Ministry of Labour in 2009 seemed keen to draw a tighter regulatory net around the labour-broking industry.[46] Similar ideas had been broached in 2004, but were shelved. In early 2010, government again backtracked. In the prevailing climate, the clamour for jobs—*any jobs*—drowned out demands for a living wage and humane working conditions.

The state of the trade-union movement

Despite (or, more likely, because of) such trends, South Africa's trade unions are unusually well represented in the workplace, certainly compared with other middle-income countries: about 33% of male and 27% of female workers belonged to trade unions in 2006 (Casale & Posel, 2009). Grouped into 16 federations, trade-union membership totalled about 3.6 million in the late 2000s, with overall membership levels having stayed relatively stable since the late 1990s. The labour movement remains fragmented along political, racial and occupational lines and includes disparate organising cultures. COSATU, with its 21 affiliated unions and 1.8 million members, is still the largest federation (NALEDI, 2006) and includes several powerful affiliates (10 of which have at least 100 000 members each.[47] Its membership is predominately blue-collar and African (Webster & Buhlungu, 2004). Several factors temper this brawn.

Union density diminished in the 2000s, most notably among female workers. Internationally, organised labour has been a major casualty of globalisation and has 'experienced a net loss in influence, members and control over and share of society's resources' (Ballard *et al*, 2006:12) and South Africa is not sidestepping that trend. Although the total number of Africans with jobs increased between 2000 and 2006, the numbers belonging to trade unions stayed relatively stable (about 2.2 million) (Casale & Posel, 2009). Such trends tend to strengthen corporatist tendencies in trade unions, while at the same time weakening their abilities to engineer and defend pacts that strongly favour their constituencies. It also has the wider political implication of consolidating support for stifling political alliances (see Chapter fourteen).

Economic restructuring has badly affected the biggest unions' traditional membership of mainly low- and semi-skilled workers. By the early 2000s, they comprised dwindling proportions of the formal work-force in almost every sector of the economy (Gelb, 2003). Union density rates in mining are high (just under 80%), but the mining work-force keeps shrinking. In the manufacturing and transport sectors, union density rates are on the decline (they were 39% and 36%, respectively, in the mid-2000s) and the rates were 25% or lower in retail, construction and finance (NALEDI, 2006). This has had a pronounced effect on COSATU, whose clout has been reshaped and diminished. Among its affiliates, between 1997 and 2003 membership shrank by 35% in the Chemical, Energy, Paper, Printing, Wood and Allied Workers Union; 27% in the Communications Workers' Union; 22% in the Farm and Allied Workers Union; 21% in the National Union of Mineworkers; and 27% in Clothing and Textile Workers' Union. One response has been to step up efforts to organise public-sector workers: membership of the National Education, Health and Allied Workers' Union (NEHAWU) grew by 44% between 1997 and 2003, while that of the Democratic Teachers' Union (SADTU) rose by 47% in the same period.[48] These developments have brought other changes, too. The profile of COSATU members—and with it, according to many analysts, the character of the trade-union federation—has changed. It now

> *represents a somewhat more established and institutionalized segment of the waged workers, while the majority of the unemployed and those surviving in the informal economy remain outside of the formal union movement* (Habib & Valodia, 2006b:234–5).

COSATU's failure to widen its base significantly beyond full-time, permanent workers fetters it politically and tactically (see Chapter fourteen). Organising the 'new working poor' is a formidable challenge. Gaining access to these workers is notoriously difficult; so, too, is convincing them that the potential benefits of formalised solidarity outweigh the immediate risks of harassment and layoffs. In addition, these workers' status is unstable; they migrate between employment, self-employment and unemployment (Webster & Buhlungu, 2004). The concept of union membership (tied, as it is, to having a job in a particular enterprise in a particular sector) needs to change. Suggestive attempts have been made on the fringes of the labour movement, and include experiments such as the Self-Employed Women's Union, formed in Durban in 1994, which sought to organise women working in the informal sector (Devenish & Skinner, 2006). But they have not acquired much momentum.

Workplace dynamics are less 'straightforward' than before. The demise of the apartheid regime removed the political undercarriage of apartheid and ruptured 'the link between the state and racial despotism in the workplace' (Webster & Omar, 2005:211). In so doing, the interplay between race and class in the workplace altered, becoming more variable, adaptive and complicated. Case studies in the mining industry, for example, show that, as Africans are promoted, decision-making powers tend to 'float up' and remain in the hands of whites. In parts of the clothing and footwear industry, the racial hierarchies hark back to the apartheid era, despite the restructuring of production. Most of the sweatshop workers (termed 'independent contractors' in the new arrangements) are African women and their clients (in effect, their 'bosses') tend to be white and Indian men (Webster & Omar, 2003).

The durability of shop-floor democracy is being questioned. Full-time union jobs, including those of shop stewards, are now relatively well paid and sometimes serve as stepping stones into management (especially in the mining sector) (Bezuidenhout & Buhlungu, 2007). Some researchers claim the ethos of serving the union and its members is eroding.[49] They note, for example, that union education work has tilted toward human-resource development and away from the more activist workers' curricula of the 1980s. Others believe that even the organisational culture of formations like COSATU has changed, as senior officials moved into Parliament, government and state institutions on ANC tickets. Some of these frailties arose from COSATU's achievements in the 1980s and 1990s,[50] including its attempts to participate in the bi- and trilateral forums that proliferated in the 1990s. Workloads increased in the national office and poor office-management systems and communication strategies took a toll on co-ordination and consultation, which aggravated tensions between rank-and-file members and leadership (as surveys confirmed), with a 'tiny minority within the federation fully understand[ing] the policies that are formulated' (Sikwebu, 1999:10). While COSATU's participation in corporatist structures brought some rewards, it also carried the political cost of stifling the social-movement unionism that had linked black trade unions so powerfully to the activism of communities in the 1980s (Pillay, 2008; Lehulere, 2005; Buhlungu, 2003) (see Chapter fourteen).[51] Disgruntlement about such changes has sparked serious strife in some unions and has led to the formation of breakaway unions.[52]

Shifts underfoot

Despite this, the trade-union movement, particularly COSATU, remains a powerful force. But, like its counterparts internationally, it is politically on the defensive on a terrain that is shifting underfoot.

Globally, the organisation of work has altered dramatically. Ideological and political interventions certainly have influenced these changes, but they emanate also from deep changes in the organisation of production. The heyday of enormous manufacturing enterprises staffed by battalions of workers is gone. Peter Evans (2007) notes, for example, that manufacturing in fact never employed more than about one quarter of South Korea's work-force (a peak that was reached briefly in the early 1990s), while in China it accounted for at most one in seven workers (in the mid-1990s and a smaller proportion since then).[53] The same trend is underway in Brazil and South Africa, where the services sector has become the largest employer. The earlier epochal shift from agricultural to industrial production laid a basis for the eventual emergence of an organised social force powerful enough to wrest (and, for several generations, defend) material, social and political concessions from the state and capital. Those arrangements are dissipating all around and their replacements hold none of the promise of that fading epoch:

> *A narrative built around the shift from an industrial to a service economy seems likely to be marked not by the creation of a new, relatively affluent working class, but by expanding inequality and stagnating wages for the majority of workers* (Evans, 2007:19).

South Africa's trade unions are yet to find their feet on this new terrain. One reaction has been to focus more effort on organising in the public sector. But their strength in that sector, which now hosts some of COSATU's strongest affiliates, has important ramifications. It has become increasingly tempting to channel worker and union militancy towards confrontations with government (as employer), militancy that previously would have been directed mainly at private capital. This risks further destabilising the workplace in state institutions, feeding enmity and rendering the smoother, more effective functioning of the state less likely. As in the private sector, workplace regimes in the public sector remain in limbo, teetering between the old and the new and are unstable, capricious and self-absorbed. Trade unions are especially muscular in the two most dysfunctional public sectors—health and education. SADTU, for example, was responsible for 42% of all working days lost due to strike action between 2004 and 2009, according to a study on labour-dispute resolution. Strike action by members of the South African Municipal Workers' Union and NEHAWU, respectively, accounted for 10% and 5% of workdays lost.[54]

The stakes are high. Recall that widespread impatience with the tactics of public-sector unions in Britain, hyped by hostile media, helped shape the ideological terrain on which Thatcherism arose. Unless carefully plotted and popularised, persistent industrial action by public-sector workers risks stoking a backlash against worker rights in particular and South Africa's rights-based order in general.

Public works — or does it?

Even resumed economic growth, the Finance Ministry conceded in early 2010, would create only about one million new jobs by 2014—slightly more than the 870 000 jobs lost in 2009 alone. The reduction in unemployment would be 'marginal', the ministry admitted.[55] Having sold South Africans on the notion that economic growth, if sufficiently spirited, was an elixir for all, this was a remarkable admission. Government's recourse was to boost to R 52 billion (USD 6.5 billion) by 2013 its spending on the Expanded Public Works Programme (EPWP) and to pay wage subsidies to employers who hire young first-time workers.

Government believes that each of these programmes will enable jobless workers to gain the work experiences and skills they need to find and stay in jobs. The assumptions are questionable. For their part, wage subsidies assume that wages are a major barrier to employment for low-skilled workers in South Africa and that, once flush with on-the-job training, these workers would be able to hold on to their jobs or find new ones. For some workers, the plot will follow that script. But, if international experience is anything to go by, many more will discover that the jobs they could not find in the first place are still not 'out there' and that their erstwhile employers prefer to retain the subsidies that attach to a new intake of youngsters rather than the newly trained cohorts. None of which is grounds for dismissing the venture, which government hopes will increase employment of school leavers by 500 000 by 2013. It could bring lasting benefit to some participants, it will almost certainly buffer most of them against poverty for the two-year period and it will provide young participants with the psychological boost of financial independence. All of which are reasons for structuring the programme in ways that demonstrably favour young (especially African) women.

Whereas wage subsidies funnel state funds into the market, public-works programmes are financed and run by the state. Their logic, though, is similar. In the immediate term, they are expected to reduce poverty. Beyond that, the experience and skills gained are meant to serve as bridges into formal employment. In Thabo Mbeki's words (2006), the EPWP would serve as 'an important bridge between the two economies and [as] a significant part of our poverty alleviation programme'.[56] In the background, as Anne McCord (2004a) noted, sat the hope that the initiative would draw people off social grants; its subtext, in other words, contrasted a 'worthy' and 'dignifying' wage with cash 'handouts'. These perspectives have survived Mbeki's departure.[57]

The public-works programme was expanded steadily in the 2000s—at face value, to good effect. Government claimed it created roughly 450 000 'work opportunities' in 2009. The R 52 billion earmarked for it in the 2010 Budget was aimed at creating 4.5 million short-term 'work opportunities' by 2014.[58] Each work stint would last an average of 100 days, calling to mind India's National Rural Employment Guarantee,[59] which entitles each rural household to 100 days of work per year. Government's stated aim is clear: it wants to reach an (narrow) unemployment rate of less than 15% by 2014. If one counts these 'work opportunities' as jobs and government throws enough money at the EPWP, then it might even reach that target. An average economic growth rate of 3% plus around three million EPWP 'jobs' (at a cost of roughly R 57 billion or USD 7.1 billion) would, by Altman and Hemson's (2007) reckoning, yield an unemployment rate of 13% by 2014. If this transpires, what, besides having paid vast sums of money for a number, will have been achieved?

Money well spent?

The shape of the EPWP reflects a compromise between government and business, on one hand and the trade-union movement, on the other. Wary of endorsing the creation of second-class workers, unions pushed for shorter stints, with training being an important component (Samson, 2007). The 'job opportunities' span activities ranging from clearing undergrowth to refurbishing schools and caring for the ill and frail. Government is also using incentives to encourage local governments to absorb more labour in their service-delivery and infrastructure projects. The duration of work and the wages vary widely. In 2006–07, for example, the average infrastructure 'opportunity' lasted 51 days and wages in the social sector fell to about R 30 per day (USD 3.70) or R 600 a month (USD 75) (Altman & Hemson, 2007), although a monthly wage in the R 1 200 to R 2 400 (USD 150 to USD 300) range is said to be the target.

The programme's potential for addressing the unemployment and poverty crises is modest. McCord's (2004) early review of EPWP performance made suggestive findings. The impact on aggregate unemployment and on the future employment performance of participants was found to be 'negligible', while labour-market participation after working in the scheme was 'very poor'. The most powerful positive effects were in improving food intake and school attendance and reducing the stigma of poverty for participating households. McCord concluded that the most realistic prospect was that the programme could *temporarily* reduce the depth of poverty experienced in participating households (2004b:11, 12).[60] There is no subsequent evidence to suggest that verdict was mistaken.

As for acting as a bridge to longer-term employment, these 'work opportunities', as even the business press notes, 'provide some work and some income for poor households and may even provide useful training', but they are 'not part of a job-creation strategy in any true sense'.[61] On average, workers receive about eight days of training, which as McCord (2007) points out, 'is not enough to differentiate you from other people in the labour market who haven't received that training'. In fact, when McCord (2005) surveyed projects in the mid-2000s, she found that many workers were not clear whether they had or had not received training.

The rhetoric and aims of the programme do not match the context in which it is being implemented (McCord, 2005). Jobs are temporary and short-term, they involve limited training and their skills-development components do not necessarily match skills requirements in a given area. Much of the labour employed is low-skilled, making it unlikely that 'marketable skills are being derived and transferred into the labour market' (IDASA, 2009:9). Intermediate and high skills are in demand in South Africa, but public-works schemes do not provide them. Observers have also noted the absence of exit or follow-up strategies for participants and criticised the tendency to measure impact as 'job opportunities created' without referring to the sustainability, earnings and quality of those opportunities (IDASA, 2007:10). Public-works programmes can be effective tools for dealing with transitional unemployment, but they are not an appropriate response in a chronic labour-market crisis such as the one in South Africa.

The ambitions invested in the EPWP need to be reconsidered: it is neither a platform for large-scale job (as opposed to 'work opportunity') creation, nor is it a sensible alternative to other forms of social protection.[62] The 'work opportunities' are a welcome temporary stopgap, but they are less a 'bridge' than a treadmill. As government chases its 2014 target, the EPWP seems less an active labour-market intervention and more an attempt to provide 'work opportunities' simply for the purpose of making available work-based income. It is valid and important to ask, as McCord (2007) does,

> whether it is appropriate for the state to tie up large amounts of financial resources in public works programmes that offer small periods of employment, or would it be better to look at alternative forms of social protection?[63]

The big picture

Several factors cloud faith in job creation as a sufficient mainstay of poverty reduction. First, there are strong and valid doubts about the job-creating potential of current trade and industrial, macroeconomic and education strategies. Skills enhancement offers limited payback, *even if* radical improvements are achieved in the education system in the short term. Beyond that, the still-dominant system of accumulation—the minerals-energy complex—is a massive barrier. A strategy that seeks to create jobs on the coat-tails of economic growth within that system holds little promise of substantial headway.

Still, in official and oppositional discourse, waged employment remains the cornerstone of social inclusion and the achievement of social rights. Barchiesi's characterisation of official discourse is accurate (2006:3):

> Its policy paradigms have given wage labour powerful disciplinary and pedagogical meanings, educating the poorest sections of the population to the idea that full citizenship revolves around individual responsibility, labour market activation, and the avoidance of 'dependency' on public spending. Conversely, the government regards with suspicion policies of generalized access to social provisions funded via redistributive transfers.

The reality is that wages and salaries are the main source of income for only 5.9 million (57%) of the 10.3 million African households, while pensions, grants and remittances are the main source of income for a further 3.9 million (38%) African households (Statistics SA, 2008c). For a very large proportion of society, job creation, achieved along the current development path, is not a viable basis for social inclusion and livelihood security.[64] Having a job is not a solid hedge against oblivion. The quest for more jobs is crucial, but it has to occur as part of the wider realisation of social rights.

Double vision: the 'two economies'

The 'two economies' creed hit the headlines in the early 2000s and has since served as a mould for the ANC's thinking about post-apartheid development. Thabo Mbeki may have been the flag-bearer of the model, but it acquired axiomatic status among ANC leaders and survived the purging of Mbeki and his acolytes. ANC intellectual Joel

Netshitenzhe stayed attached to it and President Zuma would ground his understanding of economic and employment challenges in the notion.[65]

The schema pictures the South African economy as a dichotomy, comprising two economies that are 'structurally disconnected'. The first (or 'formal') economy is described as

> the modern industrial, mining, agricultural, financial and services sector of our economy that, everyday, becomes ever more integrated in the global economy. (Mbeki, 2003b).

In this reasoning, the second (or 'informal') economy is trapped in a state of 'underdevelopment and marginalisation' and does not automatically benefit from growth in its counterpart. While the latter is seen as mature and sophisticated enough to respond positively and automatically to certain adjustments, the former is deemed to be backward and marginalised and requires 'sustained government intervention' if it is to shed that status. Due to the

> structural disjuncture that separates the 'first world' and 'third world' economies, we cannot and should not expect that there would be any mechanism inherent within the 'first world' economy that would result in the latter transferring the required resources to the former, to enable it to outgrow its 'third world' nature (Mbeki, 2003b).

Folded into the schema are eclectic traditions of thought. Loaded with the paternalism associated with old-school 'development', it harks back to the convergence theories of the 1960s (and their faith in 'catching up'), evokes key contentions of South African liberal economists (regarding the reinforcing links or lack thereof, between the apartheid system and the economy) and echoes basic precepts of World Bank thinking of the 1990s and beyond. Its binary logic (of separate and distinct 'economies') also reproduces the appealing symmetry of Mbeki's 1996 'two nations' speech to Parliament, in which he invoked a contradiction former UK Prime Minister Benjamin Disraeli had set out in his political novel, Sybil, or the Two Nations:

> Two nations between whom there is no intercourse and no sympathy; who are as ignorant of each other's habits, thoughts, and feelings, as if they were dwellers in different zones, or inhabitants of different planets; who are formed by a different breeding, are fed by a different food, are ordered by different manners, and are not governed by the same laws.[66]

Applied to South Africa by Mbeki (1998), the 'two nations' are separated by both poverty and race. One

> is white, relatively prosperous, regardless of gender or geographic dispersal. It has ready access to a developed economic, physical, educational, communication and other infrastructure [...] The second and larger nation of South Africa is black and poor, with the worst affected being women in the rural areas, the black rural population in general and the disabled. This nation lives under conditions of a grossly underdeveloped economic, physical, educational, communication and other infrastructure. It has virtually no possibility to exercise what in reality amounts to a theoretical right to equal opportunity.

So the model presumes two separate sectors, one trapped in a 'pre-modern' dimension, the other more fully developed. It distinguishes between a thriving 'first economy' that is skilled, well resourced, productive and competitive and a precarious 'second economy' that is marred by poor skills, endemic under- and unemployment and by dependency on state beneficence. This implies the need for a transition that either enables individuals in the 'informal' economy to migrate to the 'formal' economy or that transforms 'informal' economic activities into 'formal' ones. The basic assumption is vintage: the 'informal' is undesirable and inadequate and requires the beneficence of modernisation facilitated by a kindly but stern state. According to a 2007 ANC economic policy discussion document, 'the most significant vehicle for sharing growth would be to eliminate the second economy'—as if it were some tumorous appendage (ANC, 2007d:20). Operating in a favourable climate, the 'first economy', meanwhile, is best left to its own devices as it goes about its business.

The 'first economy' is said to comprise commercial agriculture, mining, manufacturing, retail, financial and related activities—all dynamic, technologically advanced and performing relatively well. This charmed zone needs to be expanded and made more accessible. 'Informal' and subsistence activities are said to constitute the 'second economy'. Separating the two is a chasm of debilities, disadvantages and malfunctions. The challenge is to span that divide and connect them by building linkages. Those languishing in the 'second economy' require means, know-how and pathways to enter the magic circle. While this occurs, support is to be provided to those still stranded in the 'second economy'—by way of social grants, by expanding the social wage and by boosting the public works programme. Mbeki's 2004 State of the Nation speech summed this up neatly. Government's response to poverty and underdevelopment would rest on three pillars:

> *Encouraging the growth and development of the first economy, increasing its possibility to create jobs; implementing our programme to address the challenges of the second economy; and, building a social security net to meet the objective of poverty alleviation* (Mbeki, 2004c:3).

The schema's policy imprints are ever-present. It features centrally in the AsgiSA economic framework (see Chapter five), which attributes poverty in the putative 'second economy' to its uncoupling from the 'first economy'; the remedy is to 'build bridges' between the two economies'. Similarly, the EPWP is styled as a 'bridge' between the 'two economies'. The paternalism of the Municipal Indigence Policy and the extension of the Child Support Grant both stem from the unhappy recognition that some households are mired in the 'second' economy and require assistance. As Hart (2006:26) notes:

> *What is significant about this discourse is the way it defines a segment of society that is superfluous to the 'modern' economy, and in need of paternal guidance [...] Those falling within this category are citizens, but second class. As such they are deserving of a modicum of social security, but on tightly disciplined and conditional terms. To qualify for a range of targeted programmes, they must not only be identified and registered, but also defined as indigent.*

The framework contains some superficial appeal.[67] The fact that more than 80% of entrants into formal-sector jobs move from other formal sector jobs, for example, seems to fit with its inside/outside paradigm (Banerjee *et al*, 2006; Devey, Skinner, Valodia, 2006). But its flaws are profound.

Numerous backward and forward linkages operate between the 'two economies', linking ostensibly informal traders and service-providers with the 'core' corporate sector. As Jeremy Cronin (2007) has remarked, 'second economy' taxi operators are integrally linked into the 'first economy' of Toyota and Caltex, while SABMiller, the second-largest brewer in the world, has as its major domestic retail outlet tens of thousands of 'second economy' shebeens in the townships.[68] The earnings, networking opportunities and resources associated with formal employment are constantly used to finance and facilitate enterprises that government assigns to the 'second economy' category.[69] Moreover, the 'first economy' relies increasingly on forms of work that otherwise may be classified as part of the 'second economy'— insecure, poorly paid and outside the regulatory framework of benefits and obligations usually associated with the 'first' or 'formal' economy (Devey, Skinner, Valodia, 2006).[70] The distinction between informal and formal work is blurry, often absent, not least in the retail sector where Kenny (2000) found that two-thirds (65%) of total employment entailed casual and subcontracted labour. Pressures of local and global competitiveness have fused the 'two economies'.

In the Ceres valley in the Western Cape, as Andries du Toit has shown (2004a), agricultural producers exploit and reproduce precariousness which, in Desai and Bond's opinion (2006:24), 'seems to be structured just as effectively as labour control during the apartheid system'. 'Far from being excluded', temporary and seasonal workers 'are thoroughly incorporated into the first economy', their poverty a function of the 'normal operations of the market' (Du Toit, 2004a:29). The privation experienced by those in the putative 'second economy' and their unsteady income-earning prospects in fact express the terms of their *incorporation* into the dominant system of accumulation, not their exclusion. They are not simply the detritus of market 'failure'. Moreover, 'many of the obstacles to accumulation from below among poor people', states Du Toit (2004c:11), are in fact 'linked very closely to the depth of corporate penetration of the economy as a whole'. The poor, in David Hallowes' summary (2008:16),

> are poor because they are integrated into capitalism, not because they are left out of it. The wealth of the 'first economy' remains very much dependent on paying workers less than a living wage, dispossessing people and externalising environmental costs.

Lineages

The 'two economies' schema calls to mind an important debate of the 1970s in which contending analyses of the relationship between capitalism and apartheid famously pitted the perspective of Harold Wolpe against that of Michael O'Dowd (1978). The schema invokes the dualism that characterised liberal economic analysis in South Africa, an important thrust of which was to exonerate South African capital from its complicity in and profiting from, the apartheid system. Wolpe (1972) challenged that perspective and reasoned that South African capitalism required and thrived on the super-exploitation made possible by the colonial and, later, apartheid system's control of pre-capitalist modes of production in the so-called native reserves (and, later, Bantustans). O'Dowd rejected that articulation. Where Wolpe detailed linkages and integration, O'Dowd saw separation and contradictions. Seen in that context, the 'two economies' schema seems mercenary. It disavows a body of intellectual work that formed the spine of radical economic, sociological and political geographic thinking in South Africa. In its place it prefers a decidedly conventional—and unconvincing— portrayal of South African capitalism. It operates, in fact, as an alibi for capital, which is entrusted with the task of keeping the economy growing. Rather than adjust the economy, the intention is 'to use the leverage of the first economy to address the second economy', in the words of former Deputy President Phumzile Mlambo-Ngcuka.[71] As Stephen Gelb (2006a:25) has noted,

> almost all the massive [post-2000] increase in infrastructure spending is aimed at reducing 'the costs of doing business' in the first economy, rather than extending infrastructure services to those in the second economy.

Instead of locating the central challenge within the patterns of capital accumulation, the problem is stood on its head. The alleged exclusion of the poor (most of them Africans) from profitable participation in a supposedly sleek and potentially benign 'first economy' becomes the chief culprit. It then follows that the groundwork of policies and conditions put in place to spur post-apartheid economic growth is not to be meddled with, as Mbeki (2003b) made clear:

> Many of the major interventions made by our government over the years have sought to address this 'first world economy', to ensure that it develops in the right direction, at the right pace. It is clear that this sector of our economy has responded and continues to respond very well to all these interventions. This is very important because it is this sector of our economy that produces the wealth we need to address the many challenges we face as a country [...] The task we face therefore is to devise and implement a strategy to intervene in the 'third world economy' and not assume that the interventions we make with regard to the 'first world economy' are necessarily relevant to the former.

The 'two economies' model is best understood as a discursive intervention that is meant to endorse and disguise a development path that requires, first and foremost, that the prerogatives of capital be serviced. It marks continuity, not departure. 'The operative question,' Hart (2006) notes,

> is not whether the First / Second Economy is an accurate portrayal of reality, but rather how it is being constructed and deployed to do political—or perhaps more accurately, depoliticizing work.

Importantly, Hart also detects an important *political* motive for hoisting the 'two economies' discourse to such prominence: the eruption of popular protests in 2001–02 and the emergence of new social movements as contesting forces (see

Chapters twelve to fourteen). It was clear to the ANC leadership that intimidation and slander alone would not curb the disgruntlement; other interventions were required. One was material and hinged to a large extent on the expansion of social grants (see Chapter eight). The other was 'intellectual' and required a plausible analysis of the quagmire of post-apartheid development—hence the 'two economies' model.

Endnotes

1   Significant numbers of these jobs were 'created' through reclassification, as previously in-house work was outsourced and thereby became classified under 'services'. This is borne out in Tregenna's (2008:33) research, which found that 'significant intersectoral outsourcing has taken place in South Africa' (cited in Mohamed, 2009).

2   Mariam Isa, 'Slump in job creation casts doubt on targets', *Business Day*, 13 December 2007.

3   See Neva Makgetla, 'Busting myths that throw SA's employment debate off track', *Business Day*, 27 May 2009.

4   The introduction in 2000 of a new labour survey (Statistics SA's September Labour Force Survey) complicated comparisons with data derived from the earlier October Household Survey (used in 1995–99). In addition, the Labour Force Survey has been re-weighted in light of the 2001 census, an exercise that itself was fraught with statistical dispute. Nevertheless, basic trends can be discerned.

5   The official definition of 'unemployment' is spartan. The Labour Force Survey includes, for example, questions about business activities (with queries about 'selling things, making things for sale, repairing things, guarding cars, brewing beer, hairdressing' and more) and whether the respondent begged 'for money or food in public'. Those answering in the affirmative are counted as 'employed'.

6   Labour Minister Membathisi Mdladlana, speaking in Parliament, quoted in Linda Ensor, 'Minister defends labour market', *Business Day*, 10 May 2008.

7   See Mariam Isa and Thabang Mokopanele, 'Job creation far too slow to halve jobless rate by 2014', *Business Day*, 27 September 2007.

8   Discussed in some detail in the section on education.

9   Rivonia Naidu, 'Thousands apply to guard schools', *Daily News*, 24 October 2008.

10 Trevor Manuel was quoted in Paul Stober, 'SA's four-letter word: JOBS. Employment isn't what it used to be', *Sunday Times*, 12 December 2004.

11 For reasons discussed in Chapter five and later in this chapter, 'formal' and 'informal' are merely descriptive terms here and do not imply rigid categories.

12 'SA unemployment edges lower, job losses halted', *Mail & Guardian*, 9 February 2010.

13 Linda Ensor, 'Back to work: State plans to spend R52bn to create jobs', *Business Day*, 18 February 2010; 'Jobs bloodbath a call to action: Labour market hit harder than economy itself', *Business Day*, 2 November 2009.

14 An estimated 40% of formal-sector workers are women, as are 80% of domestic workers. Women account for only about 20% of the formal-sector work-force. See Neva Makgetla, 'Challenge for state as recession cuts a swath through jobs', *Business Day*, 5 August 2008.

15 Linda Ensor, 'Minister defends labour market', *Business Day*, 10 May 2008.

16 Wage increases that outstrip productivity rises.

17 As shown in this chapter, the formal/informal dichotomy does not survive scrutiny. Inverted commas are merited, but they are irritating on the eye and therefore are not used here.

18 Female African workers who belong to a trade union on average earn higher wages than their male counterparts, according to Casale and Posit's (2009) research. That probably reflects the comparatively higher-skilled jobs for women in the public sector (especially in nursing and teaching).

19 According to Banerjee *et al* (2006), despite the fact that the formal sector work-force became more skilled, real wages per unit of human capital increased only slightly between 1996 and 2003. Had they not been unionised, the wages of unionised *unskilled* workers would have fallen significantly faster. Meanwhile, for higher-skilled unionised workers, wage increases did not match productivity increases.

20 Earnings in the informal sector are difficult to determine, but they are believed to be about one fifth to one half of those in the formal sector (Altman, 2005). By some estimates, just over half (51%) of workers in that sector earn less than R 500 (USD 63) per month and about 75% earn less than R 1 000 (USD 125) per month (Devey, Skinner, Valodia, 2006). The authors based their calculations on March 2004 Labour Force Survey data. They estimated that the so-called informal economy contributes 7 to 12% of gross domestic product.

21 Ann Crotty, 'How much lower do employers want wages to be?', *Business Report*, 15 June 2005.

22 Linda Ensor, 'Minister defends labour market', *Business Day*, 10 May 2008.

23 Alide Dasnois, 'Labour laws alone do not kills jobs', *Business Report*, 4 July 2005.

24 A mere 9% of working-age people in the bottom 10% of income-earners were working in the early 2000s (Aliber, 2005).

25 Linda Ensor, 'Minister defends labour market', *Business Day*, 10 May 2008.

26 Pegged at USD 2 per day.

27 Also significant are the National Economic, Development and Labour Council (NEDLAC) Act (1994), the Skills Development Act (1998) and the Social Plan Act (1998).

28 The CCMA was handling more than 400 cases a day in the late 2000s.

29 Alert to this, government opted to intervene by penalising employers with large fines for using 'illegal' workers. But on the streets and farms, this only intensified the harassment and shakedowns. Previously, the pickings available to corrupt police and other extortionists had been scant, limited by the scandalously poor earnings of most 'illegal' workers. Putting their bosses in the firing line upped the ante—and the lucre. Employers have continued exploiting foreign workers, and corrupt cops can now fleece both employers and workers.

30 Barchiesi (2009) cites findings from a survey carried out in the Pretoria area in which most respondents supported the deportation of all migrants and immigrants, irrespective of their legal status.

31 The irony is that South Africa has historically offered little basis for such a viewpoint; until the ascendancy of the trade-union movement from the early 1980s onward, wage incomes and benefits provided a paltry barrier against impoverishment.

32 Brendan Boyle, 'Manuel's revolution', *Business Times* [Johannesburg], 25 February 2007. Manuel was speaking after presenting the 2007/08 Budget. Seven years earlier, Manuel had irascibly challenged journalists on the same issue: 'I want someone to tell me how the government is going to create jobs. It's a terrible admission but governments around the world are impotent when it comes to creating jobs.' Quoted in *Sunday Independent* [Johannesburg], 16 January 2000.

33 Calculated from SA Reserve Bank data.

34 Cited in Richard Tomkins, 'Profits of doom', *Financial Times*, 13 October 2006.

35 The use of 'informalised' labour is especially extensive in business services, as well as in the mining and manufacturing industries. Subcontracting production to home-based facilities is common, especially in the clothing and footwear sectors. Because labour inspectors are not allowed access to private homes, these operations function literally outside the ambit of state regulation.

36 Prishani Naidoo and Franco Barchiesi's work being sterling exceptions.

37 Barchiesi (2006, 2007) reminds how anomalous and recent this perspective actually is when set in the context of late-colonial and post-colonial histories of South Africa and other African countries. He recalls, for example, the vital distinctions workers, until recently, drew between *mmereko* (alienated wage labour) and *tiro* (autonomous, purposeful forms of 'doing'). Popular consciousness in South Africa retains, he argues, a strongly subversive attitude toward wage labour.

38 Former Deputy Finance Minister Jabu Moleketi (also formerly a top SACP member) tabled the proposals.

39 In this case, however, the argument bore uncanny resemblance to an IMF document released a little earlier; see IMF(2004) 'South Africa: Staff report for the 2004 Article IV Consultation', IMF, Washington (cited in Makgetla, 2005).

40 For an instructive critique, see Paul Benjamin, 'Bend debate around labour flexibility back to the facts', *Business Day*, 29 June 2009.

41 Quoted in Linda Ensor, 'Back to work: State plans to spend R 52 bn to create jobs', *Business Day*, 18 February 2010.

42 Paul Benjamin, 'Bend debate around labour flexibility back to the facts', *Business Day*, 29 June 2009.

43 Editorial, 'Labours lost', *Business Day*, 17 May 2005.

44 The practice has become entangled in outbreaks of xenophobic violence. In the grape-growing town of De Doorns, in the Western Cape, 3 000 Zimbabwean migrant workers spent Christmas 2009 in tents pitched on a sports field. South African residents had driven them from their shacks the previous month amid complaints that the Zimbabweans were 'stealing jobs'. Researchers discovered that local labour brokers had instigated the attacks to get rid of competing Zimbabwean labour contractors. These brokers pocket at least R 5 (USD 0.60) of each worker's daily wage (R 60 or USD 7.50 on average) plus a commission from farmers. See 'Labour brokers fingered in De Doorns xenophobia report', *Mail & Guardian*, 17 December 2009.

45 Allister Sparks, 'At home and abroad: Losing the battle of the wealth gap', *Business Day*, 13 October 2009.

46 Wyndham Hartley, 'Clamour to ban labour broking "slavery"', *Business Day*, 26 August 2009.

47 Other federations include the black consciousness National Council of Trade Unions (NACTU), the mainly white-collar Federation of Unions of South Africa (FEDUSA), the largely white Solidarity and the Confederation of South African Workers' Unions (CONSAWU).

48 Based on data compiled in Habib and Valodia (2006b).

49 See, for example, Roskam, A (2002) 'Ensuring better governance in unions', NALEDI *Policy Bulletin*, Vol. 5, No. 3, pp. 10–11, cited in Buhlungu, Brookes, Wood (2008).

50 For a detailed discussion of union gains and positioning in the 1990s, see Marais (1998c:222–34).

51 Discussed in more detail in the Chapter fourteen.

52 Including the 2002 Volkswagen strike (Desai, 2009) and the formation of radical new unions, such as the Oil, Gas and Chemical Workers Union.

53 See Ghosh, J (2003) 'Exporting jobs or watching them disappear?' In: Ghosh, J (ed) *Work and Well-being in the Age of Finance*, Tulika, New Delhi; Carlson, J (2003) 'Manufacturing payrolls declining globally: the untold story'; both cited in Evans (2007). In China, production has shifted from labour-intensive plants in the north-east to high-tech, labour-saving plants in the south-east. Productivity growth therefore outstrips employment increases.

54 Lucky Biyase, 'A disgrace: New figures show how teachers failed', *Business Report*, 8 February 2010.

55 See Linda Ensor, 'Back to work: State plans to spend R 52 bn to create jobs', *Business Day*, 18 February 2010.

56 Or, more wordily, the programme would bring 'significant numbers of the unemployed into productive employment' and allow them to 'gain skills while they are gainfully employed and increase their capacity to earn an income once they leave the programme' (Mbeki, 2003c).

57 Linda Ensor, 'State takes a "progressive" line on jobs', *Business Day*, 22 June 2009.

58 The semantics are important. The conversion of rights and entitlements into 'opportunities' is a hallmark of 'Third Way' politics. The UK's Labour Party also refitted jobs into 'work opportunities'. Additionally, at the accelerated rate of 450 000 'work opportunities' created in 2009, an extra two million would be created in 2010–14—not 4.5 million. That target

presumably refers to the total number of 'opportunities' that would have been created since the entire Expanded Public Works Programme began.

59 An elaboration of the famous Employment Guarantee Scheme introduced in Maharashtra state in the 1970s.

60 For example, a 2003 survey of participants in two different public works programmes in Limpopo and KwaZulu-Natal found almost all the participating households in one programme and 87% in the other still fell under the poverty line. The programmes had reduced their poverty levels, but not by enough to enable them to escape from poverty. See McCord (2004).

61 Hilary Joffe, 'Turning work opportunities into proper jobs', *Business Day*, 17 November 2009.

62 An early study of projects in Limpopo and KwaZulu-Natal was even more emphatic (ODI, 2004): 'The benefits of temporary full-time employment, an instrument used elsewhere as a safety net for victims of short-term loss of livelihood, are more elusive in the South African context. Their contribution to poverty reduction and employment creation is inefficient and short-lived.'

63 This was the reasoning of the Taylor Commission, which concluded that a universal income would be more viable and affordable than large-scale public works programmes. Le Roux (2002), for example, calculated that a universal income grant of R 100 (USD 12.50) a month per person would cost about R 54 billion (USD 6.7 billion). The administrative costs and burden would be much lower than for a public works programme and a universal income programme would also be better targeted.

64 By 'jobs', I mean waged work that is of reasonable constancy and that pays a living income. It is an index of how far matters have regressed when the *Rerum Novarum* (*Of New Things*) issued by Pope Leo XIII in 1891 seems to offer some guidance: 'Let the working man and the employer make free agreements, and in particular let them agree freely as to the wages; nevertheless, there underlies a dictate of natural justice more imperious and ancient than any bargain between man and man, namely, that wages ought not to be insufficient to support a frugal and well-behaved wage-earner. If through necessity or fear of a worse evil the workman accepts harder conditions because an employer or contractor will afford him no better, he is made the victim of force and injustice.' See *Rerum Novarum: Encyclical of Pope Leo XIII on Capital and Labour.* Available at http://www.vatican.va/holy_father/leo_xiii/encyclicals/documents/hf_l-xiii_enc_15051891_rerum-novarum_en.html

65 'First 100 days, Part II', President Jacob Zuma interviewed by Erika van der Merwe, Summit Business (TV channel), 14 August 2009. Transcript available at http://transcripts.businessday.co.za/cgi-bin/transcripts/t-showtranscript.pl?1250456213

66 Cited in Everatt (2008:299). Sybil chronicled the plight of England's working classes and was published a year after Friedrich Engels' *The Condition of the Working Class in England in 1844.*

67 Some formulations hold little truck for subtlety. A 2003 document issued by the Presidency described the 'first economy' as an 'advanced, sophisticated economy, based on skilled labour, which is becoming more globally competitive'; by that definition, South Africa's 'first economy' is minute and rarified (see Policy Coordination and Advisory Services Unit, 2003). The full quote reads: 'One of the major consequences of the change in the structure of the economy is that "two economies" persist in one country. The first is an advanced, sophisticated economy, based on skilled labour, which is becoming more globally competitive. The second is a mainly informal, marginalised, unskilled economy, populated by the unemployed and those unemployable in the formal sector.' (2003:97).

68 Jeremy Cronin, 'The dangers of two-faced development', *Mail & Guardian*, 3 June 2007.

69 Lebani and Valodia (2005) found evidence of strong intra-household links between formal and informal economic activity in KwaZulu-Natal when they examined the KwaZulu-Natal Income Dynamics Survey.

70 In fact, the informal sector is still comparatively small, both in terms of output and work-force numbers. Best estimates suggest the sector absorbed about 19% of the work-force in 2002 (Kingdon and Knight, 2005). The size of South Africa's informal sector is largely a legacy of

the apartheid system which, depending on the setting, either outlawed, stymied or crushed African entrepreneurial efforts.

71 Mlambo-Ngcuka, P (2006) 'A catalyst for growth: Accelerated and shared growth—South Africa (AsgiSA)', Media briefing, 6 February. The AsgiSA policy framework adheres to the 'two economies' model and aims at a large expansion of infrastructure and skills, as well as increasing job opportunities in tourism and business-service outsourcing sectors (see Chapter five).

CHAPTER SEVEN

Poverty and inequality in the post-apartheid years

Although classified as a middle-income country, South Africa's harshly skewed allocation of income, resources and opportunities means that close to half the population lives in poverty (Meth, 2008; UNDP, 2006 & 2003), which is inordinately concentrated among Africans. Against a backdrop of modest economic growth, infrastructure development and service delivery benefiting poor households have improved, but at rates too slow to match mushrooming needs and generally on terms that follow market logic. Overall, the country's unequal social structure continues to be reproduced, with inequalities still exhibiting strong racial and spatial patterns (UNDP, 2003):

- Almost half (49%) of African *households* earned less than R 1 670 (USD 210) a month in 2005/06. By way of comparison, 2% of white households fell in that income bracket (Statistics SA, 2008a). Among *individuals*, more than half of Africans (55%) were earning less than R 400 (USD 50) per month in 2004 and 16% of them earned less than R 100 (USD 13) a month (Meth, 2006).

- The average white South African household spent R 198 600 (USD 24 800) in 2005/06—6.5 times more than the average African household (R 30 500 or USD 3 810), more than three times as much as coloured households (R 58 800 or USD 7 350), and almost twice as much as their Indian/Asian counterparts (R 104 500 or USD 13 060) (Statistics SA, 2008a).

- The gendered character of poverty is striking. Female-headed households are disproportionately likely to be poor (Woolard, 2002) and to remain so for long periods. Where female heads of households do have employment, it is usually in low-wage, piecemeal jobs.

- Much is made of the rise of an African middle class, with the consumptive habits of a new black elite routinely attracting lewd media coverage. In the wider scheme of things, though, these are marginal phenomena. Fewer than one in 10 (9%) African households had a *total monthly income* of R 7 500 (USD 940) or more in 2005/06 (Statistics SA, 2008a).

Savings levels are very low and debt levels are high. One 'financial diary' project found that more than 90% of poor households were paying off debt each month and one quarter of them was highly indebted (SALDRU, 2005). Between three-quarters and nine-tenths of surveyed households in another, localised study had no savings whatsoever (De Swardt, 2003). The baseline reality for a large proportion of South Africans, the majority of them black, is distressed and insecure with very little ability to withstand the shocks of serious illness, injury or death.

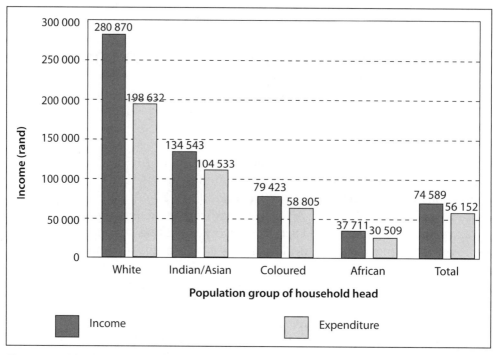

Figure 7.1: Average annual income and expenditure of South African households by population group of household head, 2005/06

SOURCE: STATISTICS SA (2008B), *INCOME & EXPENDITURES OF HOUSEHOLDS 2005/06*, STATISTICAL RELEASE P0100, PRETORIA, P. 7, 9.

Is poverty decreasing?

Poverty kept increasing in the late 1990s, as shown in several surveys and studies using different data sources (Statistics SA, 2002a; UNDP, 2003; Leibbrandt *et al*, 2004; Simkins, 2004).[1] This trend dates back to the final 15 years of the apartheid era, which had seen a significant redistribution of income from the poor to the rich: between 1975 and 1991, the incomes of the poorest 60% of the population had declined by about 35%.[2] Between 1995 and 2002, a further 1.7 to 2.3 million people, depending on the yardstick, slid 'into poverty'.

According to the UNDP (2003), the percentage of South Africans surviving on less than USD 1 (PPP)[3] a day—in other words, in destitution—doubled between 1995 and 2002, from 9.4% to 19.5%. Statistics SA data showed that from the mid-1990s to 2001, average annual household incomes and expenditures *declined*—from R 51 000 (USD 6 380) to R 45 000 (USD 5 630) and R 51 000 to R 40 000 (USD 5 000), respectively. But this decline reflected a drop in income and spending of mostly African households. In other words, Africans actually became poorer in the first years after the end of apartheid. Rampant job losses were the main cause of this trend (Statistics SA, 2002a).[4]

One data set made contrary findings. Collated by the South African Advertising Research Foundation, it found that the percentage of South Africans in the lowest 'living standard measures' category shrank from 20% to 5% between 1994 and 2001, prompting trade unionist-turned-billionaire Cyril Ramaphosa to claim that South Africans 'never had it so good' (Seekings, 2006:8). But the grounds for such cheeriness were weak. Even the Presidency eventually acknowledged that the proportion of people living below the poverty line (of R 322, or USD 40, per month) grew from 28% in 1995 to 33% in 2000 (PCAS, 2006). The picture changed in the early 2000s, when poverty levels began declining, enabling government to declare that 'our pro-poor policies are meeting with success' (Mbeki, 2006b; PCAS, 2006).[5] The actual extent of the decrease in the poverty headcount is controversial, however.

A range of calculations, some of them generated by the same researchers, is in circulation. Van der Berg and his colleagues (2005, 2007a, 2007b), for example, have variously published poverty headcounts of 21.8 million, 15.4 million and 13.1 million for 2004 and poverty headcount rates of 47%, 33% and 28% for that same year, using the same poverty line (of R 250, or USD 31, per person per month).[6] Depending on the set of figures one selects, the number of South Africans living below the poverty line fell by either 8%, 20% or 23% in 2001–04. Charles Meth's (2006, 2008) careful examination of the data indicates that the best estimate of the changes in the poverty headcount in 2001–04 was a decline from 19.4 million to 18.2 million—in other words, of 1.2 million.[7] The likely reasons for these discrepancies, he shows, range from elementary errors (such as failing to adjust the data adequately for under-reporting)[8] to the more prickly and ongoing problem of inadequate data (Meth, 2008).

Given these constraints and viewed from a policymaking perspective, which does the least harm: an overestimation of the severity of poverty or an underestimate? Doubtless there are sections of society that draw morbid satisfaction from data that seem to feed their prejudices about a 'black government'. They are a loathsome irritant. But they command no power in policymaking circles. In contrast, *underestimations* of poverty (and a mistaken confidence in the success of existing policies) have the potential of doing great harm, as Meth (2008:30) points out. Embarrassment is a price worth paying if more effective policies and actions are the likely rewards. Unfortunately, governments tend to go to great lengths to avoid the tonic of discomfort.

A heartless irony is buried in these poverty trends, as well. Several factors—including the AIDS and tuberculosis epidemics—are slowing the rate of growth in South Africa's population.[9] In 2008–09, the growth rate was estimated at 1%, down from 1.4% a decade earlier (Statistics SA, 2009b). Meth has calculated that a sustained decline in the population growth rate of 0.06% annually (not unlikely in the context of two deadly epidemics) would further reduce the poverty headcount ratio (2006:39). Since 2000, the population growth rate has been decreasing at an average 0.04% per year, which suggests that the exceptional mortality rates in the 2000s indeed may have contributed to the overall decline in the poverty headcount.

Government at first sought to attribute the drop in poverty levels to an increase in employment, before also acknowledging the key role of social grants. In fact, jobs accounted for a small part of the drop in income poverty. The best evidence indicates that South Africa currently has no better poverty-alleviating tool than its social-grant system (Lund, 2008)[10] and that the child-support grant in particular is having a powerful effect (Meth, 2006) (see Chapter eight). Trends observed in the 21 deeply impoverished Integrated Sustainable Rural Development Programme (ISRDP) and Urban Renewal Programme (URP) areas underlined the overall decrease in poverty since 2000, as well as the likely causes of that drop.[11] In the urban sites, poverty levels scarcely changed between 1996 and 2001 (29% to 27%), but they then fell to 18% in 2006. In rural areas, the drop was less steep (56% in 1996 to 48% in 2006). However, unemployment levels rose in almost all these communities (and reached an average of 79% in the rural and 63% in the urban areas)—which suggests that social grants were the main factor causing the observed decrease in their poverty levels (Everatt, Smith, Solanki, 2006).

Are pensions and grants reaching the very poorest sections of the society? Given that wages and self-employment constitute a much smaller part of the total income (about 23%) of the poorest income decile (compared with the next three or four deciles), one would expect to see social grants providing a much larger share of their income. Yet social grants constituted 34% of the income of that poorest decile, less than for the next two income deciles (Statistics SA, 2008a). Grants appeared not to be as large a source of income for the very poorest households as one might expect, which suggests that, even in 2007, they were not yet reaching the very poorest households to the extent required.[12]

Measuring poverty

These trends are based on income and expenditure data, which provide an important but partial picture of reality. Poverty is multifaceted and no single measurement adequately captures it (Magasela, 2005). It manifests in tangible computable terms, but also has important non-material dimensions (such as pride, self-respect, dignity, independence and physical security) that resist measurement and enumeration (Harriss, 2007; Du Toit, 2007).[13] This does not render the existing yardsticks meaningless, but it highlights their limitations. Frailty of measurement does not itself change reality—but it can handicap efforts to transform reality. Until 'the poor' are properly understood, targeted programmes will be hit and miss.

South African discourse defines 'the poor' in such loose terms that the phrase sometimes sheds meaning. As defined in the Reconstruction and Development Programme, for example, the 'disadvantaged' and 'vulnerable' comprised about 80% of the population. This woolliness persists in ANC policy documents. The organisation's core strategic text, its 'Strategy and Tactics' document, singles out the need to assist 'the most vulnerable in our society', which it defines as 'Africans in particular and Blacks in general' (ANC, 2007c:4). When Mbeki (2008a) proposed an anti-poverty plan in 2008, he listed the potential beneficiaries in terms that encompassed, by Everatt's count, 94% of the population. Jumbled into broad categories such as 'the poorest of the poor' or 'the most deprived', the poor, Everatt concludes, are rendered both ubiquitous and 'oddly lifeless' (2008:35).

Even if we settle on a particular measurement (say, income or expenditure levels) and fix a poverty threshold, hurdles remain. Unadjusted incomes data are notoriously prone to under-reporting biases, which is why those data are usually adjusted. Income data also tend to underestimate urban poverty since they often do not take account of the higher living expenses in those areas (Harriss, 2007). Expenditure-based measures of poverty suffer other weaknesses. For example, when Klasen (2000) constructed a composite measure of deprivation, the data closely matched those derived from expenditure surveys—except among the worst-off South Africans. The deprivation yardstick found that black South Africans, rural inhabitants and female-headed households were even more deprived than the expenditure data had revealed.[14]

Amid all this, government's approach to poverty data has been erratic and confusing. It has supported efforts to arrive at a common yardstick that would enable more accurate comparisons and trend analysis. But Hemson and O'Donovan (2006:17) also noted 'the growing tendency for government to evince an attitude of scepticism, doubt or rejection of statistical trends which do not reflect progress'.[15] Given the state's investments in reducing poverty (Swilling *et al*, 2005), the problem, it seemed, could not lie in the objective reality but in the measurement of that reality. Consequently, government officials grew fond of insisting on 'going to the poor themselves', a tautological proposition that nodded toward critical traditions in poverty research.[16] Some researchers had already travelled that route.

A 1997 participatory poverty assessment, for example, had asked persons deemed 'poor' to define their status. Most respondents associated poverty with alienation from kin and community, children going hungry, crowded and poorly maintained homes, lacking safe and efficient sources of energy, lacking jobs or earning low wages in insecure jobs and fragmented families (May, 1998). Such subjective measurements bring their own complications, however. The Indian social scientist N S Jodha's (1988) research in Rajasthan, India, for example, found villagers insisting that their lot had improved, even though money-metric measures of poverty showed they were worse off than before.[17] Neither the objective nor the subjective yardstick, it seems, necessarily trumps the other.

This also points to the limits of poverty measurement itself, especially the tendency to reify poverty as 'a state that is external to the people affected by it' (Harriss, 2007:5), as a definable space that people 'fall into', become 'trapped in' or 'escape from'. Typically, the conventional understandings rely on circular logic: indicators that are associated with poverty end up being deployed also as explanations of poverty. The ways in which poverty

> is conceptualised separates it from the social processes of the accumulation and distribution of wealth, which depoliticises it—and depoliticisation is of course a profoundly political intellectual act (Harriss, 2007:5).[18]

Once relational and distributional dimensions are considered, we enter the realm of inequality—where the issues of power and privilege and the relations that determine their distribution, move to centre-stage. Unlike poverty, inequality leaves little room for pity and charity; it invites moral and political judgements and it calls into question systemic trends. Which is why governments (South Africa's included) are more often heard sermonising about poverty than about inequality: in the 12 State of the Nation speeches given by South African presidents between 1999 and 2010, 'poverty' was spoken of 95 times; 'inequality' was mentioned 11 times, usually in relation to racial disparities.

Less poor, more unequal

Income distribution is exceptionally unequal in South Africa. By Statistics SA's reckoning, the wealthiest 10% of income earners bagged 51% while the poorest 20% of the population received 1.4% of total income in 2005/2006.[19] So skewed is income distribution that the poorest 50% pocketed a mere 10% of total income and the poorest 70% of the population got only 21%.[20] The Gini coefficient[21] stood at an astonishing 0.8, probably the worst in the world (Statistics SA, 2008b).

Once social grants were factored in, the Gini coefficient narrowed to 0.73, which illustrates their effect on inequality. Still, Statistics SA (2002a & 2008a) data show the Gini coefficient widened from 0.56 in 1995 to 0.73 in 2005/06, while Leibbrandt's (2004) estimations showed a worsening trend of 0.68 to 0.73 between 1996 and 2001 (using census data).[22] Gender inequalities are equally stark: male-headed households comprise about 58% of all households, but they earn about 80% of total annual household income.

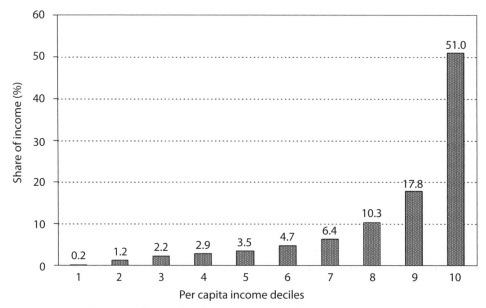

Figure 7.2: Distribution of household income across deciles, South Africa, 2005/06
SOURCE: STATISTICS SA (2008B) *INCOME AND EXPENDITURES SURVEY 2005/2006*, PRETORIA.

The racial patterns of income inequality remain so stark that one is tempted to question the demise of apartheid.[23] The wealthy are still overwhelmingly white and the poor are almost exclusively African and coloured. In 2005/06, whites accounted for 9.2% of the population but netted 45% of total household income, about eight times more than African households (and almost four times as much as coloured households and twice as much as Indian or Asian households).[24] Only 2% of white households earned less than R 20 000 (USD 2 500) a year, compared with 49% of African and 23% of coloured households (Statistics SA, 2008a).

Wealthier households also benefited disproportionately from the economic upturn of the 2000s. Between 2000 and 2005/06, the average annual household income for whites soared by 78% to R 281 000 (USD 35 100)—while that of African households increased by 45% to R 37 700 (USD 4 700) over the same period (Statistics SA, 2008a & 2002a).[25] Flip the lens to expenditure patterns and the racial inequalities are equally startling. Fewer than 8% of African households spent more than R 68 000 (USD 8 500) annually in 2005/06 (placing them in the top quintile), compared with 83% of white households and 50% of Indian or Asian households. At the other end of the scale, half (49%) of African households spent less than R 18 500 (USD 2 300) a year — as did a mere 1% of white households, 7.5% of Indian or Asian households and 26% of coloured households (Statistics SA, 2008a).

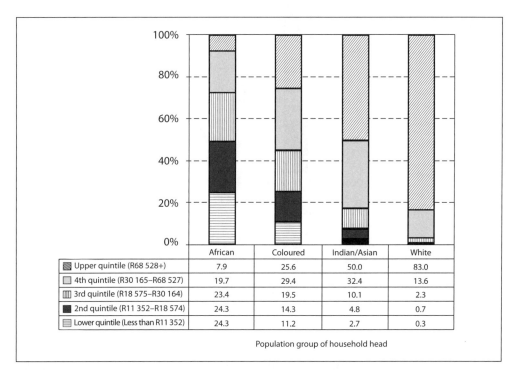

	African	Coloured	Indian/Asian	White
Upper quintile (R68 528+)	7.9	25.6	50.0	83.0
4th quintile (R30 165–R68 527)	19.7	29.4	32.4	13.6
3rd quintile (R18 575–R30 164)	23.4	19.5	10.1	2.3
2nd quintile (R11 352–R18 574)	24.3	14.3	4.8	0.7
Lower quintile (Less than R11 352)	24.3	11.2	2.7	0.3

Population group of household head

Figure 7.3: Distribution of South African households by expenditure quintiles and population group of household head

SOURCE: *STATISTICS SA (2008A) INCOME & EXPENDITURES OF HOUSEHOLDS 2005/06, STATISTICAL RELEASE* P0100, PRETORIA, P. 8.

That account hides important new trends, however. The monstrous inequality generated by the market does not neatly overlay the racial disparities engineered under colonialism and apartheid. Inequality between population groups is very high, but inequality within groups has worsened dramatically. This suggests that inequality increasingly follows class rather than racial lines of disparity (Terreblanche, 2002). By the 1980s, the racial privileges accorded to whites were being distilled and reproduced through a highly distorted market. White privilege no longer required the constant and explicit intervention of the state, as Nattrass and Seekings (2006) have argued and could be replicated through the market, which was permitting the upward mobility of some Africans. An uneven deracialisation of inequality was set in motion. Between 1975 and 1991, significant income disparities opened among Africans as class and social structures were reshaped (see Chapter two), the middle classes and professional layers grew and a tiny economic elite found its feet (Everatt, 1999). Subsequent political interventions (notably black economic empowerment and affirmative action) have accentuated those patterns.

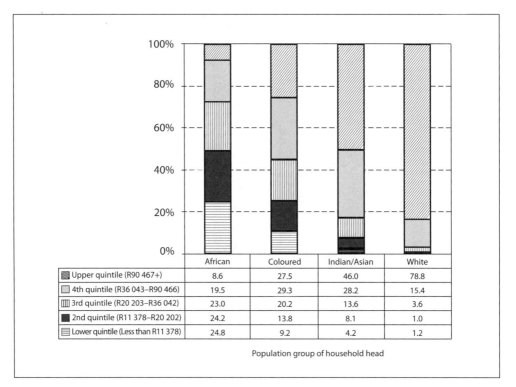

	African	Coloured	Indian/Asian	White
Upper quintile (R90 467+)	8.6	27.5	46.0	78.8
4th quintile (R36 043–R90 466)	19.5	29.3	28.2	15.4
3rd quintile (R20 203–R36 042)	23.0	20.2	13.6	3.6
2nd quintile (R11 378–R20 202)	24.2	13.8	8.1	1.0
Lower quintile (Less than R11 378)	24.8	9.2	4.2	1.2

Population group of household head

Figure 7.4: Distribution of South African households by income quintile and population of group of household head, 2006

SOURCE: STATISTICS SA (2008B) *INCOME & EXPENDITURES OF HOUSEHOLDS 2005/06*, STATISTICAL RELEASE P0100, STATISTICS SA, PRETORIA, P. 10.

The trend was already evident in the 1990s. Using census data on incomes, Whiteford and Van Seventer (2000) showed that the *between-race* share of income inequality shrank from 62% in 1975 to 42% in 1991 and 33% in 1999, while the *within-race* share grew from 38% to 58% to 67% over the same period.[26] The trend continued subsequently. The Theil index (which calculates inequality within subgroups) showed *within-race* inequality worsened from 0.35 in 1993 to 0.61 in 2006 (Presidency, 2008). Inequality is now highest within the African population group (Statistics SA, 2008b).

The trend holds even if one forsakes income data and focuses instead on characteristics such as accommodation, ownership of commodities (such as electrical appliances and cars) and use of infrastructure (such as electricity), as Bhorat *et al* (2006) showed. In that case, the *between-race* share of inequality halved between 1993 and 2004 (from 37% to 18%), while the *within-race* share grew from 63% to 82%.

The social wage debate

Poverty is about more than income and expenditure. Measuring poverty without factoring in social spending tends to exaggerate the severity of the problem (and probably skews understandings of it).[27] No doubt, social wage provisions are key facets of post-apartheid transformation and considerable achievements have been made on this front, as we discuss later. But 'the fact that income poverty is only part of the story does not mean that it is not important' (Meth, 2007b:6). Many of the services that comprise the social wage are not free and even those that are free (health-clinic visits, for example, or primary-school attendance) require other investments (taking time off work, transport costs, school uniforms and materials) which poor households struggle to make.

Defining the social wage

Government seems to regard social grants, tax relief and the provision of free basic services (including healthcare and education) as the main components of the social 'wage' or 'income'[28] (on occasion it also includes public-works programmes). At first glance, this seems sensible. Gauging the actual poverty-reducing impact of any of those components, however, is another matter.

When the Human Sciences Research Council (HSRC) in 2004 tried to measure the social wage in South Africa, it warned that the meaning of the term was 'ambiguous' and that estimates had to 'be used with caution' (2004:5,35). The actual scale of social-wage benefits, it transpired, was very difficult to determine, although *trends* in 'benefit incidence' could be identified with more confidence. Meth (2006:55) came to a similar conclusion:[29]

> It is clear that the 'social wage' in SA reduces the income required to maintain the minimum lifestyle regarded as socially acceptable. What the magnitude is of this reduction, nobody has thus far, with any reliability, been able to say.

Drawing on Guy Standing's (2002) suggestive schema, Meth (2007b) has tried to plot a path past such uncertainty by dividing the social wage into 'bankable' and 'non-bankable' elements. The former have a direct impact on disposable income. So, for example, provision of free water would reduce the amount a household previously spent on water, thus freeing disposable income for other uses. The 'non-bankable' components, on the other hand, reduce asset poverty, services poverty or time poverty—benefits that are less easily converted into monetary terms.[30]

Consider education: its benefits are taken for granted, especially in relation to the income and livelihood prospects of individuals. Countless international studies show a positive association between years of education completed and income levels. But in settings with very high unemployment, such as in South Africa, that relationship seems less clear-cut, as Meth (2007b) has shown. Here the 'bankable' benefits of subsidised or free education are called into doubt.

Using the 2004 Labour Force Survey data, Meth found that almost one third (32%) of *unemployed* black Africans aged 25–34 years were comparatively well educated (they had complete or incomplete secondary schooling). Among their counterparts who had no formal schooling or incomplete or complete primary schooling, only 7% were unemployed—as were about 3% of those who had achieved a post-secondary-school diploma or degree. Overall, the unemployed were 'better' educated than the employed. This suggests that education as a component of the social wage, does not automatically have a positive 'bankable' value.[31] Additionally, school attendance also involves other expenses that a household may not otherwise have incurred. Meth therefore argues that social spending on education should not be regarded as a 'bankable' social wage, but as a 'non-bankable' benefit; its value is not easily expressed in monetary terms.

Tracking improvements in the social wage

Access to school and healthcare and provision of water, sanitation and electricity have improved since 1994, most notably for urban and peri-urban residents. Against a backdrop of modest but (until 2009) consistent economic growth, infrastructure development also increased in the 2000s and institutional changes were made with the aim of further boosting service delivery. Local government systems were reorganised, the intergovernmental fiscal system was rearranged and an elaborate local development planning system was devised (Gwagwa & Everatt, 2005).

Official statistics show 1 600 healthcare clinics had been built and half the 400 public hospitals had been refurbished by the late 2000s. More than 90% of pregnant women visit an antenatal clinic at least once and some 80% give birth in a health facility. At least 80% of children are fully immunised by the time they are one year old (Bradshaw *et al*, 2008). About 71% of households have access to piped water (in their dwellings or on site), 83% are connected to the electricity mains and 61% have their refuse removed by the local municipality (Statistics SA, 2009d). A free basic water policy, introduced in 2001, allocates each household, regardless of its size, 15 kilolitres of free water per month (increased from the initial six kilolitres). The policy has been described as 'one of the most progressive water-rights-related legislative and policy frameworks in the world' (CALS, 2008:2).

Such progress is tempered by other factors. Firstly, the improvements are shadowed by an increase in the scale of need. The percentage of households that received a government housing subsidy, for example, doubled between 2002 and 2008 (from 5.6% to 11.2%), yet the proportion of households living in 'informal' dwellings (13%) remained virtually unchanged over that period (Statistics SA, 2009d). The paradox is easily explained. Urbanisation has increased, households are splintering and becoming smaller, and the population is growing. By government's tally, some eight million people were still without potable water in early 2007 and many more lacked access to electricity and sanitation (Mbeki, 2007b). In fact, the percentages of households connected to the electricity grid, with access to potable water and receiving refuse-removal services stayed relatively flat in the 2000s, as shown in Figure 7.5. Those data would seem to undermine the official version of events, which describes a period of belt-tightening (including stingy social spending) in the 1990s, which made possible later substantial increases in public spending and social-wage provision. According to Trevor Manuel's (2006) account,

> the fiscal consolidation of the late 1990s has provided the resources to accelerate the implementation of the RDP at a pace even the authors could not have forecast.

Yet when Bhorat and his colleagues (2006:46) reviewed service delivery in 1993–2004, they were surprised to find that household services had improved at a faster rate between 1993 and 1999 than in the period 1999 to 2004—although it was in the latter period that expenditure on service delivery was said to have increased significantly. This seemed to reflect a lag effect of the GEAR plan (see Chapter four), with the early momentum in socioeconomic improvement interrupted in the late 1990s as cutbacks 'reduced resources ... and made the implementation of existing projects more difficult' (Hemson, 2006:54).

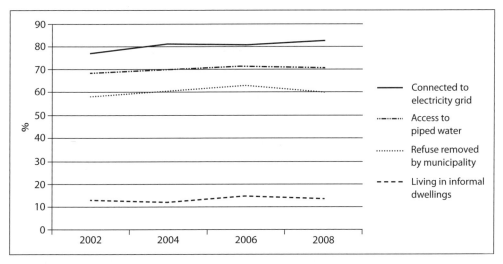

Figure 7.5: Social wage provision in South Africa, 2002–08
Source: Statistics SA (2009d)

Between 1996 and 1999, government had cut into some line functions, especially defence and economic spending. Improved tax collection also swelled government coffers and provided more leeway in budgetary decisions. But restrictions on public service hiring and wage increases had also been used to yield government 'savings', and real, year-on-year social spending (as a percentage of non-interest expenditure) indeed fell—by 2.6% in 1999/2000 and another 1.2% in 2000/01.[32]

Public-service managers who battled to balance their books under the GEAR regime complained that, rather than 'consolidate' later service provision, GEAR in the late 1990s seriously eroded institutional capacities to manage, monitor and sustain boosted service delivery. Studies in the public-health system arrived at similar conclusions (Schneider, Barron, Fonn, 2007). Putting the brakes on infrastructure spending until the early 2000s also saddled many local governments with outdated service-delivery tools and systems (IDASA, 2009), deteriorating infrastructure and major backlogs.

Secondly, dysfunctional local government, cost-recovery policies and the commo-dification of basic-needs provision undermine the improvements. Government's development interventions have been largely supply-driven; their design, pace and extent determined chiefly by fiscal constraints and institutional weaknesses. Roberts (2005:490) reminds that 'public service provision has tended to be target-driven rather than outcomes-driven'. As a result, quantity has tended to trump quality and the vital matters of maintenance and sustainability of services have slipped down the rung of priorities. Financing support from central government goes mainly toward capital expenses, leaving local municipalities, many of them cash-strapped, responsible for maintenance. The patterns of financing and the cost-recovery policies local governments follow are aggravating matters. In relation to water provision, notes the Centre for Applied Legal Studies (CALS, 2008:3–4), 'there is a definite preoccupation with cost-recovery and credit control at local government level', with

> overburdened, under-capacitated and under-funded municipalities [focusing] on generating much-needed revenue and prohibiting poor households from using 'too much' water as opposed to extending the access to an adequate supply of water to all within their jurisdiction [...] While there may be national policy in place, there is as yet no clear enforcement of the policy or national assistance to implement at the local level.[33]

Municipalities are caught in the 'growing tension between infrastructure provision' and low employment and income levels (Everatt, Smith, Solanki, 2006). Already some municipalities (typically rural and under-resourced ones) do not provide any free basic water to poor households (CALS, 2008). Water and electricity cut-offs or harsh rationing due to non-payment are rife and seriously erode the benefits of basic-services provision. David McDonald and John Pape (2002) estimated that between 5.5 million and 9.8 million people 'were affected by water cut-offs' from 1994 to 2001.[34] The HSRC (along with the Department of Water Affairs) conducted its own survey in 2003, but did not publicise the results. According to McDonald (*ibid*), who claims to have seen the data, the survey found that *at least 1.18 million people had their water cut off between mid-2002 and mid-2003. This figure would likely have been much higher if not for the introduction of 'free water' and a moratorium on cut-offs in many of the country's largest municipalities in 2002.*

That seems to validate McDonald and Pape's estimates. Other surveys suggest likewise. In the 2002 General Household Survey, 3% of respondents said their household's water had been cut off in the previous year due to non-payment, which translates to more than a million people affected (Hemson & Owusu-Ampomah, 2006).[35] Subsequent research has confirmed that the pressures placed on municipalities to recover costs has led to spates of illegal disconnections of water supplies and the imposition of flow restrictions that impede or block residents' access to these entitlements (CALS, 2008).[36] In a survey of 21 deeply impoverished areas, for instance, 17% of urban households had electricity arrears and 27% had outstanding water payments. Eleven percent had had their water services terminated and 18% had had their electricity cut off for non-payment (Everatt, Smith, Solanki, 2006):

> [I]t can reasonably be asserted that in a pro-poor state, to find that in the eight poorest urban nodes a fifth of urban households have had electricity cut off, a tenth have had water cut off and one in 50 [has been] evicted for non-payment, does indeed represent a crisis for the poor—and for the state.

Moreover, the manner in which some of this provisioning occurs is both stigmatising and exclusionary. Many municipalities use income-based indigence registers for allocating the free basic water supplies. Registering as 'indigent' is a stigmatising and onerous process, with numerous requirements. The applicant must present an identity document, usually must be a municipal account-holder (which rules out most poor tenants and excludes 'unlawful occupiers') and has to provide proof of income (or lack thereof). There are alternatives to such administratively intensive targeting. A universal approach, for example, would provide each household, irrespective of income status, with a free basic amount of water and then claw back the costs using a progressive ('the more you use, the more you pay') tariff scale that becomes steeper as use volumes increase.[37] But government seems philosophically opposed to universalist approaches (see Chapter eight).[38]

So impoverished South Africans are benefiting from social wage provisioning, but the poorest households are not necessarily at the front of the queue, as Thabo Mbeki noted in his 2005 State of the Nation address (2005): 'The public sector as a whole cannot claim to be such,' he said, 'if the benefits of free basic electricity are accruing mainly to those who are relatively well off.' When Neva Makgetla (2007:157) compared national data for 1996 and 2006, she found that 'there was little or no improvement in the share of households with access to most services in the poorest district-council areas'.[39] The total number of households with access to those services had increased, but the improvements significantly favoured households in the highest three income quintiles. Similar disparities occur even in areas classified as very poor (Everatt, Smith, Solanki, 2006). Neither national programmes nor provincial interventions fully explain such unevenness. The major factors, it seems are local governance (Everatt, Smith, Solanki, 2006) and the patterns of local-government financing (Makgetla, 2007).

Explaining the unevenness

Despite attempts at redress, disparities in local-government financing still mirror the spatial order under apartheid, which is proving to be much more intractable than anticipated. On average, the main cities budgeted about R 3 800 (USD 475) per person in 2006/07, towns in formerly 'white' areas budgeted around R 2 000 (USD 250) and towns located in what used to be Bantustans budgeted roughly R 400 (USD 50) per person. This largely reflects the financing arrangements for local governments. Various transfers from central government fund roughly 40% of local-government budgets[40], but the rest has to be raised from local rates and service fees. So the poorer the municipality, the smaller its budget and the weaker its ability to fund service provision and maintenance becomes.[41]

In especially tough times, like the 2009–10 economic recession, revenues dwindle further. Lacking the wherewithal to borrow, the poorest municipalities struggle most. Add to that the capacity problems that bedevil many municipalities (and which also undermine their efforts to implement capital projects) and popular grievances pile up.[42] South Africa is believed to have one of the highest per capita rates of protests in the world, the majority of them occurring in impoverished areas on the fringes of cities and towns. These protests are usually attributed to slow provision of housing and services. However, the anger stems also from the poor quality and uneven provision of services, the lack of democratic participation in local development, indifference towards citizens' complaints and a brash culture of self-enrichment among local officials (Atkinson, 2009; Hemson, 2007; Friedman, 2006; Pithouse, 2006) (see Chapter fourteen). Hence considerable disgruntlement is vented at local politicians and bureaucracies, which, as the Minister for Co-operative Governance and Traditional Affairs, Sicelo Shiceka, admitted, are 'perceived to be incompetent, disorganised and riddled with corruption and maladministration'.[43]

Inserted, as they are, into local power-broking and patronage circuits, South Africa's municipal bureaucracies will prove difficult to rehabilitate, especially those in peri-urban and rural areas. The ANC's mobilising base—its countrywide network of branches—relies on the muscle and connections of these local politicians. A clean-up is necessary but it is likely to be fitful and selective and will probably target out-of-favour officials, particularly those whose loyalties are deemed to rest with the ousted Thabo Mbeki and other figures that fall into disfavour (see Chapter twelve).

These realities cast doubt on the claims that a developmental state is being built. Dysfunctional institutions, hobbling management systems and practices, the widespread lack or mismatch of expertise, fiscal frailties, financial mismanagement and thousands upon thousands of vacancies plague the public sector (see Chapter eleven). In many places, local officials certainly deserve their share of the blame. But the problems run deeper, as well. 'Municipalities', IDASA analysts (2009:12) remind, are 'forced to bear the very public effect of poorly planned state policies' and are required to obey directives that force an excessive focus on 'procedure or output rather than performance or outcomes'.

Attempts to reduce poverty and boost social wage provisions have run up against formidable hindrances. Some of them are legacies of history, some stem from inappropriate policies and others emanate from malfunctioning systems or spring from misjudgements, shoddy management or sheer bad luck—as the next sections illustrate.

Slow harvest: land reform

Land reform has been slow and skimpy. Government's target, set in 1994, is to redistribute 30% of agricultural land by 2014, a deadline it almost certainly will have to extend.[44] By late 2009, only 5.2 million of the 24 million hectares of land earmarked for redistribution had been handed over to Africans. In total about 18% of South Africa's land was in the hands of Africans, ie an increase of about 5% since 1994.[45]

Part of the problem is that redistribution became conflated with black economic empowerment. Especially in the early 2000s, considerable effort went toward boosting the African presence in agribusiness, while land restitution lagged behind. In 2009, however, government drafted legislation that would enable it to expropriate land if negotiations to buy the land at a fair, market-related price failed.[46] Public pressure for more forthright action is certain to increase.

But an invigorated land-reform programme will have to contend with dynamics that tend to be neglected. It is generally assumed that a land-reform programme that promotes and supports smallholder production is a potentially potent anti-poverty strategy.[47] The evidence cautions against such expectations. Rural households draw fully 67% of their income from wages (46%) and old-age pensions or social grants (21%) (Statistics SA, 2008a). Kim Palmer and John Sender's (2006:347) review of the research evidence indicates that even if

> very poor rural households were granted access to more land, or even to credit and the necessary farm inputs, marketing facilities and extension advice, they would be unlikely and unwise to rely on own-account farming in the mix of survival strategies.

It is also tacitly assumed that small-scale agrarian production somehow bypasses class and other forms of exploitation. Yet it involves the creation of new layers of petty bourgeois rural entrepreneurs, many of them profiting from lamentable labour relations that tend to hit impoverished women and their dependents the hardest. Sender's research among poor rural households in Mpumalanga found that employment on large-scale or agribusiness farms provided 'far more reliable and secure wage earnings than those on small-scale farms' (2000:39). Given the often-appalling labour record of large farms in South Africa, that finding puts into perspective the extent of insecurity and exploitation workers on small farms endure.

More generally, land-reform efforts seem caught between different paradigms. Politically and emotionally charged, it is clearly an issue of justice and reparation. But, since it involves arable land, land reform also involves more prosaic calculations that relate to agricultural, especially food, production. For a variety of reasons (not least the removal of subsidies and tariffs), South Africa's status as a net food exporter is at risk, and there are concerns about sustaining adequate levels of agricultural production.[48] This need not entail trade-offs between land redistribution and commercial food production, but it does complicate the design of—and support for—land-reform projects.

An additional challenge arises from the fact that land reform and agrarian development are no longer strictly 'rural' issues. The redrawing of municipal boundaries has conflated the rural and the urban in many places. As a result, desperately poor residents of 'rural ghettos' are now able to stake claims on the limited resources of towns and small cities across South Africa (Hart, 2002b). This has compressed major tensions in and around the local state. Within these new political-spatial arrangements, the collapse of agrarian livelihoods—and with it, a deep crisis in social reproduction—places ever-greater pressure on cash-strapped municipalities. Hart is one of the few analysts to have peered beyond the obvious and noted how these realities potentially recast the land question and land reform, delinking them 'from agriculture narrowly defined and re-articulating [them] in terms of the social wage and broader livelihood imperatives' (2002b:25). This points to untapped possibilities for 'linking what are commonly seen as separate rural and urban struggles under the rubric of the social wage' (op cit, 26). It also adds new complexities to the state's land-reform ventures.

Necessary as it is, land reform, even if scaled up radically, will not on current evidence become a significant or effective remedy for poverty and joblessness. Case studies suggest that the economic development and livelihood-boosting potential of projects often does not materialise (Aliber, 2006).[49] New farmers often remain poverty-stricken and farm workers (including those on small and medium-sized farms) are intensely exploited. But because land reform is infused with potent political and historical meanings, government will come under increasing pressure to speed up and expand the process.

That hollow feeling: food and hunger

The most unforgiving indicator of wellbeing is a household's ability to eat regularly and healthily. Here, the latest trends seem promising: hunger appears to be a less commonplace experience than in the 1990s.

The General Household Survey includes a simple list of questions relating to hunger and those data show a steady drop in the percentage of households who said they often or always went hungry—from 6.8% in 2002 to 2.5% in 2007 (Statistics SA, 2008d). Hunger among children has also been reduced considerably, according to those data, with the percentage of children who reportedly went hungry at least 'sometimes' decreasing from 24% to 12.5% in 2002–07 (Statistics SA, 2003 &

2008d).[50] Fewer than 3% of households said their children frequently or always went hungry and the incidence of hunger in female-headed households appears to have decreased dramatically (Statistics SA, 2008d). School-feeding schemes (which provided about six million learners with a midday meal in 2006/07), social grants and the efforts of churches, NGOs and charity organisations probably deserve credit for these promising trends. Unfortunately, soaring food prices in 2008 and the economic recession of 2009 possibly reversed the declining trend.

Other surveys have painted more disturbing pictures. A robust data source[51] such as the National Food Consumption Survey (which the Department of Health conducts), found that about half (51%) of households experienced hunger at least some of the time during 2005 (Labadarios *et al*, 2007). In a 2005 Afrobarometer survey, 11% of respondents said they had gone hungry regularly in the previous year (Afrobarometer, 2005), while other large studies have indicated that between one quarter and one third of households could not afford to meet the dietary requirements of their children at any given time (Roberts, 2005). Among residents in 21 deeply impoverished areas,[52] more than 60% said they had found it 'difficult' or 'very difficult' to pay for food at some point in the previous year (similar percentages reported difficulties paying for transport, healthcare and school books) (Everat, Smith, Solanki, 2006).

Even if one accepts the Statistics SA data as the more accurate, some 2.5 million children in African households went hungry at least some of the time in 2007 (Statistics SA, 2008c)—an unconscionable reality in a wealthy country that considers itself food secure and that is a net exporter of food.

Rates of malnutrition[53] and stunting are high, with differences in the nutritional status of South Africans mirroring historical patterns of inequality. Child hunger, for example, is visited largely upon African and coloured households (Statistics SA, 2008c)[54] and child mortality rates in poorer suburbs can be twice as high as in better-off ones (Groenewald *et al*, 2007). Malnutrition afflicts women and children especially, one in three of whom are anaemic. Stunting in young children is a major problem, though it appears to be on the decrease in rural areas. It affects roughly one in five (18%) children younger than 10 years of age and almost 25% of those younger than five years (Labadarios *et al*, 2007).[55] Stunting is associated with slower development and is a very strong predictor of childhood death. At least 10% of childhood deaths in the early 2000s were attributed to malnutrition (Nannan *et al*, 2007). In the midst of a serious AIDS epidemic, however, it is difficult to know to what extent hunger is the underlying cause when children die underweight. In the early 2000s, an estimated 40% of the deaths of children in hospitals were due to AIDS (Krug & Pattinson, 2003).

A sickly society

Impressive as some of the achievements since 1994 have been, they are trammelled by the uneven quality of and access to, services. Unfortunately, there have also been some disastrous setbacks, many of them affecting the health prospects of South

Africans. Usually classified as a middle-income country, health outcomes in South Africa are worse than in many low-income countries (Coovadia *et al*, 2009). To a great extent, this represents the overhang of history. But regarding the present merely as an instance of the past would tell only part of the story. Indeed, the ANC itself admits that the quality of public healthcare has deteriorated in many areas.[56]

It is an understatement to say that the health of the population has worsened in the past decade (see Chapter ten). South Africans are dying in unprecedented numbers and at exceptional rates. Total annual deaths (from all causes) doubled between 1997 and 2006 (Statistics SA, 2005b, 2006, 2009b). Life expectancy in 2008 was 12 years lower than it was in 1996, child mortality was higher than in Iraq[57] and maternal mortality rates[58] were worse than in the early 1990s.[59] This is due largely to the AIDS and TB epidemics and the bungled manner in which they were handled (see Chapter nine). If the excess mortality caused by AIDS were removed, average life expectancy at birth would be on par with that in other upper-middle-income countries. Instead, it was 53.5 years for men and 57.2 years for women in 2009 (Statistics SA, 2009b).

The mortality rate for children younger than five years rose from 60 to 69 deaths per 1 000 live births between 1990 and 2006, making South Africa one of only 12 countries in the world where child mortality worsened in that period (Chopra *et al*, 2009). AIDS is believed to be the cause of more than half of those deaths.[60] The poor performance of programmes for preventing mother-to-child transmission of HIV was largely at fault. It is estimated that in 2008 only slightly more than half (53%) of HIV-infected pregnant women received antiretroviral (ARV) drugs to prevent such transmission. As a result, one in five children born to an HIV-infected mother also acquired the virus.[61] Without paediatric HIV treatment, the death rate among those children is very high: about half of them do not survive beyond their second birthday (Newell *et al*, 2004). Yet HIV in children is almost entirely preventable. In high-income countries, it has been virtually eliminated through the ready availability of HIV prevention, testing and treatment services. Mother-to-child transmission rates have been reduced to less than 2% and more than 80% of HIV-infected infants now live past the age of six (Resino *et al*, 2006). Similar results have been achieved in Cape Town's Khayelitsha township (Site B), where the reported rate of mother-to-child HIV transmission in 2007 was 3.5% (Médecins Sans Frontièrs *et al*, 2007).[62]

Maternal mortality in public-health institutions increased by 20% to more than 4 000 a year between 2002 and 2004, with AIDS responsible for at least half of those deaths (NCCEMD, 2009).[63] A government-appointed committee found that more than one third of those deaths 'were clearly avoidable within the healthcare system' (*op cit*, p. 3). Part of the solution would be to integrate ARV treatment more securely with prenatal care—an entirely feasible step which government finally took in late 2009.

The refusal to provide ARV drugs through the public-health system until the AIDS death toll peaked claimed an estimated 330 000 lives between 2000 and 2005, according to a Harvard School of Public Health Study (Chigwedere *et al*, 2008). A great deal of culpability belongs with Thabo Mbeki and his circle, notably former

Health Minister Manto Tshabalala-Msimang. But personalising the fiasco distorts matters. While some of the most egregious and callous decisions emanated from the Presidency and the Health Department, top ANC officials and MPs either supported them or looked the other way. The exceptions were rare and their courage earned them harassment and censure—though few colleagues objected. Vital as it is to also appreciate the deeper reasons for these failings, the ANC as a political movement (and not a mere few individuals) has to account for the shambolic handling of the AIDS and TB epidemics and the state of health in the country (see Chapters ten and twelve).

Inequality mars other realms of social policy too, including education (see Chapter ten). Primary school enrolment rose from 80% in 2002 to 87% in 2008, for example, but the percentage of learners who completed Grade 12 grew marginally (from 23% to 25%) and scarcely one third of them earned the exemption they require to study at tertiary level (Statistics SA, 2009c). The quality of education varies dramatically. State spending might be targeted at the poor, but the relative wealth or poverty of communities still determines the quality of education children receive (Chisholm, 2005).

The fetish of coping

A hallmark of the neoliberal era is the emphasis placed on the presumed pluck, grit and altruism of the poor. Household and community 'resilience', 'perseverance' and 'ingenuity' are routinely talked up, as are interventions that can 'empower' people, strengthen kinship and community safety nets and support 'coping strategies'. Like motherhood and *pap-en-vleis*,[64] all this seems beyond reproach. The resourcefulness and endurance people muster against adversity can be a marvel. But this does not remove the unsightly assumptions that lurk in the admiration for coping capacities.

A 'coping strategy' is generally understood to be a coherent set of actions aimed at overcoming an event or process that threatens the wellbeing of a household. Coping should, at the very least, result in a return to the status quo ante—and there lies the problem. Restoring a parlous and chronically insecure state of household 'viability' cannot reasonably be declared a success; a 'successful coping strategy' is an oxymoron. Implicit in the discourse of coping is an acceptance, an endorsement even, of the way things are. As Susanna Davies (1993) has pointed out in the context of famine studies, coping strategies are not about success—they are about failure. They can enable a household to survive, but not to transcend the circumstances that placed it in the path of mishap in the first place.

Tapping networks of mutual assistance and other forms of social support are vital aspects of poor persons' livelihood strategies. But these social connections tend to lack a transcendent thrust powerful enough to propel the poor out of poverty. 'Social networks and relations at best seem to stabilise incomes, but provide little in the way of longer-term accumulation or economic advance,' is the conclusion Adato, Carter and May (2006:245) reached after reviewing South African poverty trends in the 1990s.

The lineage of coping-strategy dogma is instructive. It first acquired theoretical footing during the African famines of the 1980s, as researchers tried to explain and anticipate households' responses to such disasters. They sought answers to three important questions: what strategies did households use to survive, could coping strategies be used as a kind of 'early warning system' for impending famines and what kinds of support could buttress those strategies? (Goudge & Govender, 2000). From this there emerged a relatively standard schema describing a sequence of responses that contained a 'tipping point' beyond which households would tilt into destitution and, quite possibly, dissolution.[65] By the early 1990s, studies were placing famine-related shocks in the wider context of long-term and structural vulnerability; the 'shocks', in other words, became understood as aspects of chronic hardship.[66] But coping dogma had acquired a momentum of its own, with ascendant neoliberalism providing the backdrop (Bailies, 2002).

As state obligations and resources were directed away from social provisioning, notions of community resilience and coping gained enthusiastic support among multilateral agencies and development organisations. After years of scorched-earth social policy directives, 'the community' now found itself cast in a redemptive role, as a repository of unfathomed vigour and invention. Coping dogma celebrates and schematises those qualities in ways that observe key principles of neoliberal discourse. Households' and communities' close knowledge of their circumstances and environment, for example, is said to enable them to act as rational agents within a market-governed context. By rewarding and penalising various courses of action over time, theory holds, the market not only confers a good deal of this accumulated 'knowledge' but also imbues households' and communities' actions with rationality (Rugalema, 2000). When adversity strikes, households then juggle alternatives and take decisions that might seem unpalatable, but that ultimately yield provident outcomes. Usually couched in more fragrant terms, these assumptions shape the thinking and practices of many development 'practitioners'. The fundamental, overriding narrative of amputated options and foreclosed alternatives is left untouched.

That neoliberal undertow was hidden, though—largely because of other discursive shifts in mainstream development theory. Among the talismanic interventions were Amartya Sen's efforts to extend the focus of development from material wellbeing to boosting capabilities and 'empowering' people (Sen, 1985). This drew, to an extent, on the radical participatory development and pedagogical practices propagated in the 1960s and early 1970s, with their stress on self-reliance and local empowerment.[67] Also influential was the emphasis post-colonial studies would place on agency and subjectivity, with key contributions from Arturo Escobar (1995) and John Friedmann (1992). The upshot was to shift the conceptualisation of 'the poor' from being objects (victims, beneficiaries, clients) to subjective agents capable of organising their collective wellbeing chiefly through the household, which becomes the 'central element for the production of livelihood, the principle of moral economy (trust, reciprocity, voluntarism) and the utilisation of [people's] "social power"' (Bayat,

2000:539). Neoliberal discourse would appropriate many of these important developments.

South African history applies a further twist, producing an odd fusion of *ubuntu* and neoliberalism.[68] An ethos of communalism and mutual obligation survives and is encoded in many social practices and arrangements. In particular, the guiding principles of communitarianism, mutual assistance and the bonding sense of shared destinies that underpin *ubuntu* are said to provide a bedrock for community-level resilience and solidarity. The ethos seems to be in fine fettle and is routinely enlisted in a self-conscious project of ideological recuperation that taps into popular practices, 'the capacity for innovation, reinvention of traditions and resurgence of native skills' (Ela, 1998). But that is to ignore the splintering impact of colonial and apartheid social engineering and the current spread of introverting values. 'South Africa,' as Monica Wilson noted decades ago, 'has lived on the capital of a very strong African family system and that capital has been squandered (1975:18).'[69] *Ubuntu*, in fact, is surprisingly compatible with a central thrust of neoliberalism—which is to absolve the state from its basic responsibility for social reproduction.

These ideological heritages have enormous implications for the pursuit of 'development', the design of social protection strategies and efforts to contend with the ruinous effects of the AIDS and TB epidemics. The home- and community-based care system, for instance, fits snugly in the mould of coping dogma—not least in the central roles assigned to the sphere of the home (and to women within it), which is erratically and unevenly supported by NGOs and the state (see Chapter nine). This veritable 'privatisation' coincides with the increasing subordination of social life to market forces. As more dimensions of life and work are ceded to the market, the responsibility for providence and calamity, for life and death, is being lodged with ever-smaller units of society (and is ultimately, in the neoliberal ideal, assigned to the individual).[70] This occurs within a social protection system that 'remains constrained by narrow conceptions of the state and by distrust of rights-based demands on state resources' (Hassim, 2005b:3–4). The promotion of self-empowerment and community responsibility meshes with a dominant mindset that seeks to restrict citizens' claims on the state (Barchiesi, 2005). Meanwhile, powerful dynamics are shrinking the boundaries in which obligations and entitlements circulate and the extent of support that is on offer.[71] It is in this material and ideological environment that home- and community-based care practices operate and in which households and communities are expected to 'cope'. This is not to dismiss the flowering of mutual support that *ubuntu* evokes and which home- and community-based care assumes. But it underlines the wretched inequality and exploitation these discourses cloak as 'normalcy'. Claude Ake's (2000) riposte to the celebration of 'an explosion of associational life' seems better aligned with reality:

> Some have welcomed this development as a sign of a vibrant civil society in Africa. It may well be that. However, before we begin to idealise this phenomenon, it is well to remind ourselves that whatever else it is, it is first and foremost a child of necessity, of desperation even.

Microfinance: small change

Faith in entrepreneurial zest as a route out of poverty is a choice bromide of the neoliberal era. Hernando De Soto (2000), for example, sees the shacks of slum-dwellers as potential sources of capital if they can be properly titled and registered. Shacks—an embodiment of precariousness—become the basis for unleashing the pent-up potential of these 'natural entrepreneurs'. The Grameen Bank in Bangladesh is feted almost universally (founder Mohammad Yunus won the Nobel Peace Prize in 2006) for using small loans to empower impoverished communities. Countless other 'development' ventures follow similar logic. In James Ferguson's (2007:74) phrasing,

> Neoliberal motifs of 'empowerment' restyle the unemployed as 'micro-entrepreneurs' who, perhaps with the aid of a little 'micro-credit', might use their inventive creativity to power a new kind of economic development strategy.

A kind of alchemy is envisaged. The 'informal' economy transmutes from a pool of unemployed strugglers into a site of economic growth and job creation (Ferguson, 2007).[72] Even in rural areas, orthodoxy emphasises the growth of smallholder agriculture and self-employment in rural microenterprises as a feasible exit route from poverty.[73] In the fashionable theoretical framework, as John Sender has observed, the rural poor are transformed into self-employed 'agents' struggling in imperfect markets; what they need, it is claimed, are more 'assets' to 'smooth their transition into the ranks of the petty bourgeoisie' (2000:38). Microfinance and microenterprise schemes distil neoliberal ideology quite pithily: deeper integration into the market economy and adherence to its strictures become the conditions for relief (Baylies, 2002). The magic ingredient is said to be credit—hence the explosion of microfinance ventures in poor communities. These ideas weigh heavily in the government's thinking about economic growth and development: attempts to kindle small and microenterprises are a linchpin of current economic strategy (most obviously in the AsgiSA framework).[74]

In places with chronically high unemployment, limited income-earning opportunities and pervasive ill health and early death, such as much of South Africa, it might seem churlish to question such optimism. Yet a tacit but fundamental premise of microfinance is that the viability of poor households depends on them becoming (bigger) consumers of credit. It is unclear how deeper indebtedness should boost and safeguard economic security when households are losing incomes and income-capable members and when the surviving members often are stretched to the limit.

Microfinance has become a major business in its own right and the industry commands about USD 60 billion in assets.[75] Globally, more than R 90 billion (USD 11.3 billion) was funnelled into the microfinance industry in 2008, much of it by private investors. Their outlook is disarmingly straightforward: 'We see our role as deepening the financial sector and strengthening the enterprise sector and the banks in the countries in which we work,' according to Helen Alexander of the top microfinance investment fund, ProCredit Holding.[76] Lured by the prospects of hefty profits, banks and financial institutions now tower over the microfinance sector and many of them charge interest rates worthy of loan sharks.[77]

Microfinance under the microscope

The jury seems in on the benefits the poor derive from these schemes—and the verdict is not comforting (Banerjee *et al*, 2009; Karlan & Zinman, 2009; Baylies, 2002; Mosley & Hume, 1998). 'The problem with microfinance,' according to Aneel Karnani of the University of Michigan, 'is that is simply doesn't do that much to lift the poor out of poverty.'[78] Recent, careful studies support that verdict, prompting *The Economist* magazine to admit that 'there are surprisingly few credible estimates of the extent to which microcredit actually reduces poverty'.[79]

A path-breaking study into the developmental effects of microfinance schemes in Hyderabad, India, for example, came up empty-handed. Abhijit Baneerjee and his colleagues (2009) found that microfinance '[appeared] to have no discernible effect on education, health, or women's empowerment'.[80] A similar study in the Philippines reached the same conclusion. In neither was there a measurable effect on household consumption, while the Philippines study also found no improvements in the quality of food intake or in the probability of being below the poverty line (Karlan & Zinman, 2009). Even claims about the Grameen Bank's developmental impact are in doubt.[81]

An older United States Agency for International Development (USAID) study of microfinance schemes in Zimbabwe, India and Peru found that microfinance programmes helped some very poor households meet basic needs and protect themselves against certain risks. But household incomes did not rise in the Zimbabwean case and income sources did not diversify in India, nor did food consumption improve there. The assessment also found 'limited impact on the ability to cope after [financial] shocks had occurred' (Snodgrass & Sebstad, 2002). Research on Uganda's Women's Finance Trust found that microfinance projects were not reaching the poorest households. But those households that did benefit were able to spend more money on health and education (Hoang, 2002).

What about the enterprises themselves? The wages, terms and conditions of work in microenterprises are typically hyper-exploitative. This unmasks one of the defining ruses of the microenterprise fad: its supposedly 'class-less' character. Yet, as Sender (2000:39) highlights, the entities targeted for capacity-building and other forms of support in rural and township development projects very rarely include organisations that have 'a realistic prospect of increasing the political and economic bargaining power of the lowest-paid workers'. Conceptually, 'the poor' are lumped together into an undifferentiated mass.

In practice, relatively privileged sections in 'poor' communities often are able to capture microenterprise incentives and support. Researchers frequently encounter evidence of this elsewhere in Africa. In such cases, the outcome is neither poverty reduction nor the 'formalisation' of 'informal' activities, but a recomposition of the 'informal sector' (Meagher & Bello-Mohammed, 1993).

Moreover, not many of the loans are actually used to invest in small enterprises. In the Hyderabad study, only one in five loans led to the creation of a new small business (Banerjee *et al*, 2009). Poor households mostly spend the money on essential expenses (especially food) or use them to settle other debts. Their extremely limited resource base tends to discourage additional risk-taking. In effect, the 'credit' is used like a grant—except that the household then owes the money, often at extortionate interest rates. In such cases, the credit tides a household over, but since it does not necessarily generate additional income, it adds to the overall debt load and becomes an additional encumbrance. The most 'enterprising' households seem to be the ones most adept at juggling and redistributing their multiple debt obligations, enabling them to stay one step ahead of their debt collectors. Needless to say, in such cases poverty reduction is not necessarily the outcome: research in India and Malawi found that extremely poor borrowers ended up worse off financially.[82]

In periods and places with extraordinarily high levels of morbidity and mortality, the usefulness of microcredit—as opposed to other forms of non-indebting support—must be questioned. Taking on additional debt when disposable income is shrinking seems a self-defeating option. The impoverishing effect of AIDS and TB on poor households underscores these concerns. As illness and death shrink household incomes, microenterprises that rely heavily on the custom of poor households (and which typically are operated by vulnerable households themselves) are coming under severe strain. This 'double squeeze' (less disposable income plus intensified competition) is helping stoke the anxiety and resentment that periodically takes the shape of xenophobic attacks.

The schemes seem potentially effective only when productive capacity exists and access to markets is available—conditions that cannot be assumed—and are appropriate for supporting *existing* economic activities rather than starting up new ones. But in many parts of South Africa, these conditions are absent. De Swardt's (2003) study of poor households in rural areas of the Eastern and Western Cape and in Cape Town, for example, highlighted the marginal value of self-employment as a source of income. In Mount Frere, Ceres and Langa, wage labour was by far the major source of household income, followed by social grants.

More constant forms of social protection (including expanded access to social grants) and start-up grants would seem more suitable and beneficial (Baylies, 2002; Hoang, 2002). Sender's (2000) research among poor women in rural Mpumalanga goes further and suggests that where people rely heavily on insecure wage incomes, steps to extend and protect the labour rights of casual and seasonal workers would be most appropriate.[83] Microfinance seems to be of limited benefit—even counterproductive—when macro policies and the structural environment continue to reproduce impoverishment and inequality.

Crime, violence and justice

Anxiety about crime used to be scoffed at as a symptom of white angst. But survey after survey has confirmed that personal-safety fears are ubiquitous in South Africa—even if, as journalist Doug Henwood has pointed out in the US context, 'crime, like health, wealth and wisdom, is not distributed very equally'.[84] By the mid-2000s even the Mbeki government was admitting that *we cannot claim the happiness that comes with freedom if communities live in fear, closeted behind walls and barbed wire, ever anxious in their houses, on the streets and on our raids* (Mbeki, 2007b).

Mbeki was not exaggerating. One third of black Africans feel 'personally unsafe on most days', according to the South African Social Attitudes Survey, as do about one quarter of coloured and white respondents. At least one in three South Africans say they are afraid to walk alone in their own neighbourhoods *during the day* and three-quarters are afraid to do so at night. Residents in informal settlements are the most fearful: four in 10 say they feel unsafe on most days (Roberts, 2009).

The unease is justified. Each year, around 3.5 million South Africans seek medical assistance for non-fatal injuries, half of them inflicted by another person (Seedat *et al*, 2009).[85] Almost 60 000 people die from their injuries annually, which translates into an injury death rate of 158 per 100 000 inhabitants: twice the global average. More than half of those deaths are the outcomes of assaults or attacks (more than four times the proportion worldwide). In the mid- to late-1990s, South Africa's homicide rate was among the highest in the world. It has declined since, but approximately 18 000 South Africans are still murdered each year—at a rate of about 39 per 100 000 in 2007/08 (SAPS, 2008), which was still five times higher than the global average (Seedat *et al*, 2009).[86]

Some 2.1 million serious crime cases were registered with the police in 2008/09, of which one third were 'contact crimes' that involved physical assault against victims (ranging from murder and attempted murder to sexual assault, aggravated robbery and much in between).[87] These, along with the high rates of burglaries and house robberies, stoke fear and loathing. Children are not spared the depravity: 246 children younger than 12 years were murdered, 3 600 were seriously assaulted and 7 900 were sexually assaulted in 2008/09 (SAPS, 2009).[88] Those are the cases that were reported to the authorities. Even the annual report of the South African Police Services (2009) dispenses with euphemism:

Contact crime frequently causes extremely serious and often lingering (sometimes permanent or even fatal) physical, psychological and material damage to victims, leaving lasting scars on the psyche of South African society.

The personal agonies defy description. They also register on the larger fields of politics and society—for the trauma of crime and violence undermines many of the rudiments of healthy social relations, both between people (as individuals or groups) and between citizens and the state. As summarised by Hamber and Lewis, elementary assumptions about the 'self and the world' are upended, including:

the belief in personal invulnerability ('it won't happen to me'); the view of the self as positive; the belief that the world is a meaningful and orderly place; that events happen for a reason (and) the trust that other human beings are fundamentally benign (1997:9).

Affordable and accessible counselling and support services are rare, despite the warnings of psychiatric workers that 'as a country, South Africans are exhibiting symptoms which add up to Post-traumatic Stress Disorder'.[89]

Woe to the women

Men in South Africa kill women at extraordinary rates. The homicide rate for women was 25 per 100 000 population in the early 2000s, six times the global average. Half of those 3 800 female victims were killed by their husbands or boyfriends (Abrahams *et al*, 2009).[90] Rates of murder and attempted murder of women have declined since then; nonetheless 5 400 murders or attempted murders of women were reported to the police in 2008/09 (SAPS, 2009).

Each year, more than 70 000 women and girls summon the courage to report to the police that they were raped or sexually assaulted (SAPS, 2009).[91] Many complain that police officers treat them with indifference or incredulity. Many more spare themselves that additional ordeal; it is estimated that only one in nine rapes is reported to the police (Abrahams *et al*, 2009; Jewkes & Abrahams, 2002). The rape of girls is not uncommon. In Gauteng province, 40% of rapes reported to the police in the early 2000s involved girls younger than 18 years and 15% of them involved girls younger than 12 years (Vetten *et al*, 2008).[92]

The control of women by men forms an axis of current constructions of masculinity in South Africa—and the use of violence to achieve that control and punish resistance is widely legitimated, including among women (Wood & Jewkes, 2001; Jewkes, Penn-Kekana, Rose-Junius, 2005).[93] These values probably represent one of the few truly trans-racial features of the society. Violence against women is highly prevalent, irrespective of racial grouping. In a study in three provinces in the late 1990s, one in 10 adult women said they had been physically assaulted in the previous year (Bradshaw, Bourne, Nannan, 2003), but other studies have found at least 40% of men admitting to assaulting their partners, with 40–50% of women reporting such violence (Seedat *et al*, 2009).

The violence is often sexual. In a national survey, one in 10 sexually experienced young women said they had been physically forced to have sex at some point (Pettifor *et al*, 2004), while one in four (28%) young men surveyed in a recent study said they had raped someone at some point and half of those perpetrators said they had raped more than once (Jewkes *et al*, 2009). Many women regard sexual coercion as a routine part of relationships with men (Wood & Jewkes, 1997). Mager's (1996) observations about sexual violence in the 1940s and 1950s seem apposite in contemporary South Africa:

> *In a context where male power was constructed around control over women, male aggression was readily expressed, often blurring the line between assault and sexuality for both men and women [...] Sexual violence was an outlet for power and anger; it was an expression of masculinities that depended on the submission of women.*[94]

Few people would claim that these values emerged overnight, but the extent to which they build on or violate earlier templates of gender relations is debatable.[95] It is generally agreed that intensive labour migration and urbanisation, and the growth of violent gang cultures that accompanied these developments, were instrumental in fusing notions of sexual entitlement with the valorisation of physical aggression. In that view, dominant constructions of masculinity appeared to become especially violent from the 1930s, though the trend waned and waxed subsequently (see, for example, Mager, 1999). (Among white men, the militarisation of society in the 1970s and 1980s appears to have had similar effects.)

In a context of coerced proletarianisation, many 'traditional aspects of adult manhood [became] unattainable, including a family and fulfillment of a provider role' (Coovadia *et al*, 2009:823). Notions of manhood increasingly emphasised available resources such as courage, strength, risk-taking and male camaraderie, while women and their bodies often were instrumentalised. Other researchers have pointed out that the glamorisation of such attributes also preceded the dislocation imposed by forced labour migration. But it seems safe to say that rampant joblessness and hardship, against the backdrop of severe inequality, currently again seem to invest 'manhood' with compensatory, domineering notions. The upshot is that dominant constructions of masculinity place high value on sexual conquest and the control of women (Dunkle *et al*, 2007), with physical violence often used to impose or maintain gender hierarchies and 'keep women in their place', as the perpetrators might frame it.[96]

Cycles of violence

These experiences are destructive enough in their own right, but they also drive cycles of abuse and aggression that span generations. Research evidence shows emphatically that children exposed to abuse or violence are more likely to become perpetrators or victims of violence, compared with peers who had been spared such tribulations.[97] Being a child is a punishing, often horrifying experience for many South African children. In one study, 35–40% of children said they had watched their mothers being beaten and 15% said their parents were often too drunk to care for them. There are also

> high levels of sexual, physical, and emotional abuse and neglect of children, which has major effects on their mental and physical health, and increases the likelihood that boys will become involved in crime and violence (Coovadia et al, 2009:824).

Although pervasive, violence against children is very seldom reported to the authorities (Seedat *et al*, 2009). When it is, protection or punishment is a rare consequence; in 2006, government abolished the child-protection units attached to some police stations (though subsequently it seemed to be reconsidering that move). The bulk of child protection services are now provided by NGOs—an example of the state abdicating the fundamental responsibility of protecting the most vulnerable members of society. The Children's Act, on paper an impressive attempt to improve and safeguard children's wellbeing by focusing on preventing problems, was passed in 2005. By mid-2009, only 30 of its 300 sections had been implemented.[98]

Wedged apart

Trust in the ability, even the willingness, of the police to protect citizens is low. Preoccupied with enforcing apartheid laws, the police used to neglect common-law policing in South Africa's townships. Crime flourished, but the victims often resisted seeking the assistance of a police force that was brute, unjust and widely perceived to be corrupt. Scorned, the police lacked legitimacy. Conventional law enforcement, in the sense of apprehending culprits, charging them with common-law offences and prosecuting them, was rare. Subsequently, the democratic government misjudged its supporters' attitudes to and relationships with, the police. It had assumed that the police would be redeemed once a legitimate political authority was at the helm:

> When the police's new political bosses came to power in 1994, they gave themselves the tasks of stabilizing the organization [...] and winning legitimacy for it in black communities. Perhaps the last of these tasks was misconceived. Perhaps the proper aim ought not to have been to win the police legitimacy, but authority (Steinberg, 2008b:97).

A decade on, policing in South Africa is inconsistent, ill disciplined and lacking in confidence and skill. Consequently, it is marred by arbitrariness and an inclination to violence.[99] Self-financed policing is ubiquitous. A USD 10 billion private-security industry employs at least 130 000 people, who work long hours for poor wages. Most are African men, many of them economic refugees from neighbouring countries. Security walls, electrified fences, sealed-off neighbourhoods and streets, gated communities and fortress-like cluster-housing complexes have redrawn the geography of cities and towns. An odd paradox operates. The more security is added, the less secure and the more distrustful, suspicious and intolerant people seem to become. Social distance widens even further. In some impoverished neighbourhoods, meanwhile, the glaring absence of reliable law enforcement has legitimised vigilante rampages, including lynchings.

The dispensing of people's justice forms a rich seam of the mythology of the 1980s, but contemporary vigilantism, especially in urban areas, is a much more freewheeling phenomenon that is frequently uninhibited by oversight or structured process. Also increasing are attempts to revive community policing and 'people's courts' initiatives from the past. Some appear to be nominally successful, but at a cost that often goes unrecognised. Geared at identifying and tracking down suspects, then bringing them to 'justice', these ventures do not bond communities as much as they divide them—between accusers and suspects, the guilty and the innocent, the righteous and the stigmatised.

More effective and consistent law enforcement (including a refurbished and improved detective service and more and better-trained and -resourced prosecutors and court personnel) is an obvious priority. It may also reduce some of the fear and insecurity South Africans live with. But the underlying causes of the mayhem are not momentary. They are lodged in social dynamics that support, even encourage violence: widespread livelihood insecurity amid outrageous material inequalities, harsh gender inequality, notions of manhood that valorise intolerance and sanction aggression, exposure to abuse in childhood, feeble parenting and intense alcohol and substance abuse (Seedat *et al* 2009).[100] Identifying, prosecuting and convicting perpetrators of violence will not end this scourge. But it is a fundamentally important aspect of repairing public trust in the state, in the principle of due process and in the rights-based democracy that South Africa seeks to be.

Endnotes

1   Local studies confirmed this trend. Among 1 200 African households surveyd in KwaZulu-Natal, for instance, poverty rates increased from 27% to 43% between 1993 and 1998 (Carter & May, 2001).

2   'South Africa is still suffering inequalities from racial capitalism', *Parlia-mentary Bulletin*, 14 April 1998.

3   Purchasing power parity.

4   Meanwhile, average income and expenditure in white and coloured households *increased* between 1995 and 2000 (Statistics SA, 2002a).

5   Mbeki, in response to a question during Parliamentary Question Period on 30 March 2006, cited in Meth (2006:5).

6   The R 250 per month poverty line corresponds to the USD 1 per day line—a pitilessly low and unrealistic threshold, which should be abandoned.

7   The differences between Meth's estimate and those of Van der Berg and his colleagues stem from the ways in which they compensated for under-reporting of income in household surveys.

8   Universally, significant proportions of respondents provide either no or incomplete information about their incomes. The tendency is also toward under-reporting income. Statisticians have developed various methods to adjust for those reporting errors. Note, however, that if the under-reporting is consistent over time, it need not distort the analysis of *trends* in income poverty (Seekings, 2006:9–11). However, government, in its widely circulated Mid-term Review report, publicised poverty figures that were based on data that had *not* been adjusted for under-reporting (Meth, 2008:11).

9   Note that it is the *growth* rate that is declining, not the population size.

10   The estimated 2.6 million beneficiaries in 1994 increased almost five-fold to about 12 million in 2007. Social grants expenditure comprised 3.1% of GDP in 2003/04, rising slightly to 3.3% in 2006/07, then dipping again to 3.1% in 2009/10 (IDASA, 2007).

11   Everatt, Smith and Solanki (2006) used Statistics SA's 10-element matrix to assess poverty in the 13 Integrated Sustainable Rural Development Programme (ISRDP) and the eight Urban Renewal Programme (URP) nodes they surveyed. It includes household income, employment, basic service access, literacy, incidence of female-headed households, overcrowding, dwelling type and refuse removal.

12   A caveat: subsequent increased take-up of this grant may have changed this.

13   A 1997 participatory poverty assessment, for example, sought to turn this measurement challenge on its head and asked persons deemed 'poor' to characterise their status. Respondents most commonly associated poverty with the following circumstances: alienation from kinship and community, children experiencing hunger, crowded and poorly maintained homes, lacking safe and efficient sources of energy, lacking jobs or earning low wages in insecure jobs, and fragmented families (May, 1998).

14   Cited in Woolard (2002).

15   Government occasionally has preferred market research done by the advertising industry to survey research conducted by the official statistical agency. The *Development Indicators Mid-term Review* (Presidency, 2008), for instance, based its poverty and inequality findings on All Media and Products Survey (AMPS) data.

16   Most famously associated with Robert Chambers' (1988, 1995) research in India, where he distinguished between the perceptions of professionals and the perceptions of poor people themselves. The former tended to focus on aspects of deprivation that could be measured fairly easily (usually flows of incomes and expenditures). Poor people, though, tended to emphasise material possessions, access to water and sanitation, housing, education and healthcare, debts, isolation, physical frailty or disability, status and self-respect. Chambers concluded that, in mainstream poverty research, poverty had become that which could be readily measured.

17   For a critique of Jodha's findings, see Moore, Mick Moore, Choudhary and Singh (1998), which elicited Jodha's (1999) reply.

18   For a fascinating engagement with these issues, see Du Toit (2007).

19   South African corporations (parastatal and private) have followed the global trend of handing executives and top managers scandalously inflated remuneration packages. In 2009, in the midst of the worst economic recession in more than 20 years, the chief executive of insurance giant Sanlam bagged R 27 million (USD 3.4 million), as did his counterpart at FirstRand, another financial corporation. The median package for a chief executive officer was worth R 5.3 million (USD 662 000). See 'Average CEO earns R5.3 million a year', *Business Report*, 8 October 2009. The figures were drawn from a report by Mabili consultants.

20   The poorest five million South Africans received about 0.2% of national income (via wages and social grants), while the richest five million pocketed 51% of national income. The mean household income per year of the poorest 10% was R 4 314 (USD 540) in 2005–06; for the richest 10% it was R 405 646 (USD 50 700) (Statistics SA, 2008a).

21   The Gini coefficient is a measure of inequality. Zero (0) represents complete equality and one represents complete inequality (ie one person owns the entire wealth of a society).

22   Ostensibly a pittance, social grants nevertheless reduce income inequality by around eight percentage points.

23   Nitpicking perhaps, but to a small extent these patterns have also been affected by demographic changes. White South Africans in the mid-2000s accounted for a slightly smaller share of the population compared with the mid-1990s, while Africans' share of the population grew slightly. Even if incomes remained static over that period, that shift would increase the per capita income of whites and decrease that of Africans.

24   The average income for coloured households was R 79 400 (USD 9 900) and for Indian or Asian households it was R 135 000 (USD 16 900).

25   These are based on nominal income data for each of the years and were not adjusted for inflation.

26   This is usually schematised in a Theil index, which disaggregates inequality into 'between-group' and 'within-group' components.

27   Those distortions can be politically costly. In the US, for example, it has been argued that the failure to adequately measure the impact of social spending enabled right-wing opponents of welfare to claim that welfare had failed. See Glennerster, H (2000) 'US poverty and poverty measurement: the past twenty five years', CASE Paper No. 42, Centre for Analysis of Social Exclusion, London School of Economics, October; cited in Meth (2007b).

28   Joel Netshitenzhe, *Business Day*, 26 March 2003, cited in Meth (2007b:16).

29   For more, see Meth (2006:55), where he describes as 'risible' government's attempts to value the impact of social wage. Meth and Dias' earlier analysis (2003) acknowledged improvements in the social wage, but found that some four million people became poor between 1999 and 2002 (even if the social wage was evaluated at generous levels).

30   This is why 'non-bankable' forms of social wage cannot be used to determine income inequality.

31   Most studies of the relationship between education and earnings exclude non-earners from their regression analyses, as Meth (2007b:69) points out. Keswell and Poswell (2002) analysed the 2000 Labour Force Survey (LFS) data, taking pains to avoid that pitfall and discovered that returns on education trace a convex path, falling steadily up to about Grade 10 and rising sharply after Grade 12. Meth's review of 2004 LFS data points in a similar direction.

32   Department of Finance budget Review 1998 and 1999, Pretoria; 'Development elements of give-and-take budget outflank critics', *SouthScan*, Vol. 15, No. 4, 25 February 2000.

33   For more detailed picture, see CALS, COHRE and the Norwegian Centre for Human Rights (2008) 'Mapping SA's water services at the local level: An analysis of 15 South African municipalities and their approaches to water services provision', CALS, Johannesburg. Meanwhile, Bond (2010) provides a withering analysis of water provision.

34   See also David McDonald, 'Getting the facts right', *Mail & Guardian*, 17 December 2004,

35   Three percent of the 11.5 million households (each with four inhabitants on average) equals about 1.38 million people. Make allowance for the fact that not every household has access to piped water and the number of persons affected by cut-offs would be at least one million.

36   Unless they are sensitive in design, surveys may *underestimate* the numbers of people deprived of water or electricity due to affordability. People with prepaid meters, for example, effectively 'cut themselves off' when they are unable to pay to resume their supply of water or electricity. Since no outside entity is cutting them off, many surveys miss these 'auto cut-offs'. Similarly, 'trickle' valves (that slow the flow and amount of water) are increasingly used by municipalities to prevent households from exceeding their free allotment of water—again, a form of rationing and inconveniencing that escapes the casual gaze. 'The problem of water cut-offs has not gone away', McDonald has warned, but it has been 'transformed by a new set of cost recovery systems, technologies and discourses'.

37   Instead, the current tariff pattern in Johannesburg, for examples, does the opposite. Tariff steps are steep for the first increments of consumption, then level out—a pattern that benefits high-volume users. Much more equitable would be a pattern where tariffs increase slowly for the first 50 or so kilolitres (per month), then increase more sharply as volume rises. See Bond (2010) for a stinging critique of South Africa's water policy.

38   Mkandawire (2005) provides an insightful overview of the targeting versus universalism debate.

39   Those services included electricity, piped water on site, refuse removal and flush toilets on site. Makgetla compared data from the Labour Force Survey (Statistics SA, 2004) and the October Household Survey (Statistics SA, 1996).

40   Transfers from central government tripled in the 2000s, reaching about R 50 billion (USD 6.3 billion) in 2009. But they were scheduled to level out at the end of the decade, just as the economic recession hit hard. Bear in mind that those increases were not all destined for basic infrastructure and service provision: a large share of the transfers financed the building or upgrading of stadiums, airports and related facilities for the 2010 Soccer World Cup.

41   Neva Makgetla, 'Municipal spending tells the same old story', *Business Day*, 10 December 2008.

42   The massive hikes in electricity tariffs approved in 2010 almost certainly will feed this discontent if payment defaults lead to electricity cut-offs.

43   SA Press Association, 'SA's municipalities in "state of paralysis"', *Mail & Guardian*, 10 June 2009.

44   See Muchena Zigomo, 'SA govt plans revised farm takeover law', *Mail & Guardian*, 8 October 2009.

45   That does not mean that whites own the rest. National and provincial government owns about 27% of land, while municipalities own a further, undetermined proportion. The Deeds Registry Database does not match land-ownership data against population groups. See Yolandi Groenewald, 'Who owns what land in South Africa?', *Mail & Guardian*, 23 January 2009.

46   Muchena Zigomo, 'SA govt plans revised farm takeover law', *Mail & Guardian*, 8 October 2009.

47   See, for instance, Ben Cousins (2005). 'Agrarian reform and the "two economies": Transforming South Africa's countryside', IDS Seminar Series, June 17, Institute for Development Studies, Sussex University.

48   Along with momentary factors, the removal of state support to farmers and cuts in tariffs on agricultural commodities have left local farmers vulnerable against their subsidy-supported European competitors. See Mathabo le Roux, 'ANC concedes agricultural output trumps land reform', *Business Day*, 18 October 2008.

49   Aliber's study assessed three significant land reform projects. In the Maluti-a-Phofung project in the eastern Free State 'very few new land-based livelihoods [were] being created', while a set of 10 projects on commercial farms in Theewaterskloof (Western Cape) showed very little potential of promoting economic development. 'From a rural development perspective, land reform is presently having very limited impact,' the study concluded (Aliber, 2006b:8).

50   One in five children in the Eastern Cape experienced hunger in 2007— not surprising, one would think, given that the province has some of the highest levels of child poverty and unemployment in the country. Yet so does Limpopo, but 'only' 9% of children reported going hungry there in the same year (Statistics SA, 2003 & 2008c).

51   The 'hunger' question in the General Household Survey provides 'notoriously weak data', according to the Children's Institute (2009b), not least because an adult in the household (not the children themselves) answers the question. Still, if there is a reporting bias it is probably fairly consistent across each survey year, so the overall trend in reported hunger should be fairly accurate (even if the actual levels of hunger are less so).

52   Thirteen Integrated Sustainable Rural Development Programme (ISRDP) nodes and eight Urban Renewal Programme (URP) nodes.

53   Technically there are two types of malnutrition: micronutrient and protein-energy malnutrition. The former is caused by poor diet and is especially damaging to the cognitive development and disease resistance in children and to the health of mothers in childbirth. Micronutrient malnutrition takes a large toll in lives lost and in quality of life (Academy of Science of SA, 2007).

54   In 2007, 17% of African children experienced hunger, as did 11% of children classified as coloured under the apartheid system. Among Indians and Asians the figure was 1% and among whites it was 0.1% (Statistics SA, 2008c).

55   One in 20 (5%) children younger than 10 years was severely stunted in 2005, a slight improvement since 1999, when almost 7% were severely stunted (Labadarios *et al*, 2007).

56   ANC, 'A unified, equitable and integrated National Health System that benefits all South Africans', *ANC Today*, Vol. 29, No. 9 (24–30 July).

57   Clare Kapp, 'South Africa heads into elections in a sorry state of health', *Lancet*, Vol. 373, 24 January 2009.

58   A 'maternal death' is defined as the death of a woman while pregnant or within 42 days of termination of that pregnancy due to any cause related to her pregnancy or its management.

59   When research commissioned by government confirmed these trends, the former minister of health, Manto Tshabalala-Msimang, reportedly tried to excise data describing the underlying causes (35% of infant and child deaths were attributed to AIDS) from the final document; see Tamar Kahn, 'Experts defy minister of death figures', *Business Day*, 12 March 2008. South Africa's child-mortality rate is now worse than Egypt's or Peru's, for example. There were 25 deaths of children younger than five years per 100 000 live births in Peru in 2006 and 35 in Egypt. See Victora, Black, Bryce (2007).

60   About 300 000 HIV-positive women give birth to infants each year in South Africa; see Patrick, M and Stephen, C (2007) *Saving children 2005: a survey of child healthcare in South Africa*, Medical Research Council Unit for Maternal and Infant Health Care Strategies, Cape Town.

61 These are very likely underestimates, given the poor standard of data collection and collation in the public-health system. See, for example, Schneider *et al* (2007) and Von Holdt and Murphy (2007).

62 Médecins Sans Frontièrs *et al* (2007) 'Khayelitsha annual activity report 2007–2008: comprehensive TB/HIV services at primary health-care level', Cape Town.

63 The actual number of maternal deaths is likely higher, since these statistics only capture deaths in public-health settings. The maternal death rate is at least five times higher in women with HIV, compared with their uninfected peers (Black *et al*, 2009).

64 Literally 'porridge and meat'.

65 See, for example, Walker, P (1989) *Famine early warning systems: victims and destitution*, Earthscan Publications, London.

66 See, for example, De Waal, A (1989) *Famine that kills: Darfur, Sudan, 1984–1985*, Clarendon Press; Keen, D (1994) *The benefits of famine: a political economy of famine and relief in southwestern Sudan, 1983–1989*, Princeton University Press.

67 See Hickey and Mohan (2003) for a critique of the efforts of post-development theorists to refurbish those traditions.

68 *Ubuntu* is a humanist philosophy that centres on people's allegiances and obligations to one another and which is expressed in the idea that one exists through one's fellow human beings.

69 Cited in Lund (2008:2).

70 This is what Margaret Thatcher had in mind when she declared that 'there is no such thing as society; there are individual men and women, and there are families'. Interview 23 September 1987, as quoted in by Douglas Keay, *Women's Own* magazine, 31 October 1987, pp. 8–10.

71 Mutangadura's (2000) research findings in urban and rural Manicaland, Zimbabwe, are instructive. Fully 95% of respondents said it was difficult getting relatives and friends to help with loans or child fostering. Community support mainly involved food and clothing and rarely extended to assistance in paying school or healthcare fees or rent.

72 This valorisation takes many forms. Ferguson (2007) has also pointed out the striking reclamation of the imagery of urban poverty in post-apartheid South Africa. During the anti-apartheid struggle, a standardised visual vocabulary of peri-urban poverty, despair and oppression was deployed effectively to mobilise solidarity and action against the apartheid regime. Even though impoverished and poorly serviced shack settlements endure, those imageries are now valorised as examples of mettle, creativity and community spirit: 'The same rows of tiny cinderblock houses and rusted shacks that formerly stood as proof of apartheid's bankruptcy are now increasingly understood as places of hope and possibility—sites of development, not proof of development's failure' (Ferguson, 2007:75).

73 This veritable cult of small enterprise has flourished also in industrialised countries, despite survey evidence from OECD countries that 'increases in the proportion of self-employment appear to produce *lower* not higher GDP' (Sender, 2000).

74 Two of the six 'binding constraints' that handicap the economy, according to the AsgiSA document, are 'barriers to entry, limits to competition and limited new investment opportunities' and 'the regulatory environment and the burden on small and medium enterprises (SMEs)'. See http://www.info.gov.za/asgisa/

75 Neil MacFarquhar, 'Big banks draw big profits from microloans to poor', *New York Times*, 13 April 2010.

76 Parminder Bahra, 'Microfinance comes under the microscope', *The Times* [London], 28 April 2009.

77 Neil MacFarquhar, 'Big banks draw big profits from microloans to poor', *New York Times*, 13 April 2010.

78 Parminder Bahra, 'Microfinance comes under the microscope', *The Times* [London], 28 April 2009.

79   'Microcredit may not work wonders but it does help the entrepreneurial poor', *The Economist*, 16 July 2009.

80   This was the first large-scale randomised trial of access to microfinance ever done. In it, 52 of 104 very similar slums in Hyderabad were randomly selected to receive new branches of a microfinance outfit called Spandana. The outcomes in the two groups of slums were then compared. The study is available at: http://www.povertyactionlab.org/papers/101_Duflo_Microfinance_Miracle.pdf

81   For example, a study of 1 800 households in rural Bangladesh at first glance revealed impressive outcomes: in households that had borrowed from the Grameen Bank, 62% of school-age sons were in school, compared with only 34% of their peers in households that had not borrowed. But closer examination showed there was, in fact, no causality between the loans and school enrolment; households that were more likely to have children in school were the ones most likely to sign up for microfinance. See 'Microcredit may not work wonders but it does help the entrepreneurial poor', *The Economist*, 16 July 2009. Earlier studies found that more than half the households benefiting from Grameen loans were still not able to meet their basic nutritional needs—after eight years of loans. A 1995 World Bank study found that Grameen loans had not had significant impact on rural women's wages, though it did increase men's wages. See Gina Neff, 'Microcredit, microresults', *Left Business Observer*, No. 74, October 1996.

82   See Hulme, D and Mosley, P (1996) *Finance Against Poverty*, Routledge, London.

83   Part of the problem lies with the vague and slack use of the concept 'poverty' and with the tendency to ignore differentiation within communities and households classified as 'poor'. As a consequence, projects intended to assist the most vulnerable households can end up being dominated by households that are relatively better off, as Sender (2000) found in Mpumalanga.

84   See Henwood, D (1994) 'Crime wave!', *Left Business Observer*, No. 63 (May).

85   The average on the rest of the African continent was 140 per 100 000 people; the global average is 87 per 100 000 inhabitants. The bulk of the other injury-related deaths are due to traffic accidents. These data are for various years in the 2000s and are drawn from Seedat *et al* (2009) which provides the original data sources for each of these statistics.

86   Most homicide victims are Africans, though the highest homicide rates are reported among persons classified as coloured under the apartheid system.

87   Cases registered with the police in that year included 71 000 sexual assaults, 191 000 common assaults, 204 000 assaults with intent to do grievous bodily harm and 121 000 aggravated robberies.

88   The rape of babies and toddlers is not uncommon; 511 cases of sexual assault against children younger than three years were reported to the police in 2008/09 (SAPS, 2009).

89   Quoted in *The Sunday Independent* [Johannesburg], 21 July 1996.

90   Typically, both victims and perpetrators have high blood-alcohol concentrations. Studies in the Western Cape have found that two-thirds of female victims had blood-alcohol concentrations at least twice that of the legal limit for driving (0.11g/ml). See Mathews, S *et al* (2009) 'Alcohol use and its role in female homicides in the Western Cape, South Africa', *Journal of Studies on Alcohol & Drugs*, Vol. 70, pp. 321–7.

91   The rate of reported rapes was 117 per 100 000 in 2005–06 and has decreased only slightly since the mid-1990s (SAPS, 2006).

92   In most of those cases, the perpetrators were men known to the victims. By contrast, about half of the rapes of adult women are perpetrated by strangers.

93   This is not rare. The WHO's multi-country study on violence against women, for example, found that more than 40% of surveyed women in parts of Ethiopia, Peru and Tanzania said their husbands were justified in beating them if they disobeyed them and at least 20% of them said a beating was in order if they did not complete the housework (Garcia-Moreno *et al*, 2005).

94   Cited by Marks (2002:21) who notes the similar conclusions reached by Mamphele Ramphele in her research on single-sex hostels in Cape Town where, as paraphrased by Marks, 'male violence against women was the unfortunate outcome of their own exploitation, subordination and lack of control in the wider society'; see Ramphele (1993).

95   See, for example, Delius and Glaser (2002); Ouzgane and Morrell (2005); and Hunter (2005 & 2006).

96   The gendered aspects of the 2008 pogroms were noteworthy (see Chapter thirteen). In some places, women from elsewhere in Africa were deliberately targeted for assault and rape. This reflected the highly sexualised nature of male violence and domination and the fact (evident in many other countries, as well) that women's bodies often are transformed into sites for constructing and asserting ethnic and national identities.

97   See, for example, Garcia-Moreno *et al* (2005); Dunkle *et al* (2004); and Hotaling & Sugarman (1986).

98   Evidence presented to the Parliamentary Portfolio Committee on Women, Children and People with Disabilities by the country's largest children's NGO, Childline, 26 August 2009, Parliament, Cape Town.

99   Between March 2008 and March 2009, for example, 912 people died at the hands of the police; see Wyndham Hartley, 'Big rise in numbers of deaths at hands of police, says watchdog', *Business Day*, 24 June 2009.

100   A study comparing socioeconomic inequalities and rates of violence in 63 countries found that severe income inequality, low economic development and high levels of gender inequity were strong predictors of rates of violence. Aside from income inequality, high levels of unemployment among young men were the factor most strongly associated with homicides and major assaults (Wood, 2006).

CHAPTER EIGHT

The social protection system

What is the primary aim of society? It is to maintain the inalienable rights of man. What is the foremost of these rights? The right to exist. Therefore, the first social law is that which guarantees all members of society the means of existence; all others are subordinate to that.

—*Maximilien Robespierre*[1]

Social expenditure in South Africa

South Africa has become an unusually big social spender for a middle-income country. Welfare spending in 2009/10 amounted to R 94 billion (USD 12.3 billion) or 3.5% of GDP (up from R 18 billion, USD 2.4 billion, or 2% of GDP in 2000/01).[2] The Finance Ministry regards the continued expansion of social grants as fiscally unsustainable and prefers to see grant provision and take-up tracking population growth (which has slowed to about 1%).[3] Political and social pressure, however, forced it to relent.

The number of beneficiaries increased significantly after 2000 and rose steeply after 2003, as eligibility was broadened (Seekings, 2006). The estimated 2.6 million recipients of pensions and social grants in 1994 increased to 5.85 million in 2003 and totalled almost 14 million in 2010.[4] By 2007, these transfers constituted more than 12% of the total income of African households (Statistics SA, 2009a)[5], with female-headed households particularly reliant on them. A large proportion of low-income households would probably be unviable without these grants. About one third of adult women were on the grants register in 2007, a proportion that has increased since.[6]

The main social grants

In twentieth-century welfare states, social policy and particularly social protection, was seen as a powerful instrument for transformation. It was assigned at least five complementary functions: it had to enhance protection, redistribution, production, reproduction and freedom (Mkandawire, 2007). Most of the 'late industrialising' countries approached social policy in that manner (Pierson, 2003), but in the Anglo-capitalist countries, social policy has been associated mainly with technical interventions aimed at reducing poverty and providing some protection against destitution. South Africa fits this mould and, like many other countries, it is keenly aware of the political and ideological value of social protection schemes for repairing state legitimacy and fostering political consent.

South Africa's current social protection system centres on five major grants: the Old Age Pension, Disability Grant, Child Support Grant, Foster Child Grant and the Care Dependency Grant. Each is targeted and means-tested.[7] The grants are administered by a separate national government agency, the South African Social Security Agency.

About 2.5 million persons received the old-age pension in 2009/10 (up from 2.1 million in 2006/07).[8] The qualifying age for men has been lowered to 60 years, the same as for women.[9] Often described as a poverty-alleviation tool, the pension (worth R 1 080 or USD 135 per month) enables many households that otherwise might have sunk into destitution to remain afloat—as long as the recipient is alive. In the 1990s, pensions had eclipsed migrant remittances both in terms of size and reliability as a source of economic support for poor rural households (Case & Deaton, 1998). Households receiving pensions have been shown to spend more on food and education and less on alcohol and tobacco than other households (Maitra & Ray, 2003).

Disproportionate reliance on the old-age pension as a poverty-alleviating instrument will probably backfire because of the demographic impact of the AIDS and TB epidemics. Over the next 20 to 30 years proportionally fewer adults will live to pensionable age, thus limiting the pension's spill-on benefits. Those epidemics are also depleting the pension's benefits in other respects. The epidemics' staggering toll among young adults means that the elderly increasingly are denied the intermittent financial and other support younger relatives used to provide. Yet, many of these nominally 'retired' persons, especially women, now have to perform care, fostering and child-rearing work. Given the dearth of income-earning opportunities for women and the burdens they bear, there is a strong case for lowering the qualifying age for women to 55 years (Legido-Quigley, 2003).

By 2010, more than 30% of households (compared with 17% in 2003) were receiving at least one child support grant and 9.4 million children were benefiting from this cash transfer, which has been expanded considerably in the past decade (Statistics SA, 2009a). Initially targeting children up to the age of six years, the eligibility age has been extended to 14 years, which largely accounts for the sharp increase in beneficiaries. The cabinet has agreed to gradually extend eligibility to children aged 15 to 18 years, though there is pressure (especially from Treasury) to make this means-tested grant conditional, as well.[10] Its potential benefit, however, is diminished by the amount payable: at R 250 or USD 31 per month, it barely approaches minimum child-raising costs.[11]

The numbers of people receiving the foster-child grant also increased steeply in the 2000s, a trend that will persist as the AIDS orphan crisis worsens. An estimated 1.9 million children have lost at least one parent to AIDS (Statistics SA, 2009b); most of them are cared for by families or extended kin (Richter & Desmond, 2008), some of whom receive foster-care grants. About 450 000 children benefited from the grant in 2007.[12] But the grant is entangled in a conundrum. At R 680 (USD 85) per month in 2010, it is worth 2.5 times as much as the child-support grant. A significant share of welfare resources is being funnelled into a labour- and procedure-intensive grant channel that can benefit a very limited number of children (Meintjies et al, 2003) making it an inefficient social protection mechanism.

Moreover, with AIDS sapping administrative capacity in the public sector and simultaneously increasing the need for foster care, the management of this grant—and of child-protection services in general—has come under extreme strain. Neglect and abuse of children (including orphans) are widespread enough to demand effective oversight. But the scale of need is swamping social workers, often preventing them from performing other key tasks (such as monitoring the well-being of children placed in foster care and probing cases of alleged abuse). At a minimum, the ranks of social workers (and the resources available to them) need to be increased.

Protecting orphans and vulnerable children

Financial grants can serve as powerful incentives for fostering orphans. In the context of scarce income opportunities, however, they might also tempt arrangements where some applicants provide minimal, nominal care for orphans in order to access financial support that can be used to sustain families that are already in distress (Loening-Voysey, 2002). In the literature, this is usually (and misleadingly) referred to as a 'perverse incentive'. In a society pummelled by the world's worst AIDS epidemic and by pervasive impoverishment, a social security system that is both targeted and means-tested creates incentives for people to craft ways to access one of the available grants. Those incentives, as the Department of Social Development has noted (2006:ix) 'are not necessarily perverse'. 'When poorly-designed social policy creates perverse incentives,' as Charles Meth (2008:26) puts it, 'people act rationally in taking advantage of them.'

More generally, in the South African context, targeting orphans for state support is neither equitable nor cost-efficient: it misdirects scarce and vital resources and is based on dubious understandings of children's circumstances. In impoverished communities, the differences in socioeconomic circumstances and life prospects of orphans and non-orphans are small and tend to be eclipsed by the hardship and deprivation those children share.[13] The central issue is less the 'condition' of orphanhood than the social arrangements that permit the exclusion, abandonment and abuse of children, orphaned or not. Children's needs, not their orphan status, should determine the provision of support (JLICA, 2009).

The most sensible approach would be to shift away from targeting orphans and instead adopt a universalist approach that benefits all children in need. This could be done by providing a child-support grant for all children and dropping the current means test—a variant, in other words, of the universal income grant (discussed later) (Meintjies et al, 2003). The goal would be to provide stronger social security to many more South African children, vast numbers of whom live in dire circumstances. The overriding ethic would be one of universalism and equity, rather than differential and happenstance relief.

The money or your life

Meanwhile, demand for the disability grants (worth a maximum R 1 010 or USD 126 per month in 2009) has risen to such an extent that the Treasury has grumbled about the fiscal implications. Available to 'severely physically and mentally disabled persons' between the ages of 18 and 65 years, this grant reached 1.4 million South Africans in 2008 (up from 1.08 million in 2003) (Statistics SA, 2009a).[14] AIDS is responsible for a significant part of that trend, though not all; persons living with HIV and whose CD4 counts are lower than a specified threshold also qualify for the grant.

For many impoverished, AIDS-sick beneficiaries, the grant involves an odious dilemma: once grant recipients benefit from antiretroviral (ARV) treatment, their CD4 counts rise, rendering them neither 'disabled' nor eligible for the disability grant once their eligibility status is reviewed (Nattrass, 2006a & 2006b).[15] Yet, the grant very often sustains not only the beneficiary, but entire households. A survey in Khayelitsha, Cape Town, for example, found that disability grants contributed 40–50% of the total income in those households receiving the grant (Nattrass, 2004).[16]

There is considerable anecdotal evidence that some people opt to *discontinue* ARV treatment rather than lose their disability grants—exercising a literal, pitiless choice between 'the money or your life'.[17] Besides compromising their health, this also boosts the chances that drug-resistant HIV strains could become prevalent enough to undermine the ARV treatment programme. On the other hand, as Nattrass (2006b) has highlighted, a moral conundrum arises if HIV-positive persons are allowed to retain their disability grants after their health has been restored by ARV therapy. In essence, HIV status then functions as a criterion for access to financial support, with equally needy but HIV-negative persons (without other disabilities) not qualifying for the grant. Little wonder that Guy Standing (2007:24) regards South Africa's disability grant 'as one of the worst-designed cash-transfer schemes in the world'.

Origins of the system

South Africa's social protection system dates to the early twentieth century and was assembled piecemeal. An old-age pension was introduced in the late 1920s and a disability grant followed a decade later. Initially, both explicitly excluded blacks, though this changed in the late 1930s and 1940s, when benefits were scaled according to racial categories. Other instruments, including a state maintenance grant, were added later. As the apartheid system became evermore Byzantine and obtuse, welfare functions were parcelled out to numerous state entities. By the late 1980s, 13 'national',[18] four provincial and three co-ordinating departments were nominally providing welfare services. Yet, there was virtually no form of welfare support for vulnerable African children (Lund, 2008). Fusing this jumble of bureaucracies into a relatively coherent system became one of the early achievements of the post-apartheid era. In particular, replacing the old state maintenance grant with a new child-support grant proved to be one of the most far-reaching changes in the post-apartheid social development landscape.

The ideological template on which social security would be restructured was laid out in the 1996 Lund Report (RSA, 1996) and the 1997 White Paper on Social

Welfare (RSA, 1997). Dubbed 'developmental social welfare' the new system would be geared at overcoming the racial inequity of the previous system. Similar to the overhaul of the health system, the emphasis was on preventive rather than curative interventions. The notion of 'exit strategies' was prominent and much effort went into promoting 'community development' to counteract possible 'dependency' on grants, as well as linking welfare recipients with other income opportunities.[19] Instead of the 'paternalistic old mode of welfare' came a more 'development-oriented' approach, which also saw a role for 'social assistance as one route to poverty alleviation' (Lund, 2008:13).[20] Nonetheless, it has remained targeted and means-tested (though not conditional on certain actions).

For all its transformative ambitions, the new approach reproduced key principles that had shaped welfare thinking for decades. The social security system was assigned two basic roles, each of which assumes that waged employment provides a sufficient basis for social inclusion. One part, entailing a range of social grants, is designed to assist people who, due to age or disability, cannot reasonably be expected to fend for themselves by selling their labour. The other part includes various employer- and worker-subsidised protective mechanisms (all tied to employment status). This follows convention, which prefers a system of social insurance and means-tested social assistance (Standing, 2007). It also conformed to the outlook of business. In 1997 the South African Chamber of Business had declared that government should not 'interfere' in the market but should 'put in place poverty safety nets to assist those that are in dire straits until the economy improves to the point where the majority of citizens benefit from growth'.[21]

Most of the social safety net maintained by the state therefore assumes that able-bodied adults can earn a living by performing wage labour (Nattrass, 2004). Imbedded in the system is a double fiction: the idea that employment is available to those who seek it and that wage incomes ensure wellbeing. As shown in Chapter six, in the context of very high unemployment and increasingly poor wages and terms of employment, large numbers of vulnerable workers fall between those two stools: they are not eligible for state grants, nor do they benefit from highly rationed employment-based provisions.

The substantial expansion of social protection since 1994 has been couched also in a stigmatising outlook that frets about 'dependency' and 'handouts' (discussed later). The echoes of apartheid-era social policy discourse are troubling. Alongside the dramatic breaks with the past there has remained a patronising insistence on regarding the poor as 'self-sustaining communities' that are 'able to fulfil functions that capitalism prefers not to assume [...] the functions of social security' (Wolpe, 1972:434–5).[22] This is why COSATU, for example, criticised the 'development social welfare' approach as part of a broader ideological shift that sought to 'divest the state of responsibility and [...] shift the burden from the state to poor communities'.[23] Viviene Taylor, chair of the Taylor Task Team on Social Security set up in 2000, shared the view that social security reform had to be liberated from the shackles of 'community survival and coping mechanism discourse' (see Chapter seven).[24] Alert to the changes occurring the labour market, trade unions began championing the introduction of a universal income grant in a bid to push the boundaries of social security reform.[25]

Hit and miss: means-testing and targeting

Most states are disinclined to provide cash grants that are not tied to certain conditions, a paternalistic approach that finds especially strong support among the middle classes. Internationally, therefore, most cash grants are tied to certain conditions, often involving school enrolment for children and/or health-seeking behaviour. Among the best-known examples are Brazil's *bolsa familia*[26] and Mexico's *opportunidades* scheme,[27] although Bangladesh, Colombia, Honduras and Nicaragua are among other countries that have introduced similar programmes.

Chico de Oliveira (2006:22) has criticised the *bolsa familia* for depoliticising 'the question of poverty, turning inequality into an administrative problem'.[28] Other critics see those approaches as expensive, inefficient and 'offensive to basic egalitarian principles' (Standing, 2007:12) and point to research which suggests that 'it is typically the poorest and most vulnerable who will find it most costly to comply with any conditionalities, and are therefore the most likely to be deprived of benefits if they fail to do so' (Freeland, 2007:77).[29] Moreover, studies suggest that the desired outcome (such as school attendance) tends to be linked to the receipt of money and not to the conditionality of school attendance. More families send their children to school when they can afford to do so. Conditional grants impose enormous administrative burdens on social-development bureaucracies, which typically are under-resourced, making them inappropriate in settings where state capacities and resources are at a premium.[30] Even USAID (2004) has acknowledged the positive aspects of unconditional cash grants.[31]

Means testing and targeting are administratively expensive and tend to be difficult, especially when it is tough to determine an individual's income and when that income is likely to fluctuate significantly.[32] They also run the risk of creating arbitrary divides between those who benefit from social grants and those who do not, as Everatt (2008) has shown.[33] In South Africa's case, the main social grants are not (yet) conditional. Eligibility is determined not by need, but by age or health status; those who meet these criteria are then means-tested. This means that many ineligible households that are at least as insecure as their eligible counterparts, do not qualify for social grants. The reason is obvious: the grants were not designed primarily to combat poverty. So a divide is created among poor households, separating those that have no state support from those 'very similar households that receive comparatively generous support simply because they are "lucky" enough to include grant-eligible children, elderly or disabled persons' (Ferguson, 2007:78). It is clear that these grants are having an overall poverty-reducing effect, but they achieve this through a spray-gun approach that still misses many people who are in dire straits.

In fact, in places where very large proportions of the population are poor, targeted cash transfers defy common sense, especially if transfers to the 'non-poor' can be taxed back (which they can and at minimal cost) (Mkandawire, 2005). This is basically the logic behind a universal income grant, as we discuss later. Moreover, targeting requires thresholds (usually determined by income) that are inevitably arbitrary and often fictive. Anyone who has been within touching distance of a livelihood sustained on R 15 (USD 2) a day knows that the notion of a 'poverty line' (which is among the common thresholds) is a cold-hearted fabrication. Eighteen rand a day would be marginally 'easier' than R 15 day, but it hardly banishes insecurity and vulnerability. And it certainly does not make the beneficiary 'non-poor'.

The logic of means testing, targeting and conditionality also feeds the evergreen notions of the 'deserving' and 'undeserving' poor. Historically, that line has been drawn on the basis of a person's capacity to work for a wage. Both social security and social assistance have been structured accordingly and become available usually when an accident, illness, disability or age prevents a person from selling their labour or when a person (temporarily) loses a job. The state (or another designated entity) then provides support to those who are insured against contingency risks, or it gives 'charitably' to those it deems incapable of performing labour. The principle of reciprocity may appear to be the hinge in this relationship, but the act of 'charity' is laden with power and authority and functions as a disciplinary tool that services the labour market in general and employers in particular. Crafted is a framework in which

> [t]hose who fall into a state of 'need' (poverty) are deemed to be either culpable in some sense or in 'need' of assistance to return them to the mainstream of society, capable of labour ... [F]ar from reviving the vital sense of social solidarity and universal citizenship, it divides society into saints and sinners. It has been tried before, and it has failed (Standing, 2007:25).

That framework rests on an industrial labour model that only faintly resembles current reality. Increasingly large proportions of workers toil in circumstances and for wages that are at best marginally governed by state-managed regulatory systems and protection. These circumstances are not aberrations or unfortunate instances of 'market failure': they are chronic and systemic. Joblessness accounts for a great deal of impoverishment in South Africa, but it is sobering to discover that four million people living below the poverty line belong to 700 000 households in which *at least one person works* for a wage that is too meager to lift them out of poverty (Meth, 2006 & 2008). As discussed in some detail (see Chapter six), employment does not automatically translate into wellbeing (Barchiesi, 2004).[34] Today's realities are strikingly similar to those that prevailed more than a century ago in Victorian England, when, as Karl Marx and Friedrich Engels famously noted, 'the modern labourer instead of rising with the progress of industry, sinks deeper and deeper below the conditions of existence of his class' (in Tucker, 1978:43).

But most governments have a visceral aversion to boosting social assistance. Two arguments tend to do the rounds. Firstly, doing so is deemed economically irresponsible and is seen to carry a risk of fiscal populism. Secondly, it dilutes the allocative, arbitrating and disciplinary authority of the market. These claims are often compressed into the assertion that social transfers do not amount to 'productive' spending. Hence the hand-wringing about 'dependency', the bootstrap emphasis on self-help and coping strategies, volunteerism and community solidarity and the appeal of coercive forms of social assistance such as workfare schemes and conditional grants. But perhaps the most routine objection is that social grants discourage people from working for a wage.

The impact of social protection on labour supply

Critics claim that social grants distort labour markets by discouraging persons from seeking waged employment and that they increase 'dependency' on the state. 'If you have all these nice social benefits,' ANC parliamentarian Michael Masutha fretted in 2000, 'where is the incentive to want to go back to work?'[35] The evidence for this view is contentious. South Africa's main social grants target persons who, due to age, frailty or disability, are *not* expected to fend for themselves by engaging in waged employment. Logically, the grants cannot discourage the beneficiaries from employment.

But grants often are distributed among several household and/or family members. Might they therefore interfere with the 'normal' job-seeking behaviour of those secondary beneficiaries? World Bank documents, in particular, have advanced the view that old-age pension beneficiaries tend to withdraw adult children from the labour market (Bertrand *et al*, 2003). Yet the evidence from South Africa and elsewhere suggests that, in poor settings with high unemployment rates, cash transfers tend to have a negligible impact on labour-market participation. Nicaragua's conditional cash-transfer programme (which is linked to children's school attendance and the family's participation in maternal and child-health programmes) was found to have a 'very small' impact on the labour supply of extremely poor households (Arcia, 2002). In the case of Brazil's *bolsa escola* 'those receiving the stipend are the ones who work more' (Schwartzman, 2005).[36] In South Africa research shows that persons in households with access to pensions and other social grants tend to increase their participation in the labour market faster than individuals in households that do not receive grants (Posel, Fairburn & Lund, 2004).

When Statistics SA (2009a) analysed data from the 2003 and 2007 General Household Surveys, it detected a significant drop in unemployment among both grant- *and* non-grant-recipient households. Employment gains, however, were stronger in the households that did *not* receive any grants: ostensibly grist for the mill of those expressing misgivings about the grant 'dependency' and 'perverse incentives'. Yet such a conclusion would be corrupt, for two obvious reasons. First, more than 40% of grant recipients are *unable* to work due to age or disability. Second, almost all the other grants go to adults (a very large majority of them African women, mostly younger than 35 years) who are raising or fostering children or who are tending the ill and frail. They are working, but they are not being remunerated for that care and reproductive labour. Besides, unemployment levels typically exceed

50% among young African women. Even in an economic upturn, they still have the weakest prospects of landing work that pays a living wage. In fact, women's median monthly earnings in 2007 were so low (about R 950 or USD 120) that they matched the value of the disability grant (R 960 at the time).[37] So do households receiving grants tend to be less economically active? The Statistics SA analysis (2009a:31) says no: 'The findings [...] suggest that this is not true for low-earning households.' The pattern noted earlier, it says, 'may be more related to the improved coverage of the social grants system, i.e. increased inclusivity of those who are unable to work' (Statistics SA, 2009:26).

Grants, poverty reduction and development

South Africa currently has no better poverty-alleviating tool than its social transfer system—a backhanded compliment, given the absence of an overarching anti-poverty strategy. Careful analysis of poverty trends shows that expanded eligibility and greater take-up of social grants (especially the child-support grant) have been the single-biggest cause of declining poverty levels since 2000 (Meth, 2007 & 2006; Everatt *et al*, 2006).[38] Among AIDS-affected households in Free State province, social grants were also found to reduce inequality and decrease the prevalence, depth and severity of poverty (Booysen & Van der Berg, 2005). The official statistical agency in 2008 confirmed these interpretations and attributed the increase in incomes among the poorest 30% of South Africans since 2001 mainly to social grants, terming them 'a major source of income for the poor' (Statistics SA, 2008b). The observed effects include reduced stunting in children and better nutrition levels (Aguero, Carter, Woolard, 2006), and a positive association between receipt of the child-support grant and school enrolment of young children (Case, Hosegood, Lund, 2004). According to Statistics SA (2009a) children in low-earning households receiving a cash transfer were significantly more likely to attend school compared with those in low-earning households that did not receive any such assistance.[39]

About 43% of households in 2007 received at least one social grant (up from 36% in 2003) and in one half of those households, pensions or grants constituted the *primary source of income* in that year. By way of comparison, wages were the main source of income in 38% of those households, and remittances in 9% of them (Statistics SA, 2009a).[40] It is estimated that at least 40% of jobless South Africans live in households that survive mainly on social grants, as do one in five workers in the 'informal' sector. What their circumstances would be like without these grants is difficult to imagine: in 2007, 40% of households relying on grants still found it difficult to meet their food needs consistently. (Alarmingly, almost 10% of households that relied primarily on wage incomes also failed to meet their food needs at least some of the time.)[41]

A *political* dependency has been created for the ANC government, however. Unless or until a meaningful anti-poverty strategy takes effect, social grants are the main stopgap. They address, for now, a problem most democratic regimes in deeply unequal societies face: the need to maintain *political legitimacy* and attract support from the poor majority, without sparking insubordination from the middle and upper classes (Molyneux, 2008).

There are significant disagreements, though, on how best to tackle poverty. Ranged on one side are the churches, COSATU and the SACP who demand a concerted assault on poverty by expanding welfare provisions and fitting out a fully fledged 'developmental state' (Everatt, 2008). Gathered on the other side are business, senior government officials and much of the media who broadcast antipathy to 'handouts' and 'dependency'. At the same time, though, both 'camps' share a pious faith in job creation (though they disagree on how best to achieve it) and both are wedded to the notion that, ideally, full citizenship is attained chiefly (if not solely) through waged work. But both camps tend to view the issue mainly through a productivist lens and approach grants as traditional welfarist tools. Neglected is the liberating potential of a basic or universal income.

The universal income debate

The concept of a basic or universal income grant dates back to the mid-nineteenth century. Drawing on the thinking of the French socialist Charles Fourier, the philosopher John Stuart Mill argued for such an instrument in the 1848 edition of his *Principles of Political Economy*. It would require, he wrote, that

> a certain minimum is first assigned for the subsistence of every member of the community, whether capable or not of labour. The remainder of the produce is shared in certain proportions, to be determined beforehand, among the three elements, Labour, Capital, and Talent.[42]

Typically, a universal income grant would be available to all adult citizens and would be neither conditional nor targeted or means-tested. Its appeal is self-evident, especially in settings with high levels of unemployment and poverty. Yet the concept triggers visceral resistance, for reasons that go beyond fiscal concerns.

Many West European countries introduced some form of guaranteed minimum-income scheme after the Second World War, but these were highly conditional and were means-tested. Other, conditional variants have included fixed payments to families for each child (irrespective of income level). More closely resembling a universal income grant is an instrument the state of Alaska, in the US, introduced in 1999. Known as the 'Alaska Permanent Fund Dividend' it annually pays each resident a share of the state's oil revenues (Van Parijs, 2000). A localised pilot project was launched in Namibia to illustrate the benefits of such a grant. Within six months, there was evidence of reduced child malnutrition and increased school attendance. Recipients also became more active in income-generating activities (Haarmann *et al*, 2008).[43]

South African trade unions, church organisations and NGOs (and, intermittently, the former Social Development Minister)[44] began championing a universal income in the late 1990s. Formally proposed at the 1998 Presidential Jobs Summit, the envisaged grant was pegged at R 100 per month, an amount unionists believed was politically 'winnable'. Although the grant would be spread thinner than current social transfers, its benefits would extend far wider, they claimed— and without the restrictive, rationing terms. Even if fixed at a low amount, it would have a dramatic effect in reducing the depth of poverty. Financial simulations showed that a grant of R 100 per month for all South Africans could close the poverty gap by 74% (Liebenberg, 2002)[45] and lift about six million people above a poverty line of R 400 (USD 50) per month (Gumede, 2005). Concerned about 'issues of fiscal feasibility' (Barchiesi, 2006:15) the Taylor Committee in 2002 recommended phasing in such a grant by first extending the child-support grant to all children younger than 18 years.

'It's not the money, it's the idea'

Reasons for supporting such an instrument differ widely. In one conception, the grant is seen as a way to help people weather shocks (illness, death, losing a job, etc) and access other, additional sources of income. The grant would help individuals make it through a period of joblessness, retrain and gain new skills. COSATU (2000c), for example, saw the grant as a way to 'alleviate poverty' and for 'laying the foundation for more productive and skilled communities'.[46] It would be part of a wider response to the chronic and significant need for forms of livelihood security that can survive the vagaries, even the failures, of the labour market. In this conception, the grant lacks transformative thrust: it helps brace the current system.[47] In settings such as South Africa, though, the instability and insecurity of wage labour and the steady dissolution of benefits linked to it, demand new forms of income that can *reduce* rather than reinforce dependence on the labour market.

In Ferguson's view (2007), arguments used in favour of a universal income grant merge into a blend of traditional social-democratic and more contemporary neoliberal reasoning. Often marshalled alongside statements about social solidarity, social cohesion and poverty alleviation, for example, are descriptions of the grant as an 'investment' in 'human capital'.[48] The grant then functions less as temporary relief or charity and more as a productive boost, an 'investment' that lubricates individuals' deeper integration into the market system.[49] Others have noted a tendency to portray a universal income as a substitute for other forms of social welfare (Bull, 2001). Related is the occasional claim that such a grant would enable individuals to become 'risk-takers' and, in other words, true neoliberal subjects. Even the Taylor Committee (2002:61)[50] felt that the grant would leave people

> empowered to take the risks needed to break out of the poverty cycle. Rather than serving as a disincentive to engage in higher return activities [the grant] could encourage risk-taking and self-reliance. Such an income could thus become a springboard for development.

Those approaches overlook the radical thrust of such a grant, as we show later. Meanwhile, opponents of a universal income rely on a handful of objections: it would, they claim, be 'too expensive', the effects would be minor,[51] it would distort and reduce labour supply, lower wages, foster dependency and offend the principle of 'social reciprocity'. These claims are easily answered.

The Treasury has opposed the grant from the outset, citing fiscal concerns. Former Finance Minister Trevor Manuel in 2004 claimed that introducing the grant would 'bankrupt the country'. In the next financial year (2005/06), though, revenue collection exceeded budget estimates by R 41.2 billion (USD 5.2 billion), emboldening the Finance Ministry to hand out R 19.1 billion (USD 2.4 billion) in tax cuts in the 2006/07 financial year. As Di Lollo (2006) pointed out, the surplus plus the cuts, hypothetically, could have financed a monthly income of about R 100 (USD 13) for each of the 47 million South Africans in that year.

In the South African context, though, the affordability of such a grant is not simply a fiscal question; it is a moral question, which has to be settled politically. Government approaches the matter in a curious manner: it rejects a universal income grant as 'unaffordable', yet constructs a massive welfare machine. As Everatt (2008:303) notes: 'The dominant voice within the ANC after Mandela was one that chided the poor for remaining poor, rejected [a basic income grant] but was unable to resist pressure for major cash transfers to the poor in the form of social grants.' Clearly, fiscal objections do bend to political and social imperatives.

Meanwhile the principle of 'social reciprocity', which traditionally revolves around participation in the labour market, has been reduced to little more than a fiction in places with deep, structural unemployment. When there are not jobs for one third or more of adults, the grant's potential impact on labour supply would seem to be virtually academic. As for encouraging 'dependency' and sloth, no one

> who has observed the efforts of the poor to scratch a living out of some enterprise that requires endless hours of toil will believe that R 100 per month will put an end to the aspirations of most of them for self-improvement. What cannot be called into question is the welfare improvement in, for example, workerless households, among whom the slightest risk (eg job search requiring some expenditure) threatens an already precarious existence. Their menu of choices could be considerably expanded by the existence of a secure income source, be it ever so small (Meth, 2004:22).

The real objection to an instrument such as the universal income grant lies elsewhere. It is, as former Trade and Industry Minister Alec Erwin is said to have remarked, 'not the money but the idea' that offends.[52] Former Land Affairs minister Thoko Didiza, who headed the ANC's social transformation department, understood this: 'This discussion at the moment is about the values underpinning such a grant', she told reporters in 2002.[53] Government's philosophical approach was straightforward: 'We would rather create work opportunities', explained a spokesperson. 'Only persons who were disabled or ill should get handouts.'[54] The use of the term 'handouts' is revealing. The aversion to a universal income grant seems so ingrained in the ANC that even the supposed 'left turn' at its national conference in 2007 did not gain the grant a mention in the resolutions (ANC, 2007a). Instead, the resolutions contained phrases that would sit comfortably in the programmes of centre-right parties anywhere in the world (ANC, 2007a:13–14):

Whilst many families have access to social grants and other poverty-alleviation programmes, many of these households and communities remain trapped in poverty, are dependent on the state and thus unable to access the opportunities created by the positive economic climate [...] Grants must not create dependency and thus must be linked to economic activity.

The dependency discourse remains dominant and government persists in regarding 'wage labour as the cornerstone of social discipline and inclusion' (Barchiesi, 2006:17). A Presbyterian aversion to 'giving money to the poor' endures.[55]

The radical potential of a universal income

Fighting poverty is not (simply) about the right policies and capacities; it is about the distribution of power, as Ralph Miliband (1974:187) understood:

[T]he trouble, for the poor, is that the forces operating against them are very much stronger than those working in their favour. What is involved here is not recognition, or the discovery of the right policies, or the creation of the right administrative framework, or even the good will of the power-holders. The matter goes deeper than that, and concerns the distribution of power in society.[56]

It is in this respect that social grants contain a radical, emancipating potential, which the South African debate seldom conveys. The key is to uncouple grants from the labour market, which a universal income grant can achieve. For Carole Pateman (2003:88), a guaranteed universal income is the 'emblem of full citizenship'. It becomes an opportunity for imagining, in Barchiesi's (2006:5) phrasing, 'alternative forms of social citizenship [that are] capable of liberating individuals from waged work, labour market dependence and their associated forms of social discipline'.[57] This is a potentially radical and subversive turn that confronts the 'double separation'—from the means of production and the means of subsistence—that is customarily imposed on workers. An unconditional universal income can partially counteract the imbalances of power that typify capitalist class relations:

A generous, unconditional basic income which would allow employees a meaningful exit option from the employment relation that directly transforms the character of power within the class relations of capitalist society (Wright, 2003:79).

This would not amount to an assault on capitalism per se, but the impact potentially reaches much farther than gains in social justice. It endows 'the weakest with bargaining power' (Van Parijs, 2003:10) and, once linked with other efforts to strengthen wellbeing and expand the content of citizenship, it can contribute toward significant redistribution of power, time and liberty within the parameters of that system. It is, potentially, a profoundly emancipating intervention. Its most subversive potential effect is to equip people with the freedom not to sell their labour and to withdraw, at least sporadically, from the 'race to the bottom' between low-skilled workers in high-unemployment settings. The grant thus becomes double-edged. It challenges one of the anchoring principles of Anglo-capitalism in which employment and citizenship is tightly intertwined. And it has the potential to improve the wages and terms of employment for low-skilled workers, if deployed in the context of wider efforts to protect the basic wage and working condition gains won in South Africa in the past four decades.

It has other ramifications, too. By delinking income and basic needs provision from wage labour, a universal income creates the space for critical rethinking of the relations and structures of marriage, employment and citizenship (Pateman, 2003) and for taking up socially productive activities that are not commodified. It potentially limits, perhaps even helps counter, the commodification of life—a vital intervention, particularly in a society in which the market increasingly colonises the social realm and leisure time.

Some feminists worry that such a grant might reinforce domestic regimes that subordinate and exploit women. Released from the compulsion to seek wage employment that may hold the promise of some economic independence, women may find themselves again trapped in exploitative domestic arrangements. On the other hand, Almaz Zelleke (2009) argues that a universal income could create the 'social and economic conditions required to reduce the gendered division of labor [and] could greatly reduce the poverty rate of the most vulnerable group in capitalist economies: single women and their children'. [58]

Since the 1980s, millions of women in South Africa have entered the labour market, despite their exceptionally poor job and wage prospects. The majority of those who do find employment tend to work part-time, for low wages and in highly exploitative conditions. Overall, the sexual division of labour in both the domestic sphere and labour market remains structured in ways that enable men to monopolise full-time and better-paying jobs, while women perform most of the household labour. In effect men, whether employed or not, continue to 'free ride' on women's work. A guaranteed universal income could challenge these arrangements, provide currently inaccessible economic independence and strengthen the negotiating position of women who do enter the labour market. It has an emancipating potential:

> [S]ome single mothers would use the money to work harder. They might buy better food or housing, a car to get to work, or better day care. Others would trade money for time, by quitting a second job or taking a job with a shorter commute but lower pay. The [grant] places that choice squarely where it belongs—with women (Alstott, 2000).

A universal income would boost the bargaining power of workers usually beholden to low-skills, low-wage jobs. If the bare necessities of life can be secured elsewhere, demeaning and hyper-exploitative wage labour, when available, is no longer the 'only option'. This is likely to have a more salutary effect than minimum-wage regulation; this altered power relation can also boost the collective strength of workers:

> Where workers individually have easier exit options, employers may have greater incentives to agree to new forms of collective cooperation with organisations of workers (Wright, 2003:80).

To the extent that it can buffer individuals somewhat against the coercion of demeaning, low-pay and unsafe wage labour, it potentially enhances their liberty and reduces the alienation generated in capitalist society (Van Parijs, 2000). The grant holds strong appeal also from an eco-socialist perspective, since it potentially breaks with the productivist ideology that predicates poverty reduction on faster economic growth. It potentially recasts the relationship of dependency and subservience between worker and employer. It redefines the meaning of citizenship and reasserts citizens' entitlements. It assigns to the state a fundamental provisioning role, while at the same time stripping it of the paternalism with which it customarily would fulfil such duties. And it has a potentially powerful emancipating effect. All this tends to discomfit both state and capital, which is all the more reason why the realisation of a universal income should be a central plank in any leftist project.

Dependency and shame

The ANC maintains a highly ambivalent attitude towards social grants. This is not a recent disposition, nor is it limited to conservatives in the organisation. On the one hand, grants demonstrate the ANC's commitment to shield the poor against privation, a stance that also carries political reward. There is also an awareness of the potential developmental dimensions of social protection; after all, when the ANC renamed the former Department of Social Welfare and Population Development, it settled on 'Department of Social Development'. At the same time, there is a stern, moralising disdain for nurturing so-called 'dependency' on the state.[59] Thabo Mbeki declaimed the need 'to cultivate the spirit of self-reliance among our people' (2008b), for example, ignoring the research evidence that 'poor people volunteer far more than rich people do' and that 'the poor are already the most active givers in South Africa' (Everatt, 2008:311).[60] Following a similar script, President Zuma has asserted the need 'to link the social grants to jobs or economic activity in order to encourage self-reliance among the able-bodied'.[61]

These sentiments have done the rounds in the ANC for some time, with social grants frequently referred to as 'handouts'. Few noticed at the time, but even the Reconstruction and Development Programme (RDP) declaimed the need to eradicate poverty while counselling, as if channelling garden-variety Thatcherism, that

> although a much stronger welfare system is needed to support all the vulnerable, the old, the disabled and the sick who currently live in poverty, a system of 'handouts' for the unemployed should be avoided. All South Africans should have the opportunity to participate in the economic life of the country.[62]

Common to these sorts of pronouncements is the figure of the overbearing patriarch wielding the rod of kindness. Government ministers implore communities 'to change the thinking of those who held out their hands for help but kept their sleeves down'[63] and have gone as far as to claim that land in rural areas lies fallow because people are receiving social grants.[64] A palpable distrust prevails. Former Finance Minister Trevor Manuel reportedly opposed proposals for food vouchers on the basis that there was no guarantee they would be used 'for food only, and not to buy alcohol and other things'.[65] At work is a mean-spiritedness that bears more than passing resemblance to Thomas Malthus's (1989:128-129) counsel that

> *a man who is born into a world already possessed, if he cannot get subsistence from his parents on whom he has a just demand, and if the society do not want his labour, has no claim of right to the smallest portion of food, and, in fact, has no business to be where he is. At nature's mighty feast there is no vacant cover for him. She tells him to be gone, and will quickly execute her own orders.*[66]

Such sour dispositions are especially rife among the middle classes, among whom allegations of welfare fraud are a recurring refrain.[67] A staple of talk-show myths is the belief that the child-support grant has led to an increase in teenage pregnancies and 'child farming'. Popular legend has it that, according to Biyase (2005:8), the child-support grant is sometimes nicknamed the '"thigh grant", meaning that girls "spread their thighs" to get the grant'. There is no empirical evidence for these claims. While there has been an increase in teenage fertility, the rise preceded the introduction of the child-support grant—and the rate of that increase slowed in recent years, despite the fact that the eligibility age range widened and the grant amount increased. Moreover, the rise in teenage fertility occurred across the board, including in sections of society that do not qualify for the child-support grant (Makiwane & Udjo, 2006).[68]

The 'welfare cheat' refrain is part of the censorious perspective that sees social grants as 'handouts' which, while necessary within limits, encourage an entitlement culture, foster dependency, undermine productive citizenship, destabilise the labour market and threaten fiscal rectitude. Mbeki spoke regularly of the need to provide a cushion for the poor, but invariably also sermonised about the need to 'reduce the number of people dependent on social welfare [and increase] the numbers that rely for their livelihood on normal participation in the economy' (2003). 'Certain things' had to be done to 'reduce the dependence of people on grants', including promoting small enterprise,

> *so that people don't think it is sufficient merely to hold out their hands and receive a handout, but to understand that all of us, as South Africans, have a shared responsibility to attend to the development of the country.*[69]

These sorts of pronouncements are especially jarring in places such as South Africa, which has 35% unemployment and which lacks a coherent anti-poverty strategy while outmoded, inappropriate social security mechanisms are used as makeshift poverty-reducing tools. Yet still prevailing is the faith that waged labour and entrepreneurial zest eventually shall supersede social transfers as the basis for wellbeing. Social provisioning and rights-based claims on state resources are regarded with reserve, even distaste, though a residual 'social net' would remain 'to protect the most vulnerable in our society' (ANC, 2007:2). Across the political spectrum, dominant discourse regards social inclusion and the achievement of social rights as a function of people's abilities to earn a wage or turn a profit (Barchiesi, 2006) (see Chapter six).

Lineages of a taboo

These sensibilities have a long history that spans ideological divides. Commonly associated with neoliberalism, their lineages extend further back in history and combine a celebration of the work ethic with an emphasis on 'self-help, family-based solidarity and community development' as ways of providing a modicum of social security (Barchiesi, 2006:4).

The founders of the American Republic, for example, highly valued the work ethic of yeomen and craftsmen and regarded them as the epitome of upright citizens. That liberal tradition survived, even as industrial capitalism deprived workers of autonomy and control. It was echoed in unexpected quarters. In the nineteenth century, the titans of capitalism shared with socialists like William Morris the 'belief in work itself as the single most important source of both mutual respect and self-respect', as Richard Sennett (2003:109) has observed. Nesting in such convictions were harsh judgements, not least the equation of joblessness with sloth and defective character, sentiments that

> held sway over 19th century revolutionaries and radicals as much as over bourgeois charity workers or educational reformers. Marx's contempt for the lumpen proletariat derived directly from his enemies' view of paupers—the character of the lumpen proletariat corrupted by servility and blind need (op cit, 111).

As in industrial England of the 1800s, the poor today are simultaneously pitied and besmirched as the architects of their own misery (Keating, 1981). This ambivalence stems from the distinction drawn, since time immemorial, between the 'impotent' and the 'able-bodied' poor (with the latter prone to 'dependency' on state assistance).[70] Since South Africa's social protection system hinges on that same dichotomy (see above), it also distinguishes implicitly between the 'deserving' and the 'undeserving' poor—between, as Margaret Thatcher put it,

> those who had genuinely fallen into difficulties and needed some support till they could get out of them [and] those who had simply lost the will or the habit for work and self-improvement.[71]

That distinction has been at the heart of social security policy for almost two centuries, as Meth (2004) has pointed out. It was at the crux of the English Poor Laws of 1834 and their infamous and cruel enforcement of 'less eligibility', and it gave rise to the innovation of 'deterrent poor relief' that would 'enforce the work ethic and discourage dependency'. Post-apartheid South Africa has not broken with that tradition, although, as Everatt (2008) argues, here the element of shame possibly helps to explain the attachment to a discourse on poverty that is both denigrating and embarrassed. For in South Africa, 'dependency' on state largesse seems also to evoke the racist stereotype of the feckless 'native'. Indeed, that is precisely the stereotype that lurks behind the counsel of the business press when it warns against creating 'perverse incentives' that 'reward a certain type of behaviour'.[72] For many top officials, that sense of embarrassment probably also fuses with the supercilious pride that achievement sometimes nourishes:

[T]he combination of the scars of apartheid experience, and their own success in surmounting the monumental obstacles that characterized this system of oppression, has caused them to elevate 'self-reliance' and an abhorrence of 'dependence' to mythical status (Meth, 2008:27).

It is from within these traditions that the ANC's Joel Netshitenzhe can declare (while squashing calls for a universal income grant) that 'able-bodied' South Africans should have the right to 'enjoy the opportunity, the dignity and rewards of work[73]—a remark [...] so rich in problematic ideological content that it probably merits a comprehensive analysis of its own' in Danie Brand's judgement (2003:20). This is the world of 'New Labour' in the United Kingdom, with its insistence on 'compassion with a hard edge' (Blair, 1997) and its emphasis on individual responsibility, all emblematic of social policy in the neoliberal era, which calls for risk to be 'co-managed':

That is, the individual has to make responsible provision against risks (through education and employment), the family too must play its part (through better care), while the market (through private interests) and the community (through the devolution, 'co-responsibility' and the voluntary sector) are involved in the delinking of expectations of welfare from the state (Molyneux, 2008:785–6).[74]

In the late 1990s, this thinking nested comfortably in the empowerment prescriptions broadcast by the UNDP, the World Bank and major bilateral development agencies. Thus the UNDP routinely called for efforts 'to empower the poor to participate more in the development of their communities' (2000:12), while the United Kingdom's Department for International Development (DFID) advised that 'poor people need to be empowered in their capacity to interact with other private sector agents' (1999:27).[75] Wage labour is seen as the only meaningful form of work and 'opportunities' replace rights and entitlements (which imply different relationships between citizen and state). Imperceptibly, left-wing productivism shades into the sour, right-wing view of social grants as 'handouts'. The coercive function of social provisioning becomes obvious. Key rights and entitlements are made contingent on individuals' willingness to submit themselves to the market. This outlook, as Barchiesi (2006:3) has written, assigns to

wage labour powerful disciplinary and pedagogical meanings, educating the poorest sections of the population to the idea that full citizenship revolves around individual responsibility, labour market activation, and the avoidance of 'dependency' on public spending. Conversely, the government regards with suspicion policies of generalised access to social provisions funded via redistributive transfers.

Social rights, the state and the market

Nurturing small and microenterprises therefore forms a central plank of government's economic and social development plans (see Chapters five and seven). The ANC has also mooted workfare programmes as a way to 'to link grants to economic activity [and] ensure sustainable growth' (ANC, 2007:3), a proposal that would not be out of place among the policy planks of the centre-right in Europe and North America. In 2010 the government announced plans to introduce a wage subsidy scheme to encourage employers to hire young workers, a move that fits neatly with the neoliberal contention that assistance to the poor ideally should be mediated or 'rationalised' through the market. Even the World Bank adds important provisos to its advertisements for workfare and public-works programmes as useful ways to help to address unemployment in 'developing' countries. In its 2001 'World Development Report' the Bank highlighted, for example, the ephemeral benefits of public-works programmes—a misgiving that seems not to have unsettled South African policymakers. Government announced in 2010 it would funnel R 52 billion (USD 6.5 billion) over three years into its Expanded Public Works Programme, the current flagship of its efforts to reduce unemployment (see Chapter six).[76]

Social inclusion and the realisation of social rights are filtered through policy frameworks that equate wellbeing with waged employment or entrepreneurial zeal. Ultimately, South Africans are expected to 'mature' and 'graduate out of dependence on social grants and enter the labour market' (Mbeki, 2007b & 2008b). Even the Expanded Public Works Programme, in Shireen Hassim's reading (2005:13), implies an unsavoury distinction between the 'deserving' and the 'undeserving' poor:

> There is an in-built normative choice in the emphasis on public-works programmes as opposed to expansion of the scale of welfare benefits that sets up a two-tier system of benefits with people on work-related programmes treated as 'deserving poor' and those on welfare (and particularly mothers drawing the child-support grant) as either passive dependent subjects or cunning exploiters of the system.

Typically, the sentiments are broadcast in developmentalist terms with much talk of 'enablement', 'empowerment' and building on 'traditional' community security networks and resilience.[77] These are extraordinary disavowals of reality. Poverty, as John Harriss (2007:5–6) put it, becomes

> the outcome of the behaviours of those who are affected by it, and they may in fact be judged adversely because of it [...] Poverty is a kind of social aberration rather than an aspect of the ways in which the modern state and market society function.

South Africa mimics this approach, which isolates 'poverty from the process of capital accumulation and economic development', in the phrasing of Mexican sociologist Carlos Vilas (1996:16) and reduces 'the solution to designing specific social policies' that target the 'poorest of the poor' while urging economic policies that structurally reproduce highly unequal social relations.

Current, popularised understandings of poverty—and the strategies aimed at combating it—need to be dislodged from the polarised frameworks into which they have been shoehorned, where 'welfare' is pitted against 'development', 'job creation' against 'dependency' and (an even greater conceit) a 'first economy' is contrasted with a 'second' one (see Chapter six). These dichotomies do less to illuminate reality than to justify certain policy choices and to discredit alternatives.

No doubt, more jobs are vital and feasible. But current trends offer no basis for the hope that job creation will provide a sufficient basis for social inclusion and livelihood security for a large enough part of the population. Instead, employment should be positioned among a wider array of routes and options for radically reducing both the depth and scale of impoverishment, and for enhancing liberty. Jobs are one aspect of the wider realisation of social rights, not a substitute for it.

Endnotes

1   Quoted in Labica, G (1990) *Robespierre—Une Politique de la Philosophie*, Presses Universitaires de France, Paris, pp. 53–4; cited in Di Lollo (2006:1).

2   ODI (2006) and Donwald Pressly, 'Social grants recipients to keep rising', *Business Report*, 18 February 2010.

3   Brendan Boyle, 'More support to the people', *Sunday Times*, 27 February 2005.

4   Karima Brown, 'State set to add 1-million child grants', *Business Day*, 18 February 2008; Donwald Pressly, 'Social grants recipients to keep rising', *Business Report*, 18 February 2010.

5   By way of comparison, these cash transfers contributed 1.3% of total household income for whites, 5.6% for coloureds and 2.9% for Indians and Asians (Statistics SA, 2009).

6   Hilary Joffe, 'A stretch too far: ensuring social grants work for all of SA's poor', *Business Day*, 30 January 2007.

7   For a summary of the grants and their eligibility requirements, see http://www.actuarialsociety.org.za/Portals/1/Documents/a4fd20be-0196-494f-a655-f01b71dd4bf0.pdf

8   Donwald Pressly, 'Social grants recipients to keep rising', *Business Report*, 18 February 2010.

9   This was hardly a generous gesture, as the Finance Ministry's actuaries understood. Because South Africa's AIDS and TB epidemics have radically reduced average life expectancy, take-up of the old-age pensions is unlikely to unduly burden the fiscus in coming decades.

10   The decision was announced in October 2009. Sixteen-year-olds became eligible in January 2010.

11   Set at R 1 100 (USD 138) per month in 1998, the income means-test was left unchanged for a decade, despite high inflation. It was eventually adjusted to R 2 200 (US 275) in August 2008—which, after adjusting for inflation, was the equivalent, in real terms, of the 1998 cut-off. See Katherine Hall, 'Adjusting the poverty line', *The Mercury* [Durban], 2 June 2008.

12   Many eligible households are either unaware of this grant or encounter huge difficulties in accessing it (Case *et al*, 2005). The grant (which is available until an orphan reaches 18 years of age) can be accessed only if the child has been placed in the care of foster parents by the Children's Court after a cumbersome and protracted process. Acquiring the requisite documentation is a routine problem for applicants.

13   There is evidence, however, that children orphaned by AIDS are prone to social ostracism, as well as to psychosocial difficulties (Cluver, Gardner, Operario, 2007; Simbayi *et al*, 2006). But the research does not support the contention that large-scale AIDS orphanhood is leading or will lead to rising rates of juvenile delinquency and social disorder (Bray, 2003), even though the AIDS and TB epidemics almost certainly will transform childhood into an ordeal for many more children in poor communities (Richter & Desmond, 2008; Richter, 2004).

14   Strictly speaking, there are two types of disability grants: for persons who are permanently disabled and for persons who are temporarily disabled. Grants for AIDS-sick persons would fit in the latter category. However, the recipients of permanent disability grants increased dramatically between 2003 and 2007, from 743 000 to 1.14 million. Those receiving *temporary* disability grants *decreased* in the same period, from 336 000 to 265 000 (Statistics SA, 2009a).

15   A bizarre poverty trap, in other words. A poverty trap operates, for example, when means-tested forms of income support discourage a person from increasing their income above the designated threshold in order to avoid losing the support.

16   Similar dynamics occur in Namibia, where the disability grant has become that country's second-most prevalent form of income support for poor households (Standing, 2007).

17   Once ineligibility halts access to the grant and the person's failing health again drives his or her CD4 count below 200, it can take six or more months before grant payments resume.

18   This, of course, included Bantustan administrations.

19   The blueprint for this approach was the 1992 doctoral thesis of Leila Patel (who managed the White Paper process) (Lund, 2008).

20   Francie Lund's book *Changing Social Policy* (2008) provides an illuminating account of the transformation of the unwieldy and unjust old social security system.

21   Ben van Rensburg, quoted in 'Relations sour between government and business', *SouthScan*, Vol. 12, No. 42, 14 November 1997.

22   Wolpe quoting Meillassoux, cited in Barchiesi (2006:17).

23   Neil Coleman, interview with Franco Barchiesi, 24 October 2000, Johannesburg, quoted in Barchiesi (2006:9).

24   Viviene Taylor, interview with Franco Barchiesi, 8 August 2000, Pretoria, quoted in Barchiesi (2006:14).

25   The grant, soon abbreviated to 'BIG', would be worth R 100 (USD 13) per month, an amount the federations believed was 'winnable'.

26   A combination of four earlier income-transfer schemes (including the *bolsa escola*), this means-tested scheme focuses on schooling, nutrition and health, and reaches more than 11 million households (about 44 million people) surviving below the poverty line. It almost certainly has reduced female poverty, increased school enrolment and improved learning performances and it is widely believed to have helped President Lula win re-election in 2006 (Standing, 2007). Recipients decide how to use the grants, but they have to abide by several conditions, including school attendance for children up to 15 years, attending antenatal classes for pregnant women and vaccinations for children younger than seven years.

27   It evolved out of the *progressa* scheme, introduced in 1992 in marginalised rural communities. Extended to other rural and to urban areas in 2002, this targeted and conditional scheme now reaches about three million households and has three elements: a household nutrition allowance, a schooling subsidy that increases in amount by grade (and that is higher for girls in secondary school) and an annual payment to help cover uniforms and books. Conditionality calls for school attendance of 85% or more, regular medical check-ups for the children and 'parenting classes' for the parents. It requires complex administration and is highly intrusive, but it has been shown to reduce poverty in beneficiary households and to improve both school enrolment and attendance as well as health status (Skoufias, 2001).

28   Cited in Freund (2007:673).

29   Cited in Fine (2009:18).

30   See Alison Tilley, 'Manuel not so smart when it comes to child support grant', *Business Day*, 20 February 2009. Tilley points out that international experience provides 'no evidence that it's the condition in the cash transfer that has an effect on school attendance'. Moreover, South Africa has 'no mechanisms that would allow us to measure whether children are in school, and no systems that allow transfer of that information to the South African Social Security Agency'.

31   Reviewing a 'cash for relief' programme in Ethiopia, it found that the initiative had 'allowed individuals and communities to begin making a series of decisions, giving them the power to prioritise needs for their families'.

32   This had led to the use of proxy means-testing in many places (especially in the Americas, but also in Indonesia, the Russian Federation and Turkey), but these tend not to be much more reliable (Standing, 2007).

33   Other researchers have made similar findings. Among AIDS-affected households in Free State province, uptake of available grants was weakest among the poorest households (Booysen & Van der Berg, 2005).

34   The irony is that South Africa historically has never offered much basis for such a viewpoint; until the revival of the trade-union movement in the 1970s, wage incomes and benefits provided paltry barrier against impoverishment.

35 Transcripts of the Committee of Inquiry, 6 October 2000 meeting, p. 17, cited in Barchiesi (2006:14).

36 Cited in Standing (2007:18).

37 Business journalist Hillary Joffe was correct (though not in the way she seemed to intend) when she wrote of 'disturbing findings ... that women can earn as much (or more) from grants as they can from paid work'. See Hillary Joffe, 'A stretch too far: ensuring social grants for all of SA's poor', *Business Day*, 30 January 2007.

38 According to Van der Berg *et al* (2004), the poverty headcount fell by three million in 2001–04. In his detailed examination of those findings, Meth (2006) critiques Van der Berg's claim that 'improved job creation in recent years' possibly also lowered the poverty headcount and shifts the headcount decrease closer to 1.5 million.

39 In 81% of households receiving a social grant, all school-age children were attending school in 2007, compared with 76% in the case of households that did not receive any grant. In the case of child-support grants, the association was similar but less dramatic (Statistics SA, 2009a:18).

40 These data were drawn from the 2003 and 2007 General Household Surveys.

41 Neva Makgetla, 'Grants help, but remain a second best for SA's jobless', *Business Day*, 23 February 2007.

42 Mill J S (1987) *Principles of Political Economy*, 2 ed [1849] Augustus Kelley, New York; cited in Van Parijs (2000).

43 The pilot project is in the Otjivero-Omitara area, near Windhoek. Within six months the percentage of underweight children fell from 42% to 17%, school-fee payments doubled and dropout rates fell sharply.

44 Former Minister of Social Development, Zola Skweyiya, supported the introduction of a universal income grant, but was unable to win over enough of his colleagues in government and the ANC to that position. He continued to speak in favour of such a grant, but was careful to frame that support as his 'personal view'; see, for example, Linda Ensor, 'Skweyiya calls for basic income grant for poor', *Business Day*, 10 November 2006.

45 The poverty gap refers to the total income shortfall of households living below the poverty line. A narrower poverty gap means more households would edge closer to or above the poverty line.

46 COSATU (2000c) 'Submission on comprehensive social security', Submitted to the Taylor Task Team on Social Security, Johannesburg, para. 3.2; cited in Barchiesi (2006:14).

47 A universal income grant would also seem to shed the intrusive, patronising presence of the state (vetting eligibility, setting conditions, monitoring compliance, etc), which characterises targeted, means-tested or conditional grants.

48 A staple of World Bank development thinking in the 1990s, the concept of human capital has been forced into the background. The most obvious objection is that it regards education or health, for example, not as a 'good' in its own right, but values it in terms of its contribution to economic growth and capital accumulation (euphemised as 'development').

49 Ferguson suggests that such an amalgam of arguments that do not fit the conventional oppositions of 'progressive' social-democracy and 'reactionary' neoliberalism might be creating 'new and potentially promising forms of political struggle' (2007:84). Or the situation might be rather more prosaic. Motley groupings have made these arguments, cribbing them from dominant discourses on both left and right and have tried to tailor them to the perceived biases, concerns and guiding values of their audiences.

50 Cited in Ferguson (2007:81).

51 Mbeki, for instance, was quoted dismissing the grant with the claim: 'If you give everybody R 100 a month, it will not make a difference [...] To introduce a system which indiscriminately gives R 100 to a millionaire and a pensioner does not work' (*Mail & Guardian*, 1 August 2003). At the time, more than 18 million South Africans were surviving on less than R 250 per month (Meth, 2008); an extra R 100 would have increased their incomes by at least 60%.

52   Quoted in Hart (2006:26).

53   'Didiza cautions about basic income grant', *Business Day*, 14 August 2002.

54   *Sunday Times*, 28 July 2002; cited in Desai (2005:12). The spokesperson was dismissing the Taylor Committee's proposal for a basic income grant.

55   It is heresy in South Africa (and elsewhere) to suggest, as has Maghnad Desai of the London School of Economics, that 'we should simply find the poor and give them one dollar a week [...] That would probably do more to relieve poverty than anything else'. 'People often say, "These problems are not solved by throwing money at them". I say, "Just try"' was Desai's punchline. Desai was speaking in the House of Lords, 12 June, House of Lords Hansard column 459; quoted in Hanlon (2004).

56   Thanks to Ashwin Desai (2005:13) for bringing this remark to light again.

57   This, for example, was the appeal of a guaranteed income for the Italian autonomist movement in the 1970s, who saw it 'not as a means of cutting the welfare bill, but as part of the effort to uncouple productive labour from the capitalist economy' (Bull, 2001:3).

58   For a useful compendium of both sides of this particular debate, see Pinilla-Pallejà, R. *et al* (2009).

59   Government was so obsessed with this issue that in 2005 the presidency tasked the Department of Social Development to work with the Finance Ministry to address 'issues of dependency, perverse incentives and sustainability of the social grant system' and to ensure that the grants are linked to 'reducing poverty and unemployment'. The process included a survey of 14 000 households aimed at assessing 'potential perverse incentives and dependency' (Presidency, 2005); cited in Di Lollo (2006:19–20).

60   Everatt was citing evidence published in Everatt, D and Solanki, G (2008) 'A nation of givers? Results from a national survey of social giving'. In: Habib, A and Maharaj, B (eds) *Giving and Solidarity: Resource Flows for Poverty Alleviation and Development in South Africa*, Human Sciences Research Council, Pretoria, pp. 57–9.

61   'Economic crisis will not derail state plans', *Independent Online News*, 3 June 2009. When President Zuma made the comments during his first State of the Nation address, he was merely following official ANC policy: 'We are building a developmental state and not a welfare state, given that in a welfare state dependency is profound. Our attack on poverty must seek to empower people to take themselves out of poverty, while creating adequate social nets to protect the most vulnerable in our society. Beyond poverty alleviation, interventions must seek to develop exit programmes that capacitate households and communities to empower themselves. It is the duty of the developmental state to achieve this' (ANC, 2007a:13).

62   Government of South Africa (1994), section 2.2.2.

63   Former Public Service and Administration Minister Geraldine Fraser-Moleketi, quoted in Andre Koopman, 'Poor urged to roll up their sleeves', *Cape Times*, 25 May 1999.

64   Former Finance Minister Trevor Manuel, speaking at a World Bank event in 2008. See 'Poor must take responsibility: Manuel', *The Times* [Johannesburg], 21 May 2008.

65   'Eat your words', *Daily News* [Durban], 8 May 2008; cited in Everatt (2008:298).

66   Cited in Foster (2002:143).

67   Fraud is doubtless part of the social grant landscape, though state bureaucrats appear to number disproportionately among the culprits. See, for example, Linda Ensor, 'Grants agency hit by fraud', *Business Day*, 2 October 2007.

68   South Africa's overall fertility rate has been dropping quite steeply, while teen fertility increased. This is a common trend worldwide when total fertility rates decrease, though Makiwane and Udjo (2006) also note that the rise in teenage fertility in South Africa 'coincides with the major political changes that were taking place ... and may be similar to a post-war boom'. Also matching global trends is the fact that teenage pregnancy rates dropped as education levels rose (Children's Institute, 2009a). An earlier study by the Planned Parenthood Association of SA (2003) found that about 9% of teen pregnancies were planned and that half of those (ie 4.5%) seemed possibly related to achieving eligibility for a

child-support grant. Fewer than 4% of children in the child-support grant system had teen mothers, compared with almost 9% of children not in the system.

69   Mbeki quoted in 'People must help themselves', *Business Day*, 17 March 2008.

70   Barr, N (1998) *The Economics of the Welfare State*, Oxford University Press, Oxford; cited in Meth (2004:15).

71   Cited in Meth (*op cit* 15).

72   'The risks of a shift to state welfarism', *Financial Mail*, 23 February 2007.

73   Quoted in *Sunday Times* (Johannesburg), 28 July 2002; cited in Meth (2002).

74   Cited in Fine (2009:9).

75   Both cited in Sender (1999:38).

76   See Hilary Joffe, 'Economic policy in starring role on day of few surprises', *Business Day*, 18 February 2010; Linda Ensor, 'Back to work: State plans to spend R 52 bn to create jobs', *Business Day*; 18 February 2010.

77   See, for example, Republic of South Africa (1997) and ANC (2002d).

CHAPTER NINE

AIDS and TB: like 'waiting for a tidal wave to hit'

South Africa is the epicentre of the global AIDS epidemic. One in every six people with HIV globally lives here and one in every six people who dies of AIDS is buried here.[1] Nowhere in the world, including elsewhere in Africa, have HIV infection levels soared as high as in South Africa and the other hyper-endemic countries of southern Africa. Together they account for approximately 35% of all people with HIV and 33% of all people who die of AIDS (UNAIDS/WHO, 2008).[2]

Alongside one of the world's worst tuberculosis (TB) epidemics, AIDS is changing South African society. Some of that impact is vivid and shocking, but a great deal of it is subterranean and cumulative and the full effects will only register in the years and decades ahead.

An overview

The first AIDS case in South Africa was detected in 1982, but for almost a decade the apartheid health services did little of note to contain the spread of HIV. Warped by Calvinist reflexes and racist dread, early awareness campaigns did little more than recycle stereotypes and stoke stigma (Lawson, 2008). Until very late, warnings that a serious AIDS epidemic was incubating in South Africa were ignored, disputed or dismissed. The epidemic's scale and intensity now beggars belief:

- By 2009, there were 5.2 million people in the country living with HIV—more than in any other country on Earth (Statistics SA, 2009b; HSRC, 2009);
- Some 17% of all HIV-infected persons globally live in South Africa, a country with 0.7% of the world's population;
- About 250 000 people died of AIDS in 2009 and the number of children orphaned by AIDS had reached an estimated 1.9 million (Statistics SA, 2009b);
- An estimated 1.5 million adults and 106 000 children needed antiretroviral (ARV) drugs in 2009 (Statistics SA, 2009b).

The epidemic is increasingly concentrated in and around the cities. An estimated 1.5 million people with HIV live in the predominantly urban Gauteng province: more than in the whole of Mozambique or Kenya (1.4 million each) or Zimbabwe (1.2 million). There are more people living with HIV in Durban than in all of Brazil or China and more in Cape Town than in Vietnam or Indonesia. It is likely that within the next generation, around two-thirds of people with HIV will be living in South Africa's cities (Van Renterghem, 2009); the planning and management of these urban areas will have to contend with this reality.

The epidemic initially lagged behind those in several countries to the north, partly because of the country's comparative isolation during the final decade of the apartheid era. But once HIV became firmly lodged in the society, the virus spread at an astonishing pace. As political negotiations got underway in 1990, less than 1% of women attending antenatal clinics had been infected with HIV. By the time voters went to the polls for the second-ever democratic election in 1999, HIV infections levels had rocketed to 22% and at least three million South Africans were living with HIV. By 2005 almost one in three women seeking antenatal care was testing HIV-positive (Department of Health, 2006; Shisana et al, 2005a).[3] Approximately 600 000 people were being infected with HIV each year (ASSA, 2005) and more than 250 000 people were dying of AIDS (Statistics SA, 2009b). Combined with a raging TB epidemic (discussed later) AIDS has become a ruinous part of South Africa's transition. It will influence the destinies of at least two more generations and it will change society in ways that are only dimly evident at the moment.

There are, however, glimmers of good news. Annual surveys carried out among pregnant women attending antenatal clinics showed HIV infection levels among pregnant women in 2006–08 stayed level at about 29%, indicating an epidemic that seems to have stabilised, although at extraordinarily high levels. To some extent this stability reflects the natural evolution of an HIV epidemic, which tends to reach a plateau eventually.[4] But there are also some signs that new infection rates are slowing.

HIV infection levels among young people appear to be declining (among those aged 15–24 years they fell from 10.3% to 8.6% between 2005 and 2008). When the prevalence data were subjected to mathematical analysis a 'substantial decrease' in HIV incidence among young people was found, especially among those in their teens. In other words, the rate at which teenagers are being infected with HIV seems to be slowing (HSRC, 2009). It is not yet clear whether a similar trend is underway among older South Africans. Nor is the trend visible everywhere. A 2003–07 study in KwaZulu-Natal's Hlabisa district found HIV incidence stayed steady at a very high rate of 3.4 per 100 person-years. Among women aged 20–24 years the incidence rate was an astonishing 7.7 per 100 person-years. Worse, one third of the people who became infected during the course of the study were unaware that ARV therapy existed (Bärnighausen et al, 2009).

Well into the third decade of the epidemic, there were signs that more young people were using condoms more often. But they were still taking other risks. For example, the percentage of young people with more than one sexual partner in the previous 12 months increased, as did the proportion of young women who had sex with significantly older partners (from 19% in 2005 to 28% in 2008) (HSRC, 2009). Because HIV prevalence peaks in men 30 years and older, those women faced strong odds that their partners were already HIV-infected. They could protect themselves against infection by using condoms consistently. Unfortunately, study after study in South Africa and elsewhere shows that condoms are least likely to be used when people have sex with their regular partners or spouses. So prevention campaigns seemed to be getting one basic message across: use a condom during 'casual' sex.

But a lot of sex is not of the 'casual', 'one-night-stand' variety. Promoting condoms became a way of avoiding tackling other, much more prickly factors that fuel the HIV epidemic, such as the role of sex in seeking status or esteem and in building livelihoods, the place of women in men's ideas about 'manhood' and the misogyny that pervades society.

Double blow: tuberculosis and AIDS

Ranged alongside AIDS is South Africa's TB epidemic, one of the worst in the world. South Africa is home to 28% of all people with TB (Academy of Science of SA, 2007) and only three countries have more people living with TB: China, India and Indonesia (three of the most populous countries in the world). High rates of drug resistance and HIV co-infection are aggravating the TB epidemic. The lifetime risk of acquiring TB is about 10% for a South African who is not also infected with HIV, but it approaches an astonishing 10% *per annum* in persons who are HIV-infected (Academy of Science of SA, 2007).

Both these epidemics are enmeshed with the patterns of dispossession and dislocation that have shaped modern South Africa. Migrant labour, the fragmenting and dispersal of families, the crowding of workers into congested hostels and squatter camps, poor nutrition and absent or poor health services—all this helped sow the whirlwinds of today.[5] But, as we discuss later, not all the blame belongs at the door of history. South Africa's response to these epidemics 'has been marked by denialism, ineptitude, obtuseness and deliberate efforts to undermine scientific evidence as the basis for action' (Karim *et al*, 2009:922).

The TB epidemic dates back more than a century, when it was closely associated with the growth of the mining industry and its overcrowded hostels and shocking working conditions. Returning migrant workers spread the disease from cities to rural areas. TB spread steadily and peaked in the 1960s, when 350 cases per 100 000 people were being recorded per year. National data for the next two decades were incomplete (statistics from the Bantustans were excluded). Treatment was onerous (involving 12–18 months of inpatient treatment) and the treatment programme was poorly designed and, being reliant on hospitals, often inaccessible. The racial fragmentation of health services weakened TB control and blocked proper co-ordination of the overall programme (Karim *et al*, 2009).

Between 1986 and 2006 rates of TB case notification quadrupled: from 163 per 100 000 people to 628 per 100 000 (Department of Health, 2007c). Reflecting reported cases only, those data underestimate the actual rate of TB infection. According to the WHO (2008) annual TB incidence in South Africa in 2006 was in the region of 940 per 100 000 people. Between 2001 and 2007 new TB cases more than doubled to 382 000.[6] Although uniformly serious, the TB epidemic is extraordinarily intense in certain parts of the country, notably KwaZulu-Natal, where case notification rates exceeded 1 000 per 100 000 in 2006 (Health Systems Trust, 2007b). There is also a very high burden of TB among young children.

These trends are intertwined with the AIDS epidemic. Three out of four (73%) new TB infections are in people who are also infected with HIV (Karim *et al*,

2009); high levels of immunodeficiency render people much more susceptible to TB infection. But the trends also expose one of the cardinal disappointments of the past two decades: the failure to reverse the death toll of one of the few deadly infectious diseases that *can* be treated affordably and effectively. The introduction in the mid-1990s of the DOTS (directly observed treatment, short course) strategy made treatment potentially a lot more efficient and effective.[7] A standardised recording system was created and central co-ordination of the tuberculosis control programme was improved. Implementation, though, fell far short and the AIDS epidemic sabotaged many potential gains. Between 1997 and 2005, as the DOTS strategy was being implemented, the annual number of people dying of TB increased by more than 300% (from 22 071 to 73 903). Renewed treatment efforts then saw the TB cure rate improve from 51% in 2004 to 63% in 2006 (Health Systems Trust, 2009), still some way off WHO's 85% target.

The AIDS epidemic complicates both detection and treatment of TB, but systemic flaws are also at fault. Earlier poor implementation of TB control programmes and low cure rates have led to the spread of TB drug resistance, which is now a major handicap that threatens the prospects of curbing the epidemic and treating persons with HIV.[8] Outbreaks of extensively drug-resistant (XDR) TB have been reported in each of the nine provinces since 2006, when 53 such cases were first detected at a rural KwaZulu-Natal hospital (Gandhi *et al*, 2006). All but one of those patients died within a month of diagnosis. These deadly complications are being aggravated by the AIDS epidemic,[9] but their roots lie in the poor management and implementation of TB control programmes over the years, especially 'poor prescribing practices, interrupted drug supply and poor support to patients attending [TB] clinics, along with poor infection control measures' (Academy of Science of SA, 2007:39).

Entanglements of risk

The pace and extent to which HIV spreads in any given setting is shaped by a complex set of factors, which changes over time and differs from place to place. The exceptionally high HIV infection levels in South Africa indicate that a particular combination of factors has favoured rampant HIV transmission. In rough outline, the scale and intensity of a mainly heterosexual HIV epidemic such as South Africa's depends primarily on patterns of sexual behaviour (and the social relations that shape them) and on factors that either increase or reduce the chances of HIV transmission during sex:[10]

- All else being equal, women's physiology places them at higher risk of acquiring HIV during sex, compared with their male partners (Nicolosi *et al*, 1994). In the case of girls and young women, the immaturity of their genital tracts is believed to increase their chances of infection even further. This is believed to be among the reasons why, in hyper-endemic countries such as South Africa, women are disproportionately at risk for HIV infection.
- The risk of HIV infection is higher when other sexually transmitted infections (STIs) are present, especially herpes simplex virus type 2, or HSV-2, which has

been shown to double the chances of acquiring HIV and to quintuple the odds of transmitting it (Freeman *et al*, 2006; Wald & Link, 2002). Rates of STIs are high in South Africa.

■ There is strong evidence that male circumcision dramatically reduces the risk of HIV acquisition in men during *heterosexual* intercourse[11]—by about 50%, according to randomised controlled trials in Kenya (Bailey *et al*, 2007), Uganda (Gray *et al*, 2007) and South Africa (Auvert *et al*, 2005). (This might account, in part, for the much smaller HIV epidemics in countries where male circumcision is common, such as in parts of West and North Africa.)

■ HIV viral load[12] is highest in the first few weeks after infection has occurred and rises again during late stages of infection, making people more infectious during these periods (Pilcher *et al*, 2007 & 2004; Wawer *et al*, 2005). Modelling indicates that the probability of a man infecting a female partner increases eight to 10-fold if they are having sex within three to six weeks after the man was infected (Pilcher *et al*, 2004). This probably ranks among the reasons why concurrent (or overlapping) sexual partnerships might be such critical factors in the spread of HIV (discussed later).

■ It has been suggested that malnutrition may increase a person's susceptibility to HIV infection by compromising the body's immune response (Stillwagon, 2006). Very little research has been done to confirm or discount such a link. There is evidence that malarial infection can enhance the transmission of HIV (Abu-Raddad *et al*, 2006), but malaria is comparatively rare in South Africa (and in other hyper-endemic countries such as Botswana, Lesotho and Swaziland).

■ Although the evidence is suggestive at best, there is ongoing speculation and research into the possibility that genetic factors may cause stronger predisposition to HIV infection in some groups of people.[13]

■ It has been postulated also that the predominant strain of HIV-1 in southern Africa, subtype C, is more aggressive than others, but there is insufficient evidence to confirm this.

Ultimately, the vast majority of HIV infections occur when women and men have unprotected sex. The factors discussed above increase or reduce the odds of transmission during these encounters. But the underlying dynamism of the epidemic depends on how often, with whom and on what terms one has sex. AIDS, in other words, is entangled in the social relations that govern everyday life.

Having unprotected sex with more than one partner significantly increases the chances of HIV transmission (Malamba *et al*, 1994; Wawer *et al*, 1994; McFarland *et al*, 1991). Behavioural surveys, however, suggest that men in various African countries have as many or fewer sexual partners during their lifetimes than do men in, for example, Europe or the US (Wellings *et al*, 2006; Caraël, 1995). But there is evidence that multiple partnerships in at least some African countries (including South Africa, Lesotho, Tanzania and Zambia) often are overlapping (or concurrent) rather than consecutive (or serial). This is an important variable, which may substantially increase the chances of HIV transmission.[14] Viral load (and therefore infectivity) reaches a peak within the first few weeks after infection (Pilcher *et al*, 2007 & 2004); everyone in a newly infected person's sexual network during that period faces strong odds of also becoming infected during unprotected sex.[15]

It is therefore highly plausible that *concurrent* partnerships, in combination with high viral load during acute HIV infection, variable rates of male circumcision and high rates of other sexually transmitted infections may have contributed significantly to the rapid spread and the unusually large HIV epidemics underway in South Africa and several other southern African countries (Halperin & Epstein, 2007; Epstein, 2007).

AIDS discourse for some time carried an undercurrent of discomfiting stereotypes about 'African' sexual behaviour and mores, which flattened the diversity of social and cultural systems into an imaginary 'African culture'.[16] This approach recognised that the epidemic rests fundamentally on patterns of *social* behaviour. But it both 'essentialised' social relations and assumed that they arise mainly from norms and values: that they are ideologically determined and could, in theory, be altered by forcefully promoting alternative norms and values. Both inadequate and inaccurate, this perspective neglects the deadly interplay throughout history between infectious disease, social relations *and* material conditions. HIV is closely attuned to the specificities of history and place and is highly efficient at exploiting opportunities for transmission.

A political economy of AIDS in South Africa

William Budd's (1849) assessment of cholera in nineteenth-century England—that 'the disease not seldom attacks the rich, but it thrives most among the poor'—would seem to apply to both HIV and TB. Concerned about the indifference his observations might encourage among his privileged peers, Budd sermonised that

> he that was never yet connected with his poorer neighbour, by deeds of charity or love, may one day find, when it is too late, that he is connected with him by a bond which may bring them both, at once, to a common grave.[17]

Subsequently, others have sought to establish an empirical basis for such entreaty. Richard Wilkinson and Kate Pickett (2009), for example, have shown that high levels of inequality aggravate health problems among the poor, but also cause overall health standards to deteriorate.[18] Calamities tend to zero in on the dispossessed: but an injury to some becomes, in one way or another, an injury to all.[19] Is AIDS different?

A disease of poverty?

Links between social and economic conditions and health have been asserted and detected for centuries (Berkman & Kawachi, 2000; Wilkinson, 1996).[20] Epidemiology, however, has tended to regard socioeconomic status as a causally weak 'variable' for explaining the spread of disease. Greater emphasis is usually placed on the behaviours and risks of individuals than on underlying social relations and structural conditions.

A complementary tradition—social epidemiology—regards socioeconomic status as a key determinant of health outcomes. A pivotal intervention was Thomas McKeown's (1979) thesis that improvements in health outcomes in the eighteenth and nineteenth centuries in England and Wales were due largely to socioeconomic improvements (including improved diet), rather than to medical interventions.[21] This suggested that public health is, in the final instance, best approached as a function of social conditions and of the distribution of economic, political and social resources. A similar perspective gained influence in AIDS discourse in the late 1990s.

Although typically a very private matter, sex occurs within an expansive social context that helps determine who has sex with whom, in what manner and frequency, on what terms, and what those sexual encounters mean. There is an assumption that poverty—in its own right and as a marker for other forms of deprivation—is a decisive part of that context. Paul Farmer (1996), for example, has argued that diseases like AIDS are fuelled by the 'structural violence' that reproduces poverty and deprivation. In such views, poverty may put people at higher risk of HIV infection by:

- Inducing them to adopt risky behaviours (such as commercial sex or 'transactional' sex and not using condoms) (Collins & Rau, 2000; Farmer, 1996);
- Hindering them from seeking treatment for sexually transmitted infections (which can increase the odds of contracting HIV);
- Depriving them of information and services that can enable them to take precautions to avoid becoming infected with HIV (Fenton, 2004); and/or
- Forcing them to depend on partners who may have multiple sexual partners (Campbell & Mzaidume, 2002).

Were that the case one would expect to see the worst AIDS epidemics in areas where poverty is especially severe. However, at the national level the link between poverty and HIV turns out to be weak. In many of the world's poorest countries,[22] including several in sub-Saharan Africa, national HIV prevalence among adults is yet to exceed 1–2%. Conversely, some of the worst epidemics are raging in two of Africa's richest countries, namely Botswana and South Africa (UNAIDS, 2009). Analysis of data from eight countrywide surveys in Africa[23] by Mishra and colleagues (2007) also failed to find a consistent relationship between poverty and HIV risk.[24] Their conclusion: 'HIV prevalence does not exhibit the same pattern of association with poverty as most other diseases' (Mishra *et al*, 2007).[25] But that is not the last word on the matter.

Other, localised evidence (from studies in Brazil, India, Kenya, the US, Zambia and Zimbabwe) points to a possible interplay between some forms of deprivation and HIV risk (Lopman *et al*, 2007; Dandona *et al*, 2006; Cardoso *et al*, 2005; Fonseca *et al*, 2003; Leone *et al*, 2005; Gabrysch, Edwards, Glynn, 2008). In South Africa, too, research in three townships linked HIV risk to poor education, unemployment, discrimination, crime and violence (Kalichman *et al*, 2006). So the relationship between impoverishment and HIV risk seems to vary. This does not render poverty irrelevant in a chain of causation, but poverty (especially when measured by income or assets) does seem too blunt and unreliable an instrument to expose the ways in which various forms of deprivation and insecurity (poverty among them) and HIV might interact.

Much stronger, at the national level, is an association between income inequality and HIV risk (Gillespie, Kadyala, Greener, 2007). Certainly, income disparities are unusually wide in several of the hyper-endemic countries, including Botswana, Namibia and South Africa. But income gaps are almost as wide in other regions, notably Latin America, where HIV prevalence has remained low. The relationship between income inequality and HIV transmission is not simple or consistent either.

The uneven distribution of HIV in South Africa

In South Africa, HIV infections are distributed very unevenly—between population groups, men and women, income groups and regions.

Firstly, there is a racialised pattern: HIV prevalence is considerably higher among Africans than among any other population group. A national HIV household survey in 2005 found HIV prevalence of 19.9% among African adults, 3.2% among coloureds, 1.0% among Indians and 0.5% among whites (Shisana et al, 2005a).[26]

Secondly, there is geographic variety: adult HIV prevalence in 2005 ranged from 22–23% in Mpumlanga and KwaZulu-Natal to 16–19% in the Gauteng, Free State, North West and Eastern Cape provinces, 9–11% in Limpopo and the Northern Cape and 3% in the Western Cape (Shisana et al, 2005a). In each of these provinces, prevalence can vary dramatically from district to district.

Thirdly, there are stark gender disparities. As in the rest of Africa, AIDS in South Africa disproportionately affects women. One in three women aged 25–29 years was living with HIV, as were one in four men aged 30–34 years, according to the 2008 national HIV household survey (Shisana et al, 2010). Young women (15–24 years) were *four times* more likely to be HIV-infected than young men (Shisana et al, 2005a) and HIV incidence among women in their prime childbearing ages (20–29 years) was more than six times higher than among their male peers: 5.6% compared with 0.9% (Rehle et al, 2007).

What about income levels? If a fairly direct and linear relationship exists between HIV and poverty status, HIV infection levels should be highest in the poorest parts of South Africa, which tend to be in rural areas. Throughout Africa, however, HIV prevalence tends to be lower in rural than in urban areas (Shelton et al 2005) and South Africa is no exception. Moreover, the highest HIV prevalence is not found in South Africa's poorest provinces, the Eastern Cape (16% among adults) and Limpopo (11%) (Shisana et al, 2005a).

The distribution of HIV does seem to closely mirror the spatial order established under apartheid. Although just less than 9% of the total population lives in urban informal settlements, fully 29% of the total estimated number of new HIV infections in 2005 occurred there (Rehle et al, 2007). HIV prevalence was by far the highest among persons living in urban and rural 'informal' areas, where it was 26% and

17% respectively in 2005. Urban informal settlements are areas typified by high levels of livelihood insecurity and poor infrastructure and services (Shisana *et al*, 2005a). But they are not the poorest parts of the country.

South Africa has not yet conducted a national population-based study that correlates income status to HIV prevalence, but several localised studies cast some light on the matter. They show HIV prevalence tends to be lower among employed persons in the higher skills and income groups and higher among those with the lowest skills and incomes. Given the country's history of racial discrimination and dispossession, the latter are predominantly Africans.

- A national study among educators found HIV prevalence to be highest among those with lower socioeconomic status. Among those earning R 132 000 (USD 16 500) or more a year, HIV prevalence was 5.4%, while among those earning less than R 60 000 (USD 7 500) a year, prevalence was 17.5% (Shisana *et al*, 2005b).

- HIV infection levels in South Africa's universities and colleges differ widely, depending on age, race and socioeconomic status. In a large 2009 survey, HIV prevalence was 1.5% among academic staff, compared with 3.4% among students and 12.2% among service staff. The racial discrepancies were huge. Among the 17 000 students participating in the study, HIV prevalence was 5.6% for African students, 0.8% for coloured and 0.3% for Indian students, while only one of the 3 112 white students tested HIV-positive.[27]

- Among health workers surveyed at private and public health facilities in four provinces, HIV prevalence was just under 14% among professionals, but exceeded 20% among non-professional staff (Shisana *et al*, 2003).

- Among South African workers participating in a three-country survey of 34 major companies in 2000–01, HIV prevalence was 15% for unskilled workers, 18% for their semi-skilled counterparts and 20% for contract employees, but 7% among skilled workers and 4% among management staff (Evian *et al*, 2004).

- An analysis of HIV in 22 public- and private-sector organisations in all nine provinces found HIV prevalence to be significantly lower among managers than among skilled and unskilled labourers (an average 5.3% compared with 12.4%). When the data were disaggregated by race the pattern held, though a little less firmly. Especially suggestive was the study's finding that HIV prevalence was *lower* among women than among men. In the general population, the opposite is the case. This suggests that being employed may reduce women's risk of HIV infection (Colvin, Connolly, Madurai, 2007) and it implies that being unemployed may carry a higher risk of HIV infection (discussed later).

This does not mean that HIV infections are distributed in a neat, linear pattern that corresponds to income, with HIV prevalence highest among the very poorest South Africans and then tapering off as incomes rise. Workplace studies, after all, capture patterns of infection among people with jobs, and they generally do not fall in the bottom income quintile. Indeed, a localised study in rural KwaZulu-Natal found that the odds of acquiring HIV were significantly (72%) higher for people in households which fell in the *middle 40%* of relative wealth, compared with those in the 40% poorest households (Bärnighausen *et al*, 2007). On the other hand, among women in rural parts of Limpopo province, HIV incidence has been shown to be highest among the least-educated (and, presumably, poorest) women (Hargreaves *et al*, 2007).

The upshot is that the potential interaction between various forms of deprivation and insecurity (poverty among them) and HIV risk is complex—all the more so in a society with such convoluted entanglements of race, class and gender as South Africa.

History's template

The norms governing sexual liaisons are the products of the centuries-long dominance of patriarchy (pre-dating the advent of colonialism) and the skewing and modulation of social orders during the eras of colonialism and apartheid. Subsequently, many of the factors that appear to drive South Africa's AIDS epidemic are interlocked with the economic accumulation strategies and social engineering of the past 150 years.[28]

Patterns of mobility in South Africa (and elsewhere in the region) are embedded in a labour system that was engineered to service the mining industry and later also encompassed agribusiness, urban manufacturing and various service economies. Transport networks linked harbours, cities, mining hubs and agricultural basins. The labour system involved the coerced proletarianisation of the African peasantry, with young migrant men providing cheap, relatively unskilled labour in the mining and industrial sectors. Circular patterns of migration split (mainly male) workers off from their families and communities for long periods of time. Systematic dispossession and dislocation destabilised social systems, undermined social cohesion (particularly in the urban peripheries) and generated increasingly unequal social relations, including between men and women (see Chapters one and two).

In the 1940s, the social epidemiologist Sidney Kark had already linked syphilis outbreaks to the migrant labour regimes servicing mining corporations in South Africa and to the patterns of industrialisation and urbanisation that accompanied the accumulation process (Kark, 1949; Marks, 2002). His analysis contrasted sharply with an orthodoxy that tended toward 'essentialist', often racist explanations of disease outbreaks on the continent. These typically involved bigoted stereotypes about unbridled sexual lust, poor sanitary habits and the absence of social regulation. In fact, the perceived perils of the city had led elders to impose a regime of strict sexual discipline among migrant African men, prohibiting them from consorting with 'city women' (who were stigmatised as carriers of disease) on pain of severe sanction in their home villages (Delius, 1996; Delius & Glaser, 2002). That regime waned, however, as large-scale circular migration and urbanisation accelerated in the 1920s and encompassed ever-greater numbers of women in the subsequent two decades (Bonner, 1990; Mager, 1999; Walker, Reid, Cornell, 2004).[29]

Job opportunities for migrating women were rare and survival was often achieved through combinations of piecemeal work, support from boyfriends and/or brewing homemade beer (Bonner, 1990). Rates of sexually transmitted infections soared, both in urban areas and, via returning migrants, in rural villages (Mager, 1999; Walker *et al*, 2004).[30] Sexual violence also appeared to increase, which Mager (1996 & 1999) later attributed to a 'crisis in the gendered ordering of African society' and an expression of 'desperate attempts by African men to reassert patriarchal domination in a rapidly changing world'.[31]

When the apartheid regime imposed draconian influx control measures in the mid-1950s, the migration of women was curtailed. Able-bodied men were drafted into the industries burgeoning in urban areas, while women were confined to the pre-capitalist sector, tasked with the social reproduction of labour in the county's rural hinterlands. Massive forced removals of populations meanwhile uprooted as many as three million people from the late 1950s onwards—amounting to one of the largest peacetime population movements in the twentieth century (Marks, 2002). Created over the course of several decades were 'classic conditions for the spread of disease', including sexually transmitted diseases such as HIV (Walker *et al*, 2004:71; Hargrove, 2008). Mark Lurie's (2000) observation remains apposite:

> *If one were to design a social experiment in an attempt to create the conditions conducive to the spread of HIV and other sexually transmitted diseases, you would remove several hundred thousand rural men from their families, house them in single-sex hostels, provide them with cheap alcohol and easy access to commercial sex workers and allow them to return home periodically.*

Applied to HIV, such an analysis positions the AIDS epidemic within the patterns of dispossession and development that created contemporary South Africa, making it, in many ways, 'apartheid's epidemic'. An ideal social and ideological template for the epidemic took shape and was intractably in place when HIV first entered sexual networks in South Africa (Lawson, 2008). This is a tantalising proposition, and the country's history provides it with a great deal of support. But it runs the risk of not taking sufficient account of the ways in which the epidemic's course has also been shaped by developments that accompanied apartheid's demise and by choices made subsequently.

Lives turned upside down

The economic growth path fashioned during the heydays of apartheid began unravelling in the early 1970s (Saul & Gelb, 1981; Gelb, 1991). This had dramatic social costs and, eventually, history-changing political consequences (see Chapters one and two). At household level, too, jarring changes occurred in the ways in which impoverished families built and defended their livelihoods.

Until the early 1970s rural households had depended heavily on the redistributed earnings of migrant men. But by the mid-1970s unemployment levels were rising, a trend that hardened in the following decade as economic growth stalled. Formal-sector employment was in a deep slide by the end of the 1980s, with devastating consequences for households that relied heavily on migrant-worker remittances. By the mid-1990s pensions were eclipsing migrant remittances in terms of size and reliability as income sources for large numbers of African households (Case & Deaton, 1998). Collapsing agrarian and waged livelihoods caused precariousness to increase, especially among poor women. Against this background of heightened material insecurity there had emerged an embattled layer of employed workers who were able to command 'living wages' thanks to the influence of powerful trade unions. Their redistributed wages became vital also for the subsistence of the rural households that were linked to them.

The collapse of the 'influx control' system and, eventually, the entire apartheid system enabled more people to migrate more often. By the late 1980s much of South Africa was literally on the move. Massive job losses and evictions of farm workers meant that rural livelihoods were becoming ever more parlous. Increasing numbers of young women migrated to urban and peri-urban areas in search of work, periodically returning to rural areas (Crush, 2001). By and large, men were still more likely to migrate than women (Posel & Casele, 2003), but studies in KwaZulu-Natal showed women outnumbering men among migrants in their early twenties (Hunter, 2006; Hosegood & Timaeus, 2005). This increased mobility featured strongly in the accelerated spread of HIV (Lurie et al, 1997).[32]

More women entered the labour market, but rather than being drawn in by a burgeoning demand for their labour, they were migrating in desperate bids to try and repair disintegrating rural livelihoods (which were also losing remittance support) and build new ones in urban areas. Female entrants into the labour market rose by two million between 1995 and 1999, while median wages for women fell sharply (Casale, 2004). For many, returning to rural areas was not a viable alternative. But like their predecessors in the 1930s and 1940s, these women discovered that jobs in the country's cities and towns were scarce, tightly rationed, erratic and low-paying. Three-quarters (75%) of African women younger than 30 years were unemployed. A majority of those with jobs worked in poorly paid and badly provisioned jobs (Hassim, 2005) and their wages have been falling (see Chapter six).

Despite this, African women still bear most of the responsibility for social reproduction (Hassim, 2005b). More than 40% of African households are female-headed, most of them single-parent households surviving with paltry and unstable sources of income (Coovadia et al, 2009). These households are disproportionately likely to be poor (Woolard, 2002). Livelihoods have to be assembled from various sources, including piecemeal work (very often as domestic workers or cleaning staff), petty trading and service provision and, in some cases, sexual liaisons.

Unemployment is also high and rising among young, low-skilled men. All this has had profound consequences for household formation, marriage and sexual networking patterns (Hunter, 2005a, 2005b, 2006a, 2006b, 2007) and, ultimately, for the spread of HIV. Deepening poverty has made marriage increasingly unaffordable, particularly where marriage hinges on the exchange of bride wealth. Marriage rates in South Africa overall began declining in the 1960s, but there is evidence of a more recent significant drop among Africans specifically (Hunter, 2007; Hosehood & Preston-White, 2003). Hunter's (2005b) review of census data shows that the proportion of Africans older than 15 years who had married declined from about

57% in 1960 to 30% in 2001, while the percentage of persons who had never been married grew substantially. The average age of marriage among Africans has risen (to 28 years for women in 2003). Wedlock has become an increasingly inaccessible and inflexible arrangement 'through which to organise social alliances and the flow of resources' (Hunter, 2007:695). Adaptation has occurred: cohabitation without marriage has become more common, as have female-headed households (usually with children but without cohabitating men).

Sexual networking

Although sex work is practised in all the hyper-endemic countries, it is a minor factor in their overall AIDS epidemics.[33] More profound, it seems, is the informal exchange of sex for favours, gifts, services and other forms of support, usually as part of ongoing relationships (as opposed to a one-off encounter). AIDS literature refers to this as 'transactional sex'.[34]

Transactional sex is not unique to South Africa or its neighbours (Maganja *et al*, 2007; Khan *et al*, 2008a & 2008b), but it appears to be relatively common in many of the hyper-endemic countries. There is considerable evidence that combinations of high unemployment, material insecurity and the burgeoning migration of women who are marginalised in the formal labour market sometimes force resort to sexual liaison as a survival tactic or as a lever for meeting material and other aspirations (LeClerc-Madlala, 2008 & 2003; Hunter, 2007 & 2005b; Weiser *et al*, 2007; Byron, Gillespie, Hamazakaza, 2006; Chatterji *et al*, 2005; Dunkle *et al*, 2004; Hallman, 2004; Machel, 2001; Preston-Whyte *et al*, 2000; Meekers & Calvés, 1997).[35]

Hallman's (2004) research in KwaZulu-Natal's Durban metro and Mtunzini district found that women residing in poorer households were more likely to have exchanged sex for gifts, goods or money than were women in better-off households.[36] Among young women, economic disadvantage was found to correlate with higher odds of exchanging sex, being forced to have sex and having multiple sexual partners. In his field research in Isithebe, an informal settlement near Mandeni, in KwaZulu-Natal, Mark Hunter (2005a, 2005b, 2006b) encountered women surviving on the basis of a plethora of informal-sector activities, along with liaisons with boyfriends and male 'providers'. Boyfriends and companions were expected to 'help out' with money for groceries, clothes, transport, mobile-phone credit and more. This also enabled women to remit money elsewhere: to their families, to finance children's school fees and uniforms and to invest in job searches. Shifting webs of overlapping sexual networks were maintained.

Women, especially migrant women, used these networks to stake claims on the resources of better-off, older men (often men belonging to the diminishing 'elite' of unionised workers in the area), giving rise to a 'sexual economy [that] is also an increasingly important mechanism for the redistribution of formal and informal earnings' (Hunter, 2006a:8). It seems that traditionally polygamous and patrilineal systems (in which bride wealth conferred authority and rights over women and children) often still provide a *normative* basis for such sexual networking. But they do so in the context of harsh material disparities (and the celebration of consumption) and amid notions about manhood that valorise sexual conquest and the sexual 'pleasuring' of women (Hunter, 2010). Having several simultaneous sexual relationships becomes a modified form of polygamy (Leclerc-Madlala, 2008), adapted to new material realities. Ultimately, in Hunter's analysis, South Africa's AIDS epidemic surged in a context where 'the sexual economy overlapped with the informal economy in ways that involved a much larger number of people and reflected dramatic shifts in economic circumstances and household composition' (2006a:19).[37]

These liaisons serve multiple functions and 'are not simply instrumental' (Hunter, 2006a:21). They can involve complex reciprocal arrangements and varied forms of emotional attachment and often are used to foster kinship ties (Leclerc-Madlala, 2008; Hunter, 2007). And they do not necessarily match the stereotype of 'venal', 'predatory' men exploiting 'powerless' women. Young women might also exercise *their* agency by pursuing sexual liaisons that involve various forms of material and emotional reward (Steinberg, 2008a; Leclerc-Madlala, 2008; Hunter, 2007; Nkosana & Rosenthal, 2007). They might look to older men as potential marriage partners, as sources of assistance in obtaining access to education and jobs, for meeting other needs and for addressing other aspirations and desires. They might exchange sex and companionship for gifts that signal status or increase esteem (clothes, jewellery, cellular phones, perfumes, etc) or for other forms of affirming assistance (Luke & Kurz, 2002; Longfield *et al*, 2004). In urban areas especially, these relationships are formed amid aggressively propagated cultures of consumerism, vivid inequalities and gnawing covetousness. As Suzanne LeClerc-Madlala's research (2008) shows, relationships with older men are seen to present opportunities for young women to achieve material gains, build esteem and social status and enhance their long-term life prospects. Even when pushed into such relationships, few women perceive themselves as victims. Sexuality, status and consumption are closely intertwined. Add to this the 'charge' of hormones and libido and the importance of sex in satisfying people's craving for fun, for seeking and expressing trust, bolstering self-esteem or simply escaping loneliness or boredom and it is clear that numerous computations of sexual, emotional and material motives are at work, as Jonathan Berger (2004) has reminded.

Women's agency, nevertheless, is often highly circumscribed and risky—not least when exercised in the context of aggressive constructions of masculinity that valorise sexual risk-taking and the domination of women and especially so in the midst of the raging HIV epidemic. Research shows that a young woman's chances of becoming infected increases with the age gap between her and her partner.[38] Fundamentally, transactional sex and age-mixing need to be understood in the broader context of men's generally superior economic position and access to resources (Jewkes & Wood, 2002) and of conceptions of masculinity that place high value on sexual conquest and control of women (Dunkle *et al*, 2007).

HIV, transactional sex and violence

Sexual violence, mainly against women, is an ordinate 'fact of life' in South Africa (see Chapter seven). Less well known is the close link that exists between intimate partner violence and HIV risk for women. A study at antenatal clinics in Soweto, for example, found that women who had been physically abused by their partners were most likely to be HIV-infected (Dunkle *et al*, 2004a). Even more suggestive is the evidence that men who sexually abuse women are more likely to engage in transactional sex (which may help explain the higher infection levels in women who have experienced sexual violence). When young men (15–26 years) were surveyed in 70 rural Eastern Cape villages, those who said they had sexually assaulted an intimate partner were also more likely to have engaged in transactional sex at some point (Dunkle *et al*, 2006; Jewkes *et al*, 2006).[39] Sexual violence and transactional sex both involve attempts by men to exercise control over women. There is also a strong association between alcohol use and violence, on the one hand and heightened risk for HIV infection, on the other (Kalichman *et al*, 2007), with HIV risk increasing in people who consume greater quantities of alcohol (Kalichman *et al*, 2006; Morojele *et al*, 2006). Binge drinking, a national pastime in South Africa, appears to be especially risky (Simbayi *et al*, 2004). Drinking, sex and violence become an even more destructive cocktail in the context of a raging HIV epidemic.

The AIDS epidemic is interlaced, in other words, with the circuits and terms on which power, opportunity and entitlements are distributed and desires and needs are pursued. In the case of South Africa, these remain extremely unequal. The effects of AIDS morbidity and mortality are likely to reinforce these inequalities (Marais, 2005), which are being reproduced along a development path that marginalises young people and burdens women, young and old, with most of the responsibility for social reproduction (see later). It is this combination of deprivation, need and desire, of layered inequalities, truncated capacities and excessive responsibilities that seems to provide the AIDS epidemic with much of its momentum. This suggests that a serious epidemic was almost inevitable. But was it destined to become the world's largest AIDS epidemic?

Aiding and abetting: government's AIDS response

At the beginning of the 1990s, health activists in and beyond the ANC, as well as some political leaders, had seen the writing on the wall. South Africa's comparative isolation during the final decades of apartheid had slowed the virus' arrival. Consequently, its epidemic lagged behind those in countries to its north, where the havoc was already evident. In 1990, Chris Hani, leader of the South African Communist Party, told an AIDS conference in Maputo:

> *Those of us in exile are especially in the unfortunate situation of being in the areas where the incidence of the disease is high. We cannot allow the AIDS epidemic to ruin the realisation of our dreams. Existing statistics indicate that we are still at the beginning of the AIDS epidemic in our country. Unattended, however, this will result in untold damage and suffering by the end of the century.*[40]

A year later, at a conference in Lusaka, Hani reiterated his concerns. He urged the ANC to 'learn to tackle these problems head on'; a plea he seemed to direct at those 'of us [who] might regard this as a diversion from the important task of transfer of power to the people'.[41] The prescience was eerie.

A survey conducted in 1990 had found 0.76% of pregnant women attending antenatal clinics in South Africa were infected with HIV. Public-health specialists were alarmed enough to try to model the epidemic's likely trajectory. One of the earliest efforts, a complicated actuarial model devised by Jonathan Broomberg, Malcolm Steinberg and Patrick Masobe, painted a shocking picture. It predicted that by 2000, 5.2 million South Africans would have become infected with HIV and 666 000 would have died of AIDS. By 2005, according to the model, there would have been 2.9 million cumulative AIDS deaths. The forecasts must have seemed outlandish to the untrained eye. But they turned out to have been underestimations of what lay in store.[42] Relaying those early forecasts in an article for the *London Review of Books*, R W Johnson wrote that it felt 'a bit like sitting in an oceanographic laboratory waiting for a tidal wave to hit'.

Progressive health workers did not sit on their hands. They ensured that a viable national AIDS strategy was drafted and ready when democracy was achieved in 1994. The Mandela government adopted that plan (known as the NACOSA plan)[43] and prioritised it as one of the ANC's Reconstruction and Development Programme (RDP) lead projects. Despite this neither AIDS nor TB truly became national priorities (Lawson, 2008; Marais, 2000). Double-guessing and distrust took hold early on and would hobble government's reactions to the AIDS epidemic. From the mid-1990s onward AIDS kept making headlines—but for all the wrong reasons!

A series of debacles—some embarrassing, most foolhardy and all of them avoidable—fed the appetites of the mass media and opposition parties. First came the 1996 controversy surrounding *Sarafina II* (a lavish anti-AIDS play marred, according to critics, by questionable financial management and shoddy research); then Cabinet opted to support research on a toxic industrial solvent, dimethlyformamide (Virodene), which was being peddled as a cure for AIDS. Those controversies had scarcely faded when government refused in 1998 to fund the provision of zidovudine (or AZT) for pregnant women to prevent mother-to-child transmission of HIV. A shambles ensued. The media and opposition parties feasted on the debacles. In government, a maelstrom of self-righteousness, paranoia and miscalculation began seething (Cullinan & Thom, 2009; Lawson, 2008; Marais, 2000).

A central motif was the 1997 Medicines Bill (Lawson, 2008). Although clumsily crafted, the Medicines Bill's main aim was unimpeachable: it would restructure the procurement, distribution, selection and pricing of medicines. Circulating in the ANC—and among health activists generally—was a healthy disgust at the practices and ethics of the pharmaceutical giants. Health Minister Nkosazana Dlamini-Zuma's attempt to revamp the national drug policy included an attempt to endorse a smaller range of more affordable generic drugs. Alarmed, international pharmaceutical companies ganged up against the government, deploying legal and other muscle to block the bill's passage. Even the White House tried to bully South Africa into submission. The stand-off had several facets. The government read it as a challenge to its sovereignty and to its right to improve public health. The dramaturgy was that of David and Goliath, a liberation movement's *Boy's Own* tale of brave, principled defiance. This self-gratifying sense of resisting 'imperialist bullying', of bucking the system, would colour government's AIDS policy and practice for many years hence. Economic policy was off-limits; domestic and international corporate capital had already instilled a keen aversion to heterodoxy on that front; and AIDS became the preferred theatre for anti-imperial posturing.

So from early on the AIDS response became entangled in a nationalist morality tale in which neither equivocation nor criticism would be brooked. This closeted self-righteousness would generate blunders of shocking proportions. The Virodene scandal was one. A 'cure developed in Africa, for Africans' according to one of its inventors and above all cheap (though also ineffectual), the concoction seemed heaven-sent to a government embarking on a fiscal austerity programme while at the same time broadcasting the advent of an African Renaissance. Government threw its weight behind the research (Myburgh, 2009; Govender, 2007). Lesley Lawson (2008) has documented how basic rules of scientific research and medical ethics were breached: ironically, the same kinds of transgressions that pharmaceutical giants were routinely accused of committing.

Driving government's refusal to sanction the use of the antiretroviral drug AZT, meanwhile, were disparate calculations and concerns, some legitimate, others misinformed or disingenuous. In claiming that the drug's alleged toxicity posed a threat to public health, Mbeki and other government officials seemed to draw no distinction between peer-reviewed evidence and allegations encountered on the Internet. In fact, South Africa's Medicines Control Council had registered AZT almost a decade earlier for the treatment of HIV. But there was more afoot than the weighing of scientific evidence (Coovadia, 2009). The manufacturer of AZT, Glaxo Wellcome (now GlaxoSmithKline), was also one of the pharmaceutical corporations holding the Medicines Bill to ransom. The other argument was fiscal. Nkosazana Dlamini-Zuma had already declared in 1998 that AZT 'was not cost-effective because we do not have the money' (Lawson, 2008). Her arithmetic might have been flawed. But the remark showed how strongly another set of calculations, arrived at elsewhere in the system, also shaped key AIDS-related decisions and hardened hostility toward the kinds of rights-based claims that AIDS activists later would promote so effectively. Public spending was tight and the still-extortionate prices of HIV drugs seemed to make a programme to treat AIDS and prevent infection in infants an unattractive prospect.

Losing the plot

As the HIV infection rate rocketed and the scandals multiplied, public outcry grew. Opposition parties relished the frenzy. But much of the media reporting, as Lawson shows, was crass and neglectful of important detail and context. Government circled its wagons. At times, reason seemed to prevail; too often it yielded to bewilderment.

During the early days of Manto Tshabalala-Msimang's tenure as health minister, she tried to mend some of the fences her predecessor had wrecked. But soon afterward former President Mbeki barged in with some sensible questions but hapless and misinformed propositions about the possible association between AIDS and poverty.[44] His timing was spectacularly ill-judged: Durban was hosting the biennial International AIDS Conference and national adult HIV prevalence had reached almost 20%. A global uproar ensued, compounded by increasingly outlandish claims emanating from the President's Office (Marais, 2005). Tshabalala-Msimang dug in her heels at his side; so did most of the ANC leadership. Nourished by the highest political office in the land, denialism surged:

> *There were many shades and shapes of denial of the AIDS crisis in late 20th century South Africa: from the politicians who played down the seriousness of the crisis to the ordinary people who denied their own risk and vulnerability; from the mass media, which dodged difficult and meaningful debate, to the teachers who refused to talk about safer sex. It is not surprising then, that this national state of benign denial created the space for a more malignant version to emerge* (Lawson, 2008:172).

The South African National AIDS Council, under the nominal stewardship of Jacob Zuma, mustered not a whimper in protest. The AIDS response steadily collapsed under the weight of bombast, bitterness and sophistry. Soon the AIDS saga would resemble an episode of the *Keystone Kops* scripted by Dante.

As thousands of HIV-infected South Africans fell ill and died, Mbeki denied knowing anyone with AIDS. The farcical President's Advisory Panel on AIDS ('not a scientific discussion or debate [but] just a shouting match', according to virologist Barry Shoub)[45] came and went.[46] The health minister's office distributed texts claiming that HIV had been concocted to reduce the global population (including a chapter from US writer William Cooper's *Behold a Pale Horse* screed) to key officials. Witch hunts were mounted against health officials who tried to perform their duties and provide AIDS drugs to patients and rape survivors. Scientific evidence was rubbished the one day, cherry-picked the next for snippets to prop up bankrupt arguments.

Supported by COSATU and church organisations and spearheaded by the Treatment Action Campaign (TAC), AIDS activists challenged health-service providers, government and pharmaceutical companies to do more to bring AIDS treatment to poor people. They launched petitions, staged protests, mobilised community activities and highlighted the success of pilot ARV treatment clinics (such as those run by Médecins Sans Frontières). AIDS lobby groups challenged government in court for failing to uphold the health rights enshrined in the Constitution. In 2001 the Constitutional Court ruled against the government, instructing it to provide the drug nevirapine to all HIV-positive pregnant women (Friedman & Mottiar, 2006).

Shamed and outmanoeuvred—chiefly by the TAC—the pharmaceutical corporations eventually dropped their legal challenge against the Medicines Bill. AIDS and health activists celebrated in the belief that the path had been cleared for sanctioning generic production of AIDS drugs and for levering the response to a new level. They cheered too soon. Government's intention, as Lawson (2008) shows, 'had never been to use the [Medicines Act] to get cheap AIDS drugs, and they had consistently rejected demands for ARVs to be made available in the public health system'. Indeed, by mid-2001 the government's arguments for not introducing a full-scale programme to prevent mother-to-child transmission (PMTCT) of HIV were already threadbare. Drug prices were at a new low; clinical trials had confirmed the safety and effectiveness of the drug nevirapine and the Medicines Control Council had licensed it. Still government balked and turned its guns on the TAC.

In the ANC denialism was not simply dominant, it was hegemonic (see Chapter twelve). It was being fed from a number of directions, one of which was government's determination to hold the line of fiscal stringency. For instance, when Mbeki invoked out-of-date WHO data to claim that AIDS was a minor cause of death in South Africa, the gambit was aimed at holding AIDS-related spending in check. In an August 2001 letter to Cabinet, he urged his colleagues to ensure that 'the allocation of resources reflects the incidence of death [from AIDS or HIV-related illnesses]'.[47] Denialism, Kenyon (2008:33) later noted, 'dovetail[ed] perfectly with a neoliberal ethos'.

More years—and deaths—would pass before government, backed into a corner by international ridicule and by the clout, connections and tactical savvy of the TAC, would relent. In 2003, Cabinet finally decided to provide ARV drugs for free in the public-health service and declared tuberculosis (the most common HIV co-infection) a national emergency. By 2004, the PMTCT and ARV treatment programmes were being rolled out nationally and most of the HIV drugs dispensed in the state programme were generic versions made by a local company—feats achieved largely by the activism of the TAC and health workers. For all its bluster about sovereignty and 'African solutions', the government had succeeded only in delaying those outcomes by years, at the cost of several hundred thousand lives (Chigwedere et al, 2008).

Former Health Minister Tshabalala-Msimang continued to lurch from one controversy to the next. Scientific evidence was second-guessed, evidence-based HIV interventions disparaged or ignored and quack remedies supported. Scrupulous healthcare professionals found themselves harassed and persecuted while the Health Ministry promoted untested and unlicensed traditional remedies and vitamin supplements as alternatives to the medical treatment of AIDS (Cullinan & Thom, 2009). At Tshabalala-Msimang's behest, the government's stall at the 2006 biennial International AIDS Conference in Toronto promoted garlic, beetroot and lemons as treatments for AIDS. Former UN envoy for AIDS in Africa, Stephen Lewis, described Tshabalala-Msimang's stance on AIDS as 'worthy of the lunatic fringe'.[48] She remained in her post for a decade.

Embarrassment eventually led to some changes. Government delegated responsibility for the AIDS response to then Deputy President Phumzile Mlambo-Ngcuka, who worked with then Deputy Minister of Health Nozizwe Madlala-Routledge to revive the defunct South African National AIDS Council in 2006. Madlala-Routledge, however, misread the mood; when she criticised the scandalous state of public hospitals, Mbeki dismissed her, citing alleged breaches of protocol.

But a new strategic AIDS plan was in the works, thanks to an inclusive process that involved a broad range of health workers, AIDS activists, scientists and researchers. A Tuberculosis Strategic Plan for South Africa was also adopted in 2007. The purging of Mbeki in 2008 seemed to inaugurate a new approach that would be less closeted and hostile and more evidence-based and urgent. But priceless opportunities to curb the epidemic's growth had been squandered at an inestimable cost to society.

The impact of a hyper-epidemic

By the mid-2000s, South Africans were dying in unprecedented numbers and at unusually young ages.[49] The annual number of recorded deaths increased by 100% between 1997 and 2005, when it reached 634 100 (Statistics SA, 2008d)[50]—considerably more than the entire populations of Bloemfontein or East London. Death rates for women aged 20–39 years more than tripled in that same period and for males aged 30–44 they more than doubled. People aged 30–34 years (supposedly in the prime of their lives) were accounting for about 10% of all deaths, as did infants up to four years old (Statistics SA, 2008d). Supermarket chains began peddling funeral insurance to low-income earners.

The Mbeki administration dismissed these trends. In mid-2001, for example, Mbeki claimed that AIDS was the cause of just 2.2% of deaths in the country. In a letter to his health minister he predicted 'a howl of displeasure and concerted propaganda campaign from those who have convinced themselves that HIV/AIDS is the single biggest cause of death' in the country. He had ignored the modelled estimates prepared by South African scientists.[51] Instead he based his claim on an old WHO data set, dating back to 1995, when sharp increases in mortality were only beginning to occur in South Africa, as various Statistics SA reports (Statistics SA, 2005b, 2006, 2008d, 2009b) would confirm.

Not all deaths are due to AIDS, of course. But close to half (47%) of recorded deaths in the mid-2000s were caused by the AIDS epidemic (Statistics SA, 2009b; Anderson & Phillips, 2006; Medical Research Council, 2005).[52] By the end of the decade, Statistics SA (2009b) estimated that AIDS was responsible for 43% of deaths: the introduction in 2004 of free ARV therapy via the public-health system had begun to have an impact and total deaths in 2009 decreased slightly to 614 000 (Statistics SA, 2009b). The failure to introduce a timely antiretroviral drug treatment programme in the early 2000s cost approximately 330 000 lives (Chigwedere *et al*, 2008).

The AIDS epidemic, combined with the closely related TB epidemic, has manifestly reversed health gains. Life expectancy in 2008 was 12 years lower than it had been in 1996, maternal mortality rates had worsened considerably since the mid-1990s and the child mortality rate was worse than Iraq's:

- Average life expectancy at birth in 2009 stood at 53.5 years for men and 57.2 years for women (Statistics SA, 2009b) and was less than 50 years in the Eastern Cape, Free State, KwaZulu-Natal and Mpumalanga provinces.
- The Actuarial Society (2005) has estimated that more than half of 15-year-olds would not live to their sixtieth birthday.

■ Maternal mortality increased from 117 to 147 per 100 000 between 1998 and 2004 (Barron, 2008), with AIDS responsible for almost half of those deaths (NCCEMD, 2009).

■ The mortality rate for children younger than five years rose from 60 to 69 deaths per 1 000 live births between 1990 and 2006 (Chopra *et al*, 2009). AIDS is believed to be the cause of more than half of these deaths.[53] A properly functioning programme for preventing mother-to-child transmission of HIV could prevent most of those deaths. Dual therapy (a combination of the antiretroviral drugs AZT and nevirapine) has been shown to cut HIV transmission from mothers to their newborn babies by almost two-thirds.[54]

■ Once the data are disaggregated, familiar patterns appear. The infant mortality among the poorest 20% of South Africans was 87 (per 1 000 live (normal) births), compared with 22 in the richest quintile; among Africans, it was 64 and among whites 15 (Department of Health, 2003).

■ The introduction of ARVs is saving thousands of lives, but the drugs are not reaching everyone in need. In addition, a large proportion of people who start ARV treatment only do so after becoming severely ill, which makes the treatment much less effective. Even with ARVs available in the public-health system, about 250 000 people were expected to die of AIDS in SA in 2010.

The effects of AIDS and TB epidemics as sustained and intense as those in South Africa ultimately will penetrate the breadth of society. Historical precedents and the unfolding evidence suggest that the damage will be inordinately concentrated in and around the lives of the disadvantaged.

History lessons

Infectious-disease epidemics usually claim the lives of the weak and frail: the very young, the already sick and the elderly.[55] The 1918–19 influenza epidemic was a case in point. It killed at least 20 million people globally in just over six months (though some estimates put the toll at least twice as high) (Kolata, 2000).[56] The epidemic struck with extraordinary speed and hit three distinct age groups hardest: infants and babies under five years; the elderly (especially those older than 60 years); and people between 20 and 40 years of age (Kolata, 2000). Mortality rates were high enough to cause shortages of coffins in Cape Town, where some of the deceased had to be buried in mass graves (Kilbourne, 1987). In hard-hit cities, illness and death cut into business operations. The demographic shock was severe, but short-lived. Life expectancy in the US, for instance, recovered to pre-epidemic levels within a year; in South Africa it took longer, although the impact appears not to have extended much beyond the early 1920s.

The Plague, which swept through Europe and parts of the Middle East between 1347 and 1351, was a singular, highly compressed shock—though on an unmatched scale. In four years 'King Death' claimed an estimated 25 million lives, killing at least one third of Europe's population and possibly halving England's population (Kolkata, 2000; Kelly, 2005).[57] In some cities between one half and three-quarters of the population was wiped out. Although often seen as an indiscriminate epidemic, the Plague was nothing of the sort, at least not in places like Oxford (England), where carefully maintained records showed a much higher mortality rate among the rural poor compared with local elites.[58]

The Plague shifted Western Europe's foundations and helped alter the course of its history. Average life expectancy in Western Europe prior to the Plague was around 35–40 years; in the second half of the fourteenth century, it fell to below 20 years. It took some 200 years before Europe's population reached its pre-Plague levels.[59] Routines of work and service were upended as high death rates left posts vacant and services unfulfilled. The volumes of land under cultivation shrank due to labour shortages, which also forced landowners to revise the terms of their relations with labour tenants and other workers. Agricultural rents collapsed and the wage demands of workers (especially those of artisans and other skilled workers) soared (Herlihy, 1997).

Not only did labour markets change, the status and power of its various strata radically altered as greater possibilities for social and economic mobility opened up in rigidly stratified societies. Some forms of discrimination (against women, for example) were temporarily ignored due to the need to maintain essential services.[60] The ranks of craftsmen and other professionals were drastically thinned and the professions responded by vigorously recruiting new members. That meant relaxing rules of admission (Herlihy, 1997). Gradually, a wedge of social transformation worked its way through society. In the longer term, the ructions were much more dramatic, for the Black Death unleashed 'intense social pressures which the old-order conservatism could not contain'[61] and which eventually put flame to the fuse of the English Peasants' Revolt of 1381.[62] More generally, the Plague divided, separated and polarised. In Herlihy's summary:

> The plague caused divisions between the healthy and the sick; between those in the cultural mainstream and those at its margins [...] and between the mass of society and its cultural leaders, its governors, priests, and physicians. These fissures cut across society in complex and at times pernicious ways (1997:59).

Keeping perspective

Much has been written about the anticipated cumulative effects of hyper-epidemics of AIDS on societies. Forecasts include dramatic cuts in economic growth, dysfunctional state institutions, 'derailed development' (Feldbaum, Lee, Patel, 2006; National Intelligence Council, 2000), eroded democratic governance, increasing lawlessness (Youde, 2001) and worse. Encouraging such cataclysmic forecasts is the concentrated toll AIDS takes among young adults in the prime of their productive and reproductive lives, the fact that this toll tends to cluster within households (with partners infecting each other and the virus also being transmitted to newborns) and the long-term momentum a serious epidemic can acquire. On current evidence much of the doomsaying seems overwrought. Nowhere have the epidemics caused a national economy to crash, nor have they threatened the viability of any national government (De Waal, 2007). Occasionally, though, the quest for silver linings yields startling claims. According to Allister Sparks (2003:302–3), seemingly channelling Malthus:

> AIDS is not going to reduce South Africa's overall population, but it is going to slow its growth rate. A smaller population can be better educated, and better education, especially of women who are then in a stronger position to determine their own choices, is by far the more effective method of birth control.[63]

Focusing on spectacular outcomes alone seems misdirected. Most accounts of the impact of AIDS neglect the ways in which risk and responsibility are distributed in society. In a society as unequal and polarised as South Africa's mishaps are not distributed evenly, nor are their consequences necessarily transmitted neatly from the micro-levels of individuals and households to the macro-levels of national systems and economies. Some parts of society can shield themselves against the damage; others are unable to deflect and redistribute the costs of AIDS beyond the confines of their lives. Women and girls, for example, shoulder most of the burden and they typically perform this labour without remuneration or institutional support. Their ordeals are often private, even in their own homes. The effects of illness and death also are not automatically transferred onto the balance sheets of enterprises or into the labour market. Putative workplace-related costs are often externalised through the retrenchment of ill employees, restrictive or absent health insurance, trimmed worker benefits and so on.

An analysis of the damage AIDS does requires an understanding of the ways in which the unequal distribution of privilege, risk and responsibility in societies both shapes and channels the epidemic's impact and how that impact might reinforce those patterns of inequality.

Home is where the hurt is

The impoverishing effects of AIDS illnesses are well documented, as is the fact that those effects tend to be most severe in already-poor households (Hosegood *et al*, 2007; Collins & Leibbrandt, 2007). AIDS illness incurs significant additional expenses, which poor households are least able to bear. Lost wages and other income and the costs of seeking and providing care (transport expenses, time off work, medicines etc) all eat into household income. Eventually AIDS robs households of income earners, distorts expenditure patterns, depletes savings and assets and erodes livelihoods (Whiteside, 2008).

In Free State province, researchers found that AIDS-affected households' monthly expenditures were 23–43% lower than those of unaffected households; they also spent 20–30% less on food than their peers. Their main lifeline was social grants (Bachmann & Booysen, 2006).[64] Another study conducted in four provinces, found AIDS-care-related expenses absorbed, on average, one third of monthly household income (Steinberg *et al*, 2002).[65] Mills' (2004) research in KTC, Cape Town, made similar findings: AIDS-affected households were found to be rationing food and relying on donations of fruit and vegetables. The biggest financial shock usually arrives with death. A study in Diepsloot (Johannesburg), Langa (Cape Town) and Lugangeni (Eastern Cape) found that funeral costs absorbed up to seven months of income in households suffering an AIDS death (Collins & Leibrandt, 2007). AIDS is compounding the routine distress endured by millions of South Africans.

The uniform category of 'affected households' obscures the variety and contingency of experiences and responses and veils the unequal distribution of authority, duties and resources within households. The effects are most punishing in households with the least resources, lowest incomes, least entitlements and the weakest social networks. A loosely woven safety net is available in the form of rationed and conditional social grants, but these are small and are spread thin in poor households. Women provide the bulk of care, but those aged between 18 and 60 years are not directly eligible for any social assistance from the state (except for the stigmatising indigence grant).

Shifting burdens: home- and community-based care

Home- and community-based care (HCBC) is central to efforts to cushion the effects of illness and death—and for good reason. The sheer volume of care needs would swamp the public-health system. The approach fits within the post-1994 overhaul of the health system which, along with shifting to a focus on primary healthcare, has sought to ensure that 'care in the community' becomes 'care by the community'. In the Department of Health's view, HCBC is a cost-effective, cheap and flexible way of providing basic palliative and symptomatic care (Department of Health, 2001b). HCBC involves 'the provision of health services by formal and informal care-givers in the home in order to promote, restore and maintain a person's maximum level of comfort, function and health, including care toward a dignified death' (Department of Health, 2001a:1).[66] In theory, care-givers in the home (typically women) receive support from community-based volunteers who themselves receive training and support from the formal health system. These lay health workers visit patients in their homes, provide care and counselling and link them into a functional referral system for specialised care if needed. Community volunteers are supposed to receive care kits (with gloves, basic medicine and food supplements) and are expected to provide basic care and support in order to relieve the burden on family members (Razavi & Staab, 2008).

All this is admirable. HCBC is meant to marshal the respective strengths of households, the communities they constitute and the organisations they spawn, along with the resources of the state. It is meant to slot into a 'continuum of care' that links together the various levels and zones of the public healthcare system and other role-players, thereby boosting the quality, scale and sustainability of the overall care effort (ANC, 2001; Department of Health, 2001). HCBC is seen, in other words, as a more humane and dignified form of care and a way of drawing on and enhancing communal solidarity and mutual assistance.[67] All of this is supposed to occur against a backdrop of 'integrated services' that address basic needs for food, shelter, education, healthcare and more.

The reality is rather more profane. HCBC has reduced the cost of care to the health system (and state), but it has done so in the main by displacing costs onto care-givers, patients and the neighbourhoods in which they live and work, with women bearing the brunt (Mills, 2004). Imbedded in HCBC are hoary assumptions about the respective roles of the state, the family and the women within in it. In all countries women and girls perform the lion's share of social reproduction work: raising and nurturing children; schooling them in norms and values; managing their introduction into wider society; performing domestic labour; tending the ill and much more. Upwards of 90% of care-givers in most African countries are women or girls. In the context of rigid, gendered divisions of labour they usually receive scant support from men (Akintola, 2006).[68] South Africa is no different. Consequently, HCBC has been melded into the largely invisible and taken-for-granted labour women perform in the care economy. It is unremunerated, often bereft of institutional support and very probably contributes to the feminisation of poverty.

HCBC was meant to be a cheap, cost-effective and flexible means of providing basic symptomatic and palliative care for people living with AIDS in a heavily burdened context (Department of Health, 2001). It does this, but mainly by concentrating the bulk of the material and emotional costs of AIDS care within the homes and neighbourhoods the poor, saddling women in particular with most of the burden. HCBC intensifies the exploitation of women's labour, financial and emotional reserves—a form of value extraction that subsidises the economy at every level from the household outward, yet remains invisible in political and economic discourse (Marais, 2005). Underpinning HCBC is the assumption that 'care' is what 'comes naturally' to women and that the domestic sphere is their natural habitat.[69] The esteem and meaning women draw from their labours should not be belittled. The burdens and responsibilities women bear are often extraordinary, but heaped on them is the utterly conventional expectation that the role of women in society is to serve, literally, as 'mothers of a nation'.

Assessments of self-initiated care projects in South Africa report that care-givers and patients often subsidise many aspects of care provision themselves, in addition to paying the costs of not receiving the levels of care and support they require. Essential needs (such as food and money for basic necessities) often go unmet, as Nina Hunter (2007) and Elizabeth Mills (2004) found in their research in six urban and rural communities in KwaZulu-Natal and around Cape Town, respectively. Thus the poor subsidise the poor. These realities fit well in neoliberal frameworks of social governance and resource allocation. In Mark Hunter's summary (2006:4), they involve

> new frameworks for the allocation of resources for individual and social welfare [...] between the state, the family, the market, and the voluntary and informal sectors [...] social citizenship therefore appears to be giving way to market citizenship, where citizens now become responsible for helping themselves.

Interactions with healthcare workers who do provide information, encouragement and emotional support typically have a morale-boosting and empowering effect on patients and care-givers (Giese *et al*, 2003). Until very recently, though, the overall tenor of the HCBC system has been one of piecemeal support and crisis management (Hunter N, 2007). Referral systems are in disarray, clinics frequently lack supplies and patients and care-givers often have to shuttle between clinics and hospitals to access the services or medicines they need. Dismissive staff attitudes (especially towards people living with HIV) are a regular source of complaint. Although thrust into the roles of mediators, counsellors and saviours, care-givers are often unable to provide things as basic as painkillers or a meal. Government departments and donors have been providing more home-based care kits, but training in care tasks, as well as psychological support and counselling for care-givers, has been sorely inadequate. Researchers have found that care-givers often lack sufficient knowledge about AIDS or are unaware that the person they are caring for is HIV-positive (Campbell, Nair, Maimane, 2004). Basic precautions are neglected, putting the care-givers themselves at risk of infection.

Along with the physical demands, the mental and emotional strain are immense (Hunter, 2007; Orner, 2006; Giese *et al*, 2003) and care-givers routinely admit to feeling overwhelmed and alone, stressed and tired and wracked by feelings of guilt. AIDS stigma poisons these experiences further. The overall effect is highly stressful and debilitating (Orner *et al*, 2006), not only for the care-givers but also for the community volunteers and the health and social workers that attempt to support them (Moultrie & Kleintjes, 2006). Generally, rates of depressive, panic and post-traumatic stress disorders are twice as higher for women than for men (Norman *et al*, 2006); the AIDS and TB epidemics are almost certainly aggravating those trends.

HCBC can work much better and efforts are underway to place it on a more solid footing. Certainly, it has worked elsewhere. Home- and community-based programmes in Uganda, for example, sought to professionalise care provision and greater efforts were made to co-ordinate and network the various types and levels of care-giving activities. Volunteers played a pivotal role in identifying and supporting ill persons and providing them with basic care. Supporting them, in turn, were mobile teams of professionals. The upshot, according to Akintola (2004), was 'community-oriented' programmes—qualitatively different from the 'community-based' model applied in South Africa. Further afield, there are relatively successful community health worker programmes in Brazil's Ceara state and in India's Chhattisgarh state (Sundararaman, 2007). There, too, the key ingredients have been good training, strong supervision and backup, along with an incentive and remuneration system (Schneider, Hlope, Van Rensburg, 2008).

Lessons are being learnt. Internationally the community health worker approach had fallen into disfavour, but the extraordinary demands of the AIDS epidemic saw it revived in the 2000s (Schneider, Hlophe, Van Rensburg, 2008). By 2006 there were an estimated 62 000 community health workers in South Africa, many of them providing care to persons with HIV and/or TB. In an innovative move these community health workers have been drawn into the ambit of the Expanded Public Works Programme and many are paid stipends.[70]

Institutional support is also improving, enabling the cadres of community health workers to relieve some of the strain in communities. Research by Helen Schneider and her colleagues (2008) in the Free State province suggests that these workers are beginning to span the divide between patients and the health system. However, their status as an irregular 'support labour force on the margins of the health system' still undermines their relationships with professional health workers. Ultimately, though, HCBC only works as well as the health system overall. And in South Africa this system is a paradigmatic expression of society's inequalities.

An unhealthy system

Health economists have noted that South Africa's health spending as a proportion of GDP is relatively high compared to other middle-income countries, but that the country's health status indicators are far worse than those of most other middle-income countries (McIntyre & Thiede, 2007). Indeed, South Africans spend a great deal of money on healthcare: the equivalent of close to 8% of GDP in 2008, which is slightly less than Sweden's 8.9% (World Bank, 2008). But the spending occurs in a two-tiered system, most of it funnelled into the private sector which is where most of the resources are also concentrated (see Chapter ten).

Almost 60% of the total annual health spend pays for the healthcare of about seven million, typically wealthier, South Africans who belong to private medical schemes and who use the well-resourced for-profit private health system (Statistics SA, 2008).[71] Meanwhile, at least 23 million South Africans rely entirely on an overburdened, understaffed and poorly managed public health system, while a further 10 million use the public sector but also seek private care (which they finance themselves) (McIntyre *et al*, 2007). The disparities in healthcare access and quality are unconscionable.[72]

There is a major shortage of trained, skilled doctors, nurses and support staff in the public health system. New nurses are not being trained quickly enough and in requisite numbers,[73] large numbers of doctors and nurses have opted to work abroad and there is gross misallocation of existing human resources between the public and private health sectors. As the AIDS and TB epidemics crested in the 2000s the ratio of professional nurses in the public sector shrank from 149 per 100 000 people in 1998 to 110 for every 100 000 people in 2007. The percentage of general practitioners employed in the public sector diminished from about 60% in the 1980s to 27% in 2006 (McIntyre & Thiede, 2007). The effects of these shortages are felt acutely in the clinics and community health centres on which families and communities rely.

Meanwhile the strain on the public health system is increasing. It has been projected that a country with a stable 15% HIV prevalence (as is the case in South Africa) could expect to see 1.6%–3.3% of its healthcare personnel die of AIDS each year—a cumulative mortality rate over five years of 8–16% (Tawfik & Kinoti, 2003). Even before the epidemic death toll peaked, in 1997–2001, AIDS was responsible for an estimated 13% of deaths among health workers, according to HSRC research

(Shisana *et al*, 2003). A more recent sero-survey in two public hospitals found that 11.5% of healthcare workers were HIV-positive, including nearly 14% of nurses (Connelly *et al*, 2007). Those who are aware of their HIV-positive status are likely to seek and receive antiretroviral treatment, enabling them to continue to work and live relatively normal lives. However, most South Africans with HIV are unaware that they have been infected (Shisana *et al*, 2005a) and tend to seek treatment at stages when opportunistic infections have begun ravaging their bodies and treatment efficacy is low, necessitating hospitalisation. The demands placed on public hospitals seem unrelenting, as are the workloads and stress borne by their staff, large numbers of whom cite burnout, low morale and ramshackle systems as chronic problems (Von Holdt & Murphy, 2007).

Learning to cope?

The AIDS and TB epidemics are also hollowing out an already stressed education system. Access to education has widened substantially since 1994 and there are many examples of excellent educational practice in South Africa's 26 000 public schools. But the overall quality of schooling is substandard. One third of the learners who write their final (Grade 12) examinations fail them (Presidency, 2008); overall, fewer than half the learners who enrol in Grade one stay in school up to Grade 12 (De Jager, 2009; Louw, Van der Berg, Yu, 2006). The reasons for such poor performance are complex and are discussed in Chapter ten. Not only are overall education performances poor, but the prospects of receiving a good-quality education are distributed along highly discriminatory class and racial lines. In reality, the public school system comprises two parallel education systems. One provides an education of reasonable quality that can serve as a launch pad for successful tertiary education, employment and career advancement. A small minority of learners benefit from it. The other part of the system services the majority of learners and provides sub-par education (Bloch, 2008).

AIDS almost certainly is compounding this inequality. Although the epidemic's effects on schooling are poorly researched, there is some evidence that school attendance is lower in households affected by AIDS (Steinberg *et al*, 2002).[74] But the harm probably penetrates deeper than studies reveal, especially in the many communities where HIV infection levels exceed 20%. There the epidemic's effects, obvious or otherwise, are ubiquitous. It is not known how many school students are living with HIV, but it has been estimated that more than 300 000 primary-school students are HIV-infected (Jansen, 2007). Since almost all of them will have acquired HIV during or shortly after birth, they are likely to be experiencing complicated health problems that also handicap their learning abilities. Meanwhile, HSRC research found that 13% of educators overall were HIV-infected. Among female educators aged 25–34 years 22%–24% were living with HIV (Shisana *et al*, 2005b).

Attrition was a problem for the public education system even before the epidemic peaked, with poor pay, increased workloads, lack of career-advancement prospects and dissatisfaction with work policies typically cited as reasons for leaving the profession.[75] Between 1997/98 and 2003/04, public schools were losing about 21 000 educators a year. At the beginning of that period deaths accounted for a small percentage of the attrition: about 7% in 1997/98.[76] By 2003/04, however, almost one in five (18%) teachers lost to the system had died. The increase was almost certainly due to the AIDS and TB epidemics (Shisana et al, 2005b). Fully 58% of teachers dying were younger than 40 years of age (Jansen, 2007). It has been estimated that about 30 000 educators have to be trained annually to maintain current staffing levels. Demand far outstrips supply, with management and administrative skills especially short in supply.

The cumulative effects spill wide. In a highly unequal system, the damage tends to be distributed along discriminatory lines. Impoverished and badly serviced communities will bear the brunt. Channels for quality educational advancement exist, but access is tightly rationed. It is estimated that learners in township schools on average benefit from one third as much instructional time as their counterparts in former 'white schools' enjoy (Jansen, 2007). Limited in number and imposing high school fees, the latter are schools of privilege and are inaccessible to all but a few. The vast majority of learners have to cope with learning environments that are riddled with routine dysfunction and where AIDS adds exceptional difficulties. Neither teaching nor learning can even approach being 'normal' in places where one in seven educators is living with HIV and where large proportions of learners are either themselves infected or live in households where one or more persons are battling AIDS or TB.

What might this mean for intergenerational social mobility? If the quality of public school education deteriorates further against a backdrop of continuing marginalisation of the poorest households—and of overall polarisation—social mobility will be hobbled further, trapping more South Africans in a cycle of poor education, paltry employment prospects and precarious livelihoods.

Similarly, AIDS appears to be corroding other institutions' capacities to provide predictable, consistent and acceptable standards of service. Already saddled with heavy workloads and compromised capacity, the police, correctional and judicial services, as well as managerial and administrative services at local government level, are especially vulnerable. By one tally, 233 local councillors in the 22- to 49-years-old age group died in office between early 2001 and the end of 2007 (Chirambo & Steyn, 2009).[77] Non-governmental and community-based organisations (CBOs) are also highly vulnerable to attrition. Destabilisation brought on by staff losses has been a familiar facet of CBO and NGO life since the 1990s[78] and AIDS and TB are compounding those frailties. Even in the best of circumstances NGOs and CBOs tend to rely heavily on a few key individuals in whom organisational knowledge, contacts and experience are concentrated. Losing them can be disastrous for small organisations and for the communities that rely on their services.

AIDS on the bottom line

It seems axiomatic that the AIDS and TB epidemics will affect the economy—even though the extent of the damage is not easily calculated (Barnett & Whiteside, 2002

& 2000). The direct costs of AIDS to organisations and businesses tend to manifest in the form of higher healthcare costs and more expensive workers' benefits, while indirect costs take the form of reduced productivity, loss of skills, experience and institutional memory, as well as (re)training and recruitment time and expenses. Indirect costs are significantly higher for skilled workers, as are employee benefit costs (Whiteside & O'Grady, 2003). In a serious AIDS epidemic, these are expected to add up to a hidden payroll tax, or 'AIDS tax' (De Waal, 2003).

Estimates of the epidemic's effect on South Africa's national economic output vary enormously, however. Some trivialise the damage, while others anticipate havoc. Arndt and Lewis (2000) predicted that GDP would be 17% lower in 2010, while the Bureau for Economic Research (2006) estimated that real GDP would be 3.4% less in 2010 and 8.8% lower in 2020 (compared with a no-AIDS scenario). ING Barings (2000) foresaw minimal damage; GDP would be just 2.8% less in 2015, it predicted. Other studies do not even list AIDS among the factors affecting South Africa's economy.[79] Siding with the sanguine forecasts, the Finance Ministry has been unruffled by the epidemic's impact on economic growth (though much less so about the fiscal implications of providing free ARV drugs to several hundred thousand people). In early 2006 it convened a panel of 29 top local and international economists to devise a roadmap for boosting economic growth and employment. Their final recommendations, released in mid-2008, contained not a single reference to HIV. Nor does the AsgiSA framework regard AIDS (or health generally) as a constraint on economic growth.

Mere cynicism does not explain such calm. Disagreement about the damage AIDS wreaks on economies stems partly from different understandings of the epidemic's demographic impact, the channels along which AIDS affects an economy and the nature and extent of those effects (Nattrass, 2004 & 2002).

In a serious AIDS epidemic, companies generally have four strategic options (Rosen & Simon, 2003): they can invest in HIV prevention programmes; they can provide treatment, care and support to AIDS-affected workers and their families; they can invest more in sustaining and extending their human capital base; and they can change the ways and terms on which they use labour.

A few major companies (including some large mining corporations) have introduced high-profile antiretroviral (ARV) treatment programmes for some of their employees, usually in response to pressure from trade unions. Many more sponsor some prevention activities (distributing condoms, some AIDS awareness and education, etc). All do so with great fanfare. BHP Billiton, for example, claims that 'there is an overwhelming business case' for investing in HIV workplace programmes which, it says, yield a four-fold return in the form of avoided absenteeism, retraining and rehiring and productivity gains.[80] SABMiller says its HIV efforts were 'cost-beneficial' within two years.[81]

Yet surveys also show that many companies, especially medium-sized ones, have been taking AIDS in their stride. They have considerable leeway for deflecting the effects of the epidemic—and they use it (Rosen & Simon, 2003). One study of large private and parastatal companies in southern and East Africa, for example, found that AIDS raised labour costs by about 1–2% annually (considerably less than price inflation). In South African companies, this 'AIDS tax' ranged from 0.5% (in the retail sector) to 2.4% (mining) (Rosen *et al*, 2006). The 'tax' is even lower when contract and casual labour is extensively used; in those cases, worker benefits are rare or absent and workers prone to illness can be easily dismissed and replaced. Among small and medium-sized companies, the researchers found that most were 'not terribly concerned about [AIDS] and have taken little action to address it' (Rosen *et al*, 2006:11). The bottom line, according to Rosen and her colleagues (2006:16), was that

> *the private sector has greater scope than other employers to shift the economic burden of AIDS onto government, nongovernmental organizations, households and individuals. Common practices that shift the AIDS burden from businesses to others include: pre-employment screening, reduced employee benefits, restructured employment contracts, outsourcing of less skilled jobs, selective retrenchments, and changes in production technologies.*

Companies have been cutting worker benefits. Medical benefits are now often capped at levels far too low to cover the costs of serious ill health or injury; employer contributions have been slashed, compelling workers to pay larger shares of the premiums for the same benefits. By 2000, more than one third of workers with access to medical schemes had already withdrawn from them because they could not afford to pay their contributions.[82] Regulatory changes proposed by the government could improve some workers' access to medical insurance schemes, but casual workers are unlikely to benefit. There has also been a major shift from defined-benefit retirement funds to defined-contribution funds (the latter offering meagre help to workers stricken with disease in the prime of their lives) (Barchiesi, 2004).[83]

Companies have also stepped up their use of outsourcing and casual labour and the adoption of labour-saving work methods and technologies. When surveyed in the mid-2000s almost one quarter of mining companies and almost one fifth of manufacturing companies said they were investing in machinery and equipment in order to reduce their labour dependency because of AIDS. Most of these trends precede the AIDS epidemic (see Chapter six), but they have a huge effect on working South Africans' abilities to cushion themselves and their kin against the effects of the epidemic (Nattrass, 2002).

The net effect is the steady erosion of benefits for those South Africans with jobs at a time when they and their families face increased risks of severe illness and premature death. The masses of 'casual' workers and the unemployed have to fend largely for themselves, with some indirect support channelled via the state's grant system.[84]

'Microenterprises' which typically are operated by poor households themselves, lack such evasive abilities. A disease like AIDS has a severe impact on impoverished households. Unless other (unlikely) factors compensate for those effects and boost dispensable incomes of those households, small retailers, spaza shops and service providers in impoverished neighbourhoods will see their customer base and earning potential shrink. This casts a shadow over government's hopes of fighting poverty by boosting small and micro-sized enterprises (see Chapter seven).

In such ways, many of the costs of the AIDS and TB epidemics are being 'socialised'—trapped in or deflected into the lives, homes and neighbourhoods of the poor. A massive, regressive redistribution of risk and responsibility is underway. The conventional yardsticks for measuring the impact of an epidemic such as AIDS do not capture these discriminatory dynamics.[85] They also do not capture the epidemic's effects on the non-market economies of households and communities (including child-raising, care of the frail and sick, other home-based tasks and volunteer work).[86]

An unequal epidemic in a polarised society

The same dynamics that govern the distribution of wealth, opportunities, resources and power in society also filter, dissipate and redistribute a good deal of the impact of South Africa's AIDS epidemic. This is not a 'democratic' epidemic. Alan Whiteside (2008) seems correct in arguing that the inequalities that shape the social and economic architecture of a hyper-endemic country such as South Africa also act as a barrier or filter preventing the effects of AIDS from snowballing into systemic collapse. Thus a great deal of the mayhem and tribulation wrought by AIDS is being compressed and contained within the lives and communities of the poor; the more privileged and powerful sections of society seem capable of 'gating' themselves, to a considerable extent, against the worst of the impact.

In some respects, however, the impact does spill over and travel to macro realms—in ways that are likely to further aggravate inequalities. In highly stratified labour markets (such as South Africa's) that are marked by shortages of highly skilled workers and a surplus of low- and unskilled workers, attrition in an already limited pool of skilled and highly skilled labour will tend to push up their wages and salaries. Meanwhile the surfeit of low-skill labour will continue to depress the wages of those workers. This will undermine attempts to narrow income gaps, which currently are among the widest in the world. In the mid-2000s, the poorest five million South Africans received about 0.2% of national income (via wages and social grants), while the richest five million pocketed 51% of national income (Statistics SA, 2008a).

This underlines the likelihood of deeper marginalisation of the very poor and especially of the women in their ranks. The ability to participate in networks of reciprocity, entitlement and responsibility is an essential tool of survival and advancement in impoverished settings. But participation depends on whether a person can marshal the time, energy and other means for remaining a part of the social circuitry of reciprocity (Pieterse, 2003). The poorest households, especially those headed by women, find themselves pushed back in the queue of entitlement and claims-staking. The effects feed into a loop. The more impoverished and marginalised sections of society are least equipped to manage or overcome the effects of these corroded capacities, while the more privileged sections have the means to sidestep or vault those obstacles. Inequality deepens.

Turning the tide

The most obvious first step to cushion the epidemic's impact is to provide antiretroviral treatment (ART) to all who need it. About 370 000 people were receiving ART in the public sector in 2008, according to the Department of Health. Record-keeping and monitoring systems are poor, however, making it difficult to know how accurate that tally is.[87] After examining various data sources for both the public and private sectors, Adam and Johnson (2008) estimated that 568 000 people were getting ART in 2008 in both the public and private sectors. If so, a little more than one third of the 1.5 million adults and 106 000 children in need of ART in 2008 were receiving the drugs (Statistics SA, 2009b).

Even if new HIV infections are drastically reduced, the total number of people in need of ART will likely remain the same for some time (since ARV treatment helps people live longer). Government's stated target is to have 1.4 million people on ART by 2011–12 (about 80% of those in need of ART at that stage)—an improbable outcome on current trends. It is highly doubtful whether ART access can be expanded and sustained in the medium term unless health systems and resources are strengthened considerably (Bärnighausen et al, 2007).

The infrastructure, systems and staff required to properly monitor treatment retention and loss grow increasingly inadequate as programmes are expanded. When the Free State provincial health department ran short of ARVs in mid-2009, for example, officials blamed funding shortfalls. In reality, the problem arose from weak governance and accountability systems and poor budget planning and management.[88] There is a danger that scale-up which compromises the quality of treatment and care could undermine programme benefits in the long term and lead to widespread viral resistance (Hirschhorn & Skolnik, 2008). Already, early treatment mortality is a major problem, partly because of late HIV diagnosis, late initiation of therapy and inequitable access to healthcare. This limits the overall benefits of ART programmes (Hallet et al, 2008). Tracking and monitoring ARV provision is weak and pharma-covigilance is poor. There is growing concern about patient retention, which elsewhere in sub-Saharan Africa averages at about 60% after two years. The main causes of attrition appear to be the failure to continue treatment and death (Rosen, Fox, Gill, 2007).

Looming, meanwhile, is the future affordability of ARV drugs. Given the lifelong need for treatment, the volume of people requiring ARVs will continue to grow and increasing numbers of them will at some stage need to shift to second-line regimens. It costs between R 6 000 and R 8 000 (USD 750–1 000) a year to keep a patient on ART, with drug expenses comprising about two-thirds of the total cost.[89] Generic versions of first-line ARV drugs are widely used and significant further price reductions for patented first-line ARV drugs are still possible. But most second-line ARV drugs (such as abacavir, lopinavir/ritonavir, nelfinavir, saquinavir) remain under patent and are exorbitantly priced.[90] As a hyper-endemic country, South Africa has the right to issue compulsory licences for the cheaper manufacture of such life-saving medications. To date it has recoiled from using that right, for fear of retaliation from its major trading partners. But government's fundamental duty to safeguard the lives of citizens means it will have to cross that line soon—and it is only likely to do so with success if simultaneously pressured and backed by popular mobilisation, both in South Africa and abroad.

Studies show that a bigger treatment programme would be cost-effective. It would reduce the burden on the health system in the medium term, as fewer AIDS patients would have to be hospitalised. And, all else being equal, it would reduce new HIV infections in the medium term.[91] By 2012 an estimated 2.75 million South Africans will need ARVs. If half of them were diagnosed and started treatment, roughly 600 000 deaths could be averted over the course of five years. This would cut the AIDS death rate by one third and push health spending up by a net USD 1.1 billion over those five years. With moderate economic growth over that period and if public-health spending increased from the current 3% of GDP to 5%, an ART programme with 80% coverage would absorb about the same share of the health budget as it currently does (12%–14%) (Walensky *et al*, 2009).[92]

Aside from the costs, the model of ART provision has been too restrictive. It revolved around some 400 accredited sites staffed by doctors, professional nurses and pharmacists. Each would need to have enrolled and retained 100 new patients every month until 2011 if government's ART target was to have been met (Schneider, Van Rensburg, Coetzee, 2007). This was unrealistic. ART provision has to become more diffuse, decentralised and creative (Boulle *et al*, 2008). In 2010 the government moved to lodge ART programmes in some 4 000 public health clinics and centres; in April alone 500 additional health facilities began dispensing HIV drugs.[93] It also hugely expanded its HIV testing campaign, by shifting to a policy of routinely offering HIV tests to all people who use the public health system. Hundreds of pharmacies were also beginning to offer customers free HIV tests, using government-supplied testing kits.

There is considerable room for enhancing TB treatment efforts as well, including drawing on lessons from HIV treatment provision. AIDS activism thrust patients' rights into the spotlight and challenged one of the hallmarks of medicine: the authoritarian and paternalistic relationship between healthcare systems and patients. In South Africa and elsewhere, people living with HIV have helped to draft, implement and monitor HIV programmes—to mixed degrees and sometimes irritating effect, but often with auspicious results. Among the imprints of this involvement are the relatively high rates of patient retention and treatment compliance in antiretroviral programmes that feature 'treatment literacy' training for patients (Lawn *et al*, 2007). These are generally provided by peer counsellors and offer patients an emancipating understanding of the treatment.[94] TB services, in contrast, tend to take the old-school approach; they require direct daily observation and recording of treatment compliance, often at healthcare facilities and seldom include 'treatment literacy' elements.

Given the deadly interplay between the AIDS and TB epidemics, the integration of HIV and TB services is a priority.[95] HIV-positive patients should be routinely screened for active tuberculosis and patients with tuberculosis should be offered a HIV test (and provided with ART should they test HIV-positive). Concurrent ART and TB treatment has been shown to cut the death rate among co-infected persons by more than half. Up to 10 000 lives can be saved each year by providing ART to persons who are infected with both HIV and TB and have CD4 cell counts of under 500 (Karim *et al*, 2009).[96]

Government has stepped up both its AIDS and TB responses. In December 2009 it announced that TB and HIV would be treated under one roof—an overdue move that might be tripped up by inefficiencies in the health system, but which could save many lives. South Africa accounts for more than one quarter (28%) of the world's people with both HIV and TB and 33% of all cases in sub-Saharan Africa (WHO, UNAIDS, UNICEF, 2008). Patients presenting with both TB and HIV infections will also be eligible for ART if their CD4 counts (a measure of their immunity strength) fall below 350. Also significant is the decision to provide all HIV-positive pregnant women with ARVs once their CD4 counts drop below 350. All children younger than one year will also be provided with ART if they test HIV-positive.[97]

One step forward

Treatment alone, though, will not save the day. Modelling indicates that even if 2.1 million South Africans receive ART by 2011, nearly 1.5 million people would still have died of AIDS between 2007 and 2012 (Walensky *et al*, 2008). Ultimately, the biggest challenge is to radically reduce the rate at which HIV spreads from person to person.

The basic components of a potentially successful AIDS response now form the backbone of South Africa's new AIDS Strategic Plan for 2007–11. The plan also includes a set of objectives aimed at reducing 'vulnerability to HIV infection and the impact of AIDS' by reducing gender inequality and gender-based violence, 'accelerat[ing] poverty reduction strategies and strengthen[ing] safety nets' (Government of SA, 2007:61–3).

There are tentative grounds for encouragement. National HIV surveys showed a substantial decrease in HIV incidence among teenagers between 2005 and 2008 (Shisana *et al*, 2005 & 2010). More young people were using condoms, for example. But achieving consistent and correct condom use (especially in long-term relationships) is massively difficult (Simbayi & Kalichman, 2007; De Walque, 2007; Chimbiri, 2007).[98] Even among young South Africans with concurrent partners, condom use declines rapidly with a 'main' partner and is inconsistent even with 'other' partners (Parker *et al*, 2007).

Condom promotion is an important cornerstone for HIV prevention, but reducing multiple sexual partnerships, especially concurrent partnerships, can have an even more dramatic effect on HIV transmission (Shelton, 2007; Halperin & Epstein, 2007). Uganda's 'zero-grazing' campaign is credited with a reduction of more than 50% in the number of people with multiple partners between 1989 and 1995 (Shelton *et al*, 2004) and helped reverse the country's HIV epidemic. Unfortunately, a replicable approach for reducing multiple concurrent partnerships in other countries has not yet been found (Potts *et al*, 2008). On this front, the latest trends in South Africa were not positive. The proportion of young women (aged 15 to 19 years) with partners at least five years older rose from 19% in 2005 to 28% in 2008 and the percentage of young men (aged 15 to 24 years) with more than one sexual partner in the previous year rose from 27% to 31% (Shisana *et al*, 2010). Oddly, the same national HIV survey found that accurate knowledge about how HIV is transmitted deteriorated in all age groups and researchers said participants in the survey found it hard to grasp the link between multiple partners and higher HIV risk.

King Goodwill Zwelithini's support in 2009 for a male circumcision campaign among Zulus could have telling positive effects within a decade. There is strong evidence that male circumcision dramatically reduces the risk of HIV acquisition in men during heterosexual intercourse. Modelling suggests that large-scale male circumcision could avert up to 5.7 million new HIV infections and three million deaths over the next 20 years in sub-Saharan Africa, including among women and non-circumcised men (Williams *et al*, 2006). Evidence from Botswana and Swaziland suggest male circumcision services are acceptable and desired (Westercamp & Bailey, 2007).

Gender dynamics must be factored in, however. At population level, women would gain some protection against HIV infection (via the 'herd immunity' effect) (Hallett *et al*, 2008; Williams *et al*, 2006).[99] But there are concerns that some circumcised men, aware that their risk of acquiring HIV is reduced, might be disinclined to practise safe sex, thus putting their female partners at risk. So male circumcision is not a 'magic fix', but it potentially is one of the most powerful interventions available to help protect men and women from infection. In the long term it could lead to fewer AIDS deaths and a reduced need for ART, so cushioning the overall impact of the epidemic.[100]

As with AIDS, failed prevention is the biggest hurdle facing South Africa's TB response. Public-awareness campaigns on TB remain patchy and half-hearted and elementary precautionary steps (such as preventing transmission in the waiting rooms of health facilities) are often lacking. Programmes to improve the nutrition of undernourished populations that are especially vulnerable to TB (young children, the elderly, healthcare workers and institutionalised populations such as prisoners) can have considerable impact.[101] So can simple steps, such as ensuring adequate ventilation in clinic waiting rooms,[102] the introduction of contact tracing and the provision of infection-control education to the families of persons with TB.[103] Karim *et al* (2009) have argued for the building of a social movement, along the lines of the TAC, to tackle TB and other diseases of deprivation and neglect.

It is generally accepted that HIV responses that focus exclusively on behaviour change (such as condom use) are inadequate in hyper-endemic settings. As discussed earlier, the choices they promote are often short-circuited by powerful underlying factors that lie beyond the immediate, direct control of individuals

(JLICA, 2009; Wellings *et al*, 2006). Similarly, avoiding TB infection is hardly a matter of 'personal choice'. Comprehensive approaches to HIV and TB prevention therefore also focus on tackling the social relations and structural factors that shape people's lives and choices. The most promising approach is one that resolutely promotes 'conventional', behaviour-focused interventions in the context of society-wide egalitarian strategies. South Africa's record on the latter front is disappointing and invites rampant improvement. Wider and stronger social safety that significantly and directly benefits impoverished communities (especially women) should be a priority.

In the context of the overlapping AIDS and TB epidemics, a social protection package needs to include a drastic overhaul of the current home- and community-based care systems. Stronger financial and institutional support, more user-friendly administrative procedures and a much sharper focus on using, developing and supporting existing skills in communities to boost access to social services should be one priority. That would mean expanding a para-professional cadre that can improve community access to services such as early child development and education and various forms of care provision (including, urgently, mental healthcare and support) (Altman, 2005). By 2009, government was expanding the cohorts of community health workers and community care-givers and, although still patchy, institutional support was being strengthened. These are potentially powerful steps: sharing and socialising the individualised burdens of care-givers, reducing the mental-health effects of stressed households and communities and possibly strengthening social bonds and networks. Other positive steps include the Early Childhood Development Programme and greater support for orphan care projects, though both areas remain woefully underfunded and under-resourced.

Fragmentation, introversion, erasure

An epidemic that threatens to prematurely end the lives of one fifth of a country's adult population will change society. But the nature of that change is not easy to predict. One of the most far-reaching outcomes of the 'Black Death' in England, for example, was the destabilisation of social relations, which eventually erupted in the form of peasant uprisings that reshaped society. These outcomes required a specific context however and were fed by the arrogant detachment and tactical buffoonery of elites and the vibrant self-awareness of the subaltern classes. But different outcomes unfolded in places that were at least as hard hit by the plague; in Italy, the Netherlands and in the countries of the Middle East, for example. Even epidemics of such ferocity, it seems, do not lend themselves to generalisations.

The South African struggle for liberation was a struggle for a just society and for freedom of many kinds, not least from penury and sickness, banishment and exclusion. It is onto this template of ideals that the effects of the AIDS and TB epidemics must be mapped. That these epidemics mangle is clear. But when they do so in a society with South Africa's characteristics, the adversities and distress are not distributed evenly. AIDS and TB are reinforcing the country's warped social relations. On current trends the epidemics will exacerbate inequality, worsen impoverishment and further corrode the prospects of a better life. In their wake we can expect intensified polarisation, with privilege no longer guaranteeing mere comfort and indulgence, but buying life itself and cornering the future. Many millions of people will have to contend with compromised services and with the fraying of those bonds and circuits of obligation and reciprocity that, in the past, helped stave off destitution.

The living versus the dead

Like many scourges, AIDS pits the living against the dead and the healthy against the sick. That AIDS-related stigma does so in ways that diminish and wound others is not unusual; what is atypical is the ferocity with which it is aimed at loved ones, kin and friends. Infectious diseases are met instinctively with attempts to demarcate danger and safety, to distinguish the 'pure' from the 'contaminated'. Victimisation and polarisation typically follow. All this is evident with AIDS, not just in the stigmatisation of people living with HIV but also in the virulent tendency to regard and treat women as bearers of contagion and 'disease-carriers'. A distillation of everyday obsessions (about trust, desire, belonging, betrayal, contamination, sex, death) AIDS stigma also derives its energy from the 'invisibility' of HIV[104] and the licence it provides for judgement and exclusion. Stigma cleaves. It is used to assert virtue in ourselves and deny it to others; to affirm some and condemn others. As wounding as AIDS-related stigma is, it is hardly an aberration. It is one of the devices people use to traverse society. To pretend that AIDS stigma can be 'challenged' and removed is to misunderstand how deeply embedded it is in the arrangement and exercise of social power.

There is a chance that the extraordinary tribulation unleashed by the AIDS and TB epidemics might spur new social arrangements and new forms of popular organisation and activism. But the current trends are not cheering. They point to petrifying arrangements and possibly even a kind of social contraction, as the capacities of the poor to extend generosity diminish and the reciprocal arrangements that sustain social life wane further (De Waal, 2003a).

Responsibilities and entitlements, it seems, are not being reallocated more equitably in households and communities; social roles seem to be ossifying instead of growing more pliant. Rather than trigger a re-imagining of 'womanhood' and 'manhood', AIDS is cementing squalid stereotypes. In the male imagination, the nurturer/witch, angel/whore dichotomies and the association of women's bodies with impurity and contamination retain prominence. It is women who are accused of 'bringing the disease' into homes, girls who are subjected to 'virginity testing' and women and girls who tend the sick, the frail and the survivors. Men seem to hover along the fringes of this drama, leaving women ubiquitous yet trapped between blame and the praise they earn for the forbearance shown within the confines of domestic space and duty. AIDS exposes the coercive subtext nestled in the notion of 'mothers of the nation'. Collectively assigned the duty of care, nurture and salvation women oblige with stoicism and courage, but at the cost of their autonomy and freedom. The home-based care model, so flimsily supported at present, codifies this exploitation of women's labour, finances and emotional reserves.

A similar process of 'erasure' occurs among children who endure systematic deprivation, trauma and stigmatisation. The tendency of traumatised children is less to 'explode' their hurt than to invert it and collapse into themselves, into a private twilight that might offer some solace (Richter, 2004; Stein, 2003). People at the mercy of pain and the indignities that accompany it live at the extreme limits of that experience. The necessary aversion to the phrase 'AIDS sufferers' cannot undo the reality that unthinkable numbers of people do suffer horribly and in ways that almost literally remove them, living, from the world. Their pain, as Elaine Scarry has written (1985), erases the world and them in it:

> *What from the inside is experienced as an increasingly insubstantial world may look from the outside as though the world is intact but the person is growing insubstantial, and so the experience is often represented as solid world ground on which the person no longer has a place [...] As one's world is obliterated, one's externalized self and therefore one's visibility is obliterated.*[105]

This is not mere metaphor. In north-eastern South Africa terminally ill persons are literally hidden away from society. Known as 'noisy ancestors' (*bakwale badimo*), they are deemed dead to society, yet physically alive: in effect, zombies. AIDS assigns this undead state even to healthy persons: 'If you test HIV-positive,' explains a villager, 'you are dead. They will take you as dead. They will take you as a living corpse.'[106]

Polarisation, implosion, erasure and the dismantling of the social—all this forms the undertow of these epidemics, their secret thrust. Folded into this horror is the prospect that epidemics this intense, layered atop a reality this unjust, imprison vast numbers of people in a kind of eternal now, corroding the ability and perhaps even the desire to imagine a different, better world.

Endnotes

1   Based on the Joint United Nations Programme on HIV/AIDS (UNAIDS) EPP and Spectrum estimates; see Department of Health (2009:35).

2   There were an estimated 33.4 million people, globally, living with HIV at the end of 2008; 22.4 million of these lived in sub-Saharan Africa. Fully 1.4 million of the estimated two million AIDS deaths in 2008 occurred in sub-Saharan Africa (UNAIDS/WHO, 2009). Within this region, however, the epidemic is disproportionately concentrated in southern Africa (and, to a lesser extent, East Africa).

3   HIV *prevalence* data indicate the *total* number of people infected with HIV at a particular point in time. HIV prevalence is usually expressed as a percentage of the adult (15 to 49 years old) population. These data can provide a good picture of the overall *scale* of an epidemic. But they offer a less satisfactory picture of recent developments, since they do not distinguish between people who acquired the virus very recently and those who were infected several years earlier. In places where large numbers of people receive antiretroviral (ARV) treatment, HIV prevalence becomes an increasingly unreliable yardstick for recent trends in the epidemic. In South Africa's case, rising or steady HIV prevalence in the late 2000s probably also reflected increased access to life-prolonging ARVs: more people with

HIV were living longer than before. Very large numbers of new infections continued to occur but at a rate that appeared to be slowing. HIV *incidence* data describe the rates at which *new* infections occur—the number or percentage of people infected over a specific period, usually a year.

4   Persons most at risk for HIV infection tend to become infected and die, earlier in the epidemic. Their deaths reduce the pool of people living with HIV, eventually slowing HIV prevalence growth. Everything else being equal, this pattern drives the 'natural' evolution of an AIDS epidemic. UNAIDS estimates that, without ARVs, the median survival time from sero-conversion to death is 10–12 years. Most of the people infected during the period of exponential growth in South Africa's epidemic (the first half of the 1990s) therefore would have died by the mid-2000s, at which point the epidemic should have been approaching a plateau. Indeed, official mortality data show AIDS deaths peaking in the mid-2000s.

5   See, for example, Packard (1987) and Kark (1949).

6   Clare Kapp, 'South Africa heads into elections in a sorry state of health', *Lancet*, Vol. 373, 24 January 2009.

7   DOTS, though, is no panacea. Trials (including in South Africa and Thailand) assessing its effectiveness have shown conflicting results. In countries with serious HIV epidemics the impact of the DOTS approach appears to be highly diminished. See Academy of Science of SA (2007:38).

8   There are at least 6 000 cases annually of multidrug resistant (MDR) TB, which requires complex and prolonged treatment, but also carries a high failure rate. In combination with HIV, MDR TB is decidedly aggressive and progresses very rapidly to death without antiretroviral therapy. See Academy of Science of SA (2007:39).

9   TB patients who are infected with HIV are twice as likely to have multidrug resistant (MDR) TB than are people without HIV (Booth & Heywood, 2008).

10   The vast majority of HIV infections occur during unprotected heterosexual intercourse, while a small minority occurs during unprotected sex between men and when drug injectors share contaminated injecting equipment (Gouws & Stanecki, 2008; Shisana *et al*, 2005).

11   These are important caveats. There is no evidence that male circumcision reduces the risk of HIV acquisition during anal sex between men. The evidence is mixed on whether it reduces a female partner's chances of becoming infected (Wawer *et al*, 2009; Baeten *et al*, 2009). But the so-called 'herd effect' means that wide-scale male circumcision in a country like South Africa will reduce HIV infections in both men and women; if fewer men become infected, onward transmission of the virus to their female partners will also decrease (Baeten, Celum, Coates, 2009).

12   The amount of HIV found in the blood. The viral load indicates how fast the virus will damage the immune system.

13   See, for example, Mombo, L E *et al* (2003) 'Mannose-binding lectin alleles in sub-Saharan Africans and relation with susceptibility to infections', *Genes and Immunity*, Vol. 4, No. 5, pp. 362–7; Ma, L *et al* (2005) 'Distribution of CCR2-64I and SDF1-3'A alleles and HIV status in 7 ethnic populations of Cameroon', *Journal of Acquired Immune Deficiency Syndrome*, Vol. 40, No. 1, pp. 89–95; Donfack, J *et al* (2006) 'Human susceptibility to viral infection: the search for HIV-protective alleles among Africans by means of genome-wide studies', *AIDS Research and Human Retroviruses*, Vol. 22, No. 10, pp. 925–30; Gonzalez, E *et al* (2001) 'Global survey of genetic variation in CCR5, RANTES, and MIP-1alpha: impact on the epidemiology of the HIV-1 pandemic', *Procedures of the National Academy of Science*, Vol. 98, No. 9, pp. 5199–204; Philpott, S *et al* (2003) 'CC chemokine receptor 5 genotype and susceptibility to transmission of human immunodeficiency virus type 1 in women', *Journal of Infectious Diseases*, Vol. 187, No. 4, pp. 569–75.

14   See Chen *et al* (2007) and Helleringer and Kohler (2007), among others.

15   Mathematical modelling done by Morris and Kretzschmar (2000) compared a population in which serial monogamy is the norm against one in which long-term concurrency was common. The modelling showed much more rapid HIV transmission in the population

with long-term concurrency, which resulted in an HIV epidemic 10 times larger than in the population with serial monogamy. Subsequent modelling and empirical evidence seem to confirm that overlapping partnerships (compared to serial partnerships) could increase the size of an HIV epidemic, the speed at which it infects a population and its persistence within a population (Mah & Halperin, 2008).

16   Among the often-cited examples were Caldwell *et al* (1989, 1991, 1992), although they did not always regard 'cultural patterns' of sexuality as free-floating ideological phenomena and related them to long-term changes in material conditions.

17   For more, see Smith, G D (2002) 'Commentary: behind the Broad Street pump: aetiology, epidemiology and prevention of cholera in mid-19th century Britain', *International Journal of Epidemiology*, Vol. 31, pp. 920–32. Available at http://ije.oxfordjournals.org/cgi/content/full/31/5/920#R38; and Johnson, S (2008) *Ghost Map: a Street, a City, an Epidemic and the Hidden Power of Urban Networks*, Penguin Books, London.

18   For a précis of the evidence and reasoning, see Wilkinson (2002).

19   For a sympathetic yet keen engagement with Wilkinson and Pickett, see Runciman, D (2009) 'How messy it all is', *London Review of Books*, Vol. 31, No. 20, 22 October, pp. 3–6.

20   See also Davis, M (2001) *Late Victorian Holocausts: El Niño Famines and the Making of the Third World*, Verso Books, London; Hughes, C C & Hunter, J M (1970) 'Disease and "development" in Africa', *Social Science and Medicine*, Vol. 3, No. 4, pp. 443–93; Farmer, P (1999) *Infections and Inequalities*, University of California Press; Kim, J Y *et al* (2000) *Dying for Growth: Global Inequality and the Health of the Poor*, Common Courage Press, Monroe; Leon, D A & Walt, G (2001) *Poverty, Inequality and Health*, Oxford University Press, Oxford.

21   McKeown showed that TB rates in Britain commenced a steep decline decades before effective clinical prevention and treatment interventions were developed and introduced. For discussion of his findings, see the special issue of the *American Journal of Public Health*, Vol. 92, No. 5 (May); and Szreter, S (1992) 'Mortality and public health, 1815–1914', *Recent Findings of Research in Economic & Social History* (ReFresh), No. 14:1–4.

22   For example, Afghanistan, Bangladesh, Ecuador, El Salvador, Guatemala, Laos, Mauritania, Mali, Niger, Nepal, Senegal, Somalia and Sri Lanka.

23   The countries were Burkina Faso, Cameroon, Ghana, Kenya, Lesotho, Malawi, Tanzania and Uganda.

24   Poverty was measured against an asset index.

25   For critiques of Mishra *et al* (2007), see Bingenheimer (2007) and Gillespie, Kadiyala, Greener (2007).

26   Subsequent analysis suggests that HIV *incidence* (the rate of new infections annually) among Africans older than two years was nine times higher in 2005 than among other South Africans: 1.8% compared with 0.2% (Rehle *et al*, 2007).

27   Anso Thom, 'Low HIV prevalence among SA students — study', *Health-e*, 29 March 2010.

28   This discussion does not survey all forms of HIV risk in South Africa. Small proportions of infections occur during unprotected paid sex and unprotected sex between men. There are also indications that drug injecting has become a minor factor in the epidemic. The bulk of HIV transmission, however, occurs during unprotected sex between men and women as part of some or other relationship between them (from the proverbial one-night stand to the bond of marriage and much in between).

29   It has been estimated that about one-sixth of adult women in the Ciskei region of the Eastern Cape had moved to cities and towns by 1940, as did at least one quarter of the female population of Basutoland (Bonner, 1990; Mager, 1999).

30   At the Mount Coke Hospital, near King William's Town in the Eastern Cape, for example, the prevalence of venereal disease among pregnant women increased from 1% in 1938 to over 20% in 1948.

31   Mager, A (1996) 'Sexuality, fertility and male power in the Eastern Cape', unpublished paper presented to the Societies of Southern Africa seminar, 7 November, Institute of Commonwealth Studies, London; cited in Marks (2002:20).

32   In KwaZulu-Natal, for example, astonishing levels of HIV prevalence have been found among young migrating women: one in four sexually-active 17–18-year-olds was HIV-positive, as were two in three of their 22–24-year-old peers (Coffee *et al*, 2007).

33   In particular locations, however, such as border crossings and towns along major transport routes, sex work can be a powerful driver of HIV transmission.

34   'Transactional sex' is the 'exchange of sex for material gain among women in the general population' (ie women who are not commercial sex workers); see Dunkle *et al* (2004). However, as Hallman (2004:17) points out, 'the distinction between commodified exchanges of sex and receiving gifts that are considered a normal part of a dating relationship is not always clear'.

35   In southern Zambia, for example, droughts and employment insecurity ranked high among the factors driving apparent increases in transactional sex, while in Kenya, sexual risk-taking (paid sex, multiple partners, not using condoms etc) has been shown to be significantly associated with asset poverty. A study in Botswana and Swaziland found that women who had experienced food insecurity in the previous year were 84% more likely to have engaged in transactional sex, 68% more likely to have had unprotected sex with a man who was not their primary partner and 46% more likely to have had sex with a person significantly older than them (compared with women who had not experienced food insecurity). Each of those factors is associated with increased risk of HIV infection. The association between food insecurity and risky sex was much weaker for men.

36   They were also more likely to have been forced to have sex—a correlation found in other South African studies (see below).

37   Shifts such as those described here and the insecurities they express, have also boosted HIV risk in rural areas. Earlier in the epidemic, it was returning migrants who appeared to be introducing HIV into rural areas, but there is now strong evidence that HIV transmission *within* rural areas is playing a significant role in the spread of the virus there (Coffee *et al*, 2007; Lurie *et al*, 2003).

38   For example, among South African women aged 15–24 years, HIV prevalence was found to be 30% in those with partners at least five years older, compared with 19% in those with partners less than five years older (Shisana *et al*, 2005a). HIV prevalence was approximately 16% among teenage girls (15–19 years) in rural Zimbabwe whose last partner was less than five years older than themselves, but among girls with partners 10 or more years older, it was *twice as high*. Studies from East Africa have found similar patterns. Men in their late twenties and thirties are more likely to be HIV-infected and the dependencies built into such relationships can badly curtail women's abilities to protect themselves from HIV infection. See Kelly *et al* (2003), Gregson *et al* (2002), Luke (2005), Glynn *et al* (2001).

39   The survey revealed startling levels of sexual violence. Fully 32% of the young men reported perpetrating physical or sexual violence against a female partner. One in six (16%) of them said they had raped a non-partner. Those who aggressed or assaulted women were also found to engage in significantly higher levels of HIV risk behaviour (not using condoms, having more than one sex partner, etc) and more severe violence was associated with higher levels of risky behaviour (Dunkle, 2006).

40   Quoted in Marais (2000).

41   Hani was addressing an AIDS policy conference convened by the ANC in Lusaka, Zambia, in May 1991. Quoted in Marais (2000). Mzala's denialist screeds had already been published in the ANC journal, *Sechaba*, a few years earlier (see Chapter twelve).

42   Between 2000 and 2009 alone 2.5 million South Africans died of AIDS. The model had also predicted that AIDS would help to cut South Africa's population growth rate to around 1% by 2005, which also was more or less on the money: the growth rate was 1.07% in 2008–09 (Statistics SA, 2009b).

43   NACOSA refers to the National AIDS Convention of South Africa, the consultative process that formulated a new AIDS policy between late 1992 and early 1994. For a more detailed discussion of the racist and listless manner in which the apartheid health bureaucracy had

approached AIDS in the 1980s, as well as descriptions of the NACOSA process and the plan's troubled passage into practice, see Marais (2000) and Lawson (2008).

44   Mbeki claimed to be engaged in a search for truth. However, he conducted that quest with lamentable regard for the scientific evidence and for the scientific methods used to generate that evidence. Amar Hamoudi (2000), for example, had set out to examine two questions that flowed from the claim that AIDS was a misnomer for various poverty-related conditions. Firstly, had mortality trends in the hardest-hit countries of Africa changed significantly compared with trends in other countries on the continent? And, secondly, could such discrepancies be attributed to factors other than AIDS—for example, to malnutrition, parasitic diseases, illness due to poor sanitation and unnatural causes such as violence or accidents? Focusing on southern Africa, Hamoudi found no statistically significant differences in life expectancy for southern Africa compared with the rest of Africa in 1980. Fifteen years later, however, significant differences were evident (thus answering the first question). Yet, differences in incidence of malnutrition and access to sanitation were found not to be statistically significant between southern Africa and the rest of continent, while malaria had a much less severe presence in most southern African countries compared with the tropical regions of the continent. In addition, most of the burden of mortality caused by malnutrition, diarrhoea and parasitic diseases (such as malaria) is borne by infants and young children, yet significantly higher *adult* mortality was being observed in countries with severe AIDS epidemics. Hamoudi concluded that the rising mortality rates seen in southern Africa could not be explained without factoring in the AIDS epidemic. Such elegant enquiries did not serve Mbeki's purpose, however, as we discuss later.

45   Lawson (2008:226).

46   Mbeki convened the panel in March 2000, on the eve of the International AIDS Conference in Durban. It comprised 16 HIV 'dissidents' (who claimed that HIV did not cause AIDS) and 16 'mainstream' HIV scientists, ostensibly with the mandate of informing the government on the most appropriate response to the epidemic. Among the 'dissidents' were two academics the South African denialists held in high esteem: Charles Geshekter (a scholar of African history) and David Rasnick (who trained in chemistry). Geshekter would be granted face-to-face meetings with the Health Minister to discuss HIV and HIV drugs. David Rasnick, meanwhile, was in regular email contact with Mbeki. Neither Geshekter nor Rasnick was a qualified AIDS scientist. Tellingly, Lawson (2008:211) asks why, for Mbeki and his circle, trading as they were in the discourse of anti-colonial righteousness and African sovereignty, 'two US academics—qualified in their own fields, but not in HIV and AIDS research—could be more convincing than the host of African researchers working on the issue across the continent'.

47   *Business Day*, 7 August 2001; quoted in Kenyon (2008:33).

48   Quoted in Clare Kapp, 'New hope for health in South Africa', *Lancet*, Vol. 372, October 4, pp. 1207–08.

49   This section draws on research done for the Centre for the Study of AIDS, at the University of Pretoria. Grateful thanks are owed to Mary Crewe.

50   The number of non-natural deaths stayed constant at 50 000 to 55 000 per year from the mid-1990s (Statistics, 2008d). Improvements in the death registration system probably accounted for a small part of the observed trend. An estimated 85% of male deaths and 79% of female deaths were captured in the national death registration system in 2006—an improvement over the 75% and 65% for male and female deaths, respectively, in 2001 (*op cit*). If these estimates are accurate, the actual number of deaths annually is about 20% higher than the total recorded deaths. Improved data capturing and reporting, however, cannot explain the shifts in the distribution of deaths between various age groups since the mid-1990s.

51   The Medical Research Council (MRC) estimates attributed 25% of all deaths (and 40% of deaths among adults) during 1999/2000 to AIDS which, it said, had become the leading cause of death in South Africa (Dorrington *et al*, 2001). In September 2001, the release

of the document was unexpectedly delayed, probably due to pressure from government. When the report was leaked to the media, government spokespersons declared the findings 'alarmist' and 'inaccurate'. (See 'President uses 1995 data to bolster claim that HIV/AIDS is not SA's leading killer', *Business Day*, 10 September 2001.) The leak incensed government; it reportedly demanded that the MRC undertake a forensic enquiry to identify the source.

52   A minority of death certificates list AIDS as cause of death; typically with AIDS deaths, the underlying cause of death is noted. For infants, the main underlying causes of death were 'intestinal infectious diseases, influenza and pneumonia and certain disorders involving the immune mechanism'. Among adults TB, influenza and pneumonia were the top causes of death. See Statistics SA (2008d:24–6).

53   About 300 000 HIV-positive women give birth to infants each year in South Africa; see Patrick, M and Stephen, C (2007) *Saving children 2005: a survey of child healthcare in South Africa*. Medical Research Council Unit for Maternal and Infant Health Care Strategies, Cape Town.

54   Kerry Cullinan, 'AIDS-free generation within grasp', *Health-e*, 8 December 2009. The findings emerge from a year-long study among 38 000 mothers in KwaZulu-Natal's six largest urban areas. Two years earlier, the provincial health department had battled to prevent the provision of dual therapy in Umkhanyakude district: in early 2008, a Manguzi doctor, Colin Pfaff, was charged with 'willfully and unlawfully without prior permission of [his] superiors [rolling] out dual therapy to the pregnant mothers and newborns', after he had privately raised funds to purchase the ARV drug AZT for his patients.

55   The following sections draw on research done for the Centre for the Study of AIDS at the University of Pretoria. Grateful thanks are owed to Mary Crewe and her colleagues at the centre.

56   The outbreak was known in Britain, Canada, France and the United States as the 'Spanish flu'—possibly because the epidemic received more press coverage in Spain, which was not subject to wartime censorship. In Spain, it was known as 'the French flu' in keeping with our tendency to lay blame for calamities at the doors of others. In India, the flu claimed an estimated 17 million lives, in France at least 400 000, while in the US it killed as many as 675 000 people, more than the combined number of American deaths in the First and Second World Wars, the Korean War and the Vietnam War (Kolata, 2000). In South Africa it is estimated to have killed 140 000 people in late 1918, roughly 2% of the entire population (Simkins, 2001).

57   The death toll remains difficult to peg with precision and for obvious reasons. According to Herlihy (1997), local records suggest the populations of some cities and villages in England and Italy shrank by 70–80%: 'Europe about 1420 could have counted barely more than a third of the people it contained one hundred years before (1997:17).'

58   The mortality rate at Oxford University matched that in the upper levels of English society (25–27%), while among the rural poor and those clergy that served them it was 40%. See Catto, J I, Aston, T H and Evans, R (eds) (1992) *The History of the University of Oxford: Late Medieval Oxford*, Oxford University Press, Oxford, quoted by Hugh Pennington in 'Two spots and a bubo', *London Review of Books*, 21 April 2005.

59   As with AIDS, a minority position questions the primacy of the plague in the demographic and other disruptions experienced in Western Europe during that period. Focusing on an area of Normandy (France), Guy Bois developed a fascinating Marxist analysis of the upheavals, attributing them largely to a wider crisis in the social order (of feudalism, specifically), with the plague a subordinate factor. See Bois, G (1984) *The Crisis of Feudalism: Economy and Society in Eastern Normandy c. 1300–1550*, Cambridge University Press, Cambridge. For a brief discussion, see Herlihy (1997:35–8). Parts of the denialist camp in South Africa seem similarly inclined, although their contributions have not ventured beyond declamations. Lacking a conceptual framework, analytical rigour and an informed engagement with the various types of data such an undertaking would require, the denialist output remains largely intellectually barren.

60   Growing demand for the services of priests and physicians opened the way for new entrants into those ranks, some of them brazen charlatans and others (like women physicians) ground-breakers. The church acceded to women performing pastoral functions or administering sacraments, while in the courts women were for the first time allowed to serve as witnesses.

61   Andrew Rissik, 'When all life changed', *Guardian Review,* 9 April 2005.

62   The immediate trigger was the levying of a third poll tax, but the revolt was long in the making with the 1351 Statute of Labourers having caused lasting resentment.

63   Cited in Desai (2005:17).

64   That mitigating effect often disappeared when a death occurred in the household, which suggests that many of the households were heavily reliant on a social grant paid to a single person.

65   A total of 771 households were surveyed in parts of Free State, Gauteng, KwaZulu-Natal and Mpumalanga.

66   The guidelines were drafted before government relented and introduced an ARV treatment programme through the public health system.

67   Thus the National Guideline defines it as care that 'the consumer can access nearest to home, which encourages participation by people, responds to the needs of people, encourages traditional community life and creates responsibilities' (African National Congress, 2001, cited in Mills, 2004:4).

68   Both women and men enforce these divisions of labour. Akintola's (2006) qualitative research in peri-urban parts of KwaZulu-Natal, for example, found many female care-givers were dismissive of men's care-giving abilities.

69   Care-givers complain, for example, that they are expected 'to be always around home' and have 'to do everything'; as reported in assessments of care-giving projects in Khayelitsha, Gugulethu and Delft, Cape Town (Mills, 2004).

70   Their relationship to the state, though, is noteworthy. They are employed by NGOs and CBOs which receive funding from the state. Consequently, the community health workers fall outside the regulatory framework that governs employment in the public service. In essence they are outsourced workers who lack the employment rights of formal health workers but are expected to work regular hours.

71   Almost 70% of white households belong to medical schemes compared with just 8.4% of Africans (and 22% of coloureds and 39% of Indians). The proportion of households with medical-aid membership actually dropped to 14% in the mid-2000s before rising to match its 2002 levels.

72   The disparities are most obvious around entry-level care where diagnosis and treatment is required for non-life-threatening ailments and injuries. Beyond that, at the level of tertiary care, a handful of public hospitals are still capable of providing top-quality care; conversely, some private hospitals provide shoddy (though expensive) care.

73   Between 2003 and 2005, for example, the total number of nurses registered with the South African Nursing Council rose from 130 290 to 136 619—an increase of less than 5% (Matsebula & Wilie, 2007).

74   The main reason was lack of money for school fees, uniforms and books.

75   'Survey gives hard facts about the lives of educators', *HSRC Review*, Vol. 3, No. 2, July 2005.

76   *Op cit.*

77   There may also be an effect on voter turnout; almost 400 000 deceased voters were removed from the voters' roll before the 2009 national election. See Zuma, J (2009) 'Address by the President of the Republic of South Africa, Mr Jacob Zuma, to the National Council of Provinces', 29 October 2009, Parliament, Cape Town.

78   From 1994 onward, hundreds of key NGO staff were lured into post-apartheid government departments and parastatal institutions and, later, the private sector. Along with funding difficulties, this dimmed the effectiveness and even accelerated the demise of many progressive NGOs and CBOs. Those that survived soon encountered another trend. Large

companies, keen to advertise their acquiescence to the 'new South Africa' (and under pressure to heed affirmative action requirements), began courting (black) NGO staff and snatching newly graduated talent.

79   Roy Cokayne, 'AIDS "has no major effect on economy"', *Business Report*, 13 April 2006.

80   Andre van den Bergh, BHP Billiton's regional health adviser for southern Africa, quoted in Anna Stablum, 'HIV time bomb under the mining industry', *Reuters*, 11 July 2007.

81   'Business and AIDS: Fighting the good fight', *The Economist*, 18 December 2008.

82   See 'Will your trustee fund survive AIDS?' *Old Mutual Trustee Times*, February 2000, Johannesburg, cited in Rosen & Simon (2003:132).

83   *Defined-benefit* funds provide long-term support for the spouses of deceased workers (at significant cost to companies). *Defined-contribution* funds provide a one-off payout equal to the combined amounts contributed by the employer and the worker up to the last day of employment. By 2000 almost three-quarters of 800 retirement funds had *defined-contribution* funds, up from just one quarter in 1992.

84   Mainly old-age pensions, child-support grants and disability grants. Pensions and child-support grants typically are shared widely within (and sometimes also across) households; their benefits therefore extend well beyond the designated 'beneficiary'. Disability grants are available to persons with AIDS whose conditions have deteriorated beyond certain clinical thresholds (usually a CD4 count below 200).

85   Simulation analysis sometimes detects these patterns. Such analysis of household survey data for Swaziland, for example, found a significant impoverishing effect of AIDS considerably 'beyond its impact on average per capita incomes'. The study concluded that 'the disease can throw a considerable share of the population into poverty even in cases where researchers do not expect a significant fall in income per capita'; see Salinas and Haacker (2006).

86   'Economists fail to note AIDS widening impact', *SouthScan*, 5 May 2006.

87   Official data do not reflect patients who are lost to follow-up (ie do not remain on treatment or stop and start treatment), who deregister or who die after commencing treatment.

88   Faranaaz Parker, 'AIDS policy: "Systemic problems need to be addressed"', *Mail & Guardian*, 3 December 2009.

89   *Ibid.*

90   In low- and middle-income countries the average price per person per year in 2007 of the most commonly used second-line regimen (didanosine, abacavir and ritonavir-boosted lopinavir) was USD 1 214. Prices vary though: South Africa was paying an average USD 1 600 for that regimen in 2007, while El Salvador was paying USD 3 448 (WHO, UNAIDS, UNICEF, 2008).

91   Persons on ART tend to have lower HIV viral loads, making them less infectious. Studies also show that persons on ART are more likely to avoid HIV risk behaviours.

92   This paragraph draws on research done for UNAIDS.

93   'South Africa redoubles efforts against AIDS', *New York Times*, 25 April 2010. Decentralising ART provision holds great promise. A study in Cape Town and Johannesburg townships showed that handing more responsibilities to nurses and other cadres of medical staff leads to treatment outcomes that are as good as when only doctors manage ARV provision. See Wood, R *et al* (2009) 'Nurse management is not inferior to doctor management of ARV patients: the CIPRA South African randomized trial', Fifth International AIDS Society Conference on HIV pathogenesis, Treatment and Prevention, Abstract LBPE, Cape Town.

94   These education sessions provide patients with information about HIV infection, how antiretroviral drugs work, why treatment adherence is vital, how to recognise side effects and how to blend pill-taking with daily routines. There is some evidence from the US that a DOTS approach, modified along these lines, works more effectively (Academy of Science of SA, 2007:38).

95   This is easier said than done. For example, TB infection is often more difficult to detect in persons with HIV and confident diagnosis in those cases requires sophisticated laboratory

techniques. See Corbett, EL *et al* (2003) 'The growing burden of tuberculosis: global trends and interactions with the HIV epidemic', *Archives of International Medicine*, Vol. 163, pp. 1009–1021.

96   For useful, critical summaries of feasible improvements, see Karim *et al* (2009:929–30) and, in relation to nutrition and TB, the Academy of Science of South Africa (2007:167–9).

97   'New hope for HIV+ moms', *Mail & Guardian*, 9 April 2010.

98   These failure rates are similar to those reported by adolescent males in the US (Crosby *et al*, 2005).

99   Research evidence is still scant, but a recent intriguing finding points to a possible protective effect on women as well. Circumcision in men was found to result in a statistically significant (47%) reduced risk of HIV acquisition in their female partners (Baeten *et al*, 2009b).

100   The rate of male circumcision among young men in South Africa is low. Among 15–18-year-olds it exceeds 20% in only three provinces: Gauteng (23%), Mpumalanga (27%) and Limpopo (67%). See Shisana *et al* (2010).

101   Several studies have linked improved nutrition to lower TB infection and morbidity rates. Among the more tantalising findings was the strong difference in TB morbidity between British and Russian prisoners of war (POWs) held in German camps during the Second World War. The TB rate among the British POWs was 1.25%, compared with 15%–19% among their Russian counterparts, although both groups shared the same living and working conditions. The major difference was in nutrition: unlike the Russians, the British received Red Cross food supplements (Leyton, 1946).

102   The Ubuntu clinic in Site B of Khayelitsha township, for example, has a waiting room without walls, but with heaters (for cold days) and UV lights (for destroying bacteria).

103   Health workers at Tugela Ferry, in KwaZulu-Natal, have used this approach for people diagnosed with MDR TB with excellent results (Booth & Heywood, 2008).

104   This 'invisibility' is reproduced in speech. Even the words 'HIV' or 'AIDS' are customarily denied. Instead, a person suffers from 'germs' (*twatsi*); or the 'virus of pain' (*kukoana hloko*); or the 'three letters' (*maina a mararo*) or 'was on diet' (*o ya dayeta*); see Niehaus (2007), drawing on his research in the Bushbuckridge region.

105   Scarry (1985), cited in Wright (2005).

106   Quoted in Niehaus (2007:8). The villager is not identified by name. 'AIDS seems to be marked by a peculiar compression of time,' notes Isak Niehaus (2007:10); 'Even the newly infected person is "tainted with death".'

CHAPTER TEN

False starts: the health
and education systems

A fundamental duty of the state is to secure the conditions and ensure the services that can enable citizens to live to a reasonable age, do so with dignity (which implies a fair income and humane living conditions) and bequeath to their children the realistic chance of improving the quality of their lives. The state is not the sole arbiter, nor the only source of means for achieving these goals, but they constitute the overriding reason for the state's existence. In a society with South Africa's history and dynamics, these goals pose a redoubtable challenge. Nevertheless, more than 15 years into the post-apartheid era, it is not unreasonable to gauge the progress made toward reaching them.

Rebuilding the health system

South Africa's public health system in the early 1990s was not only unjust, it was a shambles. Health infrastructure had been designed and built to fit the apartheid mould. Skewed to favour the white minority, the mix and distribution of healthcare activities (and financing) was utterly unsuited to the society.[1] More than 80% of resources went to hospitals (most of them in cities and towns) and only 11% of spending was on primary or preventive healthcare. One third of the 419 public hospitals and 4 000 clinics were in disrepair when the ANC-led government took office in 1994 (Heunis, 2004; Boulle *et al*, 2000). Correcting these imbalances was the new government's main health system priority.

A basic problem was the fragmentation of the health system, which had been segmented along several lines: racial, geographical, public/private and curative/preventive. This parcelling dated back to the early twentieth century, but acquired a crazed rigour after 1948. When the apartheid system finally collapsed there were 14 separate health departments operating in South Africa. Levels of funding for each ranged from paltry to indulgent, depending on the communities they served.

The ANC's 1994 health plan aimed to restructure this irrational and unjust system, broadly following the primary healthcare model promoted at the Alma Ata conference in 1978. The system would revolve around networks of community clinics and health centres and pregnant mothers and children younger than six years old would receive free care (ANC, 1994b). Initial progress was heartening. Disparities in provincial health funding were narrowed, the body of public health legislation was modernised, a new medicines regulatory body was established, immunisation campaigns were expanded and hundreds of health clinics were constructed or refurbished. Some of the worst regional disparities in health spending were reduced.

However, from 1997 onward provincial governments acquired greater autonomy for determining their own budgetary allocations and health-spending decisions again became subject to a mix of trade-offs and caprice. Disparities between provinces have widened since, though not by huge degrees (McIntyre & Thiede, 2007). Fees for all public-sector primary-care services were later removed, as were those for termination of pregnancy services.

The principle of shifting the focus onto primary and preventive healthcare cannot be faulted.[2] But multiple oversights and missteps (not to mention the ideological fads of the time) handicapped these efforts early on. Neoliberal dogma weighed on the public sector too and promoted the outsourcing of functions, flashy public management techniques driven from above and rampant cost cutting. In addition, economic policy rationed the resources that were available for transforming the health system and imposed 'the overriding imperatives of fiscal restraint and the crowding out of other goals' (Schneider, Barron, Fonn, 2007:305). Beyond that, the health system was not a core concern for economic planners and managers. South Africa's guiding economic strategies implicitly position health as a trickle-down outcome of economic growth; neither the 1996 GEAR plan nor the 2006 AsgiSA framework regards it as a precondition for economic and social development.[3]

Skewed spending

A large share of South Africa's gross domestic product goes toward healthcare: 8.7% in 2008 which was slightly less than Sweden's 8.9% (World Bank, 2008). Yet South Africa's health-status indicators are far worse than those of most other middle-income countries (McIntyre *et al*, 2007). In part, this reflects legacies of poor nutrition, unhealthy working and living conditions and perfunctory or inaccessible healthcare. But the patterns of health spending and resource distribution are at fault too. The private sector absorbs the bulk of healthcare spending in South Africa and captures most of the resources. Public health funding does not match the scale of need.

The country's health system has become more resolutely split: between a public health service buckling under the AIDS and TB epidemics and an inadequate primary healthcare system on the one hand and a private, profit-driven counterpart managed by financial capital on the other. Healthcare spending occurs in a two-tier system, with almost 60% of the funds paying for the healthcare of a minority (about seven million people). These constitute the 14–16% of (typically wealthier) South Africans who belong to private medical schemes and who use the well-resourced, for-profit private health system (Statistics SA, 2008c).[4] By way of comparison, in the 1970s, during the heyday of apartheid, roughly one third of all healthcare expenditure was funnelled toward the 20% of the population that carried private health insurance (Benatar, 2003):

■ Annual per capita expenditure on healthcare in the private sector in 2005 was almost six times larger than that in the public sector: R 9 500 (USD 1 190) versus R 1 300 (USD 163) (McIntyre *et al*, 2007).

■ At least 23 million people rely entirely on an overburdened, understaffed and poorly managed public health system, while another 10 million finance their own health needs but turn to the public system when stricken by serious ailments or injuries (McIntyre *et al*, 2007).

■ The maldistribution of human resources is glaring. By the end of the 1990s three out of every four medical doctors were working in the private sector (Sanders & Lloyd, 2005), compared with 62% in the early 1990s and 40% a decade earlier (Rispel & Behr, 1992). In the public sector in 2006 there was one specialist doctor for every 11 000 people; the ratio in the private sector was 1:500 (McIntyre *et al*, 2007).

The private sector operates independently from the public one, an incongruity that a proposed national health insurance system might eventually overcome. Meanwhile, the disparities in healthcare access and quality are glaring.[5] There have been attempts to temper these trends, but to limited effect: as a general rule, income determines access to healthcare, its use and its quality.

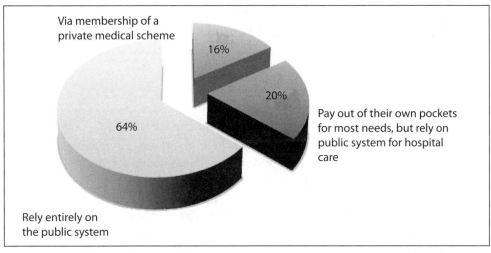

Via membership of a private medical scheme — 16%

20% — Pay out of their own pockets for most needs, but rely on public system for hospital care

64%

Rely entirely on the public system

Figure 10.1: How South Africans pay for their healthcare needs
SOURCE: DATA FROM MCINTYRE *ET AL* (2007)

Health spending in context

South Africa spent the equivalent of about 3.5% of GDP on its *public* health system in the mid-2000s—less than several other 'medium human development' countries, including Nicaragua (3.9%), Mongolia and Honduras (4% each), Namibia (4.7%), Lesotho (5.5%) and Colombia (6.7%). Conversely, *private* health expenditure absorbed the equivalent of 5.2% of GDP. It is not unusual for a country's private health spending to outstrip its public health expenditure by some margin. However, aside from Argentina (5.1%) and Paraguay (5.3%) no other 'medium human development' country with levels of income inequality similar to South Africa's devoted as large a share of its GDP to private health spending (UNDP, 2008).[6]

Real public spending on health rose modestly in the early 2000s then increased impressively in the middle of the decade.[7] However, these increases did not match population growth and per capita spending actually declined slightly (McIntyre & Thiede, 2007). The rate at which spending increased also lagged behind the overall growth in government expenditure.[8] As a proportion of overall government expenditure, public health spending shrank slightly between 2000/01 and 2007/08 (from 11.5% to 10.9%) while the expenditure share of economic services and of social security and welfare grew significantly. The bottom line, according to McIntyre and Thiede, (2007:38)

> is that public sector health care expenditure has been stagnant in real per capita terms for a considerable period of time, despite the fact that the demands on public sector services have increased dramatically due to the AIDS epidemic.

Compared with other, similar-sized economies, South Africa's public health expenditure in 2004 came to USD 307 (PPP)[9] per person—much less than the USD 836 spent in Brazil, Argentina's USD 573 or Poland's USD 562, though considerably more than Thailand's USD 193, Venezuela's USD 123 or Egypt's USD 95.[10] Per capita spending also paints a more nuanced picture of comparative health expenditures. In 1998 per capita spending in private medical schemes in South Africa was five times more than in the public health sector; by 2005 it was 6.6 times more (McIntyre & Thiede, 2007).

The private health system

Financed mainly by mining capital, the private health sector is a further reminder of the extensive and formative influence of the minerals-energy complex in South Africa (see Chapter one). The first medical schemes were earmarked for white mineworkers and dated back to 1889. For many decades, private hospitals were either on-site at large mines or non-profit mission facilities. For-profit general hospitals are a comparatively recent development, facilitated by the apartheid regime's turn toward deregulation and privatisation in the 1980s. As the regime shifted its policies onto a neoliberal footing, greater private sector involvement in healthcare provision was explicitly encouraged. Medical schemes proliferated from the mid-1980s onward, with members corralled into ever-smaller risk pools (following the risk-rating model used in private health insurance in the US). This put paid to the cross-subsidisation principle, which initially had applied to medical schemes (Van den Heever, 1997). Minimum benefits were abolished in 1993 substantially widening the scope for profit-taking. When the ANC assumed office in 1994 the private health sector was booming and only faintly regulated.

Private-sector spending on healthcare soared in the 1990s and beyond, far outstripping inflation. This was not because the mainstay of the private system (medical schemes) drew more members. In fact, access to these schemes has stayed comparatively rare: only 16% of South Africans have any form of medical aid (Statistics SA, 2005c). Among low-income earners (individuals in households earning less than R 6 000 or USD 800 a month) only 7% have any formal medical-scheme coverage (Broomberg, 2007). Memberships dipped below the seven million mark in 1997 and only reached that level again in 2005 despite economic growth and a larger middle class (Council for Medical Schemes, 2006; McIntyre *et al*, 1995). Rising subscription fees were the main cause of these trends. By the mid-1990s, medical-scheme expenditure was rising by some 30% per year (in nominal terms).[11] Driving that trend were various cost escalations, including rising administration and brokerage fees, commercial reinsurance costs and a proliferation of private hospitals.[12]

The number of for-profit hospitals grew from 161 in 1998 to 216 in 2006, with almost half of them concentrated in one province, Gauteng. The number of beds in these hospitals more than doubled between the late 1980s (approximately 11 000) and 1999 (23 700) and then increased to 27 000 in 2006 (Matsebula & Willie, 2007). Three corporations (Netcare, Medi-Clinic and Life Healthcare) own more than 80% of these beds (Van den Heever, 2007),[13] a consolidation that formed part of the wider trend of mergers and acquisitions in South Africa's economy (see Chapters two and five). In combination the private hospital oligopoly and high-end specialist care[14] have been key drivers of the increases in medical-scheme fees and appear to be bound together by various 'performance-based' reward systems (Matsebula & Willie, 2007). Hospitals attract doctors with monetary and subsidy arrangements and by installing top-end medical equipment. Following models pioneered in North America, hospitals seem to rely on doctors to generate demand for bed occupancy; the use of high-tech, high-fee equipment; and surgical procedures. Meanwhile, many specialists hold stakes in the financial performance of hospitals via share ownership. Consequently, South Africa has a very high rate of elective Caesarean sections, for example and there has been a significant increase in the use of other, expensive services, such as magnetic resonance imaging (Folland, Goodman, Stano, 2001).[15] Specialists and other practitioners also benefit from subsidised or rent-free consulting rooms at hospitals in return, it seems, for

> meet[ing] targets for use of hospital facilities, which is likely to have contributed to higher levels of hospitalization, longer periods of admission and/or increased use of diagnostic procedures than would have occurred without these financial inter-relationships (McIntyre et al, 2007:27).

The private-hospital monopoly now pockets about one third of private health spending in the country, which reflects a dramatic shift in the balance of power between medical schemes (there were 131 of them operating in 2008) and the corporate owners of private hospitals. Facilitating that shift were some key regulatory interventions, among them the Competition Commission's decision that each medical scheme had to negotiate separate terms and fees with each service provider (which boosted the power of corporations monopolising the private-hospital sector). The failure to publish a National Health Reference Price List since 2004 removed a further vestige of provider fee controls and appears to have benefited private hospitals and specialist doctors (McIntyre *et al*, 2007).[16] Medical schemes, in turn, redistributed these inconveniences. As a result, benefits are now so delicately calibrated and are managed with such meanness that medical-scheme members are responsible for about two-thirds of out-of-pocket healthcare spending (as they 'top up' inadequate policy coverage).[17]

The current dual system is both unjust and inadequate given the scale and nature of South Africa's health crisis. The volume of financial and human resources available to medical-scheme members is on the increase, while the proportion of the population served by these schemes is stagnant. Much greater cross-subsidisation of healthcare financing and spending has to be achieved.

There were attempts after 1994 to re-regulate medical schemes. Risk-rated contributions were done away with and minimum benefits were reintroduced (McIntyre, 2007). Overall, though, the regulatory interventions have been timid. South Africa still lacks effective regulation of the quantity and distribution of private healthcare providers (the vast majority of which are concentrated in urban areas) and over the quality of care provided by them (Coovadia et al, 2009; McIntyre et al, 2007).

Making the current arrangement even more objectionable is the fact that tax revenues are used to subsidise the private medical-scheme system. Medical-scheme contributions are tax-deductable—a handout to the most privileged layers of society that cost the fiscus R 10.1 billion (USD 1.3 billion) in 2005, equal to about 30% of total government spending on health in that year (McIntyre et al, 2005). In addition, a large amount of tax revenue is used to pay for civil servants' private medical insurance: the state spends 12 times more per civil servant than it does per 'ordinary' citizen who relies on the public health service (McIntyre & Doherty, 2004). The only cross-subsidies that do exist are via the tax funding of public healthcare, but these are at least partially offset by the tax-deductible status of medical-scheme contributions.

A national health insurance scheme

It is fair to say that government's appetite for taking on powerful sectors of corporate South Africa has not been prodigious. The debacles and fiascos that made headlines on the watch of successive health ministers also denuded them of the political capital they needed to confront the for-profit healthcare sector. This held especially for Manto Tshabalala-Msimang who served as health minister for the duration of Thabo Mbeki's two presidential terms. Irrespective of her intentions, her capacity to sell, steer and manage a process of healthcare reform was scuttled by her handling of the AIDS response and the rank ridicule and reproach this invited. In this sense, government's misconduct around AIDS claimed other extensive casualties, such as postponing the restructuring of an unconscionably unjust health system.

The idea of a national health-insurance (NHI) scheme dates back almost 70 years to a proposal published in the *South African Medical Journal* in 1941. At that stage, at least 30 countries around the world had already introduced compulsory NHI schemes. The South African proposal, which would have covered people of all races (except for those in rural areas), was never implemented. Instead, government set up another commission, which proposed a national health service. It, too, was not implemented. These options languished until 1995 when a committee of inquiry proposed a social health-insurance arrangement, which subsequent committees tweaked but failed to get off the ground. In the meantime, as Olive Shisana notes, the public and private sectors remained 'worlds apart; in fact they have grown even further apart in terms of financing, service provision and the size of the population served'.[18] There were fitful attempts subsequently to redesign an NHI, but none found traction until 2009, by which time countries such as Brazil, Ghana, Peru, Taiwan, Thailand and Tunisia had all introduced NHI systems.

The scheme outlined in 2009 could potentially transform the country's health system into a more equitable and accessible one. It triggered a torrent of doomsaying from the private sector, which focused its misgivings on claims of affordability and efficiency. Essentially, an NHI would be a risk-pooling mechanism that would correct the currently skewed allocation of resources between the private and public systems. Modelled on the Canadian system, it would use a financing mechanism to integrate private- and public-sector activities, relying on a system of mandatory health-insurance contributions

> in which those who can afford contribute according to their ability and those who cannot are paid for through subsidies from Government. The funds are pooled into one fund from which resources are drawn as people use services according to their need.[19]

Details were still being worked out in 2010, but the envisaged NHI is expected to involve a single-payer fund that receives funds, pools resources and purchases services on behalf of the entire population. Health services covered by the NHI would be free at the point of use and patients would be able to choose their service providers (private or public). Both private and public providers would deliver healthcare, but government would collect and allocate the money. Research commissioned by COSATU predicted significant savings over time, though the NHI would cost an extra R 46 billion (USD 5.8 billion) annually after an initial five-year phase-in period. Financing could be achieved through the tax system and by extending payroll deductions to all current full-time workers who do not belong to a medical scheme (Anon, 2009).

A great deal of debate revolves around whether the public-health system should be fixed first or whether the NHI would form an integral aspect of repairing that system. If underfunding is not the sole cause of the public system's woes, then some basic mending has to occur first. A 2008 report by the Development Bank of South Africa (DBSA) argued as much, saying

> SA's health system is performing poorly as a consequence of factors under the control of Government [...] more important than financial resources, the most important factor relates to poor leadership and structural weaknesses within the institutional framework.[20]

Underfunding, though, is an issue. The same DBSA report estimated that R 34 billion (USD 4.3 billion) extra was needed over the next decade. Although government seems committed to an NHI, its fate is unclear. Along with resistance from within government (especially from the Treasury), the for-profit health sector is intent on derailing the scheme. Doubtless, an NHI stands no chance of success unless backed with strong political leadership and popular mobilisation.

Sick system

The public system languishes, meanwhile. Officially, the country shifted toward a primary healthcare system soon after achieving democracy in 1994. But that overhaul was not completed. 'When last did you see a nurse in any school checking kids, checking their teeth, their eyesight, their ears, tonsils, whether they have been immunised, nutritional status?' Health Minister Aaron Motsoaledi asked with exasperation in early 2010.[21]

Primary healthcare strategies work best when there are enough well-trained healthcare workers with the right mix of skills, when they are distributed appropriately across the system and when the system is responsive to innovation (Sewankambo & Katamba, 2009). South Africa flunks on each of those fronts and on others.

There is a major shortage of skilled medical doctors, nurses and support staff in the public health system. Four factors underpin this situation: new nurses are not being trained quickly enough and in requisite numbers;[22] large numbers of doctors and nurses have opted to work abroad; there is gross misallocation of existing human resources between the public and private health sectors; and the AIDS and TB epidemics are stripping the system of workers.

In the 1990s there was an obvious need to boost the number of professional nurses. The primary healthcare approach would pivot on them and evidence from elsewhere in Africa suggested that a burgeoning AIDS epidemic would sap the time and health of personnel. Instead, the number of new nurses trained each year dropped from 2 629 in 1996 to 1 716 in 2004.[23] Part of the reason lay in the closure of several nursing colleges (in line with cost-containment drives) in the 1990s. An early sign of 'poor stewardship of the system at the highest level' (Schneider, Barron, Fonn, 2007:299) this foolhardy move occurred in the absence of a human-resource plan and without co-ordination between the health and education sectors.[24] Transformation efforts also saw voluntary severance packages offered to thousands of public health workers in the 1990s, most of whom retired, moved into the private sector or migrated abroad.

Short-handed

By several accounts, South Africa's public health force is now weaker than in the mid-1990s, with fewer doctors and nurses per head and huge regional disparities. In the 1970s and 1980s, the public health system churned out health professionals: the number of registered nurses, for example, rose four-fold between 1960 and 1994, from 27 000 to more than 100 000 (Van Rensburg, 2004)[25] but then stayed stagnant. As the AIDS and TB epidemics grew, the percentage of general practitioners employed in the public sector shrank from about 60% in the 1980s to 27% in 2006. The trend was similar among nurses, 79% of whom worked in the public sector in 1989, before that percentage decreased to 59% in 1999 and 42% in 2007 (Sanders & Loyd, 2005; McIntyre *et al* 2007).[26]

The impact is most detrimental in the network of district-level clinics that are supposed to be the frontline of the healthcare system. These are staffed almost exclusively by nurses. The average nurse in the public sector in 2005 served six times more people (and the average general practitioner seven times more people), compared with her counterpart in the private sector (Health Systems Trust, 2007). On average, each nurse in a public-health clinic sees 27 patients a day (Health Systems Trust, 2009)—'sees' probably being the operative word. Once administrative tasks, lunch and tea breaks and various other interruptions are factored in, it is unlikely that an average consultation lasts 10 minutes. Very few of these clinics have attending or visiting doctors; fewer than 10% of the required number of doctors were visiting and supporting clinics and community health centres in the mid-2000s.

Compounding matters is the exodus of health workers and professionals. More than 23 000 South African medical professionals were working in Australia, Canada, New Zealand, the UK and the US in the mid-2000s, according to an Organisation for Economic Co-operation and Development study.[27] Government has stated its intention to fill more vacancies, but the poaching of health workers from South Africa and other 'developing' countries will continue. The US alone, for example, will need an estimated 800 000 additional nurses over the next decade.[28] No doubt, the state of affairs in South Africa's public hospitals and clinics lends allure to a posting abroad; so need outstrips supply. Remedial efforts have been sluggish, with new nurses being trained at rates that are too low to narrow the shortfall (Ijumba, Day, Ntuli, 2004). There are about 400 nursing-education facilities in the country. More than one third of these, though, are private and it is not clear whether or to what extent, their graduates end up in the public health system (Wadee & Khan, 2007).

The upshot is that there are 40% too few enrolled nurses and 17% too few enrolled nurse assistants in public health (Daviaud & Chopra, 2008). Overall, the public health system was short of 46 000 trained personnel in the mid-2000s—a 27% vacancy rate (Day & Gray, 2005). A 2008 Development Bank of South Africa report estimated that 64 000–80 000 more doctors and nurses were needed in the public system by 2013.[29] In 2009 only 3% of registered nurses were younger than 30 years and it was estimated that as many as 40% of nurses were due to retire in the next decade.[30] Many of their younger colleagues are keen to leave the public sector and complain of poor pay and working conditions, low morale and weak and unsupportive management. A dread cycle ensues: the crisis in hospitals and clinics makes it even more difficult to recruit new nursing staff. Patients, meanwhile, grumble about health workers' dismissive and uncaring attitudes and poor work ethics.

While staff numbers and capacity ebb, care needs have surged. AIDS and TB add further stress to the system, with both the demand for health services and the toll on health staff surging. In the early 2000s, an HSRC survey of public and private healthcare facilities had already found that an estimated 28% of patients in medical and paediatric wards were HIV-positive (46% in public hospitals) and their hospital stays were almost twice as long as those of non-AIDS patients. The situation in rural Hlabisa district, in KwaZulu-Natal, seemed emblematic: as adult HIV prevalence among residents rocketed from 4% in 1992 to 35% a decade later, clinic visits increased by 88% and hospital admissions by 81% (Dedicoat et al, 2003).

It has been projected that a country with a stable 15% HIV prevalence (such as South Africa) could expect to see 1.6%–3.3% of its healthcare personnel die of AIDS each year—a cumulative mortality rate over five years of 8–16% (Tawfik & Kinoti, 2003). From 1997 to 2001, before the AIDS death toll peaked, an estimated 13% of deaths among health workers were attributed to AIDS (Shisana et al, 2003).[31] More recently, 16% of surveyed health workers were found to be living with HIV (Connelly et al, 2007). The good news is that antiretroviral (ARV) therapy can enable many of them to stay relatively healthy and productive: if they are diagnosed early enough.

Triage

Fitful attempts have been made to tackle these issues, but none are drastic enough to leave a lasting mark. A Patients' Rights Charter exists on paper and patient surveys are conducted: neither of the two human-resources plans (one dating back to 1999/2000, the other done in 2006) has led to more than stopgap, piecemeal actions to deal with the human-resource crisis (Schneider, Barron, Fonn, 2007). Newly graduated doctors are required to perform one year of community service, yet few of them seem touched enough by the experience to commit themselves to the public sector. In 2001, almost half of these doctors said they planned to move abroad and complained of poor working conditions and support during their deployment.[32]

Buckling under the strain of the AIDS and TB epidemics, the public system now relies heavily on squads of generalist community health workers, care-givers and lay counsellors, an estimated 62 000 of whom are active in providing care to persons with AIDS or TB (Booth & Heywood, 2008). Most of them are attached to NGOs and community organisations and none of their training, roles nor supervision is standardised (Coovadia et al, 2009). Task shifting, which is now vogue in 'developing' countries, is being considered. This involves delegating certain responsibilities to other healthcare workers: for example, having nurses (rather than doctors) initiate ARV treatment or allowing lay counsellors (rather than nurses) to perform rapid HIV tests and so on. Often the opposite tends to happen and nurses also end up doing the work of semi-skilled staff, as this lament from a chief nurse illustrates:

> We always have to rush: we wash, we medicate, we move on. You miss some things [...] We also have to do inventory, push patients to other departments, clean floors, take a trolley to fetch food and dish it up.[33]

Complaints about lackadaisical and uncaring nursing staff abound, but a great deal of the public health system's decrepitude emanates from its managerial ranks. In the withering but fair assessment of Coovadia *et al* (2009:831):

> *Inexperienced managers have struggled to handle the major challenges associated with transformation, and, in particular, efficient and effective management of human resources. Reports of ill discipline, moonlighting, and absenteeism are widespread. Additionally, there is a serious shortage of training, support, and supervision. There has been insufficient political will and leadership to manage underperformance in the public sector. There has also been a stubborn tendency to retain incompetent senior staff and leaders [...] Poor stewardship at the policy level and weak management and supportive supervision at the implementation level are major obstacles to improving the health system in South Africa.*

Diagnosing the problems

Karl von Holdt's (2007 & 2009) research in public hospitals in Gauteng province has unearthed a disturbing jumble of problems, many of them structural. He describes public hospitals as 'highly stressed institutions' that are all but crippled by 'staff shortages, unmanageable workloads and management failures' (Von Holdt & Murphy, 2007:315). The system has haemorrhaged experienced and skilled staff and has failed to replace them. Poor and unpredictable management, stressful working conditions and fiscal handicaps have drained morale.

Even more disturbing is the sense that the public health system seems to be in a state of decline. Poor surveillance systems have compounded the makeshift and erratic character of healthcare provision. Information systems function poorly. The collection of data is often incomplete or incorrect and their collation and analysis are weak, as are practices of using the information for planning, monitoring and evaluation (Schneider, Barron, Fonn, 2007; Von Holdt & Murphy, 2007). A recent report intended for official consumption spoke of 'serious inefficiencies in the management of the South African public health system' and noted that these 'occur[ed] at all levels'. It also highlighted 'endemic' weaknesses that stem 'from poor quality of care' (Harrison, 2010: 28–9). In Von Holdt's analysis (2009:6–7) the causes run deep:

> *[T]he ability of the health department bureaucracy to perform effectively is undermined by poor institutional and system design, characterised by incoherent structures and systems, fragmentation, failure to delegate appropriate authorities, lack of accountability, and lack of financial, technical and human capacity.*

Assembling a potentially coherent public health system from the fragmented components of the apartheid system was an enormous undertaking, but it was also fraught with anxiety, suspicion and diffidence. Creativity tends not to thrive in such climates. An institutionalised aversion to innovation and creativity has taken hold. Enterprise and invention is also stifled by the distrust that emerged between trained healthcare professionals and the managerial mandarins who were drafted in to run the new system. In addition, relationships between the provincial health department managers and their hospital counterparts are dysfunctional, as are many of the organisational structures (Von Holdt, 2009). Shortly after being appointed health minister in 2009, Aaron Motsoaledi seemed to acknowledge these dimensions when he said that 'people previously seemed to think anyone could manage a health institution [but] that's not true. You need to understand the health system [...] You can't just be a manager'.[34] That may be so, but the problems run deeper. Not only is managerial capacity in short supply in many public hospitals and higher up in the chain (Von Holdt, 2009), but the other difficulties are entangled in multiple failures at various levels and sectors of the bureaucracy. The upshot is a

> structural relationship between province and institution [that] is a disincentive for managerial innovation and responsibility, and [that] rewards subservience, over-sensitivity to rules and a lack of focus on problem-solving. It is also clear that even if it were desirable for head offices to exercise this degree of control, in many cases they lack the capacity or competency to do so. Lengthy delays and poor decisions in turn encourage passivity and lack of initiative on the part of hospital managers (Von Holdt & Murphy 2007: 322).

Operations are plagued by breakdowns, lack of systems and low management capacities. Compounding these weaknesses are textured troubles—particularly the organisational practices and culture that shape everyday decisions and actions (see Chapter eleven). Few of these problems are peculiar to the public health system, but the consequences can be literally life-robbing. Although management skills are not abundant, the bigger hindrance, according to Von Holdt and Murphy (2007), are fragmented and 'incoherent' authority structures, the nebulous positioning of managerial authority and the fuzzy and inconsistent nature of accountability. Attempts to impose a remote but overweening authority from head office level do not help matters.[35] The upshot is managerial inefficiency and 'bureaucratic inertia'. Combined with routine operational dysfunction, this carries the risk of 'a long-term erosion of public service ethos and consequent decline of the public health sector' (Von Holdt & Murphy, 2007:337).

A further problem relates to disciplinary regimes in the workplace, specifically the failure to replace the authoritarian apartheid model with a new, widely endorsed workplace order, especially for non-professional staff (Von Holdt & Murphy, 2007). As a result, labour relations are often fraught, short-fused and marred by conflicts between management and trade unions. Disciplinary measures tend to be unpredictable, puny or absent. Morale and the sense of public service are weak and work performances suffer. The overall effect is corrosive. The absence of broader accountability has meant that the imposition of (often rarefied) rules and regulations eclipses the management of people and day-to-day operations, at the expense of problem solving and service delivery. 'It sometimes seems,' writes Von Holdt (2009:7), 'that health service delivery is secondary or even incidental to the real purpose of the bureaucracy.'

On the whole, the public health system reaches more people than ever before, but dispenses services that are subpar. It has not made much headway in preventing ill health. The AIDS and TB epidemics no doubt have stood in the way of quicker improvements, but they are also symptoms of the poor stewardship that plagues the health system (see Chapter nine). In the judgement of Coovadia and his colleagues (2009:832), 'there has been a notable lack of progress in implementing core health policies developed by the ANC, and some disastrous policy choices'.

Alongside that doleful record are some important achievements. Many of them have stemmed from specific, focused programmes that operate along separate tracks. The ARV programme is probably the most eye-catching example. Those are important gains, but they do not necessarily strengthen the overall health system. Indeed, they are sometimes accused of diverting resources and of applying a technocratic rather than social perspective to health challenges. Community and non-government organisations are more active than ever in the healthcare field. In one respect this is emblematic of the neoliberal era, with civil-society groups and households stepping in to compensate for scaled-back state services and provisioning. Most obviously with AIDS care, South Africa fits this trend (see Chapter nine). But AIDS activism has also challenged traditional hierarchies and power imbalances in healthcare by promoting an informed assertiveness among patients and campaigning for patients' rights. There is still a long way to go, but this activism has begun to chip away at the almost medieval authority of healthcare providers.

Intensive care

A major overhaul is needed. An NHI system is vital if access to quality healthcare is to become more equitable. But it is not a panacea; its phasing-in must be linked to urgent, priority improvements in the public health system. A good start would be for accountability systems to encompass the top political and managerial echelons. A system of routine and random spot-checks of health facilities and care provision is long overdue. More generally, functioning management systems must be created, including basic systems for staff-performance management, individual staff accountability and procurement of supplies.

Von Holdt's (2009) prognosis calls for a new institutional design that 'overcomes fragmentation, creates clear lines of accountability and delegates authority to appropriate levels'. Health Minister Motsoaledi seemed to be thinking along such lines when he highlighted the need for managers to have experience as health professionals. But it also means that health professionals should gain greater voice and managerial authority. This, writes Von Holdt (2009:26), 'could generate a fresh dynamic in which organisational performance, problem-solving and clinical outcomes gained more weight and in turn increased the salience of skill, experience and expertise'. The work-force has to be revamped—in terms of numbers, skills and dedication. Human-resource capacity can be enhanced by in-service training; increased output from training institutions of healthcare workers who are competent to work in primary healthcare services; task-shifting; increased flexibility in health services roles; and a greater reliance on community-based healthcare workers.

Such recommendations are hardly novel: they have featured in government health policies and pronouncements since the mid-1990s, yet they have left little imprint. A major obstacle has been the sheer, deadweight inertia that can beset bureaucracies. According to Von Holdt and Murphy (2007:338),

> incompetence, the fear of disruption and the loss of control, and insufficient political will have probably all played a role [...] The accumulated weight of existing practices and procedures together with embedded hierarchies that institutionalize a specific distribution of power and privilege, tend to overwhelm processes of rational policy debate and the implementation of new policy.

Boulle *et al* (2000) have detected other factors, including the need to impose spending constraints, which created a climate of crisis and anxiety that reinforced a perceived need to maintain centralised control and which, in turn, sabotaged strategic planning and corrective steps. Managerial accountability became focused on finances, which had the perverse effect of concentrating a great deal of managerial zeal on pruning costs rather than improving healthcare. As Helen Schneider and her colleagues noted,

> GEAR and its operational presence in the Public Finance Management Act have had an enduring impact on health services, establishing cost-containment as the de facto driver of everyday practice in the health system [...] Staying within budget became and remains the key preoccupation of managers, implicitly relegating equity and other dimensions of institutional change to secondary goals (Schneider, Barron, Fonn, 2007:297).

The problems have become encrusted. Dislodging them will need the backing of powerful sections within the state (and the forbearance of the Treasury), supported by organisations and formations beyond it.

Worlds apart: the new education system

The design and rationing of education was one of the cornerstones of the apartheid system. Particularly after the introduction of 'bantu education' in 1954, the education system was intensively racialised and shamelessly racist. Education was extended to larger numbers of African learners, but it was designed primarily to serve as a tool of state control and to 'prepare' learners for their respective roles in society. Across the board teaching was highly authoritarian, with rote-learning the method of choice. For Africans in particular, the type and quality of education provided was both limited and limiting. It was students subjected to this system who later pushed resistance to new levels in the 1970s and 1980s and who put radical visions of democratic, people's education on the agenda.

One of the top priorities in 1994 was to democratise education within a single, non-racial and non-sexist system. This meant integrating no fewer than 18 education departments and reallocating educators and other resources much more equitably. Access to education would be widened and its quality enhanced; new policies and laws would be drafted; the curriculum would be redesigned; and governance systems would be democratised. These were colossal challenges. The quality baseline was scandalously low. A 1994 study showed that 80% of Africans were unable to read passages written at a Grade seven level; neither could 40% of whites (Chisholm, 2006). In addition to the decrepit state of the inherited system there were other limits. Fiscal constraints meant that the education portfolio did not receive significant increases in funding in the 1990s. Rather than increase, the education budget was to be redistributed more equitably.

The policies and legislation guiding the transformation of education emerged from negotiation and compromise (Chisholm, Motala, Vally, 2003), but they were shaped by two overriding goals: economic growth and social equity. The assumption was that these goals were fundamentally compatible and that trade-offs could be avoided. This was unduly optimistic. Included in the new Constitution, meanwhile, were provisions that would profoundly shape the transformation of education. Enshrined along with the right to basic education, for example, was a policy of multilingualism in schools and the granting of substantial powers to school governing bodies (Chisholm, 2006).

The initial changes arrived rapidly. The fragmented and dishevelled education sector was organised into one national and nine provincial departments, a new legislative framework was prepared, budget allocations were adjusted and a primary-school nutrition scheme was started. The legislative pillars were in place by 1996 and a new curriculum ('Curriculum 2005', which included human-rights education) was ready a couple of years later. New, more inclusionary textbooks were developed. An impressive architecture for democratic education had been created. Very quickly, the doors of learning were opened to all. But, as Jonathan Jansen (2004a:122) would later remark, 'what happens behind those doors is infinitely more complex'.

The doors of learning open

Education is now more widely available, but the quality of schooling is poor and the level and variety of skills being taught has not improved significantly. The education bureaucracy, according to Freund (2007:174), is 'spectacularly inefficient by comparative standards'. For impoverished learners 'the system offers neither equality of opportunity nor significant redress to compensate for the injustices of apartheid education' (Lemon, 2004:269).

Official figures show the literacy rate improving from 70% in 1995 to 74% in 2006 (Presidency, 2008). But numeracy and literacy performance is poor. In multicountry surveys, the numeracy and literacy levels of young South Africans lag behind those of many other African countries. In the 40-country Progress in International Reading Literacy Study carried out in 2006, South Africa was the worst performer.[36] According to a Department of Education national study of Grade six learners achievement 'was generally poor' (2005:75) in mathematics, language and natural science. The phrasing was charitable. In fact, only 19% of learners could do mathematics and only 37% could read and write in the language of instruction, at the appropriate grade level (*op cit*, 2).[37] Among the problems listed in the report were school fees and access to information (at school), school libraries, textbooks and learning materials.

Grade 12 pass rates increased from 58% in 1994 to 73% in 2003, but those ostensible gains have reversed since. By 2007 the pass rate had fallen to 65% (Presidency, 2008) and it kept dropping: to 63% in 2008 and 61% in 2009.[38] Even those numbers apply an undeserved gloss to reality. Only 38% of the learners who entered Grade one in 1998 were still in school to write to their final exams in 2009 (580 000 out of 1.55 million).[39] Viewed thus, the actual Grade 12 pass rate in 2009 was 21%. This was no aberration. A Western Cape study tracked learner enrolment from 1995 to 2008 and found that only 44% of those who had enrolled in Grade one even reached Grade 12 (De Jager, 2009).[40] Earlier national data showed that only about 40% of African students complete 12 years of schooling (Louw, Van der Berg, Yu, 2006). Repeat rates are high, especially for male learners (Schindler, 2005).[41]

The problems are systemic and they are evident in the quality of teaching. Complaints about poorly qualified and inexperienced educators are routine and have some basis. Of the 382 000 educators working in the public school system in the mid-2000s, about 15% (or 57 000) did not have a three-year post-school qualification (Department of Education, 2005). Conversely, professional disgruntlement is rife. Topping teachers' complaints are poor pay, increased workloads, lack of career-advancement prospects and dissatisfaction with work policies.[42] Between 1997/98 and 2003/04, roughly 5% (about 21 000) of educators left the system annually. More than half (53%) of those who headed for the exit had resigned, while a further quarter (26%) had either retired or left for medical reasons. Striking, too, was the growing role of mortality among educators: in 2003/04, almost one in five (18%) teachers lost to the system had died, compared to 7% in 1997/98.[43] This was almost certainly due to the AIDS and TB epidemics (see Chapter nine).

The best education money can buy

Notwithstanding the best of intentions, inequalities are being reproduced. The racially fragmented system is gone, but in its place a two-tier school system has emerged (Bloch, 2008). Not only are overall education performances poor, but the prospects of receiving a good-quality education are distributed along highly discriminatory class and racial lines.

One part of the system is comparatively multiracial and dispenses an education of reasonable quality that can serve as a launch pad for successful tertiary education. A small minority of learners benefit from it. The other part provides substandard education and, especially in the case of many rural and township schools, does little more than 'warehouse' learners. African schools in townships and rural areas tend to be the worst-performing ones; those that excel tend to be in (formerly white) affluent neighbourhoods. In a 2009 survey, some 11 000 of the 17 000 learners in the country's 100 top performing schools were white; only three of the schools were in 'townships'.[44]

The disparities are especially glaring around subjects such as mathematics, which require more support from teachers and tutors and more intense extra-curricular effort. Only 39% of the African students who wrote the Grade 12 mathematics examinations in 2008 passed, compared with 98% of their white counterparts. One in four (28%) of the white learners scored 80% or higher, but only 2% of their African peers managed that feat.[45]

Schooling is compulsory, but it is not free. Parents can apply to be exempted from paying school fees and about 20% of learners were benefiting from the 'no-fee' policy in 2006. That provision was then expanded. Officially, about half of primary schools belonged in the 'no-fee' category in 2010. However, schools are under huge pressure to recover costs via school fees and many are reluctant to enrol learners who cannot pay. The financial transfers from provincial departments of education are often tardy, which aggravates schools' fiscal insecurity. Delays in salary and wage payments are not unusual.

Unequal resourcing is reflected in school facilities. More than three-quarters of public schools do not have libraries and 60% lack science laboratories.[46] As a general rule, the worst-resourced and worst-performing schools are in the poorest areas, especially those once bundled into Bantustans. More than half the 1 000 schools without sanitation facilities in 2007 were in Eastern Cape province, as were almost half of 1 100 schools that lacked running water and one third of the 3 700 that somehow functioned without electricity.[47] Programmes are in place to reduce these numbers. Assessing the state of education in 2006, the Human Rights Commission found that 'the lived daily reality at school for many children in South Africa, particularly those in rural and township schools, is incongruous with the legislation and the policies of the Department of Education' (SAHRC, 2006:3).

Meanwhile, schools in wealthier areas have taken to charging higher school fees in order to maintain and improve facilities and hire more and better educators. Ironically, the right to set school fees was ceded to schools in a bid to salvage the public school system. By granting schools (and their governing bodies) this tool for investing more in facilities and staff, it was hoped that privileged (mainly white) learners would not abscond to private schools. The move succeeded, but arguably at the cost of recasting and reinforcing inequality. In Linda Chisholm's (2006:151) summary:

> Although many educational institutions have improved, they have not improved equally. Despite significant changes, class and race inequality, inflected by gender, continue to give shape to the contours of educational institutions, experiences and life-chances in South Africa.

Will spending more on education solve the problems? It is regularly claimed that South Africa outspends most 'developing' countries on the education front. In 2008, it devoted about 5.6% of GDP to that sector, but its spending is hardly out of the ordinary. Ghana, Malawi, Mexico and Senegal, for example, each allocates 5.4%–5.8% of GDP to education, while Bolivia, Ethiopia, Kenya, Malaysia and Tunisia spend at least 6%, and Cuba almost 10% of GDP (UNDP, 2007:265–8). No doubt, funding is needed to equip schools properly, repair and maintain facilities, subsidise the education of learners in poor households and provide better training for more teachers. Certainly, there is some evidence from Latin America, for example, that targeted spending on certain resources and structures, including at primary-school level, can lead to improved outcomes.[48] But many of the flaws in South Africa's tumbledown education system operate at levels that money cannot easily reach.

All mixed up?

Ask South Africans where they see hope for a genuine, non-racial future and most will look to the country's schools. Great effort has gone toward building an integrated new system that, officially, is now racially integrated. Each learner has the right to attend a school of choice. In reality, however, a small minority of the schools are integrated in any meaningful sense of the word. Most schools have only African learners and a significant number of formerly white schools remain predominantly white. Schools that used to serve only Indian and coloured communities have done better and have assimilated more African learners, compared with those in formerly white areas (Chisholm & Sujee, 2006).

Democratic participation was a touchstone of the struggles against apartheid education and was meant to become a cornerstone of the new system. Intended as a democratising tool, extensive powers were granted to stakeholder bodies (school governing boards in schools and various 'forums' in universities and colleges). Especially in formerly white schools, however, participation in these bodies became a function of social class and they served as a basis for redrawing and reinforcing lines of inequality (Jansen, 2004a).[49] Among other things, these bodies have the right to determine school fees and the language of instruction: discretionary powers that are potentially exclusionary. Intentionally or not, in many formerly white schools these powers exclude or ration enrolment by African learners. Assiduous participation in these governing bodies has turned them into 'sites of domination by white parents who claim and hold ownership of the school's ideological and material cultures' (Jansen, 2004a:125). A customary ploy is the language of instruction, which governing bodies can determine: Afrikaans-medium schools tend not to attract many African learners. Many of the more liberal English-language schools, meanwhile, look like exemplars of cosmopolitanism. Some, such as Johannesburg's Sacred Heart College, have a long, authentic history of being just that. But in many others the pretence is palpable. The real test is not whether these schools admit some African pupils; it is whether they also employ African teachers. And very few do. Jansen (2004a:122) is not being unsporting when he declares that this 'has to do with deeply engrained, racialised notions of white competence and black incompetence'.

Glaring racial polarisation therefore persists in the school system, as does sexism. In poorly resourced, mainly African schools, female learners consistently perform worse than their male counterparts. The opposite seems to happen in well-resourced, mainly white and Indian schools (Kahn, 2006).[50] Both racial polarisation and gender inequalities in education overlap firmly with class inequality. Taylor and Yu (2008:49) noted an

> *increasing concentration of socioeconomic status in the school system, rather than socioeconomic integration [...] It appears that class is displacing race as the critical factor in the determination of the composition of South Africa's schools.*

This supports Soudien's (2004) contention that the uneven integration of South African schools is fortifying class dominance. Wealthier African households are abandoning historically black schools, argues Soudien and cultivating class affinities with wealthy white households around values such as 'good schooling' and quality education. This also serves to acknowledge that many urban schools indeed 'are remaking the nation' as Chisholm (2008:260) insists, albeit along lines that are highly ambiguous and heavily inflected with racial and class inequalities.

Engines of inequality

South Africa's education system is failing in complex ways and no one remotely familiar with the sector claims to have pinpointed any easy fixes. The media lavish attention on atypical success stories: the rural school that achieves a high Grade-12 pass rate or its counterpart in an impoverished township that produces exceptional science students. These are remarkable accomplishments that merit admiration, but the accolades often obscure the deeper flaws that hobble education. Implicit in the praise for these schools and their dedicated educators is the notion that it is sheer grit and toil that separates extraordinary achievers from their lacklustre peers. In celebrating aberrations, we risk vindicating the status quo. Not that unusual determination and inventiveness are irrelevant—but their impact is filtered, even stifled, by a host of handicaps. Most schools are sunk in legacies that help to decide the facilities, skills and other resources at their disposal, as well as the quality of teaching they offer. Related is the socioeconomic environment and status of learners, which has a profound influence on education performances.

In a society as unequal and polarised as South Africa, learners are subject to a degree of determinism. Van der Berg and Louw (2006) have shown that a strong positive link exists between household resources and a learner's performance at school.[51] Similarly, Taylor and Yu's (2008) analysis found that variances in learners' reading scores correlated closely with their socioeconomic status. Strikingly, though, they also found that the social composition of a school seemed to be a decisive factor in learners' achievements. Generally, there seems to be an almost intractable 'performance threshold' in South African schools, with the two wealthiest quintiles above the threshold and the rest below it. In Jonathan Carter's (2008:27) summary:

> *At schools where resources are better they seem to be able to pass over many of the major problems, much like a ship on a high tide will float over rocks. The poorer schools are, however, not able to float over the rocks and these obstacles wreak havoc on a number of fronts.*

This points to a reinforcing cycle in which an unequal society generates an unequal education system that helps reproduce inequalities. Surveys show very low percentages of learners from the bottom household-income quintiles scoring above the national average on reading and other basic indicators. There is also persuasive evidence that the returns on primary education tend to be low, but that they increase considerably for higher levels of education (Taylor & Yu, 2008).[52] High dropout rates in conjunction with high unemployment levels, even among learners who complete Grade 12, suggest that those returns are very tightly rationed in South Africa. Simply put: the rich have both greater means and incentives to push on toward higher levels of education than do the poor. Inequality is reinforced.

Other 'ambient' factors are also at work, robbing learners of a quality education. These include the distressing prevalence of violence (at school and beyond),[53] gender inequality and the debilitating but disguised effects of the AIDS epidemic (see Chapter nine). In a scathing 2008 open letter[54] some of the country's top educationists catalogued a litany of ills:

> Too many schools are unsafe, bleak, uninspiring places where violence and abuse are rife. Teachers and their students are too often traumatized, demotivated and merely going through the motions. Schools as learning spaces, where opportunities exist for experiencing the joy of learning, exploring, experimenting and achieving, are few and far between. When they do exist, they are to be found mainly in established suburban, former white areas (Alexander et al, 2008).

More tangible factors include the wretched physical state of many schools; the lack of teaching facilities, materials and equipment; educators' limited capabilities and experience, and their sometimes faint grasp of subjects; the (in)ability to maintain discipline; feeble parental involvement in schooling; a skewed balance between actual teaching and measuring so-called 'performances'; and more (Lumby, 2003; Jansen, 2004 & 2006; Porteus, Vally, Ruth, 2002). It adds up to what Jansen (2006:26) has termed 'the inertia of black schooling'. The legacy of Bantu education and the misjudgements made around teacher-training resources in the 1990s means that teachers are often poorly qualified, poorly motivated and poorly managed. It is estimated that most teachers spend less than half the required 6.5 hours a day in class. Relations between educators and government tend to be conflictive, perhaps even more so than in parts of the private sector. Industrial action by members of the South African Democratic Teachers' Union (SADTU) was responsible for 42% of all working days lost to strikes in 2005–09.[55] According to Jansen (2006:26),

> township learners are exposed to about one third of the instructional time that learners in former white schools enjoy. This bald statistic does not even imply that what is taught is taught accurately; it is simply an observation about when teachers in township schools show up for classes.

Beyond this lie 'policy breaches', not least the outcomes-based education (OBE) approach that 'contributed to overload and massive failures amongst poorly resourced schools and teachers' (Bloch, 2008:129). The good news is that the Department of Education has recognised many of the weaknesses in the system and has launched new programmes to try to tackle some of these. But programmatic responses tend to abstract reality into technical terms that skim the surface, leaving undisturbed the powerful undertows that generate and reinforce inequality in schools.

In late 2009, government finally pronounced OBE to be dead: 'If anybody asks us if we are going to continue with OBE, we say that there is no longer OBE,' the Minister of Basic Education, Angie Motshekga told Parliament. 'We have completely done away with it.'[56] In place of OBE, potentially far-reaching reforms were pledged. The effects of the OBE experiment, though, have been jolting; OBE may be 'dead', but it will cast a long shadow over the country's education system.

A bridge too far: the folly of outcomes-based education

The new curriculum ('Curriculum 2005') introduced in 1998 embodied one of the more ambitious and radical shifts in the post-apartheid era. The old approach to school education had been highly authoritarian and indoctrinating. Centred on rote learning, it had discouraged creative and critical engagement from learners. Schools functioned basically as assembly lines for dutiful learners, each of whom was meant to emerge more or less resigned to his or her eventual role in society. The new curriculum was to have been the antithesis.

An outcomes-based approach, it was thought, would be learner-centred and democratic and would promote critical thinking, creativity and problem-solving skills. OBE represented a self-conscious attempt to break with the past and achieve a sweeping overhaul of the system. A stern line was drawn between outcomes- and knowledge-based education. The former was seen as a progressive approach capable of building a democratic and socially just system; the latter harked back to old ways and to the despotic regimes of rote-learning and useless 'knowledge'. In Stephanie Allais' (2007a:2) summary,

> What was needed was an education policy which could ensure dramatically increased provision of high quality, relevant education, in a participatory and democratic manner, without increasing the size of the state, and without spending too much money: the miracle transition needed a miracle education policy. A qualifications framework comprised of outcomes-based qualifications seemed, to many of us, to be that policy.

South Africa's OBE experiment was a mix of outcomes-based approaches debated or attempted in Australia, Canada, New Zealand and Scotland (Spreen, 2001).[57] Codified in a new National Qualifications Framework, OBE cast a seductive allure across the political spectrum and had wide support. Knowledge would not be the preserve of experts; knowledge gained outside of formal processes and institutions would be valorised and recognised; education would be more relevant to people's lives (and to industry's needs); academic freedom and creativity would be enhanced. Buttressed by a set of new laws and structures (including 25 sector education and training authorities or SETAs) the approach was an attempt to achieve social equity while also boosting the quality and range of education and providing a platform for more inclusive economic growth. The provision of education would increase and broaden, since any authorised 'provider' would be able to offer learning programmes. Skills and education gained would be better suited to the practical needs of social and economic life. Both educators and learners would have a clearer sense of what was expected of them and outcomes would provide a good basis for improving the quality of education overall (Steiner-Khamsi, 2006).[58] All this boded well for individual learners and for social and economic development. The framework became

> an emblem and instrument of the single national high-quality education and training system that democratic South Africa aspired to create (Department of Education & Department of Labour, 2002:5).

Ten years on, the framework had neither integrated education and training, nor had it led to improved education outcomes. Adult education faltered and the competency levels of school leavers appear to have dropped. Schools in wealthier neighbourhoods, though, coped fairly well—a sign of the underlying discriminatory dynamics. Being 'resource-hungry' (Harley & Wedekind, 2004), OBE was best suited to wealthier schools. In the rest, it became a quagmire.

A key feature was the design of mechanistic performance statements against which education would be measured. Linked to the approach were performance-based accountability systems, which bristled with testing and surveillance measures. What was meant to facilitate a more organic and eclectic learning process became highly regimented and heavily supervised. Over 11 000 'unit standards' were developed to flesh out the qualifications framework. Teachers foundered. The new system required teachers who were motivated, highly qualified and theoretically nimble. But it was introduced on the back of a derelict system and in the wake of training cutbacks and other forms of 'rationalisation'. Paradoxically, as Salim Vally (2010) notes, 'by focusing on outcomes, the more fundamental issue of what education is for [was] avoided'. All this was apparent early on. Yet when a review in 2000 uncovered a parlous state of affairs, it seemed only to redouble the resolve to press ahead, albeit with some modifications.

Hindsight informs us that almost all of the other countries experimenting with an outcomes-based approach had limited it to vocational training or even more narrowly. South Africa made the rare leap of applying it to the education system as a whole; New Zealand's similar attempt had turned out to be unsustainable.[59] In South Africa's case, blame has been aimed at the regimenting bureaucracy and work regime created around the framework, as well as poor co-ordination of it. In Stephanie Allais' (2003 & 2007) analysis, however, the problem ran deeper and was bolted into the model itself.

OBE seemed in tune with the impulses for social justice, redress and empowerment. But the eventual framework also distilled other ambitions and pressures. The business community's desire for a more utilitarian education system that produced and funnelled more high-demand, marketable skills into the economy sat well with the trade-union movement's push for a system that would help to reduce unemployment, for example.[60] For unions, a framework that recognised non-formal knowledge and skills held strong appeal. Meanwhile, the dominant perspective envisaged a restructured economy that could compete globally on the basis of flexible specialisation and high-quality beneficiation. This would require rapid training and skills development that could quickly overcome the apartheid legacies of deliberate under-skilling and under-education.[61] OBE seemed to fit that bill, too. A driving motive behind the framework, therefore, was the need to increase the supply of relevant skills for economic growth:

> *The common belief, shared by the mass democratic movement, business and the apartheid state, was a win-win scenario of high skills and global competitiveness. Education and training were to be the foundations of this future* (Allais, 2003:6).

But this also involved a fundamental recasting of education, with its content and value now determined chiefly by economic usefulness, positioning it firmly within neoliberal rationality.

Many of the initial champions of the approach also failed to notice the snug fit between OBE and neoliberal public-sector reforms (Allais, 2007a). The mainstays of this brand of reform have attained the status of 'common sense': parcelling state agencies into smaller units ('cost centres') that are required to operate as competitive 'service providers' and the keen pursuit of 'efficiency', 'cost-effectiveness', 'measurable results' and 'client satisfaction'. Thus OBE permitted motley service providers to enter the education 'market', especially those in the business of providing various diplomas and certificates. With educational outcomes the centrepiece of the new approach, providers could select the outcomes they would deliver and compile them into marketable packages. Consumers (the learners) could then pick from them. In this model, education sheds its status as public good and becomes a good supplied by the market, for the market. The citizen or learner is recast as a consumer or client, swamped with choices. The state hovers in the background, performing its regulatory duties (Spreen, 2004; Allais, 2007b & 2003). It will take many years to reclaim South Africa's education system from the transfiguration of OBE.

Recasting higher education

In higher education, too, a profound restructuring of tertiary education is underway. As in many other countries, market values and practices have thoroughly penetrated South Africa's academic institutions, adulterating both intellectual rigour and output. This not-so-invisible hand of the market also appears to be reinforcing inherited inequalities: strong institutions have remained intact and sturdy, while weaker ones are still marginalised (Chisholm, 2006).

Institutional autonomy has been eroded in several ways, prompting Jansen (2006:19) to warn that universities were being transformed into 'commercial centre[s]' obsessed with 'the business of (ac)counting'.[62] For Salim Vally (2007b:20), the 'debasement of higher education' is well underway, with public space turned into 'a commodified sphere'. The sharp end of this overhaul has been the 'new managerialism' of the 1980s, which penetrated the country's academic institutions with a vengeance during the 1990s. Alongside the strictures of economic policy, this fad wrought juddering changes. Institutional budgets were cut, authority became centralised (though termed, in Orwellian fashion, the 'decentralisation of functions'), 'non-core' tasks were outsourced and an alternate value system was imposed in which 'accountability trumped autonomy, quality assurance replaced trust and surveillance displaced self-management' (Jansen, 2004b). Apologists may argue that South Africa is doing nothing more than follow a global trend. But it is a doleful one in which intellectual rigour and invention is forced to stoop to the dictates of the market.

Repair work

Doubtless, there are numerous areas for improvement. It will be important not to snatch at 'quick fixes', and to recognise that some of the repairs will take years to yield rewards:

- A major blind spot is the neglect of early childhood education, which attracts a tiny fraction of the education budget. About one in six children has access to preschool education and he or she probably lives in a privileged neighbourhood. Fewer than 30% of preschools receive any state support (they rely on fees and private funding and pay their staff very low wages).[63] Programmes are being expanded but their scale and quality remain grossly inadequate.

- New accords need to be constructed between educators and other staff on the one hand and education authorities on the other, around a shared goal of improving the quality of education. That relationship has languished far too long in acrimony and conflict. Unless it is repaired, the overall system cannot be salvaged.

- New measures to slow the school dropout rate are needed—and not just for the obvious reasons. Making it halfway through secondary school may not drastically improve learners' chances of gainful employment (see Chapter six), but it could save their lives. Several studies in South Africa and beyond have shown that the more years of secondary schooling a student has, the lower his or her risk of HIV infection becomes (Hargreaves *et al*, 2007 & 2008; Bärnighausen *et al*, 2007).[64]

- Ostensibly under-resourced schools that achieve good results should be targeted with support that enables them to sustain and build on those achievements and should be linked with other such schools through peer-support systems.

- Schools that are especially disadvantaged should be targeted for immediate upgrading, starting with access to working and properly maintained sanitation facilities, water and electricity.

- Stronger socioeconomic integration must be achieved in the school system. One way to do this may be to mandate higher quotas of no-fee admissions in wealthier schools.

The Federation of Governing Bodies of South African Schools believes that between 80–90% of schools are 'dysfunctional'.[65] The reasons for such dismal performance are complex, but the costs are immense. If we are to accept Amartya Sen's (1999:18) proposition that development be judged in terms of 'the expansion of capabilities of people to lead the kinds of lives they value—and have reason to value', then the education system is failing not only citizens but the very prospect of 'development' itself.

Endnotes

1 In 1980 about 40% of doctors worked in the public sector, but they mainly treated the white population. There was one doctor for roughly 15 000 people living in the Bantustans in the early 1970s, compared with one for every 1 700 people in the rest of the country. See Rispel, L and Behr, G (1992) 'Health indicators: Policy implications', paper no. 27, Centre for Health Policy, University of the Witwatersrand, Johannesburg.

2 The approach had been codified internationally in the 1978 Alma Ata Declaration (and was ignored by the apartheid regime). Interestingly, a partial shift to a primary healthcare system had been attempted in South Africa in the mid-1940s, under the stewardship of the health minister, H Gluckman, who spearheaded the creation of several community health centres. The 1948 triumph of the National Party derailed these innovations.

3 The 16-page summary of the 2006 Accelerated and Shared Growth Initiative for South Africa (AsgiSA), for example, does not mention the word 'health' once; see http://www.info.gov.za/asgisa/asgisa.htm. AsgiSA annual reports refer only to skills constraints in the public health system.

4 Almost 70% of white households belong to medical schemes, compared with just 8.4% of Africans (and 22% of coloureds and 39% of Indians and Asians). The proportion of households with medical-aid membership actually dropped to 14% in the mid-2000s before rising to about 16%.

5 The disparities are most obvious around 'entry-level' care, where diagnosis and treatment is required for non-life-threatening ailments and injuries. Beyond that, at the level of tertiary care, a handful of public hospitals are still capable of providing top-quality care; conversely, some private hospitals provide shoddy (though expensive) care.

6 The ratio of private-to-public health spending in South Africa was about 1.5:1. In some 'low human development' countries, the ratio is considerably wider: more than 2:1 in Cambodia, Georgia, Lebanon and Vietnam; at least 3:1 in Armenia, Azerbaijan and Laos; 4:1 in Togo; and 6:1 in Burma. The data are drawn from the UNDP's *Human Development Report 2007/2008* and are based on country-reported 2004 data. 'Medium human development' and 'low human development' are classifications based on the UNDP's human development index.

7 For a breakdown of this trend, see McIntyre *et al* (2007:21).

8 For a more detailed breakdown, see McIntyre and Thiede (2007:39).

9 Purchasing power parity.

10 Calculated from data in UNDP (2008:351–4).

11 Fees charged by private healthcare providers in the 1980s were relatively closely controlled and were guided by the tariff schedule of the Representative Association of Medical Schemes. For providers, this carried the advantage of safeguarding full and direct payment from medical schemes. But it also capped doctors' incomes from consultations. A couple of developments occurred subsequently. In the late 1980s and early 1990s, more doctors registered to dispense medicines and this 'coincided' with a steep increase in spending on medicines within medical schemes 'strongly suggesting that many doctors had begun selling medicines as a mechanisms to ensure that they were able to reach their income goals' (McIntyre *et al*, 2007:49). In addition, a close relationship was forged between private hospitals and

specialist doctors (discussed below). In other words, a key tactic used to maintain or boost profit margins was to artificially induce demand.

12 The amounts spent by medical schemes for private hospital services doubled between 1997 and 2005, from R 8 billion (USD 1 billion) to R 15.9 billion (USD 2 billion) (Matsebula & Willie, 2007). Private hospitals absorbed 35% of medical scheme spending in 2005 (up from 22% in 1992/93) (McIntyre & Thiede, 2007). The private-hospital industry claims that rising costs were caused by the devaluation of the rand (hiking the cost of imported drugs and surgical supplies), the legislated elimination of risk rating, a rise in inpatient days and a shift in case-mix. This is unconvincing. On average, medical-scheme members spent 6% less in real terms on medicines between 1997 and 2005, so these were not driving the increases. Medical-scheme spending on medicines (once the single-largest category of medical scheme expenditure) shrank radically (as a proportion of total expenditure)—from 32% in 1992/93 to 16% in 2005 (McIntyre & Thiede, 2007). The drop in spending on medicines followed two important regulatory interventions. Legislation now requires pharmacists to offer patients cheaper generic substitutes for any prescribed medicine and limited price controls on medicines have been introduced (McIntyre & Thiede, 2007). A rise in inpatient days and case-mix shift could as easily be attributed to the hospital industry's overweening power (as discussed in the text). A disaggregation of hospital cost trends, done by the Council for Medical Schemes, shows hospital costs soaring from 1999 onward even when medicine costs are excluded.

13 The trend has been to invest in surgical beds and theatres which generate more revenue.

14 McIntyre *et al* (2007:46–7) argue that this concentration has been abetted by a less-than-ideal regulatory system, including decisions of the Competition Commission. Average real expenditure per beneficiary for hospital care rose from R 1 200 (USD 150) a year in 2001 to a little under R 1 800 (USD 225) in 2005, while spending on specialists rose from a little more than R 800–R 1 000 (USD 100–125) in the same period. The only other steep increase was in the use of esoteric health providers (such as chiropractors, homeopaths, traditional healers and acupuncture therapists) and psychologists and physiotherapists—which doubled to about R 800 per year in the same period (McIntyre & Thiede, 2007).

15 There were 72 magnetic resonance image (MRI) scanners in private hospitals in 2006.

16 The price list was not mandatory, but it functioned as a reference point when schemes negotiated with providers.

17 As they top up or compensate for services and commodities that are not included in their respective 'packages' of coverage. For a useful summary of this development, see McIntyre *et al* (2007:29).

18 Shisana, O, 'Shisana on the NHI', *Health-e*, 30 June 2009.

19 *Ibid.*

20 Tamar Kahn, 'Fixing state health a priority, says DBSA', *Business Day*, 27 November 2008.

21 'SA must move to a health system focused on prevention—Minister', *Health-e*, 10 March 2010.

22 Between 2003 and 2005, for example, the total number of nurses registered with the South African Nursing Council increased by less than 5% (Matsebula & Wilie, 2007).

23 Data are from the South African Nursing Council Register, cited in Subedar, H (2005) 'Nursing profession: Production of nurses and proposed scope of practice'. In: Ijumba, P and Barron, P (eds) *South African Health Review* 2005, Health Systems Trust, Durban.

24 The effects transcended the sheer 'production' of nurses. In the previous system, colleges were integrated with hospitals, and student nurses were constantly available to lend a hand in wards and elsewhere (Von Holdt & Murphy, 2007).

25 More than half were Africans. For insights into how this fitted with apartheid 'logic', see Marks, S (1994) *Divided Sisterhood: Race, Class and Gender in the South African Nursing Profession*, Witwatersrand University Press, Johannesburg.

26 The ratio of professional nurses in the public sector dwindled, from 149 for every 100 000 people in 1998, to 110 in 2007.

27 About 9 000 of them were general practitioners, almost 7 000 were nurses and the balance was listed as 'other health professionals'. See Tamar Kahn, 'SA steps up bid to retain health staff', *Business Day*, 7 June 2006. The government reportedly has reached an agreement with the UK barring the recruitment of doctors and nurses in South Africa.

28 'Poaching nurses from the developing world', *Lancet*, Vol. 367, No. 9525, p. 1791.

29 Tamar Kahn, 'Fixing state health a priority, says DBSA', *Business Day*, 27 November 2008.

30 South African Nursing Council (2007) *Statistics 2007*, South African Nursing Council, Pretoria, cited in Coovadia *et al* (2009).

31 Astonishingly, the same researchers found that four in five managers of the 220 surveyed health facilities had not seen the 2000–05 National HIV/AIDS Plan (a strategy they were meant to help implement). About half the public hospital managers and just 8% of private health sector managers said they had seen the document.

32 Reid, S (2003) 'Community service for health professionals'. In: Ijumba, P, Ntuli, A, Barron, P (eds) *South African Health Review* 2002. Health Systems Trust, Durban; cited in Coovadia *et al* (2009).

33 Quoted in Von Holdt and Murphy (2007:330).

34 Quoted in Annabel Jacoby, 'Winds of change sweep SA healthcare', *Mail & Guardian*, 27 August 2009.

35 Von Holdt and Murphy (2007) found an absence of progressive human-resource strategies in the national and provincial health departments and in the Department of Public Service and Administration. The preference instead was for old-school procedures designed to govern and control employees.

36 The 2006 Progress in International Reading Literacy Study reported in 'Pirls reading achievement', *BBC News*, 28 November 2007. See http://news.bbc.co.uk/2/hi/uk_news/scotland/7117675.stm

37 The effects of poor-quality schooling register in tertiary education and the labour market. For example, Pauw *et al* (2006) have argued that the large numbers of unemployed graduates ostensibly equipped with skills that are in short supply point to quality problems at tertiary level. Churning out more graduates is not the answer.

38 In most education systems, achievements of the majority of students are (by definition) 'average'. Graphs plotting learners' academic performances usually group most students together in the middle and yield the classic 'bell curve' pattern. A different pattern occurs in South Africa, where a small but significant number of students (almost exclusively from schools in affluent areas) perform very well, but the majority of students perform poorly, many of them very poorly. Mediocre students are few in number (Fleisch, 2008).

39 Primarashni Gower, Monako Dibetle, Thabo Motlala, 'Matric may become irrelevant', *Mail & Guardian*, 8 January 2010.

40 Cited in IDASA (2009). Using Western Cape data, where the Matric pass rate in 2008 was 79%; this meant that once dropouts were factored in, the actual pass rate was 35%.

41 See Schindler, J (2005) 'Access to education in South Africa', *Edusource Data News*, No. 49, October, cited in Chisholm (2009).

42 'Survey gives hard facts about the lives of educators', *HSRC Review*, Vol. 3, No. 2, July 2005.

43 *Ibid*.

44 Thus 65% of the learners in those top-performing schools were white, whereas whites comprise 9% of the population. In some of the Afrikaans-medium schools, more than 90% of the learners were white. See Prega Govender, 'Exclusive: We reveal SA's top schools', *Sunday Times* [Johannesburg], 17 October 2009.

45 This was despite the fact that the threshold for passing was set at a lowly 30%. 'No one gets prizes', *The Economist*, 16 January 2010.

46 Alexander, N *et al*, 'The education crisis: call in the people', Open letter, November 2008.

47 Wyndham Hartley and Hajra Omarjee, 'Government's spending priorities are not improving learning conditions', *Business Day*, 18 October 2008. Figures cited were provided by the Minister of Education during question period in Parliament.

48 Taylor and Yu (2008) cite as an example the research of Behrman, JR, Birdsall, N and Székely, M (1998) 'Intergenerational schooling mobility and macro conditions and schooling policies in Latin America', Inter-American Development Bank, Working Paper No. 386.

49 Jansen (2004a:126) notes, however, that parents' participation in African schools has been much weaker than anticipated: 'The assumption that [...] the demand for democratic participation in schools would be taken up by willing and enthusiastic parents simply did not hold in the post-apartheid context.'

50 The educational prospects of impoverished girls are being sabotaged further by their physical insecurity at school. Complaints of sexual harassment or aggression at school are common and both fellow learners and educators are the perpetrators.

51 Interestingly, teacher/learner ratios seemed only to have a significant effect in the more affluent schools.

52 This contrasts with Servaas van der Berg's (2002) less nuanced conclusion that 'the school system contributes little to supporting the upward mobility of poor children in the labour market'.

53 Sexual bullying by schoolboys is common and sexual predation by teachers is a recurring problem. See, for example, Abrahams, N, Mathews, S, Ramela, P (2006) 'Intersections of "sanitation, sexual coercion and girls' safety in schools"' *Tropical Medicine and International Health*, Vol. 11, pp. 751–6.

54 Alexander, N *et al*, 'The education crisis: call in the people', Open letter, November 2008. The signatories included Neville Alexander, Ivor Baatjes, Nhlanganiso Dladla, Andre Keet, Nobuntu Mazeka, Nomsa Mazwai, Enver Motala, Kim Porteus, Brian Ramadiro, John Samuel and Salim Vally.

55 Lucky Biyase, 'Strikes hit school children hard', *Business Report*, 7 February 2010. The data are from the Tokiso Review. Overall, public-sector strikes accounted for 63% of working days lost in that five-year period.

56 Angie Motshekga, 'Statement by Minister of Basic Education, Angie Motshekga, on Curriculum Review Process', National Assembly, *Hansard*, 5 November 2009, Cape Town.

57 In most of these instances, the debates occurred in the context of neoliberal public-sector reforms. Globally, South Africa (and Namibia) was one of the earliest adopters of this approach on such far-reaching scale.

58 Importantly, Allais (2007) also highlights the post-modernist aspects of this approach, specifically its affinities with social constructivism (and its contention that knowledge is relative and undifferentiated). Again, this seems to democratise knowledge, by dismantling the hierarchies that determine which knowledge is dispensed to whom and how that occurs. In truth, it's a form of 'deregulation' advertised as a pathway to liberty and equality. The rapport with neoliberal ideology is obvious. The disciplinary foundations of education are removed (happily so in a country where they assumed quasi-fascist forms) and the doors of learning seem to be flung open. But the big winner, it turns out, is the market. Critics of the social constructivist approach also argue that rather than liberate, it actually ends up depoliticising and vindicating the 'selectivity of curricular knowledge' (Muller, 1996; cited in Allais, 2003:11).

59 In fact, those countries that did adopt outcomes-based education did so highly selectively, as Steiner-Khamsi's (2006) study shows. In some places, the approach was associated strictly with performance-based monitoring and remuneration of teachers, for example.

60 Allais' (2003:4–5) précis of this background is useful. She contends that advice from the Metalworkers' Union in Australia (where an outcomes-based approach had been attempted) helped galvanise National Union of Metalworkers' of South Africa's (NUMSA's) strong support for the national qualifications framework. She also reminds that the National Education Co-ordinating Committee (NECC), which had originated in Soweto in the 1980s and which went on to exert formative influence on efforts to reform the education system, was much more a political than pedagogical movement. It drew inspiration from radical pedagogy (notably the Paolo Freire tradition), but it did not excel at translating this into clear curriculum

approaches. The anti-authoritarian and egalitarian promise of the national qualifications framework therefore exerted a strong pull—but it was insufficiently tempered by informed critique.

61 Generally, both sceptics and champions of globalisation agree on the cardinal role of education as a platform for global competitiveness (Spreen, 2004).

62 For a trenchant overview of the effects of this shift, see Pithouse, R (ed) *Asinamali: University Struggles in Post-apartheid South Africa*, Africa World Press, Asmara.

63 See Brian Ramadiro, 'Many did not survive: ten years of ANC education policy', *Khanya*, No. 5, April 2004.

64 In a rural KwaZulu-Natal community, for example, women were 7% less likely to acquire HIV for each year of education they had attained (Bärnighausen *et al*, 2007). This protective effect seems to occur irrespective of whether HIV education was being provided. Several other studies, including a large one in rural Limpopo province, showed that girls who attend school are less likely to have sex at an early age and are more likely to use condoms when they do (Hargreaves *et al*, 2007).

65 Verashni Pillay, 'Matric pupils receive results', *Mail & Guardian*, 7 January 2010.

CHAPTER ELEVEN

A South African development state?

Government wheeled out the developmental state 'project' in the early 2000s, as criticism of its structural adjustment policies grew shrill. By broadcasting its developmental state ambitions, the ANC government has sought to position a polarising development path within the longer narrative of national liberation, providing it with a gloss of coherence and consistency. Having extricated the economy from its 'trilemma', calmed the nerves of investors and nursed the accounts back into the black, GEAR's 'tough love' had done its job and laid a basis for resuming the march toward a better life for all. Presiding over it would be a developmental state. Or so it was claimed.

In Alan Hirsch's (2005:4) telling, for example, GEAR becomes a momentary tonic of adjustment, after which 'rapid growth of the social system' could occur. He bookends GEAR between 1996 and 1999 after which social and infrastructure spending increased. Thus the deeper neoliberal features of post-apartheid South Africa have been squirreled away in the past.[1] Swilling and his colleagues (2005) have added more frippery to this perspective. The post-apartheid state, in their reading, had blundered about in a twilight zone—one moment resembling a developmental state, the next acting like a minion of the Washington Consensus. Critics erred in tarring government's policies as 'neoliberal', they argue. Social expenditure was disappointing not because of belt-tightening, but because of institutional snarl-ups.[2] Moreover, the earnest stumbling of the early post-apartheid years yielded invaluable lessons about building and operating institutions, which eventually would serve a developmental project well. Having steadied the ship, according to this view, conditions in the early 2000s were ripe for a more full-blooded developmental drive.

But the construal relies on an idealised understanding of neoliberalism where states forsake most regulatory duties, especially in relation to the economy and stage a wholesale retreat from social provisioning.[3] This utopian arrangement has almost never transpired and certainly did not in post-apartheid South Africa. After the demise of the Washington Consensus in the late 1990s, even neoliberal theorists repudiated the extremist idealisations propagated at the Chicago School of Economics. Constant and considerable state intervention in the economy (and society broadly) is a hallmark of neoliberalism, including in the early wave of pioneering neoliberal states. In fact, what most distinguished them from their predecessors was their aggressive deployment of the state's powers and resources to advance the interests of conglomerate corporations, attack popular social formations and police society. As neoliberalism evolved, the state's social obligations again gained prominence (see Chapter five). The dichotomy that positions the neoliberal state and developmental state as two polar opposites is mistaken.

In South Africa's case, once the public debt and budget deficit had been trimmed, public investment increased in the 2000s, particularly spending on social grants and the public-works programme. At the same time, though, many of the guiding tenets of the 'GEAR era' remained in play. The post-apartheid development path, once analysed, does not escape the description 'neoliberal', nor do higher levels of public spending transform the country into a developmental state.

In search of models

In South Africa and elsewhere the craving for a new model of progress has tempted some to discover developmental states wherever they choose to look and to interpret those discoveries in conveniently flexible terms. The developmental state, as Ben Fine (2007) warns, has come close to meaning whatever we want it to mean. The discourse often seems to spin its wheels—stuck at a point where it represents a theory of state-led economic growth that lacks both 'a theory of the state' and an analysis of the actual constellations of political and economic interests that are at play.

Stripped to basics, the developmental state refers to a model of economic growth and social redistribution in which the state acts, with varying degrees of autonomy, as a major variable promoting that growth, determining its pattern and ensuring social development. The popularised image of the developmental state in South Africa is coloured by the modernising projects of the 1960s and 1970s in the 'developing' world, where interventionist states guided economic development and managed the distribution of its fruits. The imposing achievements of some states in Asia since the 1960s feature prominently, as do the longstanding though fitful attempts of countries in other regions to rapidly 'catch up' with their industrialised counterparts. But the pertinence, in the twenty-first century, of these reference points is open to dispute.

Both in the ANC and among its trade-union allies, the developmental state tends to be associated with the achievements of the newly industrialised countries of Asia.[4] The Asian 'tigers' had already attracted strong interest from South African policymakers in the early 1990s—though not as developmental states, but as icons of rapid economic growth based on manufactured exports. A decade later the attraction was undimmed, but had broadened to take in their developmental feats. More recently China's 'miracle'—along with Vietnam's rapid economic growth and the recovery of Malaysia and Thailand after the 1997 crash—attracted admiration. The appeal, however, is somewhat schizoid, split between a fixation on economic growth (especially via competitive industrialisation) and a more expansive concern with social wellbeing. Thus China earns tributes despite its widening income inequality, imploding hinterlands and exploitation of workers.[5]

Oddly, African states feature only dimly in South Africa's developmental state debates (Edigheji, 2005). Yet, as Thandika Mkandawire (2001) has shown, there is a solid case for describing some African states at various points since the 1960s as 'developmental'. Mkandawire reminds that almost half of the 20 fastest-growing economies in the 1960s and part of the 1970s were in Africa; the GDP growth rate in Côte d'Ivoire, for instance, hovered around 10% for more than a decade. More recently, Mauritius merits scrutiny as a developmental state, as might Botswana (Taylor, 2002).[6] The oversight perhaps stems from the fact that these states are not regarded as beacons of enduring success—a stance that exposes the tautology at the heart of the developmental state debate. Success, it seems, is the fundamental yardstick, more so than key characteristics and methods. Failures, partial or worse, earn little attention in the developmental state literature. Thus Indonesia, the Philippines and Thailand (not to mention any number of African pretenders) hardly earn walk-on parts in the developmental state stories (Freund, 2007b). Also neglected are the late industrialising countries of Europe even though they have manifestly passed the 'success' test and satisfy many of the other criteria for inclusion.[7]

The Asian 'blueprints'

Bearing in mind those caveats, what are the canonical ingredients of a successful developmental state? According to Chalmers Johnson's (1982) classic examination of the 'Japanese miracle' after the Second World War, the state assumes control of economic development and leads long-term macroeconomic planning and industrial development on the basis of dense ties to entrepreneurial elites. Industrial policy is centre-stage. In the first generation of 'Asian tigers' a central objective was to nurse infant industries to health by ushering investment flows towards targeted sectors and regions and subsidising labour costs. Crucial, too, was state support for companies' pursuit of productive ideas and new knowledge if they matched overarching national development objectives. Needless to say, leverage over sources of finance was vital.

Acting in this manner required several key attributes, central among them a strong and skilled state bureaucracy that was capable of acting efficiently, reliably and predictably. It monitored companies' performances and adjusted subsidies and other allocations accordingly, disciplining them if necessary. A strict meritocratic system of recruitment and advancement was used to stock this bureaucracy, which also insulated it against the narrow interests of powerful social forces.[8] This autonomy allowed the state to deploy its administrative and political resources in service of national interests (Mkandawire, 2001; White, 1998; Evans, 1995). Regimented state-capital relations were seen to sit at the heart of the East Asian developmental states, with civil society weak and largely marginalised (particularly in the formative growth phases of the 'tigers').[9]

Most discussions of the developmental state emphasise its Weberian underpinnings. Strongly interventionist, the developmental state is, however, deemed to be much less monastic than the Weberian ideal. Partially embedded with key social classes, it acquires the mix of autonomy and connectedness (or 'embedded autonomy', in Peter Evans' famous phrasing) it needs to shape and pursue strategic development goals. Instead of directing arrangements with remote edicts and compulsion, the state pursues those goals on the basis of alliances it orchestrates with key social groups,[10] but remains shielded against the churn of contestation and feuding that can preoccupy those groups. The 'ideal type' of developmental state, therefore, relies on an elite, rules-driven bureaucracy that is sufficiently detached from the 'profane' intrigues of society to discern choices and act in the national interest (Evans, 1995).[11]

The antithesis is said to be the highly personalised, predatory state that is captured by elite groupings that use it primarily to advance their own interests (Mobuto's Zaire, Bongo's Gabon or Suharto's Indonesia are often presented as paradigmatic examples). However, predatory conduct—although usually less wanton than this rogue's gallery—is to some extent a feature of all states, including the 'developed' ones (Pillay, 2008). Predatory states, by definition, loot public resources and abuse power. But most of them do so alongside at least some calculated redistribution and state provisioning, and often harbour grand developmental ambitions.[12] Although they rely preponderantly on coercion, they also try to cultivate an ideological basis for acquiescence—often a fusion of nation-building and anti-colonialism or anti-imperialism, sometimes spiked with xenophobia. Gaddafi's Libya is a strident example. They also require at least some degree of 'embeddedness' in key social groupings. The strict dichotomy between predatory and developmental states, therefore, seems unduly idealised. Most developmental state candidates exhibit both Weberian and predatory features. But Evans' broader point stands: the issue is not so much the extent, but the *kind* of state involvement in the economy and its overriding purpose.

Attempts to discern the essential features of developmental stages sometimes neglect the importance of context and timing. In East Asia, as Evans (2007) points out, the Second World War and the militant upheavals that followed it denuded the political power of landed elites. At the same time, emergent industrial elites remained politically and economically weak and multinational capital was only tentatively active in the national economies. The state's hand was therefore strong and its room for action broad. Not only did business elites support the development models pursued by the state, but their relative weakness saw them acquiesce in the state's disciplining of recalcitrant companies. The state's strength, the broad endorsement of a 'national project' and the professionalism of the state bureaucracy, for example, enabled East Asian developmental states to tax business elites at rates few of their peers in Latin America and elsewhere managed to reach.[13] The same strong hand was wielded against workers:

> *Most of the developmental states were authoritarian, and repression was an important tool in ensuring the acquiescence of labour … [Additionally] all these states devised social policies that sought to complement repression and to integrate labour into their developmental projects. Indeed in many cases social policy was deliberately designed to pre-empt the action of labour through paternalistic solutions that sought to limit welfare privileges selectively to the workforce that was vital to economic growth* (Mkandawire, 2007:24–5).

341

There were important nuances, however. Repression of labour was not uniform, with the skilled core of the labour-force often being treated more leniently than the semi-skilled sections (often dominated by women and girls). Generally, the repressive management of labour could not be sustained for long. Ironically, the success of developmental states often undermined key conditions for their existence. In South Korea, for example, corporate capital grew too strong to be 'directed' by the state.[14] Strong economic development also emboldened and enabled workers to resist repression and successfully press for greater redistribution and wider liberties (which eventually even benefited female workers). Social pacts were among the tools then used to stabilise relations.

Gillian Hart (2002a & 2002b) has highlighted additional factors, including the massive agrarian and redistributive reforms that laid a great deal of the basis for the Asian developmental states and has emphasised the paternalistic and male-chauvinist character of many of those 'success stories'.[15] Their environmental destructiveness has also drawn attention.

Earning greater appreciation recently are the social-policy dimensions of developmental states. The importance of quality, basic education in numeracy and a strong flow of quality graduates in the applied sciences, along with the wide diffusion of information and computational technology in society, is now well established. Those interventions formed a cornerstone of the successful developmental states, including in Malaysia (Freund, 2007a & 2007b). Social provisioning, though, has taken different forms. Direct social spending by the Japanese state, for example, was low (neoliberal ideologues used this to argue that 'generous' social expenditure was a luxury that should follow and not accompany, strong economic growth). Instead the state imposed on companies the duty of social provisioning (including healthcare, social security and housing) and supported these tasks with subsidies and concessions. Rather than tax and then redistribute, the state devolved many of its provisioning duties to large companies, using the tax regime as an instrument. Underpinning this were solid and highly disciplined family structures, which provided the basis for the reproduction of social relations and labour. Elsewhere, in the Nordic countries for example, social policy was understood in more extensive terms (spanning production, redistribution, protection and reproduction) with the state positioned centrally as provider.

Civil society and developmental states

The first wave of East Asian developmental states favoured technocratic approaches to development, with civil society featuring marginally. The consent and support of workers was achieved through disciplinary regimes that were authoritarian and paternalistic and through rationed redistribution of social goods and services (especially education and training, healthcare provision and housing). Subsequently, Malaysia continued in that vein, as have China and Vietnam. Does that mean that development states perform better when not 'encumbered' by democracy and an active civil society? The experiences of the 'late industrialisers' in Europe suggest otherwise. Beyond them, however, examples of flourishing democracies that can be termed developmental states are few. The most striking examples are found at the sub-national level. Most well known are the experiments in the southern Brazilian city of Porto Alegre and in the Indian state of Kerala (Abers, 1999; Heller, 2001; Williams, 2008). The developmental achievements in Kerala are impressive. A poor state, it has nevertheless dramatically reduced infant mortality, increased literacy levels and life expectancy, electrified almost every village and built a vibrant and large co-operative sector. Porto Alegre's fame derives more from the democratic content of its participatory budgeting experiment, which has been replicated in dozens of other cities.[16]

A distinguishing feature of these democratic variants has been the central role of a mobilised civil society that is capable of engaging the state as a critical—in both senses of the word—ally. 'Embedded autonomy' featured in both cases, but was achieved and sustained in very different ways and contexts. Also key in both cases was the combined activism in civil and political society in the context of devolved state power. The devolution of certain powers, responsibilities and resources created the political space in which marginalised groups could mobilise and pursue pro-poor policies, as we discuss in more detail later (Mohan & Stokke, 2005; Hickey & Mohan, 2003; Webster, 2002; Heller, 2001).

Developmental states in the twenty-first century

Developmental states exist in many variants, therefore, each profoundly shaped by its own specific history and conditions. There is no single blueprint. Botswana, Costa Rica, Mauritius and the Nordic countries could plausibly be added to the standard list of developmental states. The celebrated examples were repressive to varying degrees and uniformly paternalistic. But more recent variants show that development states can be democratic, successful and socially inclusive. They also need not be a *national* enterprise, nor do they have to hinge on industrial development, as we discuss later.

Neglected in most of the developmental state discussions and literature are two other key aspects. Firstly, gender relations were of profound importance in the East Asian developmental states (Hart, 2002). A good deal of South Korea's export success, for example, was achieved on the backs of low-paid female workers (who predominated in the parts-supplier sectors). Secondly, the ecological dimension is typically ignored. Rooted in modernisation theory and driven by unswerving ambitions of rapid economic development, developmental states have very rarely bridled at the environmental costs of their projects. If the damage done by developmental states over the past half-century has been proportionally less compared with the industrialised behemoths of the north, it is mainly a reflection of the scale of their economies, not the ethics guiding their development paths.

Strong, balanced relations between political forces and civil society are an increasingly important factor for developmental state success: 'state-society ties can no longer be focused narrowly on relations with capitalist elites' as they were in the East Asian cases (Evans, 2006:2). This thinking is qualitatively different from post-1989 orthodoxy, which values civil society mainly as a centrepiece for political democratisation and as a surrogate provider of public goods and services. Evans' proposition fits with broader shifts in leftist thought, evocatively laid out in Antonio Negri and Michael Hardt's *Multitudes*, but also evident in the resurgent interest in anarchism and its repositioning in twentieth-century history.[17] More fundamentally, the prognosis emerges out of the broad-based shift away from economic development (and employment) that is grounded in industrial 'machine production'.

The social welfare states of the twentieth century shared three definitive features: machine-based industrial development, which generated powerful, concentrated social forces (chiefly workers' movements and organisations of capital) and efficient, relatively predictable state bureaucracies. In combination, these made possible the social compacts that would anchor social-welfare states. These same features eventually characterised the most eye-catching developmental states of the twentieth century. But it is highly doubtful whether they remain a viable basis today. Stereotypes of economic development in the south (especially in Asia but also in South Africa) highlight the manufacturing sector as an engine of growth and source of mass employment. But the proportion of overall jobs created in manufacturing is shrinking—in both the industrialised north and the industrialising south.

Globally, large parts of the platform for social progress in the twentieth century are crumbling. The workers' movements, which earlier were so central to social achievements, are on the defensive and the forms of organisation that enabled them to thrive seem increasingly outmoded and inefficient. These are not momentary blips. They are symptoms of structural changes in the organising of economic production and the circuitry of capital accumulation; changes that have shifted the balance of power between private capital, the state and other social forces—typically in favour of private capital. Copying and pasting from yesteryear's iconic experiences is not an option. Among other things, this means that many of the political economic arrangements that underpinned the developmental-state idols of the twentieth century no longer seem to be available. The form of the developmental state needs to be radically rethought—which is why the modest but distinctive experiences in places like Kerala and Porto Alegre become so intriguing and suggestive.

Closer to the ground: subnational developmental 'states'

In neither Kerala nor Porto Alegre was a developmental state type of project the goal at the outset, although the pursuit of other, less grandiose (but no less ambitious) goals provided some of the ingredients.[18] Both cases involved conscious attempts to devolve and democratise state power in pursuit of social justice (Fung & Wright, 2003). Participatory processes occurred 'within a wider political project of state transformation' that sought to challenge existing power relations—rather than merely circumvent them in order to achieve technically efficient 'delivery' (Hickey & Mohan, 2003:16).

The form of 'embedded autonomy' achieved in Kerala involved strong organisations of the peasantry and working classes. About half of Kerala's population is estimated to belong to at least one popular organisation and the members of organisations affiliated to the Communist Party of India (Marxist) (CPI-M) numbered about 10 million (out of a total population of 37 million) in the 1990s. The CPI-M relied on links it built with various sections of the subordinate classes during the course of the twentieth century, as Michelle Williams (2008 & 2007) has shown.[19] Initially, this paved access to local state power and made possible the introduction of land reforms in the 1970s; later, it facilitated Kerala's experiments in decentralised participatory planning of the mid-1990s (Mohan & Stokke, 2005). Although those bonds helped the CPI-M into political office, they were not decisive enough to ensure electoral dominance. The combination of political insecurity and the CPI-M's consequent reliance on reproducing its links with well-organised social forces, schooled the party into becoming unusually responsive to popular demands. Civil society gained increasing influence in the institutions of the state and economy. At the same time, the extent and eclecticism of popular organisations meant that state 'capture' by narrow interests was difficult to achieve.

In Porto Alegre, governed since 1989 by the Workers' Party (*Partido dos Trabalhadores* or PT), citizens achieved decision-making powers over public resources through a participatory budget process, which shapes major decisions regarding the types of services and upgrading in the city. Participatory budgeting emerged as part of an alternative political strategy that the Workers' Party spearheaded in a bid to undercut the power of clientelist networks and to pursue local state power. Several analysts have highlighted the role of a democratic socialist party that had developed a political culture of tolerance, diversity and respect for civil liberties and that comprised a variety of social groups (including a powerful workers' movement) (Heller, 2001; Abers, 2001).[20] There was a clear correlation between successful cases of participatory budgeting and areas with high membership of the PT (Schneider & Goldfrank, 2002).

The social basis for the Porto Alegre experiment differed starkly from that in Kerala. In the latter the absence of a strong capitalist class and the presence of dense, well-established networks of popular organisations were vital factors. That advantage was not available in Porto Alegre, where consent had to be built along a variety of routes. The Workers' Party (and the city administration) therefore tried to assemble a support base that went beyond the poor and working-class sectors and included parts of the middle classes (Abers, 2001 & 2003). The latter tolerated or supported participatory budgeting because it offered a possible break with a legacy of corruption and waste and a progression to efficiency and transparency (Schneider & Goldfrank, 2002). Progressive elements of the middle classes also backed the democratising and social-justice ambitions of the process. Meanwhile, those parts of the business elite that stood to benefit from some of the projects (particularly the construction industry) chose not to oppose the initiatives, thus splitting and undercutting the influence of conservative reaction. Careful political and discursive manoeuvring helped bring this about. The upshot, according to Abers

(2001:37), was that 'instead of being a political burden that brought on opposition, participatory, redistributive policies were actually an asset that helped generate political support'.[21] A win-win scenario was created: a reminder that strategies can be crafted in which elites and subordinate groups can pursue (or at least slipstream behind) the same radical agenda (Hickey & Mohan, 2003; Moore & Putzel 1999).

Highlighted in those experiments are features that will be key in this new era: the economic and social centrality of human capabilities, the state's responsibility for expanding those capabilities (especially through effective provision of healthcare and education) and the need to create new institutional spaces and arrangements for popular participation in the political and economic management of society. Also prominent is the potential importance of the many variants of the solidarity economy.

The importance of bureaucratic capacity, meanwhile, stands undiminished: 'State capacity will have an even greater role to play in societal success in the coming century than it did in the last century' (Evans, 2007:5). Still cardinal are state institutions that are capable of operating effectively and predictably with the active consent of the most powerful social forces. Equally important is the underlying balance of forces, which cannot be detoured with mere political voluntarism. Any debate about the shape and prospects of a South African developmental state needs to take account of this profoundly changed context in which such a quest would occur.

A South African developmental state?

The question of whether South Africa is, or can become, a developmental state can be approached along two paths: by examining which of the features deemed essential for such a quest are present or imminent and by assessing if it is already conducting itself in the manner of a developmental state.

The South African state's handling of the AIDS and TB epidemics—and the health crisis generally—offers a paradigmatic example of how *not* to be a developmental state. It is not unreasonable to propose that protecting citizens from dying in unusually large numbers at unusually early ages belongs high on the list of a state's duties, developmental or otherwise. Yet the government doggedly denied proven life-prolonging treatment to stricken citizens and managed key disease-prevention campaigns in a manner that can generously be termed 'listless'. Contrast that with Brazil where, despite the strength of the Catholic Church prevention programmes were put into effect with gusto, the state decisively supported the industrial capacity for manufacturing generic antiretroviral drugs, international patenting regimes were challenged and treatment was provided extensively and early (Okie, 2006).

Many of the conditions for acting as a capability-enhancing developmental state were available to South Africa. A production drive of generic drugs, underwritten by the state (and on terms favourable to it) was entirely feasible. South Africa's pharmaceutical industry was sophisticated enough to do this and keen to snatch market shares from their multinational competitors. Global activism had created strong ambient support for generic production and by 2002 the Doha round of global trade talks had endorsed countries' rights to sidestep patent rights under certain conditions (all of which applied in South Africa's case). Government's stand-off with major multinational pharmaceutical corporations over the country's Medicines Act showed that it *did* occasionally have the nerve to confront powerful capitalist interests.[22] And backing that defiance was the strongest social movement to emerge since the end of apartheid: the Treatment Action Campaign (TAC), along with COSATU and an array of international organisations and major powers of the south (including Brazil). Government stared down the pharmaceutical corporations, but then refused to provide antiretroviral treatment through the public health system (Lawson, 2008). It spurned a sterling opportunity for an industrial policy venture led by the state and with manifest benefits for social wellbeing and great potential for economic growth. Instead, it flung its weight behind a homespun snake-oil remedy concocted from industrial solvents[23] and withdrew deeper into lockdown mode, dismissing established science in favour of quackery and indulging in Afrocentric posturing (Cullinan & Thom, 2009; Marais, 2005). Rather than ally itself with progressive, well-organised social movements (the TAC, COSATU and others) around these issues, it demonised them and sustained that hostility for several years (see Chapter nine). All this happened as government claimed to be building a developmental state.

Relations with organised social forces are tetchy and inconsistent and the state is flimsily embedded in the grassroots of society, as the incessant spate of community protests remind. Still dominant in the state is an 'instrumentalist understanding of state power' that tends toward domesticating or marginalising popular organisations (Evans, 2001:134); a longstanding tendency also noted by other analysts (Gumede, 2005; Marais, 2001; Fine & Davis, 1990). Meanwhile, the state's sway in relation to capital is weak. A powerful financial sector has emerged alongside the imperious minerals-energy complex. Economic restructuring undertaken in the 1990s has undermined the state's leverage over the handful of conglomerates that dominate the economy, leaving it weaker perhaps than at any point in the previous half-century. South African corporate capital is now so globalised, sophisticated and socially remote that the 'embedded autonomy' the state seeks seems unlikely (see Chapter five). Deep social interventions with long-term pay-offs are largely absent and efforts to reduce poverty are spotty and heavily reliant on redistributive payments (Freund, 2007a). South Africa seems no different from the many other countries where

> *deeply established reliance on local private economic elites, the growing centrality of transnational capital to local accumulation and the proliferation of alliances between local and transnational capital have transformed the political landscape.*
> (Evans, 2007:24)

In addition, the familiarity, trust and comfort fostered between South Africa's major corporations and the state prior to 1994 have not transferred into the post-apartheid era. Nor have the informal channels for dialogue and engagement been adapted to the new era. This is not surprising in a country as racially divided as South Africa and where corporations are still controlled largely by whites. But it introduces a great deal of inefficiency into state-capital relations and widens the scope for misunderstandings and blunders.

More positively, key institutions remain under the (nominal) control of the South African state. Weakened by the demise of the Washington Consensus globally in the late 1990s and beaten back by the trade-union movement locally, South Africa's privatisation drive slowed to a crawl in the early 2000s. As a result, the state has retained control over major entities, including the Industrial Development Corporation, the South African Development Bank, a great deal of the rail and harbour system and infrastructure, a large portfolio of TV and radio stations and the sole electricity supplier, Eskom. Unfortunately, its failure to exercise such control effectively and efficiently became obvious to all during the blackouts of early 2008, when a 'perfect storm' of coal-supply mishaps, scheduling errors, surging demand and strategic miscalculations caused weeks of electricity cuts that shut down large parts of the mining and manufacturing industries and all but halted commercial activity in the urban centres. The fiasco brought an unnerving reminder of the muddled and reactive nature of energy policymaking in South Africa. It also spoke to deeper failings, which cast doubt on the grand hopes staked on a developmental state.

Things we learn when the lights go out

Around 2000 Eskom had swaggered with plans to expand electricity production and provision across the continent; less than a decade later, it was incapable of keeping the lights on in the country's industrial and financial heartland. Electricity demand had outstripped even reserve generating capacity, bringing the system to a standstill. Neither Eskom nor its overseers in government has been subjected to a thorough and public top-level inquiry to give account for the debacle.

Significant investment had created an oversupply of electricity in the 1980s, but demand soared from the early 1990s onward. The number of homes plugged into the electricity grid had increased dramatically (up from 1.2 million in 1990 to four million in 2007), while generating capacity dwindled (from 45 000 megawatts in 1994 to 37 000–40 000 megawatts in 2008) according to Earthlife Africa (2009). A failure to invest in the energy sector post-1994 was the single biggest factor in the crisis. Reserve capacity sank well below the 15% safety margin. A confluence of factors then tipped the system over the brink.

Prominent in the background was the ANC's penchant in the 1990s for partially privatising several state utilities, with Eskom among those targeted. Various models were considered, the most favoured one entailing splitting Eskom into three operations, which would yield funding to expand electricity-generating capacity. Having lost most of the economic policy battles in the 1990s, the ANC's alliance partners chose to dig in against the privatisation plans. International developments favoured them. Reacting to a combination of popular struggles and privatisation failures in the late 1990s (particularly in the water and energy sectors), World Bank dogma shifted towards the promotion of public-private partnerships, with key roles reserved for the state. Government put Eskom's restructuring—and with it key financing decisions, including its recapitalisation—on hold. Despite soaring electricity demands no new electricity-generating capacity was added to the grid between 2002 and 2006. Several years earlier R 300 billion (USD 40 billion) had been earmarked for a multiyear infrastructure investment programme, but Eskom barely featured in it. It was either an extraordinary error of judgement[24] or a basic failure of co-ordination, especially on the part of the Presidency and the Ministry of Finance (government's two most powerful entities).

Secondary factors featured. These included a reliance on low-quality and wet coal (transported in open trucks and carriages in the rainy season) and an unusual coincidence of scheduled power-plant refurbishments and unscheduled repairs, which reduced generating capacity even further. 'Capacity constraints' may have contributed to some of the scheduling errors that removed some power stations from the supply grid for maintenance work and shortages of skilled technicians have been cited as a reason why repairs took longer than anticipated. But, as Ben Fine (2008b) reminds, a lack of capacity is a poor explanation for why certain fundamental steps—such as financing the upgrade and expansion of generating capacity—were not taken at all. At the root of the crisis lay a very basic failure of stewardship on the part of the state (specifically government, Parliament and the national energy regulator) which, even subsequently, remained in reactive mode as Eskom led the way in planning the recuperation of the electricity sector and plotting financing strategies.

Beneath the hood

South Africa is generally seen to have well-developed state administrations and a sophisticated judicial system, all buttressed by a surprisingly liberal Constitution and Bill of Rights. Civil-society organisations are large in scope and many in number and seem capable of discouraging arbitrary abuses of power. But there is considerable evidence of dysfunction, even failure, in the state, especially at local levels. By its own account, this constitutes one of the ANC's biggest political headaches (Southall, 2006). The malaise extends to several institutions of the central state, most notably in the education and health sectors, but also in the criminal-justice system and beyond—so much so that the state's capacity to direct and manage key developmental duties is called into doubt.

Leftist promoters of a developmental state in South Africa customarily shrug off such concerns and instead lay emphasis on political will, policy frameworks and financial resources. The internal workings of institutions are seldom scrutinised and the relational dynamics between the state and social forces are seldom closely examined. Thus the remarkable rehabilitation of the South African Revenue Service (SARS), under the stewardship of Pravin Gordhan, is routinely paraded as evidence that willpower and resources beget success. Along with the Treasury, SARS is one of the few state structures that resembles the ideal Weberian bureaucracy in post-apartheid South Africa.[25] However, if the aim is to repair institutions tasked with serving citizens, SARS is a most inappropriate model. A highly centralised, top-down institution of compulsion, it operates in authoritarian fashion and wields formidable punitive powers.[26] It is no coincidence that SARS was rehabilitated with a (former) Leninist at the helm.[27] In that respect it hardly exemplifies the principles or ethos of a 'democratic state' that services citizens, nor is it evident as to how it serves as an exemplar for salvaging, say, the sprawling, decentralised web of institutions that comprise the public health system.

One of the most revealing recent probes into the internal functioning of state structures has been Karl von Holdt's study (2009 & 2007) of South Africa's ailing public hospitals. His research and analysis is a jarring riposte to many of the flippancies in circulation about a developmental state. Crucially, he situates the post-apartheid bureaucracy within the history of modernity in South Africa, the colonial patterns it assumed and the subsequent efforts to undo those patterns. The contemporary dilemmas of the South African state, therefore, are not mere imprints of the past, but are shaped also by the efforts to overcome the past. This calls into play an examination of organisational cultures and Von Holdt obliges admirably. He identifies five such features that undermine or unsettle the bureaucracy's ability to adhere to the Weberian principles usually operating at the core of developmental state bureaucracies:

- Black class formation (achieved partly through affirmative action);
- Ambivalence toward skills and expertise;
- Importance of 'face';
- Disciplinary failures; and
- Rituals of budgetary discipline.

It is worth considering these in more detail. The combination of affirmative action and rationed skills has created an unsettling churn in the civil service, as professionals react to numerous opportunities (and incentives) for shifting from post to post. Since vacancies must be advertised, promotions cannot be used to reward strong work performances. The high turnover rate (estimated at 32% nationally and 38% provincially across the public service; Naidoo, 2008) therefore is only loosely related to individuals' work performances. Employment equity legislation, which encourages the hiring of black employees (and which services the broader bid to rapidly expand an African elite), also fuels this restless quest for upward mobility.[28] This occurs in and probably reinforces, a managerial culture of 'upward' deference and 'downward' despotism, a classic feature of rigid, hierarchical structures.

Skills have been an important part of the ideological and technological arsenal of domination in South Africa and the discourse around work, capacity and efficiency remains freighted with that history. This engenders, in turn, a risk of encouraging and legitimating a cavalier attitude toward skills and expertise—a sensibility not everyone is able to resist. Yet a lack of skills and expertise is often one of the culprits when structures lapse into dysfunction. Von Holdt (2009:13) argues that 'it is not only the scarcity' of skills that creates such situations, 'but also the ambivalence toward them'.

Racist prejudice assumes incompetence and forecasts failure. Endless demurrals notwithstanding, that sensibility still clots the air when the post-apartheid state is assessed. Consciously or not, the media's constant search for drama and sensation feeds and validates this bigotry and encourages a reflexive defensiveness among its targets. One outcome is an overemphasis on 'the importance of authority, reputation and "face" in the state' (Von Holdt, 2009:14) and an inclination toward wounded dramatics. This was plainly evident in the debacles that plagued the AIDS response and in the siege mentality the ANC and government adopted around them (Lawson, 2008; Marais, 2005).[29] More routinely, it encourages 'elaborate rituals of power and respect' that feed a culture of excessive deference (Von Holdt, 2009:15). Improvisation, invention and defiance do not thrive in such atmospheres and basic operations often suffer.[30]

Breakdowns in discipline remain common in the public service. These episodes are infused with a long history of resistance against the authoritarian workplace regimes imposed under apartheid. In parts of the public health system, bitter and violent strikes in the early 1990s broke that order, but it has not been replaced with a new, widely endorsed workplace order, especially for non-professional staff (Von Holdt & Murphy, 2007). Similar developments have played out in other sections of the state. As a result, labour relations are often fraught, short-fused and marred by conflicts between management and trade unions. Disciplinary measures tend to be unpredictable, feeble or absent. Corruption appears to be widespread, as is pilfering. The overall effects are deeply corrosive.

Finally, there is the need to maintain budgetary discipline. Generally sensible, this becomes problematic when it outweighs the duty of providing quality services to the public. Underbudgeting is common, not only when the Treasury applies the screws but because budget allocations often bear faint relation to the actual operations and expenses of various units. This stems not from human error, but from budgetary procedures. Budgets are compiled at head-office level and are based on historical allocations and fashionable prerogatives (that may have nothing to do with the actual duties and functions of a given structure). Budgetary mismatches, cost overruns and service or supply breakdowns are therefore not unusual. Staff relations and morale are among the casualties.

Management skills are not abundant. But the bigger hindrances are fragmented and 'incoherent' authority structures, the nebulous positioning of managerial authority and fuzzy accountability. Attempts to impose a remote but overweening authority from head-office level do not help matters.[31] The result is managerial inefficiency and 'bureaucratic inertia'. Combined with routine operational dysfunction, warn Von Holdt and Murphy (2007:337), this brings the risk of 'a long-term erosion of public service ethos and consequent decline of the public health sector'. Von Holdt (2009:22) stops short of concluding that these observed realities have eclipsed the 'normal Weberian functioning of the bureaucracy', but finds little grounds for optimism about South Africa's prospects of emulating some of the more successful developmental states:

The bureaucracy is characterised by contradictory rationales, purposes and meanings which make it difficult to establish efficient routines or to grasp the real problems and seek innovative solutions. In this environment it is much easier to seek refuge in existing routines, rules, procedures and hierarchies than to acknowledge and tackle dysfunctionality.

Some of the underlying complications, such as affirmative action, are necessary. Similarly, there are arguments to be made in favour of incubating an African economic elite. But is not clear how or whether these kinds of undertakings are compatible with an effectively functioning state in the classical Weberian sense. Imposed through colonial conquest in South Africa, modernity was heavily invested with colonial and racialised forms. The post-apartheid state is not merely a further 'moment' in that history: it is deeply marked simultaneously by that history and by attempts to 'establish zones of sovereignty, self-definition and empowerment' that could move it beyond that history. Consequently, the state, more than usual, is permeated with struggles 'over the selective appropriation and rejection of different aspects of modernity' (Von Holdt, 2009:24).[32]

All this seems to undercut the reveries about a developmental state. But that does not rule out less grandiose (yet possibly more radical) developmental feats. The experiments in Kerala and Porto Alegre therefore seem doubly pertinent in South Africa. Citing Peter Evans' (1995) analysis of state bureaucracies in Brazil and India, Von Holdt (2009) suggests that, like theirs, South Africa's state bureaucracy falls in an intermediate category that is neither a patrimonial caricature nor the coherent and lubricated 'developmental ideal type'. This 'inbetweenness' might work to its advantage when engaging with complex and divided social structures. Or it might be that the state, particularly at the local level, is too brittle, unstable and self-absorbed to exploit such opportunities. Or it might be that the unsettled nature and context of the local state favours, even invites, such experiments.

Decorative development

South Africa does not suffer a dearth of organising, least of all in poor communities—but does this translate into vibrant, positive engagements with the state around local development? Introduced in the mid-1990s was a system of local governance that allows and, to varying extents, enables citizens to participate in local development. The Integrated Development Planning (IDP) process, in particular, was meant to facilitate deeper participation.[33]

As community protests underline, the consensual embrace sought by the state is often weak. It prefers a relationship that encloses it, corporate interests and the public in a predictable cycle of rituals and routines. The public's role tends to be perfunctory and is ideally channelled through organisations and formations that are capable of supporting and advancing the state's agenda without imposing additional fiscal and institutional burdens. Consultation occurs and a degree of inclusivity is attempted, but within regimented and hidebound processes (Marais, Everatt, Dube, 2007).

In many communities the modes of engagement promoted by the state are actively rejected, circumvented and ignored. Those residents and activists are responding to the fact that popular participation in local governance and development is irresolute and momentary, taking the shape of sporadic 'inputs' that decorate particular stages of planning and programming cycles. When they do occur, report-backs are perfunctory. For the most part, the IDP framework has elaborated such gestures and rituals without deepening democratic participation (Marais, Everatt, Dube, 2007; Moodley, 2007; Hicks, 2006; Friedman, 2006; Mathekga & Buccus, 2006; Williams, 2005). Rigid frameworks and barriers rid public inputs of weight and influence, while community-level power imbalances and political tussles shape processes and the framing of issues, options and priorities. Many practical and surmountable factors worsen matters (Marais, Everatt, Dube, 2007).[34] In Gwagwa and Everatt's assessment (2005:7), community participation generally is 'wedged at the level of consultation during planning and possibly also subsequent involvement in the running and maintenance of projects'.

Moreover, local development and governance seldom challenge the 'immanent' patterns of development and power—and South Africa is no different in this respect. Proposed projects or initiatives might reflect real needs, but they do not challenge or alter the underlying patterns of development (Hickey & Mohan, 2003). Instead they explore options within parameters of 'feasible' or 'realistic' possibilities. 'This,' Swilling and Russel (2002:73) remind us, 'is the political economics underlying the word "governance".' Yet a fundamental measure of genuine democracy and freedom is the ability to challenge the architecture of the status quo and of the arrangements that lock 'things as they are'. Without such disruptive potential, democracy is a shadow play and development remains a commandist and technical affair.[35]

Edgar Pieterse (2003:2) sees the 'technocratic rationality' that governs municipal processes as an important reason why the democracy-boosting claims of the local state are so unconvincing. Development challenges are approached as technical puzzles that need to be solved within relatively conservative frameworks. Notwithstanding the dramaturgy of 'inclusion' and 'consultation' citizens tend to be reduced to the status of objects. Local development exemplifies the often-awkward fit between ostensibly good and democratic governance. The need for sound institutions, limpid plans and reliable systems is self-evident. But popular accountability and democratic participation too often becomes a casualty of that pursuit.

The answer is not a trade-off between good and democratic governance. Rather, as the local state is discovering, both governance *and* development suffer when democracy becomes ritualistic and cramped. Rarefied and insulated processes might tick off some of the remote criteria for 'good' governance, but the test of lived reality often exposes the outcomes as flawed and inadequate.

Politics of local development

The local state is a feverishly contested zone. Since political influence opens the door to entrepreneurial or even plundering opportunities, there are often powerful motives for rationing and controlling popular participation and, especially, oversight. In many places ostensible 'development partnerships' with the state are the preserve of well-connected organisations and individuals. The case of Tladi-Moletsane, in Soweto, is instructive, partly because its inequalities mirror those in many ostensibly poor communities. Researchers found that better-off residents dominated the political and civic structures, which maintained scant contact with community structures in nearby informal settlements. There was 'virtually no evidence' of productive partnerships between civil-society organisations and local government that benefited the poor (Everatt *et al*, 2004:27). Their disheartening conclusion was that 'politics and activism have come to be seen as avenues for the ambitious, not mechanisms for effecting change' (*op cit*, 26). Participation tends to express other, predictable lines of exclusion, too, as Sithole *et al* (2007) have shown in their three-year study of women's participation in local development projects in three KwaZulu-Natal municipalities (eThekwini, Hibiscus Coast and Msinga). Substantial numbers of women attended project meetings, but these were dominated by a handful of assertive men. Overall, the culture of participation is restrictive.

Genuinely democratic arrangements are unpredictable and not easily controlled. Once extended beyond formalities, they involve highly political and politicised practices that can be restive and unpredictable. In Patrick Heller's reading, this is what transpired in the celebrated cases of participatory governance in Porto Alegre and Kerala. State reform there was 'messy, nonlinear, and driven by distinctly conflictual processes'—yet successful. It occurred and matured as part of a 'continuous process of learning and feedback, made possible by policy networks that have blurred the boundaries between state and society' (Heller, 2001:157).

Those experiences shared some cardinal features. They put great emphasis on inclusiveness and accountability; they used extensive outreach and created institutional arrangements to enable widespread and intensive public participation; they took special steps to impart skills and build capacity (both among citizens and officials); and they entailed and enabled sustained popular involvement in the prioritising, planning and monitoring of public projects and investments (Mohan & Stokke, 2005; Heller, 2001; Abers, 2001).

Key, as well, was the combined activism in civil and political society, in the context of devolved state power. This created the political space in which marginalised groups could mobilise and pursue pro-poor policies (Hickey & Mohan, 2003; Fung & Wright, 2003; Heller, 2001). Decentralisation was used as part of wider political projects of democratising state power and challenging existing power relations in pursuit of social justice—as opposed to circumventing them in a bid to achieve technically efficient, ameliorating 'delivery' (Hickey & Mohan, 2003).

The experiments all emphasised tangible socioeconomic needs and formed part of redistributive development strategies. But the character of the political formations spearheading the processes was decisive. These were strong, leftist political parties that were committed to 'wider project[s] of redistributive politics and social justice' (Hickey & Mohan, 2003:16) and that forged productive, though prickly, relationships with civil-society networks. In neither Kerala nor Porto Alegre was popular participation simply the outcome of an untroubled marriage between committed political elites and enthusiastic civil society activists (Mohan & Stokke, 2005).

Can South Africa replicate such experiments? The apartheid state's approach to civil-society organisations of the poor was relatively simple. Those that shunned oppositional activities and focused on 'betterment' and 'upliftment' were deemed functional to the notion of 'separate development' and met with indifference from the state or even received nominal aid. Those that sought to challenge its dominance were crushed. Fostered was an utterly alienated and deeply distrustful relationship towards the state. In the two decades prior to 1994, as the wave of oppositional organising crested, many of the most powerful popular organisations of the poor threw their weight behind the burgeoning struggle to capture state power (see Chapter two).[36] That binary tradition of oppositionality/collaboration has proved difficult to overcome.[37] South African organisations of the poor therefore do not have the political heritage that citizens in Kerala were able to draw on—what Heller (2002:148) has described as a

> long history of effective demand-making in general and of making representations (both through conventional parliamentary as well as extraparliamentary channels) that can now be fully exploited with more responsible and accountable local government.

The types of popular organising that emerged in South Africa, the tactics used and the sharp dichotomy drawn between state and civil society, are inappropriate for the kinds of engagements that are now required. Moreover, it is questionable as to what extent the ANC's conception of power and positioning of popular organisations within developmental initiatives allows for forms of development that involve and require mobilisation. Similar tendencies are found on the ANC's left. The SACP had pushed for the devolution of power and resources to local government institutions, a move that potentially holds great scope for community-led development initiatives. Yet, as Williams observes (2007:13–14), it balked at catalysing and supporting those opportunities, choosing instead to focus

> its activities on particular ways in which the ANC-led state could effect change rather than enhancing efforts to empower citizens to participate in effecting transformative politics [...] After ensuring the institutional spaces were created, the SACP failed to develop initiatives that would ensure citizen involvement in these newly created institutions.

By contrast, social movements in Kerala and Porto Alegre retained their autonomy from the state (without yielding their influence) and were able to help shape and drive processes of democratic decentralisation. Another important factor was the disentangling of political power from economic power. In Kerala, the ascendant radical political elites were not entwined in the acquisitive circuits of the (landed) economic elites. This accorded them a structural distance that enabled them to avoid 'capture' (Hickey & Mohan, 2003) and to pursue redistributive agendas on the basis of alliances with subordinate classes. Porto Alegre and Kerala became examples of what Amartya Sen (1999:291) has termed 'processes of participation' that are 'constitutive parts of the ends of development in themselves'. Not only does local development in South Africa currently seem to lack that political economic 'space', but it also is cast mainly as a technocratic process aimed at achieving quicker and more efficient 'development', with politics seen as 'part of the problem' rather than 'part of the solution'.

Endnotes

1   Also ignored in this sort of perspective is the fundamental need for moral compatibility between means and ends. If equality is the goal, then the instruments used to achieve it must enhance equality. GEAR patently violated that principle.

2   'A shortage of funds was never the problem,' according to the authors (2005:75).

3   The 'shock therapy' assaults on Russia and a few other Eastern European countries in the mid-1990s probably came the closest to emulating the neoliberal state as an 'ideal type'—but in the absence of functioning markets!

4   For a discussion of the manner in which those experiments were promoted by the World Bank and other international financial institutions, see Fine (2007). The developmental state 'story' actually extends deeper in history (at least as far back as Bismarck's Germany) and far beyond Asia (including the 'late industrialisers' of Europe and some African countries in the 1960s), as Thandika Mkandawire (2001) has shown.

5   Ching Kwan Lee (2007), for example, has questioned China's status as a developmental state, pointing to rising urban poverty rates, increasing income inequality (the Gini coefficient rose from 0.31 in 1979 to 0.49 in 2007), widening urban/rural disparities (the urban/rural income ratio stretched from 1.8:1 in 1984 to 6:1 in 2006), ballooning informal work-forces in the cities and soaring numbers of landless peasants (who numbered 40 million by 2004). In the mid-1990s the average hourly manufacturing wage in China was USD 0.64; in Mexico it was USD 4. Vast numbers of vulnerable migrant workers are not paid in full or at all, for their labour. Lee describes these trends as the 'Latin Americanization' of China's experiment. Its economic output remains impressive, but turbocharged GDP growth alone does not make a developmental state. The trends are not continuing unabated, though. In contrast to scholars such as Marc Blecher (2002), Lee's research has revealed powerful currents of workers' discontent and resistance, especially from those who have lost their jobs. Popular protests have forced the state to introduce reforms and embark on a rhetorical shift away from 'growth and efficiency' toward notions of a 'harmonious society' and equity. Alongside this, nationalist ideology is being used more assiduously.

6   Ian Taylor (2002) has set out a thoughtful case for considering Botswana in this light.

7   For a partial corrective, see Pierson, C (2003) '"Late industrialisers" and the development of the welfare state', Background paper, UNRISD, Geneva.

8   A predictable reward system also fostered internal cohesion inside the bureaucracy. These characteristics did not emerge overnight. A very long tradition of intensive training and mentoring and strict entrance examinations for civil servants, had existed in the Asian cases, including in China and Vietnam. In broad terms, Japan's bureaucratic model traces back more than a millennium, even though the meritocratic model was not applied consistently or firmly during the ensuing 1 000-plus years; Korea's dates back to the eighth century, as noted by Evans (1995).

9   Only slightly mischievously, Ben Fine has tabulated three features of east Asian 'developmental state' success stories: they were not designed by economists, the managers of these experiments did not know they were building a developmental state until told so by Western social scientists and the 'miracles' usually went pear-shaped when returning US-trained economists reached critical levels of influence (Fine, 2007:13).

10 Omano Edigheji's 2005 paper is part of an ongoing debate about the relevance for African states of developmental state models derived from the post-Second World War East Asian experiences. For more on developmental states generally, see Woo-Cuming, M (ed) (1999) *The Developmental State*, Cornell University Press, New York; Kevane, M and Englebert, P (1999) 'A developmental state without growth: explaining the paradox of Burkina Faso in comparative perspective' in Karl, W, Bass, H and Messner, F (eds) *African Development Perspectives Yearbook 1997/98*, Lit Verlag, Munster; Leftwich, A (1995) 'Bringing politics back', *Journal of Development Studies*, Vol. 31, No. 3, February; Mkandawire, T (1998) 'Thinking about developmental states in Africa', Paper presented at the UNU-AERC workshop on 'Institutions and Development in Africa', UNU Headquarters, Tokyo, Japan, 14–15 October.

11 Peter Evans and James Rauch have schematised the strong association between economic growth and the extent to which state bureaucracies exhibit Weberian features; see Evans, P and Rauch, J (1999) 'Bureaucracy and growth: a cross-national analysis of the effects of "Weberian" state structures on economic growth', *American Sociological Review*, Vol. 64, pp. 748–65.

12 Afghanistan counts among the few exceptions.

13 See Fitzgerald (2006), cited in Evans (2007), where the East Asian and Latin American tax efforts are compared.

14 Ben Fine, 'SA needs more equitable developmental state', *Business Report*, 30 July 2007.

15 Powerful family systems were vital in the Asian experiences, as were land reform and agrarian policies that anchored families more or less sustainably in the countryside (while providing migrant labour for industrial growth in urban areas). Also important was the geopolitical context in which the states operated, which shaped the external political support and economic largesse they could draw on.

16 It pioneered the process in 1989 and Montevideo (Uruguay) copied it the following year. Since then almost 2000 cities in Latin America, the Caribbean, Africa and Europe have introduced variants of the participatory budgeting process (Bloj, 2009).

17 See, for example Michael Schmidt and Lucien van der Walt's (2009) *Black Flame: The Revolutionary Politics of Anarchism and Syndicalism*, AK Press.

18 In fact, in none of the more conventional developmental states was the *intention* of building a development state broadcast beforehand. Typically, the intention did not even exist.

19 This did not occur without ructions and resistance. For example, some of the CPI-M-aligned trade unions were reluctant to support the popular participation projects pushed by the social movement factions in the CPI-M (Heller, 2001). Williams (2008 & 2007) provides a detailed analysis of the politics of the Kerala experience, counter-posing it with the political choices made by the SACP in South Africa. Since the 1960s, the CPI-M pursued a protest politics aimed at dismantling existing systems of political and economic control. This entailed support for, and strong relations with, popular organisations—but within a strategic outlook in which the state would ultimately direct and control civil society once power was achieved. The similarity with the SACP's outlook during the apartheid era is obvious. However, in the 1990s the CPI-M shifted its practice by pursuing a campaign of democratic decentralisation which ultimately boosted the role of civil society. Rhetorically, the SACP also strongly supported popular, grassroots participation in South Africa's transformation, though its practice tended more toward neglecting, even sidelining popular politics. 'Neither party,' notes Williams (2007:24), 'pursued the anticipated politics arising from their protest politics.' A key reason, she proposes, was the strength of the capitalist class in the respective settings—well developed, ideologically cocksure and tactically sophisticated in South Africa, but weak and immature in Kerala. The balance of forces between the main contesting classes, in other words, was of paramount importance.

20 Its official ideology, for example, hinged on two mottos: grassroots participation (*participacao popular*) and 'inverting priorities' (*invertendo prioridades*, moving government policies away from favouring elites). In Rio Grande do Sul state, the rural-based Landless Movement, allied with trade unions and progressive churches, backed participatory budgeting—to the

point of helping shoulder some of the expenses when opposition parties prevented the state government from financing participatory budget hearings (Schneider & Goldfrank 2002).

21 In more detail, Abers ascribes the success to the Porto Alegre administration's ability to (a) implement its ideals in ways that incorporated the interests of a 'critical mass' of poor, middle-class and business groups; (b) engage certain business sectors in the implementation of participatory projects; (c) build a reputation as a competent, non-corrupt, transparent and socially responsible administration; and (d) exploit frustration with traditional forms of governance.

22 Lesley Lawson's *Side Effects* (2008) provides an excellent account of that confrontation.

23 For detailed discussion of this tawdry affair, see Myburgh (2009), Lawson (2008) and Epstein (2007).

24 It is likely that the omission was not an oversight and that the recapitalisation of Eskom was still tied to partial privatisation plans which, for the time being, had been put on hold.

25 Pillay (2008) has suggested that the National Prosecuting Authority and especially its Directorate of Special Operations (the Scorpions, later disbanded by the Zuma administration) also exemplified many of the features of the Weberian state. He regards the attacks launched against the Scorpions and the judiciary by Zuma's supporters (including COSATU and the SACP) as signs of 'a clash between a Weberian state struggling to be born and patrimonial, clientilistic relations that refuse to die' (2008:11). Responsible for bringing complex criminal cases to the courts, the Scorpions also brought corruption charges against Zuma. His supporters maintained that the unit was used as political tool to scuttle Zuma's presidential bid. No impartial body has yet provided evidence that the Mbeki presidency had instrumentalised the unit.

26 Not even the South African Police Service, as Jonny Steinberg (2008) shows in his book *Thin Blue*, can be described in such terms; its authority is challenged openly on the streets, it often finds itself outwitted and outgunned by its foes and its ability to enforce the law is spotty.

27 Gordhan now heads the Finance Ministry, another highly illiberal state institution.

28 Additionally, as Von Holdt (2009) points out, it runs the risk of leaving posts vacant if no qualified black candidates can be attracted.

29 Psychoanalysis would take this a step further. Pre-emptive 'reactions' to anticipated abuse threaten to lock the subject in the grasp of that which she/he seeks to resist. In this sense, 'face' becomes an act of both defiance and submission.

30 Sadly, the public health sector offers several frightful illustrations. The 2007 sacking of Deputy Health Minister Nozizwe Madlala-Routledge for criticising her government's handling of the AIDS crisis and acknowledging scandalous hospital conditions in Eastern Cape province, the harassment of hospital doctors providing antiretroviral prophylaxis to rape survivors in Mpumalanga province and the abuse spewed at AIDS activists by the Mbeki administration are but a few examples. A more recent episode involved charges that were brought against a doctor for dumping a portrait of a provincial minister of health (Neliswa 'Peggy' Nkonyeni) in a trashcan after hearing her tell staff that white doctors were only interested in profits. The doctor was also suspended. After a lengthy and disruptive process, the charges were dropped when it was discovered that the portrait had not been damaged. Nkonyeni herself was later charged with corruption and fraud, but those charges were dropped when a key witness declined to testify, reportedly citing 'stress'. Nkonyeni has since become speaker of the KwaZulu-Natal provincial parliament and provincial treasurer. See David Beresford, 'Health reform in South Africa', *Guardian* [London], 15 October 2009; 'ANC welcomes dropping of charges against Nkonyeni', *Mail & Guardian*, 13 August 2009.

31 Von Holdt and Murphy (2007) found an absence of progressive human-resource strategies in the national and provincial health departments and in the Department of Public Service and Administration. The preference instead was for old-school procedures intent on governing and controlling employees.

32 These struggles can be liberating and can generate new conditions for advance. But in the short term they are messy, volatile and disruptive. In this respect, South Africa's particular

history contrasts sharply with those of the Asian developmental states, which 'had their own indigenous histories of meritocratic bureaucracy based on indigenous technologies of writing; it may perhaps be argued that such societies were in the process of establishing their own versions of modernity before contact with Europe and these remained a resource of great value in establishing their own modern developmental states'. (Von Holdt, 2009:25)

33 This section draws on research findings on public participation in local development, as part of a project for the Gauteng Provincial Government; see Marais, Everatt, Dube (2007).

34 They include poor publicising of issues and meetings, inconvenient meeting times, poor meeting facilitation, poor explanation of processes, the language used in documents and meetings, inadequate report-backs, questionable quality and commitment among local councilors, etc. See Marais, Everatt, Dube (2007) for a detailed discussion of these other hurdles, with suggestions for overcoming them.

35 Service organisations capable of providing valuable technical, strategic and advocacy support to communities are thin on the ground, making it very difficult for communities to engage with highly technical processes. Added to this, many NGOs focus on service-delivery work that positions them as implementing partners of the state and encourages modes of operation that disempower the communities they claim to be serving (Gwagwa & Everatt, 2005).

36 See, for example, Friedman (1992).

37 These traditions are discussed in more details in Chapters two and fourteen.

CHAPTER TWELVE

Last man standing: the Mbeki-Zuma battle

I stood on a hill and I saw the Old approaching, but it came as the new.
It hobbled up on new crutches which no one had ever seen before and stank of new
smells of decay which no had ever smelt before.

—Bertolt Brecht, *from* Parade of the Old New, *in Bertolt Brecht,*
Poems 1913–1956, *Methuen, London (1987), pp. 323*

Taking shape in the mid-1990s were three developments that would decisively shape South Africa's transition from apartheid. It was not yet plain to the eye, but the AIDS and tuberculosis epidemics had acquired an inexorable momentum. HIV infection rates were increasing exponentially and epidemiologists tracking the epidemic warned that it would require extraordinary efforts to prevent it from spinning out of control. Instead a long fiasco ensued. The full consequences are still unfolding, but their outlines are momentous, as shown in Chapter nine. These two epidemics and the ways in which they have been handled, will define South African society for many decades ahead.

The second development had deeper, structural origins, but reflected the respective strengths of the social forces contesting the direction of transformation. In 1996 the ANC government barged an economic adjustment programme past its allies. Portrayed as an unavoidable response to economic frailties and global pressures, the Growth, Employment and Redistribution (GEAR) plan elaborated and consummated the neoliberal adjustment path the apartheid regime had initiated hesitantly in the 1980s. The centrepiece of a wider programme of adjustment, GEAR enabled South Africa's largest corporations to restructure, consolidate and globalise their operations. It entrenched their dominance in the local economy, helped fuel the turbocharged surge of the financial sector and wedged open the economy for speculative international capital. As discussed in Chapters five to eight, the consequences have been formative and are not easily undone. They have already underscored the deficiencies of the organised left. The social and political costs, as the ANC is discovering, are portentous and will strain the organisation's ability to retain the loyalty of its constituencies and the consent of others.

The other development was more specific and was entirely the outcome of decisions taken by a handful of top and, for the most part, trusted politicians. Midway through the Mandela presidency, as belts were being tightened and social provisioning capped, government decided to run up an eye-watering bill for military hardware. The spree seemed inexplicable. South Africa lacked military foes (particularly those likely to attack it across open waters) and an austerity drive was underway. From early on an odour of wrongdoing hung about the deal. Perfunctory official investigations claimed to detect nothing untoward, but local court cases and international investigations leave no doubt that more than a few hands were dirtied on a deal that would cost South African taxpayers tens of billions of rands, disgrace the country's top leaders, split Africa's oldest liberation movement, drag key institutions into the muck and pollute the state. Extensively covered in the media and dissected by Gevisser (2007), Feinstein (2007) and Johnson (2008a), the arms deal scandal deserves a brief recap.

The arms deal

Worth USD 9.75 billion and involving contracts with British, French and German arms manufacturers to supply the South African military with jet fighters, training aircraft, frigates, submarines and more, the arms deal was South Africa's largest-ever procurement (Calland, 2006).

Arguments in favour of the spree were eclectic. Industrial offsets, it was claimed, would create dozens of thousands of jobs and attract vast amounts of investment: little of either materialised. The purchases, argued others, would placate a military top brass still dominated by functionaries from the apartheid era. Yet there is no evidence that the military pushed for the deal and ANC politicians overrode its recommendations for specific purchases. The air force's fighter aircraft, said others, were obsolete and scarcely airworthy. But that did not explain the decision to buy frigates and submarines.

Thabo Mbeki had chaired (from 1996 to 1999) the cabinet subcommittee that assembled and approved the arms purchase. According to his biographer, Mark Gevisser (2007:675), Mbeki was unexpectedly enthusiastic about the deal, showing 'an ardour quite remarkable in one so sceptical of military expansionism'. There is no evidence that Mbeki benefited personally from the arms deal, but there is evidence that large bribes were paid, though exactly how much and to whom remains to be discovered.

The scandal broke in mid-2000, when a draft report from the Auditor General indicated concerns about the process. A parliamentary committee (the Standing Committee on Public Accounts or SCOPA) then probed further and published its own interim report in late 2000 listing serious concerns that merited proper investigation. Among the suspected wrongdoings was the payment of bribes (or 'incentives'), a standard procedure in arms deals. Among those suspected of succumbing was Defence Minister Joe Modise[1] who allegedly received several million rands from arms bidders. The fighter-plane tender was highly questionable. The South African Air Force had selected the Italian Aeromarcchi planes, arguing that they were both more cost-effective and technically superior to the rival candidates. But Mbeki's subcommittee struck price considerations from the tender criteria and the contract went to British/Swedish BAE Systems, which was contracted to supply 24 Hawk jet trainers and 28 Gripen fighter planes (Johnson, 2008a; Gevisser, 2007; Feinstein, 2007). The United Kingdom's Serious Fraud Office would later uncover a network of companies that had allegedly been used to pay bribes totalling some 75 million British pounds in relation to the arms deal (Feinstein, 2007).[2] Other evidence suggested that BAE had made a R 5 million donation to the Umkhonto we Sizwe Veteran's Association; its 'life president' was Joe Modise. One of the arms-deal bidders allegedly also bought Modise a large number of shares in an arms company called Conlog, which he went on to chair weeks after ending his tenure as defence minister. Conlog stood to benefit from the arms deal (Feinstein, 2007; Gevisser, 2007).[3]

Other winning tenders also invited suspicions of impropriety. The South African Navy had indicated preference for the cheaper Spanish Bazan corvettes, yet the contract went to a German consortium supplying the Meka A200 frigates. Several plausible reasons have been given for favouring the German tender,[4] but evidence uncovered by German investigators in mid-2006 suggested that ulterior motives were also at work. When German authorities raided offices of ThyssenKrupp, parent company of the frigate and submarine contractors, they reportedly found evidence that bribes worth R 130 million (USD 17 million) had been paid to senior South African politicians. The Germans implicated Chippy Shaik, then head of acquisitions in the South African Defence Force and his brother, Schabir Shaik, an ANC veteran and 'adviser' to Jacob Zuma.[5] The corruption charges against Zuma were tied up with that contract. Thomson-CSF, a French arms company later known as Thales, which won the contract for the combat suites on the German frigates, was suspected of funnelling payments to Zuma (Feinstein, 2007).[6]

ANC Member of Parliament Andrew Feinstein (2007) and a handful of colleagues tried valiantly to engineer trustworthy investigations into the deal, but stonewalling and intimidation stymied these attempts and SCOPA found itself 'filibustered ... into the ground' (Calland, 2006:106).[7] A more docile official investigation, appointed by Parliament, claimed to find 'no evidence ... of any improper or unlawful conduct by the government'. That probe was widely seen as a 'whitewash'.[8] Painstaking evasive action and cover-ups at all ends of the debacle make it unlikely that the full truth will ever be known. Most of the focus has been on individual enrichment, but there is a distinct possibility that pay-offs were also used to bankroll the running of the ANC and finance its election campaigns (Southall, 2008). According to Feinstein (2007:228–9):

> If even a small fraction of the allegations emerging from the investigations in Germany and the United Kingdom are correct, the corruption in the South African arms deal will be seen to have been direct and extensive. The ANC went to such extreme lengths to prevent an unfettered investigation into the deal because they needed to conceal the corruption involving the head of procurement in the Defence Force at the time of the deal, at least two senior ANC leaders and probably the party itself.

The arms scandal almost ended the political career of one ANC leader—then, incredibly, helped him scupper the political career of the sitting president. But the scale and scope of wrongdoing and the likely extent of complicity, are so extensive that the scandal almost certainly will claim other eminent casualties in the years ahead.

Face-off: Zuma versus Mbeki

It was a journalist who ferreted out details of Jacob Zuma's entanglement in the scandal. In November 2002, Sam Sole obtained from the Durban High Court registrar a file detailing a challenge Schabir Shaik had lodged against the lawfulness of raids on his premises. Shaik had been charged with corruption. Tucked into the file was the search warrant for those raids and among the names appearing in the warrant was that of Zuma, by then deputy president.[9] Sole's newspaper article revealed to the world that the National Prosecuting Authority (NPA) was probing Zuma on possible corruption charges.[10] Shaik, who had acted as a middleman on a deal with a German subcontractor in the arms deal, was later found guilty and sentenced to 15 years in prison for fraud and corruption.[11] Presented in court was evidence that Zuma had received regular payments from Shaik, prompting the judge to describe the relationship between him and Zuma as one of 'mutually beneficial symbiosis' and involving 'inappropriate behaviour'.[12] The implication was that Zuma was embroiled in corruption.

The intrigue soon thickened to murk. The director of the NPA, Bulelani Ngcuka, first stated that a *prima facie* case of wrongdoing existed against Zuma, but that the evidence was not strong enough to merit charging him with a crime. Mbeki responded by relieving the deputy president of his duties in 2005—only to be rebuffed by the ANC's National Working Committee. Zuma was then charged with 16 counts of fraud, racketeering, corruption and money-laundering, a move that seemed certain to torpedo his political career. But this was merely the first act of the drama: many twists lay ahead. Portraying himself as a fall guy, Zuma turned the drama inside out. Instead of fading from the scene as a shamed ANC veteran accused of pocketing backhanders from arms dealers, Zuma would be transformed into an embodiment of political virtue and ANC tradition, hounded by a conniving comrade-turned-villain, Thabo Mbeki.

The pantomime would captivate South Africans for years. Lazarus-like, Zuma turned adversity into advantage. He would weather a rape trial in 2006, outlast attempts to prosecute him for corruption and attract cultish adoration in the ANC. Eventually, the country's largest left-wing formations would help muscle him into the presidency in a drawn-out commotion that would badly damage the judiciary, corrode partitions between party and state, puncture the integrity of numerous politicians and institutions, precipitate a *putsch* against a two-term president and split the ANC.

Take no prisoners (on the road to Polokwane)

The gladiatorial clash between Mbeki and Zuma was staged in December 2007 in the northern city of Polokwane, which hosted the ANC's 52nd national conference.

Held every five years nowadays, these conferences decide key party policies, pick members of the ANC's main structures and elect top office-bearers. Preceded by months of caucusing, wheedling and dickering, the conferences are largely choreographed, but the procedures were dynamic enough to leave space for some surprises. This time, though, all manner of contradictions and contests had been compressed into a mighty, personalised battle. Soul-searching was not on the agenda. Polokwane was to be the stage for a mutiny Mbeki could no longer avoid—or survive. Acolytes had spent months touring branches, imploring ANC members and hectoring backroom confabs. Both sides were profligate with promises and doom-saying. An organisation schooled in concealing strife and plastering cracks with comprises was clawing itself to shreds in full public glare.

The face-off pitted a seemingly indefatigable Zuma against an impenitent Mbeki. The immediate pretext was Mbeki's bid to gain election as ANC president for a third term. Usually, the ANC president also becomes the organisation's national presidential candidate. But since South Africa's Constitution imposes a two-term limit, Mbeki would have to have vacated the presidency if elected ANC president again. His plan, though, was to usher Phumzile Mlambo-Ngcuka in as South Africa's first female president, while he would continue to wield decisive influence from behind the screen. It was a pompous, foolhardy manoeuvre.

Even as proceedings got underway in Polokwane, Mbeki's supporters clung to the belief that he would survive Zuma's challenge. Hardly any observers shared their optimism. Mbeki had trampled on too many egos and careers and had burnt too many bridges to repel this attack. He and his circle stood accused of abusing their power and authority, sidelining the ANC and inflaming tensions inside the organisation, humiliating key allies, mismanaging major issues and using state structures to settle scores. The AIDS fiasco had squandered goodwill inside and beyond South Africa, as had Pretoria's indifferent response to Zimbabwe's descent into despotism and misery. Inside the Tripartite Alliance[13] he was deemed guilty of cardinal sins: ramming the GEAR plan into policy, steering South Africa onto a neoliberal course and supervising the emergence of a bumptious black elite while jobs vaporised and inequality deepened. Polokwane was to be a purgative intervention, clearing the way for dramatic renewal and, the Alliance left believed, change.

Mbeki was fair game. In the run-up to the conference, supporters were abandoning him in droves. Overnight, many were converted into ardent champions of Zuma, around whom gathered a catholic cluster of bedfellows that included COSATU, the SACP, the ANC Youth League, a majority of ANC provincial structures and a horde of individuals of various political stripes and income brackets. There had been hesitant moves to steer a third, compromise contender into the race, but none of the likely candidates (including Tokyo Sexwale and Cyril Ramaphosa) wanted to risk a scenario in which they merely made up the numbers. They decided to bide their time and assess their prospects afresh in 2012 and 2017.

Mbeki and his remaining supporters were routed at the Polokwane conference. An astonishing reversal of fortunes had occurred. With the ANC's top leadership purged of Mbeki acolytes, the SACP and COSATU celebrated a 'massive victory for the left'. They had fumbled a similar, though less ambitious, move at the ANC's 1997 national conference in Stellenbosch (Marais, 1999b). This time, riding on the coat-tails of Zuma, their luck had turned—or so they thought. The ANC, the Alliance left claimed, had recovered the radical values that had lit its path after the famed 1969 Morogoro consultative conference. A lame duck president Mbeki had 15 months to see out until the April 2009 national election. A deadlock of sorts threatened. The ANC had replaced many of its office-bearers, but the state's managers dated from Mbeki's heyday. This was not US-style gridlock, but the mood was intemperate and sour. Fancying themselves as the godfathers (in more ways than one) of the 'Zuma project', COSATU and the SACP were especially fidgety. Ahead, though, lurked a major problem: Zuma still faced corruption charges.

Everybody hates Thabo

Mbeki had not only tumbled from grace among ANC activists; he retained little sympathy in the rest of society. His belligerent manner had alienated many of his earlier admirers in the media and corporate elite. Among the public, as opinion polls showed, his approval ratings had nosedived.[14] Eventually the vainglory, the intrigues and injuries, the scratchy reactions to criticism and the ambience of paranoia that marked the Mbeki presidency had created a critical mass of dismay. Such was the loss of trust that all manner of alleged improprieties attributed to him or his inner circle were now treated as credible.

The charge sheet was long and, given Mbeki's reputation for indelicate interventions, hardly groundless. After railroading the GEAR plan in 1996, he had led an attempt by the ANC to prevent the publication of the final report of the Truth and Reconciliation Commission. State institutions had allegedly been manipulated to cement his control, sideline opponents and cow critics. The South African Broadcasting Corporation's board had been stacked with his lackeys and he was accused of using the NPA to stage a witch hunt against Zuma. Beyond that, fealty was said to carry tempting rewards, while dissent invariably invited penalties. State procurement contracts, in particular, had become the quick and easy route to enrichment for black businesspeople (giving rise to the neologism 'tenderpreneurs') and Mbeki supporters seemed to hog the trough when tenders were decided.

But in the public's eye, the death knell, according to Adam Habib (2009), was Mbeki's apparent indifference to the suffering of ordinary people. His AIDS denialism in a country where the death rate had doubled between 1997 and 2006, the refusal to acknowledge the pervasiveness and severity of violent crime and the witch hunts against those (such as former Deputy Health Minister Nozizwe Madlala-Routledge) who admitted and sought to tackle some of the dysfunction in state institutions—all this stuck in the craw of South Africans. Pretoria's pandering to Robert Mugabe's Zanu-PF government in Zimbabwe was especially galling.

Outwitted in Harare

The ANC government's 'quiet diplomacy' approach (redolent, in name and manner, of the Reagan administration's 'constructive engagement' with the apartheid regime in the 1980s) helped buffer Harare against censure and criticism from within the Southern African Development Community (SADC). It also abetted Zimbabwe's slide toward becoming a lawless kleptocracy.[15]

The land seizures in the early 2000s received tacit approval from Pretoria (along with some murmuring about the violence accompanying the confiscations). Scandalously, ANC observers then declared Zimbabwe's rigged March 2002 election 'free and fair'. Calls for public condemnation, sanctions and other forms of pressure were routinely rebuffed. Critics of Pretoria's indulgence of Zanu-PF highlighted the contradiction between Mbeki's African Renaissance avowals and Zimbabwe's sordid implosion. But for conservative South Africans there was also an undertow of dread. To them, Zimbabwe looked like a premonition, a sign of things to come in South Africa. When push came to shove, they and many liberals reasoned, Africanist solidarity would trump the defence of democracy and of human and civil rights.[16] Frequently aired in the media, this *Schadenfreude* was infuriating. Mbeki had a point when he complained about the anomalous concern white South Africans displayed toward Zimbabwe:

> A million people die in Rwanda and do the white South Africans care? Not a bit [...] You say to them, Look at what is happening in the Congo. No, no, no, let's talk about Zimbabwe. Why? It's because 12 white people died![17]

Sentiments such as those were often interpreted as somewhat irrational, as proof that South Africa's policy toward Zimbabwe was based on an intensely racialised and temperamental reading of the crisis. But racial or ideological solidarity did not explain the coddling approach. Pretoria was less preoccupied with Mugabe's rule than with the alternative. The ANC harbours deep distrust for the opposition Movement for Democratic Change (MDC), which it regards as an 'intruder' into the narrative of liberation. Its support base lies mainly among the urban working classes—in a country where the peasantry had been largely responsible for liberation. Worse, in the ANC's view, the MDC had been co-opted by conservative elements (including white agri-business) that sought to roll back change. Feeding this was a conceit which few national liberation movements have managed to shake off: the conviction that change has to emerge from *within* the movement. As far as the ANC was concerned Zimbabwe's destiny belonged with Zanu-PF. This is why it looked the other way as Zanu-PF cheated and thrashed its way to electoral victories and why the eventual co-optation of the MDC as a junior, hamstrung partner in government was seen as acceptable.

Throughout, Pretoria was angling for a way to replace the dominant Mugabe faction in Zanu-PF with a less obdurate and more accommodating grouping. Given Mugabe's advanced age, this seemed a mere matter of time. No doubt Zanu-PF's intelligence machinery ensured that Pretoria was spooned enough encouraging 'intel' to convince it that the 'transition' was forever imminent. Thus, Zanu-PF outsmarted its South African counterparts at almost every turn.[18] Pretoria's ham-fisted strategy facilitated enormous suffering among Zimbabweans, hundreds of thousands of whom fled to South Africa. The consequences inside South Africa were also unhappy. Xenophobia in South Africa predates Zimbabwe's implosion, but it appears to have hardened as desperate Zimbabweans tried to fashion a living in precarious neighbourhoods in South Africa.

Uses of an ogre

It was against this background that factions in the ANC's two most important allies—the SACP and COSATU—had begun plotting Mbeki's downfall. Freighted with a grand sense of destiny, but pummelled to the sidelines of the transition, these formations bore stinging grudges against the Mbeki camp. His treatment of them had been ungracious and he had helped ensure that their influence on economic policy was perfunctory, at best. From their perspective, the South African 'revolution' was being steered up the proverbial creek and required rescue. In Jacob Zuma they thought they had found the means to oust Mbeki and revive the 'revolution'. The SACP saw Mbeki as the helmsman of the country's abbreviated transformation, with party analysts picturing him as the mastermind and political manager of a '1996 class project' that had 'hijacked' the South African 'revolution'. Such grudges merely disguised the extent of the left's setbacks.

In truth, the Alliance left had suffered a succession of defeats on several fronts,[19] very few of which could be attributed strictly to Mbeki's hand. But the habit of personalising complex political economic dynamics was well established on the Alliance left and Mbeki had become its villain of choice. COSATU and the SACP, a rapidly growing faction inside the ANC and much of the public at large had found the ideal scapegoat: a distant, self-involved leader seemingly incapable of admitting to error and intoxicated with his sense of destiny. His banishment would spare the ANC the self-reckoning it owed itself and the country.

As the Zuma campaign dodged obstacles and gained momentum, sympathy for Mbeki drained away. Writers, pundits and self-promoters catalogued his flaws and sought to explain his fall from grace. Some crafted tantalising analyses, none more so than Mark Gevisser's 2007 biographical exegesis, *Thabo Mbeki: The Dream Deferred*. For him, Mbeki's great strength (and eventual undoing) was his need to commute between different realms, his 'in-between-ness'. Proud and deeply knowledgeable about his heritage, he was also cosmopolitan in his interests and affinities: 'I come of those who taught me that we could both be at home and be foreign,' as he declared in his celebrated 'I am an African' speech (Mbeki, 1996). This capacity to navigate within and between different worlds afforded him a perspective very few of his peers could match. When harnessed to a sprightly intelligence, it yielded a politician capable of calculations that dazzled as often as they bemused.

Less burdened than many of his peers by the deadweight of doctrine, he was among the first in the ANC to recognise the limits and perils of the insurrectionary path pursued in the 1980s. More importantly, he was politically dexterous enough to bring most of his colleagues around to that realisation. In the 1980s, he was already outgrowing the brittle nostrums of the SACP. A master of the artful manoeuvre, he was one of the architects of the political settlement and helped plot the moderate course the ANC would adopt after 1994 (Gevisser, 2007; O'Malley, 2007; Sparks, 1994).

That same cast of mind and set of skills would enable him later to 'modernise' the ANC into a variant of the 'Third Way' experiments attempted in Britain and Germany (see Chapter thirteen) and facilitate the restructuring of corporate capitalism in South Africa.[20] It also nursed in him a detachment that encouraged chariness and not infrequently degenerated into contempt. Dug in among confidantes and lackeys, many of them overawed and outwitted, there was always the risk that Mbeki would retreat into vengeful sulks and disdainful flailing when reality failed to bend to this will. It is tempting to regard him as a compound of (Britain's) Tony Blair, (Brazil's) Cardoso and (Malaysia's) Mahatir. But by mid-2008, his final disgrace only a few weeks away, Mbeki's closest resemblance was with Richard Nixon on the eve of his retirement in San Clemente (Lelyveld, 2009): defiant, bitter and all but abandoned. Transformed into an ogre he cut a sorry figure.

A full-throated campaign of demonisation had done for him. His capacity for contrition was too poorly developed and his errors too numerous to save him from ignominy. Soon, like the scapegoats of the Stalinist era, Mbeki would find himself remembered largely as a spectral rogue. Credit for the accomplishments of the previous decade was redirected elsewhere, while blame of practically every sort was routed to his door.

It is easy (and convenient) to forget the messianic aura that had surrounded him in the latter half of the 1990s, the pride he evoked inside and on the fringes of the ANC and the nervous respect white corporate elites felt toward him. This was always shadowed by discomfort. Some carped about his 'style of leadership', his tendency to hector critics, his unforgiving tenor of management and his stern maintenance of political discipline. But mostly this was tolerated, if not outright endorsed, as long as the 'job got done'. The 'job' was to oversee South Africa's economic adjustment and manage a realistic project of social progress. GEAR was seen to be fundamentally important in that venture and corporate South Africa openly admired Mbeki's role in engineering its passage into policy and defending it against all-comers.

Whereas the Mandela presidency had excelled at soothing nerves and appeasing foes, Mbeki introduced a political executive that was equally capable of cowing and seducing. It bled the 'new' National Party and Inkatha Freedom Party dry by co-opting individuals as ANC MPs or enticing them into other liaisons and it trapped the opposition Democratic Alliance in its discourse of minority rancour. Corporate South Africa would earn occasional rebukes, but none as withering as those aimed at ostensible allies who tried to challenge his gambits (Gevisser, 2007; Gumede, 2005). Even before being elevated to the presidency, some ANC officials (always privately and anonymously) had warned that 'if you're in his way, he'll put you down'. His style, one top ANC member confided in 1997, was

> to sidestep debate and collective decision-making. His standard line is that the matter at hand is very complex and needs more thought — then, when the meeting's over, he swings into action, him and the little bureaucratic clique he's surrounded him himself with. They're not up-front, they won't debate you on an issue, but they'll move behind the scenes (Marais, 1997).

If anything, this manner intensified in the 2000s, when it was increasingly directed at left-wing critics. Corporate elites smirked as COSATU and the SACP were shunted from influence and as the independent left, particularly the new social movements clawing their way to prominence in the early 2000s, were rubbished as 'counter-revolutionaries' and wreckers. Even circumspect intellectuals were called on the carpet. The SACP's Jeremy Cronin opted to issue a humiliating apology for a sensible and insightful interview he gave to the Irish academic Helena Sheehan in 2002, in which he had warned of the possible 'Zanufication' of the ANC.[21] When ANC stalwart Pallo Jordan in May 2000 proposed a motion in Parliament condemning Zanu-PF's transgressions in Zimbabwe, he was also forced to recant. Reflecting on that incident, Andrew Feinstein, an ANC MP at the time, remarked that 'this was totally out of character for the ANC, but was the beginning of an insidious change' (2007:121).

That verdict requires a mawkish outlook on history. The episodes were unseemly, yet hardly out of step with ANC tradition, which holds that criticism occurs inside the organisation and preferably behind closed doors (Calland, 2006). This is often forgotten. The same organisation had detained Jordan for six weeks in a military training camp in Angola in mid-1983; he had criticised the ANC's security apparatus in a private conversation.[22] A more rounded picture of the organisation seeps through in the memoir of Pregs Govender, a former trade unionist who was elected to Parliament as an ANC member in 1994. She recalls the shocked reaction of a close comrade after one of her first encounters with ANC discipline, in 1988 in Durban: 'God, they operate like the bloody Mafia. If I had not seen them in action, I would not have believed the things they get up to (Govender, 2007:103).'

Mbeki no doubt exemplified such intolerance, but he was the sharp end of a long tradition. This was no despot suddenly lording a fiefdom; he was operating within an organisational culture that sanctioned tight discipline, tolerated euphemised criticism and, most of all, valued and rewarded loyalty. What became distinctive in the 'Mbeki era' was the clumsy and arbitrary manner in which discipline was imposed, with his ornery conduct sometimes verging on parody. In April 2001, for example, Mbeki dispatched the Minister for Safety and Security to announce, at a special media conference, that a 'plot' had been uncovered to oust and possibly harm the President. Three top ANC figures were fingered: Cyril Ramaphosa (former leader of the National Union of Mineworkers, who had led the ANC's negotiating team in the early 1990s and was then transformed into a business mogul), Tokyo Sexwale (former premier of Gauteng province, then a spectacularly wealthy businessman) and Matthews Phosa (former premier of Mpumalanga province, also a businessman). The allegations were outlandish (Gevisser, 2007; Gumede, 2005),[23] but they were in keeping with the air of persecution that hung about the Mbeki presidency—a paranoia that fed an abrasive and intolerant manner that would typify his decade in power.

Loyalty, particularly of the deferent sort, was prized, but dissent (especially among allies and fellow travellers) frequently attracted the boorish attentions of his enforcers. Nonetheless, it is important to retain perspective. As menacing as Mbeki's inner circle may have seemed to ANC careerists and hangers-on, they operated within a democratic system, with a diverse and often harrying press, a rich array of non-governmental bodies and statutory watchdogs and an independent judiciary. Naturally, the system was not inoculated against intrigue and interference. But generally, even those ANC members and officials with misgivings ultimately *chose* the route of obsequiousness. Instead, what was being served up was a cartoonish melodrama in which a haughty despot supposedly ran roughshod over all.

Made to order: the Zuma challenge

Zuma's candidacy was moulded as the antithesis of Mbeki's reputation. Reputedly drawn toward compromise rather than browbeating, Zuma's leadership style was said to contrast attractively with the domineering manner of his rival. His conciliatory talents had helped bring peace to his home province, KwaZulu-Natal, long wracked by internecine violence. Lacking formal schooling beyond Grade five, he projected a common touch and would easily be advertised as a 'man of the people', yet he commanded substantial political smarts (Gordin, 2008). Those attributes had earned him formidable support in KwaZulu-Natal, where his 'mix of personal magnetism and attachment to African, traditionalist values' (Southall, 2008) was widely appreciated.

His 'struggle' credentials were also imposing. An activist since his teens, he reportedly joined the SACP in 1963 and was imprisoned on Robben Island with Nelson Mandela. Released after a decade, he helped to set up underground ANC structures in KwaZulu-Natal before going into exile in 1975, where he served in the ANC's security department, the dreaded *Mbokodo* ('the boulder that crushes'). That stint coincided with one of the ANC's darkest periods, its quelling of rebellions by restive MK guerrillas in its Angolan camps, most infamously the 1983 Quadro mutiny (which led to the execution of several guerrillas).[24] Whatever Zuma's role was in those events, his tenure as head of the ANC's intelligence department would arm him with connections and information that almost certainly lubricated his career path.

But the most crucial factor in Zuma's rise was the decision by COSATU and the SACP to back his candidacy through thick and thin. The move stemmed from a succession of defeats centrist and conservative sections of the ANC had inflicted on the Alliance left since the mid-1990s and was rooted in the belief that any prospects for radical change ultimately rested with the ANC (see Chapters thirteen and fourteen).

The odd couple: the Alliance left and Zuma

COSATU and the SACP reckoned that Zuma would enable them to pry the ANC from Mbeki's grip and strengthen their waning influence on the transition. The stakes seemed too high and the pay-off too tantalisingly close for the two organisations to take the long view and build a broad popular front (and risk further peeving the ANC). The tactics fitted well with the SACP's history of 'entryism', but they were a departure for COSATU. A mass organisation demonstrably capable of mobilising millions around campaigns (and of getting the vote out for an ANC that had grown moribund at branch level), COSATU was not as accustomed to taking shortcuts. It is possible, though, that the federation's decade-long exposure to corporatist deal-making had whet its appetite for such an approach.

Even when elbowed to the sidelines of policymaking in the 2000s, COSATU in particular had fought the 'good fight' on several fronts. The federation had contested government's indulgent stance towards Zanu-PF in Zimbabwe, its disastrous handling of the AIDS epidemic, its macroeconomic policies and its flirtation with privatisation. The outcomes were mixed. Privatisation was temporarily stalled (through huge effort, including several large strikes) and government was forced to provide antiretroviral treatment through the public health system (with COSATU ranged alongside the Treatment Action Campaign and international outrage). On the other hand, policies on Zimbabwe and the economy stood defiantly unchanged. It was this mixed yield that probably persuaded COSATU leaders to change tactics. If they could win some ground, even in the suffocating embrace of a hostile and dismissive ANC leadership, COSATU strategists calculated, what might they achieve with a friendlier administration and a firmer presence in policymaking? The irony is that COSATU's spotty returns became an argument for snuggling deeper into the ANC's bosom.

Selling Zuma to the left

Zuma's credentials as a leftist were imperceptible. A makeover was required to transform him into a standard-bearer for the interests of the working classes. COSATU and the SACP invested enormous energy and resources in the enterprise of selling Zuma and sparing him a possible conviction and jail sentence. (Re)branded as a man of the people and champion of the poor, Zuma would become their lever with which to unseat Mbeki and regain a more decisive say in government. It was not an easy sell.

In 2004, even after Zuma had been invited to address COSATU's national conference, he was hardly a popular figure among the federation's rank-and-file. Less than 1% of respondents in one internal survey felt he would best represent workers' interests; even Tony Leon, then leader of the free-market Democratic Alliance party, seemed preferred to Zuma (Buhlungu, 2006).[25] As late as 2006, communists were still deeply divided on Zuma. The dissent was neutralised with purges and harassment; much of it fed with media leaks. The intolerance became tragicomic: in Gauteng province, for example, top provincial SACP officials were suspended for attending (and, in one instance, merely being invited to) a workshop exploring the possibility of creating a broad left front. Other dissenters (including former SACP Treasurer, Phillip Dexter and former COSATU President, Willie Madisha) were ousted vengefully.[26]

The 'making of JZ' was an educating spectacle. Such was the dismay about Mbeki that few allegations or smears seemed entirely implausible or unlikely. The effort and tactics steadily paid off. Before long, COSATU's General-Secretary could boast that only 'a tsunami' would halt Zuma's rise to power.[27] When Zuma arrived at COSATU's national congress in mid-2006, he caused pandemonium as delegates leapt onto chairs and tables to regale him with his trademark song, *'Awuleth' Umshini Wami'*:

> *Delegates mobbed the podium, displaying the congress labels showing to which of COSATU's 21 unions they belonged [...] Others spoke into their cellphones amid the singing, spreading the news of Zuma's arrival to friends. Men hugged one another as they danced ...*[28]

Meanwhile, the ANC Youth League threw its weight behind Zuma, as did the ANC Women's League. Thousands of others in the party bided their time, waiting to see which way the scales would tilt. And tilt they did, to and fro.

Shatterproof

While Zuma was struggling to shake the corruption allegations, more ignominy arrived in late 2005 when he was charged with raping a prominent HIV-positive activist, the daughter of a long-time family friend, at his Johannesburg home. The 2006 rape trial was a sordid affair. Both Zuma's defence and the judge's handling of the case creaked with chauvinism. The 64-year-old polygamist's testimony included the startling admission that he had not used a condom despite knowing that his accuser was HIV-infected. Instead, he told the court, he had showered afterward to prevent HIV infection. At the time, he headed both the National AIDS Council and the Moral Regeneration Campaign.[29]

His defence invoked Zulu 'tradition' (or fictive versions of it) along with claims that he could not be a rapist because he found sex easy to acquire.[30] Outside the court bussed Zuma supporters (many sporting '100% Zulu boy' T-shirts) harangued the young rape accuser with taunts and threats. Many of them (and not a few onlookers further afield) believed the trial was part of a conspiracy to prevent Zuma from challenging Mbeki for the ANC presidency at the 2007 national conference. Photographs of his accuser were set alight as crowds chanted 'burn the bitch'. Not once did Zuma chasten his supporters or distance himself from their conduct.[31] After admitting evidence on the accuser's (but not the defendant's) sexual history, the judge acquitted Zuma. His accuser was forced to flee the country. Neither the SACP nor COSATU flinched.

Meanwhile, the NPA remained dogged in its attempts to bring Zuma to court on corruption charges, an enthusiasm that suited Mbeki well—but which Zuma eventually would outlast. Zuma's campaign was as tenacious as it was canny. The corruption charges became an assembly point for a coalition of the aggrieved. The courts provided a public stage for this drama as his lawyers fought complex tactical battles that dragged the case out while strengthening the notion that he was the victim of a vendetta. The hitch, as Roger Southall (2008) has pointed out, was that the statutory independence of the NPA meant that there was no guarantee it would restrict its hunt for arms-deal wrongdoings to a few token culprits. So when the

NPA gave notice of its independence by issuing a warrant for the arrest of police chief Jackie Selebi (although on charges unrelated to the arms-deal), Mbeki seemed panicked and suspended the NPA's boss, Vusi Pikoli, in October 2007.[32] The Zuma camp construed the move as yet more evidence of Mbeki's manipulation of the NPA.

This theme of victimisation would define Zuma's campaign, which followed the conventions of a soap opera. Backroom scheming was vital, but much of the contest was also waged in the open—and his legal woes provided an ideal stage. He was cast as the humble servant of the masses; Mbeki was the vindictive tormentor skewering his former 'comrade' with trumped-up charges and witch hunts. Allegations, spiced with plausible reasoning and circumstantial evidence, were recycled ad nauseum. Illiberal tactics became a staple as Zuma's supporters maligned, bullied and censured his critics. Supporters railed against the NPA and the judiciary, which were denigrated as 'counter-revolutionary' and accused of trying to harm the state and topple the ANC leadership.[33]

The accusers were not lowly journeymen, but top figures, including the ANC's secretary-general, Gwede Mantashe, its chief whip, Nathi Mthethwa, along with SACP and COSATU leaders. COSATU General Secretary Zwelinzima Vavi, in June 2008, told a funeral gathering that 'because Jacob Zuma is one of us, and he is one of our leaders, for him we are prepared to lay [down] our lives and to shoot and kill'.[34] Corruption charges still hung over Zuma at the time. ANC Youth League chief, Julius Malema, fumed that the ANC had to 'intensify the struggle to eliminate the remnants of counter-revolution' which, according to him, included the industrious but politically marginal opposition Democratic Alliance and 'a loose coalition of those who want to use state power to block the ANC President's [Zuma] ascendancy to the highest office of the land'. The fraud and corruption charges brought against Zuma constituted an 'unprecedented attack on the ANC's leadership' and represented a 'counter-revolutionary agenda', he said.[35] Earlier, he had told a rally in Free State province that 'we are prepared to take up arms and kill for Zuma'.[36] Paranoia had blighted Mbeki's presidency; now it was being used to grease the advance of his successor.

Off the hook

The tactics and perseverance paid off in September 2008. Pronouncing on yet another appeal brought by Zuma's defence team, Judge Chris Nicholson ventured beyond the immediate facts of the case before him (a technical challenge brought by Zuma) and declared that there had been political interference in the case against the ANC president.[37] For months Zuma's champions had harangued the courts and slandered white judges[38]; now Nicholson was hailed a veritable hero.

Zuma's strategy had been one of attrition: wear down the prosecution and courts until a political solution could be conjured. Finally it was paying off. The ANC's National Executive Committee (heartily stocked with Zuma supporters after the 2007 Polokwane conference) was hastily convened and regaled with arguments for Mbeki's immediate removal as president, reportedly including a 90-minute speech in which Cyril Ramaphosa catalogued a three-decade charge sheet against Mbeki (Johnson, 2008b). The committee opted to swing the axe. Days later Mbeki was gone from office—the victim of a *putsch* unconvincingly disguised as the democratic process at work.

The rush to remove Mbeki from the presidency was both unseemly and unnecessary. The Constitution prevented him taking office for a third term and there had been neither any indication that he might seek to amend that provision nor any chance of success. Seven more months and he would have been clearing his desk anyway. But such was the spite and impatience that ANC leaders usurped a power that actually rests with Parliament. The Constitution invests in Parliament (not the ruling party) the authority to end the tenure of a sitting President (Southall, 2008).[39] Mbeki could have insisted that the issue be put to vote in Parliament. Sparing himself further public disgrace, he chose not to.

Kgalema Motlanthe, former general-secretary of the National Union of Mineworkers, was shoved into the caretaker president's seat—a temporary compromise aimed at preventing a split in the ANC. The ruse failed. Former ANC Chair Mosiuoa Lekota and former Gauteng Premier Mbhazima Shilowa, almost certainly acting on the advice of Mbeki, lead a breakaway that became the Congress of the People (COPE) party, splitting the ANC. In the wings, Zuma waited. Elected ANC president at the Polokwane conference, he would become South Africa's president when the ANC triumphed in the following national election in April 2009. Against all odds, he had buried Mbeki and sidestepped his corruption charges. On the chat circuit there were worries about a possible descent into 'populism' and concern that Zuma would not be able to hold the Alliance left at bay. But the overall mood was expectant, even hopeful.

Weeks before the 2009 national elections, the acting national director of the NPA withdrew the corruption charges. The explanations were very weak and came couched in wispy and elliptical reasoning.[40] But the decision stood: Zuma was off the hook. His defence team had used every conceivable legal tactic to sink the case; in the end, the state itself, in the shape of the NPA, was made to ride to the rescue.[41] Adversity had been turned to decisive advantage. A criminal prosecution that could have landed Zuma in prison had become a key factor in his rise to the presidency.[42] And the same state that had been accused of conducting a witch hunt against him, had spared him a possible stint in prison.

Observers, including thoughtful ones, were deeply troubled by the events. Achille Mbembe (2009), for example, declared that 'South Africa effectively said goodbye to the idealism that had marked its first decade of democratic existence'. But many others sought—and found—positives in the drama, including Roger Southall (2008), who saw 'a strong case for arguing [that] South African politics are now more open and potentially democratic, than they have been at any time since 1994'. That may be so, but the credit did not belong with the Mbeki-Zuma feud, as we discuss later in this chapter.

Many observers saw in the breakaway COPE the promise of a party that might grow strong enough to joggle loose South Africa's monopolised electoral system.

If more is better, then COPE's creation has enhanced South Africa's democracy.[43] A mere seven months after its creation, COPE netted just over 7% of the vote in the 2009 national election, the third-highest tally (behind the Democratic Alliance's 17% and the ANC's 66%, but ahead of the Inkatha Freedom Party's 5%). But the veneer soon rubbed off. Along with the Mbeki loyalists and foot soldiers, COPE was also a haven for sundry malcontents and disgraced politicians, not to mention the fifth columnists the ANC dispatched to sign up with the new party. Ructions, squabbles and resignations (some of which was probably instigated from within the ANC) became routine.

Unlikely as it may seem, the split probably also *strengthened* the ANC's hand, at least in the short term. Instead of providing progressive voters with real electoral choice (the notion peddled by pundits), COPE provided the ANC with vital respite, allowing it to set about repairing and reinforcing its pre-eminence. By shedding figures and supporters so manifestly associated with the Mbeki era, the ANC was able to deepen and embellish a central fiction of the Zuma campaign and presidency—that most everything untoward and flawed since 1994 carried the stamp of Thabo Mbeki and his circle. It presented the ANC with an alibi for the defects and foibles for which the organisation should bear collective responsibility.

What was the Mbeki-Zuma duel really about?

Understandings of the Mbeki-Zuma battle and the Polokwane 'triumph' divided along three lines. One group saw it as a victory for the Alliance left and a prelude to resuming a more thoroughgoing 'national democratic revolution', led by an activist developmental state. Another regarded it as a much more profane affair, a perfect storm in a teacup that involved settling scores, grasping at power and influence and jostling for space at the trough of patronage. The third took the more mundane view and saw the debacle as a cleansing act, reclaiming the ANC from a supercilious clique that was running the party—and soon the country—into the ground. Each view was compatible with the others and none seemed entirely off the mark. But they missed core parts of the puzzle.

In key respects, the succession battle was an undignified jostle for positions, leverage and influence. Individuals who had been slighted, wounded or marginalised during the Mbeki years now found common purpose with 'comrades' nursing old grudges, those whose entrepreneurial or political ambitions had been thwarted, whose ineptitude or greed had upended their careers or those who had been shut out for their politics or principles. Hence the many uncomplimentary nicknames for the Zuma camp: 'coalition of the wounded', 'gallery of scoundrels', 'gang of the aggrieved' and worse. But the intensely personalised nature of the debacle was a clue that more was afoot.

Invincible?

Election results portray an unassailable ANC that virtually monopolises South Africa's political democracy. Even after shedding the rump of officials and supporters who went on to form the COPE party, the ANC in 2009 netted 66% of the popular vote. Five years earlier, its share of the vote had been 69.7%; in 1999 it was 66.4% and in 1994, 63.1%. How does a political party increase its electoral dominance in a society of rampant hardship, where the disjuncture between the circumstances of the majority and those of a tiny luxuriating minority is so extreme?

In one respect, the ANC's electoral supremacy is an index of its ability to reproduce its stature and appeal and to position itself credibly within a narrative of liberation and deliverance that spans generations (see Chapter thirteen). But delve into voting trends and the ANC's dominance at the polls seems to offer a less than emphatic picture of political sentiments.

Since 1994, the percentage of voting-age persons who actually cast votes has fallen precipitously—from 86% (1994) to 72% (1999) to 58% (2004). The percentage of eligible voters who abstained rose by more than 300% over that period. So a little more than half of South Africans entitled to vote actually went to the polls in 2004, for example. And the percentage of total eligible voters who cast votes for the ANC shrank from 54% in 1994 to 39% in 2004 (Schulz-Herzenberg, 2007). Those abstentions did not come only at the ANC's expense. In fact, the strong drift away from solid partisan support for a particular political party has hit opposition parties even harder. 'Levels of ANC partisanship among black South Africans have fluctuated between 62% and 42%, decreasing steadily since 1994', notes Schulz-Herzenberg (2007:121), but these 'have not been counterbalanced by shifts to opposition parties'. In 1999, for example, 1.6 million fewer South Africans voted for the ANC than five years earlier; but opposition parties together also attracted two million fewer votes than in 1994. This points to a more pervasive alienation from formal politics, especially among young first-time voters, whose turnout on election day in 1999 was considerably lower than that of any other age group (Levin, 2000).[44]

Schulz-Herzenberg (2007:121) also suggests that 'many voters support [the ANC], not because they are loyal partisans, but because they do not regard opposition parties as feasible alternatives'—a one-dimensional reading that neglects the complex bonds that exist between the ANC and its supporters. That relationship is not binary (on/off, for/against) but is shaded, shifts over time and is expressed in multiple forms (see Chapters thirteen and fourteen).

Another approach would be to recognise that election results are merely one gauge for public sentiment. Supplementing them are other forms of democratic expression, including the surge of community protests in the 2000s. Those protests are mistakenly interpreted as clear-cut acts of defiance and opposition to the ANC. But they have exposed vulnerabilities which the ANC, by the mid-2000s, could neither ignore nor dismiss.

Even if a small percentage of the protests were 'genuine' expressions of discontent—as they indisputably were—there was cause for alarm. Yet, as community protests mushroomed around the country, the ANC netted 66% of the vote in the 2006 local elections and wound up controlling 75% of the 238 local councils, including five of the six metropolitan councils. Six years earlier, it had won

59% of the vote and controlled 68% of the councils (Ndletyana, 2007). Independent candidates, including those associated with new social movements, fared woefully. In Johannesburg, for example, the Operation Khanyisa Movement, the political extension of several new social formations (see Chapter fourteen), contested 109 wards and won none; it received 883 out of 482 000 ballots cast. Even restiveness that sparks organised grassroots protests does not necessarily translate into condemnation of the ANC, as community activist Trevor Ngwane, mastermind behind the ill-fated Operation Khanyisa Movement, recognised when he noted that

> people vote for the ANC, despite their discontent with the party. This reflects the contradictions within the workers. They may be unhappy with the system, but are somewhat attached to it (Ndletyana, 2007:105).

This paradox is a reminder of the complex ways in which supporters relate to the organisation. For them, the ANC exists in several incarnations. One is that of an abstraction; a compilation of ideals, values, practices and traditions that have evolved over the course of a century. These are embodied in an organisational structure, the ANC and are entrusted to the custodianship of its leaders and officials.

The religious overtones are obvious, with secular structures and activities operating in service of virtually 'sacred' ideals. It is in this sense that the ANC is seen to transcend the individuals that constitute it. As a repository of ideals and distillation of history, the ANC therefore is, to an extent, inoculated against the misdemeanours of its officials. A protest in a rural town does not automatically imply condemnation of the 'metaphysical' entity—the idea of the ANC—or even of its leaders. Rather, it is an appeal for intervention, for accountability, for upholding values and ideals, and for bringing into line local individuals and structures that are seen to be desecrating the organisation and its history. When Zuma states that the ANC will rule until 'Jesus comes back' he is not only hyperbolising[45]; he is tapping into this mystique of an organisation that is invested with millenarian duties.

At the same time, the ANC of course also assumes the literal form of an organisation which, in government, commands resources, controls institutions and manages an expansive project of economic and social development. At local level, it therefore is also crystallised in the activities of local officials and structures. Protests then indict the ANC insofar as its leaders ignore or disparage the protests. These leaders are not always quick to grasp this. As late as 2005, Cabinet ministers were claiming that a 'third force' was engineering the community protests springing up around the country (Ndletyana, 2007). Often a central demand is for the president to meet with the community to hear their grievances first-hand. The assumption is that the ANC leadership, once alerted to the facts, will call the transgressors to book and act promptly and fairly. Paradoxically, a protest can also be a backhanded vote of confidence in the organisation—but only as long as the organisation takes up the grievances and acts to resolve them.

It was in this respect that the ANC became increasingly vulnerable in the 2000s. Its capacity to serve the public and address the causes of discontent, as well as its inclination to do so, were taking severe strain, accentuating the dissonance between the 'idea' of the ANC and its secular reality.

Salvage operation

Thousands of protests every year attest to the crummy performance of the state and the indifferent conduct of many local politicians and officials. When polled in 2007, only 35% of black respondents said that they trusted their local government, down from an already lowly 46% in 1998.[46] The ANC's ability to reproduce power and consent, let alone loyalty, in its core constituencies was in question (see Chapter thirteen). Internal polling and focus-group data confirmed the low-level disquiet.

The protests also underlined a serious organisational weakness: at branch level, the ANC was atrophying. Not only was the ANC-dominated local state dishevelled, underfinanced and unresponsive in many communities, but ANC branches were often unable to pre-empt, soothe or resolve the restiveness. Worse, local ANC activists and officials were sometimes implicated in the protests.

The deterioration of ANC branches (in numbers and work rates) had troubled the top brass since the late 1990s, though there was a view that preferred less activist and more technocratic, instrumentalised roles for these branches (Gumede, 2005). By the mid-2000s, the implosion of branch structures (and their capture by local elites) had become a serious liability. Mbeki launched the *Mvuselelo* programme to review the party's branch structures. There were three aims. One was to try to rebuild and strengthen the party's political legitimacy and authority at local level. Another was to improve the flow of intelligence and analysis from potential hotspots to central structures of the ANC. And the third was to repair the capacity to improve service delivery. It was too little, too late. The Zuma campaign would capitalise on the turmoil and insecurities.

Indeed, the ANC's self-criticism in the run-up to the 2007 Polokwane conference seemed withering. There were admissions about 'accumulated weaknesses' and about the corrosive effects of 'social distance, patronage, careerism, corruption and abuse of powers; ineffective management of the interface between the movement and the state' and more (ANC, 2007a:2). Underlying this was growing concern in the ANC that both the speed and quality of social progress was inadequate. Indeed, Hemson and O'Donovan's (2005) review of the targets set in the Reconstruction and Development Programme in the mid-1990s found that most remained unmet a decade later. But at work in the recrimination was a powerful subtext: this is what the 'Mbeki era' wrought, it claimed.

Yet the self-criticism was hardly novel; much of it repeated appraisals aired regularly since the late 1990s in organisational documents and in the speeches and writings of Mbeki and other top ANC figures. The malaise was well entrenched. Thus the ANC secretary-general's report presented to the 2002 national conference had lamented the emergence of 'unacceptable tendencies such as gate-keeping, factionalism, corruption and the use of branches as spheres of influence to enable individuals to access resources and dispense patronage' (ANC, 2002a). Mbeki had castigated the 'careerists who have inserted themselves into our movement' and who 'have brought unfamiliar and unacceptable practices into our organisation' (ANC, 2002b), while the 'Balance of forces' discussion document complained of 'a range of anti-people behaviours amongst [the ANC's] cadres, including corruption and using positions in the movement to access resources' (ANC, 2002c). Jacob Zuma appropriated these critiques and aimed them at the incumbent administration. Reclaiming and reasserting core ANC values became a central theme in the salvage operation.

As much as the overt backlash against Mbeki's reign and the jostling for space at the state trough, these developments explained the engineering of Zuma's rise and Mbeki's fall. An underlying frailty in the ANC's dominance was becoming evident and it called for recuperation. A vital aspect of consolidation would be to shift the public's image of the state as distant, self-serving and inefficient. Perhaps most galling has been the sense of rampant unfairness—that the fruits of liberation are not being distributed fairly. Not only does daily life reiterate the scandal of inequality, but rightful access to elementary sources of wellbeing (an income, a house, a social grant, a set of personal documents) too often seem to require connections, pay-offs or favours. Meanwhile, the state's ability to guard citizens' physical security or at least ensure that justice is administered fairly and consistently is also widely distrusted.

So Zuma's triumph—first at Polokwane and then at the polls in April 2009—is best understood in the context of a broader restorative project aimed at repairing the ANC's authority and pre-empting further harm to its pre-eminence. Achieving this, as COSATU and the SACP perhaps understood most clearly, meant saving the ANC from itself. In their view, the organisation remained the most powerful and attractive vehicle for achieving progressive objectives in the short to medium term. But it had also become riddled with patronage and corruption, which extended much deeper than a few aberrant 'chancers'. Great damage was being done to the ANC's image and moral stature and to the government's capacity to deliver on its promises. The upsurge of protests in the 2000s signalled that chronic social instability lay much closer than anticipated.

From the Alliance left's perspective, too, a salvage operation was required. But that same imperative—of regrouping and stabilising the ANC—also fenced in the radical potential many leftists detected in the Polokwane victory. Those boundaries of permissible change are not immovable, but they are formidable—as COSATU and the SACP have discovered (see Chapters thirteen and fourteen). Unfortunately, the manner of their support for Zuma also compounded problems. Bent on ousting Mbeki and helping Zuma to sidestep a possible prison sentence, they gave licence to intolerance, intimidation and retaliation—transgressions they claimed to rail against. The feuds and vengefulness they helped stoked will plague the ANC and the state for many years.

From early on, the Zuma administration assiduously tried to reposition the state as a servant of the public. Ministers detailed the failings and flaws of their institutions with a candour that is rare in politics and vowed to improve matters drastically. Understandably, the health and education sectors were targeted especially for remedial action. Speedier betterment and deliverance was pledged on all fronts. The 'Mbeki detour', they announced, was over. All this came couched in a commitment to uphold the ANC's core values and honour its traditions: to get 'back to basics'.

The contrast with the Mbeki era was glaring and deliberately so. Mbeki had been alert to the novelty, the 'newness' of a conjuncture that seemed to promise liberation in South Africa and was reluctant to treat old formulas as reliable guides to the future. New realities, he reasoned, required fresh thinking and strategies. His reflex was to fuse varied, sometimes contradictory analyses and reference points into schema that seemed appropriate in the contemporary context. The outcomes were paraded with much pomp and pretence, but they were basically homespun hybrids—the handiwork of South Africa's first postmodern president.

Postmodern president

Mbeki's readings of the shifting balance of forces (geopolitically and inside South Africa) in the 1980s, his handling of the diplomatic adventures that followed, his engineering of the structural adjustment programme, his subduing of the organised left in the late 1990s and early 2000s—all this emerged from a conviction that many core verities of the 'old' left stood in the way of progress or, worse, were recipes for disaster. Elsewhere, many other leaders of social-democratic parties had challenged key programmatic principles of their parties and sought to drag them into a brave neoliberal world. They managed to either repudiate or adulterate many of the progressive traditions of their parties, in the process hastening their parties' declines as they tried to march in step with history.

The same evisceration of tradition was not possible in South Africa, a society still tremulous with the prospect and need for radical change. Moreover, the idea of transformation remained bound up with the language, rhetoric and analytical tools of the old left. The adaptation and renewal Mbeki and others sought had to be couched in these idioms (which partly explained their contradictory flavour): hence the constant pairing of frosty rhetoric with savvy propositions, of weary clichés with invention. An example was the segue from GEAR to the 'developmental state', a flourish that allowed government to market a putative shift as both change and consolidation (see Chapter eleven). Mark Gevisser's (2007) analysis of Mbeki emphasises this emotional and intellectual refusal to divorce himself entirely from the pull of the old and familiar. Thus he sought to express new ideas using the grammar and imagery of African nationalism and the coarsened socialism absorbed during exile.

Such an overview, however, does disservice to the hybrid politics Mbeki practised and the sometimes-shapely patchwork of visions he conjured. The vaunted African Renaissance,[47] which had its heyday in the late 1990s and early 2000s, exemplified such ambiguity. Erected as a launch pad into the future, the 'project' in many respects also stood flatfooted in the past. A blend of romantic pan-Africanism and the exigencies of the neoliberal era, it was adorned with vintage claims and aspirations. Central to the discourse was a compound of Africanist nostalgia, pride and hope, and post-colonial indignation, which could tap popular defiance with rhetoric drawn from the Bandung era. This discourse rhapsodised essentialisms.

But the discourse was also 'globalist', tilted toward an indeterminate horizon of opportunities and possibilities. South Africa's economic interests were linked 'to

Africa through the register provided by the meta-narrative of globalisation with its seemingly endless vistas, shrinking horizons and economistic logic' (Vale & Maseko, 1998:8). Mbeki could announce that Africa 'must be in the forefront of challenging the notion of "the market" as the modern god',[48] yet the African Renaissance template in fact envisaged a modulated, friendlier version of that same system. Wedged into it were injunctions that typically peppered World Bank admonishments. It even assigned 'white' domestic capital an integral role in the revival, not just of South Africa, but of an entire continent. Malleable without sacrificing its core appeal, the African Renaissance managed to nod in several directions at once, revealing not only its hegemonic function but also its class character.[49] This was not simply a matter of deceit, of 'talk left, walk right', as some analysts maintained. It was Kwame Nkrumah meets Tony Blair. And it would leave many heads spinning and many hopes unmet.

Mooring points

So Mbeki's fall also marked a rejection of an opaque, confusing new world and the serpentine (sometimes circular) paths he had tried to navigate through it. 'New conceptions,' as Antonio Gramsci once pointed out, 'have an extremely unstable position among the popular masses.'[50] In this sense, Polokwane and Zuma represented a mutiny against the spirit of the times, a yearning for a world with solid mooring points.

The paradox is that Mbeki's reign had brought society to this point and had created the basis for moving beyond it. Recuperation was needed and feasible, but it could not occur with Mbeki presiding. The legions of wounded and aggrieved in and around the ANC had grown too large and embittered and the prospects for reconciliation were too thin. Hubris and paranoia had taken a heavy toll. Different qualities and sensibilities were now required. A grand purifying gesture was needed. Indeed, once sacrificed, Mbeki would be of even greater use to the organisation and the cause he had served since his early youth—even if that realisation might never dawn on him. Because so much of the malaise and discontent implicated the ANC (as a political organisation and in government), piling all manner of blame on his vanquished and 'disgraced' figure became an exorcism of sorts, a basis for moving forward.

That special 'something'

Zuma's resurrection and eventual triumph was possibly the most sophisticated and sustained piece of political theatre South Africans had ever experienced. Rattled by community protests and discontent, the ANC managed to funnel those disruptive energies into an ostensible process of cleansing and renewal, of putting the 'revolution' back on track. It consolidated its status as the pre-eminent political force in South Africa, resoundingly winning the 2009 national election. It was an exemplary feat, though not necessarily an enduring one.

As orchestrated and theatrical as Zuma's challenge was, the many millions of citizens supporting him were not mere dupes. Zuma functioned as a lightning rod for disparate frustrations and ambitions. The campaigning, cajoling and chequebooks of political fixers and opportunists, committed activists, generous patrons and slighted politicians and the might of the ANC's alliance partners, had all helped engineer his ascent. But his campaign tapped an intense restiveness and disorientation inside and around the ANC, which South Africa's new social movements had failed to mobilise or channel (Hart, 2007) (see Chapter fourteen). An understanding of the ANC post-Mbeki has to proceed from an appreciation of the sensibilities and sentiments that provided Zuma with his groundswell of support.

As varied as supporters' motives were, they shared a longing for certitude, for a world in which the ground ceases to shift under their feet, for a return to basics: hence the rousing appeal of Zuma's retro dramaturgies and the resonance of his common-man posturing. Polokwane, they hoped, would reset the controls and steer the transition back to the future. Zuma's (literal) song-and-dance, the canny exploitation of the news media's thirst for sensation, the endless media leaks—all this shifted South African politics deeper into the realm of affectation and sentiment.[51] He convincingly affected the 'common touch' and hammered the part of the upright victim; part of the ANC elite for more than 30 years, he was nonetheless able to style himself as an anti-elitist. He was a 'simple man' capable of grand deeds.[52] Jacob Zuma became South Africa's Ronald Reagan.

The morality tale played on an elemental (and very male) sense of decency. It pitted the urbane, aloof chicanery of Mbeki against the down-to-earth earnestness of Zuma: the conniver against the compromiser; the frosty intellectual against the man-of-the-people; reckless innovation against tradition; the man who quotes dead poets against the man who sings and dances. A stirring pantomime was constructed from archetypes. Mbeki became the cunning pretender whose desire to make history eclipsed his obligation to serve the people; a prince who was perhaps *with* the people, but who palpably was not *of* them. Zuma would represent the inverse: a stalwart leader free of airs and who understands the honour of service; who chooses unity over division and who appreciates the need to stay rooted in revered traditions—a man who knows and accepts his place in history.

In politics, of course, going back to the roots is the time-honoured avowal of the challenger. In promising both renewal *and* recuperation, it plays to all sides of the room. Inevitably it harks on matters of tradition and principle—an obvious line of attack after a period of modernising and innovation. Zuma embodied continuity with a past before freedom fighters donned suits to talk their way into power—to a time when right was right, wrong was wrong and struggle separated the two. Laid upon his shoulders was the task of restoring a movement to its historic pre-eminence and destiny. The stereotypes he peddled had heft because (as stereotypes do) they emitted a ring of 'truth' and offered handholds that could make the world seem a little less dizzying.[53] These theatrics fed on notions of authenticity—of what the 'real' ANC stands for, what liberation is really about—and on the idea that Zuma was more *authentically* 'of the ANC' than Mbeki ever was.

'*Awuleth' Umshini Wami*', the song associated with Zuma's rise, was emblematic. Dating from the 'struggle era', Zuma sang the song for the first time in South Africa[54] in early 2005 during the corruption trial of his close friend, Schabir Shaik. With its exhortatory refrain, 'bring me my machine gun', it became a staple of Zuma's campaign performances and a favourite among his supporters. Liz Gunner (2008:38), in an intriguing essay, reminds us that Zuma unleashed the song at a time of

> widespread anxiety and dissatisfaction concerning the nature of governance in South Africa. When the public, in all its fragmented plurality, was sated with images of suited politicians and the distancing language of technocracy, when the dancing bodies and the performed language of the struggle were a distant echo ...

In evoking the militancy and conviction of struggle and a simpler time when the lines of battle seemed clear, this excavated struggle symbol represented a bulwark when all that was solid seemed to be dissolving into the air. The song linked Zuma with the history and ideals of liberation and heaved with the subtext that the 'revolution' had been sidetracked and required rescue. It bore other, more disturbing undertones. Phallic, violent and vengeful, the machine gun hardly exemplifies the humanism Zuma also likes to profess he possesses. Repeatedly sung outside the courtroom where he faced rape charges, the song's symbolism was as obvious as it was objectionable. Nevertheless, it 'became the means by which a group of the marginalised within the [ANC] seized back agency and the power to determine the flow of change in the new era' (Gunner, 2008:30).

The Zuma campaign excelled at communicating these kinds of subtexts, even under duress. Zuma's rape trial was to have been the death knell to his leadership bid, even his political career; strangely, it seemed to have the opposite effect. Zuma's defence claimed that the sex had been consensual because the accuser had given off 'certain signals'. In the background were whisperings that the accuser had contrived the allegations and, worse, had been put up to it. All this found receptive ears in a sexist society, as Zuma's supporters made plain outside the court building.

Less obvious was the resonance of Zuma's explanation for why he had had unprotected sex with his rape accuser, although he knew she was HIV-positive. For a Zulu man to leave a woman in a state of arousal, his defence claimed, was tantamount to violating her. He was obliged to 'satisfy' her. Journalists rounded up 'experts' to ridicule the cultural authenticity of the claim. But that mattered little because, as Mark Hunter (2010) and Jonny Steinberg noticed, it rang true for many ordinary young African men.[55] In a political economy where, for millions of young men, manhood cannot viably be asserted through earning a wage and fending for one's family (due to high unemployment) or through progeny that bears one's name (because so many young men lack the means to finance marriage), there has arisen 'a veritable cult around pleasuring women'.[56] Wittingly or not, Zuma's courtroom defence referenced that reality, as Steinberg pointed out:

> [Young black men] surely had not expected the matter of pleasuring women ever to find a place in politics. Now, their prospective president was talking of it in open court, in relation to his own life, as an expression of his own personal code. It was massively exciting, a moment of extraordinary recognition between young men and

an ageing leader ... Zuma is not just sexually competent: he is also a patriarch, a man with a meaningful vocation, and a father of children who bear his name. People love him because they trust that he will deliver at least a sliver of his own fate to them.[57]

It was not only young men who were touched by Zuma's allure. In his thoughtful essay, Hunter (2010) has reminded that many of Zuma's supporters outside the courthouse were women, raising perplexing questions around the intersection of gender rights (and the rights discourse generally) with race, culture and class in post-apartheid South Africa, a matter we turn to in the next chapter.

These were some, perhaps surprising, examples of the deeper resonance of Zuma's rise, a feat that tapped into everyday, 'mundane' concerns that in fact open onto larger contests about the values and priorities that (should) underpin South African society. The Zuma phenomenon became a stage for asserting a variety of authenticities—about the meaning of being a Zulu man, a Zulu, a man, an 'African', a 'South African'. This is the Pandora's box the Zuma campaign dared to nudge open. South Africa will find it difficult to replace the lid.

Endnotes

1   Modise was defence minister from 1994 to 1999.
2   This included three million British pounds paid to Modise's political adviser at the time. See 'Arms deal: Who got R 1 billion in pay-offs?', *Mail & Guardian*, 12 January 2007.
3   Via Logtek and Applied Logistics Engineering, in which Congol was a stakeholder (Feinstein, 2007).
4   The industrial counter-trade offer (a standard sop in arms deals) appeared to be stronger and the German ships were deemed more suitable to the rough seas off the South African coast.
5   At least some of the deals seemed incestuously entangled. A third Shaik brother, Mo, whom Mbeki had dispatched to Hamburg in 1997 as consul general, had midwived the German frigate deals.
6   Aspects of this alleged arrangement emerged in the Shaik trial, as Feinstein relates (2007:218): 'The chronology accepted by the court was that Shaik had met with Thomsons on 3 March 2000 to confirm a deal that involved an annual payment of R 500 000 to Jacob Zuma. In return, Zuma would assist their efforts in relation to the deal and, crucially, from my perspective, protect them from any investigation into the transaction.'
7   A useful summary also appears in Gevisser (2007:675–85), while Johnson (2008a) provides a more extensive (and even more troubling) overview.
8   Feinstein (2007) claims he and a colleague had been presented with evidence of a paper trail showing at least R 10 million in payments made directly to Modise, for example. Investigators in the parliamentary probe had uncovered the evidence, but complained to Feinstein that they were ordered to drop those leads.
9   See 'From Oilgate to Bosasa: 10 reports that shook SA', *Mail & Guardian*, 23 December 2009.
10   Sam Sole, 'Scorpions probe Jacob Zuma', *Mail & Guardian*, 29 November 2002.
11   Six months after Mbeki was removed from office, Shaik was released from prison on medical parole, having served a little more than two years of his 15-year sentence. The decision was widely ridiculed. See 'Opposition slams release of Schabir Shaik', *Mail & Guardian*, 15 March 2009.
12   Quoted in Feinstein (2007:219).
13   Comprising the ANC, COSATU and SACP.
14   Mbeki's approval rating rose from the low 30s in 2002 to a high of 66% in both 2004 and 2005, before declining in 2006, as the campaign against him mounted. That decline accelerated

towards the end of 2007 and reached a low of 32% in June 2008. See TNS Research Surveys, 'People's perceptions of the week's events and their fall out' (media release), 26 September 2008. Available at www.tnsresearchsurveys.co.za.

15 COSATU, to its credit, consistently offered support to the Zimbabwean opposition, spoke loudly against Zanu-PF's abuses and dispatched delegations to Harare to present memoranda to the government. But its principled stance failed to sway its allies in the ANC.

16 One may wonder why the same moral energy was not summoned in the case of the Democratic Republic of Congo (DRC). Indeed, the Mbeki administration did not sit on its hands in relation to the DRC (or Burundi, Sudan or Côte d'Ivoire). But Zimbabwe and the DRC occupy very different corners of the white South African psyche.

17 Interview with Allister Sparks (2003:327), quoted in Gevisser (2007:440).

18 Zanu-PF, for instance, was alert to the resonant force of the 'land issue' inside South Africa, where the restitution of land seized by white settlers has proceeded at sloth-like pace. In August 2000, for example, Mugabe and Mbeki announced on television that the land occupations by 'war veterans' would be halted. Within hours, Mugabe recanted, gambling that Mbeki would not force the issue by threatening sanctions against a neighbour that was 'redistributing land to the people'. His calculation was correct. It is also no accident that the border between South Africa and Zimbabwe remained more or less porous as conditions inside Zimbabwe worsened. A kind reading could interpret this as a humanitarian gesture, though it is likely that more cynical calculations were also at play. Significant proportions of those fleeing to South Africa were probably MDC supporters; refugees and migrants were not able to support the party at the polls.

19 In fact, the SACP was hardly out of the loop when the ANC and South Africa's ruling elites tested the negotiating waters in the mid-1980s. In 1985, all but five of the ANC's 29 NEC members belonged to the SACP, according to Gevisser's (2007) tally. As late as 2002, Thabo Mbeki's cabinet included six members of the SACP's central committee: Sydney Mufamadi, Jeff Radebe, Geraldine Fraser-Moleketi, Charles Nqakula, Ronnie Kasrils and Essop Pahad. The premiers of two of the most powerful provinces (Gauteng and Eastern Cape) were top SACP members and the party was well represented in several other provincial cabinets.

20 For discussion of those affinities, see Marais (2001a).

21 The reference was to the degeneration of the ruling Zanu-PF party in neighbouring Zimbabwe into an autocratic and corrupt entity.

22 See Marais (1992b).

23 Even more surprising was the press statement from Jacob Zuma a few days later, confirming that he had no designs on the presidency. No one, at least publicly, had suggested as much. Clearly, something was afoot.

24 The ANC conducted three internal inquiries into the mutinies and their handling by the security department, the most comprehensive of which was the Motsuenyane Commission report. Almost no reliable information about Zuma's role or lack thereof in those events has come to light. A recent biography (Gordin, 2008) quoted Zuma as saying that details of the 'operational events of those days' were the 'property of the ANC, not his'. See David Beresford, 'Glimmers of horror as Zuma's missing years come to light', *Sunday Times* [Johannesburg], 22 February 2009; and Marais (1992b).

25 Almost 20% opted for Nelson Mandela, 15% for COSATU General-Secretary Zwelinzima Vavi, 10% for SACP General-Secretary Blade Nzimande and 7% Thabo Mbeki.

26 Dexter eventually resigned from the SACP, while Madisha was expelled from the party and was sacked as COSATU president. Others, including leading figures in the Young Communist League and the Gauteng SACP structures (such as Mazibuko Jara, Vishwas Satgar and Zico Tamela) were sidelined or suspended, as was veteran trade unionist Pat Horn.

27 Quoted in Pillay (2008:17).

28 *The Citizen*, 21 September 2006; cited in Gunner (2008:32).

29 'In the absence of a cure for AIDS, preventing infection remains critical. We want to appeal to each and every person in our country that they must exercise their individual and collective

responsibility to take care of their own lives,' Zuma had told a Moral Regeneration Campaign rally in 2002.

30 'I don't struggle to have liaisons with women', he told the court in isiZulu (*angisona isishimane*).

31 Some of Zuma's supporters aired sentiments so reactionary that they verged on satire. Ostensibly referring to Zuma's rape accuser, ANC Youth League chief Julius Malema reportedly told Cape Town students in January 2009: 'When a woman didn't enjoy it, she leaves early in the morning [...] Those who had a nice time will wait until the sun comes out, request breakfast and taxi money. You can't ask for taxi money from somebody who raped you.' See Franny Rabkin, 'Malema lawyers to argue fairness of rape comments about Zuma accuser', *Business Day*, 5 June 2009.

32 Pikoli contested his suspension, but to no avail. The Zuma administration seemed no less keen on an NPA chief who was reluctant to brook outside interference; Pikoli's removal was confirmed.

33 Wyndham Hartley, '"No truth" in claims about elite unit', *Business Day*, 22 May 2008.

34 Vavi apologised for the statement after complaints were laid with the South African Human Rights Commission. See '"Kill for Zuma": I regret it, says Vavi', *Mail & Guardian*, 22 July 2008.

35 Quoted in 'Malema: Counter-revolutionaries must be "eliminated"', SA Press Association, 14 July 2008.

36 'We are prepared to kill for Zuma—ANCYL', SA Press Association, 17 June 2008. He later apologised for the remark.

37 The immediate matter before the judge was whether the NPA had failed in its obligation to allow Zuma to make legal representations against its decision to prosecute him. Judge Nicholson held that the NPA had failed in that obligation; but it was his additional remarks that sealed Mbeki's fate.

38 Judge Hilary Squires was labelled an 'apartheid judge' after he had declared (in 2005) that Zuma had been in a corrupt relationship with Schabir Shaik. He had not, however, pronounced on Zuma's innocence or guilt, nor had he ruled out the possibility that the NPA might prosecute Zuma again in the future.

39 Many South Africans believe mistakenly that the ruling party elects the country's president, when in fact it only elects its candidate for president. The country's president is elected by vote in Parliament. Likewise, Parliament has the authority to terminate a president's tenure by vote. The ANC's NEC removed Mbeki as ANC president and he then agreed to step down as South Africa's president—in effect, as Southall (2008) argues, reducing the presidency 'to an extension of the ruling party'.

40 The NPA cited tape recordings that suggested some political interference had occurred. But it provided no indication that the case against Zuma had been created where none existed, nor that evidence had been invented. The tapes only suggested that the timing of a second round of charges against Zuma (shortly before the Polokwane conference) might have been influenced by political pressure. But the NPA was unable to show that the timing entailed any *legal* prejudice against Zuma. The NPA simultaneously dropped charges against the arms dealer Thint, a decision that was even more spurious. See Paul Hoffman, 'Error in reasoning leaves Zuma decision open to attack', *Business Day*, 7 April 2009; Steven Friedman, 'Off the hook—but NPA puts quality before law in dock', *Business Day*, 7 April 2009.

41 The tactic, very likely, was to delay Zuma's court case long enough for a 'political solution' to be imposed.

42 There was another, profane calculation most commentators ignored: the surest way for Zuma to avoid seeing justice run its course and possibly culminate in his conviction, was by becoming president. Italy's Silvio Berlusconi had already blazed that trail.

43 In South Africa's case, this is a dubious notion. Leaving aside the ANC, the Democratic Alliance, COPE and the Inkatha Freedom Party, none of the 22 other parties contesting the 2009 election polled more than 1% of the vote.

44 Whereas upward of 90% of voters 30 years and older registered for the election, only 48% aged 18–20 years registered. Among those 20–30 years old, 77% registered (see Levin, 2000).

45 'Even God expects us to rule this country because we are the only organisation which was blessed by pastors when it was formed', Zuma reportedly told an ANC rally in Khayelitsha. 'It is even blessed in Heaven. That is why we will rule until Jesus comes back.' Similar remarks were made during the 2009 election campaign. See Siyabonga Mkhwanazi, 'ANC to rule until Jesus comes back', *Independent Online*, 5 May 2008. Available at http://www.iol.co.za/index.php?set_id=1&click_id=13&art_id=vn20080505052937761C818044

46 Public confidence in state and private institutions overall had risen smartly in the early 2000s, reaching 63% in 2004, before dropping to under 50% in 2007. Religious organisations consistently earn the most trust. The data are from national Human Sciences Research Council surveys. See Wyndham Hartley, 'Public trust in institutions at new low', *Business Day*, 8 April 2008.

47 The actual African Renaissance 'project' ran out of steam and appeal by the early 2000s, its idealism punctured by government's seeming indifference to developments in Zimbabwe and its AIDS stance. The 'dream', though, lives on. Staging the 2010 Soccer World Cup in South Africa was promoted as part of a continental revival, of 'putting Africa on the map'.

48 Quoted in Ferial Haffajee, 'Renaissance incorporated', *Mail & Guardian*, 2 October 1998.

49 Engen Petroleum Ltd even boasted of its intention 'to link the splendours of Africa through a continuous network of Africa-tourism routes from the Cape to Cairo—a route colonialists failed to achieve, but which is within our grasp' (Lodge, 1999a:98). Corporate South Africa was equally accepting of other concepts woven into the African Renaissance, not least *ubuntu*. An ethos of reciprocity and mutual aid, it centres on the idea that people realise themselves through others. Motivational speakers and consultants, corporate human resource planners and advertising agencies eagerly assimilated the concept into their attempts to help modernise and revitalise South African capitalism. The African Renaissance vision was eminently hospitable to such opportunism.

50 Gramsci quoted in Hall (1987:21).

51 Besides the Mbeki-Zuma stand-off, many examples can be cited. ANC Youth League leader Julius Malema has developed an especially strong knack at such performance politics and perhaps more than any other contemporary South African politician understands the power of pantomime in politics.

52 A 'simple man', fond of the 'grand life', critics charge. In early 2010, for instance, the state had a mammoth R 15.5 million (USD 1.9 million) annual budget for Zuma's family (three times more than the spousal support office budget in 2005/06). This offends some sensibilities, but not all. It is as easily portrayed as a man of means living up to his patriarchal responsibilities towards a family that includes three wives (he has been married five times in total) and at least 20 children. See 'Furore over budget for Zuma's budget', *Mail & Guardian*, 18 March 2010.

53 Terry Eagleton (2006:9), in his review of Ewen and Ewen's book *Typecasting: On the Arts and Science of Human Inequality* (2006), captures this allure well: 'Stereotypes are sometimes thought to be offensive because they are fixed and inflexible,' he writes, 'but the fixed is not necessarily to be regretted ... The belief that the malleable is always preferable to the immovable is a postmodern cliché.'

54 The song originated in the Angolan training camps of Umkhonto we Sizwe reportedly in a base known as Cetshwayo (named after the Zulu king). See Gunner (2008:42).

55 Johnny Steinberg, 'Of blocked paths, borrowed dreams and Zuma's appeal', *Business Day*, 20 May 2009.

56 This hit the headlines again in early 2010, when it emerged that the 67-year-old Zuma had fathered a child out of wedlock with the 34-year-old daughter of a local football kingpin. See Versashni Pillay, 'All the president's children', 4 February 2010, *Mail & Guardian*.

57 Steinberg went on to note: 'While Zuma was on trial, the young men I spent time with were interested primarily in one piece of news: that he had lasted 34 minutes in bed. They were deeply impressed.'

CHAPTER THIRTEEN

Power, consent and the ANC

Any government managing a democratic transition has to narrow the distance between its avowals and the realities of citizens' lives. The ANC government has made headway since 1994, but the progress slowed in the 2000s as the underlying conditions, compromises and choices shaping the transition reduced the momentum of change. The theatrical face-off between Mbeki and Zuma, the Polokwane 'rebellion', and the sense of consolidation and renewal (or 'continuity and change', as the ANC preferred) bought the organisation valuable time to replenish its authority, repair the legitimacy of the state and try to mend the makeshift hegemony built in the 1990s. It is a huge undertaking, in circumstances that are hardly auspicious.

More than a third of adults and more than half of young people are jobless. Income inequalities are wider than ever before; only social grants separate many millions of South Africans from destitution. The AIDS and TB epidemics are mangling communities, killing close to 300 000 people a year, typically in torturous ways. Although commendably effective in some respects, the state is decrepit and under-resourced in many others, especially at local level, where hundreds of communities have tired of promises and excuses, not to mention corruption and incompetence.

There are enormous opportunities for improvement and the ANC and the government have broadcast their determination to do the repairs. In 2010, after almost 20 years of the AIDS epidemic, government finally launched an AIDS campaign that did more than go through the motions. The disastrous outcomes-based education approach was abandoned. A national health insurance scheme was being (re)crafted. These and other life-changing and life-saving shifts are hugely important and can be augmented with many other feasible initiatives.

But the formative compass points of the transition have stayed unadjusted, despite the efforts of the ANC's allies on the left. The inequities and precariousness that decide the fate of millions continue to be reproduced underfoot. As long as that persists, the biggest challenge—for the ANC, the state and capital—is how to reproduce and maintain power and achieve social and political stability. The left, meanwhile, faces an inverse predicament: how to shape, support or, where necessary, counter those endeavours in ways that greatly enhance equality, social justice and emancipation. Before considering these dilemmas in more detail, it is helpful to recall briefly the road travelled.

Rewind: the road travelled

The South African economy was running aground in a morass of constraints in the 1980s. International boycotts and sanctions cramped access to investment capital and new technologies. As economic growth puttered along, the state's reform programmes put huge strain on the fiscus, with the wage bill for the state bureaucracy consuming about 60% of the national budget by 1988 (roughly a quarter of GDP) (O'Meara, 1996). The deficit was ballooning. There had been spasmodic attempts at neoliberal reforms, but those were shelved, as anti-apartheid resistance grew more militant and intense. When capital controls were introduced in the mid-1980s, corporate capital found itself doubly constrained: penned in a stagnant economy, but unable to expand abroad.

The state was incapable of introducing and managing the extensive restructuring that was required in the economic, political and social dimensions (see Chapters one and two). It blundered along, combining fierce repression with a series of cursory, half-baked 'reforms'. Many in the liberation movement still eyed an all-out victory,[1] but its top strategists understood the likelihood that the conflict might be resolved along other lines. By 1988–89, it was clear that a deadlock had been reached. The political management of the system had broken down, but the liberation movement was also unable to apply the death blow. Until this political impasse could be resolved, economic restructuring was not feasible. A new basis for social and political stability had to be constructed. In Andrew Nash's (1998) phrasing:

> [B]ig capital needed a government which expressed the aspirations of the majority, but only in the limited and modified form made possible by the repression of the mid-1980s revolt, the international context after the collapse of Stalinism, and the gradual transformation of the liberation movement itself as it became increasingly dependent on the support (or neutrality, or unwillingness to aid the apartheid state) of bourgeois institutions.

The trajectory of post-apartheid South Africa would answer broadly to those prerogatives. On the economic front, a neoliberal path was adopted. This entailed more than mere 'adjustment' to overcome a set of momentary constraints. The economy was restructured on the terms of conglomerate capital, enabling it to wriggle free of a thicket of constraints, restructure and globalise its operations and embark on a fresh round of accumulation. The trade-off, the ANC hoped, would be the resurgence of brisk economic growth and corporate support for a 'disciplined' programme of socioeconomic redress.

ANC leaders also recognised the potential compatibility of corporate ambitions with the creation of a black, hopefully 'patriotic', bourgeoisie. This, they believed, would yield a 'win-win', 'middle-road' scenario, in which positive changes would accumulate on a bedrock of political and social stability. It was vital, therefore, to visibly and quickly address contesting interests and demands—principally those of the African majority, which (particularly in the 1980s) had organised itself into a formidable array of popular organisations. Demonstrable reconstruction and development had to occur, the most egregious features of the old order had to be removed and the more radical demands for change had to be subdued or disciplined.

Ultimately, the new state could persevere along this path only to the extent that the overall balance of forces allowed. The details of the post-apartheid development path were not, therefore, preordained by some 'law of necessity'. Nor were they the sleight-of-hand shenanigans of a tiny elite. They were a provisional outcome made possible by, as Stuart Hall put it, 'the relations of forces favourable or unfavourable to this or that tendency' (1996:422). There was no simple, *direct* causality running from economic factors to political effects and policy choices; these also reflected the strengths and tactics of contesting forces.

Numerous interlocking dynamics have shaped those relations of forces, including the geopolitical shifts triggered by the end of the Cold War, the ideological and strategic impact of the collapse of Eastern-bloc socialism and the ideological ascendancy of neoliberalism (and the related restructuring of the global division of labour) (see Chapter four). Among them, too, were the moves made to establish an adequate platform of stability for a post-apartheid system, the organisational and strategic weaknesses of popular formations and the decompression of class differences among the African majority generally and within the ANC specifically. It is on this terrain that an 'unstable balance' was created, propped on an evolving alliance of classes and interests and expressed in the sequence of policies and practices that now constitute South Africa's development path. Crucially, this 'balance' is not unilaterally and coercively imposed: it requires the resolute cultivation of consent and the withering of dissent, feats that were becoming increasingly insecure as the 2000s progressed.

No specific alliance of forces has yet achieved hegemony, but neither is the situation one of mere flux, despite the received wisdom. Claims to the contrary would have to account for the remarkable consistency in economic policies (particularly the undeviating subservience to corporate capital). A tentative and unsteady hegemonic project operates, but it is highly improvised and in constant need of adaptation and repair. This wavering equilibrium manifestly favours domestic (and international) corporate capital. Indeed, the economic policies chosen thus far have shifted the balance of power further in their favour, particularly those sections that have managed to insert themselves deeper into the global system. Parts of the state (and, much more so, the ANC) are now also entangled in that circuitry. Simply turning back the clock is not an option.

The major winners have been a few dozen conglomerates, especially those active in the financial sector and/or tied to the minerals-energy complex. Significant benefits, however, do cascade beyond them and across other layers of society. The equilibrium therefore rests on interventions and trends that are also beneficial to a range of other social strata—chiefly the middle classes and the organised working classes. These benefits hinge on links with the state—and the jobs, contracts, tenders, subsidies and other support that emanate from it. But beyond this, the gains are not being distributed equally. Punishing costs are being imposed on the poor. Tempering these somewhat are state interventions to expand the social wage, the cash grant system and public-works programmes—protection schemes that became *political* imperatives in the 2000s.

This is not exactly the 'win-win' scenario for which the ANC thought it had signed up—but it does reflect the prevailing balance of forces; it is not merely the handiwork of back-room schemers and elite dealmakers. The failure to decisively achieve a development strategy that, in the first instance, addresses popular needs cannot be attributed simply to 'sell-outs' or 'betrayals'. It expresses the weakness of a popular alternative hegemonic project and attests to the comparative strength of an unstable hegemonic work-in-progress that nevertheless has managed to assemble a tentative and prickly '"unity of classes" on the basis of "specific economic, political and ideological practices" that enable the ruling class to lead and not just dominate' (Hall, 1996:423).[2]

Hegemonic struggles

In capitalist societies it is preferable for power to remain largely invisible and banal, blended into the 'everyday', spread across the fabric of social life and 'naturalised' as habits, conventions and common sense. The exercise of power then becomes indistinguishable from 'the way things are', galvanising it with widespread consent. Such consensual rule is not peculiar to capitalist societies, but in them the inclination is toward emphasising consensus over coercion (Eagleton, 1994). The basis of power becomes an arrangement of principles, values, avowals and activities that can acquire the status of 'common sense' and that can enable a dominant class 'to escape the confines of its own corporate interests and to enlarge its political action to the point where it can understand and advance the aspirations of the subordinate classes' (Pellicani, 1981:30). Thus it involves compromises, requires agility and entails constant work at seducing and winning over diverse social forces and disabling opposition. When successful, hegemony is achieved.

Achieving hegemony, in Terry Eagleton's (1994:198) summary, means establishing 'moral, political and intellectual leadership in social life by diffusing one's own "world-view" throughout the fabric of society as a whole, thus equating one's own interests with those of society at large'. This involves more than mere 'legitimation, false consciousness, or manipulation of the mass of the population' (Bottomore, 1983:202). As an ideological map it has to enable a class to co-ordinate its own class interests with those of subordinate groups in order to obtain their active consent. Hegemony, therefore, in Roger Simon's (1991:22) phrasing, 'is a relation, not of domination by means of force, but of consent by means of political and ideological leadership'. It involves the consent—spontaneous and cultivated—given by large parts of the population 'to the general direction imposed on social life by the dominant fundamental class' (Gramsci, 1971:12). So, a social group does not only exercise power and govern, it has to *lead* as well.

Ideology is the cement that binds together an eventual alliance of diverse classes and social strata. But it also has to neutralise or undercut the ability of an alter-hegemonic project to emerge, which is why the fatalistic notions that 'nothing one does makes a difference' or that 'there is no alternative' are such potent aspects of a dominant ideology. Crucially, the ingredients of this ideological compound are not created anew. They are assembled from the themes, values, traditions, practices and aspirations that arise from the specific history of a society and from strata within it. Those ingredients transcend class. The ideological platform on which consent is built has to be 'constructed at the intersection of [...] multiple subject positions which, though overdetermined by class struggle, cannot be said to be directly determined by it or reducible to its effects' (Mercer, 1980:126). Naturally, this cannot affect essentials and, in the last instance, the fundamental interests of the dominant class have to prevail. But no class can achieve hegemony if it restricts itself purely to the pursuit of its class interests. The project has to be equipped with an elasticity that allows subordinate classes to align themselves to it—and benefit from it. It therefore has to operate also in the *national-popular* dimension and take into account the popular values, demands and struggles of people (Simon, 1991). In South Africa the struggle for national liberation—and the symbols and concepts that surround it—forms one such central theme. Increasingly, the affective appeal of cultural traditions and authenticity is being tapped. It is on such a basis that a broad bloc of varied social forces can be assembled. In all this, Gramsci (1971: 181–2) insisted, the state plays a crucial role in the

> *process of formation and superseding of unstable equilibria [...] between the interests of the fundamental group and those of the subordinate groups—equilibria in which the interests of the dominant group prevail, but only up to a certain point, ie stopping short of narrowly corporate economic interests.*

As a practical example, one might consider the rise of Thatcherism in Britain. Margaret Thatcher could be said to have operated squarely in the Gramscian mode, as David Coates argued:

> *In the heyday of her dominance, Thatcherism re-established the link between values and policies in UK public life [...] Like all successful political forces in democratic societies, Thatcherism took many of the central values and aspirations held by us all (values of liberty and individual rights, aspirations for prosperity and progress), tied them to a series of operating principles (in her case, overwhelmingly the principle of the unfettered market), and then steadily, resolutely and with great self-confidence, applied that operating principle, in the pursuit of those values and aspirations, to policy area after policy area (1996:73).*

So hegemony is constantly being built and refurbished—and it is constantly contested, with each 'side' striving 'to strengthen its own pattern of alliances, to disorganise the alliances of the other, and to shift the balance of forces in its favour' (Simon, *op cit*).

Power, state and society

Gramsci separated out one set of institutions, the apparatuses of the state, on the basis of it having a monopoly on the legitimate exercise of force.[3] The remainder makes up civil society—and it is on that terrain of relations and institutions that hegemonic struggle is primarily waged. The field of politics, in other words, extends across the entirely of civil society, all the way into the kitchen and bedroom. Social relations in civil society are relations of power and this power is amassed and exercised along numerous lines (class, race, gender, ethnicity, age, place, religion, income, language, disability, etc). The social relations that constitute capitalist society therefore are embodied in a huge variety of entities and phenomena, including political parties, trade unions, the mass media, religious bodies, sport and cultural formations and spectacles, advertising and celebrity cults, to mention a few. Ultimately, as Simon (1991:76) reminds, 'the decisive struggle for state power ... can only be won on the basis of a decisive shift in the balance of forces in civil society'.

The distinction between state and civil society is not rigid; these zones are interlinked in complex ways. This allows for an understanding that locates civil society in rules, transactions and struggles that connect the state and society (Beckman, 1993), creating a 'complex "system" which has to be the object of a many-sided type of political strategy' (Hall, 1996:429). So the state does not represent the site of pure, concentrated power in society. Neither is it simply a set of administrative and coercive institutions through which a dominant class imposes and defends its prerogatives over subordinate classes. Instead of functioning as the central instrument for precarious domination via coercion and material force, the state is central to the *ideological* conquest of society. One of its most important functions, according to Gramsci, 'is to raise the great mass of the population to a particular cultural and moral level or type which corresponds to the needs of the productive forces for development, and hence to the interests of the ruling class' (1971:258). In Hall's interpretation, the state

> is the point from which hegemony over society as a whole is ultimately exercised (though not the only place where hegemony is constructed). It is the point of condensation—not because all forms of coercive domination necessarily radiate outwards from its apparatuses but because, in its contradictory structure, it condenses a variety of different relations and practices into a definite 'system of rules'. It is, for this reason, the site for conforming (that is, bringing into line) or 'adapting the civilization and the morality of the broadest masses to the necessities of the continuous development of the economic apparatus of production' (1996:428).

The dominion of a ruling class is therefore grounded in the ability of the state to nurture the active consent of broad sections of society, in concert with other social forces. It is not the sole marshalling agent of consent, but it is an essential one. Not a *thing* to be captured, smashed or overthrown, the state is revealed as a strategic field or zone where 'the bloc of social forces which dominates over it not only justifies and maintains its domination but wins by leadership and authority the active consent of those over whom it rules' (Hall, 1996:429). Power, in a Gramscian understanding, therefore, amounts to 'hegemony armoured by coercion'.[4] This means that the struggle for socialism, say, requires more than 'winning' state power; it has to be extended across the whole of society (Simon, 1991). Once hegemony is achieved, it is no longer a 'ruling class' that leads, but a 'historic bloc'.[5] This is an important distinction. It recognises that, although class remains a 'determining level of analysis', whole classes cannot unproblematically and directly be translated

> onto the political-ideological stage as unified historical actors. The 'leading elements' in a historic bloc may be only one fraction of the dominant economic class—for example, finance rather than industrial capital; national rather than international capital. Associated with it, within the 'bloc', will be strata of the

subaltern and dominated classes, who have been won over by specific concessions and compromises and who form part of the social constellation but in a subordinate role [...] Each hegemonic formation will thus have its own, specific social composition and configuration. This is a very different way of conceptualising what is often referred to, loosely and inaccurately, as the 'ruling class' (Hall, 1996:424).

The achievement of hegemony is a rare feat and of indeterminate duration: 'Hegemony is not a state of grace, which is installed forever [and] it's not a formation that incorporates everybody (Hall, 1987:21).'[6] Such periods represent the achievement of unity that is sufficient for a society 'to set itself a new historical agenda, under the leadership of a specific formation or constellation of social forces' (Hall, 1996:424). It is a mistake to liken that achievement to 'crossing the finishing line'; hegemony is a process, not a singular accomplishment. Its basis constantly has to be replenished, adapted and reproduced and the project itself fluctuates between strong and weak phases.

Work in progress

If we apply this frame of analysis to South Africa, what do we discover? We can detect in post-apartheid South Africa the outlines of a provisional and wavering hegemonic project. Centred politically on the ANC, it has managed to achieve the tentative co-ordination of the interests of a divergent range of classes and strata. But the ability to continue doing so weakened seriously in the 2000s, for reasons discussed earlier. Key among these is the continuing reproduction of inequality; difficulties in improving the wellbeing of impoverished South Africans at the pace and on the scale required; the weakening of the ANC as a mobilising and disciplining presence in communities; COSATU and the SACP's flirtation in the early 2000s with a possible break from the ANC; the absence of charismatic and trustworthy leadership (which, in the person of Thabo Mbeki, largely dissolved in the mid-2000s); the dented legitimacy of the state (particularly at local level); and the emergence of raucous dissent at community level. The ANC, in particular, found itself on unsteady, potentially precarious terrain. The political undercarriage of the transition was taking strain. The mid-1990s dazzle of mythmaking ('Rainbow Nation') and the overwrought idealism of the late-1990s ('African Renaissance') had dulled. Even the profit-gouging, debt-fuelled binges of the well-to-do in the 2000s had a panicky feel about them, a sense that good times could not—would not—last for long.

The true significance of the Zuma-Mbeki battle, the jousting at the ANC's 2007 Polokwane conference and the subsequent ousting of Mbeki as president lay in the attempts to address some of these weaknesses, repair the ANC as a political and ideological force capable of marshalling broad-based consent, restore the state's legitimacy and patch up an unravelling hegemonic project. That venture is equipped with imposing advantages, not all of which have been deployed yet. But it is hamstrung by weaknesses that render it unstable and in constant need of overhaul. Its central pillars are a rules-based system of governance and policies that are geared at efficiency, stability and growth, a manifest commitment to private ownership and a market-driven economic system and the ability to foster and sustain social unity. That requires modulating capital's 'modernising' drive in ways that enable the allocation of gains also to other social layers—not least to an emergent African bourgeoisie, the black middle classes, organised workers and much more difficult, the vast layers of society that are economically disenfranchised.

The ideological building blocks of hegemony in post-apartheid South Africa are, therefore, necessarily eclectic, even contradictory. These include the consensus that the social and political arrangements of apartheid were unacceptable; recognition that the Charterist movement (and specifically the ANC) channels and embodies the values of aspirations of liberation; endorsement of a relatively liberal system of political democracy; general agreement that economic growth is a priority and benefits everyone (eventually) and that this is best achieved in a market economy; veneration for the pursuit of prosperity (and wealth); unanimity on the need to reduce poverty (but with certain caveats); acceptance of the need for some welfare safety net (preferably only in the short term) but wide support for the notion that 'dependency' on the state must be avoided; and more. Crucially, they do not fit together seamlessly. At various points, tensions and contradictions emerge between these elements, which are constantly also adapted and adjusted. These notions are not only projected across society, they are also generated within it. In Stuart Hall's (1987:19) précis of Gramsci,

> we think that the world will collapse as the result of a logical contradiction: this is the illusion of the intellectual—that ideology must be coherent, every bit of it fitting together, like a philosophical investigation. When, in fact, the whole purpose of what Gramsci called organic (ie historically effective) ideology is that it articulates into a configuration different subjects, different identities, different projects, different aspirations. It does not reflect, it constructs a 'unity' out of difference.

The South African left has been virtually immobilised by such conundrums. It labours at highlighting the contradictions of the ANC policies and affirmations, as if the absence of perfect harmony condemns them to disintegration. The real issue is what kind of unity is sought, on what terms is it constructed and where its fault lines lie.

The fact that this hegemonic project encompasses professed ideals, pledges and deeds that (seem to) benefit a wide range of classes and interests does not obscure its overriding bias toward the key *desiderata* of capital—particularly financial capital and conglomerates anchored in the minerals-energy complex, which required (and got) substantial economic liberalisation and active state support for expansion abroad. Prominent among the prerogatives of the former was capital account liberalisation and a positive monetary policy. On that front, the ANC government has delivered with gusto. The latter requires that the state desist from directive interventions in their investment decisions, as well as provide a political-ideological and economic framework that enables them to globalise their activities in pursuit of higher returns than the national economy seems to offer.

But the project is also saddled with noteworthy weaknesses and contradictions. Not least is the fact that its fate hinges on the ability to maintain—and overcome—an unsteady balance between servicing the requirements of the classes that stand at its hub and addressing the needs of a range of subordinate, but restive layers of society. This has entailed significant, sometimes risky, choices and adjustments. The most dramatic was the imposition of the GEAR plan, which subordinated the realisation of socioeconomic rights to the achievement of economic growth. A mollycoddled market, it was hoped, would generate sufficient jobs and trickle down enough wealth to reduce the onus placed on the state, thus relieving it somewhat from the welfarist role of ponderous provider and allowing it to act as a more agile catalyst and promoter of innovation. The thinking was angled at achieving a distinctive but diluted social democracy in which the seeding of opportunities replaced the realisation of rights. This sought-after arrangement has not materialised.

In addition, there are other challenges that deserve some elaboration. The project is being managed primarily out of and across a state that is riddled with internal conflict and contradictions, even more so after the Mbeki-Zuma battles. This enormously complicates the process of engineering consent also *within* the state. Meanwhile, the ability to foster popular consent via state activities is spasmodic and is undermined by dysfunction in state institutions and the failure of many public servants to perform their duties in a reliable, predictable and adequate manner. Corruption adds to the difficulties.[7]

Some of the symbolic tools deployed in the project also have divisive effects. At one level, there are proficient efforts to manufacture consent across disparate sections of society—the hallmark of a potentially successful hegemonic venture. On this front, the accent on 'efficiency', good governance and 'realistic' policies combines with state-supervised efforts to distribute or facilitate gains across wide zones of society. Simultaneously, the *uneven nature of those gains* requires that the 'allegiance' of the African majority be shored up through other means. Loud condemnations of poverty are a vital part of such a repertoire—as long as palpable inroads are made against poverty. As shown in Chapter seven, such achievements were modest until 2000 and irresolute afterwards. Government's response was to expand both the social-grants system and public-works programme. Affirmative action policies have also served on this front, although their effect is both bonding and divisive, since they alienate sections of the non-black working and middle classes and are of little direct benefit to vast numbers of unskilled and poorly educated Africans. One response has been to step up support for small enterprises and boost rural development—to little demonstrable effect, however. In other words, each of these manoeuvres has also had the effect of highlighting underlying contradictions.

Finally, some of the reference points of this work-in-progress (the historic avowals of the Congress movement, the Freedom Charter, the RDP, etc) are also implicit indictments of it—since they can be used to highlight failures to meet popular demands. But that same double-edged dynamic also hampers an alter-hegemonic project. Potentially key formations in such a project are locked into a political alliance with the main custodian of those traditions and commitments, the ruling ANC. They share many of the symbolic tools and reference points with the ANC and are yet to fashion a distinctive discursive arsenal.

Not yet pushed into prominent service, meanwhile, is a range of other elements that could repair broad *ideological* unity across large parts of society. These include popular but conservative social values, 'law and order' drives, distrust of the liberal individualist features of the political system and a revamp of nationalist values along more chauvinist lines. We discuss these in some detail later.

How far has the hegemonic project progressed? An answer is aided by the schematic distinction Gramsci drew of three key phases of maturity: the 'economic corporate', the 'class corporate' and the 'hegemonic' stages, as outlined by Hall (1996:423). In the first phase, common though parochial interests become manifest and serve as a springboard for action. The main protagonists, however, are oblivious to the need and the possibilities for engineering wider class solidarities. South Africa clearly has surpassed that stage. The 'class corporate' phase sees the achievement of such solidarities—but only in the economic realm. The moment of hegemony is approached when such an alliance transcends

> the corporate limits of purely economic solidarity, [encompasses] the interests of other subordinate groups, and begins to 'propagate itself throughout society', bringing about intellectual and moral as well as economic and political unity, and 'posing also the questions around which the struggle rages ... thus creating the hegemony of a fundamental social group over a series of subordinate groups' (Hall, 1996:423).[8]

For short periods since 1994, South Africa has seemed to hover between the 'class corporate' and 'hegemonic' stages. At the time, the 1995–96 'Rainbow Nation' heyday resembled such a period. In retrospect, its material basis was too shallow, the ideological elements too overcooked and the state in too much disarray to merit that assessment. The imposition of a structural adjustment plan that serviced key prerogatives of corporate capital seemed to consolidate the 'class corporate' stage after 1996, especially once coupled with the modernising drive and idealistic visions associated with the early years of Mbeki's presidency. But the bid for hegemony was undermined by the feeble pace at which ordinary citizens' wellbeing improved, the shocking growth in inequality, government's handling of the AIDS and TB epidemics and its hostile reactions to criticism.

Reform from above

This analysis assumes that a hegemonic project commenced in the early 1990s, remains underway and is geared to service, in the first instance, the needs of corporate capital, along with an emergent layers of new 'junior capitalists' and the African middle classes.

An alternative reading, however, may describe the post-apartheid trajectory as a 'passive revolution': a determined effort by the ruling class to redirect 'historical processes to reproduce capitalism' (Satgar, 2008:42). This is achieved through a process of extensive 'reforms from above' that is carried out largely through the agency of the state and that requires the sidelining of popular organisations. Vishwas Satgar (2008) has provided an appealing depiction of the South African transition in such terms, with left formations neutered and the potential for working class-led hegemony blocked.

This 'passive revolution', he argues, 'redirected and coopted South Africa's national liberation project and struggle for socialism' and 'fostered a non-hegemonic historic bloc in support of this class project' (Satgar, 2008:66). Leading this 'historic bloc' is a 'transnational fraction of South Africa's ruling class', which has succeeded in advancing its own interests while 'blocking fundamental transformation' and unleashing 'a new form of elite politics' that has 'reduced democracy to narrow electoralism' (*ibid*). Popular organisations were co-opted, absorbed or demobilised, while the trade-union movement in particular was corralled into corporatist arrangements that blunted its potentially revolutionary edge. Overall, the prospect of a concerted popular challenge was reduced significantly.

The 'passive revolution' schema paints a tantalising but simplistic picture. It evokes a picture of a historical momentum towards socialism that was derailed with political negotiations and the eventual settlement 'hijacking' and then subduing a more radical process. Yet the notion that a decisive movement toward a socialist transition was underway in the late 1980s (let alone whether it had any prospect of realisation) is far-fetched. As Satgar (2008:44) himself observes, citing Gramsci, 'change happens within the "limits of the possible"'—and those limits were more constricting than the rhetoric of the day conveyed (see Chapter two).[9] The picture also distorts the composition and the state of the popular movement. It is a mistake to romanticise that movement as wholly radical and leftist. Like the ANC, it embraced a wide range of political views. Even the organisational weight of COSATU in that movement did not tilt it firmly to the left, given the different political and ideological positions within that trade-union federation.

When formal political 'talks' got underway, the main components of the Mass Democratic Movement stood bruised and woozy, battered by successive states of emergency and relentless security crackdowns. The momentum of the working-class movement had also been checked (not only by the overambitious 1987 miners' strike,[10] which took a heavy toll, but by job losses that were eating into union ranks generally). Many hundreds of smaller groupings remained active, but they were hardly at the top of their game. Much of the initiative for eye-catching, jarring acts of resistance had shifted in the late 1980s to groups of young activists and militants that evaded tactical co-ordination and discipline, some of which were combining criminal pastimes with ostensibly political agendas. South Africa circa 1988–89 was not ripe for revolution; it had lumbered into a stalemate. Soon, the left would find itself outsmarted, outmanoeuvred and, eventually, muscled out of the navigational centre of the transition. Fifteen years later, it still had not recovered sufficiently to mount a counter-offensive on the basis of popular mobilisation. Instead, its strongest formations (COSATU and the SACP) chose a timeworn Leninist route, as if selecting the inside track could help them outrun history (see Chapters twelve and fourteen).

There is no doubt that demobilisation and absorption of popular groupings occurred in the early to mid-1990s. This was not simply an engineered process, nor was it unusual. Typically, in democratic transitions, as the political system becomes democratised, extra-institutional mobilising and organising tend to decline. In addition, many of these organisations had benefited from the enormous amounts of funding that flowed to anti-apartheid organisations in the 1980s. Most funders saw them in instrumental terms as ways to hasten the end of apartheid and apply particular (political and normative) inflections to a post-apartheid order. In 1994, a great deal of that funding either dried up or was redirected towards other programming priorities. Hundreds of organisation had to close their doors. No doubt, the ANC encouraged funders to funnel their largesse through it, the 'government-in-waiting'—although this probably was more of a lunge for funds than an underhanded ploy. The ANC also 'encouraged' many organisations to merge with its structures. Sometimes, such a move made perfectly good sense to both parties, though a degree of 'persuasion' was required in other instances. In sum, the 'structural adjustment' of progressive civil society in the early 1990s was a more consensual and complicated affair than is conveyed in a tale of sheer manipulation and emasculation.[11]

Depicting the South African transition as an example of 'reform from above' also plays down the extent to which popular energies and organisations eventually helped to shape the terms of the political settlement and bring about key new arrangements.[12] Were they simply instrumentalised? Not exactly. The details of the political settlement were certainly not hammered out at town hall meetings. Popular passions—usually condensed into a perceived threat of bedlam—helped to focus the minds of negotiators, with the disciplining effect strongest on the National Party and the far right (Gevisser, 2007; O'Malley, 2007). But reality was also more textured. While it is true that the settlement and its main elements were achieved beneath the spectre of uprising and tumult (and possibly civil war), it also took shape against the backdrop of ongoing struggles, campaigning and politicking by popular organisations. Their influence varied from sector to sector, but was telling in some (the labour regime, community media and education, among others). Even after 1994, hundreds of organisations participated in consultations and deliberative forums as sector policies were designed. The extent to which they were able to decide or influence outcomes depended on a host of factors, but the picture of neglect and disregard oversimplifies reality. The labour movement, for example, found its political weight trimmed by onrushing globalisation, shifts in the utilisation of labour and its co-optation into corporatist structures—but it was by no means crippled. Safeguarding the accomplishments has not been easy; some became morphed or mangled as priorities shifted, turf wars were waged and the vagaries of implementation and management took their toll. But many of the achievements survived and *still* contain the potential for more radical breakthroughs.

Since 'passive revolution' involves 'a non-hegemonic form of class rule' (Satgar, 2008:40), the analysis also presumes an absence of consent and ideological leadership in post-apartheid South Africa. But this is manifestly not the case. One of the great feats of the transition has been the marshalling of sufficient consent to avoid social instability and political rupture. The consent is highly conditional and moody and its depth or intensity fluctuates. This is no surprise. In a society as unequal and fractured as South Africa, mustering consent requires ungainly and unstable balancing acts. The 'bulwarks' and 'trenches' of civil society in which consent is reproduced demand constant attention and mending.

The consent is replenished in various ways: for example, by situating the state, its policies and practices within the symbolic world of national liberation and African nationalism (and by auto-critiquing itself in the same terms); by retaining the discourse of 'national democratic revolution' and couching its endeavours in it; by denying dissenters and opponents a place in these conceptual and normative 'worlds'; by extending social provisioning; and so on. Satgar (2008:41) correctly refers to the concept of 'national democratic revolution' as a 'false abstraction' that does disciplinary duty rather than illuminates the post-apartheid political economy.[13] Yet seduction and discipline are precisely its main functions. It may be defective as a conceptual tool, but it is eminently useful for shoehorning an assortment of contradictions into a narrative of progress and deliverance and for affirming the pre-eminence of the ANC and its main allies. It is one of several ideological devices that are used to marshal consent for a hegemonic work-in-progress.

Finally, in Gramsci's exposition, a passive revolution is attempted when an incumbent hegemonic project falters badly and is faced with the real likelihood of being eclipsed by a counter-hegemonic project that is organised around another class. But the apartheid system had been imposed and elaborated with systematic, brutal coercion; it did not involve the achievement of hegemony. Beyond the white minority, consent was for all practical purposes absent; from the early 1970s onward, outright and increasingly intense rebellion constituted normality. The apartheid regime's acceptance of a settlement was based on the recognition that domination mainly by force had become unviable. The regime's 'total strategy'[14] had been premised on the need to try to marshal consent beyond whites and the reforms of the 1980s were geared at trying to achieve this. These never got out of the starting blocks. In the mid-1980s, it was not hegemony that was unravelling, but the sheer ability to continue to govern through coercion. Around the same time, black workers had arrived at a point of vibrant self-awareness of their corporate interests as a class and were creating powerful organisations to advance those interests. Also developing was a more expansive consciousness that linked the interests of workers to those of other subordinated social groups and classes. A stalemate was reached, which brings us to one of Gramsci's (1971:178) most-cited formulations:

> [C]risis occurs, sometimes lasting for decades. This exceptional duration means that incurable contradictions have revealed themselves (reached maturity) and that, despite this, the political forces which are struggling to conserve and defend the existing structure itself are making every effort to cure them, within certain limits, and to overcome them. These incessant and persistent efforts ... form the terrain of the 'conjunctural' and it is upon this terrain that the forces of opposition organize.

In South Africa, that crisis dates back to the late 1970s, when capital accumulation was faltering and its political and ideological basis began to crumble (see Chapter two). These two developments were dynamically linked. The economy was able to absorb diminishing portions of the labour surplus, while social protection against growing precariousness was absent. Political and social demands grew bolder, fuelled by (and causing the failure of) piecemeal attempts to dilute resistance. Between 1990 and 1995 the political and ideological aspects of the crisis were addressed in far-reaching ways, recasting the terrain on which the economic crisis could be tackled. Doing duty on the latter front was a series of profound adjustments. Property rights were entrenched, the expatriation of profits was allowed and corporate capital was able to restructure and extend its operations across the continental and global fields. Opportunities for social mobility multiplied visibly, even though not nearly as extensively as the mass media would pretend. Crucially, this occurred against the backdrop 'illusion that upward mobility is available to everybody who takes advantage of the available opportunities' (Buhlungu, 2006b:85).

Prospects for hegemony

The prospects of the hegemonic work-in-progress seemed less healthy in 2010 than a decade earlier. Several dimensions of the underlying crisis—particularly the morbid coupling of economic growth and profit-taking with surging precariousness—remained largely untouched. Inequality widened and poverty deepened in 1990–2000, with unemployment also increasing. The ANC and the state would respond primarily in three ways:

- Against a backdrop of African-nationalist idealism, it helped engineer the emergence of a black capitalist elite (see Chapter five). This occurred in two phases: the false start of 1993–98, followed by the less rickety but still highly exclusive revamp in the 2000s. That idealism (coupled to concepts such as the 'national democratic revolution') also provided an ideological basis for cementing the cross-class alliances that had enabled the ANC to become South Africa's pre-eminent liberation organisation. Affirmative action would play an important role, as would the introduction and defence of progressive labour laws. These processes, however, dismayed whites and other minorities, who much preferred the soft, undemanding 'inclusive' gestures of the mid-1990s and who felt more comfortable with the non-threatening makeover of non-racialism as multicultural 'tolerance'.

- The ANC and government headed off challenges from the left by stifling dissent and bullying critics. In particular, it took the rod to its alliance partners, COSATU and the SACP. The overriding mode was disciplinary. Drubbings replaced dialogue, and critics were censured rather than co-opted. This checked the Alliance left's ambitions, but only temporarily. A paranoiac sensibility spread; first in the presidency, then across government and the ANC. Political management became ham-fisted and impulsive. Reflexes of denigration and dismissal won out, allowing miscalculations and mistakes to become debacles that drained public trust and eroded the confidence of key allies.

- The state refurbished and expanded the social protection system in order to cushion growing desperation and misery, despite a strong, visceral distaste for 'welfare' and 'dependency' (see Chapter eight). Although this constituted one of the most dramatic interventions in the post-apartheid era, it was not trumpeted as such, since it conflicted with deeply held conceptions of citizenship and the relationship between the state and citizens. The underlying assumption was that the economic adjustments (codified in GEAR and its AsgiSA successor, remodelled black economic empowerment, and efforts to kick-start a small-enterprise boom) would eventually supplant extensive reliance on social protection.

The current situation therefore encompasses more than the political and economic problems of the day; it includes the compendium of efforts made to conserve and defend the existing system. In Simons' summary of Gramsci's thinking:

> If the crisis is a deep—and organic—one, these efforts cannot be purely defensive. They will consist in the struggle to create a new balance of political forces, requiring a reshaping of state institutions as well as the formation of new ideologies; and if the forces of opposition are not strong enough to shift the balance of forces decisively in their direction, the conservative forces will succeed in building a new system of alliances which will [establish] their hegemony. Beneath the surface of the day-to-day events, an organic and relatively permanent structural change will have taken place (1991:39).

Attempts at recasting and managing the crisis have brought temporary respite, but not enough to prevent the protests, enmity and embarrassments that began accumulating in the early 2000s. The political and ideological management of the transition required repairs. Those developments provided the context in which the Mbeki-Zuma struggle, the *putsch* against Mbeki and the ANC split is best understood—as part of the adjustments required to prevent this hegemonic work-in-progress from rattling apart. The ANC acted to prevent a situation emerging in which 'social classes become detached from their traditional parties' and where their political formations and the people leading them 'are no longer recognised by their class [...] as its expression' (Gramsci, 1971:210)—where the ANC and the state it dominates would no longer be able to perform their vital roles in mobilising consent.

The Mbeki-Zuma duel made it possible to channel the swirl of discontent within the ANC and among its presumed constituencies *away* from the organisation and deflect it onto a vilified band of 'pretenders'. The split in the ANC consummated that flourish. Celebrated by liberal South Africans as a progression in the democratisation process, the split was actually a step backward. The creation of the COPE party, stocked with Mbeki supporters, made it even easier for the ANC to exonerate itself from the debacles of the previous decade and parry blame and criticism toward the 'Mbeki camp'.[15] The split, in other words, validated the contrivance that the ANC stood unsullied and pure. And Zuma's triumph temporarily re-authenticated the ANC's status as the custodian of liberation and was meant to replenish popular trust in its determination and ability to fulfil that role. His campaign hammered home this message: he understood his place in the larger scheme of things; he would *serve* as leader. Many observers, however, would interpret this as indecisiveness (Southall, 2010).

The ANC still commands enough attributes and means to continue patching together this project; no other political or social force rivals it in this respect. But as long as the central terms of the project—the pre-eminence of capital accumulation over the wellbeing of citizens—stays unchanged, hegemony is unlikely to be achieved. The underlying crisis will remain unresolved and will generate increasing instability. How this unfolds will depend on the character and prospects of a possible alter-hegemonic project and on the versatility of the current bid for hegemony, structured around the ANC-led state.

Building consent

The ANC's history confirms its skill at nurturing and consolidating loyalty and trust. By the late-1980s, it had established its status as a government-in-waiting and confirmed its ideological supremacy over the internal opposition. The route towards a 'better life for all' (the party's later election slogan) was seen to pass through the 'broad church' of the ANC, where the specific meanings different constituencies attached to this vision seemed to achieve harmony. Through deed and affirmation, it lodged itself in the popular imagination as the vessel for redressing all manner of grievances and for realising a rich assortment of ambitions and interests. Paradoxically, the apartheid system assisted in this process. Its ideology of exclusivity summoned a counter ideology of inclusivity. The unifying and inclusive character of the ANC therefore played counterpoint to a system that violently tried to enforce the converse.

Key to these feats was an ideology of struggle and ideals that were supple enough to accommodate contradictory impulses and to persuasively present shifts as distillations of a consistent historical vision of change. In the 1990s, especially after 1994, an inclusive ethos was projected across society, where it formed a mantle of reconciliation, consensus-making and nation-building. Putative commonalities and shared interests were highlighted in a crucial quest for stability. The perspectives were widely embraced and propagated by the main political parties, organised business and the vast majority of the media. They also enjoyed what one might term 'organic authenticity', in the sense that they resonated (and made 'sense') among most ordinary South Africans. A rich stock of spectacles and gestures amplified this endorsing mood. Sports events such as the Rugby World Cup and the African Nations Cup and startling images such as those of white army generals saluting President Nelson Mandela, the new South African flag billowing beneath air-force helicopters at the 1994 presidential inauguration or Mandela sipping tea with the widow of apartheid architect, Hendrik Verwoerd, were examples.

At least as dramatic was the translation of this mood of appeasement and 'unity' into government policies. By late 1994, the Reconstruction and Development Programme (RDP) bore the stretch marks of a bid to accommodate the divergent interests of contesting social and economic forces. So much so that conservative commentators could approvingly remark that 'all signs now are that our policy makers see that the objectives of the RDP are wholly compatible with the three words [privatisation, liberalisation and convertibility] which so interest the money men'.[16] Adjusted in line with the conciliatory principles that propped the political settlement, the RDP was seen by government as a partnership of 'everyone, every organisation, every opinion-making group that can contribute ... that's the protection this government needs to ensure that if anything goes wrong, it will be our collective responsibility'.[17]

Whatever the radical intentions injected into the programme initially, it became the product of many hands, minds and motives, leaving it 'beset by enough fragmented voices, multiple identities and competing discourses to leave even postmodern analysts confounded' (Bond, 1999). Intellectuals with ties to the earlier UDF (see Chapter two) had pushed the more radical elements in the RDP, but they were not at the heart of power inside the ANC (Freund, 2007b). Promoted as a national endeavour, the RDP embraced, but also transcended, parochial interests. As a road map of transformation, it promised to lead just about everyone to their respective promised land: 'With a little ingenuity,' noted Thabo Rapoo, 'anything can be made to fit in with the goals of the RDP (1995:5)'. Not quite, though. No matter the ingenuity applied, massive job losses could not be reconciled with the goal of creating jobs and moving towards full employment. Likewise, the guarantee of a living wage could not be made to fit a reality in which many employed workers live in poverty; nor could a commitment to reduce income disparities square with a reality of widening gaps. But Rapoo was correct in the sense that the RDP had become more than a blueprint for transformation; it became a template for many of the compromises that would define the transition and for reproducing consent around them.

So the *function* of the RDP had changed. In this revised role it was neither the paragon of, nor a mere sop to, the ideals that had brought the ANC to power. It expressed concessions that would define the post-apartheid development path—trade-offs that were spurred by a perceived need to not jeopardise stability, but that also reflected a balance of forces that favoured capital. The RDP distilled these realities. The question often posed by the left—'who killed the RDP?'—was replaced by the liturgical reminder that 'the RDP died for us all'. The variegated interests of capital and of the subaltern classes were not only blurred, but were made to appear contingent on each other.

Closely related was the programme's other, subsequent function: as an ideological reference point that seems to confirm the continuity between Freedom Charter ideals and post-apartheid realities. That political resonance prevents it from being erased from memory, even though it has been shorn of *literal* meaning. Hence the RDP, although interred since 1996, still features in official rhetoric. It became a form of shorthand for the values and principles that had animated the anti-apartheid struggle and which the ANC pledges still to be upholding. Michael McDonald (2005) has gone even further and suggested that the RDP's abandonment might even have stabilised the ANC in power—by pushing into the background the socialist aspirations that stir inside it and laying greater emphasis on the party's cardinal unifying strength, African nationalism.

The discourse of reconciliation had helped foster consent and sap resistance. Inside the ANC, the ideological basis for camaraderie also required an overhaul. With the unifying impetus of the anti-apartheid struggle flagging, a new 'language' of unity was needed—one that could resonate among the different layers and interest groups that constitute the party's constituencies. As a canopy of values, avowals and ideals, that discourse had to cultivate fellowship and trust.

Repair work

The dominant discourse after 1994 orbited around postulated common interests and destinies, but as dismay increased over GEAR and other signs of acculturation to a neoliberal order, the boundaries of dissent were patrolled more diligently. An emphasis on loyalty and patriotism emerged and the noxious notion that 'if you are not with us, you are against us' prevailed. There was a populist undertone, with invective aimed at an assortment of targets: 'undisciplined' teachers; corrupt bureaucrats and businesspeople; elitist black business ventures; and motley 'sinister' forces bent on scuttling the democratic revolution. A fair share of the spleen was aimed at leftist critics, whose analyses and complaints were sometimes ridiculed as expressions of 'a psychosis which dictates that a message of failure and pessimism must necessarily be communicated, overriding the nuisance of facts' (Mbeki, 1998b).[18] Often these rebukes were cast in the language of the (old) left.

Cribbed from dusty hymnals, the ANC's rhetoric stayed doggedly retro—reflecting the fact that a sizeable part of its activist base inclines toward the left. Many of these are COSATU shop stewards and/or members of the SACP.[19] Party discussion papers creak with Marxist-Leninist jargon, even when utterly conventional policies are being extolled. As noted, these phrases function less as analytical tools than as signalling devices, for many in the ANC appreciate their use as symbols of affinity rather than literal descriptions. Thus the reconfiguration of elite dominance can proceed under the mantle of a 'national democratic revolution'. Crucially, this can occur because that discourse, along with that of national liberation generally, is invested with great 'moral weight and connect[s] with specific histories, memories, embodied experiences and meanings of racial oppression, racialised dispossession, and struggles against apartheid' (Hart, 2007:20).

Another theme was a more forthright focus on the racism and other iniquities that define society. This shift spoke more directly to the realities Africans still encounter—where the hand of appeasement is routinely shunned, racism remains rife and privilege is defended with steely resolve. Mbeki spearheaded the shift, which most observers misunderstood as a retreat toward 'narrow' Africanism (discussed later). In fact, it was part of a subtler juggling act. Mbeki would launch stirring attacks on racism and remonstrate against whites for refusing to promote greater equity and reconciliation, while also condemning the 'seemingly insatiable and morally unbound greed' of the black elite. 'Those responsible for or who were beneficiaries of the past absolve themselves of any obligation to do away with an unacceptable legacy,' he told parliamentarians in June 1998.[20] Similar themes became a hallmark of government pronouncements, though few politicians emulated Mbeki in tailoring the same rebukes for different audiences. To the African poor, they announced the ANC government's unflinching empathy with their plight. To white South Africans, they warned that the indulgence of their privilege could not continue unless some form of reciprocation occurred. To the left, they declared that the party's progressive instincts were intact.

Facts on the ground

Such flourishes would dissolve in the face of reality, were it not for the visible gains that have accrued to a variety of classes and social strata. These accomplishments are commonly misread.

Scanning post-1994 South Africa, only a jaundiced eye will fail to recognise evidence of the benefits allocated to specific classes—the organised working classes, the existing and emerging black middle classes and the aspirant African bourgeoisie, not to mention the largesse clasped by the incumbent elites. All this is shadowed by unsightly realities, but these do not erase the ways in which, for instance, many of the historical demands of the labour movement acquired legislative force early in the transition. The affirmative action thrust of the Employment Equity Act, for example, resonates beyond the workplace and authenticates the ANC's status as historical guardian of African nationalist ideals and the post-apartheid state's determination to advance those ideals. For the majority of South Africans, it has a powerfully legitimating impact (even though it carries the cost of unsettling minorities).

Also pertinent are measures to aid African entrepreneurs. The state's record on supporting the emergence and survival of small and medium-sized enterprises is spotty. But the efforts advertise a 'unity of purpose' that extends beyond the state and includes major capitalist organisations (that contribute to small-business funds, marshal skills-building ventures and stage entrepreneurial training). This signals a commonality of interests that joins the fate of African entrepreneurs to that of both capital and the ANC-led state. This evolving *ménage a trois* is most obvious in the entanglements of black economic empowerment (BEE) and is decisively influencing the transition.

Since transformation within a capitalist system is incompatible with a situation in which the economy remains almost exclusively in white hands, BEE has been cast as an aspect of the 'national democratic revolution' and of attempts to address the 'national question'. As discussed in Chapter five, an African capitalist elite is expected to operate as a wellspring of a 'patriotic' capitalism that reconciles the hunt for profit with improvements in the living standards and opportunities of the black poor. The conceit sits squarely in the African-nationalist tradition,[21] but it brings to mind the similar approach adopted under the mantle of Afrikaner nationalism. The upshot is a more intimate nexus between African capitalists and the state, perhaps analogous to the apartheid state's levering of the Afrikaner bourgeoisie (O'Meara, 1983 & 1996). Along with the ANC's 'redeployment' of figures into the parastatal and private sectors, this has had made a new elite stratum heavily dependent on political links at all levels of government. A convoluted system of patronage, conniving and commuting between the state and private sector has taken root within the ambit of BEE. The elitist nature of such 'upliftment' attracts much moralistic disapproval. But the rise of an African capitalist class not only kindles the ambitions of the tiny coterie of individuals able to capitalise on the new opportunities, it also decorates the private yearnings of millions more. Publicly denigrated but privately envied, African-elite advancement carries strong symbolic meaning.

Circling the wagons

Deployed alongside such ideological tools are more literal 'disciplinary' mechanisms for discouraging organised dissent in the ANC and government. South Africa's system of proportional representation ties individual politicians' careers to party machineries and prevents them from building careers based on popular constituency support. The apparatchiks who control the ANC's election lists also control the fates of its politicians.[22] These centralised pathways of power and accountability are reinforced by a constitutional clause that deprives a parliamentarian of her seat if she abandons her party. Democratic processes inside the party (and the political system generally) therefore fit into a matrix of rules and powers that sets stern limits on dissidence and nonconformity. The resulting disciplined loyalty is largely self-administered; the wages of transgression are known to all, as a 1997 episode during an ANC caucus meeting illustrated:

> [ANC MP] Barbara Hogan kept prefacing her remarks with the phrase that she 'did not want to cause any trouble'. To his credit, Mbeki intervened and said he was worried that she felt it necessary to say this. Was there, he asked, a more general feeling that the ANC leadership did not welcome dissent? 'Yes-s-s,' the MPs whispered in chorus (Lodge, 1999a:117).

By all accounts, the reins were tightened further once Mbeki took charge of the executive. A firmer political line was laid down and policed and debate in the ANC's parliamentary caucus waned. By 2000, in Andrew Feinstein's (2007:123) telling, the caucus

> reflected a more disciplined, choreographed and constrained party, a party fearful of its leader, conscious of his power to make or break careers, conscious of his demand for loyalty, for conformity of thinking.

But this style of governance is mistakenly equated with Mbeki's presidency. The premium placed on discipline, loyalty and 'restraint' is an enduring feature of the ANC and traces back to organisational traditions and styles that, perforce, characterised the ANC in exile and in the underground struggle (see Chapter twelve). For the most part, activists were schooled in the need for discipline and obedience. Those sensibilities remain strong. The ANC is seen as larger than the sum of its parts—a mindset that explains the servile manner in which most censured figures accept their fates. Any of the ANC's older supporters lodge the very fate of the African majority with the organisation. An almost mystical trust prevails.

The parameters of obedience shift; space for criticism and heterodoxy narrows or widens depending on dynamics inside the ANC. But vested, in the final instance, with party leadership are powers that engender self-enforced discipline and compliance and that militate against the emergence of open, organised blocs and platforms that can promote specific interests. Until the mid-2000s, formidable degrees of consent, loyalty and unity were the outcome. Potential centrifugal dynamics were restrained. The outcome was a party that, at once, seemed rooted in a codex of principles and traditions, but which was also capable of considerable manoeuvrability.

This capacity to impose internal discipline and authority weakened during the Mbeki-Zuma battle, as feuding and plotting intensified. Squabbling divided the organisation at all levels, most raucously at branch level, but the altercations have also polluted the state. The push to unseat Mbeki gave licence to all manner of skirmishing, much of it conducted in the open. In the process, the ANC sacrificed its enviable ability to present a unified and (usually) dignified image to the world. Internal discipline has not entirely disappeared, but the strife has badly destabilised the ANC organisationally. A great deal of effort is now required to contain the centrifugal impulses that have been released.

Avoiding accountability

The standard leftist explanation for South Africa's neoliberal drift is the pithy but tired notion of a 'sell-out'. Within the Tripartite Alliance this was embellished into the '1996 class project' contrivance, with Mbeki and his circle supposedly 'hijacking' the 'national democratic revolution' (see SACP, 2010). The thinking assumes that another, dominant trajectory of transformation was short-circuited. In the folklore of the liberation movement, that trajectory is traced back to the ANC's 1969 Morogoro conference and a purported hegemony of leftist forces subsequently within the ANC. These are facile notions, as Zuma (2009b) himself would confirm as he beat back the Alliance left's attempts to snatch greater influence: 'As soon as we start associating government policy with one individual, we risk forgetting that these policies are developed collectively and reflect an organisational position.'

Yet, as Zuma barged his way to the presidency, his allies promoted an account that painted the Mbeki era as an aberration in which a tight-knit, authoritarian clique supposedly seized command and reduced the ANC and its parliamentarians to an assembly of drones. AIDS denialism became the folly one man managed to impose on an entire movement; so, too, the indulgence of Mugabe's ruinous reign in Zimbabwe. The ramshackle state of public health and education, the lumbering pace of social development, the failure to create jobs in meaningful numbers—it all indicted Mbeki and his 'camp'. When township protests erupted again in mid-2009, with Zuma now in the president's seat, blame would still be aimed at councillors elected during Mbeki's tenure. The protestors, claimed Tokyo Sexwale, the new minister for human settlements, 'are simply saying leaders in the past have done things wrong and they want to tell us'.[23] This would become a familiar refrain.

The centralisation of authority achieved by Mbeki has been discussed extensively (Mangcu, 2008; Gevisser, 2007; Feinstein, 2007; O'Malley, 2007; Calland, 2006;

Gumede, 2005). The executive was restructured in 1999, expanding the power of the presidency. Directors-general, for instance, would sign contracts with the presidency rather than their respective line-function ministers.[24] Also augmented was the power of the executive in relation to the provinces, a response to the dismal auditing reports and spotty performance of most provincial governments during the 1990s. In addition, new draft legislation would be presented to a policy unit in the presidency before being reviewed by Cabinet. Based in the president's office and reporting to him, this gate-keeping structure was vested with 'power at least equal to that wielded by ministers'.[25] Also created was a new cabinet portfolio, that of 'Minister in the Office of the President', essentially a fixer and henchman. First to hold the post was one of Mbeki's most loyal lieutenants, Essop Pahad, who did duty as 'office manager, political adviser, go-between and fixer' (Jacobs, 1999:6).

Inside government, power also shifted along another axis. Whereas other ministries had to jockey for influence on the basis of their performances, relations with the presidency and their ability to sway opinion in the cabinet, the Finance Ministry emerged as a super-ministry. It stood alone in its ability to fortify its authority primarily *outside* government, by invoking the reactions of the market to its policies. A higher investment or credit rating from Standard & Poor, a supportive remark by an IMF chief or a bull-run on the Johannesburg Stock Exchange—these 'extraneous' factors dramatically boost the ministry's weight in policy jousting inside government. To a great extent it reproduces its power separate from the rest of the machinery of government.

Three points should be borne in mind. Firstly, there were sound arguments for most of the governance adjustments, many of which followed closely the recommendations of a public commission of inquiry. That commission had found that adequate co-ordination was lacking across national departments and between them and their provincial counterparts and it pinpointed the need to overhaul poor policy formulation and decision-making systems (Gumede, 2005). Chief among its recommendations was the conversion of the presidency into 'the core of the system of governance', a move in line with global trends.

Secondly, the moves sat squarely in the paradigm of good governance and spoke to the imperatives of efficiency, cost-effectiveness, enterprise and rectitude. Demanded, therefore, were robust systems, institutional harmony, oversight mechanisms and transparency. After becoming president, Zuma would scarcely tinker with most of these arrangements. And, thirdly, the image of an imperial presidency running roughshod over an entire government and a venerable liberation movement does not account for how particular sets of policies were introduced and sustained for such long periods and could survive the departure of the supposed clique of culprits. It is beyond dispute that browbeating and intimidation featured prominently in Mbeki's repertoire, but intolerance and chicanery does not explain 15 years of economic orthodoxy, spanning the tenure of three different presidents and maintained in the face of demonstrable damage and loud opposition.

It seems more plausible to blame the AIDS fiasco on autocratic whimsy. Yet, during that drawn-out debacle, which earned South Africa global ridicule, no

ANC figure of note broke ranks, including intellectual stalwarts usually revered for their independence of thought and courage of convictions. Andrew Feinstein's (2007:125–8) account of a speech Mbeki gave to the 260 members of the ANC parliamentary caucus at the end of September 2000 is telling. The soliloquy soon turned to AIDS, with the president recycling hoary denialist claims (the virus has never been isolated, the pharmaceutical industry invented the idea that HIV causes AIDS so they could sell drugs, etc). Applause interrupted him. Then he pilloried the Treatment Action Campaign, which, he told MPs, was 'funded by pharmaceutical companies in the US', according to Feinstein's careful notes.[26] The ANC, Mbeki continued,

> mustn't be scared to take on a lobby that is too strong [...] we must be prepared to respond to these challenges and be aware of the links between the AIDS agenda and the IMF agenda.

When Mbeki sat down, the room erupted in cheers, 'interspersed with cries of "Viva Thabo Viva"' (op cit, 126). Pregs Govender, in her memoir, claims she raised her hand to ask a question, but 'comrades seated nearby glanced sideways at me, their eyes urging me to put my hand down. The chairperson looked away, saying there was to be no discussion' (2007:223)—hardly the stuff of show trials and Siberian exile. This was not coercion but seduction and 'self-discipline', spiked with intimidation. Still, she was one of the rare ANC MPs who would try and use her position to contest the ANC's refusal to provide antiretroviral treatment.

So there was wide complicity in the shambles and a good deal of it was heartfelt. Those with misgivings could hardly shelter behind the ANC's tradition of democratic-centralism, which demands subservience once leadership takes a position on a matter; to ridicule the AIDS epidemic and deny treatment to the afflicted was never a policy of the ANC. Members had every right to challenge pronouncements and practices that scoffed at an epidemic that was killing hundreds of thousands of people a year. The vast majority of ANC leaders and members chose not do so. The head of the National AIDS Council, Jacob Zuma, uttered no protest. 'The question of why the government's unresponsiveness never became a burning issue for the movement and its basic constituency,' Lelyveld (2009) points out, 'can't be seen simply as a function of one man's over-rationalised hang-ups.' The bemusement about 'Mbeki's denialism' needs to be directed at the ANC writ large.

Of course, this calls into question the vigour of democratic practice, the nature of debate and the handling of dissent inside the ANC, particularly in its upper tiers—matters that implicate the organisation as a whole, its traditions and its culture of governance. But it also suggests that the sources of support for apparently incongruous, even 'irrational', positions and practices can run deeper than is commonly recognised. Interpreting them simply as the outcome of stern discipline or compulsion is often mistaken and almost always misleading.

It is therefore worth pausing to examine the ANC's AIDS denialism, precisely because it seems so irrational, yet persisted for so long. What emerges is a picture that upends a favourite stereotype about the 'Mbeki era'—that it exemplified cold, detached, technocratic reasoning. The unlikely endurance of denialism is also a reminder that a history as debasing as South Africa's will continue to intrude in the present, often in ways that perplex.

Roots of denial

It should surprise no one that popular understandings of AIDS have been coloured with stereotypes and prejudice, including 'pathologising discourses' in which black sexuality is constructed as unbridled and insatiable (Steinberg, 2008a). These stereotypes date back to the early periods of colonialism and featured strongly also in medical science—vividly, for example, during South Africas syphilis panics of the 1930s and 1940s, when African men were typified as voracious sexual predators.[27] For centuries, this kind of imagery served as a screen against which Western cultures constructed their own, contrasting self-portraits of restraint, purity and rationality, as Frantz Fanon famously observed. The linking of race, libido and death in colonialist discourses—and the apparent complicity of medical and social science in this—still resonates loudly in South Africa.[28] It hovers as a kind of 'contemporary past', a history that refuses to be consigned to the past:[29]

> I, for my part, will not keep quiet while others whose minds have been corrupted by the disease of racism, accuse us, the black people of South Africa, Africa and the world, as being, by virtue of our African-ness and skin colour, lazy, liars, foul-smelling, diseased, corrupt, violent, amoral, sexually depraved animalistic, slaves—and rapists (Mbeki, 2004).[30]

When, in 2000, Mbeki set about questioning the causal relationship between HIV and AIDS, he was not the first to do so. Similar doubts dated back more than a decade and had fuelled numerous conspiracy theories, including the claim that HIV was part of a plot to exterminate blacks.[31] In 1988, the ANC's lionised young intellectual Mzala was already writing in the ANC's *Sechaba* mouthpiece that HIV had been concocted in the 'laboratories of the military-industrial complex' of the US and that theories of the African origins of AIDS were 'yet another justification for ... racist prejudice'.[32] Similar sentiments circulated widely in Africa and the US. By the time Mbeki began pontificating on AIDS, the epidemic was already doubling as a stage for other battles (against pharmaceutical corporations, for instance), for asserting 'third world nationalism' and for reiterating the neglected encounters between Western science and Africa. The bilious 'Castro Hlongwane, caravans, cats, geese, foot and mouth, and statistics' tract (Anon, 2002) exemplified this. Possibly penned by Mbeki, it dismissed what it termed the 'HIV/AIDS thesis' as:

> informed by deeply entrenched and centuries-old white racist beliefs and concepts about Africans and black people [...] Driven by fear of their destruction as a people because of an allegedly unstoppable plague, Africans and black people themselves have been persuaded to join and support a campaign whose result is further to entrench their dehumanization.[33]

Interventions of this sort confirmed that memories of encounters with colonial power and science linger strongly in South Africa. One example was the *rinderpest* epidemic that struck the east coast of the country in late 1896. Following on the heels of other setbacks (including droughts), rinderpest scythed through black and white cattle-farming communities in what was then Natal and Zululand (Carton, 2003). Dubbed *umaqimulana*, the disease felled huge numbers of cattle and prompted various responses. On the one hand, there were attempts to enforce customs deemed to shield against this apparently supernatural force; on the other hand, there were the panicked demands from white commercial farmers that the contagion be halted before it also decimated their herds.[34] If the quarantine measures applied by the authorities were resented, the subsequent vaccination of black-owned cattle by roaming teams of veterinarians, court officials and police stoked deep distrust about the true motives of the exercise. Western medical science was experienced as an invasive and destabilising force. The fact that vaccinated cattle showed temporary symptoms of *rinderpest* and that the most effective serum at the time protected cattle for only four months (after which the beasts were again susceptible to infection), deepened suspicion about this 'white man's disease' (Carton, 2003:4). Measures ostensibly taken to 'protect' African farmers seemed to achieve the opposite, leaving them worse off.

Similar distrust shaped reactions to flu vaccination efforts in the Eastern Cape during the 1918 influenza epidemic. The vaccine was widely feared as a genocidal tool, 'a device of the Europeans to finish off the Native races of South Africa and as it had not been quite successful, they were sending out men with poison to complete the work of extermination' (Carton, *op cit*). The parallel with claims circulating on the fringes of AIDS scepticism are obvious.

In the decades that followed, the use of science-based knowledge by the authorities in South Africa intensified. Sometimes it took the relatively 'neutral' form of promoting new cultivation, irrigation or contouring techniques in agriculture or livestock vaccination requirements. But it was also expressed as a blend of racism and Malthusianism that gave rise to the apartheid state's 'family planning' initiatives among black South Africans. In extremist form, it would manifest in the chemical and biological warfare experiments of Wouter Basson and his search for ways to surreptitiously induce infertility in Africans.[35] South African history therefore fed a fervent suspicion about disease, science and power—and about the loathsome ways in which they can converge. AIDS became a lens that focused these misgivings and that invited the denialism of Mbeki and others. Orthodox AIDS science was ridiculed as yet another instance of the putrefied fusion of colonial oppression, Western medicine and imperialist exploitation.

So the AIDS debacle did not centre on a debate about the substance and quality of knowledge; it was about how knowledge is inflected with power, prejudice, memories and resistance. Indeed, Schneider and Fassin (2002:S49) have described South African 'denialism' as a form of 'defiance' against 'official scientific knowledge' and an 'identification with those on the margins, whether of science or society'. That reading misses some of the eclectic functions of denialism. For this was no rebellion against authority; it was authority pronouncing. Nowhere else in the world were denialist doubts issued from such lofty heights and with such insistence. More appropriate than the folksy image of the underdog squaring off against massed power would be comparisons with other occasions when the state backed quack science (the Lysenko debacle in the 1930s in the Soviet Union, for instance, and the meddling of the George W Bush administration in the US around climate science).[36]

But the broader point stands. In South Africa, denialism functioned as a grammar for overarching political and ideological compulsions and tussles. It provided a platform for pinpointing and denouncing racism and served as a vent for the sublimated passions that had been stifled during the 1990s, when stability, conciliation and calm were the priorities. It seemed to signal, in an impudent outburst, the end of that interlude, a reminder that history still bulged with unfinished business and that there were 'truths' that would not remain unspoken.

Denialism therefore also performed a therapeutic role. It substituted for other confrontations and made it possible to speak about some of the ignominy that shapes so much of South African (and African) history, to condemn the racism and the indignities that millions still endure and to advertise a determination to end those blights.[37] The crude, flailing nature of denialist pronouncements was, at one level, a mark of pained earnestness. But this sincerity also exposed it as a hypocritical and self-indulgent gesture, for the rebellious thought was never extended into other realms. The economic orthodoxies preached in Washington, Chicago and London were embraced, not challenged. In fact, it is tempting to wonder whether the ANC's AIDS denialism can be fully understood separately from other, decisive accommodations with 'Western' orthodoxy. Karl von Holdt (2009:24) suggests that government's imposition and effective defence of neoliberal economic policies can be understood in psychoanalytic terms. It looks, he says,

> like the successful replication of the authentic 'European' model of the modern state; yet it may as plausibly be seen as a neocolonial internalisation of the 'racial gaze' in the form of the policy prescriptions of the Washington Consensus institutions for the developing world.

Around AIDS the opposite happened. It is as if the embrace of economic and technocratic orthodoxy in post-apartheid South Africa demanded, psychologically, a theatrical act of resistance, for which AIDS became the stage.

This brief detour cannot exhaust the phenomenon of AIDS denialism in South Africa, but it underscores its multifaceted and magnetic appeal, an allure that reached beyond a handful of powerful individuals. The choices made in post-apartheid South Africa—even such frothy ones as AIDS denialism—express complex dynamics that roil beneath the surface.

The exposition also highlights a key fiction of Zuma's rise: that the flaws and failures were aberrations or miscalculations imposed against the run of history by a band of pretenders.

A year into the Zuma presidency, the charade was evident. Some admirable changes were underway. The decrepit state of the public health system was acknowledged and the AIDS response seemed to acquire new vigour. The outcomes-based approach in education was condemned.[38] Yet many of the policies and programmes associated with Mbeki's 'reign of error' had survived both the Polokwane 'rebellion' and Zuma's rise to power. And, as we show later, many of those touted subsequently as proof of a 'leftward shift' in fact had originated during Mbeki's terms as president.

Paying the price

The Zuma victory came at the cost of importing the ANC's divisions into the state (Southall, 2008). Institutions have been 'cleansed' of perceived Mbeki influence, with a special emphasis on the intelligence and prosecutorial apparatuses. The dyspeptic and intolerant conduct of the Mbeki administration had already primed a backlash of reprisals; indeed, the tactics used to hoist Zuma into the presidency fuelled and legitimised cycles of requital that, by 2010, had not yet run their course. Reprisals have targeted provincial premiers, mayors, councillors, activists, government officials and businesses deemed 'close to Mbeki'. Some ANC branches were even dissolved after having voted against Zuma at the 2007 Polokwane conference.

Especially coveted was control of the security and intelligence apparatuses, including the National Prosecuting Authority (NPA). Tasked with investigating and prosecuting serious breaches of law (including organised crime), the NPA was in the thick of the Mbeki-Zuma struggle. The victors exacted revenge by disbanding its investigative arm (the Scorpions), despite an impressive record, replacing it with a new Directorate for Priority Crime Investigations (the Hawks) and restaffing it. Zuma loyalists now also staff the top tiers of the state's intelligence structures. Meanwhile, the judiciary has suffered damage and jostling within it has taken on racial overtones. The significant presence of progressive white jurists in the top tiers of the judiciary (particularly the Constitutional Court) since 1994 is probably drawing to a close.

Most of these moves were predictable and, comparatively speaking, hardly unusual. But they have entrenched a sense of arbitrariness in institutions where professionalism, consistency and predictability are at a premium. And they signal to state officials that fealty trumps proficient public service.

Damage control

The apparent 'crusade' against Zuma handed to the ANC many of the discursive tools and flourishes it needed to reconsolidate its pre-eminence, replenish its consent and help to repair the makeshift and unsteady hegemony assembled in the 1990s.

Some of the appeal is reactionary and could provide a basis for an anti-liberal backlash against rights and practices which, in a socially conservative society such as South Africa's, are easily caricatured as 'luxuries' that are alien to dominant traditions and values. The view circulates at the highest tiers; according to one of Zuma's ministers, Sicelo Shiceka, the 'Eurocentric' Constitution requires review.[39] There are several easy targets, all of which are 'rights-based'. Same-sex marriages and gay rights, for example, are easily rubbished as 'un-African' and unduly permissive and present welcome, distracting targets (as politicians in Malawi, Uganda and elsewhere can attest).

Even more popular is government's 'tough on crime' posture, which features little by way of substantive improvements in police training, policing techniques and prosecutorial efficiency. Fingered instead is the allegedly overindulgent treatment of criminals, whose rights are said to trump those of law-abiding citizens—a hoary staple that still plays well. 'Laws that bite' are needed to curb violent crime, according to Zuma.[40] 'We do not have a normal crime rate [...] It is violent and abnormal, and requires extraordinary measures to deal with it,' he told 1 000 police-station commanders gathered at the Voortrekker monument near Pretoria in September 2009.[41] When people's lives are threatened, he said, the police 'have no choice but to use force':

> We have allowed [people's] rights to be trampled on by the rights of criminals. We will not tolerate this anymore, and once you are a criminal who has taken a life, we need to question your rights.

Signalling its 'no-nonsense' approach, government renamed the oxymoronic Department of Safety and Security, settling for the more literal Department of Police. A push to restore the death penalty (abolished in 1994) is very likely, although one can argue that the 'shoot to kill' approach promoted by top government officials already goes a step further by assigning to police officers the status of both judge and executioner in situations they deem to be 'life-threatening'.[42] 'Shoot the bastards' was the sentiment attributed to Deputy Police Minister Fikile Mbalula.[43] He has pushed for converting the police into a paramilitary force, with military ranks and modes of discipline. When former government minister Kader Asmal condemned the notion as 'craziness', Mbalula unbuttoned his populist rhetoric and accused Asmal of using his elderly status 'to stifle radical criticism and policy positions'.[44] Sentiments usually associated with hobnailed rule were now being paraded as radicalism.

In truth, the system hardly indulges arrested suspects. In 2008–09, 912 suspects died in police custody (up from 792 the year before), according to the Independent Complaints Directorate, which told Parliament that it was investigating more than 11 000 official complaints lodged against the police.[45] Two-thirds of the accused remain in custody in overcrowded and dangerous conditions until their cases are concluded—despite the fact that there is an almost 50% chance 'of any given case ending in the charges being withdrawn'. According to researcher Jean Redpath, 'it is difficult to imagine a less rights-friendly legislative environment around bail than the present one'.[46] South Africa has already got one of the highest incarceration rates in the world: 400 out of every 100 000 persons are behind bars, roughly the same rates as in Thailand and the Ukraine. Judges are also handing down stiffer sentences: by 2002, the number of prison sentences of 10 years or longer had increased by at least 67% compared with 1995 (Sekhonyane, 2004).[47] This hardly jibes with the commonplace notions of 'molly-coddled criminals'. Nonetheless, the clamorous pursuit of 'law and order' (the term now preferred in the ANC) and crackdowns on 'common' criminals play well in the context of justifiable fear and insecurity (see Chapter seven).

Anti-crime populism is dangerously corrosive. Inevitably it fixes liberal concepts of individual rights in its firing sights and risks opening a path for the selective application of the rule of law (and of the principles of due process, the presumption of innocence, the right to fair trial and of punishment fitting the crime). Such regression also popularises the notion that rights are contingent, accrue only to certain strata of society and can be revoked or restricted on the basis of suspicion, legal record or more extensive normative criteria. If such populism is allowed to flourish (and there is every indication that it will), it provides licence for action against anyone who convincingly can be tarred as miscreant, lawbreaking or subversive—including protestors, activists and dissenters. A greasy slope is in preparation.

By 2009, Zuma had been coached to bite his tongue on such matters. But there was ample earlier evidence that his views on several social issues ranged from conservative to downright reactionary. In September 2006 he condemned same-sex marriages as 'a disgrace to the nation and to God'. 'When I was growing up,' Zuma was quoted as saying, 'an *ungqingili* [a gay person] would not have stood in front of me. I would knock him out.'[48] Later he warned that he might support legislation making it illegal for children not to be in school: 'If they don't stop roaming the streets instead of being in school, we will take them to far-away colleges and forcefully educate them. We are building a nation,' he reportedly told ANC members in Soweto. Punitive steps were also needed to reduce teenage pregnancies, he suggested.[49]

The roles and rights of women will feature prominently in these unfolding struggles. Already roused to self-awareness is a deeply conservative set of assumptions about women's 'place' in society. South Africa's high rates of violence against women express those values in a horrifically forthright way. But there is considerable room for mobilising a more generalised enforcement of an order in which men and women 'know their place' and act accordingly. Conservative interpretations of tradition and Christian scripture will serve as the pretexts and templates for these interventions.[50]

Such sentiments are not as anomalous as liberals and progressives want to believe. After surveying attitudes towards women among residents in 21 of the country's most impoverished urban and rural communities, Everatt (2008:315) concluded that 'post-apartheid South Africa is failing to produce citizens with values that match the democratic Constitution'. Hostile attitudes to gender equality and women's reproductive rights and endorsement of violence against women were commonplace and were more likely to be found among men younger than 35 years. Education levels seemed not to account for these views, nor did media access. The ANC is likely to tap into these sentiments as part of its efforts to forge an affective bond with constituencies that may feel increasingly ambivalent towards lofty rights that seem to leave such faint imprint on their daily lives.

In a broader sense, these assertions of conservative impulses all speak to a visceral unease and insecurity, that sense of 'things falling apart' that formed the basis of the Zuma triumph.[51] They announce a palpable need for consolidation, for mooring society to values that reflect more faithfully a dominant sense of 'who we are'. They are linked, therefore, to highly normative (and essentialist) notions of 'decency', 'normality', identity and authenticity, of who is 'truly South African', who constitutes the citizenry and on what basis they do so. And they contrast starkly with the notions of belonging proposed during the 'Mbeki era'.

Nationalism and the boundaries of belonging

Daily experiences of inequality and injustice generate a churn of restiveness in South Africa. Sporadically this vents as protests and other forms of dissent. It befalls the ANC to manage these uproars. The tried and trusted way of doing this is by affirming and valorising bonds that can muffle discord. South Africa pulses with vast, expectant collectivities that orbit around racial identities, notions of 'South African-ness' and ethnic chauvinism. The most tempting epoxy is race, but it is also the riskiest in a society with South Africa's history and demographics. Nationalism—particularly African nationalism, with its strong racial inflections—is more appealing.

Since the late 1990s, many observers have claimed to detect a shift toward a narrower, more pinched variant of African nationalism. According to Peter Kagwanja (2008), for example, the political settlement was propped on the principle of 'civic or liberal nationalism' and its highly inclusive notions of 'belonging'. By and large, these were neither invented afresh nor drafted in from elsewhere: the Freedom Charter provided a resonant reference point. But these liberal visions have dissolved as organising principles, it is claimed and have yielded to a less accommodating 'ethno-nationalism'. The blame is customarily placed at Mbeki's door.

An eventual recourse towards a jingoist 'Africanism' cannot be ruled out, but the turn taken under Mbeki was not simply to a narrow chauvinism. It formed part of a more ambitious confrontation with the politics of identity and terms of belonging. It took the form of a discourse that updated the African nationalism of the late 1940s and early 1950s, establishing perimeters and conditions for inclusion that were not strictly racial, while at the same time pivoting on the interests and histories of the African majority. Grandly, it sought to align a model of inclusive nationalism to the exigencies of both a racially divided society and the global capitalist order. More than other South African politician in recent memory, Mbeki engaged the idea of being 'South African' not only from a political angle (as an aspect of stability), but from an ethical and philosophical vantage point.

During the 'Rainbow Nation' period of the mid-1990s, the terms of belonging had been undemanding. They proposed a cosmopolitan basis for post-apartheid South Africa, structured around the principle of 'live and let live'. In the abstract—and for many South Africans—this seems appealing. But it is unsatisfactory in a society with a history as brutal and jaundiced as this; a history that, in many ways, still constitutes the present and decides the future.

The 'Rainbow Nation' hinged on a double fiction: on the notion that existential history could be consigned to the past and that the acknowledgement that 'bad things happened' offered a sufficient basis for a viable, 'reconciled' and fraternal society. The Truth and Reconciliation Commission pushed this conceit to its limits, by not only acknowledging the horrors but (re)exposing and narrating them to society (Marais, 1998c). The problem with this is that 'bad things' did not only happen (in the past tense), *they happen still*. As a stabilising interlude, the obliging cosmopolitanism of the 'Rainbow Nation' made sense, but it lacked a normative content, hinging instead on an undemanding tautology: 'Here we are, we are here, therefore we are.'

Central to Mbeki's imagery was the proposition that 'we are who we strive to become'. And it demanded of white South Africans, in particular, a reckoning. They could not merely assert their belonging, nor could it arise from the mere fact of 'being here'; it had to be constituted through deeds. Moreover, he tried to lodge the idea of 'South African-ness' within a larger, enveloping conception of being 'African'.

Mbeki expounded this thinking most evocatively in his 1996 'I am an African' speech.[52] Being 'African', he contended, was not a category defined by race, colour or historical origins; the definition was open-ended. It meant, in Ivor Chipkin's (2007:102) close reading, 'being able to define for oneself who one is and who one should be'. In Mbeki's (1996) words: 'We are assembled here today to mark [our] victory in acquiring and exercising [our] right to formulate [our] own definition of what it means to be African.' In this vision, an African and a South African are *free* individuals. We build our belonging.

But at the same time, in Mbeki's exposition, these identities also require an understanding of colonial history and racist power. They emerge from the ability to recognise and to seek to release oneself from the restraints and imprints of history, to see oneself through liberated eyes. But they are also tied to particular, generic experiences; they attach not simply to individuals, but to *categories* of people. The vision, therefore, also revolves around an essentialist and determinate idea of 'being African' and 'being South African'. One's identity is then constituted by an active refusal of the 'white gaze'—an act which, paradoxically, also chains the identity to the target of resistance, defining it in terms of that which it rejects. Rather than an *outcome* of freedom, 'being African' and 'being South African' then stays entangled in a *quest* for freedom, which involves memorialising histories and asserting and valorising fixed, immanent attributes.

So at the core of Mbeki's vision of South African-ness stood this fundamental contradiction. On one hand it tilted toward pan-African notions of nationalism, the Negritude associated with Aimé Césaire and the masculine black consciousness of Steve Biko (Chipkin, 2007). On the other it was aligned with a logic that detached the nation from essentialisms of heritage, race and language, and it became an act of political will:

> In no way must I strive to bring back to life a Negro civilization that has been unfairly misrecognized. I will not make myself the man of any past. I do not want to sing the past at the expense of my present and my future [...] My black skin is not the repository of specific values (Fanon, cited in Chipkin, 2007:115).

This was a work-in-progress, full of inconsistencies and sometimes undermined by crude reflexes. Often, flat 'Africanist' chords would be struck, drowning out these other, more complex themes. But no other South African politician had ventured nearly as far into the fundamental question of who belongs and on what terms they do so. In the public arena, however, this contradictory but rich exploration became conflated with literal interventions such as affirmative action. Whites took loud affront at the insistence that the past required, if not a reckoning, at least acknowledgement and some form of active recompense. Potentially expansive parameters for citizenship were flattened into chauvinistic understandings of 'Africanism'. The question of what constitutes a 'South African' therefore remains unresolved. Post-Mbeki, the debate has been resumed, but in surreptitious ways and on conservative terms.

Sections of the left outside the Tripartite Alliance, meanwhile, nurse hopes that African nationalism has reached the end of its lifespan in South Africa, having already exhausted itself elsewhere on the continent. Some of the new social movements of the 2000s, for example, predicted an eventual break with a 'debased' nationalism that serviced the new elites, but bamboozled the masses:

> Mbeki and his main allies have already succumbed to the class (not necessarily personalistic) limitations of post-independence African nationalism, namely acting in close collaboration with hostile transnational corporate and multilateral forces whose interests stand directly opposed to Mbeki's South African and African constituencies (Bond, 2002:1).

The heritage of such claims is often traced to Frantz Fanon's *Wretched of the Earth* (1963) and its indictment of post-independence betrayals in Africa:

> During the struggle for liberation the leader awakened the people and promised them a forward march, heroic and unmitigated. Today, he uses every means to put them to sleep, and three or four times a year asks them to remember the colonial period and to look back on the long way they have come since then. Now it must be said that the masses show themselves totally incapable of appreciating the long way they have come. The peasant who goes on scratching a living from the soil, and the unemployed man who never finds employment do not manage, in spite of public holidays and flag, new and brightly coloured though they may be, to convince themselves that anything has really changed in their lives [...] The intellectuals who on the eve of independence rallied to the party, now make it clear by their attitude that they gave their support with no other end in view than to secure their slices of the cake of independence. The party is becoming a means of private advancement.[53]

But nationalism has far from run its course in post-apartheid South Africa. It retains great potency and potential, even if what Fanon called 'national consciousness' remains poorly developed. The versions of nationalism pushed into service until now have been largely genteel—embracing rather than estranging. Pursued in their place, on current evidence, will be more profane and resonant varieties of nationalism—ones inflected with racial and ethnic chauvinism, for example, or with narrow, exacting interpretations of culture and tradition, or with antipathy toward the 'alien luxuries' of liberal constitutionalism.

During its 'Zuma era', the ANC has flirted with such permutations and it may yet give rein to a few. The Mbeki camp was vanquished by a 'back-to-the-future' discourse that tapped deep into nationalist traditions and impulses—in ways that accommodate different variants and understandings of nationalism. Crucially, these variants are now seen in 'essentialist', fixed terms, not as evolving constructs. What is being sought is compatibility between them, not a new fusion. The left seems oblivious to these shifts. Rather than announce the death or decrepitude of nationalism, the left needs to engage it, contest its meanings and uses and transform its content into an emancipatory humanism.

When Jacob Zuma barbeques with prominent white Afrikaners (including, pointedly, the composer of a popular ode to Anglo-Boer War hero Jacobus de la Rey) or visits impoverished Afrikaner neighbourhoods, he is making more than a non-racial gesture. These are also statements about the compatibility (even the similarity) between ostensibly distinct nationalisms that are rooted in the same soil—and an expression of a resurgent, overhauled popular nationalism that draws links between different encounters with imperialism and colonialism. Zuma's confabs with Afrikaners are inclusive gestures, which, at the same time, are also cliquish and exclusionary. They are trapped in the paradox of all nationalisms: by constituting an 'us', they presuppose a 'them'. Affirmed in these instances is the old chestnut that Afrikaners and Africans, like it or not, are bound by a mutual, passionate attachment to the soil of a land called South Africa. That bond implies the presence, however, of others, whose loyalties run shallow and fickle. Nationalism's embrace is always potentially chauvinistic; it sanctions other possible interventions that cleave or banish on the basis of attributed characteristics.

The bonding and disciplinary force of African nationalism remains perhaps the cardinal ideological turnkey of South Africa's transition. It lays the basis for the overwhelming electoral victories of the ANC, can blanket fissures of discontent and situate policies and deeds in an idealised historical narrative. At its core is the declared goal of empowering and reclaiming the dignity of Africans. There are other important facets—including non-racialism and combating poverty—but they have secondary status. Socialist *inflections* are possible within the dominant discourse of African nationalism, but the larger ambitions of the ANC-aligned socialist left seem misplaced. In Freund's (2007a:171) appraisal,

> the failure to articulate a vision of a socialist South Africa beyond the words of the Freedom Charter from the 1950s was not merely a useful way of keeping the ANC united; it also blocked the possibility of such a vision attaining any reality beyond pious hopes.

Folded into that observation are towering challenges for the South African left—for shifting the balance of forces requires a much more thoughtful and delicate engagement with nationalism than the left typically seems willing to muster. In Gillian Hart's (2007:16) summary,

> [T]he ANC government's embrace of GEAR constitutes a re-articulation of race and class that is also very much part of an activist project of rule. Elements of this project include the consolidation of conservative forces working in alliance with white corporate capital to create a black bourgeoisie nominally more responsive to

'development'; creating the conditions in which the coalition in control of the state can hold not only its agencies but also non-state bodies to its principles; and inciting not only the black bourgeoisie but the population more generally to embrace freedom and democracy by becoming 'entrepreneurs themselves'.

There are huge risks in such undertakings. The ANC's mystique and appeal derives not only from its struggle pedigree, but from the 'redemptive vision of liberation' (Gevisser, 2007:655) it blazons and the radical postures it affects. Hence the demonstrative use of Marxist-Leninist clichés (often in defence of policies that postpone, even undermine, social justice[54]) and the melange of neoliberal tropes and African-nationalist liberation ideology, a discourse aimed at reconciling idealism and expediency. The discourse of national liberation and its Holy Grail of deliverance also vitalise fearsome demands on the ANC and the state. It is a narrative with whip in its tail. Held centre-stage, national liberation therefore is both 'the lynchpin of ... hegemonic power and a key source of vulnerability' (Hart, 2007:21). It affirms the pre-eminence of the ANC as the custodian of transformation, but it also renders it vulnerable to charges of betrayal.

Policing the borders

These struggles over authenticity and belonging (and the *terms* of belonging) exploded into the open in the most unforgiving ways in early 2008. Sporadic attacks against foreigners had been occurring since the mid-1990s. But in April and May 2008, community after community turned on foreigners in their midst, killing 62 people, injuring hundreds more and driving tens of thousands from their homes.[55] The targets were people from elsewhere in Africa and, to a small degree, south Asia. Months later, thousands of refugees, migrants and immigrants were still stranded in makeshift camps and shelters, too fearful to return to their homes.

The pogroms occurred almost exclusively on urban peripheries, in informal settlements and in zones of intense 'informal' trading—in other words, settings where scarcity and intense competition converge. All these areas had high concentrations of foreigners, were largely 'out of bounds' for the police and poorly integrated into local governance systems and had weak political structures. To borrow a phrase from the 1980s, these are the domains of 'surplus peoples' somehow assembling livelihoods beyond the circuits of the formal system and in them, perforce, a 'do-it-yourself' sensibility prevails. The structures and processes of the formal system tend to shun or neglect these zones: demands are ignored, needs are misunderstood and grievances accumulate, creating a churn of insecurity and resentment.

The immediate pretexts for the attacks involved grievances about jobs and housing.[56] The attacks were, to some extent, organised, but there is no evidence that they were orchestrated. In most cases, they were preceded by small and makeshift meetings, which proved sufficient to assemble the mobs and spark the rampages. The mobilisers differed from place to place. Hostel dwellers reportedly played a role in many of the attacks in and around Johannesburg, while rival small traders took an active hand elsewhere, as did motley groups of young men apparently keen on fashioning opportunities for looting. But large numbers of residents (men and women) participated in the attacks, which often followed planning meetings organised by local leaders (Misago *et al*, 2010).[57]

A groundswell of hostility against migrants and refugees from elsewhere in Africa and Asia had already become evident by the mid-1990s, when the South African Catholic Bishops' Conference was moved to speak out against xenophobia. In a national survey in 1998, the Southern African Migration Project (SAMP) found that one quarter of South Africans wanted all migration and immigration halted, almost half supported strict limits on immigration and one fifth wanted to see all foreigners deported. A year later, migrants and immigrants were targeted in a series of attacks in Alexandra, in the north of Johannesburg. As transformation proceeded at a shuffle and more migrants and refugees entered the country, the sense of cramped insecurity grew. By 2006, in another SAMP survey, two-thirds of the respondents said foreigners were using up 'their' resources and half accused them of introducing diseases such as AIDS into the country. When quizzed in successive 'Social Attitudes Surveys', the percentage of South Africans saying no foreigners were welcome in the country rose from 33% to 47% between 2003 and 2007 (HSRC, 2007).

The harassment, extortion and exploitation of refugees, migrants and immigrant workers had become institutionalised. Routinely rounded up and shaken down, their coerced bribes supplemented the earnings of thousands of grasping 'public servants' in police stations, Home Affairs offices and beyond. Media reports and anecdotal tales had reinforced caricatures of African migrants as conmen, criminals and 'chancers' and of their Asian peers as gougers and exploiters. This routine denigration of foreigners legitimised their status as 'deserving' targets of outrage and expropriation.

What is uncomfortably 'South African' about these episodes is how similar the discourse of xenophobia is to that of apartheid (difference, separation, expulsion) and how closely the slurs picturing persons from elsewhere in Africa as 'lazy', 'thieving' and 'disease-carrying' match the staples of white racism. A society rotted with bigotry and humiliation had found a target for a chauvinism that seems to span cleavages of race and class. There is more at stake here than scapegoating, though.

The tendency toward introversion, parochialism and enclosure is a hallmark of our times—and of the destabilising aspects of globalisation. Its flows of goods, cultures, ideas and people occur alongside burgeoning uncertainty and insecurity. Emphatic claims of authenticity and entitlement are a typical response, with anxiety usually displaced onto victimised, proximate and, oddly, familiar sections of society (Appadurai, 2006). By targeting and devalorising the 'other', the attackers were asserting a particular claim about 'us', about who has rights and entitlements in South Africa and who therefore can make legitimate claims on the state. They were expressing notions of belonging and citizenship that sit comfortably within a pinched and sour nationalism.

These boundaries of inclusion and exclusion usually coincide with the geopolitical frontiers that separate nation-states. But the pogroms also targeted people deemed

Shangaan, Pedi or Venda (in fact, almost one in four persons killed were South African citizens)—a reminder that these margins are as easily drawn along lines of ethnicity, language, religion or race.

Much was made of the eruption of sympathy and cross-sectional mobilisation that answered the pogroms—and justifiably so. But the goodwill and effort of churches, the Treatment Action Campaign, community activists, some ANC branches and lone councillors could not hide other, less appealing patterns. Almost as shocking as the pogroms themselves was the initial inertia of the central government (and ANC leadership) and the paranoia and conspiracy-mongering that informed its pronouncements.[58] In some places, attacks were quickly halted, even prevented, by local councillors and community structures. But in too many, local political structures seemed clueless and out of touch. And the threadbare status of imbedded civil society in communities that are poor became even more glaring.

The pogroms therefore were an episode—an engagement—in the larger, unresolved business of nation-building, of assembling a particular myth of 'South African-ness'. In a society forged in a cauldron of outrageous discrimination, they will not be an isolated outrage. The pogroms were not an aberration, a fickle blip in South Africa's jaunt toward better times. They spoke unpleasant truths about South African society and about the flimsy basis on which the post-apartheid transition has been built.

Pandora's box

There is within the ANC a view of the movement as the embodiment of transcendent ideals. As a political entity, the ANC is seen to function as a kind of secular vessel for destiny itself, which, for most ANC supporters, probably resembles a form of Afro-nationalist liberation, while for a minority it extends deeper toward some hybrid of national liberation and socialism. Fundamentally, it means that the ANC exceeds the individuals and structures that constitute it: 'Criticise us as individuals, not the ANC as an organisation of the people', as Zuma told a prayer service in early 2007.[59] The religious overtones are glaring and were underlined a year later when Zuma addressed an ANC rally in Khayelitsha, Cape Town:

> God expects us to rule this country because we are the only organisation which was blessed by pastors when it was formed. It is even blessed in Heaven. That is why we will rule until Jesus comes back.[60]

This is more than idle hyperbole. A conception that invests a political organisation with such mystic authority sits uncomfortably in a political system that pivots on a Constitution and Bill of Rights and that demands the separation of party and state. In effect, the political system contains two potentially conflicting sources of authority. The one—the national liberation movement—is hailed as a distillation of the aspirations and ideals and the struggles and sacrifices of the African majority. The other—the Constitution—is seen as an intellectual construct, rooted in the European Enlightenment. Their respective normative content overlaps substantially, but there are also considerable points of (potential) friction.

423

As the ANC struggles to reinforce its authority and sway in the years ahead, it will be tempted to exploit at least some of those abrasive aspects. It is notable that one of the Zuma camp's biggest gripes against Mbeki involved the filters and barriers he maintained between the 'movement' and the state. Mbeki's motive was a mix of tactical pragmatism and principle, but the effect was to bolster the structural logic of the post-apartheid political system. Under Zuma, the commitment to that division seems to have relaxed—to the point where one of his ministers, bizarrely, could criticise an institutional arrangement in which government 'was stronger than the party, so government was accountable to itself, there was no oversight'.[61]

The signs are not encouraging. None of these struggles—around the Constitution, individual rights, social citizenship or the terms of belonging—have been settled. But there are strong hints of a drift away from the constitutionalism that has helped anchor and distinguish South Africa's transition. At least as troubling is the organised left's sanguine response. When, at the height of the Mbeki-Zuma struggle, COSATU and the SACP attacked the judiciary with such relish, they were not simply condemning the apartheid era hangovers in its ranks, but also acting out a crude notion of the law as a mere instrument of power (very different from recognising that the law is *inflected* with power).[62] Misgivings about the progressive role of the Constitution and the courts circulate also among some of the new social movements, which have watched government effectively disregard several watershed judgements handed down by the Constitutional Court. The 2000 Grootboom case, for instance, was hailed as a landmark affirmation of socioeconomic rights, when the Constitutional Court ruled that government had to provide suitable alternative accommodation to people evicted from their homes. Eight years later, though, the housing activist who had spearheaded the case, Irene Grootboom, died in a shack.[63] A palpable sense of 'hollow rights' and a 'paper Constitution' is emerging and it potentially gives licence to populist experiments that trade heavily on notions of tradition and culture.

Wittingly or not, the Zuma campaign stoked tensions between a back-to-basics populism and rights-based, constitutional democracy. Among the central refrains, for instance, was the claim that he was more open to discussion and debate and therefore was more of a democrat than Mbeki. Equating discussion with democracy is a risky move, since it encourages the claim that public opinion (or the 'will of the people') is, in the final instance, decisive. But, were that the case, 'there would be no need for constitutional adjudication', as former Chief Justice Arthur Chaskalson has pointed out[64] and the rights-based foundation of post-apartheid South Africa would crumble. South Africa has entered a murky period where popular sentiment potentially trumps at least some of the liberal and progressive values inscribed in the Constitution.[65]

Reinventing authority, rebuilding power

What the ANC is struggling to pre-empt is a crisis of authority, a general crisis of the state in which all sorts of fundamental propositions about constitutional, social, moral and economic issues explode into an uproar of polemics. It is at that point that the centre finally gives. The ANC has to repair (perhaps even construct) a normative framework that can calm these mordant energies. Doing so requires a set of propositions that resonate, that exude an authenticity for 'ordinary' South Africans.

Thatcherism in Britain tapped into the disorientation, insecurities and disquiet of 'ordinary' Britons and their aspirations and hopes, and addressed itself to the various 'collective fantasies' that dominated the public imaginary (Hall, 1987:19). These 'fantasies' are not a given, nor are they fabricated anew; they are modelled and elaborated from heartfelt sentiments and sensibilities and are then fashioned into new, unifying shapes. Our identities—'who we are' and who we 'belong with'; our cultural, sexual and family lives; our ethnic, linguistic and other allegiances; our moral maps—are deeply politicised and brim with contradictions. If it is to be successful, a political project has to engage, modulate and connect them into a practical politics. In the early twenty-first century, this is the *central* task confronting the ANC and the state, for the state remains crucial for 'articulating the different areas of contestation, the different points of antagonism, into a regime of rule' (Hall, 1987:20). Notions of custom and tradition will feature prominently in that endeavour. Already they are being stitched into more literal frameworks of authority and power.

The powers invested in traditional authorities in the 2000s are an important aspect of this shift. They mark a conscious attempt by the ANC to extend and strengthen its authority via traditional leaders. At the forefront is a trio of legislative interventions: the Communal Land Rights Act (2004), the Traditional Leadership and Governance Framework (2003) and the Traditional Courts Bill (2008).

Traditional authorities pushed hard after 1994 for greater authority over land and other aspects of people's lives. This encountered strong opposition among top cadres in the ANC, who still regarded culture and custom with distaste as tools of colonial rule (Comaroff & Comaroff, 2005). But in the 2000s, the duality of 'citizen and subject' (Mamdani, 1996) acquired a new lease of life. The authority of traditional councils over land was extended, undercutting the long-held claims of many families, individuals and other groupings. In some cases, villagers were placed under the authority of traditional leaders with whom they had no historical links. Many of the boundaries of tribal authorities enforced were, in fact, established by the apartheid state and involved the displacement and forced removal of people (Peters, 2009). Similarly, the Traditional Courts Bill would operate on a template established under apartheid—specifically the tribal authorities created by the Bantu Authorities Act of 1951 (and which became key building blocks of the Bantustan system).[66]

It is generally accepted that customary courts are potentially valuable institutions that can link millions of South Africans with access to more affordable and accessible forms of justice than the formal court system.[67] But the Traditional Courts Bill would override many customary dispute-resolution processes and sidelines community councils. Proposed in their place is an authoritarian and centralised system that vests great powers directly with 'senior traditional leaders'. Bestowed upon traditional leaders would be the right to order any 'subject' stripped of customary entitlements or even community membership.[68]

According to researcher Aninka Claassens, the Bill

provides traditional leaders with the unilateral power to create and enforce customary law within the bounded jurisdictional areas it confirms. Instead of focusing on what unites people, it reinforces the constructs of ethnic difference and insider-outsider status ... [and] undermines the consensual character of customary law.[69]

Traditional leaders were the only rural constituency consulted in the drafting of the Bill—an odd 'oversight', given that the Bill also undermines one of the resolutions the ANC adopted at its 2007 Polokwane conference.[70] There is a manifest gender bias in this Bill and the other two Acts, which authorise 'increasing discrimination [against women] under the growing authoritarian control of traditional leaders and of male family elders, all in the name of "custom"' (Claassens & Cousins, 2008:164).

At work is a potent interplay of political expediency, patronage and accumulation. Senior figures in the ANC hope to use such concessions to assemble alliances through which the organisation's authority can be projected and cemented in rural areas. Already, the state finances traditional leaders and royal families to the tune of R 140 million (USD 18.5 million) a year.[71] The statutory interventions have also widened opportunities for accumulation. The Communal Land Rights Act, for example, has facilitated land-grabs by traditional leaders. Several communities have brought court challenges accusing chiefs of seizing or subjecting communal land to commercial deals with outside investors (Claassens & Cousins, 2008). The Department of Land Reform and Rural Development has been hoping that such latitude might unlock the economic potential of rural areas by providing investors and some residents with bankable tenure. In late 2009, a High Court declared 14 sections of the Communal Land Rights Act unconstitutional, forcing legislators back to the drawing board.[72] It will take more than court verdicts to defuse this reanimation of conservative, anti-democratic 'traditional' authority over the lives and livelihoods of citizens.

Under Zuma, the ANC and the state seems to be dabbling with a normative framework for belonging that would be both more conservative and more permissive than those that marked the Mandela and Mbeki eras. Such an approach would combine social conservatism (invested with essentialist notions of culture, tradition and values) with licence for acquisitiveness and immoderation[73] and potentially generate a tide of populist nationalism.

A possible prototype has proved to be unexpectedly productive in the hands of ANC Youth League and its leader, Julius Malema, who in the early part of the Zuma presidency commanded disproportionate public attention and, it seemed, political sway. Skilled at both the flamboyant smear and troglodyte slur, and keyed into the normative grammar of lumpen radicalism, Malema's populism might be a taste of things to come. Certainly, the ANC leadership seemed happy to capitalise on his lurid political performances, as he broadcast sentiments that played well, but which would have been considered too risqué or uncouth if uttered by his political elders. Zuma praised him as 'a good leader' who 'understands the people', and anointed him as 'a leader in the making':

Some of us are no longer young and when we go across the mountain in terms of age, we are happy that when we go on the organization will remain in the hands of [those] who will think of the people.[74]

Zuma's flattery was partly earnest and partly recognition that Malema could represent a potent template, capable of combining barefaced accumulation with radical posturing and populist savvy. Smartly positioned in an extensive patronage network, Malema, according to journalist Jacob Dlamini, was a 'true political don and one of the biggest influence-peddlers' in the country.[75] The ANC hierarchy in early 2010 was already discovering that his ambitions and means outstripped the flashy but auxiliary role in which they preferred him. The impressions of journalist Tim Cohen, after going toe-to-toe with Malema in a public debate, were telling:

He was just masterful. He had the sense of poise and instant likability of a great speaker, combined with the feel for where the audience is that makes for the best kind of stand-up comic [...] His speech may have been filled with inaccuracies, misinterpretations and the conflation of facts and events. Yet his balance was spot-on; he didn't speak down nor up to his audience [...] Is the ANC transforming itself into a Peronist movement, I wondered; that confused mix of nationalistic capitalism and socialistic populism? It's possible.[76]

That reading may seem unduly despondent. But, the Alliance left's buoyant hopes notwithstanding, the ANC's most pronounced drift, post-Mbeki, has been in a conservative direction. It has showed its willingness to revisit key beacons of social progressivism, the powers of traditional leaders are being augmented, the fears and insecurities of citizens are being exploited and the status of the Constitution as the foundation of the post-apartheid order is unsure.

The ANC's ethnical moorings are doddery and its political character increasingly indeterminate. Ideologically, too, it is increasingly indistinct. Rather than acting as a coherent and cohesive organisation it now functions as a field, a zone in which motley interests and ambitions (including progressive ones) can be pursued. This places an even greater premium on retaining power—not for any single goal, but in order to facilitate the pursuit of disparate objectives. It can no longer credibly claim to be the custodian and manager of a coherent 'liberation project', which is why it has to broadcast that claim ever louder and in new ways. This formlessness forces it to invoke claims of authenticity that can position it more firmly within the narrative of national liberation.

The ANC's central biggest problem is how to reproduce and retain consent in an economy which structurally is incapable of providing jobs on remotely the scale and quality required, where public service is proving elusive, inequality is widening, precariousness and misery is routine and a palpable sense of unfairness is rampant. Power and consent can then only nominally depend on material change, forcing greater recourse to ideology, to the language and symbols of the liberation struggle and to rousing affirmations about entitlement and belonging. In a society this unequal and unjust, there is a serious risk that chauvinist, exclusionary notions of belonging, citizenship and rights will prove politically rewarding. Figures such as Malema therefore are not to be understood in literal terms. They *represent* one possible manner of reproducing power and consent in these circumstances. In the person of Malema, South Africans have been introduced to an idea, a construct which significant sections of the ANC believe offers a way forward out of the impasse in which the the organisation finds itself.

Endnotes

1   For example, in 1989, months before the Berlin Wall fell, the SACP adopted a new programme, 'The Path to Power', in which it still positioned insurrectionary action as the key strategic route forward.

2   The concept of hegemony used here corresponds to that found in Antonio Gramsci's later writings where it 'applied to the strategies of *all* classes' and 'to the formation of all leading historical blocs, not the strategy of the proletariat alone', in Stuart Hall's phrasing (1996:425).

3   Gramsci used the term 'political society' for the coercive capacities and relations that defined various institutions of the state—the military, police, judicial and penal system, as well as the tax collection, social security, finance and trade and industry—all of which rely in the final instance on the state's coercive powers. Crucially, the state cannot be reduced simply to its monopoly on coercion; it also plays vital educative and formative roles. 'Political society' therefore is not the same as the 'state', but refers only to 'coercive relations embodied in the state apparatuses' (Simon, 1991:71).

4   As Gramsci (1971:238) famously remarked, 'when the state trembled a sturdy structure of civil society was at once revealed'.

5   Distinct from a power bloc which describes only the moment of force and coercion.

6   This is why Gramsci preferred the word 'moment' to the word 'victory', which suggests a definitive triumph. Once achieved, hegemony has to be positively sustained. Even then, as Hall reminds, 'this extraordinary degree of organic unity does not guarantee the outcome of specific struggles' (1996:423).

7   Corruption in state structures typically earns the headlines, but there is every reason to assume that corruption is at least as rife in the private sector. Private-sector corruption also drains confidence in the state, given the prevalence of public-private partnerships and contracting-out by the state.

8   Stuart Hall quoting Gramsci (1971:182).

9   Recall, as well, that South Africa reached this phase well after the post-war tide of national liberation had ebbed, as leftist anti-imperial struggles were running out of steam (the FMLN vanquished in El Salvador, and the Sandinistas defeated in Nicaragua, for example) and as the key benefactor of these struggles (the Soviet Union) withdrew from many of the geopolitical chess games of the Cold War. This was hardly a time of boundless opportunities for leftist advance.

10 The August 1987 miners' strike, in hindsight, was a classic example of overreach. The National Union of Mineworkers' (NUM) demands were ambitious and reflected the heady expectancy of the day (the ANC had declared 1987 'the year of advance to people's power'). Some 250 000 miners walked off the job. Mining corporations' financial losses were eye-watering, but they approached the strike as an endgame. By week three, they had sacked 40 000 miners and NUM sued for peace. It won reinstatement of the dismissed workers and some other concessions, but its wage demands lay trampled. Padraig O'Malley (2007:242) called the strike 'a shot across the bow' of the system, but misses the way in which mining corporations exploited it as a chance to restructure their labour forces. A little more than a decade later, half the mining work-force had lost their jobs (Wilson, 2001).

11 It is useful to recall another trend that became evident after 1994: a steep drop in party membership, especially among African voters, only about 10% of whom belonged to the

political party in 1999 (according to a HSRC poll), compared with 24% in 1994. See 'Mass fall-off in African party political activity', *SouthScan*, Vol. 15, No. 4, 25 February 2000.

12 For Gramsci, the archetypal 'passive revolution' was the Italian *Risorgimento*, which led to the unification of Italy in the nineteenth century and established the ascendancy of the bourgeoisie in that country. Driving unification was the monarchy and army of the independent state of Piedmont. Rather than side with the struggles of peasants, the Moderate Party (representing the emerging bourgeoisie of northern Italy) forged an alliance with southern landowners and helped to achieve a 'revolution from above'.

13 During the course of the 1990s, the national democratic revolution was virtually emptied of substance. As Ivor Chipkin (2007:108) outlined, it no longer pinpointed capitalism as the cause of poverty but a particular, 'skewed' version of that system. And the driving force of the revolution would no longer be the working classes, but the state allied with an enlightened 'black bourgeoisie' and a harnessed capitalist class in general. For another trenchant critique of the concept, see Alexander (2010).

14 This was heavily inspired by the writings of French strategist Andre Beaufre, the former commander of French forces in Algeria. According to Frankel's book *Pretoria's Praetorians* (1984:46), the 'total strategy' was 'essentially Beaufre writ large in the particular counter-revolutionary context of South Africa' (cited in O'Meara, 1996:259).

15 Though not entirely cleansed, of course. Former Mbeki supporters who had stayed on in the ANC would provide convenient targets for ongoing rebuke and blame.

16 Kevin Davie writing in *Business Times* [Johannesburg], 9 October 1994.

17 Former 'RDP Minister', Jay Naidoo, quoted in the *Cape Times*, 4 July 1994.

18 Remarkably, Mbeki would also lament the lack of substantive debate in South Africa: 'I worry about the level of debate in the country. Truly, what I feel has happened is that the ending of apartheid government, and therefore the removal from our national agenda of a matter that had persisted for a very long time, has exposed a lack of depth in many people's thinking about the new challenges that face us. That worries me.' See 'Face to face with the president', *Sunday Times* [Johannesburg], 6 February 2000.

19 Richard Calland (2006:143) quotes an 'ANC leader' admitting: 'Thank god for the communists. Without them we would fall apart. They work hard and are very committed.'

20 'Mbeki champions poor against black and white elites', *SouthScan*, Vol. 13, No. 12, 12 June 1998.

21 It also fits comfortably in the SACP's Colonialism of a Special Type thesis. Consider this assertion from the SACPs 1962 Programme: 'The special character of colonialism in South Africa, the seizing by Whites of all the opportunities which in other colonial countries have led to growth of a national capitalist class, have strangled the development of a class of African capitalists [...] The interests of the African commercial class lie wholly in joining the workers and rural people for the overthrow of White supremacy.' See various authors (1970:135).

22 A great deal of this power is concentrated in the ANC's 'deployment committee' which operates under the aegis of the ANC's national working committee and functions as a powerful lever for patronage and discipline. Its deployment decisions allow the organisation to extend its (disciplinary) reach into top tiers of the state (including nominally 'independent' statutory bodies) and into pockets of civil society. The criteria for those decisions are flexible enough to disguise the actual motives for decisions, which can be explained in terms of a need to achieve a balance in terms of gender, racial, ethnic and even internal/exile representation.

23 *Sunday Times* [Johannesburg], 26 July 2009.

24 The terms of those contracts were adapted to the results-oriented and performance-based principles of managerialism. For a critical review of the 'new managerialist' approach in South Africa, see Paine (1999:44–51).

25 Howard Barrell and Barry Streek, 'The hidden face of government', *Mail & Guardian*, 12 November 1999. Instead of line-function ministers submitting draft policies directly to the Cabinet, the drafts went to the PCAS, which then advised the presidency on their feasibility and desirability. Once the president's office approved the draft, it was put before Cabinet. The advantage was that experts could detect flaws and inconsistencies in new policies and draft

legislation before they went to Cabinet. Unlike Cabinet ministers, the chief directors of the advisory unit were not accountable to Parliament and no portfolio committee could summon them to explain decisions; they reported to the president. For detailed descriptions of the overhaul of the presidency, see Calland (2006:22–41).

26 His note-taking was so accurate that, after he had leaked the notes to the *Mail & Guardian*, the meeting room was swept for eavesdropping bugs; see Feinstein (2007:125–8).

27 This section draws on work done for the Centre for the Study of AIDS, at the University of Pretoria.

28 Medical science generally was an important adjunct of colonial projects, especially after the rise of bacteriology, which made possible the development of relatively effective drugs and treatments for many afflictions encountered in Africa, Asia and the Americas. England's London School of Hygiene and Tropical Medicine and France's Pasteur Institute were particularly active on those fronts.

29 For an incisive review, see the essays collected in *South African Historical Journal*, No. 45 (2001), pp. 1–190.

30 See Thabo Mbeki, 'Dislodging stereotypes' (Letter from the President), ANC Today, 4(42), 22–8, October 2004. Mbeki was reacting in Parliament to a question from an opposition Democratic Alliance politician about HIV and the role of rape in the epidemic. The response, which runs to three pages of text, makes only cursory reference to HIV and to rape—the latter euphemised as a 'contact crime', a clinical choice of language that contrasted with the impassioned declamations about racism. There was a hint here of one of the overlooked hallmarks of South African 'denialism'—the overbearing male-ness of a discourse that is typically silent about gender injustices and inequality, and their role in the epidemic. At its core, this is a discourse by men about men, with women a shadowed presence. Lisa Vetten's remarks about Mbeki's statements on rape seem apt here: '[I]n repeatedly and exclusively confining the debate to African men, Mbeki is deflecting attention away from the sexual predatoriness [sic] of men generally, regardless of colour [...] not once in these debates have the words "gender inequality" appeared in the President's writings or utterances [...] No *onus* is placed on South African men generally to examine and change their unequal relations with women.' See Lisa Vetten, 'Mbeki and Smith both got it wrong', *Mail & Guardian*, 29 October 2004.

31 Some South African periodicals ran articles to this effect—as *Drum* magazine, for example, did in 1991; see Walker *et al* (2004).

32 Mzala (1988) 'AIDS—Misinformation and racism', *Sechaba*, October, and (1988) 'AIDS and the imperialist connection', *Sechaba*, November; both cited in Gevisser (2007:731). Many of the AIDS conspiracy theories seem only a little less exotic than those concocted by 'scientists' during the fourteenth century Plague. Academics at the medical faculty of the University of Paris, for example, acting under orders from the monarchy, contrived a meticulous astrological explanation for the Black Death: 'With a careful thesis, antithesis, and proofs', Barbara Tuchman (1978) wrote, they 'ascribed it to a triple conjunction of Saturn, Jupiter, and Mars in the 40th degree of Aquarius said to have occurred on 20 March 1345'. Intricate conspiracy theories were spun, fed with false confessions obtained under torture. The eye of suspicion fell on lepers and other social outcasts, but settled most firmly on Jews and to tragic effect. Pogroms swept across Western Europe; more than 350 massacres of Jews were recorded during the Black Death. 'As ever,' as Andrew Rissik (2005) observes, 'what matters wasn't what was true, but what seemed at the time to make wider sense.' And so it has been with AIDS, too.

33 Electronic versions of the document reportedly bore an embedded signature which suggested that they were written on Mbeki's computer. See Howard Barrell, 'Would the real AIDS dissident please declare himself', *Mail & Guardian*, 19 April 2002. According to the Mark Gevisser, Mbeki had an updated version of the screed delivered to him in August 2006: 'Some of the new language in the document was stronger than ever,' Gevisser noticed (2007:736).

34 By some accounts the *rinderpest* had a hand in changing social attitudes and behaviour, especially of young women. By denuding the social and material capital that cattle represented, the disease shifted social relations. For many, *lobola* or bridewealth became unaffordable and this released some women from the regimented strictures of the prevailing social order. Elders complained of rising promiscuity among women, which some feared would prolong the epidemic. A romanticised past of purity, discipline and obedience was ruptured. Noteworthy, too, was the prophet Nontetha Nkwenkwe's claim that the epidemic was divine punishment for sexual promiscuity and debauchery (Carton, 2003). There were many later examples where public-health measures seemed indistinguishable from other efforts to extend the control of the colonial (or apartheid) state over black South Africans, including the 'de-verminisation' campaigns in Durban and the clearly discriminatory quarantining operations during an outbreak of the plague. See Youde (2005) and Carton (2003).

35 The analogy was not lost on Mbeki who, in 2000, reportedly railed against South Africans being used as 'guinea pigs' for dangerous antiretroviral drugs which he likened to 'biological warfare of the apartheid era'. He was referring to the provision of the drugs in the Western Cape, at that stage governed by the Democratic Alliance. AIDS 'denialism' featured routinely also as a party political tool, at all ends of the spectrum. Mbeki's remarks in this case were made shortly before the municipal elections. See Drew Forrest, 'Behind the smokescreen: The record reveals President Thabo Mbeki's true stance on AIDS', *Mail & Guardian*, 26 October 2000.

36 Reflecting on his experiences as president of the Medical Research Council, Dr Malegapuru Makgoba in 2002 suggested as much: 'The politicization of scientific research, trying to do research according to political ideology and along party political lines, and trying to manage, recruit and appoint staff along these lines have never worked successfully anywhere where excellent science is being done. This approach has been a death knell to science [...] Innocuous as it may currently appear, the long-term effects of this are devastating and will take too long to rectify. I think it is therefore critical that we nip this pernicious problem in the bud early on. These are the challenges I faced and resisted and will resist for as long as I live. We should always remember what Lysenko did to Soviet science and the future generation of Soviet scientists.' See 'Dr Makgoba—a passion for excellence', *MRC News*, August 2002, Vol. 33, No. 4, p. 6. For a caustic summary of the Bush administration's conduct, see Mooney, C (2005) *The Republican War on Science*, Basic Books, New York.

37 By denouncing racism and (neo)colonialism, affirming Africans' right and duty to describe their own realities and define their own futures, rejecting the imageries of Africa conjured by the West, denialism also operated in the wider orbit of a putative 'African Renaissance'.

38 That ill-fated experiment, however, was not Mbeki's brainchild (as discussed above).

39 Shiceka was Minister of Co-operative Governance and Traditional Affairs. See Maureen Isaacson, 'Turnaround minister is custom-made', *Sunday Independent* [Johannesburg], 2 August 2009.

40 Quoted in Timoty Trengrove-Jones, 'Zuma hits dark notes as he catches popular mood', *Business Day*, 12 March 2008. Apparently referring to the death penalty, Zuma said: 'If people are saying we need to relook this matter and they are saying we want a referendum, I don't think we can't have a referendum'.

41 Graeme Hosken and Sapa, 'Police have no time to fire warning shots', *Independent Online News*, 30 September 2009. Government has amended Section 49 of the Criminal Procedure Act, which determines when police may use deadly force in the apprehension of a suspected criminal. It was also considering altering provisions on a person's right to remain silent and changing the definition of a suspect.

42 In 2009 there were several instances where police shot and killed unarmed civilians, not all of them criminal suspects. Typically, the police officer would claim that the deceased had appeared to brandish a weapon or had appeared to pose a threat. Government has been unapologetic, saying it was inevitable that innocent bystanders would be killed in the crossfire of a 'war against crime'. See Wyndham Hartley, 'Mbalula says civilian deaths are "unavoidable"', *Business Day*, 13 November 2009.

43 Emsie Ferreira, '"Shoot the bastards", Mbalula says of criminals', *Mail & Guardian*, 12 November 2009.

44 See Wyndham Hartley, 'Mbalula says civilian deaths are "unavoidable"', *Business Day*, 13 November 2009.

45 Wyndham Hartley, 'Big rise in number of deaths at hands of police, says watchdog', *Business Day*, 24 June 2009.

46 Jean Redpath, 'Why getting bail is harder than one might think', *Business Day*, 21 April 2008. Her article summarised a research report produced by the Open Society Foundation.

47 The US is the most enthusiastic incarcerator, with 686 prisoners per 100 000 population in 2003. The data are from the International Centre for Prison Studies.

48 Sumayya Ismail, 'Mixed reaction to Zuma apology', *Mail & Guardian*, 28 September 2006. Zuma was forced to apologise for the remarks, an indication that a rightward drift will not pass unchallenged.

49 Thabo Mkhize, Dominic Mahlangu, Nkululeko Ncana, 'Zuma wows huge crowd as Lekota prepares to launch new party', *The Times* [Johannesburg], 3 November 2008.

50 In mid-2009 an elite group of religious figures, the National Interfaith Leadership Council, with close ties to the ANC, said it would target legalised abortions and same-sex marriages. At least four of the group's members are ANC MPs, including ANC chief whip Mathole Motshekga and former Western Cape premier Ebrahim Rasool. See Mandy Rossouw, 'Zuma's new God squad wants liberal laws to go', *Mail & Guardian*, 11 September 2009.

51 They also spawn a paradox. The insecurity and frustration shaping daily life is seen as linked to the state's apparent failure to protect and provide for citizens. Yet, the state, if savvy enough, can sometimes invert those sentiments in its favour and harvest (for the time being) even greater legitimacy.

52 Full text available at: http://www.soweto.co.za/html/i_iamafrican.htm

53 Cited in Hart (2007).

54 The compatibility between Marxist-Leninist schooling and neoliberal practice has been noticed often. As Slavoj Zizek states, 'Indeed one could argue that, when the Communist regimes collapsed, the disillusioned former Communists were better suited to run the new capitalist economy than the populist dissidents [...] the ex-Communists were able without difficulty to accommodate themselves to the new capitalist rules.' See Slavoj Zizek, 'Post-wall', *London Review of Books*, 19 November 2009, p. 10.

55 The attacks began in Alexandra and then spread to other areas in and around Johannesburg. Violence in Kwazulu-Natal, Mpumalanga and Cape Town soon followed (Hadland, 2009).

56 Blaming crime on foreigners is a pastime in every society. Similarly, foreigners are also routinely accused of 'stealing jobs' and 'stealing' women from South African men. Foreigners are also accused of swamping scarce rental housing or illegally buying their way into occupancy. Ignorance or misunderstanding feeds some of these claims. Often occupancy is based on legitimate ownership by permanent residents or on subletting. In fact, the 'emergency' and 'upgrading' sections of current housing policy do not discriminate against foreigners—although the 'subsidy' system does exclude them. For examples of these perceptions and complaints, see Thembelihle Tshabalala and Monako Dibetle, 'Inside the mob', *Mail & Guardian*, 22 May 2008.

57 A careful study of the attacks in Alexandra reported that local leaders' role was not only limited to the planning of the violence; they led and were actively involved in carrying out the attacks. The members of the [study's] men's focus group were surprised when asked what leaders had done to stop the violence. One answered: 'No, you are missing the point. Leaders were with us at all times. They directed us on where to go and when.' (Misago *et al*, 2010).

58 A common claim was that a mysterious 'third force' orchestrated the attacks. The ANC's Gauteng spokesperson, for instance, insisted that a 'hidden hand' was involved, while the provincial community safety ministry claimed it had 'concrete evidence' of 'third force' involvement. The evidence was never produced. See 'Another night of terror in Gauteng', *Mail & Guardian*, 20 May 2008.

59 'ANC must return to God: pastor', *The Citizen*, 5 February 2007.
60 'ANC to rule until Jesus comes back', *Cape Times*, 5 May 2008. He had aired the same theme before; see 'ANC will rule SA until Jesus comes back, says Zuma', *Business Day*, 15 March 2004; and 'Zuma: ANC could rule forever', South African Press Association, 28 October 2007.
61 Minister of Co-Operative Governance and Traditional Affairs, Sicelo Shiceka, quoted in Maureen Isaacson, 'Turnaround minister is custom-made', *Sunday Independent* [Johannesburg], 2 August 2009.
62 The manner of the SACP and COSATU's support for Zuma roundly compromised their stances on several key issues. As Richard Calland (2006:155) points out, by setting up a legal support fund for Zuma, they 'undermined the credibility of their anti-corruption stance'. In August 2005 COSATU's central committee urged a 'political solution' to the crisis and demanded that the charges against Zuma be dropped, effectively calling for executive interference in the judicial process—exactly what they were railing against in the first place.
63 Niren Tolsi, 'Freedom's prisoners', *Mail & Guardian*, 23 December 2009.
64 In his judgement in *The Constitutional Court v Makwanyane*, when he rejected the argument that the death penalty should be reinstated because the majority of South Africans want it.
65 The 2005 decision to legalise same-sex marriage is a case in point. Public sentiment opposed the move, as did the majority of ANC members. ANC MPs had to be instructed to vote in favour of the Civil Union Bill, which passed into law on 30 December 2005.
66 Tribal authorities were converted into 'traditional councils' under the Traditional Leadership and Governance Framework Act of 2003. See Aninka Claassens, 'What's wrong with the Traditional Courts Bill?', *Mail & Guardian*, 30 May 2008. The Bill's text is available at: http://www.info.gov.za/view/DownloadFileAction?id=80588
67 Aninka Claassens, 'What's wrong with the Traditional Courts Bill?', *Mail & Guardian*, 30 May 2008.
68 Sindiso Mnisi, 'Terror in the name of tradition', *Mail & Guardian*, 26 February 2010.
69 Aninka Claassens, 'What's wrong with the Traditional Courts Bill?', *Mail & Guardian*, 30 May 2008.
70 The resolution called for steps to 'ensure that the allocation of customary land be democratised in a manner which empowers rural women and supports the building of democratic community structures at village level ... The ANC will further engage with traditional leaders ... to ensure that disposal of land without proper consultation with communities and local government is discontinued' (ANC, 2007a).
71 Thus the state pays about 900 senior traditional leaders annual salaries of at least R 140 000 (USD 18 500), while the 11 kings receive nearly R 800 000 (USD 106 000) each. See Donwald Pressly, 'Traditional leaders now cost tax payers R 140m', *Business Report*, 26 November 2008.
72 'Land Act is against the constitution, court rules', *Business Day*, 31 October 2009.
73 This, after all, was an organisation that could raise R 29.5 million (USD 4 million) in a single fundraising dinner and which was headed by a patriarch with three wives and at least 20 children. See Buddy Naidu, 'Zuma gets R 29.5 million pledge for ANC', *The Times* [Johannesburg], 12 October 2008.
74 Quoted in Carien du Plessis, 'Zuma calls Malema "leader in the making"', *Pretoria News*, 26 October 2009.
75 Jacob Dlamini, 'While SA laughs, Malema spreads his tentacles', 19 November 2009, *Business Day*.
76 Tim Cohen, 'The bearable lightness of debating Malema', 1 November 2009, *The Daily Maverick*. Available at http://www.thedailymaverick.co.za/opinionista/2009-10-23-The-bearable-lightness-of-debating-Malema

CHAPTER FOURTEEN

Left behind:
challenge and protest

The first step towards liberation is, in a way, the awareness of defeat.

—*Slavoj Zizek*[1]

The line-up of popular organisations that had confronted the apartheid system changed dramatically in the early 1990s. Many dissolved or morphed into ANC structures; others tried to change tack, with mixed results. Almost all had been active allies or fellow travellers of the exiled ANC. But most had evolved not as internal adjuncts of the 'government-in-waiting', but out of grassroots and interest-based struggles waged by workers, women, youth, students, black professionals and rural peasants. Mostly the restructuring of popular organisations occurred consensually and 'naturally'. It was also in the ANC that career paths beckoned and where political and other ambitions seemed most likely to be satisfied. But mere self-interest could not explain the high degrees of consent that accompanied the moves. That was rooted in one of the ANC's most remarkable feats: the mystique and authority it had achieved over much of the internal popular movement during the 1980s.

The gravity field of national liberation

The ANC had become adept at a key aspect of any hegemonic project: it developed and deployed an array of ideological precepts and symbols and asserted their pertinence to the lived realities of millions of South Africans. The Freedom Charter had been resurrected and popularised as the programme for change; the liberation struggle was personified in the form of Nelson Mandela; the colours, flags, songs and slogans of the ANC became ubiquitous features of resistance activities.

The idea of 'the people' was 'turned into a formalism whose singular consciousness was homogenised by the movement which spoke in its name', while a 'plurality of opinions' was 'negated by the singular notion of public opinion', as Robert Fine noted (1992:80). The armed struggle, too, functioned impressively in this process. The impact of armed attacks lay less at the level of military strategy than as cathartic, galvanising signifiers of resistance and as a symbolic rebuttal of the apartheid system's power. Overall, the ideological field through which millions of citizens experienced reality was dramatically altered. Canonised within the Charterist movement, the 'language' of national liberation structured analysis and rhetoric and acted as a sort of 'common sense' that attracts, inspires and seems to make sense of the world. The ANC had positioned itself as the 'mother ship of liberation'.

A rich variety of organisations survived (even if the terms of their survival were not entirely hearty). The trade-union movement did not succumb to absorption, but its strongest organisations (those affiliated to COSATU) had entered the political and ideological force field of the ANC. In 1994, they went further—releasing their top leaders to take up seats in Parliament as ANC members and dispatching hundreds more into provincial and local government structures. The hope was that these emissaries would advance workers' interests from their new vantage points. That prospect soon faded, as party discipline compelled them to toe the ANC line or risk losing their seats. COSATU's 'Trojan horse' in the ANC turned out to be little more than a pack animal for the ruling party—yet it would repeat the manoeuvre with unnerving enthusiasm in the mid-2000s during the Mbeki-Zuma battle.

The SACP, of course, was more familiar with such entryism; but it, too, was jostled badly off-balance in the 1990s. The disorientation stemmed partly from the 1989 collapse of the system it had adulated—even though, organisationally, the SACP recovered surprisingly well (in the mid-1990s it was probably the only communist party on the planet with growing membership). The real damage was political, as the party found it increasingly difficult to exert decisive influence on the ANC, especially in government.

The SACP, COSATU and the other main organisations of the left remained caught in the gravity field of national liberation, which still evinces key conceptions associated with the Bandung era.[2] One is the unequal relationship maintained between victorious liberation organisations and other popular formations, with the former harnessing the energies and resources of the latter. The central guiding principle remains the notion that the transformation process, in Samir Amin's (1990:113) summary, 'does not involve popular initiative as a starting point but simply popular support for state actions'. Related is the fixation on state power, with the state understood not in Gramscian terms, but as a fortress of power.[3] That perspective militates against the need for an authentic plurality of forces that could become allied in struggle without surrendering their autonomy or their ability to act in the interests of their respective constituencies. Instead, it relegates those forces to the status of instruments or condemns them as 'opportunist', 'ultra-leftist', 'counter-revolutionary' and worse.

Historically, within a discourse that conflates 'the masses' with the main liberation organisation (and it, eventually, with the new liberated state), all this seemed acceptable. As long as the successful liberation movement could build and consolidate hegemony after decolonisation or democratisation, the costs seemed modest: the draining of progressive civil society, the weakening of authentically independent organisations and the stifling of popular expression and initiative. Once the organisation's hegemony waned, however, the inclination to resort to new forms of authoritarianism grew, as many post-colonial societies attest.

The SACP, meanwhile, seemed even more emphatically caught in that orbital path. In fact, it had understood its role in such terms since the late 1920s. The reasoning traced back to the party's so-called 'Native Republic' policy[4], the related 'two-stage theory' (first winning and consolidating national liberation, then the struggle for socialism) and the colonialism of a special type (CST) thesis. In 1962, the SACP indigenised the 'two-stage theory' by defining the South African situation as CST:

> On one level, that of 'White South Africa', there are all the features of an advanced capitalist state in its final stage of imperialism [...] But on another level, that of 'Non-White South Africa', there are all the features of a colony [...] It is this combination of the worst features both of imperialism and colonialism, within a single national frontier, which determines the special character of the South African system (SACP, 1962:129).

Harold Wolpe noted that CST 'purports to rest on class relations of capitalist exploitation [but] in fact treats such relations as residual', according them 'little or no role in the analysis of relations of dominance and exploitation, which are instead, conceived as occurring between "racial", "ethnic" and "national" categories'.[5] Indeed CST was a 'self-consciously pragmatic' effort to devise an 'ideological midpoint at which both nationalists and communists could meet' (Everatt, 1991). It served as the theoretical platform for the ANC/SACP alliance and, although appearing to reconcile the tension between national and class struggle, it asserted the imperative of the former, with the latter relegated to an ancillary role. It is in the CST theory that one finds embedded the strongest roots of the ANC's dominion over the traditional left.

Give and take

The SACP's decision to struggle under the mantle of African nationalism and within a multiclass ANC was not foolhardy. It created a basis for mobilising disparate social forces into an encompassing front that eventually helped to produce the deadlock of the late 1980s and cleared the path for subsequent breakthroughs. The marshalling of this broad front and the cementing of ANC authority over it enabled the democratic movement to meet one of the prerequisites for a negotiated settlement: the existence of a powerful political force capable of 'delivering' its constituencies to the bargaining table and sticking to an eventual deal. But there were steep costs attached.

One has been the muffling of ideological and strategic plurality in the Congress movement, with the socialist left targeted especially. Under the dome of the national liberation struggle, sundry interests and forces could be enlisted in a common struggle. That this served the anti-apartheid movement well is beyond dispute. But differences and contradictions also became flattened under the canopy of inclusive identities: 'the people' or the 'oppressed majority' or 'the poor', for instance. At times, the process encouraged outrageous propositions—such as Tom Mboya's description, lacking even a hint of irony, of the main liberation movement as 'the mouthpiece of an oppressed nation' whose 'leader embodies the nation'.[6] In the post-liberation phase, inclusivity was increasingly maintained at the expense of heterodoxy, strategic autonomy and contestation. This house-trained status was maintained with a high degree of consent. An especially cringe-worthy example was the SACP's (1997) explanation for its (initially muted) criticism of the 1996 structural adjustment plan, GEAR (emphasis added):

> *Our first objective has been to* keep the debate on macro-economic policy wide open. *We have taken up this objective both out of principle* (we want to set an example of comradely debate and discussion), *and out of concern with the actual content of GEAR. We fully appreciate the huge financial market pressures on government* (and therefore upon all of us), *and we appreciate the temptations that may exist to declare this or that policy 'non-negotiable', to show 'toughness' and 'determination'. But it is simply* not helpful *to declare any policy, particularly one that has not emerged out of an effective process, 'non-negotiable'.*

The flinching tone defies comment. To be fair, the SACP subsequently grew bolder, earning itself repeated rebukes from ANC leaders. By the early 2000s, the boundaries of dissent in the Tripartite Alliance were being patrolled so sternly that COSATU and SACP flirted with the possibility of shifting themselves into another orbit, even splitting from the ANC. The manner of reprimand was illuminating. Leftist critics who complained of slow transformation were lumped with conservatives as 'those who seek to spread the gospel of failure' or were accused of being duped by enemies of change. Thabo Mbeki, addressing the SACP's national congress in July 1998, would rail against

> *those who [...] seem so ready to use the hostile messages of the right and thus join forces with the defenders of reaction to sustain an offensive against our movement* (1998b:8).

Vivid in such clunky declamations were the terms of unity, the limits of tolerance and the boundaries of permissible dissent within the ANC and the Alliance left. Far from becoming a driving force of change, the Alliance was assigned two main functions: one *therapeutic*, the other *disciplinary*. Its formal processes would funnel contestation away from the public realm and into a zone where disagreements could be aired, managed and contained, and where consent could be nourished via selective compromises. Debate and criticism would be allowed, but in a tightly managed context, both kindling and stifling hopes that unpopular policies and practices could be contested and changed.

That faith is not entirely unwarranted. The Alliance was a valuable site for holding off challenges against the new labour regime and for curbing the privatisation drive of the late 1990s. Partly because of this, COSATU members' loyalty to the alliance with the ANC was still high in the mid-2000s, even though it was slipping. Surveys among COSATU shop stewards showed about two thirds (66%) backed the Alliance in 2004 (down from 70% in 1998 and 82% in 1994) (Pillay, 2006). But the battles COSATU had won could not erase the fact that larger battles were being lost. The ANC leadership had rammed the GEAR plan through without substantive debate and then kept it off the agenda in Alliance meetings until 1998 (using the time-honoured method of postponing meetings). When both COSATU and the SACP in frustration took their dissent to the public, they earned a matronly dressing-down:

> *We must not engage in fake revolutionary posturing so that our mass base, which naturally wants speedy transformation and the fulfilment of its material needs on an urgent basis, accepts charlatans who promise everything that is good while we know that these confidence tricksters are telling the masses a lie* (Mbeki, 1998b).

The evergreen faith vested in the Alliance is shored up by other factors, too. One is the habitual counsel that the only alternative to the current arrangement is divorce, a prospect that tends to have a vitalising effect on sagging confidence levels inside the Alliance. A break-up, insists Jeremy Cronin (2002), would also split each of the ANC, COSATU and SACP and end up strengthening conservative forces inside the ANC. Indeed, a surprising variety of political tendencies cohabit in each of the Alliance partners. Orbiting deferentially around the ANC and its discursive axis of 'national democratic revolution', the Alliance enables those differences to become 'reconciled' around various compromises. Finally, the Alliance also serves as a life-support system for the SACP, as Mbeki occasionally would remind:

> *The idea that any of our organisations can build itself [sic] on the basis of scavenging on the carcass of a savaged ANC is wrong. This is because the death of the ANC, which will not happen, would also mean the death of the rest of the progressive movement of our country* (Mbeki, 1998b).

In the late 1990s, the SACP stood exposed as a surprisingly heterogeneous outfit, marked by what Jeremy Cronin generously called 'a considerable degree of necessary ideological fluidity'. It had become a hybrid of social democrats skilled at commuting between Thatcherite positions and popular affirmations, dyed-in-the-wool Stalinists, a rump of paint-by-numbers socialists and a band of left-wingers intent on transforming the party into a democratic socialist entity appropriate for the twenty-first century. Less than a decade later, it had alienated or purged several of these currents and reverted to old ways—running a tight ship and seeking to insert itself deeper and more decisively into the ANC's circuitry by helping to engineer Jacob Zuma's rise to power.

The SACP's influence on the transition had grown faint, but it shrewdly turned that state of affairs (and the intolerant chidings issued from the presidency) to its advantage, using it to recuperate its status as a principled and unwavering force of the socialist left. Unintentionally, Mbeki became the SACP's strongest recruiter. The party tailored its analysis of the transition accordingly, singling out as the chief obstacle 'the 1996 class project' allegedly managed by Mbeki and his circle (SACP, 2010). Vanquishing him became a central objective and Jacob Zuma was identified as the man for the job. The Zuma campaign became symbiotically linked to the demonisation of Mbeki, a ploy that carried the advantage of enormous superficial appeal, as shown in Chapter twelve. The party fed off Mbeki to the last. It again struck out on the path of entryism and the prospect of quick paybacks. In one respect the choice reflected the lasting damage the collapse of 1989 had done to the party. The world had shifted beneath its feet, but almost two decades later, it still lacked the confidence and imagination to adapt to the new realities. So it reverted to type.[7]

COSATU and the SACP take a shortcut

During the exile decades, machinations and intrigues had enabled the ANC-aligned left to extend its influence in the liberation movement. The approach seemed to pay off most famously with the assertion of a 'working-class bias' at the ANC's 1969 Morogoro consultative conference. As Dinga Sekwebu (2007) has reminded, the Morogoro shift had the international convergence of forces at its back. The late 1960s had marked a heyday of anti-colonial and anti-imperialist struggles and bristled with expectancy. In fact, the Morogoro tilt derived almost no momentum from realities within South Africa's resistance struggle: in 1969, the trade-union movement inside the country had not yet re-emerged, the ANC's armed struggle existed largely in name only and mass protest in the country had not occurred for almost a decade.

In the mid-2000s, there doubtless existed an 'objective' need for a left turn, but neither the internal nor external balances of forces favoured a sustained shift to the left. Moreover, a leftward shift would now entail more extensive achievements than those that had yielded the Morogoro breakthrough. It would require mobilising and organising support across society and transforming that into an institutional presence and influence within the ANC, from branch level upward. Shoehorning individuals into top national positions was no substitute. Instead of seeking hegemony within and around the ANC and bolstering it with control of key provinces and structures, COSATU and the SACP chose to rig and ride the bandwagon of a new ANC leader. The engineered rise of Zuma and the palace coup that unseated Mbeki became their short cut.

Zuma's tide of support comprised an assortment of demands, aspirations and grasping ambitions that would require deft and firm political management. This diverse (and opportunistic) support base would confront him with many of the same dilemmas that had flummoxed his predecessor. Zuma lacked the defining ingredient of the Mbeki years, however: the intellectual confidence to envision a distinctive *project* and the arrogance to believe that he could preside over it. For COSATU and the SACP, that shortcoming seemed god-sent; it would create space and indeterminacy they could exploit.

By the Alliance left's initial reckoning, its renewed struggle for the 'soul of the ANC', channelled through the medium of Jacob Zuma, brought handsome rewards. It touted as proof resolutions adopted at the ANC's 2007 Polokwane conference and a number of subsequent proposals and initiatives. These included an agreement to discuss inflation targeting; assigning to Parliament the right to amend money bills; the appointment of a former trade-union leader to the position of Minister of Economic Development; loosening the Treasury's monopoly over budget allocations; the creation of a planning commission to harmonise departmental activities with government's strategic objectives; a proposal on prescribed investments; and plans to set up a national health-insurance scheme.

None of this, as Steven Friedman noticed, was particularly left-wing. Many centrist and centre-right governments elsewhere have taken similar steps: 'Adjustments that were considered normal when they were taken by conservative Western governments are painted here as portents of revolution.'[8] Some of the 'evidence' for the alleged shift also provided an unwitting commentary on how low the bar was being set. 'We are now once more coming to appreciate that transformation of healthcare and education or rural development, are critical ingredients for making any sustainable growth,' Jeremy Cronin asserted in late 2008.[9] Dozens of World Bank documents have broadcast the same sentiments since the late 1990s.

Saddled with huge political debts and besieged by the demands of its bankrollers, fixers and foot soldiers, the Zuma presidency's top priority has been to try and steady the ship. It is faced with a tough but traditional exercise in political management—pacifying the motley interests, ambitions, claims and entitlements that orbit around it. Restrained social-democratic ventures would be used to appease the clamour to step up the fight against poverty. Social protection packages would be strengthened; public-works programmes showcased; and corrective interventions attempted in the dysfunctional zones of education and health. The AIDS response would be repaired. Moves to introduce a national health-insurance (NHI) scheme would serve as a talismanic radical initiative and be advertised as proof of the desire to push transformation past the cramped perimeters of the Mbeki era.

With the exception of the NHI, though, none of those moves are left-wing; all fit comfortably on the policy menus of centrist and centre-right governments around the world. The post-Mbeki 'leftward shift' was as much a media creation (spiced with much Red scare-mongering) as a figment of the wounded Alliance left. The corporate world, whose business it is to spot impending peril, understood this from early on. Moreover, it had received its own assurances from Zuma that the boat would not be rocked. COSATU and the SACP 'participate in the evolution of policy, but they do not determine which way policy must go', Zuma told *Bloomberg.com* in late 2008. The ANC, he said, sets policy, and 'that should be a comforting thing to investors. Even if it was not Zuma, if it was anybody else, you should not worry about the ANC, and I think we have a track record'.[10]

COSATU and the SACP had been pushing for an arrangement in which 'the Alliance [would] be in full control of key government decisions' (COSATU, 2001). During his campaign, Zuma had certainly lent succour to those ambitions, telling COSATU's twentieth anniversary rally in Durban, for example, that 'the Alliance must drive Government' (Calland, 2006:156). But even at Polokwane two years later, the bid to boost the authority of COSATU and the SACP got short thrift. Alliance partners, one key resolution asserted, were free 'to discuss and arrive at their own decisions on how they seek to pursue their strategic objectives', but 'the ANC will continue to determine, in its own structures and processes, how best to advance its own strategic objectives' (ANC, 2007a).

Indeed, the CEO of Business Leadership South Africa and former vice-president of Anglo American, Michael Spicer, found 'no significant policy changes' and saw 'no indication of ANC interest in intervening to restrict property rights or to enhance significantly the regulation of business'.[11] Friedman's reading seemed accurate: 'This is not a leftward shift. It is an attempt to prevent one by doing what Mbeki failed to do—bringing the alliance partners into the discussion in the hope of defusing tension.'[12]

Investment bankers were soon showering plaudits on Zuma for his 'very solid decisions' and for being 'a pragmatist'.[13] Zuma chose to replace Trevor Manuel as finance minister with Pravin Gordhan, who had overhauled South Africa's tax-collection system. In his first 'mini-budget' in late 2009, Gordhan made it even easier to ship capital abroad. Tito Mboweni, another bugbear for the left, vacated his office as head of the central bank, but made way for Gill Marcus, a former deputy who had helped him to introduce the controversial inflation-targeting policy before becoming chair of one of the country's largest banks.[14] In terms of new, more progressive policies, the Alliance left had little to show for its pro-Zuma exertions, except for some changes made to industrial policy (see Chapter five). The continuity was underlined by the fact that many of the policy improvements and institutional adjustments mooted or pursued by the Zuma government originated in the Mbeki era:

- Attempts to refurbish industrial strategy started well before Mbeki's departure;
- The NHI proposal builds on a process first mooted in the mid-1990 (in a resolution at the ANC's 1997 Mafikeng conference), with substantive work starting in the early 2000s (see Chapter ten);
- Plans for a contributory social security system also date from the Mbeki era (and were reiterated as early as 2002 at the ANC's Stellenbosch conference);
- A more flexible monetary policy capable of spurring 'job creation, investment and poverty eradication' has been ANC policy since 2002;
- A prescribed investment proposal seeks to tighten a voluntary commitment made at the 2004 Growth and Development Summit;
- The creation of a planning commission is an extension of 'Mbeki's style' of governance, with decisions and co-ordination centralised in the presidency;
- The Expanded Public Works Programme was conceived and implemented by the Mbeki administration; and
- Substantial expansion of the social grant system began during Mbeki's second term.

In truth, the Polokwane resolutions on economic policy were generously vague and accommodated any number of interpretations. There was repeated mention, for example, of the need for a 'new and more equitable growth path' (ANC, 2007a), but little indication of what that would mean. The left's push for new economic policies also remained short on details. After an economic summit in October 2008, as the recession bit, the ANC, COSATU and SACP mustered a half-hearted declaration that 'macroeconomic interventions need also to be constantly monitored in this turbulent situation'. There was a need, it said, for 'both continuity and change' and whilst some policies 'require review ... in many cases persisting problems relate to poor institutional coherence and coordination within the state'.[15] This was a far cry from the fighting talk in the immediate aftermath of Polokwane, when COSATU would publicly chide Zuma for suggesting that relaxing labour laws might reduce poverty.[16]

Exasperated, but punching above its weight, COSATU pushed on. Its attempts to elevate the Economic Development Ministry to pre-eminence were stymied, as were the efforts to shift control of the Development Bank to that Ministry. Soon after, Ebrahim Patel (COSATU's main man in Zuma's Cabinet) was informed that his remit was to help co-ordinate, not to make policies, although he did manage to acquire control over the Industrial Development Corporation.

Pegged back

Two years after thrusting Zuma to victory at Polokwane and less than a year after helping the ANC to achieve yet another crunching electoral victory, COSATU and the SACP found themselves pegged back once again. Hopes of a 'working-class bias' had thinned. The new ANC National Executive Committee included even more businesspeople than the one elected in 2002 during Mbeki's heyday (SACP, 2008a). The Alliance left's influence on government was not nearly as telling as it had presumed. This reflected both an overall balance of forces (domestically and internationally) that did not favour the left and its surprisingly light organisational weight inside the ANC. Despite its Polokwane 'triumph', the Alliance left in 2010 could claim to control only one province (the Eastern Cape) and its grip there wavered. The rash posturing seemed to stand in inverse proportion to the left's institutional weight inside the ANC.

The Alliance left also did not reckon with the heterogeneity of Zuma's support base and the weight of acquisitive and conservative forces within it. Early on, sceptics were warning that patronage politics were providing a great deal of the momentum behind Zuma's challenge and that the Mbeki-Zuma battle was a tussle for control of the spoils of liberation. In that view, the SACP and COSATU had blundered into collusion with emergent black business interests whose eyes were trained not on a more progressive agenda but on the pickings of state power; the succession battle, in that view, was about securing space at the trough. The new order, wrote Achille Mbembe (2009), was in the hands of 'a gang of adventurers, wheeler-dealers and politicians looking for perks and ways to launder dirty money [who] have attached themselves to the party machine'.

By late 2009, Zuma had drawn the line. He chastised the ANC's left-wing allies, warning them against drifting into 'the borderline between constructive criticism and being in opposition to the African National Congress, the leader of the Alliance' (Zuma, 2009). The tone was friendlier, but the sentiments echoed positions Mbeki and, prior to him, Mandela had taken. COSATU and SACP leaders stood flummoxed by a question they had chosen to ignore as they trekked across the land, stumping for Zuma: why exactly should the transition from Thabo Mbeki to Jacob Zuma have opened new vistas for radical change? In what ways did the 'new conjuncture' favour breakthroughs that were not on the cards in the 1990s? It had no answer to these questions, besides the refrain that the Zuma presidency would be less self-absorbed and pompous and more open to debate and engagement. But radical transformation does not happen because a president leaves his door ajar.

'I never thought I would face this moment so soon,' COSATU General-Secretary Zwelinzima Vavi told an SACP special congress in late 2009. 'We do not struggle so others can be our rulers; these victories belong to us', he complained. Zuma himself soon disabused him of the latter claim, reminding the gathering that the ANC led the Tripartite Alliance. As for the SACP, it 'should play its historical role and provide robust and profound intellectual and ideological debate to the alliance', said Zuma, paying the party a backhanded compliment. Both the sentiment and the language, as Anthony Butler corrected noted, were 'strongly reminiscent of Mbeki's'.[17] In case the overall message did not register, Zuma went on to invoke the legacy of Albert Luthuli, whose social conservatism had grated the left during his 1952–67 tenure as ANC president.

COSATU and the SACP went into this eyes open and aware that it faced a real prospect of being outmanoeuvred. In a 2008 discussion document, the SACP (2008b:5) had discerned two distinct scenarios. In one, the 'many positive features of Polokwane' would be 'taken forward'. In the other, the left would fail to achieve hegemony, and an alliance of

> 'floor-crossers', 'compradorists' and 'fugitives from justice' [would coalesce] around a programme of awarding influential posts, tenders and contracts to themselves, while the factional destabilisation [...] of the state, including the criminal justice system, persists.

The left, it warned, will have been 'used for the electoral campaign and then dumped, with some individuals co-opted, while the rest are marginalised—perhaps more brutally than before'. Folded into that warning was both admirable prescience and troubling amnesia. In its drive to unseat Mbeki and hoist Zuma to power, it was the Alliance left that had contributed to the 'factional destabilisation' of the state and undermined the criminal justice system. It had sought to use the Zuma candidacy (not the reverse) as a shortcut to try to undo some of the setbacks it had suffered since the mid-1990s. It wilfully chose the route of theatrical campaigning around a half-baked messianic figure over the painstaking slog of building a genuinely democratic left movement that could challenge for hegemony. Entryism and trying to lever influence by proxy is no substitute.

A balancing act

The trade union movement—COSATU, in particular—remains the largest, best-organised and well-resourced social movement in the country. Whether it is the ideal agent for radical social transformation is another matter. The federation shifted to 'strategic unionism' in the 1990s, as it sought to shape the economic and socioeconomic terms of the transition (through its participation in the National Economic Forum and, later, in the National Economic, Development and Labour Council, among others). Subsequently, it tried to merge these two approaches into a form of 'social unionism' that could channel its organised power, mobilising capacity, socioeconomic policies and participation in political and social alliances into shaping national, economic and social development (COSATU, 1997). This confirmed COSATU's commitment to a corporatist route (that would centre on social pacts between it, the state and business) and an overall pursuit of strategic compromises. It also cemented COSATU's political alignment with the ANC.

The heyday of this approach was in the mid-1990s, when the union movement notched up a series of important accomplishments (see Chapters five and six). But its limits were soon apparent, as COSATU sought, but failed, to check the quickly maturing strategic alliance that was being forged between the post-apartheid state and capital. Webster and Adler's (1999) claim that a 'class stalemate' prevailed was unduly optimistic and underestimated the extent to which COSATU's political weight and influence was waning. By 2000, COSATU was in strategic

> disarray, its relationship with the ANC was bad and getting worse, it was increasingly confronted by assertive critics, and an organizational alternative was emerging on the political scene. The labour federation was in need of a new strategic path (Habib & Valodia, 2006b:244).

The Zuma presidency, like its predecessor, seems to be working from an assumption that the structural weight—and therefore also the political power—of the trade-union movement indeed remains diminished and will continue to weaken. Instead of institutionally grounding expansive compromises around the state, labour and capital, labour's standing is being downgraded to an 'interest group'. This opens scope for the political leadership to assemble a set of policies, which, although not integrated and harmonious enough to constitute a programme, creates some possibilities for addressing certain 'priority problems' on the basis of broad consent, while managing the fundamental adjustments required by capital.[18]

This is an arrangement that is less about class compromise than about class struggle. The challenge is to restructure social relations in ways that achieve productivity, competitiveness and growth in a new global division of labour that demonstrably favours capital, but without inducing social instability. The affinity with the 'Third Way' experiments in the north should be obvious. A key feature of these was the de-ideologising of politics. Traditional categories of 'conservative' and 'progressive', left and right, were declared outmoded and became compressed under new headings, notably that of 'realism'. The illusion was of organised interests dissolving and society becoming the sum of individuals living in it[19]—an 'illusion' because the underlying sway of corporate interests persisted. Accompanying all this was a heightened accent on patriotism and generous use of 'inclusive' gestures and dramaturgies.

Sketched here are broad 'tendencies' that become patterned depending on the specificities of societies. In Britain, New Labour proceeded on the scorched terrain left by almost two decades of Thatcherite adjustment. In France and Germany, social democrats supervised a diluted version that had to contend with a socially embedded trade-union movement capable of stronger defensive actions. South Africa lacks the corporatist foundation for a managed class compromise and it doesn't have much to show for its attempts thus far to institutionalise such a compromise. That is not surprising, given the context of mass unemployment, mediocre economic growth (the benefits of which are distributed extremely unequally), rationed provisioning by the state and the constricted strength of the trade-union movement. A corporatist arrangement cannot hold in such conditions—but neither can the organised working class easily go on sustained attack.

For the union movement, one option would be to seek a new corporatist accommodation with the state, under which the government consults the trade-union movement more earnestly on a wider range of policies in return for certain compromises (such as wage restraints that could allow government to channel savings into agreed-upon social initiatives) (Simon, 1991). This was the risky route the Labour governments chose in Britain in the 1970s—risky because it hinged on the ability to improve living standards and expand social reforms, which depended in turn on robust economic growth (which did not materialise). At the same time, the South African trade-union movement's ability to extract meaningful concessions outside such a framework is cramped. It could stand its ground against regressive changes to the labour regime and privatisation and campaign for social policy improvements on the basis of new, more expansive alliances. But it has not replenished its leverage by forging links with other social movements. Dinga Sekwebu's complaint in 1999 was still valid a decade later:

> COSATU has been unable to successfully link up with and strengthen other organisations. There has been no revival of the mass democratic movement [...] COSATU does not appear to take the emergence of sector networks (for example, the rural development network) seriously. [It] also seems contemptuous of single-issue coalitions (for example, on debt) and other NGOs [...] Although always strongly denied, a tendency has developed within COSATU to approach issues from a narrow 'workerist' perspective (1999:7).

The decision to renew a struggle 'for the soul of the ANC' partly reflected the trade-union movement's turn of fortune. Still, in a society where one party monopolises electoral politics, working within and through it does seem the most sensible and realistic route for influencing change. COSATU's '2015 programme', sketched early in the 2000s, tasked it with doubling its membership to four million and conducting (with the SACP) intensive political and ideological training of cadres who could also become more active in ANC ranks. The objective was for a self-conscious, politicised layer of workers to dominate the structures of the ANC. The other leg of this strategy required boosting the authority and power of the Tripartite Alliance, so that it became the hub of government policy (COSATU, 2006a & 2003; SACP, 2008b).[20]

Zuma's challenge presented COSATU with an opportunity to move that strategy through the gears. But, argues Devan Pillay (2008b), the decision to help to engineer Zuma's ascent and the manner of doing so, actually betrayed a conservatism that had seeped into the union federation's strategic thinking and which reflected its weakening as a political force. '[T]he changing nature of its membership and relations of patronage within the Alliance,' writes Pillay (2008b:13), 'has forced it to remain within the limiting embrace of Alliance politics.'

For good reason, unionists abhor the term 'labour aristocracy', but intense differentiation within the working classes is an undeniable reality. COSATU, for example, represents 65% of organised workers but only 14% of all workers

445

(COSATU, 2006a). Its membership profile has changed: the majority of members are now skilled, supervisory and clerical workers (especially since the successful membership drives among public-sector workers in the 1990s) (Pillay, 2008b).[21] Belonging to a union is manifestly associated with higher wages. In the first half of the 2000s, union members on average earned three times as much as their non-union counterparts (Casale & Posel, 2009). This profile, along with the emergence of what Sakhela Buhlungu (2006) has termed 'entrepreneurial unionism', partly explains the failure to organise the most vulnerable sections of workers. Faced with the slog of organising vulnerable workers (and *keeping* them organised in an inconstant environment), inertia becomes an easier and more attractive option. The traditional methods of organising industrial shop floors do not yield the same results in these new settings (see Chapter six).

This poses uncomfortable questions and points to displeasing prospects. If ultra-vulnerable workers cannot be organised as workers, then on what basis can solidarity be achieved? The risk is that if notional class consciousness fails as a basis for marshalling solidarity, other affinities that pivot on difference and enmity gain traction: race, nationality, ethnicity, urban versus rural and more. Pillay (2008b) believes this can be avoided by (re)building a politics of contestation that brings together the realms of production and consumption. He argues for resurrecting the spirit and practice of the 1980s to forge a path where

> a 'popular-democratic' approach combines the best of 'workerism'—namely its emphasis on class politics and participatory democracy (in the form of deep-rooted accountable democratic structures that empower working class people in a real sense)—as well as the best of 'populism', which hegemonizes a progressive politics throughout society (2008b:30).

But COSATU's loyalty to the Alliance tends to discourage links with other left formations and initiatives. Critics such as Oupa Lehulere (2005:7–8) have disapprovingly compared the federation's fierce support for Zuma with its stand-offish attitude toward the new protest movements in the 2000s:

> [W]hen it came to taking the leadership of the mass struggles that have unfolded in various parts of the country [...] COSATU has not displayed a fraction of the energy it has displayed in defending former deputy-president Zuma. For the struggling masses in dusty townships no songs of praise, no SMS campaigns, no trust funds to bail out those accused of public violence, no funeral funds for those killed in combat, no T-shirts in honour of the water that no longer runs, of energy cuts in the heart of winter.

In the meantime, radical politics is marginalised in zones beyond the ANC and its Alliance partners. A replay of 1980s social movement unionism, when shop-floor and community militancy was fused in the heat of an anti-apartheid struggle, does not seem likely. The combustible and unifying context that prevailed then is not available. Collaboration and networking will have to be achieved on new terms and those inevitably have implications for COSATU's relationship with the ANC. Breaking the Alliance, Adam Habib (2004) has suggested, would add more 'substantive uncertainty' to the political system—an element he believes is necessary if the current trajectory of change is to bend in a more progressive direction. It might also usher the ANC's left-wing allies into the political wilderness ... where new bonds, alliances and strategies would have to be sought.

Popular activism beyond the Alliance

A complaint frequently heard in the mid-1990s was that 'the masses of our people have withdrawn from the public space and have pulled back from popular involvement'.[22] Indeed, a great number of anti-apartheid formations were either absorbed or co-opted by the ANC or post-apartheid state. Many of the non-governmental organisations (NGOs) that supported these formations also dissolved or were prodded toward development 'delivery' (Marais, 1998c). For some, this seemed perfectly 'natural': after all, the custodian of liberation was ready to take up its duties. The trend was less sinister than it seemed. The demobilisation of popular organisations is a fairly common phenomenon in democratic transitions; as political systems become democratised, extra-institutional mobilising and organising tends to flag.

Conducted by political elites, the political negotiations in the early 1990s had offered few entry or marshalling points for grassroots-based organising (as opposed to mobilising). Members' enthusiasm dwindled, only to be sporadically revived when deadlocks in the negotiations prompted calls for mass action. Organisational capacity at grassroots level waned. After 1994, this was exacerbated as thousands of key activists and figures in progressive organisations left to participate in Parliament and in the transformation of state structures, taking a great deal of institutional memory and experience with them.[23]

Dazed and confused

Conceptual confusion added to the difficulties. The popular sector was often (and mistakenly) equated with 'civil society', which became seen as a *countervailing* sphere, distinct from the state, where liberal-democratic rights and freedoms could be promoted. Or it was viewed as a zone where the failure of the state to live up to its developmental duties could be remedied. Both conceptions cast it in explicit tension with the state and they cut to the heart of some of the dilemmas facing the popular sector.[24] Disaffection with the old statist routes of transformation became coupled with the perception of the state as a threat or an irrelevance. The complex interconnectedness of the state and civil society was mistaken for relations of exter-nality and exclusion, neglecting the ways by which the exercise and reproduction of state power interweaves state and civil society (see Chapter thirteen). South African leftists have found it very difficult to step clear of this template.

This compounded the confusion popular organisations had about their 'new' roles and, particularly, their relationship to the democratic government and state. The oppositional idiom of organising that had prevailed during the anti-apartheid era was obviously inappropriate in the context of the new democracy. But organisations that had cut their teeth in the anti-apartheid struggle were poorly equipped for activities based on the principle of 'critical support'. The weakness was rooted in two core features of anti-apartheid resistance. Firstly, efforts to exploit spaces and frailties in the state had been denounced as collaborationist and were rejected in favour of outright conflict or opposition. Hardly any experiences of engagements with and within state apparatuses were allowed to accumulate (see Chapter two). Secondly, change had been 'conceptualised as starting with a seizure of state power and from there the transformation of society would flow in a very centralised manner', in Enoch Godongwana's words.[25] 'The irony,' Jeremy Cronin admitted, 'is that we fought for decades to arrive at a point where we seem unable to devise a clear strategy to move forward.'[26]

The ANC and government urged a shift from 'resistance to reconstruction'. But such remarks only highlighted the conundrums popular organisations faced as they tried to reposition themselves. Many popular organisations experienced financial and political pressure to partner with the private sector and/or the state and focus their work on 'delivery'. Often, though, the pressure to 'deliver' and the dependencies and imbalances in these contractual relationships, yielded drab collaborations that stifled the hallmarks of popular development efforts: democratic practices, participatory processes, capacity-building, experimentation and transferable skills and experiences. 'Technicism, as a new, core trait of NGO endeavours', noted Shamim Meer, was eclipsing the 'political nature of development' (1999). The pressure for quick, quantifiable outputs left little space or inclination for the more laborious, 'old-fashioned' notions of democratic participation and popular invention and accountability.

Off balance: the civics movement

The civic movement was an early casualty of this disorientation and was knocked badly off balance. Regarded in the 1980s as one of the most promising 'new social movements' to have emerged in South Africa, it seemed rudderless in the mid-1990s—'fragmented' and lacking, according to Jeremy Seekings (1997), 'coherence and a sense of direction and purpose'. With foresight, Monty Narsoo in 1993 had proposed that civics adopt a 'programmatic' role, in which they would 'lobby, pressure, negotiate and form alliances to press for the programmes they want and then, with other interests and institutions, state and private, monitor the implementation of those which are agreed' (1993:17). But that proved difficult. The mobilising skills honed during the anti-apartheid struggle were poor stand-ins for the facilitation, lobbying and management abilities highlighted in Narsoo's prognosis.

Also perplexing civics was their relationship to the ANC, with which the South African National Civics Organisation (SANCO) was joined in a political alliance at national level. But representing local community interests required autonomy (CORE, 1999), a stance sometimes attempted though not always with sincerity. In the run-up to local government elections, for example, some civic leaders would become loud advocates of 'autonomy' and 'independence'—usually *after* local

ANC branches had chosen not to nominate them as ANC election candidates. Other weaknesses were becoming evident, too. In Johannesburg, researchers linked 'the flagging authority, legitimacy and representivity of civics' to their association with powerful local elites amid 'increasing social differentiation' (CASE, 1998b:17).

SANCO was foundering. Shorn of donor support, it had even formed an investment arm to generate funding, while its official focus shifted to 'skills development, education and employment' (Kobokoane, 1997).[27] A vital and potentially influential platform and channel for community concerns, demands and initiatives stood denuded, leaving a vacuum in many areas. At the same time, grassroots party political activism also took a hard knock. Stripped of active members, some ANC branches existed in name only by the late-1990s. Its Dobsonville branch in Soweto, for example, saw its membership evaporate from 4 500 in 1993 to 27 in 1997. A November 1999 poll found that political party membership among Africans had dropped from 24% in 1994 to only 10%.[28]

SANCO tried several postures, eventually settling on the role of loyal sidekick to the ANC. Many were troubled by this departure from the radicalism of the 1980s civics tradition. Tensions had also grown between local SANCO affiliates and the ANC. The grievances varied, but misgivings about SANCO's 'unhealthy' deference toward the ANC were a recurring theme.[29] In Zuern's (2006:189–90) summary,

> *SANCO had experienced a sharp decline as a national civic structure; it suffered multiple public crises and many of its former local branches simply ceased to operate and those that continued to exist were often dormant until a local crisis occurred ... [Its] claim to represent the masses of community residents across the country was often greeted with strong scepticism if not outright disbelief.*

Taking the gap

SANCO's retreat into subservience underlined broader concerns that the 'struggle organisations' of the 1980s were poorly equipped for the new reality in which an ally—the ANC—was administering a neoliberal adjustment programme (Desai, 2002). COSATU was caught up in that exact dilemma (see earlier). But left activists who had been sidelined during the mid-1990s seemed more alert to the opportunities for a new wave of social movement activism that would seek to bypass the behemoths of the liberation struggle.

As the outlines of the post-apartheid order became more evident, diverse new community-based organisations and pressure groups began emerging.[30] They included the Treatment Action Campaign (TAC, formed in 1998), the Concerned Citizens Group (1999), the Western Cape Anti-Eviction Campaign (2000), the Soweto Electricity Crisis Committee (SECC), the Landless People's Movement, the Coalition of South Africans for the Basic Income Grant (2001) and the Education Rights Project (2002). These formations targeted different aspects of the new order, including access to basic services (and the impact of privatisation and cost-recovery policies); labour practices; landlessness and homelessness; environmental destruction; gender equity; sexual minorities; and migrants.

Almost all of them were pursuing goals that had formed major planks in the national liberation struggle[31] and most claimed to be upholding the ideals of the Freedom Charter and principles and commitments outlined in the Reconstruction and Development Programme. They positioned themselves consciously within the narrative of national liberation and typically made explicit reference to the rights codified in South Africa's Constitution. Beyond that, though, there was no obvious or easy fit between them.

Protests had flared sporadically since the late 1990s, but an upsurge started in 2001, with the Bredell land occupations near Johannesburg. The drama 'signified a profound moral crisis for the post-apartheid state' (Hart, 2006:25). In the middle of a bitterly cold Highveld winter, the authorities tried to expel the occupying households. Media interest was intense and, coincidentally or not, the South African currency commenced a steep dive as the drama escalated. The state ordered a crackdown using the 1959 Trespass Act, an apartheid law kept on the statute books after 1994. An urgent eviction was secured from the courts and the expulsions of several thousand people proceeded, sparking outrage (Huchzermeyer, 2003). New formations, such as the Landless People's Movement (LPM), the Anti-Privatisation Forum (APF) and the Anti-Eviction Campaign (AEC) capitalised on the events. Mobilising support, they resolved to use two impending international spectacles to showcase the depth of principled opposition to government's alleged betrayal of popular ideals.

At the 'World Conference of Racism', held in Durban in September 2001, these 'new social movements' jostled enthusiastically for attention, but earned mostly bemusement. Within a year, though, at the 'World Summit on Sustainable Development' in Johannesburg, the ANC and its allies were visibly jittery in the face of a mobilisation that had grown much quicker and larger than anticipated. A protest march drew some 20 000 mostly leftist critics of the ANC government, dwarfing and embarrassing a counter-march staged by the ANC, COSATU and the SACP. Less than a decade after the demise of apartheid, organised popular protest had erupted, apparently with affinities toward the alter-globalisation protests sweeping the globe. Theorists Antonio Negri and Michael Hardt (2004), for example, endorsed these

> protests against local officials and the South African government, which they claim has, since the end of apartheid, deepened the misery of the poor, [protests that] also target neoliberal globalisation as the source of their poverty ...

A giddy expectancy was at work among left-wing activists and analysts, some of whom saw in the rise of these new movements the potential of an early departure from national liberation tradition and its alleged route of betrayal. The line between analysis and agitprop, however, was often faint. Protests were talked up as proof of growing disgruntlement with the government, of a potential shift in allegiances and the beginnings of a 'counter-hegemonic movement'. 'Are we on the eve of a new 1973–76', John Appolis asked rhetorically in 2004, of 'a new phase of more sustained mass struggles?'[32] The expectancy was overcooked.

A taxonomy of the new social formations

There is some doubt whether the label 'new social movement' suits the formations that emerged from the late 1990s onward. Charles Tilly's (1985:736) suggestion that a social movement is best understood as a political campaign or challenge 'in the name of a social category that lacks an established political position' is attractive. But it is not very useful in the South African context, where many of the protestors either support the ANC (albeit with misgivings), vote for it or even belong to it.[33]

Other theorists have proposed additional criteria, including high degrees of popular participation and the avoidance of institutional channels (Jelin, 1986). Whatever definition is chosen, none is likely to encompass all of these contemporary forms of popular and radical engagement. TAC, no doubt the most successful of the new formations, for instance, is best described as a national association, although it was organised also at local level. Entities such as the SECC, meanwhile, are local community-based structures with distinct leaderships and memberships. The environmental movement, meanwhile, is loosely clustered around distinct organisations (Earthlife Africa, Groundwork and the Environmental Justice Networking Forum) although, according to Jacklyn Cock (2006:204), it

> has no coherent centre and no tidy margins; it is an inchoate sum of multiple, diverse, uncoordinated struggles and organizations [and is] characterized by a radical decentralisation of authority, with no governing body, official ideology or mandated leaders, minimal hierarchy and horizontal forms of organizing.

For all their differences, these formations share three features: they target alleged failures of the state, they are political entities and they rely heavily on the support of middle-class activists with anti-apartheid struggle pedigrees and access to institutional resources and solidarity networks (Ballard et al, 2005). On the whole, they were established with the explicit political aim of organising and mobilising the poor and marginalised and contesting or engaging the state and other social actors around the implementation of neoliberal social policies (Habib, 2005:683).

Despite their variety, the formations can be grouped usefully along two lines: their tactics and relations with the state and the scope of their goals. Although they seek to challenge government policies through political action and impertinent initiative, their tactics are eclectic and pliant. They include what Bayat (2000) has termed rebellion through 'quiet encroachment' (hooking households into the electricity grid, for example), forthright opposition (wrecking prepaid water meters, reconnecting cut off water and electricity supplies, even disconnecting the Johannesburg mayor's electricity supply) and extracting concessions from the state.

Among the more militant groups is the SECC, which emerged when local government shifted to cost-recovery policies for water and electricity provision in impoverished communities. In the early 2000s, the SECC claimed to be reconnecting electricity supplies to hundreds of households each month (Egan & Wafer, 2006).[34] Equally militant is the APF, which grew into a larger network spread across Gauteng and the North West province comprising more than 20 affiliates and four political groups. For its part, *Abahlali baseMjondolo*, the country's largest shack-dwellers' organisation, consciously situates itself 'outside the system'. It rejects party politics and advocates election boycotts and focuses on building and networking a series of sustainable communes.[35] TAC, on the other hand, has been more tactically agile, combining critical support for the ANC government (which it also backed in legal stand-offs with the pharmaceutical industry) with extra-legal actions (smuggling in cheaper antiretroviral drugs, for instance), court challenges, lobbying and popular mobilisation to press home its demands. This tactical variety reflects the ambivalence of some of these formations toward the post-apartheid state.

Politically the formations tend to group along two lines: those making extensive, rights-based claims of citizenship more or less within the current liberal-democratic framework and those that seek to mount a challenge against the current order. Some formations (and most of their supporters) regard the state as legitimate, but reject key policies of the ANC government (Buhlungu, 2006b). The TAC exemplified this stance and contested official policies at national level, while mobilising and engaging in activism at local levels. Most other entities classified as 'new social movements' focus on grassroots activism rather than engaging the state through formal channels and institutions. A few seem willing to contest local elections, using them as stages for promoting their positions and mobilising support and perhaps even for gaining access to local state structures and resources. Others take a harder line and condemn the state for continuing to do the bidding of a (reconfigured) elite and for becoming increasingly polluted by cronyism and corruption. They see declining voter turnout in elections as proof that increasing numbers of South Africans are losing faith in 'the system'. Extracting concessions from the state is seen as self-defeating and participating in its formal processes is

> incapable of fundamentally transforming social relations [since] South Africa has already entered into the terrain of a low-intensity and commodified democracy [...] where elections have become the political playground of those with access to capitalist patronage and where electoral choice is reduced to different shades of grey (McKinley, 2006:423).

That analysis plays out in several ways. Proponents see themselves as the subjects of an upstanding struggle tradition that stretches back long before 1994 and that is rooted in a 'principled internationalism, a socialist vision and an independent mass-based mobilisation and struggle as an ideological and organisational alternative to the capitalist ANC' (McKinley, 2004:20).[36] At work here is an almost Quixotic determination to achieve a socialist order in which a democratic state would serve the working and subaltern classes. These movements therefore position themselves within a long tradition of radical left struggles in South Africa that 'has not been extinguished', in the view of Peter Dwyer (2006:92), for whom 'it has continued throughout the 1990s and into the new millennium, and can be understood as a "new wave" of popular protest'.

Less easily pigeonholed are the groupings active around landlessness and the environment. Rather than focus criticism on the alleged betrayals of the ANC in power, the environmental justice movement places a moral imperative at the centre of its activities (an approach the TAC used to great effect). Its starting point, according to Cock (2006: 205), is to ask 'what is morally correct?', rather than what is politically, legally or scientifically possible. Slowly gaining ground in this movement is an eco-socialist approach to politics and development.[37] The Landless People's Movement (LPM), meanwhile, has styled itself in Afro-centric terms (not surprising given the history of land dispossession in South Africa) and seems drawn toward radical populism. It supported, for instance, the land grabs orchestrated by Zanu-PF in Zimbabwe, hailing them as a form of resistance against neocolonialism. A 'mix of different class and social forces that the hegemonic bloc has been incapable of entirely absorbing into its own project' (Greenberg, 2006:136), the LPM has the advantage of tackling an issue that is packed with great emotive power and potential for widespread support, but is also threaded with racialised notions of identity, tradition and culture.

There has also emerged a fresh approach that rejects an 'outmoded' obsession with state power. These groups do not so much oppose the state as ignore it. They are what Andile Mngxitama (2009) has called 'the principled boycotters': activists who position themselves outside, but play off against the dramatics of institutional power and representation. Their most recent points of reference are the counter-cultural currents of the international alter-globalisation movement, but they also announce the very delayed arrival in South Africa of the spirit of 1968. The 'Nope' initiative (its name a play on the new political party COPE, which split from the ANC in late 2008), for instance, called for a boycott of the 2009 national election, with slogans like 'Our dreams don't fit on your ballots' and 'A better lie for all' (a cheeky play on the ANC's election slogan).[38] These are tiny collectives, but they have introduced a sense of irreverence and play long absent from activism (though Mngxitama traces their heritage to the boycott politics of black-consciousness leader Steve Biko in the 1970s).

'With us, or against us'

The ANC-led government much prefers more compliant critics—such as SANCO, which adopted a tractable role as junior partner, helping local government to deliver services.[39] The organisation became demonstrably submissive, endorsing government's cost-recovery development model and sermonising on the need to support government programmes generally. In 2002, it elected senior ANC figures to its national leadership.[40] Whereas the TAC had developed a nuanced and sophisticated relationship with the ANC and government, SANCO lapsed into pantomime. Many observers and civil activists were dismayed and dismissed SANCO as an 'empty shell' and a 'moribund ally'.[41]

Although styling itself as a broker between communities and government, it more often played the role of sidekick to the state. In the early 2000s, for instance, Eskom officially negotiated a write-off of electricity payment arrears in Soweto with SANCO. In fact, SANCO acted less as an honest broker than as a 'sweetheart' partner of a government that was trying to undercut community restiveness and the mobilising potential of new social movements. Behind the scenes, government had arranged the deal with Eskom, but staged it as a SANCO feat 'to publicly demonstrate the benefits of alignment with the ruling party' (Habib, 2005).[42] Occasionally (in Tshwane/Pretoria for instance), SANCO would use its alliance with the ANC and connections with the local state to press home community demands. The tactic of quietly supporting community activism while using its ANC links to broker local deals held some promise for SANCO. But mostly it used its relationship with the ANC to tranquilise rather than invigorate citizens' activism, as Elke Zuern (2006) has detailed. It was a short-sighted ploy.

The new formations, meanwhile, were being targeted with florid slurs. Some officials pilloried them as part of a 'criminal culture' bent on sabotaging the government's programmes.[43] Others labelled them renegade 'ultra-leftists', allegedly in cahoots with the (centre-right) Democratic Alliance and motley foreign interests opposed to South Africa's 'national democratic revolution'.[44] The occasionally baroque posturing of some groups (including the APF and LPM) did not always serve them well in defence. But the state's reaction was spirited enough to confirm its vulnerability to the criticisms and politics of these formations. Permission to stage marches is often refused and it is not unusual for the police to harass protestors and detain movement leaders. 'The ANC regards us—not the other official political parties—as their true opposition,' says *Abahlali baseMjondolo* leader Sbu Zikode, 'because we are closer to the pain on the ground.'[45]

Yet the hostility also seemed exaggerated. Most of the formations are small, many are highly localised and almost all rely heavily on the energy and resources of a handful of activists.[46] Objectively, they pose no foreseeable threat to the ANC. The enmity seems fed from two main sources. Firstly, there is the indignation of a liberation movement that sees itself as the embodiment of 'the oppressed masses' and the historic vehicle for transformation. Any challenge to that monopoly invites aggression. The antagonistic grandstanding of some activist figures feeds that disposition. Secondly, the movements underscore elemental worries for the ANC: they announce that neither its political authority nor its status as the avatar of African aspirations are shockproof indefinitely.

COSATU, still the largest (and most powerful) social movement, has not refrain from the mud-slinging, although it has tried to be more discerning in its criticisms. It drew a line between what it termed 'ultra-left' groups (with an 'anti-ANC' agenda) and 'the rest of civil society' (Buhlungu, 2006b). Wedged between COSATU and 'ultra-left' groups are disagreements 'on basic principles' that preclude collaboration, since the 'ultra-left argues that the ANC has completely sold out to capital and thus squandered the revolutionary potential unleashed by the waves of struggle against apartheid' (COSATU, 2001).[47] There is more to the hostility, though. COSATU, too, has projected itself as a 'big brother' capable of supporting and advancing the struggles of communities in general. The new social movements challenged that status (Buhlungu, 2006b) and spotlit the strategic dilemmas that continue to faze the federation.

COSATU claimed it remained steeped in a social movement tradition, but the evidence had grown so faint, argued Oupa Lehulere (2005), that alliances between it and the new social movements of the 2000s were inadvisable—certainly as long as COSATU stayed formally allied to the ANC.[48] The federation looked askance at these new formations, partly because its relationship with the ANC forced it to triangulate its options. In the prickly climate of the early 2000s, ties with groups brashly critical of the ANC risked hardening the animosity between it and the ANC. Links with the emergent social movements were rejected (COSATU even expelled the APF from its offices in 2003) and unionists advocating a break with the Alliance were disciplined. COSATU's support for the TAC was the lone exception and it was possible mainly because the TAC throughout insisted on its loyalty to the ANC and the government.

Deprived of links and alliances with a large, 'old' social movement, the new formations, meanwhile, seem trapped on the margins. Buhlungu's verdict that the APF has been 'extremely unsuccessful in re-appropriating some of the political capital and symbolism of the anti-apartheid struggle' (2006b:84) seems valid for many of the new social movements. 'The task of building a counter-hegemonic movement from scratch in a post-colonial society entails more than pointing out the shortcomings of the existing social order,' he noted (2006b:85–6). It requires converting the dissatisfaction 'into a coherent programme for an alternative social order' (*op cit*, p. 86).

In this respect, ironically, the new social movements have been operating squarely within a core tradition of the anti-apartheid struggle—delegimitising one's foes and filling the future with broad mobilising avowals. It worked then, but it is not up to the task in a democratic setting. Even 15 years into the post-apartheid era, sheer denunciation of the ANC is a weak and counter-productive mobilising discourse. The organisation continues to dominate the ideological realm and to a large extent monopolises both the semantics and grammar with which future options are envisioned. Although not ceaseless, those ideological advantages are priceless—and they help to explain why the most successful of South Africa's new crop of social movements was an entity that both challenged government and co-operated with it.

Working the system: the Treatment Action Campaign

An independent association of organisations and individuals, the TAC used the discourse of human and socioeconomic rights (a discourse shared by the liberation struggle) to force far-reaching changes in government policy, raise public awareness of HIV and AIDS treatment and mobilise grassroots activities against the epidemic. This was a trying feat. Government was in no mood for shrewd contrariness and demonised the organisation and its leaders. Government seemed more comfortable with clear lines distinguishing friends and foes, which had prevailed under apartheid and in the authoritarian socialist countries of Eastern Europe—that is, the TAC was either an ally or a foe. TAC, though, was adept not only at challenging the state, but at baiting, wheedling and bargaining with it. It was a great advertisement for the rewards of working both inside and beyond the institutions of the state.

Some of its tactics harked back to the apartheid era (Friedman & Mottiar, 2006), but the overall mix was new. Especially astute was the ambivalent relationship the TAC struck with government, positioning itself simultaneously as critic and watchdog while insisting on its status as a supporter of the ANC. TAC was the most successful of the new social movements and the most distinctive. Its starting point was the assumption that it could 'win gains from this system' and that 'far-reaching reform is possible', in the words of Mark Heywood.[49] It sought to 'work the system'. It saw potential merit in the law, recognised potential allies among political elites and pinpointed 'winnable' goals that could be achieved through a blend of conflict and co-operation (Friedman & Mottiar, 2006). Combining court-based challenges with direct action and grassroots mobilisation and forging tactical alliances with other social formations (including with COSATU and organised religion), the TAC devised the most successful adaptation of liberation struggle traditions seen since 1994. Indeed, many, perhaps most, TAC activists were also ANC members. Unlike many of the new social movements, the TAC therefore recoiled from conflict with a democratically elected, legitimate government. But as government's intransigence hardened, TAC leaders took the difficult step of challenging it with a civil disobedience campaign in 2003. The move succeeded and is credited with swaying Cabinet to approve the mass provision of free antiretroviral drugs through the public health system (Lawson, 2008).

Contributing to that breakthrough were other factors, too. In Zackie Achmat, the TAC had a charismatic and media-savvy figurehead. Instead of flinging condemnations at government, the TAC positioned morality centre stage. It worked hard at appealing 'to a sense of compassion and fairness across many of the social barriers that are often assumed to impede a common morality' (Friedman & Mottiar, 2006:31) and at occupying the moral high ground. Rather than accentuate differences and antipathies, it tried to build a basis for transcending them, if only temporarily. By shifting tactics throughout, it maintained enough initiative and momentum to keep attracting fresh activists into its ranks. These feats occurred in a particular global context in the early 2000s, where a very visible and voluble AIDS constituency was temporarily allied with the alter-globalisation movement, especially with its attack on the intellectual property rights regime (with pharmaceutical multinationals a major target). TAC plugged into this global circuitry of highly networked and dramatic activism. It drew on its data and analysis, its contacts and resources and the media attention it garnered—and it reciprocated with enthralling social drama and spectacle (Marais, 2005).

The TAC helped to legitimise and validate progressive rights-based demands. Largely due to its efforts, health (and specifically AIDS) became the only arena in which the state's monopoly on policymaking authority has been visibly and successfully challenged in a sustained way since 1994, as Greenstein (2003) observed. Subsequently, the TAC has focused on helping the antiretroviral 'roll-out' succeed—in the guise of a watchdog, as well as through grassroots mobilisation, education and training. Its heyday had passed by the mid-2000s, however.

It is unclear as to what extent the TAC experience offers a template for groups pursuing more extensive and radical social change. Association-based support mechanisms tend to be less amenable to radical social mobilisation (Pieterse,

2003). A mix of factors enabled the TAC to overcome those limits in the late 1990s and early 2000s, but it has struggled to reposition itself into a broader health or social justice movement—a difficulty some see as proof of the limits of a rights-based challenge that seeks to use the system against itself. Eventually, they argue, the system regains its equilibrium, appropriates the concessions and disarms the challenger. The challenger can regroup and recast new demands, but the ambient factors that enable success are not necessarily available at each phase of renewal.

It may also be that public health generally is a less combustible mobilising issue than anticipated. Many of the hardships and grievances associated with a disease such as AIDS tend not to be experienced as communal issues but as 'private', 'domestic' matters—with AIDS attaching an additional premium of stigma and shame (see Chapter nine). Public outrage and solidarity is less easily mustered and channelled into campaigns.

Efforts to bring about a NHI system, however, may push past those limits and become a powerful wedge for the left. The potential benefits for the majority of South Africans are huge. Although powerful, the interests opposed to it are fractious and can be pried apart with smart tactics. It presents the left (inside and beyond the ANC) with an attractive opportunity to display the political maturity and tactical nous it will need to start reversing a long string of defeats. But the left's savvy has spoiled. More than a decade of defeats and humiliations boosted its intemperate instincts and fed it a taste for brawls that has threatened to scupper isolated radical interventions such as the NHI scheme.

'Movement beyond movements'

The impulse toward control and subordination did not serve the ANC well. By the mid-2000s, many of its branch structures were anaemic and incidental to the daily realities of communities and their political authority was being questioned. The ANC's aversion to criticism and its preference for docile allies meant that potentially useful interlocutors lacked the legitimacy they needed to broker compromises and remedies. A surge of community protests would test its political authority.

Local protests erupted in force after the 2004 national elections. Inchoate and sparked by disparate gripes and demands, there were at least 6 000 such protests in 2004/05 and at least as many every year since. The hotspots were in Gauteng, KwaZulu-Natal and the North West province.[50] Most of the protests seemed to flare around 'service delivery' issues and were directed at local government officials and councillors. Gillian Hart has called this phenomenon a 'movement beyond movements' (2007:6) that reflects disgruntlement at the ANC's record in managing social progress, but which also exemplifies 'the failure of the first round of post-apartheid [new social movements] to tap into huge reservoirs of popular anger and discontent'. Few of these formations seemed to grasp this: the protests also indict their impulse to package and channel discontent into narrow, highly ideologised narratives of opposition against a 'sell-out' ANC.

The protests are complex and eclectic phenomena. Bundled into them are numerous motives, grievances and ploys. Common to most is indignation at the distant manner and scornful conduct of some local officials and the failure to involve residents meaningfully in the decisions that shape their neighbourhoods and lives. At an elemental level, they invoke the 'people-driven development' extolled in the RDP and represent a form of popular participation. The demand for specific services or redress is often in the foreground, but underpinning it is a democratic impulse that the state has been unable to engage fruitfully. Protestors focus their wrath on local power brokers, municipal politicians and business cliques, which they accuse of anything from indifference and incompetence, to cronyism and corruption. In some cases, the protests are entwined with feuding inside the ANC and SACP or are stoked by individuals who have fallen foul of local party machineries. In many places, groupings that include local ANC and SACP activists spearhead protests. Mostly, as Steven Friedman pointed out, 'the protestors are demanding public service, not delivery'.[51]

All this is symptomatic of the troubled domain of the local state. Some of its functionaries fail to represent constituents or to meet their needs, while others are self-seeking and opportunistic. Many others struggle valiantly, despite institutional constraints, to help improve communities. The caricature of indifference and incompetence is only one part of the picture, as all but the angriest and most wronged constituents recognise. Fiscally hamstrung, local councils' stock of experience, management capacity and warm bodies is hardly bountiful. Management skills are often lacking and poor political and managerial leadership are common problems. Infrastructure and services are introduced unevenly and at a fitful pace, which magnifies the impression of favouritism and the sense of unfairness (Hemson, Carter, Karuri-Sebina, 2009). Hence, the protests often express a paradox: they seem to stem less from an abject failure to provide services and entitlements, than from the *partial* success of those efforts. Very often the poor quality, upkeep and maintenance of infrastructure is at issue. The reasons for these failings are numerous (see Chapter seven).

Many of the protests are attempts to shape or gain a voice in local development processes that lock out or ignore certain constituencies. Community participation in local development is sanctioned in legislation and structures (such as ward committees) and processes have been created ostensibly to facilitate deeper democratic participation. But the local state seems uncomfortable with processes that transcend decorative 'consultations' and 'report-backs'. The participation that does occur is mostly momentary and highly regimented and takes the form of sporadic 'inputs' that garnish various stages of planning and programming cycles (Marais, Everatt, Dube, 2007; Hicks, 2006; Friedman, 2006; Williams, 2005). Ward committees were meant to deepen participation. Instead they 'have largely become vehicles for party activists rather than voters' and have been sucked into the domains of political parties and local cliques. They have become, charges Friedman, 'a phoney form of representation that is [now] part of the problem'.[52]

Deepening democracy in and around the local state requires invention and experimentation; approaches bureaucracies tend to recoil from. Conventional, formalistic processes will not encapsulate the more marginalised sections of communities (Friedman, 2006). The 'organic' circuitry of urban life is highly tensile, in contrast to the rigidities that define conventional forms of representation and participation. Its mechanisms are often opaque and problematic to outsiders and do not easily accede to the rules and customs of formal engagements (Ferguson, 2007; Gotz & Simone, 2001). Relatively stable and predictable partners, orbiting around identified interests, can be rare (Everatt *et al*, 2004). There is enormous room and need for deepening democracy in poor communities, but it is not easily achieved everywhere.

The gravity of the situation is dawning on government. Sicelo Shiceka's title—Minister of Co-operative Governance and Traditional Affairs—hints at an awareness that drastic repairs are needed. 'The relationship between the communities and local government is irretrievably broken,' he admitted in mid-2009.[53] His deputy, Yunus Carrim, has been equally candid: local government 'just ain't working', he told the press.[54] But government seemed attracted to remedies that either tinker with current structures (expanding ward committees, for instance) or repeat the bureaucratic ritual of 'organisational restructuring' (in this case, reviewing the powers and functions of the three spheres of government). Genuinely democratising local governance and development still seems a bridge too far (see Chapter eleven). Compounding matters is the fact that, at branch and district levels, the ANC is dishevelled, rife with factionalism and poisoned with patronage and expediency. Some in the ANC attribute many of the community protests to this organisational decrepitude, yet the preferred reaction is to strengthen the disciplining hand of ANC headquarters, rather than the more painstaking work of moral and political recuperation.

Keeping perspective

In other quarters, meanwhile, the protests are romanticised as a rolling rebellion against the ANC government and its policies and practices at local levels. They doubtless express a great deal of discontent—but of many sorts. The protests stem from many dynamics, not all of which signal failure of the state or rejection of the ANC or the stirrings of an alter-hegemonic movement. Reading them as an index of opposition misses the nuanced and contradictory ways in which citizens relate to political organisations. Even outright anger at the ANC does not necessarily signal complete estrangement and hostility.

A process is underway in which citizens are questioning their own loyalties, scrutinising a revered political organisation and reclaiming traditions of insubordination that the liberation movements had harnessed previously. It already has deprived the ANC of unquestioning devotion in many poor African communities. Structural weaknesses in the ANC's relationship with the citizenry are being revealed. These (and other) shifts provided the undertow for the ANC's own adjustment exercise, which became dramatised as the Mbeki-Zuma struggle (see Chapter twelve). These developments, however, can take any number of turns, only a few of which herald progressive outcomes. Much depends on the choices the ANC makes, on whether COSATU steps clear of the holding pen of the Tripartite Alliance and on whether left formations outside that Alliance are mature and sophisticated enough to capitalise on the many opportunities for advance.

Broadly speaking, the new social or protest movements potentially fulfil several roles. They can seek to push through reforms and innovations by 'working the system' from within and without (as the TAC did), they can help build alternative hegemonic activities capable of challenging the post-apartheid development path and they can seek to construct radical alternatives in the interstices of the system. All those options are mutually compatible—and all hold some radical potential. But many of the new formations are angled toward more distant horizons, pitting them against the ANC government, its political tradition and narrative of struggle. Some are drawn toward a break with conventional politics and talk of building new, genuinely democratic forms of organisation, of unleashing new forms of activism. For them, the task is not to smash the system; the system is already broken. Beginning in 2009, an ambitious effort was underway to draw together these and other currents of activism under the mantle of a Conference of the Left, an open-ended process that seeks to divert from the main liberation tradition by 'focusing on building power from the bottom up' and not fixating on the state.[55]

There is room and a need, for each and all of these approaches. Yet this compatibility is not commonly acknowledged. It is not merely a matter of which form of activism achieves the most demonstrable gains most quickly or reflects the most pristine analysis. The crucial issue is whether such different approaches (and their respective political logics) are seen to be so irreconcilable (with one another and with other formations of the left, including trade unions) that collaboration, networking or alliances are shunned. In this case, their energies and invention will stay inchoate and marginal and they will function as a destabilising irritant that gives licence to reaction. Whatever the choices made, there is a long process of experimenting, building and adapting ahead. There are no shortcuts left.

Endnotes

1   'An interview with Slavoj Zizek', *Left Business Observer*, No. 105, August 2003. Available at http://www.leftbusinessobserver.com/Zizek.html

2   With an important twist: in South Africa, the standard formula of that era—development first, then democracy—was turned on its head. The reason was obvious: in the South African context, decolonisation became democratisation, the central historical demand of the ANC.

3   In conceptions of struggle that converge on the seizure or destruction of the state, history is deemed to compress around a point of triumph, beyond which a kaleidoscope of new possibilities arc out. It is easy to forget just how pervasive and appealing such perspectives were: in El Salvador they lasted until the *offensiva ultima* of 1989.

4   This was directly linked to the SACP's (called the CPSA at the time) membership of the Communist International (or Comintern), which at its second congress in July/August 1920 had adopted Lenin's 'Theses on the national and colonial question'. Emphasised in them was the need for an alliance of national and colonial liberation movements with working-class organisations. Handed down to the CPSA at the sixth congress of the *Comintern* in 1928 was a harder line: socialism could arrive only after a phase of bourgeois nationalism had passed, the so-called 'two stage theory'. Not all South African communists received the dictum happily,

but it became a central part of the dogma that would define the party's strategy for the rest of the century. See Ellis and Sechaba (1992:17–22).

5 Wolpe, H (1975) 'The theory of internal colonialism: the South African case'. In Oxaal, I *et al* (eds) *Beyond the Sociology of Development*, London; cited by Bundy (1989:9–10).

6 Quoted in Cronin (1994b:15).

7 For more detailed discussion of the SACP's performance in the 1990s, see Marais (1998c, 1999a & 2001a).

8 Steven Friedman, 'Time to recognise that red scare is a red herring', *Business Day*, 4 November 2009.

9 Jeremy Cronin, '"Leftward shift" is a return to the essence of the RDP', *Business Day*, 30 October 2008.

10 Quoted in Ken Fireman and Stewart Bailey, 'Zuma says crisis may force less South African spending', *Bloomberg.com*, 24 October 2008.

11 Michael Spicer, 'Why business can take heart from Polokwane', *Business Day*, 24 January 2008.

12 Steven Friedman, 'Sorting illusion from reality in ANC's "shift to the left"', *Business Day*, 24 October 2008. Friedman was being kind. Even before the Polokwane 'triumph', the ANC's economic transformation co-ordinator, Michael Sachs, was recalling that 'whenever the ANC meets, COSATU will declare a shift leftwards. This is what the federation said when the ANC had its National General Council in Port Elizabeth in 2000. COSATU also referred to a shift after the Stellenbosch national conference in 2002. Similar pronouncements were made when we had another NGC in 2005'. Quoted in Sikwebu (2007:44).

13 Nasreen Seria, 'Zuma may be African Lula as anti-inflation move lures investors', *Bloomberg. com*, 28 August 2009.

14 She became chair of the ABSA Group and ABSA Bank in July 2007.

15 ANC, COSATU, SACP, 'Declaration of the Alliance Economic Summit', 20 October 2008.

16 When Zuma in February 2008 mooted a more flexible labour policy, for example, COSATU forced him to backtrack quickly and embarrassingly. The trade-union federation was wrong to assume that this was a sign of things to come, though. Zuma, with corruption charges still hanging over his head, understood the need to endear himself to COSATU. See Hajra Omarjee, 'Cosatu whips Zuma into line over labour reform', *Business Day*, 29 February 2008.

17 Anthony Butler, 'Zuma, like Mbeki, has no more use for the left', *Business Day*, 14 December 2009.

18 There is strong similarity with the underlying logic of the 'third way' experiments in the United Kingdom and parts of Western Europe. These were based on an analysis that the class compromises that had undergirded the post-war welfare systems were neither available nor viable and belonged to a particular (and, in hindsight, short-lived phase of capitalist development). The key component of those choreographed class compromises had disappeared: the ability to organise workers into strong, coherent and 'centralised trade unions in the context of large, dominant and stable firms' (Zuege, 1999:88).

19 Or, as Peter Mandelson and Roger Liddle (1996:18) put it in their book, *The Blair Revolution: Can New Labour Deliver?*: '[W]hereas the old Left saw its job as to represent the unions, pressure groups and the working class, and the Right saw its role to protect the rich together with powerful corporate interests, New Labour stands for the ordinary families who work hard and play by the rules.'

20 Cited in Pillay (2008:26).

21 There are significant exceptions, especially in the retail sector, where the South African Commercial, Catering and Allied Workers' Union (SACCAWU) has won important gains for vulnerable workers.

22 Sangoco (1996), '1996 NGO Week' report, p. 9.

23 The extent of this withdrawal from organising and networking is sometimes exaggerated. Compared with many middle-income countries, South Africa boasts a large and diverse array of non-profit organisations. These range from burial societies and *stokvels*, to issue- or project-specific neighbourhood committees (crime watches etc), co-operatives of many stripes

and colours, service delivery organisations, faith-based organisations and trade unions. A minority of them can be described as 'progressive' or 'radical'. Still, of the more than 100 000 non-profit organisations tallied in the early 2000s, some 20 000 were active in development and housing, almost 21 000 in social services, 6 000 in health and more than 3 000 worked on environmental issues. Nearly 1.5 million people participated in these activities (Swilling & Russel, 2002).

24 Instead of the term 'civil society', this section prefers the term 'popular sector' to refer to formations, organisation and movements that are self-consciously committed to transform society along just and equitable lines. They occupy a small but significant part of the field of civil society, which is dominated by voluntary, survivalist structures and by the institutions and activities of capital.

25 Author's interview, October 1994.

26 Author's interview, November 1994.

27 Cited in Ballard, Habib, Valodia (2006a).

28 See 'Mass fall-off in African party political activity', *SouthScan*, Vol. 15, No. 4, 25 February 2000.

29 SANCO's clumsy handling of criticism did not help matters. In 1998, prominent SANCO figures in Gauteng broke away to form a new federal civic structure. SANCO's Transkei region had already split in the previous year, and similar rumblings emanated from the Northern Cape and Eastern Cape.

30 Ballard, Habib, Valodia (2006b) provide a handy overview of these new social movements.

31 The environmental organisation Earthlife Africa is an important exception. Formed much earlier (in 1988), it pursued issues that barely registered within the mainstream liberation tradition.

32 Cited in Buhlungu (2006:75).

33 Cited in Ballard, Habib, Valodia (2006a:2).

34 SECC's membership profile is eclectic. The 're-connectors' are young men, but most members are middle-aged and elderly women, who tend to lead the various branches. Men, however, tend to dominate leadership structures.

35 *Abahlali baseMjondolo* (isiZulu for 'shack dwellers') emerged out of a road blockade protest in Durban in early 2005 and now operates also in Cape Town and Pietermaritzburg. See http://www.abahlali.org/

36 Cited in Ballard, Habib, Valodia (2006a:398).

37 See, for example, Trevor Ngwane, 'Socialists, the environment and ecosocialism', *MRZine*, 20 November 2009. Available at http://mrzine.monthlyreview.org/2009/ngwane201109.html

38 Nope's 'A better lie for all' poster featured a portrait of Schabir Shaik, ANC veteran and close friend of Jacob Zuma, who was convicted and jailed for fraud in 2005. A mock poster for the opposition Democratic Alliance party depicted leader Helen Zille, with the slogan 'A botox future: It's all cosmetic'. Nope's boycott call stated: 'Our call is simple: say something, write something, show something, jam something, break something, spray something, mobilise something, mock something, paint something, fight for something [...] The theme is your dreams and what we will do together in giving a place in the world for them. Take our name, or make up your own. Embrace our manifestering, or write your own.' See http://www.nope.org.za/

39 The cosy relationship promised additional rewards for the ANC. With hundreds of its township branches in disrepair, it hoped SANCO activists could assist in election campaigning and mending the organisations grassroots presence.

40 Former Minister of Public Enterprises Jeff Radebe and Deputy Minister of Minerals and Energy Susan Shabangu.

41 Drew Forrest, 'Social movements: "ultra-left" or "global citizens"?', *Mail & Guardian*, 31 February 2003; cited in Ballard, Habib, Valodia (2006a:16).

42 In truth, credit for the write-offs belonged with the SECC. Zuern (2006:191) quotes an anonymous SANCO leader gloating about the tactics: 'As a civic movement we grab those

people that support Trevor [Ngwane], look at their issues and actually change them. We can strategise [...] Let the credit come to SANCO and then SANCO will take the credit back to government.'

43 See, for instance, Radebe, J (2001) 'Speech of Jeff Radebe, Minister of Public Enterprises', Workshop on service delivery framework, 30 November, Megawatt Park (Johannesburg), and Moleketi, J and Jele, J (2002) 'Two strategies of the national liberation movement in the struggle for the victory of the national democratic revolution', Discussion document, ANC, Johannesburg. Both cited in Egan and Wafer (2006).

44 See, for example, the ANC Political Education Unit's document 'Contribution to the NEC/NWC response to the "Cronin Interviews" on the issue of neoliberalism', issued in September 2002 and Dumisani Makhaye's 'Left factionalism and the NDR: the ANC must respond to the professionals of the "left"'. Those with longer memories knew that this was not a new turn. Addressing the ANC's national conference in December 1997, Nelson Mandela had lashed at critical civil groupings and accused them of collaborating with foreign donors to undermine the ANC and transformation efforts.

45 Quoted in Niren Tolsi, 'Freedom's prisoners', *Mail & Guardian*, 23 December 2009.

46 Andile Mngxitama, for example, has spotted similarities between the leading roles assumed by largely middle-class (often white and Indian) activist-intellectuals in the new social movements in the 2000s and in trade unions in the 1970s, respectively. Mngxitama disapproves, describing it as the 're-inscription of racial domination in the service of a greater good' (2004:3). Unwittingly, the APF has underlined such parallel by trying to model itself on the trade-union movement that emerged in the early 1970s. See APF Gauteng (2003) 'Celebrate May Day, celebrate the 30 years of Durban strikes' pamphlet, 1 May; cited in Buhlungu (2006b:82 & 85).

47 Some of the antipathy involves particular disputes with the APF, which COSATU believes was 'hijacked' by anti-ANC activists. The South African Municipal Workers' Union insists it created the APF, which was then launched by COSATU. Relations with the trade-union federation soured badly, however, even though COSATU had been vocal in opposing neoliberal policies. Also puzzling, as Sakhela Buhlungu (2006b:77) notes, was the APF's failure to make inroads with other working-class formations (such as the National Council of Trade Unions).

48 Lehulere's essay sparked an emotive debate, part of which was compiled in the *Khanya* journal, No. 11, December 2005.

49 Quoted in Friedman and Mottiar (2006:27).

50 The data are from the SAPS Crime Combating Operations, Visible Policing Unit. Between 2004/05 and 2007/08, Mpumalanga had the lowest number of protest actions.

51 Steven Friedman, 'People are demanding public service, not service delivery', *Business Day*, 29 July 2009.

52 Steven Friedman, 'Fixing the toy telephone will not still the grassroots clamour', *Business Day*, 26 August 2009.

53 Quoted in Maureen Isaacson, 'Turnaround minister is custom-made', *Sunday Independent* [Johannesburg], 2 August 2009.

54 Karima Brown, 'SA's provinces under fire', *Business Day*, 22 August 2009.

55 See Mmanaledi Mataboge, 'New life for the left?', 3 December 2009, *Mail & Guardian*.

Acronyms

AIDS	Acquired immune deficiency syndrome
ANC	African National Congress
ANCYL	ANC Youth League
APDP	Automotive Production and Development Plan
APF	Anti-Privatisation Forum
ARV	Antiretroviral
ART	Antiretroviral therapy (or treatment)
AsgiSA	Accelerated and Shared Growth Initiative for South Africa
BEE	Black economic empowerment
CBO	Community-based organisation
COPE	Congress of the People Party
COSATU	Congress of South African Trade Unions
CPSA	Communist Party of South Africa
CSIR	Council for Scientific and Industrial Research
CST	Colonialism of a special type
DA	Democratic Alliance
DBSA	Development Bank of South Africa
DEP	Department of Economic Policy (of the ANC)
EPWP	Expanded Public Works Programme
FDI	Foreign direct investment
FOSATU	Federation of South African Trade Unions
GATT	General Agreement on Tariffs and Trade
GDP	Gross domestic product
GEAR	Growth, Employment and Redistribution strategy
HCBC	Home- and community-based care
HIV	Human immunodeficiency virus
HSRC	Human Sciences Research Council
IDASA	Institute for Democracy in South Africa
IDP	Integrated Development Planning
IFP	Inkatha Freedom Party
ILO	International Labour Organisation
IMF	International Monetary Fund
ISI	Import substituting industrialisation
ISP	Industrial Strategy Project
ISRDP	Integrated Sustainable Development Programme
LPM	Landless People's Movement
LTMS	Long-Term Mitigation Scenario
MDC	Movement for Democratic Change (in Zimbabwe)
MDM	Mass Democratic Movement
MEC	Minerals-energy complex

MERG	Macro-Economic Research Group
MK	Umkhonto we Sizwe
NACTU	National Council of Trade Unions
NCCS	National Climate Change Strategy
NEC	National Executive Committee (of the ANC)
NECC	National Education Crisis Committee
NEDLAC	National Economic Development and Labour Council
NEHAWU	National Education, Health and Allied Workers' Union
NEF	National Economic Forum
NEM	Normative Economic Model
NHI	National health insurance
NIEP	National Institute of Economic Policy
NP	National Party
NPA	National Prosecuting Authority
NPO	Non-profit organisation
NSMS	National Security Management System
NUMSA	National Union of Metalworkers of South Africa
NUM	National Union of Mineworkers of South Africa
OBE	Outcomes-based education
OECD	Organisation for Economic Co-operation and Development
PAC	Pan-Africanist Congress
PPP	Purchasing power parity
PWP	Public Works Programme
RDP	Reconstruction and Development Programme
SACOB	South African Chamber of Business
SACP	South African Communist Party
SACTU	South African Congress of Trade Unions
SADC	Southern African Development Community
SADTU	South African Democratic Teachers' Union
SAMP	Southern African Migration Project
SANCO	South African National Civics Organisation
SARS	South African Revenue Service
SAYCO	South African Youth Congress
SCOPA	Standing Committee on Public Accounts
SECC	Soweto Electricity Crisis Committee
STI	Sexually transmitted infection
TNC	Trans-national corporation
TRC	Truth and Reconciliation Commission
UDF	United Democratic Front
UNAIDS	Joint United Nations Programme on HIV/AIDS
UNDP	United Nations Development Programme
URP	Urban Renewal Programme
WHO	World Health Organization
WTO	World Trade Organization

Bibliography

Abers, R. N. (2003) 'Reflections on what makes empowered participatory governance happen'. In: Fung, A. & Wright, E. O. (eds) *Deepening Democracy: Institutional Innovations in Empowered Participatory Governance,* London, Verso.

Abers, R. N. (1999) 'Practicing radical democracy: Lessons from Brazil', *Plurimondo*, Vol. 1, No. 2, pp. 67–82, July–December. Available at http://www.nsl.ethz.ch/index.php/en/content/download/387/2479/file

Abrahams, N. *et al* (2009) 'Mortality of women from intimate partner violence in South Africa: a national epidemiological study', *Violence and Victims*, Vol. 24, No. 4, pp. 546–56.

Abrahams, N., Mathews, S. & Ramela, P. (2006) 'Intersections of sanitation, sexual coercion and girls' safety in schools', *Tropical Medicine and International Health*, Vol. 11, pp. 751–6.

Abrahams, N. *et al* (2004) 'Sexual violence against intimate partners in Cape Town: prevalence and risk factors reported by men', *Bulletin of the World Health Organization*, Vol. 82, pp. 330–7.

Abu-Raddad, L. J. *et al* (2006) 'Dual infection with HIV and malaria fuels the spread of both diseases in sub-Saharan Africa', *Science*, Vol. 314, No. 5805, pp. 1603–6.

Academy of Science of South Africa (2007) 'Scientific inquiry into the nutritional influences of human immunity with special reference to HIV infection and active TB in South Africa', Academy of Science of South Africa, Pretoria.

Actuarial Society of South Africa (2005) *ASSA 2003 AIDS and demographic model*, ASSA, Cape Town.

Adam, M. & Johnson, L. (2009) 'Estimation of adult antiretroviral treatment coverage in South Africa', *South African Medical Journal*, Vol. 99, No. 9, September.

Adato, M., Carter, M. R., May, J. (2006) 'Exploring poverty traps and social exclusion in South Africa using qualitative and quantitative data', *Journal of Development Studies*, Vol. 42, No. 2, pp. 226–47.

Adelzadeh, A. (1999) 'The costs of staying the course', *Ngqo!* (June), NIEP, Johannesburg.

Adelzadeh, A. (1996) 'From the RDP to GEAR: the gradual embracing of neo-liberalism in economic policy' (research paper), Johannesburg.

Adelzadeh, A. & Padayachee, P. (1995) 'The RDP White Paper: reconstruction of a development vision?' *Transformation* (February), Durban.

Adesina, J. O. (2007) 'Social policy and the quest for inclusive development: research findings from sub-Saharan Africa', Social Policy and Development Programme Paper No. 33, May, UNRISD, Geneva.

Adler, G. (1998) 'Social partnership: a dead end for labour', *SA Labour Bulletin*, Vol. 22, No. 1 (February), Johannesburg.

Africa Watch (1991) *The Killings in South Africa*, Human Rights Watch, New York.

African National Congress (2005) 'Development and underdevelopment: learning from experience to overcome the two economy divide', National General Council discussion document, 29 June–3 July.

African National Congress (1999) *ANC Election Manifesto*, Johannesburg.

African National Congress (1994) 'Reconstruction and Development Programme: a policy framework', (base document), *Umanyano*, Johannesburg.

African National Congress Department of Economic Policy (1992) 'ANC policy guidelines for a democratic South Africa' (as adopted at the National Conference), 28–31 May.

African National Congress Youth League (1996) 'Organisational and leadership issues in the ANC: A perspective of the ANC Youth League' (discussion document), Johannesburg.

Afrobarometer (2005) 'Lived poverty in South Africa', Afrobarometer briefing, Cape Town.

Aguero, J. M., Carter, M. R. & Woolard, I. (2006) 'The impact of unconditional cash transfers on nutrition: the South African Child Support Grant' (paper), July. Available at http://www.cgdev.org/doc/events/11.07.06/unconditional%20cash%20transfers.pdf

Aitchison, J. (2003) 'The origins of the Midlands war: the Natal conflict from 1975 to 1989'. In: Greenstein, R. (ed) *The Role of Political Violence in South Africa's Democratisation*, Community Centre for Social Enquiry, Johannesburg.

Ake, C. (2000) *The Feasibility of Democracy in Africa*, Codesria, Dakar.

Akintola, O. (2006) 'Gendered home-based care in South Africa: More trouble for the troubled', *African Journal of AIDS Research*, Vol. 5, No. 3, pp. 237–47.

Alexander, N. (2010) 'South Africa: an unfinished revolution?', 4th Strini Moodley Annual Memorial Lecture, 13 May, University of KwaZulu-Natal.

Alexander, N. (2009) 'Let us return to the source: in quest of a humanism of the 21st century', *Pambazuka News*, 22 October, Issue 454. Available at http://pambazuka.org/en/category/features/59678

Alexander, N. (2002) *An Ordinary Country: Issues in the Transition from Apartheid to Democracy in South Africa*, University of Natal Press, Pietermaritzburg.

Alexander, N. (1993) 'Nation-building: an interview', *Work in Progress*, No. 93 (November), Johannesburg.

Aliber, M. (2006a) 'Case studies of redistributed land reveal patchy results', *HSRC Review*, Vol. 4, No. 4, pp. 4–6.

Aliber, M. (2006b) *Rural municipality case studies: land reform, farm employment and livelihoods: summary of research reports*, HSRC, Pretoria.

Aliber, M. (2005) 'Overcoming underdevelopment in South Africa's second economy: synthesis of the 2005 Development Report', UNDP, HSRC, DBSA. Available at http://www.sarpn.org.za/documents/d0001597/HSRC_underdevelopment_July2005.pdf

Aliber, M. (2003) 'Chronic poverty in South Africa: incidence, causes and policies', *World Development*, Vol. 31, No. 3 (March), pp. 473–90.

Allais, S. (2007a) 'What's wrong with the NQF?' (presentation to Wits/Umalusi seminar), 29 August, University of the Witwatersrand, Johannesburg.

Allais, S. (2007b) 'Education service delivery', *Progress in Development Studies*, Vol. 7, No. 1, pp. 65–78.

Allais, S. (2003) 'The national qualifications framework in South Africa: a democratic project trapped in a neoliberal paradigm?' (seminar paper), 14 March, Randse Afrikaanse Universiteit, Johannesburg.

Alstott, A.L. (2000) 'Good for women', *Boston Review*, October–November. Available at http://bostonreview.net/BR25.5/alstott.html

Altbeker, A. (2007) *A Country at War with Itself*, Jonathan Ball Publishers, Johannesburg.

Altman, M. & Hemson, D. (2007) 'The role of expanded public works programmes in halving unemployment' (research paper), August, Employment Growth and Development Initiative, Human Sciences Research Council, Pretoria.

Altman, M. (2005) 'The state of employment'. In: Daniel, J., Southall, R. & Lutchman, J. (eds) *State of the Nation: South Africa 2004–2005*, HSRC Press, Cape Town.

Altvater, E. (2007a) 'The social and natural environment of fossil capitalism'. In: Panitch L. & Leys, C. (eds) *Socialist Register 2007: Coming to Terms with Nature*, Monthly Review Press, New York.

Altvater, E. (2007b) 'A Marxist ecological economics', (review of Paul Burkett, *Marxism and Ecological Economics: Toward a Red and Green Political Economy*), *Monthly Review*, January. Available at http://www.monthlyreview.org/0107altvater.htm

Amin, S. (2010) 'The battlefields chosen by contemporary capitalism' (seminar paper), World Social Forum, 25–29 January, Porto Alegre. Available at http://seminario10anosdepois.wordpress.com/2009/12/01/the-battlefields-chosen-by-contemporary-imperialism/#more-37

Amin, S. (1998) 'The challenge of globalization' (paper), Third World Forum, Dakar.

Amin, S. (1997) 'For a progressive and democratic new world order' (conference paper), Afro-Asian Solidarity Organization conference, April, Cairo.

Amin, S. (1996) 'Regionalisation in the Third World' (paper), Third World Forum, Dakar.

Amin, S. (1993a) 'Social movements in the periphery'. In: Wignaraja, P. (ed) *New Social Movements in the South: Empowering the People*, Zed, London.

Amin, S. (1993b) 'SA in the Global Economic System', *Work in Progress*, No. 87 (March), Johannesburg.

Amin, S. (1992) 'The perils of Utopia', *Work in Progress*, No. 86 (December), Johannesburg.

Amin, S. (1985) *Delinking*, Monthly Review Press, New York.

Amin, S., Arrighi, G., Frank, A. G. & Wallerstein, I. (1990) *Transforming the Revolution: Social Movements and the World-system*, Monthly Review Press, New York.

ANC (2007a) *ANC 52nd National Conference 2007 Resolutions*, ANC, Johannesburg.

ANC (2007b) 'Social transformation policy discussion document', April, ANC, Johannesburg.

ANC (2007c) 'Strategy and tactics of the ANC: building a national democratic society', (as adopted by the 52nd National Conference of the African National Congress), 16–20 December 2007, Polokwane.

ANC (2007d) 'Economic transformation for a national democratic society' (policy discussion document), March, ANC, Johannesburg.

ANC (2002a) 'Secretary-General's report: organisational report to the 51st National Conference of the African National Congress', 16 December, Stellenbosch.

ANC (2002b) 'Address of the President, Thabo Mbeki, at the opening of the 51st National Conference of the African National Congress', 16 December, Stellenbosch.

ANC (2002c) 'The balance of forces' (discussion document), 51st National Conference of the African National Congress, 16 December, Stellenbosch.

ANC (2002d) 'Draft resolutions of the National Policy Conference', Umrabulo, 17 (October 2002).

ANC (2001) *A national guideline on home-based care and community-based care*, African National Congress, Johannesburg.

ANC (1994) *A National Health Plan for South Africa*, African National Congress, Johannesburg.

ANC National Executive Committee (1992) 'Negotiations: a strategic perspective', *African Communist*, No. 131 (Fourth Quarter), Johannesburg.

ANC Department of Economic Policy (1990) 'Discussion document on Economic Policy', Johannesburg.

ANC/SACP/COSATU (1995) 'The need for an effective ANC-led political centre', endorsed Tripartite Alliance strategic perspectives paper published in *African Communist*, No. 142 (Third Quarter), Johannesburg.

Anderson, B. A. & Phillips, H. E. (2006) *Adult Mortality (Age 15–64) Based on Death Notification Data in South Africa: 1997–2004*, Report No. 03-09-05, Statistics South Africa, Pretoria.

Anderson, B. (1998) 'From miracle to crash', *London Review of Books*, Vol. 20, No. 8 (16 April), London.

Anderson, P. (2000) 'Renewals' (editorial), *New Left Review*, Second series No. 1 (January–February), pp. 1–24.

Anon (2009) 'Costs/benefits estimates for National Health Insurance: a summary of analysis submitted to the Congress of SA Trade Unions' (research paper), 7 June.

Anon (1998) 'The current global economic crisis and its implications for SA' (discussion paper approved at Tripartite Alliance summit meeting), October, Johannesburg.

Anon (1997) 'Compromising positions', *Development Update*, Vol. 1, No. 1 (June), Johannesburg.

Anon (1994) 'The RDP White Paper: special feature', *RDP Monitor*, Vol. 1, No. 2 (August/September), Johannesburg.

Anon (1990) 'Prospects for a negotiated settlement', *African Communist*, No. 122 (Third Quarter), Johannesburg.

Appadurai, A. (2006) *Fear of Small Numbers: An Essay on the Geography of Anger*, Duke University Press, Durham.

Appolis, J. (2006) 'The transformation of the South African trade union movement and its challenges'. In: Gunnarsen, G. *et al* (eds) *At the End of the Rainbow? Social Identity and Welfare State in the New South Africa*, Copenhagen, Denmark [e-Book]. Available at http://www.fredsakademiet.dk/library/getimg.pdf

Arcia, G. (2002) 'Macroeconomic impacts of social safety nets', (briefing note for Consulting Assistance on Economic Reform II), Discussion Paper No. 82, Centre for International Development, Harvard University.

Arndt, C. & Lewis, J. (2000) 'The macro implications of HIV/AIDS in South Africa: a preliminary assessment', *South African Journal of Economics*, Vol. 68, No. 5, pp. 856–87.

Arrighi, G. (2005) 'Hegemony unravelling—2', *New Left Review*, Second series, No. 33 (May/June), pp. 83–117.

Arrighi, G. (2003) 'Tracking global turbulence', *New Left Review*, Second series, No. 20 (March/April), pp. 5–72.

Arrighi, G. (1997) 'Globalisation, state sovereignty and the "endless" accumulation of capital' (paper), Fernand Braudel Center.

Arrighi, G. & Silver, B.J. (1999) *Chaos and Governance in the Modern World System*, University of Minnesota Press, Minneapolis.

Atkinson, D. (2007) 'Taking to the streets: has developmental local government failed in South Africa?' In: Buhlungu, S. *et al* (eds) State of the Nation 2007, HSRC Press, Cape Town.

Austin, G. & Morris, G. (2005) 'The status of solar water heating for domestic hot water supply in the low-income sector in South Africa', Agama energy, Stellenbosch.

Auvert, B. *et al* (2005) 'Randomised, controlled intervention trial of male circumcision for reduction of HIV infection risk: the ANRS 1265 trial', *PLoS Medicine*, Vol. 2, No. 11, p. 2298.

Bachmann, M.O. & Booysen, F.L.R. (2006) 'Economic causes and effects of AIDS in South African households', *AIDS*, Vol. 20, pp. 1861–7.

Baeten, J. M., Celum, C. & Coates, T. J. (2009) 'Male circumcision and HIV risks and benefits for women', *Lancet*, July 18, Vol. 374, pp. 182–3.

Baeten J.M. *et al* (2009) 'Male circumcision and risk of male-to-female HIV-1 transmission: a multinational prospective study in African HIV-1 serodiscordant couples', *AIDS*, December [ePub ahead of print].

Bailey, C. *et al* (2007) 'Male circumcision for HIV prevention in young men in Kisumu, Kenya: a randomised controlled trial', *Lancet*, Vol. 369, pp. 643–56.

Baker, P., Boraine, A. & Krafchik, W. (eds) (1993) *South Africa and the World Economy in the 1990s*, David Philip, Cape Town.

Balibar, E. & Wallerstein, I. (1991) *Race, Nation, Class: Ambiguous Identities*, Verso, London.

Ballard, R., Habib, A. & Valodia I. (2006a) 'Introduction: from anti-apartheid to post-apartheid social movements'. In: Ballard, R., Habib, A. & Valodia I. (eds) *Voices of Protest: Social Movements in Post-apartheid South Africa*, University of KwaZulu-Natal Press, Pietermaritzburg.

Ballard, R., Habib, A. & Valodia, I. (2006b) 'Social movements in South Africa: promoting crisis or creating stability?'. In: Padayachee, V. (ed) *The Development Decade? Economic and Social Change in South Africa, 1994–2004*, HSRC Press, Cape Town.

Ballard, R. *et al* (2005) 'Globalization, marginalization and contemporary social movements in South Africa', *African Affairs*, Vol. 104, No. 417, pp. 615–34.

Banerjee A. *et al* (2009) *The miracle of microfinance: evidence from a randomized evaluation*, Poverty Action Lab, Massachusetts Institute of Technology. Available at: http://www.povertyactionlab.org/papers/101_Duflo_Micro finance_Miracle.pdf

Banerjee, A. *et al* (2006) 'Why has unemployment risen in the new South Africa?' Centre for International Development Working Paper No. 134, October, Harvard University.

Barchiesi, F. (2009) 'That melancholic object of desire: work and official discourse before and after Polokwane' (paper presented to 2009 Congress of the South African Sociological Association), July, Johannesburg.

Barchiesi, F. (2008) 'Hybrid social citizenship and the normative centrality of wage labor in post-apartheid South Africa', *Mediations*, Vol. 24, No. 1, pp 52–67.

Barchiesi, F. (2007) '"Schooling bodies to hard work": wage labor, citizenship, and social discipline in the policy discourse of the South African State' (paper presented to the International Conference on The Poverty Challenge: Poverty Reduction in (South) Africa, India and Brazil), 26–29 June, Durban. Available at: http://works.bepress.com/franco_barchiesi/9

Barchiesi, F. (2006) 'The debate on the basic income grant in South Africa: social citizenship, wage labour and the reconstruction of working-class politics' (paper presented at the Harold Wolpe

Memorial Trust's 10th Anniversary Colloquium: Engaging Silences and Unresolved Isues in the Political Economy of South Africa), 21–23 September, Cape Town.

Barchiesi, F. (2005) 'Social citizenship and the transformations of wage labour in the making of post-apartheid South Africa, 1994–2001' (PhD dissertation), University of Witwatersrand, Johannesburg.

Barchiesi, F. (2004) 'Classes, multitudes and the politics of community movements in post-apartheid South Africa' (paper presented at the How Class Works conference), 10–12 June, State University of New York, New York.

Barnett, T. & Whiteside, A. (2002) *AIDS in the 21st Century: Disease and Globalization*, Palgrave MacMillan, London.

Barnett, T. & Whiteside, A. (2000) *Guidelines for Studies of the Social and Economic Impact of HIV/AIDS*, UNAIDS Best Practice Collection, UNAIDS, Geneva.

Bärnighausen, T. *et al* (2009) 'HIV incidence time trend and characteristics of recent seroconverters in a rural community with high HIV prevalence: South Africa', 16th Conference on Retroviruses and Opportunistic Infections, Abstract 173, Montreal.

Bärnighausen, T. *et al* (2007) 'The socioeconomic determinants of HIV incidence: evidence from a longitudinal, population-based study in rural South Africa', *AIDS*, Vol. 21, No. 7, pp. S29–S38.

Barrel, H. (1991) 'The turn to the masses: the African National Congress' strategic review of 1978–79', *Journal of Southern African Studies*, Vol. 18, No. 1 (March), York.

Barrel, H. (1990) *MK: the ANC's Armed Struggle*, Penguin, Johannesburg.

Barrett, J. (1993) 'New strategies to organise difficult sectors', *SA Labour Bulletin*, Vol. 17, No. 6 (November/December), Johannesburg.

Barrientos, A. & De Jong, J. (2006) 'Reducing child poverty with cash transfers: a sure thing?', *Development Policy Review*, Vol. 24, No. 5, pp. 537–52.

Baskin, J. (ed) (1996a) *Against the Current: Labour and Economic Policy in South Africa*, Ravan Press, Johannesburg.

Baskin, J. (1996b) 'Unions at the crossroads', *SA Labour Bulletin*, Vol. 20, No. 1 (February), Johannesburg.

Baskin, J. (1995) 'South Africa's new LRA', *SA Labour Bulletin*, Vol. 19, No. 5 (November), Johannesburg.

Baskin, J. (1991) *Striking Back: A History of Cosatu*, Ravan Press, Johannesburg.

Bayat, A. (2000) 'From "dangerous classes" to "quiet rebels"', *International Sociology*, Vol. 15, No. 3, September, pp. 533–57.

Baylies, C. (2002) 'The impact of AIDS on rural households in Africa: a shock like any other?' *Development and Change*, Vol. 33, No. 4, pp. 611–32.

Beaudet, P. (1991) 'Civics: a new social movement?' (paper), CIDMAA, Montreal.

Beaudet, P. & Marais, H. (eds) (1995) *Popular Movements and the Struggle for Transformation in South Africa*, Alternatives, Montreal.

Beaudet, P. & Theade, N. (eds) (1994) *Southern Africa after Apartheid?* MacMillan, London.

Bethlehem, L. & Makgetla, N. (1994) 'Wages and productivity in South African manufacturing', *SA Labour Bulletin*, Vol. 18, No. 4 (September), Johannesburg.

Beckman, B. (1993) 'The liberation of civil society: neoliberal ideology and political theory', *Review of African Political Economy*, No. 58, pp. 20–33.

Bell, C., Devarajan, S. & Gersbach, H. (2003) 'The long-run economic costs of AIDS: theory and an application to South Africa', World Bank Policy Research Paper No. 3152, Washington DC.

Bell, T., Cassim, R. & Farrell, G. (1999) 'Competitiveness and growth in South Africa' (paper presented at the TIPS Annual Forum), 19–22 September, Johannesburg.

Bell, T. & Farrell, G. (1997) 'The minerals-energy complex and SA industrialization', *Development Southern Africa*, Vol. 14, No. 4, pp. 591–613.

Bello, W. (1998a) 'The end of a "miracle": speculation, foreign capital dependence and the collapse of the Southeast Asian Economies' (paper), Third World Network, Penang.

Bello, W. (1998b) 'The end of the Asian Miracle' (paper), Third World Network, Penang.

Benatar, S.R. (2004) 'Health care reform and the crisis of HIV and AIDS in South Africa', *The New England Journal of Medicine*, Vol. 351, No. 1, pp. 81–92.

Berger, J. (2004) 'Resexualizing the epidemic: desire, risk and HIV prevention', *Development Update*, Vol. 5, No. 3, December, Johannesburg. Available at http://www.sarpn.org.za/documents/d0001195/2-Re-sexualising_the_Epidemic-Jonathan_Berger.pdf

Berkman, L. & Kawachi, I. (eds) (2000) *Social Epidemiology*, Oxford University Press, New York.

Bernstein, H. & Woodhouse, P. (2007) 'Africa: eco-populist utopias and (micro-) capitalist realities'. In: Panitch L. & Leys, C. (eds) *Socialist Register 2007: Coming to Terms with Nature*, Monthly Review Press, New York.

Berry, A. (2006) 'The impacts of globalization and liberalization on inequality', *Trade & Industry Monitor*, Vol. 37, pp. 21–31.

Bertrand, M., Mullainathan, S. & Miller, D. (2003) 'Public policy and extended families: evidence from pensions in South Africa', *The World Bank Economic Review*, Vol. 17, No. 1, pp. 27–50.

Bezuidenhout, A. & Buhlungu, S. (2007) 'Old victories, new struggles: the state of the National Union of Mineworkers'. In: Buhlungu, S. *et al* (eds) *State of the Nation: South Africa 2007*, HSRC Press, Cape Town.

Bhorat, H., Naidoo, P. & Van der Westhuizen, C. (2006) 'Shifts in non-income welfare in South Africa: 1993–2004' (paper presented at the Conference on Accelerated and Shared Growth in South Africa: Determinants, Constraints and Opportunities), 18–20 October, Development Policy Research Unit & Trade and Industrial Policy Strategies, Johannesburg.

Bienefield, M. (1994) 'The new world order: echoes of a new imperialism', *Third World Quarterly*, Vol. 15, No. 1, Oxfordshire.

Bingenheimer, J.B. (2007) 'Wealth, wealth indices and HIV risk in East Africa', *International Family Planning Perspectives*, Vol. 33, No. 2, pp. 83–4.

Bird, A. & Schreiner, G. (1992) 'Cosatu at the crossroads: towards tripartite corporatism or democratic socialism', *SA Labour Bulletin*, Vol. 16, No. 6 (July/August), Johannesburg.

Biyase, M. (2005) 'A simple analysis of the impact of the child support grant on the fertility rate in South Africa' (research paper). Available at http://www.essa.org.za/download/2005Conference/Biyase2.pdf

Black, V. *et al* (2009) 'Effect of human immunodeficiency virus treatment on maternal mortality at a tertiary center in South Africa: a 5-year audit', *Obstetrics & Gynecology*, Vol. 114, No. 2, pp. 292–9.

Blackburn, R. (2008) 'The subprime crisis', *New Left Review*, No. 50 (March/April), London.

Blackburn, R. (1998) 'Themes' (editorial), *New Left Review*, No. 229 (May/June), London, p. iv.

Blackburn, R. (ed) (1992) *After the Fall: The Failure of Communism and the Future of Socialism*, Verso Books, London.

Blair, T. (1997) 'Address to the Labour Party Annual Conference', Prime Minister's Press Office, London.

Bloch, G. (2008) 'The complexity of systems change in education'. In: Maile, S. (ed) *Education and Poverty Reduction Strategies: Issues of Policy Coherence*, Colloquium proceedings, HSRC Press, Cape Town, pp. 125–35.

Bloj, C. (2009) 'The budgeting process and the implications for social policies and poverty reduction: alternatives to traditional models' (background paper for UNRISD Flagship Report on Poverty), July, UNRISD, Geneva.

Bobak, M. & Marmot, M. (2009) 'Societal transition and health', *Lancet*, Vol. 373, No. 9661, pp. 360–2.

Bobbio, N. (1990) *Liberalism and Democracy*, Verso Books, London.

Bobbio, N. (1979) 'Gramsci and the conception of civil society'. In: Mouffe, C. (ed), *Gramsci and Marxist Theory*, Routledge, London.

Boden, T. A., Marland, G. & Andres, R. J. (2009) 'Global, Regional, and National Fossil-Fuel CO_2 Emissions', Carbon Dioxide Information Analysis Center, US Department of Energy, Oak Ridge. Available at http://cdiac.ornl.gov/trends/emis/tre_regn.html

Bohmke, H. (2005) 'Social movements, *toenadering* with COSATU: what's new in the "ultra-left"?' (discussion paper), September, Durban.

Bond, P. (2010) 'South Africa's "rights culture" of water consumption: breaking out of the liberal box and into the commons?' In: Johnston, B. R. *et al* (eds) *Water, Cultural Diversity and Global Environmental Change: Emerging Trends, Sustainable Futures?* UNESCO [forthcoming].

Bond, P. (2009a) 'In power in Pretoria? Reply to Johnson, R. W.', *New Left Review*, No. 58 (July–August).

Bond, P. (2009b) 'Interpretations of the global financial crisis and their implications for South Africa' (paper presented to the University of Johannesburg Sociology and Anthropology Seminar series), 6 February, Johannesburg.

Bond, P. (2009c) 'Labour influence in the new South African government' (discussion paper), September, University of KwaZulu-Natal, Durban.

Bond, P. & Desai, A. (2006) 'Explaining uneven and combined development in South Africa'. In: Dunn, B. (ed) *Permanent Revolution: Results and Prospects 100 Years On*, Pluto Press, London.

Bond, P. (2002) 'Thabo Mbeki's new partnership for Africa's development: breaking or shining the chains global apartheid?', *Foreign Policy in Focus* Discussion Paper, March.

Bond, P. (1999) *Elite Transition: From Apartheid to Neoliberalism in South Africa*, Pluto Press, London.

Bond, P. *et al* (1996) 'The state of neoliberalism in South Africa: economic, social and health transformation in question', *International Journal of Health Services*, Vol. 26, No. 4.

Bond, P. (1996b) 'An international perspective on the "people-driven" character of the RDP', *African Communist*, No. 144 (Second Quarter), Johannesburg.

Bond, P. (1996c) 'The making of South Africa's macro-economic compromise'. In: Maganya, E. (ed), *Development Strategies in South Africa*, IFAA, Johannesburg.

Bond, P. (1994a) 'Reconstruction and development during structural crisis', *African Communist*, No. 138 (Third Quarter), Johannesburg.

Bond, P. (1994b) 'The RDP, site of socialist struggle', *African Communist*, No. 137 (Second Quarter), Johannesburg.

Bond, P. (1994c) 'Election in South Africa', *International Viewpoint* (May), Paris.

Bond, P. (1991a) *Theory of the economy*, Pambile pamphlet series, Johannesburg.

Bond, P. (1991b) *Commanding Heights and Community Control: New Economics for a New South Africa*, Ravan Press, Johannesburg.

Bond, P., Pillay, Y. & Sanders, D. (1996) 'The state of neo-liberalism in South Africa: economic, social and health transformation in question', *International Journal of Health Services*, Vol. 26, No. 4.

Bonner, P. L. (1990) 'Desirable or undesirable Basotho women? Liquor, prostitution and migration of Basotho women to the Rand, 1920–45'. In Walker, C. (ed) *Women and Gender in South Africa to 1945*, David Philip, Cape Town.

Booth, P. & Heywood, M. (2008) 'Making progress against HIV/AIDS? The state of South Africa's response to the HIV and TB epidemics' (briefing document prepared for COSATU), October. Available at http://www.genderjustice.org.za/newspaper-articles/external-resources/making-progress-against-aids/details

Booysen, F. & Van der Berg, S. (2005) 'The role of social grants in mitigating the socio-economic impact of HIV/AIDS in two Free State communities', *South African Journal of Economics*, Vol. 73, Suppl. 1, pp. 531–640.

Booysen, F. *et al* (2004) *The socio-economic impact of HIV/AIDS on households in South Africa: pilot study in Welkom and Qwaqwa, Free State province*, Centre for Health Systems Research and Development, University of the Free State.

Booysen, F. & Bachmann, M.O. (2002) 'HIV/AIDS, poverty and growth: evidence from a household impact study conducted in the Free State province, South Africa' (paper presented at the Annual Conference of the Centre for the Study of African Economies), 18–19 March, St Catherine's College, Oxford.

Boulle, A. *et al* (2008) 'Antiretroviral therapy and early mortality in South Africa', *Bulletin of the World Health Organization*, Vol. 86, pp. 678–87.

Boulle, A., Blecher, M. & Burn, A. (2000) 'Hospital restructuring'. In: Ntuli, A. *et al* (eds) *South African Health Review 2000*, Health Systems Trust, Durban.

Bourdieu, P. (1998) 'The essence of neoliberalism: Utopia of endless exploitation', *Le Monde Diplomatique*, December. Available at http://mondediplo.com/1998/12/08bourdieu

Bottomore, T. (1983) *A Dictionary of Marxist Thought*, Harvard University Press, Cambridge.

Bourguignon, F., Ferreira, F. & Leite, P. (2003) 'Conditional cash transfer, schooling, and child labour: micro-simulating Brazil's *Bolsa Escola* program', *World Bank Economic Review*, Vol. 17, No. 2, pp. 229–54.

Bowles, P. & White, G. (1993) 'Central Bank independence: a political economy approach and the implications for the South,' *Journal of Development Studies*, Vol. 31, No. 2, pp. 235–265.

Bradshaw, D. (2008) 'Determinants of health and their trends', *SA Health Review 2008*, Medical Research Council, Cape Town.

Bradshaw, D. *et al* (2008) 'Every death counts: use of mortality audit data for decision making to save the lives of mothers, babies, and children in South Africa', *Lancet*, Vol. 371, pp. 1294–304.

Bradshaw, D. *et al* (2004) 'Unabated rise in number of adult deaths in South Africa', *South African Medical Journal*, Vol. 94, No. 4, pp. 278–9.

Bradshaw, D. & Nannan, N. (2004) 'Health status'. In: Ijumba, P., Day, C. & Ntuli, A. (eds) *The South African Health Review 2003/2004*, Health Systems Trust, Durban.

Bradshaw, D., Bourne, D. & Nannan, N. (2003) 'What are the leading causes of death among South African children?' *MRC Policy Brief*, No. 3, December, Medical Research Council.

Brand, D. (2003) 'Between availability and entitlement: the Constitution, *Grootboom* and the right to food', Centre for Human Rights, University of Pretoria, Pretoria.

Brenner, R. (2008) 'Devastating crisis unfolds', *Against the Current*, January.

Brenner, R. (2004) 'New boom or new bubble?' *New Left Review*, Second series, No. 25 (January/February), pp. 57–102.

Brenner, R. (1998) 'The economics of global turbulence: a special report on the world economy, 1950–1998', *New Left Review*, No. 229, pp. 1–264.

Brittain, V. (1994) 'Africa, the lost continent', *New Statesman & Society* (8 April), London.

Broomberg, J. (2007) 'Consultative investigation into Low Income Medical Schemes (LIMS)' (final report), Department of Health, Pretoria. Available at http://www.medicalschemes.com/publications/ZipPublications/Low%20Income%20Medical%20Scheme%20Publications/LIMS%20Final%20Report%20Draft%2028-2-06.doc

Budd, W. (1849) *Malignant Cholera: Its Mode of Propagation and its Prevention*, John Churchill, London.

Budlender, D., Rosa, S. & Hall, K. (2005) 'At all costs? Applying the means test for the Child Support Grant', September, Centre for Actuarial Research, Save the Children (Sweden), Children's Institute, Cape Town. Available at http://www.sarpn.org.za/documents/d0001821/index.php

Budlender, D. (1997) *The Women's Budget*, IDASA, Cape Town.

Budlender, D. *et al* (1992) 'Women and resistance in South Africa: review article', *Social Dynamics*, Vol. 18, No. 1, Cape Town.

Buhlungu, S. (2008) 'Trade unions and democracy in Suth Africa: union organizational challenges and solidarities in a time of transformation', *British Journal of Industrial Relations*, Vol. 46, No. 3, pp. 439–68.

Buhlungu, S., Southall, R. & Lutchmann, J. (2007) *State of the Nation: South Africa 2007*, HSRC Press, Cape Town.

Buhlungu, S. (ed) (2006a) *Trade Unions and Democracy: COSATU Workers' Political Attitudes in South Africa*, HSRC Press, Pretoria.

Buhlungu, S. (2006b) 'Upstarts or bearers of tradition? The Anti-Privatisation Forum of Gauteng'. In: Ballard, R., Habib, A. & Valodia, I. (eds) *Voices of Protest: Social Movements in Post-apartheid South Africa*, University of KwaZulu-Natal Press, Pietermaritzburg.

Buhlungu, S. (2003) 'The state of trade unionism in post-apartheid South Africa'. In: Daniel, J., Habib, A. & Southall, R. (eds) *The State of the Nation 2003–2004*, HSRC Press, Cape Town.

Buhlungu, S. (1997) 'Flogging a dying horse? COSATU and the Alliance', *SA Labour Bulletin*, Vol. 21, No. 1 (February), Johannesburg.

Bull, M. (2001) 'You can't a build a new society with a Stanley knife', *London Review of Books*, Vol. 23, No. 19, pp. 3–7.

Bundy, C. (1999) 'Truth ... or Reconciliation', *Southern Africa Report* (August), Toronto.

Bundy, C. (1993) 'Theory of a special type', *Work in Progress*, No. 89 (June), Johannesburg.

Bundy, C. (1991) 'Marxism in South Africa: context, themes and challenges', *Transformation*, No. 16, pp. 56–66.

Bundy, C. (1989) 'Around which corner? Revolutionary theory and contemporary South Africa', *Transformation*, No. 8, pp. 11–23.

Bundy, C. (1987) 'History, revolution and South Africa', *Transformation*, No. 4, pp. 60–75.

Burbach, R., Nunez, O. & Kagarlitsky, B. (1997) *Globalization and its Discontents: The Rise of Postmodern Socialism*, Pluto Press, London.

Burchell, G. (1993) 'Liberal government and techniques of self', *Economy and Society*, No. 22, pp. 267–82.

Bureau of Economic Research (2006) 'The macroeconomic impact of AIDS under alternative intervention scenarios (with specific reference to ART) on the South African economy', June, BER, University of Stellenbosch, Stellenbosch.

Bureau for Economic Research (2004) 'The impact of HIV/AIDS on selected business sectors in South Africa' (research report), BER, University of Stellenbosch, Stellenbosch.

Burger, R. & Yu, D. (2006) 'Wage trends in post-apartheid South Africa: constructing an earnings series from household survey data', Economic Working Paper 04/06, Bureau for Economic Research, University of Stellenbosch.

Burkett, P. (2007) 'Capital and nature: an interview with Paul Burkett', *MRzine*, 24 April. Available at http://www.monthlyreview.org/mrzine/aguiar240407.html

Business Map (1999) *SA Insider: South African Investment Report 1998,* Johannesburg.

Butler, A. (2007) 'The state of the African National Congress'. In: Buhlungu, S. *et al* (eds) *State of the Nation: South Africa 2007*, HSRC Press, Cape Town.

Butler, J. (2004) *Precarious Life: The Powers of Mourning and Violence*, Verso Books, London.

Byron, E., Gillespie, S. R. & Hamazakaza, P. (2006) 'Local perceptions of risk and HIV prevention in southern Zambia', RENEWAL Working paper. Available at http://www.ifpri.org/renewal

Caldwell, J.C., Caldwell, P. & Quiggin, P. (1989) 'The social context of AIDS in sub-Saharan Africa', *Population Development Review*, Vol. 15, No. 2, pp. 185–234.

Caldwell, J. C., Caldwell, P. & Orubuloye, I. O. (1991) 'The destabilization of the traditional Yoruba sexual system', *Population Development Review*, Vol. 17, No. 2, pp. 229–62.

Caldwell, J. C., Caldwell, P. & Orubuloye, I. O. (1992) 'The family and sexual networking in sub-Saharan Africa: historical regional differences and present-day implications', *Population Studies*, Vol. 46, No. 3, pp. 385–410.

Calland, R. (2006) *Anatomy of South Africa: who holds the power?* Zebra Press, Cape Town.

Calver, A.D. *et al* (2010) 'Emergence of increased resistance and extensively drug-resistant tuberculosis despite treatment adherence, South Africa', *Emerging Infectious Diseases*, Vol. 16, No. 2, pp. 264–71.

Campbell, C., Nair, Y. & Maimane, S. (2004) 'Home-based careers: a vital resource for effective ARV roll-out in rural communities?', *AIDS Bulletin*, Vol. 14, No. 1.

Caraël, M. (1995) 'Sexual behavior'. In Cleland, J. & Ferry, B. (eds) *Sexual Behavior and AIDS in the Developing World*, Taylor & Francis, London.

Carnoy, M. & Chisholm, L. (2008) 'Towards understanding student academic performance in South Africa: a pilot study of grade 6 mathematics lessons in Gauteng province' (prepared for the Spencer Foundation), April.

Carter, J. (2008) 'Education in South Africa: some points for policy coherence'. In: Maile, S. (ed) *Education and Poverty Reduction Strategies: Issues of Policy Coherence*. Colloquium proceedings, HSRC Press, Cape Town, pp. 19–38.

Carter, M.R. & May, J. (2001) 'One kind of freedom: poverty dynamics in post-apartheid South Africa', *World Development*, Vol. 29, No. 12, pp. 1987–2006.

Carton, B. (2003) 'The forgotten compass of death: apocalypse then and now in the social history of South Africa', *Journal of World History*, Vol. 37, pp. 199–218.

Casale, D. & Posel, D. (2009) 'Unions and the gender wage gap in South Africa', Working Paper No. 113, School of Development Studies, University of KwaZulu-Natal.

Casale, D., Muller, C. & Posel, D. (2005) 'Two million net new jobs: a reconsideration of the rise in employment in South Africa, 1995–2003', DPRU Working Paper No. 05/97, Development Policy Research Unit, University of Cape Town.

Casale, D. (2004) 'What has the feminization of the labour market bought women in South Africa? Trends in labour force participation, employment and earnings, 1995–2001', Development Policy Research Unit Working Paper, 04(84), Cape Town.

Casale, D., Muller, C. & Posel, D. (2004) '"Two million net new jobs": a reconsideration of the rise in employment in South Africa, 1995–2003' (unpublished paper), Department of Economics, University of KwaZulu-Natal.

Case, A., Hosegood, V. & Lund, F. (2005) 'The reach and impact of child support grants: evidence from KwaZulu-Natal', Development Southern Africa, Vol. 22, No. 4, pp. 467–82.

Case, A. & Deaton, A. (1998) 'Large cash transfers to the elderly in South Africa', The Economic Journal, Vol. 108, No. 450 (September), pp. 1330–61.

Castells, M. & Portes, A. (1989) 'World underneath: the origins, dynamics, and effects of the informal economy'. In: Portes, A., Castells, M. & Benton, L.A. (eds) The Informal Economy: Studies in Advanced and Less Advanced Developed Countries, Johns Hopkins University Press, Baltimore, pp.11–37.

Castree, N. (2006) 'Commentary', Environment and Planning, Vol. 38, No. 1, pp. 1–6.

Centre for Applied Legal Studies [CALS] (2008) 'Submission to Parliament on free basic water', August, University of Witwatersrand, Johannesburg. Available at http://www.pmg.org.za/files/docs/080813cals.doc

Chabane, N. (2006) 'The changing face and strategies of big business in South Africa: more than a decade of political democracy', Industrial and Corporate Change, Vol. 15, No. 3, pp. 549–77.

Chambers, R. (1995) 'Poverty and livelihoods: whose reality counts', Discussion Paper No. 241, Institute of Development Studies, Sussex University, Brighton.

Chambers, R. (1988) 'Poverty in India: concepts, measurement and reality', IDS Working Paper, Sussex University, Brighton.

Chari, S. 2005. 'Political work: the Holy Spirit and the labours of activism in the shadow of Durban's refineries'. In: From Local Processes to Global Forces, Centre for Civil Society Research Reports, Vol. 1, University of KwaZulu-Natal, Durban.

Chatterji, M. et al (2005) 'The factors influencing transactional sex among young men and women in 12 sub-Saharan African countries', Social Biology, Vol. 52, Nos. 1–2, pp. 56–72.

Chen, L. et al (2007) 'Sexual risk factors for HIV infection in early and advanced HIV epidemics in Sub-Saharan Africa: systematic overview of 68 epidemiological studies', PLoS ONE, Vol. 2, No. 10: e1001.

Chersich, M. F. & Rees, H. V. (2008) 'Vulnerability of women in southern Africa to infection with HIV: biological determinants and priority health sector interventions', AIDS, Vol. 22, Suppl. 4, pp. S27–40.

Chigwedere, P. et al (2008) 'Estimating the lost benefits of antiretroviral drug use in South Africa', Journal of Acquired Immune Deficiency Syndrome, Vol. 49, No. 4, pp. 410–15.

Children's Institute (2009a) 'HIV and health: teenage pregnancy' (fact sheet), Children's Institute, University of Cape Town. Available at http://www.childrencount.ci.org.za

Children's Institute (2009b) 'Nutrition: child hunger' (fact sheet), Children's Institute, University of Cape Town. Available at http://www.childrencount.ci.org.za

Chimbiri, A. M. (2007) 'The condom is an "intruder" in marriage: evidence from rural Malawi', Social Science and Medicine, Vol. 64, No. 5, pp. 1102–15.

Chipkin, I. & Manfunisa, J. (2005) 'Ten-year review of local government' (paper prepared for the Department of Provincial and Local Government by the HSRC) HSRC, Pretoria.

Chirambo, K. & Steyn, J. (2009) AIDS and local government in South Africa: examining the impact of an epidemic on ward councillors, IDASA, Cape Town.

Chisholm, L. (2008a) 'The meaning of racial redress in South African schools, 1994 to 2006'. In: Habib, A. & Bentley, K. (eds) Racial Redress and Citizenship in South Africa, HSRC Press, Cape Town, pp. 230–62.

Chisholm, L. (2008b) 'Migration, citizenship and South African history textbooks', *South African Historical Journal*, Vol. 60, No. 3, pp. 353–74.

Chisholm, L. (2006) 'South Africa's new education system: great intentions—harsh realities'. In: Gunnarsen, G. *et al* (eds) *At the End of the Rainbow? Social Identity and Welfare State in the New South Africa*, pp. 143–152.

Chisholm, L. & Sujee, M. (2006) 'Tracking racial desegregation in South African schools', *Journal of Education*, Vol. 40, Copenhagen, Denmark [e-Book]. Available at http://www.fredsakademiet.dk/library/getimg.pdf

Chisholm, L. (2005) 'The state of South Africa's schools'. In: Daniel, J., Southall, R. & Lutchman, J. (eds) *State of the Nation: South Africa 2004–2005*, HSRC Press, Cape Town, pp. 201–26.

Chisholm, L., Motala, S. & Vally, S. (2003) (eds) *South African Education Policy Review*, Heinemann, Johannesburg.

Chopra, M. *et al* (2009) 'Saving the lives of South Africa's mothers, babies, and children: can the health system deliver?' *Lancet*, Vol. 374, No. 9692, pp. 835–46.

Christie, R. (1984) *Electricity, Industry and Class in South Africa*, Macmillan, London.

Claassens, A. & Cousins, B. (2008) *Land, Power and Custom: Controversies Generated by South Africa's Land Rights Act*, University of Cape Town Press, Cape Town.

Clarke, G. *et al* (2007) *South Africa: an assessment of the investment climate*, Africa Private Sector Group, World Bank, Department of Trade and Industry [South Africa], and Citizen Surveys.

Clark, S. J. *et al* (2007) 'Returning home to die: circular labour migration and mortality in South Africa', *Scandinavian Journal of Public Health Supplement,* No. 69, pp. 35–44.

Cluver, L., Gardner, F. & Operario, D. (2007) 'Psychological distress among AIDS-orphaned children in urban South Africa', *Journal of Child Psychology and Psychiatry*, Vol. 48, No. 8, pp. 1–9.

Cock, J. (2007) *The War Against Ourselves: Nature, Power And Justice*, Wits University Press, Johannesburg.

Cock, J. (2006) 'Connecting the red, brown and green: the environmental justice movement in South Africa'. In: Ballard, R., Habib, A. & Valodia, I. (eds) *Voices of Protest: Social Movements in Post-apartheid South Africa*, University of KwaZulu-Natal Press, Pietermaritzburg.

Coffee, M., Lurie, M. N. & Garnett, G. P. (2007) 'Modelling the impact of migration on the HIV epidemic in South Africa', *AIDS*, Vol. 21, pp. 343–50.

Cohen, D. (2002) 'Human capital and the HIV epidemic in sub-Saharan Africa', Working Paper No. 2, International Labour Organisation, Geneva.

Coleman, N. (1999) 'The relevance of workfare to South Africa', *South African Labour Bulletin*, Vol. 23, No. 2 (April), pp. 41–4.

Coleman, N. (1999a) 'The basic income grant', *SA Labour Bulletin*, Vol. 23, No. 2 (April), Johannesburg.

Coleman, N. (1999b) 'The relevance of workfare to SA', *SA Labour Bulletin*, Vol. 23, No. 2 (April), Johannesburg.

Collins, D. L. & Leibbrandt, M. (2007) 'The financial impact of HIV/AIDS on poor households in South Africa', *AIDS*, Vol. 21, Suppl. 7, pp. S75–81.

Collins, J. & Rau, B. (2000) 'AIDS in the context of development', UNRISD Programme on Social Policy and Development, Working Paper No. 4, UNRISD & UNAIDS, Geneva.

Collins, D. & Ray, M. (1997) 'The September Commission: Confronting the future', *SA Labour Bulletin*, Vol. 21, No. 5 (October), Johannesburg.

Collins, D. (1994) 'Worker control', *SA Labour Bulletin*, Vol. 18, No. 3 (July), Johannesburg.

Colvin, M. & Connolly, C. (2006) 'The epidemiology of HIV in South African workplaces' (presentation to UCLA Business & AIDS in South Africa seminar), 21–23 June, Zimbali, South Africa.

Colvin, M., Connolly, C. & Madurai, L. (2007) 'The epidemiology of HIV in South African workplaces', *AIDS*, Vol. 21, Suppl. 3, pp. S13–19.

Comaroff, J. & Comaroff, J. (2005) 'The struggle between the Constitution and "Things African"', *Interventions: International Journal of Postcolonial Studies,* Vol. 7, No. 3, pp. 299–303.

Commission on Growth and Development (2008) 'The Growth Report: Strategies for sustained growth and inclusive development', World Bank, Washington DC. Available at http://cgd.s3.amazonaws.com/GrowthReportComplete.pdf

Community Constituency in NEDLAC (1996) 'Return to the RDP' (discussion document), Johannesburg.

Connell, D. (1995) 'What's left of the South African Left?', *Against the Current* (September), Detroit.

Connelly, D. *et al* (2007) 'Prevalence of HIV infection and median CD4 counts among healthcare workers in South Africa', *South African Medical Journal*, Vol. 97, No. 2, pp. 115–20.

Coovadia, A. (2009) 'Courting morality: the fight to prevent mother-to-child HIV transmission'. In: Cullinan, K. & Thom, A. (eds) (2009) *The Virus, Vitamins and Vegetables: The South African HIV/AIDS Mystery*, Jacana, Johannesburg.

Coovadia, H. *et al* (2009) 'The health and health system of South Africa: historical roots of current public health challenges', *Lancet*, Vol. 374, No. 9692, pp 817–34.

Cope, N. (1990) 'The Zulu petit bourgeoisie and Zulu nationalism in the 1920s', *Journal of Southern African Studies*, Vol. 16, No. 3 (September), York.

Corbett, E. L. *et al* (2003) 'The growing burden of tuberculosis: global trends and interactions with the HIV epidemic', *Archives of International Medicine*, Vol. 163, pp. 1009–21.

CORE (1999) 'Study on the history of the non-profit sector in South Africa' (research paper for the Johns Hopkins Non-Profit Sector Project), Johannesburg.

Cornia, G. A. & Menchini, L. (2006) 'Health improvements and health inequality during the last 40 years', UNU/WIDER Research Papers 2006/10, WIDER, Helsinki.

COSATU (2006a) 'Consolidating working class power: for an intensification of the jobs and poverty campaign' (political discussion document), 9th National Congress, Johannesburg.

COSATU (2006b) *State of Affiliates Report* (Book 7), 9th National Congress, Johannesburg.

COSATU (2005) 'COSATU position paper for ANC National General Council on Development and Underdevelopment', June, Johannesburg.

COSATU (2003) 'Consolidating working class power for quality jobs: towards 2015!' (paper), Johannesburg.

COSATU (2001) 'Central Executive Committee political discussion document', July, Johannesburg. Available at http://www.cosatu.org.za/show.php? include=docs/discussion/2001/cecpol.htm&ID =2170&cat=Central%20Exec

COSATU (2000a) *Public response by COSATU to the 2000/2001 budget* (March), Johannesburg.

COSATU (2000b) 'Accelerating transformation: COSATU's engagement with policy and legislative processes during South Africa's first term of democratic governance', Johannesburg.

COSATU (2000c) 'Submission on comprehensive social security'. (submitted to the Taylor Task Team on Social Security), Johannesburg.

COSATU (1998) 'COSATU's response to the 1998/99 budget' (parliamentary submission), 12 March, Cape Town.

COSATU (1997) *Report of the September Commission*, Johannesburg.

Cottle, E. (1999) 'Jobs Summit fails to deliver', *SA Labour Bulletin*, Vol. 23, No. 1 (February), Johannesburg.

Council for Medical Schemes (2006) *Annual Report 2005–06*, Council for Medical Schemes, Pretoria.

Crankshaw, O. (1993) 'On the doorstep of management', *SA Sociological Review*, Vol. 6, No. 1, Pretoria.

Creamer, K. (1998) 'A labour perspective on job creation', (Speech to Industrial Relations Association of South Africa) 3 November, Cape Town.

Cronin, J. (2009) 'The present economic crisis in the world capitalist system—and prospects for the left' (paper presented to the Chris Hani Institute seminar on The Current Financial Crisis and Possibilities for the Left), 28 January.

Cronin, J. (2002) 'An interview with Helena Sheehan'.

Cronin, J. (1995a) 'The RDP needs class struggle', *African Communist*, No. 142 (Third Quarter), Johannesburg.

Cronin, J. (1995b) 'Challenging the neo-liberal agenda in South Africa', *Links*, No. 4 (January–March), Broadway.

Cronin, J. (1994a) 'Sell-out, or the culminating moment? Trying to make sense of the transition' (paper presented to University of Witwatersrand History Workshop), July, Johannesburg.

Cronin, J. (1994b) 'The present situation and the challenges for the South African Left' (discussion document), July, Johannesburg.

Cronin, J. (1994c) 'Towards a people-driven RDP', *African Communist*, No. 138 (Third Quarter), Johannesburg.

Cronin, J. (1992) 'The boat, the tap and the Leipzig way', *The African Communist*, No. 130, Johannesburg.

Cronin, J. & Naidoo, J. (1994) 'Implementing and co-ordinating the RDP through government, the Alliance, democratic mass and community-based formations, and institutions of civil society' (paper), Johannesburg.

Cronin, J, & Nzimande, B. (1997) 'We need transformation, not a balancing act—looking critically at the ANC Discussion Document', *African Communist*, Vol 146 (First Quarter), Johannesburg.

Crook, R. & Manor, J. (1998) *Democracy and Decentralisation in South Asia and West Africa: Participation, Accountability and Performance*, Cambridge University Press, Cambridge.

Crotty, J. (2003a) *The effects of increased product market competition and changes in financial markets on the performance of nonfinancial corporations in the neoliberal era*, Political Economy Research Institute, Research Brief 2003–05, July.

Crotty, J. (2003b) 'The neoliberal paradox: the impact of destructive product market competition and impatient finance on nonfinancial corporations in the neoliberal era', *Review of Radical Political Economics*, Vol. 35, No. 3, pp. 271–9.

Cruikshank, B. (1999) *The Will to Empower: Democratic Citizens and Other Subjects*, Cornell University Press, Ithaca, New York.

Crush, J. (2001) *Spaces of Vulnerability: Migration and HIV/AIDS in Southern Africa*, Migration Policy Series No. 24, South African Migration Project, Kingston. Available at http://www.queensu.ca/samp/sampresources/samppublications/policyseries/policy24.htm

CSIR (2009) 'The state of water in South Africa: are we heading for a crisis?' *Natural Environment*, Vol. 7, No. 1, April, pp. 1–5.

Cullinan, K. & Thom, A. (eds) (2009) *The Virus, Vitamins and Vegetables: The South African HIV/AIDS Mystery*, Jacana, Johannesburg.

Daly, H. (1995) 'The steady-state economy: alternatives to growth-mania'. In: Kirkby, J., O'Keefe, P. & Timberlake, L. (eds), *The Earthscan Reader in Sustainable Development*, Earthscan Publications, London, pp. 331–42.

Daly, H. (1977) *Steady-state Economics: The Economics of Biophysical Equilibrium and Moral Growth*, W. H. Freeman, San Francisco.

Daviaud, E. & Chopra, M. (2008) 'How much is not enough? Human resources requirements for primary health care: a case study from South Africa', *Bulletin of the World Health Organization*, Vol. 86, No. 1, January, pp. 46–9.

Davidson *et al* (1976) *Southern Africa: The New Politics of Revolution*, Penguin, Harmondsworth.

Davies, R. & Van Seventer, D. E. (2007) 'An assessment of the Accelerated & Shared Growth Initiative', *Trade & Industry Monitor*, Vol. 38, pp. 121–30.

Davies, R. (1997) 'Engaging with the GEAR' (SACP discussion paper), March, Cape Town.

Davies, R. (1995) 'The international context', *African Communist*, No. 139/140 (First Quarter), Johannesburg.

Davies, R. (1992a) 'Integration or co-operation in a post-apartheid South Africa' (paper), Centre for Southern African Studies, Cape Town.

Davies, R. (1992b) 'Emerging Southern African perspectives on regional co-operation and integration after apartheid', *Transformation*, No. 20, Durban.

Davies, R., Keet, D. & Nkuhlu, M. (1993) *Reconstructing Economic Relations with the Southern African region: Issues and options for a democratic South Africa*, MERG, Cape Town.

Davies, R., O'Meara, D. & Dlamini S. (1985) *The Struggle for South Africa: A Reference Guide to Movements, Organizations and Institutions*, Zed, London.

Davies, S. (1993) 'Are coping strategies a cop out?' *IDS Bulletin*, Vol. 24, No. 4, pp. 60–72.

Davis, M. (2006) *Planet of Slums,* Verso Books, London.

Davis, M. (2004) 'Mega-slums', *New Left Review*, Second series, No. 26 (March/April), pp. 5–34.

Day, C. & Gray, A. (2008) 'Health and related indicators'. In: Barron, P. & Roma-Reardon, J. (eds) *South African Health Review 2008*, Health Systems Trust, Durban. Available at: http://www.hst.org.za/publications/841

Day, C. & Gray, A. (2005) 'Health and related indicators'. In: Ijumba, P. & Barron, P. (eds) *South African Health Review 2005*, Health Systems Trust, Durban.

Deaton, A. (2004) *Health in an age of globalization* (mimeo), Princeton University, Princeton.

Deaton, A. & Drèze, J. (2002) 'Poverty and inequality in India: a re-examination', Working Paper No. 107, Centre for Development Economics, Delhi School of Economics, Delhi. Available at http://www.cdedse.org/pdf/work107.pdf

Dedicoat, M. *et al* (2003) 'Changes in the patient population attending a primary healthcare clinic in rural South Africa between 1991 and 2001', *South African Medical Journal*, Vol. 93, pp. 777–8.

De Jager, L. (2009) 'The South African education system, 2009 and beyond' (discussion paper), Cape Town.

De Landa, M. (1991) *War in the Age of Intelligent Machines*, Zone, New York.

Delius, P. & Glaser, C. (2002) 'Sexual socialization in South Africa: a historical perspective', *African Studies*, Vol. 61, No. 1, pp. 27–54.

Delius, P. & Walker, L. (2002) 'AIDS in context: introduction', *African Studies*, Vol. 61, No. 1, pp. 5–12.

Delius, P. (1996) *A Lion Amongst the Cattle*, Ravan Press, Johannesburg.

Department of Education (2005a) *Grade 6 Intermediate phase systematic evaluation report*, December, Department of Education, Pretoria.

Department of Education (2005b) *Teachers for the future: meeting teacher shortages to achieve education for all*, Department of Education, Pretoria.

Department of Education & Department of Labour (2002) *Report of the Study Team on the Implementation of the National Qualifications Framework*, Departments of Education and Labour, Pretoria.

Department of Environmental Affairs and Tourism (2007) *Long Term Mitigation Scenario*, DEAT, Pretoria.

Department of Environmental Affairs and Tourism (2004) *National Climate Change Strategy*, DEAT, Pretoria.

Department of Finance (1996) *Growth, Employment and Redistribution: A Macroeconomic Strategy*, Department of Finance, Pretoria.

Department of Health, South Africa (2009) *The National HIV and Syphilis Prevalence Survey, South Africa, 2008*, National Department of Health, Pretoria.

Department of Health, South Africa (2008) *The National HIV and Syphilis Prevalence Survey, South Africa, 2007*, National Department of Health, Pretoria.

Department of Health, South Africa (2007a) *The National HIV and Syphilis Antenatal Prevalence Survey, South Africa, 2006*. Department of Health, Pretoria.

Department of Health, South Africa (2007b) *HIV & AIDS and STI Strategic Plan for South Africa: 2007–2011*, Department of Health, Pretoria.

Department of Health, South Africa (2006) *The National HIV and Syphilis Prevalence Survey, South Africa, 2005*, National Department of Health, Pretoria.

Department of Health (2007c) *Tuberculosis Strategic Plan for South Africa, 2007–2011*, Department of Health, Pretoria.

Department of Health, South Africa (2003) *South Africa Demographic and Health Survey 2003*, Department of Health, Pretoria.

Department of Health, South Africa (2001) *An enhanced response to HIV/AIDS and Tuberculosis in the Public Health Sector: Key components and funding requirements, 2002/2003–2004/2005*, Department of Health, Pretoria.

Department of Health, South Africa (1998) *South Africa Demographic and Health Survey 1998*, Department of Health, Pretoria.

Department of Minerals and Energy, South Africa (2003) *White Paper on Renewable Energy*, DME, Pretoria.

Department of Social Development, South Africa (2006) *Report on Incentive Structures of Social Assistance Grants in South Africa*, Department of Social Development, Pretoria.

Department of Social Development, South Africa (2002) *Transforming the Present—Protecting the Future: Consolidated Report* (Taylor Report), (report of the Committee of Inquiry into a Comprehensive System of Social Security for South Africa), Department of Social Development, Pretoria.

Department of Water Affairs and Forestry, South Africa (2009) *Water for Growth and Development Framework* (version 7), Department of Water Affairs and Forestry, Pretoria.

Department of Water Affairs and Forestry, South Africa (2006) *South Africa's Water Sources: 2006*, Department of Water Affairs and Forestry, Pretoria.

Department of Water Affairs and Forestry, South Africa (1998) *National Water Resources Strategy*, Department of Water Affairs and Forestry, Pretoria.

Department of Water Affairs and Forestry, South Africa (1998) *Waste Generation in South Africa: Baseline Studies* (Waste Management Series), Department of Water Affairs and Forestry, Pretoria.

Department of Welfare, South Africa (1996) *Report of the Lund Committee on Child and Family Support*, Department of Welfare, South Africa.

Desai, A. (2009) 'Productivity pacts, the 2000 Volkswagen strike, and the trajectory of COSATU in post-apartheid South Africa', *Mediations*, Vol. 24, No. 2, pp. 29–50.

Desai, A. (2005a) 'Finding the holy grail? Making poverty in the 21st century' (summary paper), University of KwaZulu-Natal. Available at http://www.sarpn.org.za/documents/d0001284/P1523-Holy-grail_Desai.pdf

Desai, A. (2005b) 'Shadow boxing? COSATU, social movements and the ANC government', *Khanya*, No. 11, December.

Desai, A. (2002) *We are the Poors: Community Struggles in Post-apartheid South Africa*, Monthly Review Press, New York.

Desai, A. & Bond, P. (2006) 'Explaining uneven and combined development in South Africa'. In: Radice, H. & Dunn, B. (eds) *100 Years of Permanent Revolution: Results and Prospects,* Pluto Press, London.

De Soto, H. (2000) *The Mystery of Capital: Why Capitalism Triumphs in the West and Fails Everywhere Else*, Basic Books, New York.

De Sousa Santos, B. (2006) *Another Production is Possible: Beyond the Capitalist Canon*, Verso Books, London.

De Swardt, C. (2003) 'Unravelling chronic poverty in South Africa: some food for thought' (paper presented at the conference Staying poor: Chronic Poverty and Development Policy), 7–9 April, University of Manchester.

Devenish, A. & Skinner, C. (2006) 'Collective action in the informal economy: the case of the Self-Employed Women's Union, 1994-2004'. In: Ballard, R., Habib, A. & Valodia, I. (eds) *Voices of Protest: Social Movements in Post-apartheid South Africa*, University of KwaZulu-Natal Press, Pietermaritzburg.

Devereux, S. & Sabates-Wheeler, R. (2004) 'Transformative social protection', IDS Working Paper 232, October, Institute of Development Studies, Brighton.

Devey, R., Skinner, C. & Valodia, I. (2006) 'Definitions, data and the informal economy in South Africa: a critical analysis'. In: Padayachee, V. (ed) *The Development Decade? Economic and Social Change in South Africa, 1994–2004*, Human Science Research Council Press, Cape Town.

De Waal, A. (2007) *AIDS and Power*, Zed Books, London.

De Waal, A. (2003) 'Why the HIV/AIDS pandemic is a structural threat to Africa's governance and economic development', *Fletcher Forum of World Affairs*, Vol. 27, No. 2, pp. 6–24.

De Walque, D. (2007) 'Sero-discordant couples in five African countries: implications for prevention strategies', *Population and Development Review*, Vol. 33, No. 3, pp. 501–23.

Dew-Becker, I. & Gordon, R. J. (2005) 'Where did the productivity go? Inflation dynamics and the distribution of income' (paper presented at the 81st Meeting of the Brookings Panel on Economic Activity), September 8–9, Washington DC.

Dexter, P. (1996) '75 years of the South African Communist Party', *SA Labour Bulletin*, Vol. 20, No. 4 (August), Johannesburg.

Dexter, P. (1995a) 'The big myth—sunset clauses and the public service', *African Communist*, No. 139/140 (First Quarter), Johannesburg.

Dexter, P. (1995b) 'The RDP: ensuring transformation through the state and popular transformation', *SA Labour Bulletin*, Vol. 19, No. 4 (September), Johannesburg.

Dexter, P. (1994) 'Make the RDP make the Left', *Work in Progress*, No. 95 (February/March), Johannesburg.

DFID (1999) 'Economic well-being', International Development Target Strategy Paper (consultation document), December, Department for International Development, London.

Di Lollo, A. (2006) 'A critical examination of the concept of welfare dependency: its assumptions, underlying values and manifestation in social policy, internationally and in South Africa' (Masters thesis), Department of Social Development, University of Cape Town, Cape Town. Available at http://web.uct.ac.za/depts/politics/depnews/PG_Notices/THESES/Di%20Lollo%20A%20 dissertation%202006.doc

Dlamini, K. (1999) 'Globalisation: can unions reinvent themselves?' *SA Labour Bulletin*, Vol. 23, No. 1 (February), Johannesburg.

Dugard, J. (2003) 'South Africa's low-intensity conflict'. In: Greenstein, R. (ed) *The Role of Political Violence in South Africa's Democratization*, Community Agency for Social Enquiry, Johannesburg.

Dunkle, K.L. *et al* (2007) 'Transactional sex with casual and main partners among young South African men in the rural Eastern Cape: prevalence, predictors and associations with gender-based violence', *Social Science & Medicine*, Vol. 65, No. 6, pp. 1235–48.

Dunkle, K. L. *et al* (2006) 'Perpetration of partner violence and HIV risk behaviour among young men in the rural Eastern Cape, South Africa', *AIDS*, Vol. 20, No. 16, pp. 2107–14.

Dunkle, K. *et al* (2004a) 'Transactional sex among women in Soweto, South Africa: prevalence, risk factors and association with HIV infection', *Social Science and Medicine*, Vol. 59, No. 8, pp. 1581–92.

Dunkle, K. L. *et al* (2004b) 'Gender-based violence, relationship power, and risk of HIV infection among women attending antenatal clinics in South Africa', *Lancet*, Vol. 363, No. 9419, pp. 1415–21.

Dunkle, K. L. *et al* (2004c) 'Prevalence and patterns of gender-based violence and revictimization among women attending antenatal clinics in Soweto, South Africa', *American Journal of Epidemiology*, Vol. 160, pp. 230–9.

Du Toit, A. (2007) 'Poverty measurement blues: some reflections on the space for understanding "chronic" and "structural" poverty in South Africa', Q-Squared Working Paper No. 33, February, Toronto.

Du Toit, A. (2005) 'Hungry in the valley of plenty', *Mail & Guardian*, 15 April.

Du Toit, A. (2004a) 'Social exclusion discourse and chronic poverty: a South African case study', *Development and Change*, Vol. 35, No. 5 (November), pp. 987–1010.

Du Toit, A. (2004b) 'Why poor people stay poor: the challenge of chronic poverty', *New Agenda*, No. 16.

Du Toit, A. (2004c). 'The sociology of "chronic" poverty in South Africa: challenges for action and research' (paper presented at the 2004 conference of the South African Sociological Association), Johannesburg.

Dwyer, P. (2006) 'The Concerned Citizens Forum: a fight within a fight'. In: Ballard, R., Habib, A. & Valodia, I. (eds) *Voices of Protest: Social Movements in Post-apartheid South Africa*, University of KwaZulu-Natal Press, Pietermaritzburg.

Eagleton, T. (2006) 'Have you seen my Dada boss?', *London Review of Books*, Vol. 28, No. 23, 30 November, pp. 9–10.

Eagleton, T. (1994) 'Ideology and its vicissitudes in western Marxism'. In: Zizek, S. (ed) *Mapping Ideology*, Verso Books, London.

Earthlife Africa (2009) *Climate Change, Development and Energy Problems in South Africa: Another World is Possible*, Earthlife Africa & Oxfam International, Johannesburg.

Economist Intelligence Unit (2007) *South Africa Annual Report*, Economist Intelligence Unit, London.

Edigheji, O. (2005) 'A democratic developmental state in Africa?' (concept paper), Centre for Policy Studies, Research Report 105, May, Centre for Policy Studies, Johannesburg.

Edmonds, E., Mammen, K. & Miller, D. (2003) 'Rearranging the family? Income support and elderly living arrangements in a low income country', Mimeo, University of Dartmouth.

Edwards, C. (1998) 'Financing faster growth in South Africa: the case for reforming the financial sector', *Transformation*, No. 35, Durban.

Egan, A. & Wafer, A. (2006) 'Dynamics of a "mini-mass movement": origins, identity and ideological pluralism in the Soweto Electricity Crisis Committee'. In: Ballard, R., Habib, A. & Valodia, I. (eds) *Voices of Protest: Social Movements in Post-apartheid South Africa*, University of KwaZulu-Natal Press, Pietermaritzburg.

Ela, J-M. (1998) 'Looking to a new Africa', *Le Monde Diplomatique*, October, Paris.

Ellis, S. & Sechaba, T. (1992) *Comrades Against Apartheid: the ANC and the South African Communist Party in Exile,* James Currey, London.

Elson, D. (2002) 'Social policy and macroeconomic performance: integrating "the economic" and "the social"'(research paper), July, UNRISD, Geneva.

EPRI (2004) 'The Social and Economic Impact on South Africa's Social Security System' (report commissioned by the Directorate: Finance and Economics), Economic Policy Research Institute, Cape Town.

Epstein, H. (2007) *The Invisible Cure: Africa, the West and the Fight against AIDS*, Penguin Books, London.

Epstein, G. (2005) 'Introduction: financialization and the world economy'. In: Epstein, G. (ed), *Financialization and the World Economy*, Edward Elgar, Chelthenham.

Erwin, A. (1999a) 'Interview with Alec Erwin', *Global Dialogue*, Vol. 4, No. 1 (April), Johannesburg.

Erwin, A. (1999b) 'Address by Minister Alec Erwin: Trade and Industry Budget Vote', 9 March, Cape Town.

Erwin, A. (1994) 'The RDP: a view from the tripartite alliance', *SA Labour Bulletin*, Vol. 18, No. 1 (Jan/Feb), Johannesburg.

Erwin, A. (1990) 'South Africa's post-apartheid economy: planning for prosperity', *SA Labour Bulletin*, Vol. 14, No. 6, Johannesburg.

Erwin, A. (1989) 'Thoughts on a planned economy', *Work in Progress*, No. 61 (September/October), Johannesburg.

Escobar, A. (2002) 'The problematization of poverty'. In: Schech, S. & Haggis, J. (eds) *Development*, Blackwell Publishers, Oxford.

Escobar, A. (1995) *Encountering Development: The Making and Unmaking of the Third World*, Princeton University Press, Princeton.

Esterhuysen, P. (ed) (1994) *South Africa in Subequatorial Africa: Economic Integration*, Africa Institute of South Africa, Pretoria.

Etkind, R. & Harvey, S. (1993) 'The workers' ceasefire', *SA Labour Bulletin*, Vol. 17, No. 5 (September/October), Johannesburg.

Evans, P. (2007) 'In search of the 21st century developmental state' (paper), July, University of California, Berkeley.

Evans, P. & Rauch, J. (1999) 'Bureaucracy and growth: a cross-national analysis of the effects of "Weberian" state structures on economic growth', *American Sociological Review*, Vol. 64, pp. 748–65.

Evans, P. (1995) *Embedded Autonomy: States and Industrial Transformation*, Princeton University Press, New Jersey.

Everatt, D. (2009) *The Origins of Non-racialism: White Opposition to Apartheid in the 1950s*, Wits University Press, Johannesburg.

Everatt, D. (2008) 'The undeserving poor: poverty and the politics of service delivery in the poorest nodes of South Africa', *Politikon*, Vol. 35, No. 3, pp. 293–319.

Everatt, D. & Solanki, G. (2008) 'A nation of givers? Results from a national survey of social giving'. In: Habib, A. & Maharaj, B. (eds) *Giving and Solidarity: Resource Flows for Poverty Alleviation and Development in South Africa*, Human Sciences Research Council, Pretoria.

Everatt, D., Smith, M. J. & Solanki, G. (2006) 'Baseline Survey of the 21 ISRDP and URP Nodes: Topline Report and Data Tables', November, Department of Social Development, Johannesburg.

Everatt, D., Gotz, G. & Jennings, R. (2004) *Living for the Sake of Living: Partnerships Between the Poor and Local Government in Johannesburg*, UNRISD, Geneva.

Everatt, D. (2003) 'Analysing political violence on the Reef, 1990 to 1994'. In: Greenstein, R. (ed) *The Role of Political Violence in South Africa's Democratization*, Community Agency for Social Enquiry, Johannesburg.

Everatt, D. & Maphai, V. (2003) 'The real state of the nation: South Africa after 1990', *Development Update*, Special edition, Interfund, Johannesburg.

Everatt, D. (1999) 'Yet another transition? Urbanisation, class formation and the end of national liberation struggle in South Africa' (paper), Woodrow Wilson Institute, Washington.

Everatt, D. (1992) 'Consolidated CASE reports on the Reef violence' (paper), CASE, Johannesburg.

Everatt, D. (1991) 'Alliance politics of a special type: the roots of the ANC/SACP alliance, 1950–1954', *Journal of Southern African Studies*, Vol. 18, No. 1 (March).

Evian, C. *et al* (2004) 'Prevalence of HIV in workforces in southern Africa, 2000–2001', *South African Medical Journal*, Vol. 94, No. 2, pp. 125–30.

Falon, P. *et al* (1994) 'South Africa: economic performance and policies', Informal Discussion Papers on Aspects of the Economy of South Africa No. 7, World Bank, Washington.

Fanon, F. (1963) *The Wretched of the Earth*, Grove Press, New York.

Feinstein, A. (2007) *After the Party: A Personal and Political Journey Inside the ANC*, Jonathan Ball Publishers, Johannesburg.

Feldbaum, H., Lee, K. & Patel, P. (2006) 'The national security implications of HIV/AIDS', *PLoS Medicine*, Vol. 3, No. 6, e171.

Fenton, L. (2004) 'Preventing HIV/AIDS through poverty reduction: the only sustainable solution?' *Lancet*, Vol. 364, pp. 1186–7.

Ferguson, J. (2007) 'Formalities of poverty: thinking about social assistance in neoliberal South Africa', *African Studies Review*, Vol. 50, No. 2, September, pp. 71–86.

Ferguson, J. (2006). *Global Shadows: Africa in the Neoliberal World Order*, Duke University Press, Durham, North Carolina.

Ferguson, J. (1990) *The Anti-Politics Machine: 'Development', Depoliticization and Bureaucratic Power in Lesotho*, Cambridge University Press, Cambridge.

Fig, D. (2007) 'Technological choices in South Africa: ecology, democracy and development'. In: Buhlungu, S. *et al* (eds) *State of the Nation: South Africa 2007*, HSRC Press, Cape Town.

Fine, B. (2009) 'Social policy and the crisis of neoliberalism' (paper prepared for the conference on The Crisis of Neoliberalism in India: Challenges and Alternatives), 13–15 March, Tata Institute of Social Sciences, Mumbai.

Fine, B. (2008a) 'Engaging the MEC: or, a lot of my views on a lot of things' (workshop paper presented at the University of KwaZulu-Natal), June, Durban.

Fine, B. (2008b) 'The Minerals-Energy Complex is dead: long live the MEC?' (paper presented to the Amandla! Colloquium), April, Cape Town.

Fine, B. (2008c) 'Submission to the COSATU panel of economists, on "The final recommendations of the international panel of growth"' (the Harvard Panel), 26 June, London.

Fine, B. (2007) 'State, development and inequality: the curious incidence of the developmental state in the night-time' (draft paper for presentation to Sanpad conference), June 26–30, Durban.

Fine, B. & Rustomjee, Z. (1998) 'Debating the South African minerals-energy complex: a response to Bell and Farrell', *Development South Africa*, Vol. 15, No. 4, Summer, pp. 689–701.

Fine, B. & Rustomjee, Z. (1996) *The Political Economy of South Africa: From Mineral-Energy Complex to Industrialization*, Hurst & Co., London.

Fine, A. & Webster, E. (1989) 'Transcending traditions: trade unions and political unity', *South African Review 5*, Ravan Press, Johannesburg.

Fine, R. (1992) 'Civil society theory and the politics of transition in South Africa', *Review of African Political Economy*, No. 55, Sheffield.

Fine, R. & Davis, D. (1990) *Beyond Apartheid: Labour and Liberation in South Africa*, Ravan Press, Johannesburg.

Fine, R. & Davis, D. (1985) 'Political strategies and the state: some historical observations', *Journal of Southern African Studies*, Vol. 12, No. 1 (October), York.

Fiske, E. B. & Ladd, H. (2005) *Elusive Equity: Education Reform in Post-Apartheid South Africa*, Brookings Institution Press & HSRC Press, Washington & Cape Town.

Fitzgerald, E.V. K. (2006) 'Tax reform in a globalized world' (paper presented at UN/DESA/FONDAD conference on Policy Spaces for Developing Countries in a Globalized World), 7–8 December, New York.

Flatters, F. (2005) 'The economics of MIDP and the South African motor industry' (research paper), Trade and Industrial Policy Strategies, Johannesburg. Available at http://www.tips.org.za/files/ff_economics_of_midp.pdf

Fleisch, B. (2008) *Primary Education in Crisis: Why South African Schoolchildren Underachieve in Reading and Mathematics*, Juta & Co., Cape Town.

Floyd, R. *et al* (1999) 'Admission trends in a rural South African hospital during the early years of the HIV pandemic', *Journal of the American Medical Association*, Vol. 282, pp. 1087–91.

Folbre, N. (1986) 'Hearts and spades: paradigms of household economics', *World Development*, Vol. 14, No. 2, pp. 245–55.

Folland, S., Goodman, A. & Stano, M. (2001) *The Economics of Health and Health Care,* Pearson, Cape Town.

Forsythe, P. & Mare, G. (1992) 'Natal in the New South Africa'. In: Moss, G. & Obery, I. (eds), *South African Review No. 6*, Ravan Press, Johannesburg.

Foster, J. B. (2002) *Ecology Against Capitalism*, Monthly Review Press, New York.

Foster, J. B. (1998) 'Science in a skeptical age', *Monthly Review*, Vol. 50, No. 2, June.

Foster, J. (1982) 'The Workers' Struggle: where does FOSATU stand?', *South African Labour Bulletin*, Vol. 7, No. 8, pp. 67–86.

Foundation for Global Dialogue (1998) 'South Africa and Africa: Reflections on the African Renaissance,' Occasional Paper No. 17, Johannesburg.

Frank, A. G. (1991) 'No escape from the laws of world economies', *Review of African Political Economy*, No. 50, Sheffield.

Freeland, N. (2007) 'Superfluous, pernicious, atrocious and abominable? The case against conditional cash transfers', *IDS Bulletin*, Vol. 38, No 3, pp. 75–8.

Freund, B. (2008) 'The significance of the Mineral-Energy Complex in the light of South African economic historiography'(seminar paper), 28 August, University of KwaZulu-Natal, Durban.

Freund, B. (2007a) 'South Africa as a developmental state', *Africanus*, November, pp. 170–5.

Freund, B. (2007b) 'South Africa: the end of apartheid and the emergence of the "BEE elite"', *Review of African Political Economy*, No. 114, pp. 661–78.

Freund, B. (1994a) 'The magic circle', *Indicator SA*, Vol. 11, No. 2 (Autumn), Durban.

Freund, B. (1994b) 'South Africa and world economy', *Transformation*, No. 23, Durban.

Friedman, S. (2006) 'Participatory governance and citizen action in post-apartheid South Africa' (discussion paper), DP/164/2006, Institute for Labour Studies, Geneva. Available at http://www.ilo.int/public/english/bureau/inst/publications/discussion/dp16406.pdf

Friedman, S. & Mottiar, S. (2006) 'Seeking the high ground: the Treatment Action Campaign and the politics of morality'. In: Ballard, R., Habib, A. & Valodia I. (eds) *Voices of Protest: Social Movements in Post-apartheid South Africa*, University of KwaZulu-Natal Press, Pietermaritzburg.

Friedman, S. (1999) 'Power to the provinces', *Siyaya!* (Autumn), Cape Town.

Friedman, S. (1993a) *The Elusive Community: The Dynamics of Negotiated Urban Development*, Centre for Policy Studies, Johannesburg.

Friedman, S. (ed) (1993b) *The Long Journey: South Africa's Quest for a Negotiated Settlement,* Ravan Press, Johannesburg.

Friedman, S. (1992) 'Bonaparte at the barricades: the colonisation of civil society', *Theoria,* No. 79, pp. 83–95.

Friedman, S. (1991) 'An unlikely Utopia: state and civil society in South Africa', *Politikon,* Vol. 19, No. 1 (December), Durban.

Friedman, S. (1987a) *Building Tomorrow Today: African Workers in Trade Unions, 1970–1984,* Ravan Press, Johannesburg.

Friedman, S. (1987b) 'The struggle within the struggle: South African resistance strategies', *Transformation,* No. 3, Durban.

Friedmann, J. (1992) *Empowerment: The Politics of Alternative Development,* Blackwell, Cambridge, Massachusetts.

Fung, A. & Wright, E. O. (2003) 'Thinking about empowered participatory governance'. In: Fung, A. & Wright, E. O. (eds) *Deepening Democracy: Institutional Innovations in Empowered Participatory Governance,* London, Verso.

Galbraith, J. K. (2008) 'Policy and security implications of the financial crisis: a plan for America', *Challenge,* November–December.

Galbraith, J. K. (1999) 'The crisis of globalization', *Dissent,* Vol. 46, No. 3 (Summer), New York.

Gall, G. (1997) 'Trade unions & the ANC in the "New South Africa"', *Review of African Political Economy,* No. 72, Sheffield.

Gandhi, N. R. (2006) 'Extensively drug-resistant tuberculosis as a cause of death in patients co-infected with tuberculosis and HIV in a rural area of South Africa', *Lancet,* Vol. 368, pp. 1575–80.

Garcia-Moreno, C. *et al* (2005) 'WHO Multi-country Study on Women's Health and Domestic Violence Against Women', World Health Organization, Geneva,

Gausset, O. (2001) 'AIDS and cultural practices in Africa: the case of the Tonga (Zambia)', *Social Science and Medicine,* Vol. 52, No. 4, pp. 509–18.

Gelb, S. (2008) 'SA and the world', *Financial Mail,* 5 December. Available at http://free.financialmail.co.za/projects08/sa2009/gsa.htm

Gelb, S. (2006a) 'Macroeconomic policy in South Africa: from RDP to GEAR to AsgiSA'. In: Gunnarsen, G. *et al* (eds) *At the End of the Rainbow? Social Identity and Welfare State in the New South Africa,* pp. 15–26. Copenhagen, Denmark [e-Book]. Available at http://www.fredsakademiet.dk/library/getimg.pdf

Gelb, S. (2006b) 'A South African developmental state: what is possible?' (paper presented at the Harold Wolpe Memorial Trust 10th Anniversary Colloquium, Engaging Silences and Unresolved Issues in the Political Economy of South Africa), 21–23 September, Cape Town.

Gelb, S. (2005) 'An overview of the South African economy'. In: Daniel, R., Southall, R. & Lutchman, J. (eds) *State of the Nation: South Africa 2004–2005,* Human Sciences Research Council, Cape Town.

Gelb, S. (2003) *Inequality in South Africa: Natures, Causes and Responses,* The Edge Institute, Johannesburg.

Gelb, S. (1999) 'The politics of macroeconomic policy reform in South Africa', Symposium (18 September), History Workshop of the University of the Witwatersrand, Johannesburg.

Gelb, S. (1998) 'The Politics of Macroeconomic Policy Reform in South Africa' (conference paper), 16 January, Cape Town.

Gelb, S. (1994) 'Development prospects for South Africa' (paper presented to WIDER workshop on Medium Term Development Strategy, Phase II), Helsinki, 15–17 April.

Gelb, S. (ed) (1991) *South Africa's Economic Crisis,* David Philip, Cape Town.

Gelb, S. (1990) 'Democratising economic growth: alternative growth models for the future'. *Transformation,* No. 12, Durban.

Gelb, S. (1987) 'Making sense of the crisis', *Transformation,* No. 5, Durban.

Gelb, S. & Saul, J. (1981) *The Crisis in South Africa,* Monthly Review Press, New York.

Gevisser, M. (2007) *Thabo Mbeki: The Dream Deferred,* Jonathan Ball, Johannesburg.

Ghosh, J. (1997) 'India's structural adjustment: an assessment in comparative Asian context' (seminar paper), Jawaharial Nehru University, New Delhi.

Gibson, B. & Van Seventer, D. (1995) 'Restructuring public sector expenditure in the South African economy' (paper), DBSA, Midrand.

Gibson, D. *et al* (2008) 'The state of our environment: safeguarding the foundation for development'. In: Kagwanja, P. & Kondlo, K. (eds) *State of the Nation: South Africa 2008*, HSRC Press, Cape Town.

Giese, S. *et al* (2003) 'Health and social services to address the needs of orphans and other vulnerable children in the context of HIV/AIDS', (report submitted to the National HIV/AIDS Directorate), Department of Health, January, Cape Town.

Gill, S. (1999) 'The geopolitics of the Asian crisis', *Monthly Review* (March), New York.

Gillespie, S., Kadiyala, S. & Greener, R. (2007) 'Is poverty or wealth driving HIV transmission?' *AIDS*, Vol. 21, Suppl. 7, pp. S5–16.

Glyn, A. (2005) 'Global asymmetries', *New Left Review*, Second series No. 34 (Jul/Aug), pp. 5–39.

Glynn, J. R. *et al* (2001) 'Why do young women have a much higher prevalence of HIV than young men? A study in Kisumu, Kenya, and Ndola, Zambia', *AIDS*, Vol. 15, Suppl. 4, pp. 51–60.

Go, D., Kearney, M., Robinson, S. & Thierfelder, K. (2005) *An Analysis of South Africa's Value-Added Tax*, Research Working Paper No. 3671, World Bank, Washington D C.

Godfrey, S. & Theron, J. (1999) 'Labour standards versus job creation: the impact of the BCEA on small business', *SA Labour Bulletin*, Vol. 23, No. 5 (October), Johannesburg.

Godongwana, E, (1994a) 'Cosatu approaches a crossroads', *Southern Africa Report*, Vol. 9, No. 5 (July), Toronto.

Godongwana, E. (1994b) 'Industrial restructuring and the social contract', *SA Labour Bulletin*, Vol. 16, No. 4 (March/April), Johannesburg.

Godongwana, E. (1992) 'Industrial restructuring and the social contract: reforming capitalism or building blocks for socialism?', *SA Labour Bulletin*, Vol. 16, No. 4 (March/April), Johannesburg.

Godsell, B. (1994) 'The Reconstruction and Development Programme: a view from business', *SA Labour Bulletin,* Vol. 18, No, 1 (January/February), Johannesburg.

Goldstein, A.E. (2001) 'Business governance in Brazil and South Africa: how much convergence to the Anglo-Saxon model?' *Brazilian Journal of Political Economy*, Vol. 21, No. 2 (82), April–June, pp. 3–23.

Gordin, J. (2008) *Zuma: A Biography*, Jonathan Ball, Johannesburg.

Gordon, D. M. (1988) 'The global economy: new edifice or crumbling foundations?' *New Left Review*, No. 168 (March/April), London.

Gorz, A. (1999) 'A new task for the unions: the liberation of time from work'. In: Munck, R. & Waterman, P. (eds) *Labour Worldwide in the Era of Globalisation: Alternative Union Models in the New World Order*, Macmillan, Houndmills, pp. 41–63.

Gorz, A. (1973) 'Reform and revolution'. In: *Socialism and Revolution,* Anchor, New York.

Gotz, G. & Simone, A. (2001) 'The implications of informality on governmentality: the case of Johannesburg in the context of sub-Saharan urbanization', May 2001, ESF/N-AERUS workshop. Available at http://www.ucl.ac.uk/dpu-projects/drivers_urb_change/urb_governance/pdf_partic_proc/ESF_NAERUS_Gotz_Implications_Informality_Governmentality.pdf

Goudge, J. & Govender, V. (2000) *A review of experience concerning household ability to cope with the resource demands of ill health and health care utilisation*, Equinet Policy Series No. 3, June.

Gouws, E. & Stanecki, K. (2008) 'The epidemiology of HIV infection among young people aged 15–24 years in southern Africa', *AIDS*, Vol. 22, Suppl. 4, pp. S5–16.

Govender, P. (2007) *Love and Courage: A Story of Insubordination,* Jacana, Johannesburg.

Govender, P. *et al* (1994) *Beijing Conference Report: 1994 Country Report on the Status of South African Women*, Cape Town.

Government of South Africa (2007) *HIV & AIDS and STI Strategic Plan for South Africa, 2007–2011,* April, Government of South Africa, Pretoria.

Government of South Africa (1994) *RDP White Paper*, Cape Town.

Gowan, P. (2003) 'US: UN', *New Left Review*, Second series No. 24 (November/December), pp. 5–30.

Gramsci, A. (1971) *Selections from the Prison Notebooks,* Lawrence & Wishart, London.

Gray, R. H. *et al* (2007) 'Male circumcision for HIV prevention in young men in Rakai, Uganda: a randomized trial', *Lancet*, Vol. 369, pp. 657–66.

Gray, R. H. *et al* (2000) 'Male circumcision and HIV acquisition and transmission: cohort studies in Rakai, Uganda', *AIDS*, Vol. 14, No. 15, pp. 2371–81.

Gray, J. (1998) *False Dawn: The Delusions of Global Capitalism*, Granta, London.

Green, D. (2008) *From Poverty to Power,* Oxfam International, Oxford.

Greenberg, S. (2006) 'The Landless People's Movement and the failure of post-apartheid land reform'. In: Ballard, R., Habib, A. & Valodia, I. (eds) *Voices of Protest: Social Movements in Post-apartheid South Africa*, University of KwaZulu-Natal Press, Pietermaritzburg.

Greener, R. (2004) 'The impact of HIV/AIDS on poverty and inequality'. In: Haacker, M. (ed), *The Macroeconomics of HIV/AIDS,* International Monetary Fund, Washington.

Greenfield, G. (1999) 'Who's unemployed now? Technocratic "solutions" to the unemployment crisis' (paper), Hong Kong.

Greenfield, G. (1998) 'Flexible dimensions of a permanent crisis: TNCs, flexibility and workers in Asia' (paper), Hong Kong.

Greenstein, R. (2003a) 'State, civil society and the reconfiguration of power in post-apartheid South Africa' (paper presented at WISER seminar), 28 August, University of Witwatersrand, Johannesburg.

Greenstein, R. (ed) (2003b) *The Role of Political Violence in South Africa's Democratization,* Community Agency for Social Enquiry, Johannesburg.

Gregson, S. *et al* (2002) 'Sexual mixing patterns and sex-differentials in teenage exposure to HIV infection in rural Zimbabwe', *Lancet*, Vol. 359, pp. 1896–1903.

Groenewald, P. *et al* (2007) *Cause of death and premature mortality in Cape Town, 2001–2004*, Medical Research Council, Cape Town.

Gumede, W. (2008a) 'Modernising the African National Congress: the legacy of President Thabo Mbeki'. In: Kagwanja, P. & Kondlo, K. (eds) *State of the Nation: South Africa 2008,* HSRC Press, Cape Town.

Gumede, W. (2008b) 'South Africa: Jacob Zuma and the difficulties of consolidating South Africa's democracy', *African Affairs*, Vol. 107, No. 427, pp. 261–71.

Gumede, W. (2005) *Thabo Mbeki and the Battle for the Soul of the ANC*, Zebra Press, Cape Town.

Gunner, L. (2008) 'Jacob Zuma, the social body and the unruly power of song', *African Affairs,* Vol. 108, No. 430, pp. 27–48.

Gupta, J. *et al* (2008) 'Physical violence against intimate partners and related exposures to violence among South African men', *Canadian Medical Association Journal,* Vol. 179, No. 6, pp. 535–41.

Gwagwa, L. & Everatt, D. (2005) 'Community-Driven Development in South Africa, 1992–2004', Africa Region Working Paper Series No. 92, October, World Bank, Washington.

Haacker, M. (2002) 'The Economic Consequences of HIV/AIDS in Southern Africa', IMF Working Papers, IMF, Washington. Available at http://www.imf.org/external/pubs/ft/wp/2002/wp0238.pdf

Haarmann, C. *et al* (2008) 'Towards a basic income grant for all: basic income grant pilot project assessment report', September, Basic Income Grant Coalition, Windhoek. Available at http://www.bignam.org/

Habib, A. (2009) 'Substantive uncertainty: South Africa's democracy becomes dynamic', *Pambazuka News*, 16 April, Issue 428. Available at http://www.pambazuka.org/en/category/features/55638

Habib, A. & Valodia, I. (2006a) 'Reconstructing a social movement in an era of globalization'. In: Ballard, R., Habib, A. & Valodia I. (eds) *Voices of Protest: Social Movements in Post-apartheid South Africa*, University of KwaZulu-Natal Press, Pietermaritzburg.

Habib, A. & Valodia, I. (2006b) 'Reconstructing a social movement in an era of globalization: a case study of COSATU'. In: Ballard, R., Habib, A. & Valodia I. (eds) *Voices of Protest: Social Movements in Post-apartheid South Africa*, University of KwaZulu-Natal Press, Pietermaritzburg.

Habib, A. (2005) 'State-civil society relations in post-apartheid South Africa', *Social Research*, Vol. 72, No. 3, pp. 671–92.

Habib, A. (2004) 'The politics of economic policy-making: substantive uncertainty, political leverage and human development', *Transformation*, No. 56, pp. 90–103.

Habib, A. & Taylor, R. (1999) 'Daring to question the alliance: a response to Southall and Wood', *Transformation*, No. 40, pp. 112–20.

Habib, A. (1996) 'Myth of the Rainbow Nation: prospects for the consolidation of democracy in South Africa', *African Security Review*, Vol. 5, No. 6 (Working Paper Series), Pretoria.

Hadland, A. (ed) (2009) 'Violence and xenophobia in South Africa: developing consensus, moving to action' (research report), HRSC, Pretoria.

Haidt, J. (2006) *The Happiness Hypothesis: Putting Ancient Wisdom to the Test of Modern Science,* Random House, London.

Hall, D. (2008) 'Economic crisis and public services', Public Services International Research Unit, Note 1, December, University of Greenwich, London. Available at http://www.psiru.org/reports/2008-12-crisis-1.doc

Hall, S. (1996) 'Gramsci's relevance for the study of race and ethnicity'. In: Morley, D. & Chen, K. (eds) *Stuart Hall: Critical Dialogues in Cultural Studies*, Routledge, London.

Hall, S. & Jacques, M. (eds) (1989) *New Times: The Changing Face of Politics in the 1990s*, Macmillan, London.

Hall, S. (1987) 'Gramsci and us', *Marxism Today*, June, pp. 16–21.

Hallett, T. B. *et al* (2008) 'Understanding the impact of male circumcision interventions on the spread of HIV in Southern Africa', *PLoS ONE*, Vol. 3, No. 5, e2212.

Hallman, K. (2004) *Socioeconomic disadvantage and unsafe sexual behaviors among young women and men in South Africa*, Population Council, Washington.

Hallowes, D. (2008) 'A critical appraisal of the LTMS', September, Earthlife Africa, Johannesburg. Available at http://www.earthlife.org.za/wordpress/wp-content/uploads/2008/12/ltms-final-web.pdf

Halperin, D. T. & Epstein, H. (2007) 'Why is HIV prevalence so severe in southern Africa?', *The Southern African Journal of HIV Medicine,* Vol. 8, No. 1, pp. 19–25.

Halperin, D. T. & Epstein, H. (2004) 'Concurrent sexual partnerships help to explain Africa's high HIV prevalence: implications for prevention', *Lancet*, Vol. 364, pp. 4–6.

Hamber, B. (1998) 'Who pays for peace? Implications of the negotiated settlement for reconciliation, transformation and violence in a post-apartheid South Africa' (paper), Johannesburg.

Hamber, B. & Lewis, S. (1997) 'An overview of the consequences of violence and trauma in South Africa' (occasional paper), Centre for the Study of Violence and Reconciliation, Johannesburg.

Hamoudi, A. (2000) 'HIV, AIDS and the changing burden of disease in southern Africa: a brief note on the evidence and implications', HEARD research report, June, Durban.

Hani, C. (1992) 'Hani opens up' (interview), *Work in Progress*, No. 82 (June), Johannesburg.

Hanlon, J. (2004) 'It is possible to just give money to the poor?', *Development and Change*, Vol. 35, No. 2, pp. 375–83.

Hanlon, J. (1994) 'Making People-driven Development Work', Report of the Commission on Development Finance for SANCO, Johannesburg, SANCO.

Hanlon, J. (1986a) *Apartheid's Second Front: South Africa's War against its Neighbours,* Penguin, Middlesex.

Hanlon, J. (1986b) *Beggar Your Neighbours,* James Currey, London.

Hardt, M. & Negri, A. (2004) *Multitude: War and Democracy in the Age of Empire,* Penguin Press, New York.

Hargreaves, J. R. *et al* (2008) 'The association between school attendance, HIV infection and sexual behaviour among young people in rural South Africa', *Journal of Epidemiology and Community Health,* Vol. 62, No. 2, pp. 113–19.

Hargreaves, J. R. *et al* (2007) 'Explaining continued high HIV prevalence in South Africa: socioeconomic factors, HIV incidence and sexual behaviour change among a rural cohort, 2001–2004', *AIDS*, Vol. 21, Suppl. 7, pp. S39–48.

Hargrove, J. (2008) 'Migration, mines and mores: the HIV epidemic in southern Africa', *South African Journal of Science,* Vol. 104, Nos. 1 & 2, pp. 53–61.

Harley, K. & Wedekind, V. (2004) 'Political change, curriculum change and social formation, 1990 to 2002'. In: Chisholm, L. (ed) *Changing Class: Education and Social Change in Post-Apartheid South Africa,* HSRC Press, Cape Town, pp. 195–220.

Harrison, D. (2010) 'An overview of health and health care in South Africa, 1994–2010: priorities, progress and prospects for new gains' (discussion document commissioned by the Henry J. Kaiser Foundation to help inform the National Leaders' Retreat), 24–26 January, Muldersdrift.

Harriss, J. (2007) 'Bringing politics back into poverty analysis: why understanding of social relations matters more for policy on chronic poverty than measurement', Q-Squared Working Paper No. 34 (April), Centre for International Studies, University of Toronto.

Harriss, J. (2000) 'How much difference does politics make? Regime differences across Indian states and rural poverty reduction', LSE Working Paper Series 1, No. 1. Available at http://www.lse.ac.uk/

Harris, L. (1993a) 'One step forward', *Work in Progress,* No. 89 (June), Johannesburg.

Harris, L. (1993b) 'South Africa's social and economic transformation: from no middle way to no alternative', *Review of African Political Economy,* No. 57, Sheffield.

Harris, L. (1990) 'The economic strategies and policies of the African National Congress', *McGregor's Economic Alternatives,* Juta & Co., Cape Town.

Hart, G. (2007) 'The provocations of neoliberalism: contesting the nation and liberation after apartheid' (revised version of the Antipode lecture delivered at the Association of American Geographers meeting), 20 April, San Francisco.

Hart, G. (2006) 'Beyond Neoliberalism? Post-apartheid developments in historical and comparative perspective'. In: Padayachee, V. (ed) *The Development Decade? Economic and Social Change in South Africa: 1994–2004.* HSRC Press, Pretoria, pp. 13–32.

Hart, G. (2002a) *Disabling Globalization: Places of Power in Post-Apartheid South Africa,* University of Natal Press, Pietermaritzburg.

Hart, G. (2002b) 'Reworking apartheid legacies: global competition, gender and social wages in South Africa, 1980–2000', Social and Development Programme Paper No. 13, December, UNRISD, Geneva.

Hart, G. (1994) 'The new economic policy and redistribution in Malaysia: a model for post-apartheid South Africa?', *Transformation,* No. 23, Durban.

Harvey, D. (2007) 'Neoliberalism as creative destruction', *The Annals of the American Academy of Political and Social Science,* No. 610, pp. 21–44.

Harvey, D. (2005) *A Brief History of Neoliberalism,* Oxford University Press, Oxford.

Harvey, D. (2000) 'Reinventing geography', *New Left Review,* Second series, No. 4 (July/Aug), pp. 75–97.

Harvey, D. (1995) 'Globalization in question', *Rethinking Marxism,* Vol. 8, No. 4, pp. 1–17.

Hassim, S. (2006) 'The challenges of inclusion and transformation: the women's movement in democratic South Africa'. In: Ballard, R., Habib, A. & Valodia I. (eds) *Voices of Protest: Social Movements in Post-apartheid South Africa,* University of KwaZulu-Natal Press, Pietermaritzburg.

Hassim, S. (2005a) 'Turning gender rights into entitlements: women and welfare provision in post-apartheid South Africa', *Social Research,* Vol. 72, No. 3, pp. 621–46.

Hassim, S. (2005b) 'Gender, Welfare and the Developmental State in South Africa', May, UNRISD, Geneva. Available at http://www.sarpn.org.za/documents/d0001335/P1593-UNRISD_Hassim_May2005.pdf

Hassim, S. (1991) 'Gender, social location and feminist politics in South Africa', *Transformation,* No. 15, Durban.

Health Systems Trust (2009) *District Health Barometer, 2007/08,* Health Systems Trust, Durban.

Health Systems Trust (2007a) *South African Health Review 2005/06,* Health Systems Trust, Durban.

Health Systems Trust (2007b) *District Health Barometer 2006/2007,* Health Systems Trust, Durban.

Heller, P. (2001) 'Moving the state: the politics of democratic decentralization in Kerala, South Africa, and Porto Alegre', *Politics & Society,* Vol. 29, No. 1, pp. 1–28.

Helleringer, S. & Kohler, H. P. (2007) 'Sexual network structure and the spread of HIV in Africa: evidence from Likoma Island, Malawi', *AIDS,* Vol. 21, No. 17, pp. 2323–32.

Hemson, D. (2007) 'Can participation make a difference? Prospects for people's participation in planning', *Critical Dialogue,* Vol. 3, No. 1, pp. 9–15.

Hemson, D. (2006) 'Tomorrow will be better than today: delivery in the age of hope'. In: Gunnarsen, G. *et al* (eds) *At the End of the Rainbow? Social Identity and Welfare State in the New South Africa,* Copenhagen, Denmark [e-Book]. Available at http://www.fredsakademiet.dk/library/getimg.pdf

Hemson, D., Carter, J. & Karuri-Sebina, G. (2009) 'Service delivery as a measure of change: state capacity and development'. In: Kagwanja, P. & Kondlo, K. (eds) *State of the Nation: South Africa 2008,* HSRC Press, Cape Town.

Hemson, D. & O'Donovan, M. (2006) 'Putting numbers to the scorecard: presidential targets and the state of delivery'. In: Buhlungu, S. *et al* (eds) *State of the nation: South Africa 2005–2006,* HSRC Press, Cape Town.

Hemson, D. & Owusu-Amponah, K. (2006) 'The "vexed question": interruptions, cut-offs and water services in South Africa'. In: Pillay, U., Roberts, B. & Rule, S. (eds) *South African Social Attitudes: Changing Times, Diverse Voices,* HSRC, Pretoria, pp. 150–75.

Hemson, D. & Owusu-Ampomah, K. (2005) 'A better life for all? Service delivery and poverty alleviation', In: Daniel, J., Southall, R. & Lutchman, J. (eds) *State of the Nation: South Africa 2004–2005,* HSRC Press, Cape Town.

Herlihy, D. (1997) *The Black Death and the Transformation of the West,* Harvard University Press, Cambridge.

Heunis, J.C. (2004) 'Hospitals and hospital restructuring in South Africa'. In: Van Rensburg, H.C.J. (ed) *Health and Health Care in South Africa,* Van Schaik, Pretoria.

Hickey, S. & Mohan, G. (2003) 'Relocating participation within a radical politics of development: citizenship and critical modernism' (paper presented to the conference on Participation: From Tyranny to Transformation? Exploring New Approaches to Development), 27–28 February, University of Manchester.

Hicks, J. (2006) 'Assessing the effectiveness of community-based involvement' (background paper), Centre for Public Participation, Durban. Available at http://www.cpp.org.za/main.php?include=docs/community.html&menu=_menu/pubs.html&title=Documents

Hill, G. (1999) 'The kwaito revolution', *Siyaya!,* No. 4 (Autumn), Cape Town.

Hindson, D. (1991) 'The restructuring of labour markets in South Africa: 1970s and 1980s'. In: Gelb, S. (ed) *South Africa's Economic Crisis,* David Philip, Cape Town.

Hindson, D. & Morris, M. (1992) 'Political violence: reform and reconstruction', *Review of African Political Economy,* No. 53, Sheffield.

Hirsch, A. (2005) *Season of Hope: Economic Reform under Mbeki and Mandela,* University of KwaZulu-Natal Press, Pietermaritzburg.

Hirschhorn, L. R. & Skolnik, R. (2008) 'Making universal access a reality—what more do we need to know?' *Journal of Infectious Diseases,* Vol. 197, pp. 1223–5.

Hirst, P. (1996) 'Global markets and the possibilities of convergence' (paper presented to the Conference on Globalization and the New Inequality), November, Utrecht University.

Hlatswayo, M. (2005) 'From socialist politics to business unionism', *Khanya: A Journal for Activists,* No. 8, pp. 16–18.

Ho, M. W. *et al* (2009) *Green Energies: Renewables by 2050,* ISIS & Third World Network, London & Penang.

Hoang, D-H. T. (2002) *Microfinance projects and their impact on the health of the poor,* June, University of Washington School of Public Health and Community Medicine.

Hobsbawm, E. (1996) 'Identity politics and the Left', *New Left Review,* No. 217 (May/June), London.

Hobsbawm, E. (1995) *Age of Extremes: The Short Twentieth Century,* Abacus, London.

Holloway, J. (1994) 'Global capital and the national state', *Capital and Class,* No. 52, London.

Holm, D. *et al* (2008) 'Potential of renewable energy to contribute to national electricity emergency response and sustainable development', Renewable Energy Briefing Paper, March, TIPS, Johannesburg.

Hoogeveen, J. & Özler, B. (2006) 'Not separate, not equal: poverty and inequality in post-apartheid

South Africa'. In: Bhorat, H. & Kanbur, R. (2006) *Poverty and Policy in Post-Apartheid South Africa,* HSRC Press, Pretoria.

Horn, P. (1991) 'Conference on women and gender in Southern Africa: another view of the dynamics', *Transformation,* No. 15, Durban.

Hosegood, V. *et al* (2007) 'Revealing the full extent of households' experiences of HIV and AIDS in rural South Africa', *Social Science and Medicine,* Vol. 65, No. 6, pp. 1249–59.

Hosegood, V. *et al* (2007) 'The effects of HIV prevalence on orphanhood and living arrangements of children in Malawi, Tanzania and South Africa', *Population Studies,* Vol. 61, No. 3, pp. 327–36.

Hosegood, V. (2008) 'Demographic evidence of family and household changes in response to the effects of HIV/AIDS in southern Africa: implications for efforts to strengthen families' (research paper for Joint Learning Initiative on Children and HIV/AIDS final report). Available at http://www.jlica.org/resources/publications.php

Hosegood, V. *et al* (2007) 'The effects of HIV prevalence on orphanhood and living arrangements of children in Malawi, Tanzania and South Africa', *Population Studies,* Vol. 61, No. 3, pp. 27–36.

Hosegood, V. & Timæus, I. M. (2005) 'The impact of adult mortality on the living arrangements of older people in rural South Africa', *Ageing and Society,* Vol. 25, pp. 431–44.

Hosegood, V. & Preston-Whyte, E. (2003) 'Marriage and partnership patterns in rural KwaZulu-Natal, South Africa' (paper presented to the Population Association of America on the Social Consequences of AIDS conference), 8–12 May, Atlanta.

Hotaling, G. T. & Sugarman, D. B. (1986) 'An analysis of risk markers in husband to wife violence: the current state of knowledge', *Violence and Victims,* Vol. 1, pp. 101–24.

Houghton, D. H. (1967) *The South African Economy,* Oxford University Press, Cape Town.

HSRC (2007) *South African Social Attitudes Survey 2007,* Human Science Research Council, Pretoria.

HSRC (2002) *Nelson Mandela/HSRC study of HIV/AIDS: South African national HIV prevalence, behaviour risks and mass media household survey 2002,* HSRC, MRC, CADRE, ANRS, Pretoria.

Huchzermeyer, M. (2003) 'Land invasions, evictions and the law in South Africa'. In: Alfonsin, B. & Fernandes, E. (eds) *Memorias des IX Semenario Internacional 'Derecho y Espacio Urbano',* IRGLUS, Urban Management Programme, Working Paper 101, Quito.

Hulme, D., Moore, K. & Shepherd, A. (2001) 'Chronic poverty: meanings and analytical frameworks', Working Paper No. 2, Chronic Poverty Research Centre, University of Manchester, Manchester. Available at http://www.chronicpoverty.org/uploads/publication_files/WP02_Hulme_et_al.pdf

Hulme, D. & Mosley, P. (1996) *Finance Against Poverty,* Routledge, London.

Human Rights Watch (2001) *Scared at School: Sexual Violence Against Girls in South African Schools,* Human Rights Watch, New York.

Human Rights Commission (1991) *The New Total Strategy,* Human Rights Commission, Johannesburg.

Hunter, M. (2010) 'Rights and redistribution: thinking about the state, gender, and class in South Africa after the Zuma rape trial'. In: Freund, B. (ed) *Development Dilemmas* (forthcoming).

Hunter, M. (2007) 'The changing political economy of sex in South Africa: the significance of unemployment and inequalities to the scale of the AIDS pandemic', *Social Science & Medicine,* Vol. 64, No. 3, pp. 689–700.

Hunter, M. (2006a) 'Was the scale of the South African AIDS pandemic inevitable? Rethinking the political economy of sex in contemporary South Africa' (draft paper), Dartmouth College.

Hunter, M. (2006b) 'Fathers without *amandla*?' In: Richter, L. & Morrell, R. (eds), *Baba? Fathers and Fatherhood in South Africa,* HSRC, Pretoria, pp. 99–107.

Hunter, M. (2005a) 'Cultural politics and masculinities: multiple-partners in historical perspective in KwaZulu-Natal', *Culture, Health & Sexuality,* Vol. 7, No. 4, pp. 389–403.

Hunter, M. (2005b) 'Building a home: unemployment, intimacy and AIDS in South Africa' (PhD thesis), University of California, Berkeley.

Hunter, N. (2007) 'Crises in social reproduction and home-based care', *Africanus,* November, University of South Africa.

Hunter, N. (2006) 'Crises in social reproduction in a developmental state: home-based care in KwaZulu-Natal', Working paper, School of Development Studies, University of KwaZulu-Natal, Durban.

Hussy, D. (2000) 'Where to now?' (briefing document for the National Land Committee), February, Johannesburg.

IDASA (2009) 'What should we be discussing as we head to the polls?' (background paper), 20 March, PIMS, IDASA, Cape Town.

IDASA (2007) 'Budget 2007: poverty amidst plenty' (research report), February, IDASA, Cape Town. Available at http://www.idasa.org.za/gbOutputFiles.asp?Write Content=Y&RID=1784

IDASA (2000) 'Submission to the Portfolio Committee on Finance on the 2000/01 Budget', IDASA Budget Information Service (March), Cape Town.

Ijumba, P., Day, C. & Ntuli, A. (2004) *South African Health Review 2003/2004*, Health Systems Trust, Durban. Available at http://www.hst.org.za/publications/423

ILO (1996) *Restructuring the Labour Market: The South African Challenge* (ILO Country Review), Geneva.

Industrial Strategy Project (1994) 'Industrial strategy for South Africa: the recommendations of the ISP', *SA Labour Bulletin*, Vol. 18, No. 4 (January/February), Johannesburg.

ING Barings (2000) *Economic Impact of AIDS in South Africa: A Dark Cloud on the Horizon*, ING Barings, Johannesburg.

INTERFUND (1999) *Annual Review: The Voluntary Sector and Development in South Africa 1997/98*, Johannesburg.

INTERFUND (1997) *Annual Review: The Voluntary Sector and Development in South Africa 1996/97*, Johannesburg.

Intergovernmental Panel on Climate Change (2007) *Fourth Assessment Report: Special Report on Emissions Scenarios.*

Jacobs, S. (1999) 'An imperial presidency?' *Siyaya!* (Summer), Cape Town.

Jameson, F. (1992) *Postmodernism, or the Cultural Logic of Late Capitalism*, Duke University Press, Durham, North Carolina.

Jansen, J. (2007) *Bodies Count: AIDS Review 2006*, Centre for the Study of AIDS, University of Pretoria.

Jansen, J. (2006) 'Accounting for autonomy'. In: Pithouse, R. (ed) *Asinamali: University Struggles in Post-Apartheid South Africa*, Africa World Press, Asmara.

Jansen, J. (2004a) 'Race and education after ten years', *Perspectives in Education*, Vol. 22, No. 4, pp. 117–28.

Jansen, J. (2004b) 'Changes and continuities in South Africa's higher education system, 1994–2004'. In: Chisholm, L. (ed) *Changing Class: Education and Social Change in Post-Apartheid South Africa*, HSRC Press, Cape Town, pp. 293–314.

Jardin, C. & Satgar, V. (1999) 'COSATU and the Tripartite Alliance', *SA Labour Bulletin*, Vol. 23, No. 3 (June), Johannesburg.

Jewkes, R. *et al* (2009) *Understanding men's health and use of violence: interface of rape and HIV in South Africa*, June, Medical Research Council, Pretoria.

Jewkes, R. *et al* (2006) 'Rape perpetration by young, rural South African men: prevalence, patterns and risk factors', *Social Science & Medicine*, Vol. 63, No. 11, pp. 2949–61.

Jewkes, R., Penn-Kekana, L. & Rose-Junius, H. (2005) '"If they rape me, I can't blame them": reflections on the social context of child sexual abuse in South Africa and Namibia', *Social Science & Medicine*, Vol. 61, pp. 1809–20.

Jewkes, R. & Abrahams, N. (2002) 'The epidemiology of rape and sexual coercion in South Africa: an overview', *Social Science & Medicine*, Vol. 55, pp. 153–66.

Jewkes, R., Penn-Kekana, L. & Levin, J. (2002) 'Risk factors for domestic violence: findings from a South African cross-sectional study', *Social Science & Medicine*, Vol. 55, pp. 1603–18.

Jewkes, R. & Wood, K. (2002) 'Dangerous love: reflections on violence among Xhosa township youth'. In: Morrell, R. (ed) *Changing Men in Southern Africa*, University of Natal Press, Durban.

JLICA (2009) 'Home Truths: Facing the Facts on Children, AIDS and Poverty', (final report of the Joint Learning Initiative on Children and HIV/AIDS, JLICA). Available at http://www.jlica.org/resources/publications.php

Jodha, N.S. (1999) 'Poverty Debate in India', *Economic and Political Weekly*, Vol. 24, No. 31, 31 July–6 August, Delhi.

Jodha, N.S. (1988) 'Poverty debate in India: a minority view', *Economic and Political Weekly*, Special number, November, Delhi.

Joffe, A., Kaplan D., Kaplinsky, R. & Lewis, D. (1994a) 'Meeting the global challenge: a framework for industrial revival in South Africa'. In: *South Africa and the World Economy in the 1990s*, Cape Town, David Philip.

Joffe, A., Kaplan D., Kaplinsky, R. & Lewis, D. (1994b) 'An industrial strategy for a post-apartheid South Africa', *Institute for Development Studies Bulletin*, Vol. 25, No. 1, Sussex.

Johnson, C. (2001) 'Local democracy, democratic decentralisation and rural development: theories, challenges and options for policy', *Development Policy Review*, Vol. 19, No. 4, pp. 521–32.

Johnson, C. (1982) *MITI and the Japanese Miracle*, Stanford University Press, Stanford.

Johnson, C. & Start, D. (2001) 'Rights, claims and capture: understanding the politics of pro-poor policy', Working Paper No. 145, May, Overseas Development Institute, London.

Johson, R. W. (2008a) *South Africa's Brave New World: The Beloved Country since the End of Apartheid*, Penguin Books, London.

Johnson, R. W. (2008b) 'End of the road', *London Review of Books*, Vol. 30, No. 22, 20 November, pp. 13–16.

Johnson, R.W. (1991) 'AIDS in South Africa', *London Review of Books*, Vol. 13, No. 17, September, pp. 8–10.

Jordan, P. (2006) 'The ANC in South Africa's political landscape: from underground freedom movement to governing party'. In: Gunnarsen, G. *et al* (eds). *At the End of the Rainbow? Social Identity and Welfare State in the New South Africa*, Copenhagen, Denmark [e-Book]. Available at http://www.fredsakademiet.dk/library/getimg.pdf

Jordan, P. (1992a) 'Strategic debate in the ANC: a response to Joe Slovo', *African Communist*, No. 131 (Fourth Quarter), Johannesburg.

Jordan, P. (1992b) 'Has socialism failed? The South African debate', *Southern Africa Report* (January), Toronto.

Jourdan, P., Gordhan, K., Arkwright, D. & De Beer, G. (1997) 'Spatial development initiatives (development corridors): their potential contribution to investment and employment creation' (paper), January, Pretoria.

Jukes, M., Simmons, S. & Bundy, D. (2008) 'Education and vulnerability: the role of schools in protecting young women and girls from HIV in southern Africa', *AIDS*, Vol. 22, Suppl. 4, pp. S41–56.

Kagwanja, P. (2008) 'Introduction: uncertain democracy—elite fragmentation and the disintegration of the "nationalist consensus" in South Africa'. In: Kagwanja, P. & Kondlo, K. (eds) *State of the Nation: South Africa 2008*, HSRC Press, Cape Town.

Kahn, B. (1991) 'Exchange rate policy and industrial restructuring'. In: Moss, G. & Obery, I. (eds) *South African Review No. 6*, Ravan Press, Johannesburg.

Kahn, M. (2006) 'Matric Matters'. In: Reddy, V. (ed) *Marking Matric: Proceedings of a Colloquium*, HSRC Press, Cape Town.

Kalichman, S. C. *et al* (2007) 'Alcohol use and sexual risks for HIV/AIDS in sub-Saharan Africa: systematic review of empirical findings', *Prevention Science*, Vol. 8, No. 2, pp. 141–51.

Kalichman, S. C. *et al* (2006) 'Associations of poverty, substance use and HIV transmission risk behaviors in three South African communities', *Social Science and Medicine*, Vol. 62, No. 7, pp. 1641–9.

Kaplan, D. (2008) 'Industrial policy in South Africa: targets, constraints and challenges', *Trade & Industry Monitor*, Vol. 39, pp. 33–43.

Kaplan, D. (1991) 'The South African capital goods sector and the economic crisis'. In: Gelb, S. (ed) *South Africa's Economic Crisis*, David Philip, Cape Town.

Kaplan, D. (1990) 'Recommendations on post-apartheid economic policy', *Transformation*, No. 12, Durban.

Kaplinksy, R. (1994) 'Economic restructuring in South Africa: the debate continues: a response', *Journal of Southern African Studies*, Vol. 20, No. 4 (December), York.

Kaplinsky, R. (1991) 'A growth path for a post-apartheid South Africa', *Transformation*, No. 16, Durban.

Karim, S. S. A. *et al* (2009) 'HIV infection and tuberculosis in South Africa: an urgent need to escalate the public health response', *Lancet*, Vol. 374, No. 9693, pp. 921–33.

Karis, T. & Carter, G. M. (eds) (1977) *From Protest to Challenge: A Documentary History of African Politics in South Africa, 1882–1964*, Hoover, Stanford.

Karis, T. & Gerhardt, G. M. (eds) (1977) *Challenge and Violence 1953–1964*, Vol. 3 of *From Protest to Challenge: A Documentary History of African Politics in South Africa 1882–1964*, Hoover Institution, Stanford.

Kark, S.L. (1949) 'The social pathology of syphilis in Africans', *South African Medical Journal*, No. 23, pp. 77–84. Reprinted in *International Journal of Epidemiology* (2003), Vol. 32, No. 2, pp. 181–6.

Karlan, D. & Zinman, J. (2009) 'Expanding credit access: using randomized supply decisions to estimate the impacts', *Review of Financial Studies*, Vol. 23, No. 1, pp. 433–64.

Katz, M.M. (chair) (1994) *Interim Report of the Commission of Inquiry into certain aspects of the Tax Structure of South Africa*, Pretoria.

Keane, J. (1988a) *Civil Society and the State*, Verso, London.

Keane, J. (1988b) *Democracy and Civil Society*, Verso, London.

Keet, D. (1992) 'Shop-stewards and worker control', *SA Labour Bulletin*, Vol. 16, No. 5, Johannesburg.

Kelly, J. (2005) *The Great Mortality: An Intimate History of the Black Death*, HarperCollins, London.

Kelly, R. J. *et al* (2003) 'Age differences in sexual partners and risk of HIV-1 infection in rural Uganda', *Journal of Acquired Immune Deficiency Syndrome*, Vol. 32, pp. 446–51.

Kelly, J. (1999) 'Outsourcing statistics', *SA Labour Bulletin*, Vol. 23, No. 3 (June), Johannesburg.

Kenny, B. (2000) '"We are nursing these jobs": the implications of labour market flexibility on East Rand retail sector workers and their households' (paper presented at the Annual South African Sociological Association), Cape Town, July.

Kenny, B. & Webster, E. (1999) 'Eroding the core: flexibility and the re-segmentation of the South African labour market', *Critical Sociology*, Vol. 24, No. 3, pp. 216–243.

Kentridge, M. (1993) *Turning the Tanker: The Economic Debate in South Africa*, Centre for Policy Studies, Johannesburg.

Kenyon, C. (2008) 'Cognitive dissonance as an explanation of the genesis, evolution and persistence of Thabo Mbeki's HIV denialism', *African Journal of AIDS Research*, Vol. 7, No. 1, pp. 29–35.

Keswell, M. & Poswell, L. (2002) 'How important is education for getting ahead in South Africa?' Working Paper No. 22, Centre for Social Science Research, University of Cape Town.

Khan, M.R. *et al* (2008a) 'Mobility and HIV-related sexual behavior in Burkina Faso', *AIDS Behaviour*, Vol. 12, No. 2, pp. 202–12.

Khan, M.R. *et al* (2008b) 'Incarceration and risky sexual partnerships in a southern US City', *Journal of Urban Health*, Vol. 85, No. 1, pp. 100–13.

Khan, F. & Pieterse, P. (2006) 'The Homeless People's Alliance: purposive creation and ambiguated realities'. In: Ballard, R., Habib, A. & Valodia, I. (eds) *Voices of Protest: Social Movements in Post-Apartheid South Africa*, University of KwaZulu-Natal Press, Pietermaritzburg.

Khan, F. (1999) 'SANGOCO economics project base discussion document' (paper prepared for SANGOCO), Cape Town.

Kilbourne, E. (1987) *Influenza*, Plenum Medical Book Co., New York.

Kim, J. *et al* (2008) 'Exploring the role of economic empowerment in HIV prevention', *AIDS*, Vol. 22, Suppl. 4, pp. S57–71.

Kingdon, G. & Knight, J. (2005) *Unemployment in South Africa, 1995–2003: Causes, Problems and Policies*, Global Poverty Research Group. Available at http://www.gprg.org

Kirby, J., O'Keefe, P. & Timberlake, L. (1995) *The Earthscan Reader in Sustainable Development,* Earthscan Publications, London.

Klasen, S. (2000) 'Measuring poverty and deprivation in South Africa', *Review of Income and Wealth,* Vol. 46, No. 1, pp. 33–58.

Kleinert, S. & Horton, R. (2009) 'South Africa's health: departing for a better future?' *Lancet,* Vol. 374, No. 9692, pp. 759–60.

Kolata, G. (2000) *Flu: The Story of the Great Influenza Pandemic of 1918 and the Search for the Virus that Caused It,* MacMillan, London.

Kraak, G. (1997) 'Coasting in neutral', *Development Update,* Vol. 1, No. 2, INTERFUND, Johannesburg.

Kraak, G. (1996) *Development Update: An INTERFUND Briefing on the Development and Voluntary Sector in South Africa in 1995/96,* INTERFUND, Johannesburg.

Krug, A. & Pattinson, R. C. (2003) *Saving children: a survey of child healthcare in South Africa,* Child-PIP Group and the MRC unit for Maternal and Infant Health Care Strategies, Pretoria. Available at http://www.mrc.ac.za/maternal/savingchildren.pdf

Krugman, P. (1995) *Peddling Prosperity: Economic Sense and Nonsense in the Age of Diminished Expectations,* W. W. Norton & Co., New York.

Krugman, P. (1992) 'Towards a counter-counter revolution in development theory', *Proceedings of the World Bank Annual Conference on Development Economics.*

Labadarios, D. (ed) (2007) *The National Food Consumption Survey (NFCS): Fortification Baseline, South Africa, 2005,* Department of Health, Pretoria.

Labadarios, D. *et al* (2000) *The National Food Consumption Survey (NFCS): Children Aged 1–9 years, South Africa, 1999,* Department of Health, Pretoria.

Laclau, E. (1990) *New Reflections on the Revolution of our Time,* Verso, London.

Laclau, E. & Mouffe, C. (1985) *Hegemony and Socialist Strategy: Towards a Radical Democratic Politics,* Verso, London.

Lambert, R. (1987) 'Trade unions, nationalism and the socialist project in South Africa', *South African Review No. 4,* Ravan Press, Johannesburg.

Lanchester, J. (2007) 'Warmer, warmer', *London Review of Books,* Vol. 29, No. 6, 22 March, pp. 3–9.

Latouche, S. (1997) 'Paradoxical growth'. In: Rahnema, M. & Bawtree, V. (eds) *The Post-Development Reader,* Zed Books, London, pp. 135–42.

Lawn, S. D. *et al* (2007) 'Promoting retention in care: an effective model in an antiretroviral treatment service in South Africa', *Clinical Infectious Diseases,* Vol. 45, p. 803.

Lawson, L. (2008) *Side Effects: The Story of AIDS in South Africa,* Double Storey Books, Cape Town.

Lebani, L. & Valodia, I. (2005) 'Self-employment in the informal economy and formal employment linkages: an empirical enquiry based on the KwaZulu-Natal income dynamics survey' (paper), School of Development Studies, University of KwaZulu-Natal, Durban.

Leclerc-Madlala, S. (2008) 'Age-disparate and intergenerational sex in southern Africa: the dynamics of hypervulnerability', *AIDS,* Vol. 22, Suppl. 4, pp. S17–25.

LeClerc-Madlala S. (2003) 'Transactional sex and the pursuit of modernity', *Social Dynamics,* Vol. 29, No. 2, pp. 213–33.

Lee, C. K. (2007) *Against the Law: Labor Protests in China's Rustbelt and Sunbelt,* University of Califonia Press, Berkeley.

Legassick, M. (2007) 'Flaws in South Africa's "first" economy', *Africanus,* November, pp. 98–128.

Legassick, M. & De Clerq, F. (1978) 'The origins and nature of the migrant labour system in Southern Africa', *Migratory Labour in Southern Africa,* UN Economic Commission for Africa.

Legge, D. Sanders, D. & McCoy D. (2009) 'Trade and health: the need for a political economic analysis', *Lancet,* Vol. 373, No. 9663, pp. 527–29.

Legido-Quigley, H. (2003) 'The South African old-age pension: exploring the role on poverty alleviation in households affected by HIV/AIDS' (conference paper for the 4th International Research Conference on Social Security), 5–7 May, Antwerp.

Legum, M. & Satgar, V. (2005) *The Dual Economy: First-class Citizens, Second-class Citizens?* Monograph 3, Isandla Institute, Cape Town.

Lehulere, O. (2005) 'The new social movements, COSATU and the "new UDF"' (discussion paper), August, Khanya College. Available at http://www.liberationafrique.org/spip.php?article816

Leibbrandt, M., Levinsohn, J. & McCrary, J. (2005) 'Incomes in South Africa since the fall of apartheid', National Bureau of Economic Research Working Paper No. 11384, May, Cambridge MA. Available at http://www.nber.org/papers/w11384

Leibbrandt, M. *et al* (2004) 'Measuring recent changes in South African inequality and poverty using 1996 and 2001 census data', CSSR Working Paper No. 84, Centre for Social Science Research, University of Cape Town.

Lelyveld, J. (2009) 'How Mbeki failed', *New York Review of Books,* Vol. 56, No. 6, 9 April.

Le Roux, P. (2003) 'Financing a Universal Income Grant in South Africa', *Social Dynamics,* Vol. 28, No. 2, pp. 98–121.

Le Roux, P. *et al* (1993) 'The Mont Fleur Scenarios', University of Western Cape, Cape Town.

Levin, M. (2000) 'Youth and the elections', *Development Update,* Vol. 3, No. 2, Johannesburg.

Lewis, D. (1991) 'The character and consequences of conglomeration in the South African economy', *Transformation,* No. 16, Durban.

Lewis, D. (1986) 'Capital, the trade unions and the national liberation struggle', *Monthly Review,* No. 37.

Leys, C. (2010) 'Morbid symptoms: current healthcare struggles'. In: Panitch, L. & Leys, C. (eds) *Morbid Symptoms: Health Under Capitalism—Socialist Register 2010,* Monthly Review Press, New York.

Leys, C. (1994) 'Confronting the African tragedy', *New Left Review,* No. 204, London.

Leyton, G. B. (1946) 'Effects of slow starvation', *Lancet,* Vol. 2, pp. 253–5.

Liebenberg, S. (2002) 'Universal access to social security rights: can a basic income grant meet the challenge?' *ESR Review,* Vol. 3, No. 2 (September).

Lienhardt, C. (2001) 'From exposure to disease: the role of environmental factors in susceptibility to and development of tuberculosis', *Epidemiologic Reviews,* Vol. 21, No. 2, pp. 288–300.

Lipietz, A. (1989) 'The debt problem, European integration and the new phase of the world crisis', *New Left Review,* No. 178 (December), London.

Lipietz, A. (1987) *Mirages and Miracles: The Crises of Global Fordism,* Verso, London.

Lipton, M. (1986) *Capitalism and Apartheid: South Africa 1910–1986,* Wildwood House, Aldershot.

Lodge, T. (1999a) *South African Politics since 1994,* David Philip, Cape Town.

Lodge, T. (1999b) *Consolidating Democracy: South Africa's Second Popular Election,* Witwatersrand University, Johannesburg.

Lodge, T. (1989) 'People's war or negotiation? African National Congress strategies in the 1980s', *South African Review No. 5,* Ravan Press, Johannesburg.

Lodge, T. (1987) 'The African National Congress after the Kabwe Conference', *South African Review No. 4,* Ravan Press, Johannesburg.

Lodge, T. (1983) *Black Politics in South Africa since 1945,* Longman, Harlow.

Lodge, T. & Nasson, B. (1991) *All Here, and Now: Black Politics in South Africa in the 1980s,* David Philip, Cape Town.

Loening-Voysey, H. (2002) 'HIV/AIDS in South Africa: caring for vulnerable children', *African Journal of AIDS Research,* No. 1.

Lopman, B. *et al* (2007) 'HIV incidence and poverty in Manicaland, Zimbabwe: is HIV becoming a disease of the poor?' *AIDS,* Vol. 21, Suppl. 7, pp. S57–66.

Louw, M., Van der Berg, S. & Yu, D. (2006) 'Educational attainment and intergenerational social mobility in South Africa', Working paper No. 9, Department of Economics, University of Stellenbosch.

Luke, N. (2005) 'Confronting the "sugar daddy" stereotype: age and economic asymmetries and risky sexual behavior in urban Kenya', *International Family Planning Perspectives,* Vol. 31, No. 1, pp. 6–14.

Luke, N. (2003) 'Age and economic asymmetries in the sexual relationships of adolescent girls in sub-Saharan Africa', *Studies in Family Planning,* Vol. 34, No. 2, pp. 67–86.

Luke, N. & Kurz, K. M. (2002) *Cross-generational and transactional sexual relations in sub-Saharan Africa: prevalence of behavior and implications for negotiating safer sexual practices,* AIDSmark, Washington.

Lumby, J. (2003) 'Transforming schools: managing the change process'. In: Thurlow, M., Bush, T. & Coleman, M. (eds) *Leadership and Strategic Management in South African Schools,* Commonwealth Secretariat, London.

Lund, F. (2008) *Changing Social Policy: The Child Support Grant in South Africa,* HSRC Press, Cape Town.

Lurie M. N. *et al* (2003). 'The impact of migration on HIV-1 transmission in South Africa: a study of migrant and non-migrant men and their partners', *Sexually Transmitted Diseases,* 30:149–56.

Maass, P. (2009) *Crude World: The Violent Twilight of Oil,* Allen Lane, London.

MacDonald, M. (2005) *Why Race Matters,* Harvard University Press, Cambridge, Massachusetts.

MacEwan, A. (1994) 'Globalisation and stagnation' (seminar paper), Centro de Investigaciones Interdisciplinares en Humanidades, National Autonomous University of Mexico, Mexico City.

Machel, J.Z. (2001) 'Unsafe sexual behaviour among schoolgirls in Mozambique: a matter of gender and class', *Reproductive Health Matters,* Vol. 9, No. 17, pp. 82–9.

Macroeconomic Research Group (MERG) (1993) *Making Democracy Work,* Centre for Development Studies/Oxford, Cape Town.

Magasela, W. (2005) 'Towards a Constitution-based definition of poverty in post-apartheid South Africa'. In: Buhlungu, S. *et al* (eds) *State of the Nation: South Africa 2005–2006,* HSRC Press, Cape Town.

Magdoff, H. & Sweezy, P. (1990) 'Investment for what?' *Monthly Review,* Vol. 42, No. 2 (June), New York.

Mager, A. (1999) *Gender and the Making of a South African Bantustan: A Social History of the Ciskei, 1945–1959,* James Currey, Oxford.

Mah, T. & Halperin, D. T. (2008) 'Concurrent sexual partnerships and the HIV epidemic in sub-Saharan Africa: the evidence to move forward', *AIDS and Behavior,* Vol. 14, No. 1, pp. 11–6.

Maharaj, G. (ed) (1999) *Between Unity and Diversity: Essays on Nation-Building in Post-Apartheid South Africa,* David Philip, Cape Town.

Maitra, P. & Ray, R. (2003) 'The effect of transfers on household expenditure patterns and poverty in South Africa', *Journal of Development Economics,* Vol. 71, No. 1, pp. 23–49.

Makgetla, N. S. (2007) 'Local government budgets and development: a tale of two towns'. In: Buhlungu, S. *et al* (eds) *State of the Nation: South Africa 2007,* HSRC Press, Cape Town.

Makgetla, N. S. (2005) 'Development and underdevelopment in context'. In: Edigheji, O. (ed) *Trajectories for South Africa: Reflections on the ANC's 2nd National General Council's discussion documents, Special edition of Policy: Issues and Actors,* Vol. 18, No. 2, Centre for Policy Studies, Johannesburg, pp. 27–33.

Makiwane, M. & Udjo, E. (2006) 'Is the child support grant associated with an increase in teenage fertility in South Africa?' Evidence from national surveys and administrative data, final report, December, HSRC, Pretoria.

Malthus, T. (1989) *An essay on the principle of population; or a view of its past and presents effects on human happiness: with an inquiry into our prospects respecting the removal or mitigation of the evils which it occasions,* Cambridge University Press, Cambridge.

Mamdani, M. (1996) *Citizen and Subject: Contemporary Africa and the Legacy of Late Colonialism,* Princeton University, Princeton.

Mandela, N. (1998) 'Address by President Nelson Mandela to Parliament', 6 February, Cape Town.

Mandela, N. (1997) 'Address by President Nelson Mandela to the closing session of the 50th National Conference of the ANC', 20 December, Mafikeng.

Mandela, N. (1994) 'Inaugural address to a joint sitting of Parliament', 24 May, Cape Town.

Mandela, N. (1991) 'Continuation lecture', 6 December, University of Pittsburgh, Pittsburgh.

Mandla, C. (1985) 'Let us move to all-out war', *Sechaba,* November.

Maganja, R.K. *et al* (2007) 'Skinning the goat and pulling the load: transactional sex among youth in Dar es Salaam, Tanzania', *AIDS Care,* Vol. 19, No. 8, pp. 974–81.

Mangcu, X. (2008) *To the Brink: The State of Democracy in South Africa,* University of KwaZulu-Natal Press, Pietermaritzburg.

Mann, G. (2009) 'Colletti on the credit crunch: a response to Robin Blackburn', *New Left Review*, No. 56 (March/April).

Manuel, T. A. (2009) 'Budget speech 2009', 11 February, Cape Town. Available at http://www.info.gov.za/speeches/2009/09021114561001.htm

Manuel, T. A. (2006) 'Budget Speech 2006 by Minister of Finance Trevor A Manuel', 16 February, Cape Town. Available at http://www.info.gov.za/speeches/2006/06021515501001.htm

Manuel, T. A. (2000) 'Budget speech', 23 February, Cape Town.

Manuel, T. A. (1999) 'Budget speech', 17 February, Cape Town.

Manuel, T. A. (1998a) 'Speech by Minister Trevor Manuel to Parliament on the subject for discussion: Currency volatility and its effect on the South African economy', 22 July, Cape Town.

Manuel, T. A. (1998b) 'Address to Societe Generale Frankel Pollak 21st Annual Investment Conference', 24 February, Johannesburg.

Manuel, T. A. (1996) 'Speech by Mr T. A. Manuel, Minister of Finance', Bureau for Economic Research conference, 8 October, Cape Town.

Marais, H. (2010) 'Turning off the tap: understanding and overcoming the HIV epidemic in southern Africa', (research paper), Nelson Mandela Foundation, Johannesburg.

Marais, H., Everatt, D. & Dube, N. (2010) 'Analysing the depth and quality of public participation in the Integrated Development Planning process in Gauteng', *Politikon* [forthcoming].

Marais, H. (2007a) 'The uneven impact of HIV in a polarized society', *AIDS*, Vol. 21, Suppl 3, pp. S21–9.

Marais, H. (2007b) 'AIDS in Africa: how the poor are dying' (book review), *International Journal of Urban and Regional Research*, Vol. 31, No. 4, pp. 882–4.

Marais, H. (2007c) 'Getting back to basics: a review of the ANC's Social transformation policy document', June, Centre for Policy Studies, Johannesburg.

Marais, H. (2005) *Buckling: The Impact of AIDS in South Africa*, Centre for the Study of AIDS, University of Pretoria, Pretoria.

Marais, H. (2003) 'The shattered mould: patterns of violence in the post-apartheid era'. In: Greenstein, R. (ed) *The Role of Political Violence in South Africa's Democratization*, Community Agency for Social Enquiry, Johannesburg.

Marais, H. (2001a) *South Africa: Limits to Change—The Political Economy of Transition*, 2 ed, UCT Press & Zed Books, Cape Town & London.

Marais, H. (2001b) 'Principle and expediency: South Africa and the African Renaissance' (seminar paper), April, Dakar.

Marais, H. (2000) *To the Edge: An Examination of South Africa's National AIDS Response 1994–1999* (annual review), Centre for the Study of AIDS, University of Pretoria, Pretoria.

Marais, H. (1999a) 'Blinded by the light: the left in South Africa's transition' (seminar paper), Centro de Investigaciones Interdisciplinarias en Humanidades, National Autonomous University of Mexico, Mexico City.

Marais, H. (1999b) 'His masterful voice', *Leadership* (October/November), Cape Town.

Marais. H. (1999c) 'Banking on change', *Siyaya!*, No. 4 (Autumn), Cape Town.

Marais, H. (1998a) 'Reinforcing the mould: the character of regional integration in Southern Africa' (research paper), Third World Forum & Institute for Global Dialogue, Dakar & Johannesburg.

Marais, H. (1998b) 'Saving the Non-Aligned Movement from itself', *Global Dialogue*, Vol. 3, No. 3 (December), Institute for Global Dialogue, Johannesburg.

Marais, H. (1997a) 'Leaders of the pack', *Leadership*, August, pp. 52–63.

Marais, H. (1997b) 'The Mbeki "enigma"', *Southern Africa Report*, Vol. 13, No. 1 (November), Toronto.

Marais, H. (1996) 'Who killed Bambi? The death of the RDP', *Weekly Mail and Guardian* (July 12), Johannesburg.

Marais, H. (1994a) 'Radical as reality', *African Communist*, No. 138 (Third Quarter), Johannesburg.

Marais, H. (1994b) 'The skeletons come out of the cupboard', *Work in Progress*, No. 91 (August/September), Johannesburg.

Marais, H. (1993b) 'The new barbarians (the criminalisation of youth)', *Work in Progress*, No. 90 (July/ August), Johannesburg.

Marais, H. (1992a) 'The sweeping inferno', *Work in Progress*, No. 83 (July/August), Johannesburg.

Marais, H. (1992b) 'What happened in the ANC camps?', *Work in Progress*, No. 82 (June), Johannesburg.

Marais, H. & Narsoo, M. (1992) 'And justice for all?', *Work in Progress*, No. 85 (October), Johannesburg.

Mare, G. (1992) *Brothers Born of Warrior Blood: Politics and Ethnicity in South Africa,* Ravan Press, Johannesburg.

Mare, G. & Hamilton, G. (1987) *An Appetite for Power: Buthelezi's Inkatha and South Africa,* Ravan Press, Johannesburg.

Marie, B. (1996) 'Giants, teddy bears, butterflies and bees: ideas for union organizing', *SA Labour Bulletin*, Vol. 20, No. 1 (February), Johannesburg.

Marie, B. (1992) 'Cosatu faces crises', *SA Labour Bulletin*, Vol. 16, No. 5 (May/June), Johannesburg.

Marks, S. (2002) 'An epidemic waiting to happen?' *African Studies*, Vol. 61, No. 1, pp. 13–26.

Marks, S. & Trapido, S. (1991) 'Introduction', *Journal of Southern African Studies*, Vol. 18, No. 1 (March), York.

Martin, H. & Schumann, H. (1997) *The Global Trap: Globalisation and the Assault on Democracy and Prosperity,* Zed, London.

Marx, A. W. (1992) *Lessons of Struggle; South African Internal Opposition, 1960–1990*, Oxford University, Cape Town.

Marx, K. & Engels, F. (1848) *Manifesto of the Communist Party* (English edition of 1888). In: Tucker, C. (1978) *The Marx-Engels Reader,* 2 ed, W. W. Norton & Co., New York. Full text available at http:// www.gutenberg.org/etext/61

Maseko, S. & Vale, P. (1998) 'South Africa and the African Renaissance'. In: *South Africa and Africa: Reflections on the African Renaissance,* (Foundation for Global Dialogue), Occasional Paper No. 17, Johannesburg.

Matsebula, T. & Willie, M. (2007) 'Private Hospitals', *SA Health Review 2007,* Health Systems Trust, Durban.

Matzopoulos, R. *et al* (2006) 'Estimating the South African trauma caseload', *International Journal of Injury Control and Safety Promotion,* Vol. 13, pp. 49–51.

Matzopoulos, R., Norman, R. & Bradshaw, D. (2004) 'The burden of injury in South Africa: fatal injury trends and international comparisons'. In: Suffla, S., Van Niekerk, A. & Duncan, N. (eds) *Crime Violence and Injury Prevention in South Africa: Developments and Challenges,* MRC-UNISA Crime, Violence and Injury Lead Programme, Tygerberg, pp. 9–21.

Mavimbela, V. (1997) 'The African Renaissance: A Workable Dream' (roundtable paper), Foundation for Global Dialogue, July, Johannesburg.

May, J. (1998) *Experience and Perceptions of Poverty in South Africa,* Praxis Publishing, Durban.

Mayekiso, M. (1994) 'Taking the RDP to the streets' (address to SANCO Southern Transvaal RDP conference) May, Johannesburg.

Mayosi, B. M. *et al* (2009) 'The burden of non-communicable diseases in South Africa', *Lancet*, Vol. 374, No. 9693, pp. 934–47.

Mbeki, G. (1996) *Sunset at Midday: Latshon' ilang 'emini!,* Nolwazi Educational, Johannesburg.

Mbeki, G. (1992) *The Struggle for Liberation in South Africa: A Short History,* David Philip, Cape Town.

Mbeki, T. (2008a) 'State of the Nation Address of the President of South Africa, Thabo Mbeki', February, Cape Town.

Mbeki, T. (2008b) 'Address during the Community Development Worker Indaba', 14 March, Gallagher Estate, Midrand.

Mbeki, T. (2007a) 'Letter from the President', *ANC Today,* Vol. 7, No. 45.

Mbeki, T. (2007b) 'State of the Nation Address of the President of South Africa, Thabo Mbeki to the Joint Sitting of Parliament', 9 February, Cape Town.

Mbeki, T. (2006) 'State of the Nation address of the President of South Africa, Thabo Mbeki, to the Joint Sitting of Parliament', 3 February, Cape Town. Available at http://www.info.gov.za/speeches/2006/06020310531001.htm

Mbeki, T. (2005) 'Address of the President of South Africa to the 2nd Joint Sitting of the 3rd Democratic Parliament', 11 February, Cape Town. Available at http://www.info.gov.za/speeches/2005/05021110501001.htm

Mbeki, T. (2004a) 'Aluta Continua!' (letter from the President), ANC Today, Vol. 4, No. 47, 26 November–2 December 2004. Mbeki, T. (2004b) 'Dislodging stereotypes' (letter from the President), ANC Today, Vol. 4, No. 42, 22–28 October 2004.

Mbeki, T. (2004c) 'Address of the President of South Africa, Thabo Mbeki, to the First Joint Sitting of the Third Democratic Parliament', 21 May, Cape Town. Available at http://www.info.gov.za/speeches/2004/04052111151001.htm

Mbeki, T. (2003a) 'State of the Nation address to the Joint Sitting of the Houses of Parliament', 8 February, Cape Town.

Mbeki, T. (2003b) 'Bold steps to end the "Two Nations" divide' (letter from the President), ANC Today, Vol. 3, No. 33, 22–28 August.

Mbeki, T. (2003c) 'Speech to the National Council of Provinces', 11 November, Parliament, Cape Town.

Mbeki, T. (2002) 'Health, human dignity and partners for poverty reduction', (letter from the President), ANC Today, Vol. 2, No. 14, 5–11 April.

Mbeki, T. (2000) 'State of the Nation Address at the Opening of Parliament', 4 February, Cape Town.

Mbeki, T. (1999a) 'Speech of the President of the Republic of South Africa, Thabo Mbeki, at the 54th session of the United Nationals General Assembly', 20 September, New York.

Mbeki, T. (1999b) 'State of the Nation Address', National Assembly, 25 June, Cape Town.

Mbeki, T. (1998a) 'Statement of Deputy President Thabo Mbeki on Reconciliation at the National Council of Provinces', 10 November, Cape Town.

Mbeki, T. (1998b) 'Statement of the President of the African National Congress, Thabo Mbeki, at the 10th Congress of the South African Communist Party', 2 July, Johannesburg.

Mbeki, T. (1998c) 'Statement of the President of the ANC at the Meeting of the Central Committee of Cosatu', 23 June, Johannesburg.

Mbeki, T. (1998d) 'Statement of the Deputy President on the Occasion of the Debate on the Budget Vote of the Office of the Depuly President', 3 June, Cape Town.

Mbeki, T. (1998e) 'Statement of Deputy President Thabo Mbeki at the Opening of the Debate in the National Assembly, on "Reconciliation and Nation Building"', National Assembly, 29 May, Cape Town. Available at http://www.dfa.gov.za/docs/speeches/1998/mbek0529.htm

Mbeki, T. (1998e) 'Address to NUM Congress', 28 March, Johannesburg.

Mbeki, T. (1997) 'Address to "Attracting Capital to Africa" Summit', April 19, Chantilly, US.

Mbeki, T. (1996) 'I am an African' (speech issued by the Office of the Deputy President), 8 May, Pretoria.

Mbembe, A. (2009) 'A government for all South Africans?', Le Monde Diplomatique, June. Available at http://www.mondediplo.com/2009/06/06southafrica

Mboweni, T. (1994) 'Formulating policy for a democratic South Africa: some observations', Institute for Development Studies Bulletin, Vol. 25, No. 1, Sussex.

McCord, A. (2007) 'Why the public works programme is failing the poor', Delivery, February–April.

McCord, A. (2005) 'A critical evaluation of training within the South African national public works programme', Journal of Vocational Education and Training, Vol. 57, No. 4., pp 563–86.

McCord, A. (2004a) 'Policy expectations and programme reality: the poverty reduction and labour market impact of two public works programmes in South Africa', Working Paper No. 8, Overseas Development Institute (ODI), London. Available at http://www.odi.org.uk/resources/download/4074.pdf

McCord, A. (2004b) 'Public works and overcoming underdevelopment in South Africa' (paper presented at the Overcoming Under-development in South Africa's Second Economy conference), 29 October, UNDP, HSRC, DBSA, Pretoria.

McCoy, D. *et al* (1998) *An evaluation of South Africa's Primary School Nutrition Programme,* Health Systems Trust, Durban.

McDonald, D. & Pape, J. (2002) *Cost Recovery and the Crisis of Service Delivery in South Africa,* HSRC Press, Cape Town.

McGrath, M. & Whiteford, A. (1994) 'Disparate circumstances', *Indicator SA,* Vol. 11, No. 3 (Winter), Durban.

McGreggor, R. (1985) *Investors' Handbook,* Purdey Publishing, Johannesburg.

McIntyre, D. & Thiede, M. (2007) 'Health care financing and expenditure'. In: Harrison, S., Bhana, R. & Ntuli, A. (eds) *SA Health Review 2007,* Health Systems Trust, Durban.

McIntyre, D. & Doherty, J. (2004) 'Healthcare financing and expenditure: progress since 1994 and remaining challenges'. In: Van Rensburg, H. (ed) *Health care in South Africa,* Van Schaik Publishers, Pretoria.

McIntyre, D., McLeod, H. & Thiede, M. (2005) *Comments on the National Treasury* (discussion document on the proposed tax reforms relating to medical scheme contributions and medical expenses), Health Economics Unit, Cape Town.

McKeown, T. (1979) *The Role of Medicine: Dream, Mirage or Nemesis?* Basil Blackwell, Oxford.

McKeown, T. & Record, R. G. (1962) 'Reasons for the decline of mortality in England Wales during the nineteenth century', *Population Studies,* Vol. xvi, pp. 94–122.

McKeown, T. & Brown, R. G. (1955) 'Medical evidence related to English population changes in the eighteenth century', *Population Studies,* No. 9, pp. 119–41.

McKinley, D. (2009) 'The crisis of the left in contemporary South Africa' (paper), Amandla Publishers. Available at http://www.amandlapublishers.co.za/special-features/debating-left-strategies/151-the-crisis-of-the-left-in-contemporary-south-africa

McKinley, D. (2006) 'Democracy and social movements in South Africa'. In: Padayachee, V. (ed) *The Development Decade? Economic and Social Change in South Africa, 1994–2004,* HSRC Press, Cape Town.

Meagher, K. Y. & Bello-Mohammed, Y. (1993) 'Informalisation and its discontents: coping with crisis and adjustment in Nigeria's informal sector' (draft report prepared for the UNRISD project on Crisis, Adjustment and Social Change), UNRISD, Geneva.

Mearns, A. (1883) 'The bitter cry of outcast London'. In: Keating, P. J. (ed) (1981) *Into Unknown England 1866–1913: Selections from the Social Explorers,* Fontana, Glasgow.

Médecins Sans Frontièrs *et al* (2007) 'Khayelitsha annual activity report 2007–2008: comprehensive TB/HIV services at primary health care level', Cape Town.

Medical Research Council (2005) *South African national burden of disease study 2000,* Medical Research Council, Cape Town. Available at: http://www.mrc.ac.za/bod/reports.htm

Meekers, D. & Calvés, A-E. (1997) '"Main" girlfriends, girlfriends, marriage and money: the social context of HIV risk behavior in sub-Saharan Africa', *Health Transition Review,* Vol. 7, pp. 361–75.

Meelis, T. & Makgetla, N. (2005) 'Impact of Trade on Economic Structure', *Trade and Industry Monitor* (December), Vol. 32, pp. 2–6.

Meer, S. (1999) 'Election '99: how far have we come? A balance sheet of the transition', *Development Update,* Vol. 3, No. 1, Johannesburg.

Meintjies, H. (2010) 'Orphans of the AIDS epidemic? The extent, nature and circumstances of child-headed households in South Africa', *AIDS Care,* Vol. 22, No. 1, pp. 44–9.

Meintjies, H. (2003) 'Children "in need of care" or in need of cash?' (joint working paper), December, Children's Institute & the Centre for Actuarial Research, University of Cape Town.

Mercer, C. (1980) 'Revolutions, reforms or reformulations?' In: Alan Hunt (ed), *Marxism and Democracy,* Lawrence and Wishart, London.

Meth, C. (2008) 'The (lame) duck unchained tries to count the poor', Working Paper No. 49, School of Development Studies, University of KwaZulu-Natal, Durban.

Meth, C. (2007a) 'What is pro-poor growth? What are some of the things that hinder its achievement in South Africa?' (research report prepared for Oxfam GB), May, Johannesburg.

Meth, C. (2007b) 'Social income in South Africa' (draft paper), May, University of KwaZulu-Natal, Durban.

Meth, C. (2006) 'Income poverty in 2004: a second engagement with the recent van der Berg et al figures', Working Paper No. 47 (September), School for Development Studies, University of KwaZulu-Natal.

Meth, C. (2004) 'Ideology and social policy: "handouts" and the spectre of "dependency"', *Transformation*, Vol. 56, pp 1–29.

Meth, C. & May, J. (2004) 'The state of underdevelopment in South Africa: what does a quantitative assessment of poverty, inequality and employment reveal?' (paper presented at Overcoming Underdevelopment in South Africa's Second Economy Conference), 28–29 October, Pretoria. Available at http://www.dbsa.org/

Meth, C. & Dias, R. (2003) 'Increases in Poverty in South Africa, 1999–2002' (paper presented at the DPRU/TIPS Forum), September, Johannesburg.

Mhone G. & Edigheji, O. (2003) *Governance in the New South Africa: The Challenges of Globalization*, University of Cape Town Press, Cape Town.

Michie, J. & Padayachee, V. (eds) (1997) *The Political Economy of South Africa's Transition: Policy Perspectives in the Late 1990s*, Dryden, London.

Miliband, R. (1996) 'The New World Order and the Left', *Social Justice*, Vol. 23, Nos. 1 & 2 (Spring–Summer), San Francisco.

Miliband, R. (1983) *Class Power and State Power: Political Essays*, Verso, London.

Miliband, R. (1974) 'Politics and poverty'. In: Wedderburn, D. (ed) *Poverty, Inequality and Class Structure*, Cambridge University Press, Cambridge.

Mills, E. A. (2004) 'HIV/AIDS and the "continuum of care": an ethnographic study of home-based care in KTC', University of Cape Town.

Mills, G., Begg, A. & Van Nieuwkerk, A. (1995) *South Africa in the Global Economy*, SAIIA, Johannesburg.

Ministerial Task Team (2004) 'Final recommendations concerning the implementation of Social Health Insurance in South Africa: Report 1', Department of Health, Pretoria.

Misago J. P. *et al* (2010) 'May 2008 violence against foreign nationals in South Africa: understanding causes and evaluating responses' (research report), April, Forced Migration Studies Programme & Consortium for Refugees and Migrants in South Africa, Johannesburg.

Mitchell, C. (2005) 'Mapping a southern African girlhood in the age of Aids'. In: Chisholm, L. & September, J. (eds) *Gender Equity in South African Education 1994–2004*, HSRC Press, Cape Town.

Mkandawire, T. (2007) 'Transformative social policy and innovation in developing countries', *European Journal for Development Research*, Vol. 19, No. 1, pp. 13–29.

Mkandawire, T. (2005) *Targeting and universalism in poverty reduction*, UNRISD, Geneva. Available at http://www.unrisd.org/

Mkandawire, T. (2002) 'Globalisation, equity and social development', *African Sociological Review*, Vol. 6, No. 1, pp. 115–37.

Mkandawire, T. (2001) 'Thinking about the developmental states in Africa', *Cambridge Journal of Economics*, Vol. 25, No. 3, pp. 289–314.

Mngxitama, A. (2009) 'Why Steve Biko would not vote', *Pambazuka News*, 16 April. Available at http://www.pambazuka.org/en/category/comment/55639

Mngxitama, A. (2004) 'Race and resistance in post-apartheid South Africa: towards a progressive race narrative' (paper presented at the Race, Racism and Empire Conference), 29 April–1 May, York University, Toronto.

Mohamed, S. (2010) 'The state of the South African economy'. In: Southall, R. *et al* (eds) *South Africa Review 2010*, [forthcoming].

Mohamed, S. (2009) 'Financialization, the Mineral-Energy Complex, and South African labour' (paper presented to the 5th Global Labour University Conference), 22–24 February, Mumbai.

Mohamed, S. & Roberts, S. (2007) 'Questions of growth, questions of development', *New Agenda: South African Journal of Social and Economic Policy*, Issue 28.

Mohammed, S. & Finnoff, K. (2004) 'Capital flight from South Africa, 1980 to 2000', 'African Development and Poverty Reduction: The macro-micro linkage' (forum paper), 13–15 October, Somerset West, South Africa.

Mohan, G. & Stokke, K. (2000) 'Participatory development and empowerment: dangers of localism', *Third World Quarterly*, Vol. 21, No. 2, pp. 247–68.

Molyneux, M. (2008) 'The "Neoliberal Turn" and the new social policy in Latin America: how neoliberal, how new?', *Development and Change*, Vol. 39, No. 5, pp. 775–97.

Moll, T. (1991) 'Did the apartheid economy "fail"?' *Journal of Southern African Studies*, Vol. 17, No. 2 (December), York.

Moll, T. (1990) 'From booster to brake? Apartheid and economic growth in comparative perspective'. In: Nattrass, N. & Ardington, E. (eds), *The Political Economy of South Africa*, Oxford University, Cape Town.

Moodley, S. (2007) 'Public participation and deepening democracy: experiences from Durban, South Africa', *Critical Dialogue*, Vol. 3, No. 1, pp. 3–8.

Moody, K. (2004) 'Workers of the world', *New Left Review*, Second series, No. 27 (May/June), pp. 153–60.

Moore, M., Choudhary, M. & Singh, N. (1998) 'How can we know what they want? Understanding local perceptions of poverty and ill-being in Asia', IDS Working Paper No. 80, Institute of Development Studies, Sussex University, Brighton.

Morley, D. & Chen, K. (1996) *Stuart Hall: Critical Dialogues on Cultural Studies,* Routledge, London.

Morojele, N.K. *et al* (2006) 'Alcohol use and sexual behavior among risky drinkers and bar and shebeen patrons in Gauteng province, South Africa', *Social Science & Medicine*, Vol. 62, pp. 217–27.

Morris, M. (1993a) 'The legacy of the past' (paper), December, University of Economics, Prague.

Morris, M. (1993b) 'Who's in, who's out? Side-stepping the 50% solution', *Work in Progress*, No. 86, Johannesburg.

Morris, M. (1993c) 'Methodological problems in tackling micro and macro socioeconomic issues in the transition to democracy in South Africa' (paper), May Slovak Academy of Sciences, Bratislava.

Morris, M. (1991) 'State, capital and growth: the political economy of the national question'. In Gelb, S. (ed) *South Africa's Economic Crisis,* David Philip & Zed Books, Cape Town and London.

Morris, M. (1976) 'The development of capitalism in South Africa', *Journal of Development Studies,* Vol. 12, No. 3.

Morris, M. & Hindson, D. (1992) 'Political violence: reform and reconstruction', *Review of African Political Economy,* No. 53, Sheffield.

Morris, M. & Padayachee, P. (1989) 'Hegemonic projects, accumulation strategies and state reform policy in South Africa', *Labour, Capital and Society,* Vol. 22, No. 1.

Morris, M. & Kretzchmar, M. (2000) 'A microsimulation study of the effect of concurrent partnerships on the spread of HIV in Uganda', *Mathematical Population Studies,* Vol. 8, No. 2, p. 109.

Mosley, P. & Hulme, D. (1998) 'Microenterprise finance: is there a conflict between growth and poverty alleviation?', *World Development,* Vol. 26, No. 5, pp. 783–90.

Moss, G. & Obery, I. (eds) (1991) *South Africa Review No. 6,* Ravan Press, Johannesburg.

Moss, G. & Obery, I. (eds) (1987) *South Africa Review No. 4,* Ravan Press, Johannesburg.

Moultrie, A. & Kleintjes, S. (2006) 'Women's mental health in South Africa', *SA Health Review 2006,* Health Systems Trust, Durban.

Murphy, M. (1994) 'A shaky alliance: Cosatu and the ANC', *Indicator SA,* Vol. 11, No. 3 (Winter), Durban.

Murray, R. (1971) 'The internationalisation of capital and the nation state', *New Left Review*, No. 67 (May/June), London.

Mutangadura, G. B., Mukurazita, D. & Jackson, H. (1999) *A review of household and community responses to the HIV/AIDS epidemic in the rural areas of sub-Saharan Africa,* UNAIDS, Geneva.

Mutangadura, G. B. (2000) 'Household Welfare Impacts of Adult Females in Zimbabwe: Implications for Policy and Program Development' (paper presented at the IAEN Symposium), 7–8 July, Durban.

Myburgh, J. (2009) 'In the beginning there was Virodene'. In: Cullinan, K. & Thom, A. (eds) *The virus, vitamins and vegetables: the South African HIV/AIDS mystery,* Jacana Books, Johannesburg.

Myer, L. *et al* (2006). 'Distinguishing the temporal association between women's intravaginal practices and risk of human immunodeficiency virus infection: a prospective study of South African women', *American Journal of Epidemiology,* 163(6):552–60.

Mzala (1990) 'Is South Africa in a revolutionary situation?, *Journal of Southern African Studies*, Vol. 16, No. 3 (September), York.

Mzala (1988) 'AIDS—misinformation and racism', *Sechaba* (October).

Mzala (1988) 'AIDS and the imperialist connection', *Sechaba* (November).

Mzala (1987) 'Towards a people's war and insurrection', *Sechaba* (April).

Mzala (1981) 'Has the time come for arming the masses?', *African Communist*, No. 102 (Third Quarter), Johannesburg.

Naidoo, V. (2008) 'Assessing racial redress in the public service'. In: Bentley, K. & Habib, A. (eds) *Racial Redress and Citizenship in South Africa,* HSRC Press, Cape Town.

Naidoo, P. & Veriava, A. (2007) *Re-membering movements: trade unions and new social movements in Neoliberal South Africa,* Research Report No. 28, Centre for Civil Society, University of KwaZulu-Natal, Durban.

NALEDI (2006) 'The State of COSATU—Phase 1 Report', National Labour and Economic Development Institute, Johannesburg.

Narsoo, M. (1993) 'Doing what comes naturally: a development role for the civic movement', *Policy: Issues and Actors,* Vol. 6, No. 2 (June), Centre for Policy Studies, Johannesburg.

Narsoo, M. (1991) 'Civil society: a contested terrain', *Work in Progress*, No. 76 (February), Johannesburg.

Nash, A. (1998) 'South Africa: is the revolution over?' *New Socialist,* Vol. 2, No. 1 (March–April).

National Committee on Confidential Enquiries into Maternal Deaths [NCCEMD] (2009) 'Saving mothers 2005–2007: Fourth report on confidential enquiries into maternal deaths in South Africa', Expanded Executive Summary, Department of Health, Pretoria.

National Institute for Economic Policy (1994) *Making the RDP Work: Draft Submission for the RDP White Paper,* NIEP, Johannesburg.

National Intelligence Council (2000) *Global Trends 2015: A Dialogue about the Future with Nongovernment Experts,* December, National Intelligence Council, Washington DC.

Nattrass, N. (2006a) 'Trading off income and health: AIDS and the disability grant in South Africa', *Journal of Social Policy,* Vol. 35, No. 1, pp. 3–19.

Nattrass, N. (2006b) 'Disability and welfare in South Africa's era of unemployment and AIDS', Working Paper 147, Centre for Social Science Research, University of Cape Town, Cape Town.

Nattrass, N. (2004) *The Moral Economy of AIDS in South Africa,* Cambridge University Press, Cambridge.

Nattrass, N. (2002) 'AIDS growth and distribution in South Africa', CSSR Working Paper No. 7, Centre for Social Science Research, University of Cape Town. Available at http://www.cssr.uct.ac.za/publications/working-paper/2002/007

Nattrass, N. (1996) 'Gambling on investment: competing economic strategies in South Africa', *Transformation*, No. 31, Durban.

Nattrass, N. (1994a) 'Economic restructuring in South Africa: the debate continues', *Journal of Southern African Studies*, Vol. 20, No. 4 (December) York.

Nattrass, N. (1994b) 'The limits to radical restructuring: a critique of the MERG report', *Third World Quarterly*, Oxfordshire.

Nattrass, N. (1994c) 'Politics and economics in ANC economic policy', *African Affairs* (July), London.

Nattrass, N. (1991) 'Controversies about capitalism and apartheid in South Africa: an economic perspective', *Journal of Southern African Studies*, Vol. 17, No. 4 (December), York.

Nattrass, N. & Ardington, E. (eds) (1990) *The Political Economy of South Africa,* Oxford University, Cape Town.

Nattrass, J. (1988) *The South African Economy: Its Growth and Change,* Oxford University, Cape Town.

Navarro, Z. (1998) 'Participation, democratizing practices and the formation of a modern polity—the case of "participatory budgeting" in Porto Alegre, Brazil (1989–1998)', *Development,* Vol. 41, No. 3, pp. 68–71.

Ndletyana, M. (2007) 'Municipal elections 2006: protests, independent candidates and cross-border municipalities'. In: Buhlungu, S. *et al* (eds) *State of the Nation: South Africa 2007,* HSRC Press, Cape Town, pp. 289–311.

Nel, P. (1999) 'Conceptions of globalisation among the South African elite', *Global Dialogue,* Vol. 4, No. 1 (April), Johannesburg.

Netshitenze, J. (1998) 'The state, property relations and social transformation' (ANC discussion paper), Pretoria.

Newell, M. L. *et al* (2004) 'Mortality of infected and uninfected infants born to HIV-infected mothers in Africa: a pooled analysis', *Lancet,* Vol. 364, No. 9441, pp. 1236–43.

Nicolau, K. (2000) 'Digging deep', *Ngqo!* (NIEP bulletin), Vol. 1, No. 2 (February), NIEP, Johannesburg.

Nicolaou, K. (1999) 'Pandora's box', *Ngqo!* (NIEP bulletin), Vol. 1, No. 1 (June), NIEP, Johannesburg.

Nicolosi, A. *et al* (1994) 'The efficiency of male-to-female and female-to-male sexual transmission of the human immunodeficiency virus: a study of 730 stable couples', Italian Study Group on HIV Heterosexual Transmission, *Epidemiology,* Vol. 5, No. 6, pp. 570–5.

Niddrie, D. (1990) 'The duel of dual power', *Work in Progress,* No. 67 (June), Johannesburg.

Niehaus, I. (2008) 'Death before dying: understanding AIDS stigma in the South African Lowveld' (research paper), Brunel University.

Nii-Amoo Dodoo, F., Zulu, E. M. & Ezeh, A. C. (2007) 'Urban-rural differences in the socioeconomic deprivation-sexual behavior link in Kenya', *Social Science and Medicine,* Vol. 64, pp. 1019–31.

Nkuhlu, M. (1993) 'The state and civil society in South Africa' (conference paper), August, Cape Town.

NnKo, S. *et al* (2000). 'Tanzania: AIDS care—learning from experience', *Review of African Political Economy,* Vol. 27, No. 86, pp. 547–57.

Nolan, P. (2002) 'Industrial policy in the 21st century: the challenge of the global business revolution'. In: Chang, H-J. (ed) *Kicking Away the Ladder: Development Strategy in Historical Perspective,* Anthem Press, London.

Norman, R. *et al* (2007) 'The high burden of injuries in South Africa', *Bulletin of the World Health Organization,* No. 85, pp. 695–702.

Norval, A. J. (1962) *Industrial Progress in South Africa,* Juta & Co., Cape Town.

Nyawuza (1985) 'New "Marxist" tendencies and the battle of ideas in South Africa', *African Communist,* No. 103 (Fourth Quarter).

Nzimakwe, T. I. (2008) 'Addressing unemployment and poverty through public works programmes in South Africa', *International NGO Journal,* Vol. 3, No. 12, pp. 207–12.

Nzimande, B. (1997) 'The state and the national question in South Africa's national democratic revolution' (paper), Harold Wolpe Memorial Trust conference, Cape Town.

Nzimande, B. (1992) 'Let us take the people with us: a reply to Joe Slovo', *African Communist,* No. 131 (Fourth Quarter), Johannesburg.

Oberg, S. & Gallopin, G. (1992) 'Quality of life', Working Paper 92–21, February, International Institute for Applied Systems Analysis, Laxenburg, Austria. Available at: http://www.iiasa.ac.at/Publications/Documents/WP-92-021.pdf

O'Dowd, M. (1978) 'The stages of economic growth and the future of South Africa'. In: Schlemmer, L. & Webster, E. (eds), *Change, Reform and Economic Growth in South Africa,* Ravan Press, Johannesburg.

OECD (2008) *South Africa: Economic Assessment 2008,* OECD Publications, Paris. Available at http://www.finance.gov.za/publications/other/OECD%20-%20South%20Africa%20Economic%20Assesment.pdf

Okie, S. (2006) 'Fighting HIV—lessons from Brazil', *New England Journal of Medicine,* Vol. 354, No. 19, pp. 1977–81.

Old Mutual (2003) 'Old Mutual Healthcare Survey 2003', Old Mutual, Cape Town. Available at http://www2.oldmutual.com/CR/reports/ccr/2003/indicators/economic/customers/needshtm

Oliveira, Chico de (2006) 'Lula in the labyrinth', *New Left Review,* No. 42, pp. 5–22.

O'Malley, P. (2007) *Shades of Difference: Mac Maharaj and the Struggle for South Africa,* Penguin Books, Johannesburg.

O'Meara, D. (1996) *Forty Lost Years: The Apartheid State and the Politics of the National Party, 1948–1994*, Ohio University Press, Ohio.

O'Meara, D. (1983) *Volkskapitalisme: Class, Capital and Ideology in the Development of Afrikaner-Nationalism 1934–1948*, Ravan Press, Johannesburg.

Orner, P. (2006) 'Psychological impacts on caregivers of people living with AIDS', *AIDS Care,* April, Vol. 18, No. 3, pp. 236–40.

Osborne, P. (1991) 'Radicalism without limit? Discourse, democracy and the politics of identity'. In: *Socialism and the Limits of Liberalism,* Verso, London.

Ouzgane, L. & Morrell, R. (2005) *African Masculinities: Men in Africa from the Late Nineteenth Century to the Present,* Palgrave MacMillan & University of KwaZulu-Natal Press, New York & Pietermarizburg.

Over, M. M. *et al* (1996) *Coping with AIDS: summary of the research results of the economic impact of adult mortality from AIDS and other causes on households in Kagera, Tanzania,* World Bank, Washington DC.

Overseas Development Institute (2006) 'Social Grants: South Africa', Policy Brief 1 (February), Overseas Development Institute, London.

Overseas Development Institute (2004) 'Public works as a solution to unemployment in South Africa? Two different models of public works programmes compared', Briefing Paper No. 2 (November), Economic and Statistics Analysis Unit, ODI, London.

OXFAM (2009) 'Blind optimism: challenging the myths about private health care in poor countries', OXFAM Briefing Paper, February, Oxford. Available at http://www.oxfam.org/sites/www.oxfam.org/files/bp125-blind-optimism-0902.pdf

Pacala, S. & Socolow, R. (2004) 'Stabilization wedges: solving the climate problem for the next 50 years with current technologies', *Science,* Vol. 305, No. 5686, pp. 968–72. Available at http://www.sciencemag.org/cgi/content/full/305/5686/968

Packard, R.M. (1987) 'Tuberculosis and the development of industrial health policies on the Witwatersrand, 1902–1932', *Journal of Southern African Studies*, Vol. 13, pp. 187–209.

Padayachee, V. (2006) *The Developmental Decade? Economic and Social Change in South Africa, 1994–2004,* HSRC Press, Cape Town.

Padayachee, V. (2005) 'The South African Economy, 1994–2004', *Social Research,* Vol. 72, No. 3, pp. 549–80.

Padayachee, V. (1995) 'Debt, development and democracy: the IMF and the RDP', *Review of African Political Economy,* Sheffield.

Padayachee, V. (1994a) 'Can the RDP survive the IMF?' *Southern Africa Report,* Vol. 9, No. 5 (July), Toronto.

Padayachee, V. (1994b) 'Dealing with the IMF: dangers and opportunities', *SA Labour Bulletin,* Vol. 18, No. 1 (January/February), Johannesburg.

Padayachee, V. (1994c) 'Debt, development and democracy: the IMF in post-apartheid South Africa', *Review of African Political Economy,* No. 62, pp. 582–97.

Padayachee, V. & Valodia, I. (2001) 'Changing Gear? The 2001 budget and economic policy in South Africa', *Transformation,* No. 46, pp. 71–83.

Paine, G. (1999) 'Dark side of a hot idea', *Siyaya!* (Summer), Cape Town.

Palma, J.G. (2006) *Globalizing inequality: 'centrifugal' and 'centripetal' forces at work,* ST/ESA/2006/DWP/35, United Nations Department of Economic and Social Affairs, New York.

Palmer, K. & Sender, J. (2006) 'Prospects for on-farm self-employment and poverty reduction: an analysis of the South African Income and Expenditure Survey 2000', *Journal of Contemporary African Studies,* Vol. 24, No. 3, pp. 347–76.

Panitch, L. (1994) 'Globalization and the state' (paper), Universidad Nacional Autonoma de Mexico, Mexico City.

Parker, W. *et al* (2007) *Concurrent sexual partnerships amongst young adults in South Africa,* CADRE, Johannesburg. Available at http://www.comminit.com/en/node/269915/36

Patel, R. (2007) *Stuffed and Starved: Markets, Power and the Hidden Battle for the World's Food System,* Portobello Books, London.

Pateman, C. (2003) 'Democratizing citizenship: some advantages of a basic income'. In: Wright, E. O. (ed) *Redesigning Distribution: Basic Income and Stakeholder Grants as Alternative Cornerstones for a More Egalitarian Capitalism,* Verso Books, London.

Patrick, M. & Stephen, C. (2007) 'Saving children 2005: a survey of child healthcare in South Africa', Medical Research Council Unit for Maternal and Infant Health Care Strategies, Cape Town.

Pauw, K., Oosthuizen, M. & Van der Westhuizen, C. (2006) 'Graduate unemployment in the face of skills shortages: a labour market paradox' (paper presented at Accelerated and Shared Growth in South Africa: Determinants, Constraints and Opportunities DPRU/TIPS Conference).

Peck, J & Tickell, A. (2002) 'Neoliberalizing space', *Antipode,* No. 34, pp. 380–404.

Peden, M., McGee, K. & Sharma, G. (2002) *The Injury Chart Book: A Graphical Overview of the Global Burden of Injuries,* World Health Organization, Geneva.

Peden, M. & Butchart, A. (1999) 'Trauma and injury'. In: Crisp, N. & Ntuli, A. (eds) *South African Health Review 1999,* Health Systems Trust, Durban, pp. 331–44.

Pellicani, L. (1981) *Gramsci: An Alternative Communism?* Hoover Institution, Standford.

Peters, P. E. (2009) 'Review of Land, Power and Custom', *Journal of Peasant Studies,* Vol. 36, No. 2.

Pettifor, A. E. *et al* (2004) *Sexual Power and HIV Risk, South Africa,* Centers for Disease Control and Prevention, US.

Petras, J. (1997) 'Intellectuals: a Marxist critique of post-Marxists' (draft paper), February, New York.

Philips, S. (2004) 'The Expanded Public Works Programme' (paper presented at the Overcoming Underdevelopment in South Africa's Second Economy conference), 28–29 October, UNDP, HSRC, DBSA.

Phillips M. & Coleman, C. (1989) 'Another kind of war: strategies for transition in the era of negotiation', *Transformation,* No. 9, Durban.

Pierson, C. (2003) '"Late industrialisers" and the development of the welfare state' (background paper for the Social Policy in a Development Context Project), United Nations Research Institute for Social Development (UNRISD), Geneva.

Pieterse, E. (2003) 'Rhythms, patterning and articulations of social formations in South Africa'. In: Everatt, D. & Maphai, V. (eds) *The Real State of the Nation: South Africa after 1990,* Development Update special edition, Interfund, Johannesburg.

Pigou, P. (2003) 'The state and violence'. In: Greenstein, R. (ed) *The Role of Political Violence in South Africa's Democratization,* Community Agency for Social Enquiry, Johannesburg.

Pilcher, C.D. *et al* (2004) 'Brief but efficient: acute HIV infection and the sexual transmission of HIV', *Journal of Infectious Diseases,* Vol. 189, No. 10, pp. 1785–92.

Pillay, D. (2008a) 'The stunted growth of South Africa's developmental state' (paper presented to the Global Labour University conference), April, Campinas University, Brazil.

Pillay, D. (2008b) 'COSATU, the SACP and the ANC post-Polokwane: looking left but does it feel right?', *Labour, Capital and Society,* Vol. 41, No. 2, pp. 5–37.

Pillay, D. (2006) 'COSATU, alliances and working class politics'. In: Buhlungu, S. (ed) *Trade Unions and Politics: COSATU Workers after 10 Years of Democracy,* HSRC Press, Cape Town.

Pinilla-Pal
leja, R. *et al* (2009) 'Should feminists endorse basic income?', *Basic Income Studies,* Vol. 3, No. 3 (January). Available at http://www.bepress.com/bis/announce/20090128/

Piot, P., Greener, R. & Russell, S. (2007) 'Squaring the circle: AIDS, poverty and human development', *PLoS Medicine,* Vol. 4, No. 10, pp. 1571–5.

Piryana, B., Ramphele, M., Mpumlwana, M. & Wilson, L. (1991) *Bounds of Possibility: The Legacy of Steve Biro and Black Consciousness,* David Philip & Zed, Cape Town & London.

Pithouse, R. (2006) 'Rethinking public participation from below', *Critical Dialogue,* Vol. 3, No. 2.

Planned Parenthood Association of South Africa (2003) 'Teen-parent programme: a baseline survey and needs assessment for adolescents and teen parents in South Africa' (final report), November.

Polanyi, K. (1944) *The Great Transformation: The Political and Economic Origins of our Time,* Beacon, Boston.

Policy Coordination and Advisory Services (PCAS) Unit (2006) 'A Nation in the Making: A discussion document on macro-social trends in South Africa', Presidency of the Republic of South Africa, Pretoria.

Policy Coordination and Advisory Services (PCAS) Unit (2003) 'Towards a Ten-Year Review', October. Presidency of the Republic of South Africa, Pretoria. Available at www.info.gov.za/otherdocs/2003/notused/10yrbook.pdf

Porteus, K., Vally, S. & Ruth, T. (2002) *Alternatives to corporal punishment: Growing discipline and respect in our classrooms,* Wits Education Policy Unit, Witwatersrand University, Johannesburg.

Posel, D., Fairburn, J. & F. Lund (2004) 'Labour migration and households: a reconsideration of the effects of the social pension on labour supply in South Africa' (paper presented at the Ninth Annual Conference on Econometric Modelling for Africa), 30 June–2 July, Stellenbosch.

Postman, N. (1992) *Technology: The Surrender of Culture to Technology,* Vintage, New York.

Potts, M. *et al* (2008) 'Reassessing HIV prevention', *Science,* No. 320, pp. 749–50.

Poulantzas, N. (1978) *State, Power, Socialism,* Verso, London.

Poulantzas, N. (1976) *The Crisis of the Dictatorships: Portugal, Greece, Spain,* New Left Books, London.

Poulantzas, N. (1973) *Political Power and Social Classes,* New Left Books, London.

Powers, K.A. *et al* (2008) 'Rethinking the heterosexual infectivity of HIV-1: a systematic review and meta-analysis', *Lancet,* Vol. 8, No. 9, pp. 553–63.

Prasad, E. *et al* (2003) 'Effects of financial globalization on developing countries: some empirical evidence', (working paper), March, International Monetary Fund, Washington DC.

Presidency (2008) *Development indicators: mid-term review,* Government of South Africa, Pretoria.

Presidency (2006) 'Accelerated and shared growth initiative for South Africa (AsgiSA)', summary, Government of South Africa, Pretoria. Available at http://www.info.gov.za/asgisa/asgisa.htm

Presidency (2005) *Government's Programme of Action: 2005 (Social Cluster),* Government of South Africa, Pretoria.

Preston-Whyte. E. *et al* (eds) 'Survival Sex and HIV/AIDS in an African City'. In: Parker, R. G. *et al* (2000). *Framing the Sexual Subject: The Politics of Gender, Sexuality and Power,* San Francisco, University of California.

Price, R. M. (1991) *The Apartheid State in Crisis: Political Transformation in South Africa, 1975–90,* Oxford University Press, London.

Przeworksi, A. *et al* (1995) *Sustainable Democracy,* Cambridge University Press, Cambridge.

Ramin, B. (2009) 'Slums, climate change and human health in sub-Saharan Africa', *Bulletin of the World Health Organization,* Vol. 87, No. 12, December, pp. 885–964.

Ramphele, M. (1993) *A Bed Called Home: Life in the Migrant Hostels of Cape Town,* David Philip & Ohio University Press, Cape Town & Athens, Ohio.

Rapoo, T. (1995) *Making the Means Justify the Ends: The Theory and Practice of the RDP,* Centre for Policy Studies, Johannesburg.

Raskin, P. *et al* (2007) 'Great transition: where do we want to go?' In: Cleveland, C.J. (ed) *Encyclopedia of Earth,* Environmental Information Coalition, National Council for Science and the Environment, Washington, D C. Available at: http://www.eoearth.org/article/Great_Transition:_Where_Do_We_Want_To_Go

Razavi, S. & Staab, S. (2008) 'The social and political economy of care: contesting gender and class inequalities' (background paper for Expert Group Meeting on Equal sharing of responsibilities between women and men, including caregiving in the context of HIV/AIDS), 6–9 October, United Nations Office, Geneva.

RDP Office (1995) *Key indicators of poverty in South Africa,* Ministry in the Office of the President, Pretoria.

Reitz, M. (1995) 'Divided on the "demon": immigration policy since the election' (paper), Centre for Policy Studies, Johannesburg.

Rehle, T. *et al* (2010) 'Trends in HIV prevalence, incidence, and risk behaviors among children, youth, and adults in South Africa, 2002 to 2008', 17th Conference on Retroviruses and Opportunistic Infections, San Francisco, abstract 37.

Rehle, T. *et al* (2007) 'National HIV incidence measures—new insights into the South African epidemic', *South African Medical Journal*, Vol. 97, No. 3, pp. 194–9.

Rehm, J. *et al* (2003) 'The global distribution of average volume of alcohol consumption and patterns of drinking', *European Addiction Research*, Vol. 9, No. 4, pp. 147–56.

Republic of South Africa (1997) *White Paper for Social Welfare. Principles, guidelines, proposed policies and programmes for developmental social welfare in South Africa,* Department of Welfare and Population Development, Pretoria.

Resino, S. *et al* (2006) 'Clinical outcomes improve with highly active antiretroviral therapy in vertically HIV type-1-infected children', *Clinical Infectious Diseases,* Vol. 43, No. 2, pp. 243–52.

Richter, L. & Desmond, C. (2008) 'Targeting AIDS orphans and child-headed households: a perspective from national surveys in South Africa, 1995–2005', *AIDS Care,* Vol. 20, pp. 1019–28.

Richter, L. (2004) 'The impact of HIV/AIDS on the development of children', in Pharoah, R. (ed) *A generation at risk? HIV/AIDS, vulnerable children and security in southern Africa,* Monograph 109 (December), Institute for Security Studies, Pretoria.

Rifkin, J. (1995a) *The End of Work: The Decline of the Global Labour Force and the Dawn of the Post-market Era,* Putnam, New York.

Rifkin, J. (1995b) 'The end of work?' *New Statesman & Society,* 9 June, London.

Roberts, B. (2009) 'Age of hope or anxiety? Dynamics of the fear of crime in South Africa', HSRC policy brief (March), Pretoria. Available at http://www.hsrc.ac.za/Document-2718.phtml

Roberts, B. (2005) '"Empty stomachs, empty pockets": poverty and inequality in post-apartheid South Africa'. In: Daniel, J., Southall, R. & Lutchman, J. (eds) *State of the Nation: South Africa 2004–2005,* HSRC Press, Cape Town.

Roberts, S. (2005) 'Industrial development and industrial policy in South Africa: a ten-year review' (paper presented at the Conference on South African Economic Policy Under Democracy: A Ten Year Review), 28–29 October, Stellenbosch.

Rodrik, D. (1999a) *The New Global Economy and Developing Countries: Making Openness Work,* Johns Hopkins University, Baltimore.

Rodrik, D. (1999b) 'Making openness work' (speech), 18 March, Overseas Development Council, Washington.

Rodrik, D. (1997) 'Sense and nonsense in the globalisation debate', *Foreign Policy,* No. 107, Washington.

Rodrik, D. (1996) 'Why do more open economies have bigger governments?' Working Paper 5537 of the National Bureau of Economic Research, Cambridge, Massachusetts.

Romm, J. (2008) 'The cold truth about climate change', *Salon.com,* 27 February. Available at http://www.salon.com/news/feature/2008/02/27/global_warming_deniers/print.html

Rose, N. (1999) *The Powers of Freedom,* Cambridge University Press, Cambridge.

Rosen, S., Fox, M. & Gill, C. (2007) 'Patient retention in antiretroviral therapy programs in sub-Saharan Africa: a systematic review', *PLoS Medicine,* 2007, 10:e29.

Rosen, S. *et al* (2006) 'The private sector and HIV/AIDS in Africa: taking stock of six years of applied research', Health and Development Discussion Paper No. 7, June, Center for International Health and Development, Boston.

Rosen, S. *et al* (2004) 'The cost of HIV/AIDS to businesses in Africa', *AIDS,* Vol. 18, No. 2, pp. 317–24.

Rosen, S. & Simon, J. (2003) 'Shifting the burden: the private sector's response to the AID pandemic in Africa', *Bulletin of the World Health Organization,* Vol. 81, No. 2, pp. 133–7.

Rosenberg, M. L. *et al* (2006) 'Interpersonal violence'. In: Jamison, D. T. *et al* (eds) *Disease Control Priorities in Developing Countries,* Oxford University Press, New York, pp. 755–770.

RSA (1997) 'White paper for Social Welfare: principles, guidelines, proposed policies and programmes for developmental social welfare in South Africa', *Government Gazette No. 18166,* 8 August, Department of Welfare and Population Development, Pretoria.

RSA (1996) 'Report of the Lund Committee on Child and Family Support', August, Department of Welfare and Population Development, Pretoria.

Rudin, J. (1997) *Challenging Apartheid's Foreign Debt,* Alternative Information and Development Centre, Cape Town.

Rueschemeyer, D., Skocpol, T. & Evans, P. B. (1985) *Bringing the State Back In,* Cambridge University Press, Cambridge.

Rugalema, G. (2000) 'Coping or struggling? A journey into the impact of HIV/AIDS in Southern Africa', *Review of African Political Economy,* Vol. 27, No. 86, pp. 537–45.

Runciman, D. (2009) 'How messy it all is', *London Review of Books,* Vol. 31, No. 20, 22 October, pp. 3–6.

Rustin, M. (2004). 'A practical utopianism?' *New Left Review,* Second series No. 26 (March/April), pp. 136–47.

SACP (2010) 'Building working class hegemony on the terrain of a national democratic struggle' (SACP Central Committee discussion paper), September, Johannesburg.

SACP (2008a) *'Bua Komanisi!'* Information Bulletin of the Central Committee of the SACP, Vol. 7, No. 2, November, SACP, Johannesburg.

SACP (2008b) 'The SACP and state power: the alliance post-Polokwane—ready to govern?' Information Bulletin of the Central Committee of the SACP, Vol. 7, No. 1, September, SACP, Johannesburg.

SACP (2006) 'Is the ANC leading a national democratic revolution or managing capitalism?' (discussion document), SACP, Johannesburg. Available at http://www.sacp.org.za/main.php?include=docs/docs/2006/anc.html

SACP (2002a) 'The current phase of the national democratic revolution' (discussion document), SACP 11th Congress, 24–28 July. Available at http://www.sacp.org.za/main.php?include=11thcongress/chapter1.html

SACP (2002) 'The SACP and the present political and ideological terrain', (discussion document), SACP 11th Congress, 24–28 July. Available at http://www.sacp.org.za/main.php?include=11thcongress/chapter4.html

SACP (2000) 'Declaration of the SACP Strategy Conference', May, SACP, Johannesburg. Available at http://www.sacp.org.za/main.php?include=docs/docs/2000/declaration.html

SACP (1999) 'State, reform and revolution' (document presented at the Special Strategic Conference), 3–5 September, Johannesburg.

SACP (1998) 'Forward to the SACP 10th Congress!' (draft programme discussion documents), Johannesburg.

SACP (1997) 'New confidence on the left' (editorial), *African Communist* (Third Quarter), Johannesburg.

SACP (1996) 'Let us not lose sight of our strategic priorities' (secretariat discussion document), October, Johannesburg.

SACP (1995) 'Strategy and tactics document', 9th SACP Congress, Johannesburg.

SACP (1994) 'Defending and deepening a clear left strategic perspective on the RDP' (discussion document), *African Communist,* No. 138 (Third Quarter), Johannesburg.

SACP (1962) 'The road to South African freedom: programme of the South African Communist Party', *African Communists Speak,* Nauka, Moscow.

SACP & COSATU (1999) 'Trade unions and day-to-day struggles to build socialism' (paper), Johannesburg.

Sader, E. (2005). 'Taking Lula's measure', *New Left Review,* Second series, No. 33 (May/June), pp. 59–82.

SAHRC (2006) *Report on the right to basic education,* South African Human Rights Commission, Johannesburg.

SAIRR (1992) *Race Relations Survey 1991/92,* South African Institute for Race Relations, Johannesburg.

SAIRR (1985) *A Survey of Race Relations in South Africa,* South African Institute for Race Relations, Johannesburg.

SALDRU (2005) 'The financial diaries: investigating the financial lives of the poor (findings in brief)', Centre for Social Science Research, University of Cape Town.

Salinas, G. & Haacker, M. (2006) 'HIV/AIDS: the impact on poverty and inequality', IMF Working Paper WP/06/126, May, International Monetary Fund, Washington.

Samson, M. (2008) 'Wasted citizenship? The role of reclaimers in South African municipal waste management' (paper presented to 12th General Assembly of CODESRIA: Governing the African Public Sphere'), 7–11 December, Yaoundé.

Samson, M. (2007) 'When public works programmes create "second economy" conditions', *Africanus,* November, pp. 216–27.

Sanders, D. & Chopra, M. (2006) 'Key challenges to achieving health for all in an inequitable society: the case of South Africa', *American Journal of Public Health,* Vol. 96, No. 1, pp. 73–8.

Sanders, D. & Lloyd, B. (2005) 'Human resources: international context'. In: Ijumba, P. & Barron, P. (eds), *South African Health Review 2005,* Health Systems Trust, Durban, pp. 76–87.

SANGOCO, Commission on Gender Equality & SA Human Rights Commission (1998) *The People's Voices: National Speak Out on Poverty Hearings—March to June 1998,* Johannesburg.

SA Reserve Bank (2006) *South African Reserve Bank Quarterly Bulletin,* No. 240, June, Pretoria.

SA Reserve Bank (1998) *Annual Economic Report,* Pretoria.

SA Reserve Bank (1994) *South African Reserve Bank Quarterly Bulletin,* March, Pretoria.

SA Reserve Bank (1991) *South African Reserve Bank Quarterly Bulletin,* September, Pretoria.

Sassen, S. (2009) 'Too big to save: the end of financial capitalism', *openDemocracy,* 2 April. Available at http://www.opendemocracy.net

Sassen, S. (1997) 'The global economy: its necessary instrumentalities and cultures' (paper), University of California.

Sassen, S. (1996) *Losing Control? Sovereignty in an Age of Globalization,* Columbia University Press, New York.

Satgar, V. (2008) 'Neoliberalized South Africa: labour and the roots of passive revolution', *Labour, Capital & Society,* Vol. 41, No. 2, pp. 39–69.

Satgar, V. (1997) 'Workplace forums and autonomous self-management: a perspective on transformation from below', *African Communist* (Third Quarter), Johannesburg.

Saul, J. (1994a) '(Half full) or half empty? Review of the RDP', *Southern Africa Report,* Vol. 9, No. 5, July, Toronto.

Saul, J. (1994b) 'Thinking the thinkable: globalism, socialism and democracy in the South African transition'. In: Miliband, R. & Panitch, L. (eds) *Socialist Register 1994,* Merlin, Toronto.

Saul, J. (1993) *Recolonization and Resistance in Southern Africa in the 1990s,* Between the Lines, Toronto.

Saul, J. (1992) 'Structural reform: a model for revolutionary transformation of South Africa?', *Transformation,* No. 20, pp. 1–16.

Saul, J. (1991) 'South Africa between barbarism and structural reform', *New Left Review,* No. 188, pp. 3–44.

Saul, J. & Gelb, S. (1981) 'The Crisis in South Africa: Class Defence and Class Revolution', *Monthly Review,* New York.

Schmidt, J. & Hersh, J. (2006) 'Neoliberal globalization: workfare without welfare', *Globalizations,* Vol. 3, No. 1, pp. 66–89.

Schneider, F. & Frei, Bruno, S. (1985) 'Economic and political determinants of FDI', *World Development,* Vol. 13, No. 2, pp. 161–75.

Schneider, H., Hlope, H. & Van Rensburg, D. (2008) 'Community health workers and the response to HIV/AIDS in South Africa: tensions and prospects', *Health Policy and Planning,* Vol. 23, pp. 179–87.

Schneider, H., Van Rensburg, D. & Coetzee, D. (2007) 'Health systems and antiretroviral access: key findings and policy recommendations', Centre for Health Systems Research and Development, University of Free State, Bloemfontein. Available at http://www.ufs.ac.za/faculties/content.php?id=5709&FCode=01&DCode=161

Schneider, H., Barron, P. & Fonn, S. (2007) 'The promise and the practice of transformation in South Africa's health system'. In: Buhlungu, S. *et al* (eds) *State of the Nation: South Africa 2007,* HSRC Press, Cape Town, pp. 289–311.

Schneider, H., Oyedele, S. & Dlamini, N. (2005) 'HIV impact surveillance system: burnout and associated factors in health professionals in four hospitals', Witwatersrand School of Public Health & Gauteng Department of Health, December (unpublished).

Schneider, H. & Fassin, D. (2002) 'Denial and defiance: a socio-political analysis of AIDS in South Africa', *AIDS,* Vol. 16, Suppl. 4, pp. S545–S51.

Schneider, A. & Goldfrank, B. (2002) 'Budgets and ballots in Brazil: participatory budgeting from the city to the state', *IDS Working Paper 149,* Institute for Development Studies, Brighton.

Scholte, J. A. (1997) 'Global capitalism and the state', *International Affairs,* Vol. 73, No. 3.

Schreiner, G. (1994) 'Restructuring the labour movement after apartheid', *SA Labour Bulletin,* Vol. 18, No. 3 (July), Johannesburg.

Schreiner, J. (1993) 'Breaking the mould', *Work in Progress,* No. 93 (November), Johannesburg.

Schrire, R. (ed) (1992) *Wealth or Poverty? Critical Choices for South Africa,* Oxford University, Cape Town.

Schulz-Herzenberg, C. (2007) 'A silent revolution: South African voters, 1994–2006'. In: Buhlungu, S. *et al* (eds) *State of the Nation: South Africa 2007,* HSRC Press, Cape Town.

Schwartzman, S. (2005) 'Education-oriented social programs in Brazil: the impact of *Bolsa Escola'* (paper presented at Global Conference on Education Research in Developing Countries), Global Development Network, 30 March–2 April, Prague.

Secombe, W. (1999) 'Contradictions of shareholder capitalism: downsizing jobs, enlisting savings, destabilizing families'. In: Panitch, L. & Leys, C. (eds) *Socialist Register 1999: Global Capitalism versus Democracy,* Merlin, Suffolk.

Seedat, M. *et al* (2009) 'Violence and injuries in South Africa: prioritizing an agenda for prevention', *Lancet,* Vol. 374, No. 9694, pp. 1011–22.

Seekings, J. (2006a) 'Facts, myths, and controversies: the measurement and analysis of poverty and inequality after apartheid' (paper prepared for the After Apartheid Conference), 11–12 August, Cape Town.

Seekings, J. (2006b) 'Employment guarantee or minimum income? Workfare and welfare in developing countries', Centre for Social Science Research Working Paper No. 152, University of Cape Town.

Seekings, J. & Natrass, N. (2005) *Class, Race and Inequality in South Africa,* Yale University Press, New Haven.

Seekings, J. (1997) 'SANCO: strategic dilemmas in a democratic South Africa', *Transformation,* No. 34, Durban.

Seekings, J. (1993) *Heroes or Villians?* Ravan Press, Johannesburg.

Seekings, J. (1991) 'Trailing behind the masses: the United Democratic Front and township politics in the Pretoria-Witwatersrand-Vaal Region, 1983–1984', *Journal of Southern African Studies,* Vol. 18, No. 1, pp. 93–114.

Sefularo, M. (2009) 'First Ivan Thoms memorial lecture', 22 March, University of Cape Town.

Segal, L. (1991) 'The human face of violence: hostel dwellers speak', *Journal of Southern African Studies,* Vol. 18, No. 1 (March), York.

Sekhonyane, M. (2004) 'First things first: rehabilitation starts with alternatives to prison', *SA Crime Quarterly,* March, No. 7, pp. 33–6.

Sen, A. (1999) *Development as Freedom,* Oxford University Press, Oxford.

Sen, A. (1985) *Commodities and Capabilities,* Elsevier, Amsterdam.

Sender, J. (2000) 'Struggles to escape poverty in South Africa: results from a purposive rural survey' (June), School of Oriental and African Studies, University of London, London. Available at http://www.soas.ac.uk/economics/research/workingpapers/file 28867.pdf

Sender, J. (1995) 'Economic restructuring in South Africa: reactionary rhetoric prevails', *Journal of Southern African Studies,* Vol. 20, No. 4 (December), York.

Sengul, M. *et al* (2007) 'Climate change and carbon dioxide (CO_2) sequestration: an African perspective', *International Journal of Environmental Studies,* Vol. 64, No. 5, pp. 543–54.

Sennett, R. (2003) *Respect: The Formation of Character in an Age of Inequality,* Penguin Books, London.

September Commission (1997) *Report from the September Commission,* COSATU, Johannesburg.

Sevenhuijsen, S. *et al* (2003) 'South African Social Welfare Policy: an analysis using the ethic of care', *Critical Social Policy,* Vol. 23, No. 3, pp. 299–321.

Sewankambo, N. K. & Katamba, A. (2009) 'Health systems in Africa: learning from Africa', *Lancet,* Vol. 374, No. 9694, pp. 957–9.

Shelton, J. D. (2007) 'Ten myths and one truth about generalised HIV epidemics', *Lancet,* Vol. 370, No. 9602, pp. 1809–1811.

Shelton, J. D., Cassell, M. M. & Adetunji, J. (2005) 'Is poverty or wealth at the root of HIV?' *Lancet,* Vol. 366, No. 9491, pp. 1057–8.

Shelton, J. D. *et al* (2004) 'Partner reduction is crucial for balanced "ABC" approach to HIV prevention', *British Medical Journal,* Vol. 328, No. 7444, pp. 891–3.

Shisana, O. *et al* (2010) 'South African National HIV Prevalence, Incidence, Behaviour and Communication Survey, 2008: The Health of our Children', HSRC Press, Cape Town.

Shisana, O. *et al* (2005a) 'South African National HIV Prevalence, HIV Incidence, Behaviour and Communication Survey', Human Sciences Research Council, Pretoria. Available at http://www.hsrc. ac.za/media/2005/11/20051130_1.html

Shisana, O. *et al* (2005b) 'The Health of our Educators: A Focus on HIV/AIDS in South African Public Schools', HSRC Press, Cape Town.

Shisana, O. *et al* (2003) 'The Impact of HIV/AIDS on the Health Sector: National survey of health personnel, ambulatory and hospitalised patients and health facilities', HSRC Press, Cape Town.

Shubane, K. & Madiba, P. (1992) *The Struggle Continues? Civic Associations in the Transition,* Centre for Policy Studies, Johannesburg.

Sikwebu, D. (2007) 'COSATU and the ANC national conference: can Limpopo be another Morogoro?' *South African Labour Bulletin,* Vol. 31, No. 4, October/November.

Sikwebu, D. (1999) 'June 2nd aftermath: defining a role for COSATU', *SA Labour Bulletin,* Vol. 23, No. 4 (August), Johannesburg.

Simbayi, L. C. & Kalichman, S. C. (2007) 'Condom failure in South Africa', *South African Medical Journal,* Vol. 97, No. 7, p. 476.

Simbayi, L. C. *et al* (2006) 'Baseline surveys of psychosocial issues affecting orphaned and vulnerable children in two South African municipalities', HSRC Press, Cape Town.

Simbayi, L.C. *et al* (2004) 'Alcohol use and sexual risks for HIV infection among men and women receiving sexually transmitted infection clinic services in Cape Town, South Africa', *Journal Stud. Alcohol,* 65:434–42.

Simkins, C. (2004) 'What happened to the distribution of income in South Africa between 1995 and 2001?' (unpublished paper).

Simkins, C. (2001) 'Can South Africa avoid a Malthusian positive check?' *Daedalus,* Vol. 130, No. 1, pp. 123–50.

Simkins, C., Woolard, I. & Thompson, K. (2000) *An Analysis of the Burden of Taxes in the South African Economy for the Years Between 1995/96 and 1999/2000,* Department of Finance, Pretoria.

Simkins, C. (1987) *The Prisoners of Tradition and the Politics of Nation Building,* SAIRR, Johannesburg.

Simon, R. (1991) *Gramsci's Political Thought,* Lawrence & Wishart, London.

Simone, A. (1994) 'Local institutions and the governance of community development in South Africa' (author's draft), Foundation for Contemporary Research, Cape Town.

Sinclair, S. (2005) *The GATS and South Africa's National Health Act* (research paper), November, Canadian Centre for Policy Alternatives, Ottawa.

Sitas, A. (2004) '30 years since the Durban strikes: black working-class leadership and the South African transition', *Current Sociology,* Vol. 52, No. 5, pp. 830–49.

Sithole, P., Todes, A. & Williamson, A. (2007) 'Gender and women's participation in municipality-driven development: IDP and project-level participation in Msinga, eThekwini and Hibiscus Coast', *Critical Dialogue,* Vol. 3, No. 1, pp. 31–7.

Skinner, C. & Valodia, I. (2007) 'Two economies? A critique of recent South African policy debate'. In: Bond, P., Chitonge, H. & Hopfmann, A. (eds) *The Accumulation of Capital in Southern Africa: Rosa*

Luxemburg's Contemporary Relevance, Rosa Luxemburg Foundation & Centre for Civil Society, Berlin & Durban.

Skoufias, E. (2001) *Progresa and its impact on the human capital and welfare of households in rural Mexico: a synthesis of the results of an evaluation by IFPRI,* International Food Policy Research Institute, Washington, DC.

Skweyiya, Z. (2007) 'Address by the minister of social development, Zola Skweyiya, on the occasion of the debate on the President's State of the Nation address', 13 February, Cape Town.

Slovo, J. (1992) 'Negotiations: what room for compromises?' *African Communist,* No. 130 (Third Quarter).

Slovo, J. (1990) 'Has socialism failed?', *SA Labour Bulletin,* Vol. 14, No. 6 (February), Johannesburg.

Slovo, J. (1986) 'SACP: one of the Great Pillars of our Revolution', *African Communist,* No. 107 (Second Quarter).

Slovo, J. (1976) 'South Africa: no middle road'. In: Davidson, B., Slovo, J. & Wilkinson, A. (eds) *Southern Africa: The New Politics of Revolution,* Penguin, London.

Smith, N. (2007) 'Nature as accumulation strategy'. In Panitch L. & Leys, C. (eds) *Socialist Register 2007: Coming to terms with nature,* Monthly Review Press, New York.

Snodgrass, D. & Sebstad, J. (2002) 'Clients in context: the impacts of microfinance in three countries—a synthesis report', USAID, Washington DC.

Solomon, R. & Benatar, M.B. (2004) 'Health care reform and the crisis of HIV and AIDS in South Africa', *New England Journal of Medicine,* Vol. 351, No. 1, pp. 81–92.

Soudien, C. (2004) '"Constituting the class": an analysis of the process of "integration" in South African schools'. In: Chisholm, L. (ed) *Changing Class: Education and Social Change in Post-Apartheid South Africa,* HSRC Press, Cape Town, pp. 89–114.

South African Government (1994) 'White Paper on Reconstruction and Development: A Strategy for Fundamental Transformation' (September), Pretoria.

South African Institute of Race Relations (2007) *South Africa Survey 2007,* SAIRR, Johannesburg.

South African Police Service (2009) *Crime Situation in South Africa 2008/2009: Annual Report,* SAPS, Pretoria.

South African Police Service (2006) *Crime Statistics 2005/2006,* SAPS, Pretoria.

Southall, R. (2010) 'Jacob Zuma: a year of drift', *Morung Express,* 11 May.

Southall, R. (2008) 'Thabo Mbeki's fall: the ANC and South Africa's democracy', *openDemocracy,* 14 October.

Southall, R. (2007a) 'The ANC state, more dysfunctional than developmental?' In: Buhlungu, S. *et al* (eds) *State of the Nation: South Africa 2007,* HSRC Press, Cape Town.

Southall, R. (2007b) 'The ANC, black economic empowerment and the state-owned enterprises: a recycling of history?' In: Buhlungu, S. *et al* (eds) *State of the Nation: South Africa 2007,* HSRC Press, Cape Town.

Southall, R. (2006) 'Introduction: can South Africa be a developmental state?' In: Buhlungu, S. *et al* (eds) *State of the Nation: South Africa 2006,* HSRC Press, Cape Town.

SouthScan bulletin (various issues), London.

Sparks, A. (2003) *Beyond the Miracle,* Jonathan Ball, Johannesburg.

Sparks, A. (1994) *Tomorrow is Another Country: The Inside Story of South Africa's Negotiated Revolution,* Struik, Johannesburg.

Speth, J. G. (2008) 'Global warming and modern capitalism', *The Nation,* 6 October, New York.

Spreen, C. A. (2004) 'Appropriating borrowed policies: outcomes-based education in South Africa'. In: Steiner-Khamsi, G. (ed) *The Global Politics of Educational Borrowing and Lending,* Teachers College Press, New York, pp. 10–13.

Spreen, C. A. (2001) 'Globalization and educational policy borrowing: mapping outcomes-based education in South Africa' (PhD thesis), Columbia University, New York.

Stadler, A. (1987) *The Political Economy of Modern South Africa,* David Philip, Cape Town.

Standing, G. (2008) 'How cash transfers boost work and economic security', DESA Working Paper No. 58 (April), Department of Economic and Social Affairs, United Nations, New York.

Standing, G. (2003) 'CIG, COAG and COG: a comment on the debate'. In: Wright, E. O. (ed) *Redesigning Distribution: Basic Income and Stakeholder Grants as Alternative Cornerstones for a More Egalitarian Capitalism,* Verso Books, London, pp. 142–57.

Standing, G. (2002) *Beyond the New Paternalism: Basic Security as Equality,* Verso Books, London.

Stanners, W. (1993) 'Is low inflation an important condition for high growth?' *Cambridge Journal of Economics,* No. 17, Cambridge University, Cambridge.

Statistics SA (2009a) *Social grants: In-depth analysis of the General Household Survey data 2003–2007, GHS series Vol. 1,* Statistical Release P0318.1, July, Pretoria.

Statistics SA (2009b) *Mid-year population estimates 2009,* Statistical Release P0302 (July), Pretoria. Available at http://www.statssa.gov.za/publications/P0302/P03022009.pdf

Statistics SA (2009c) *Quarterly Labour Force Survey: Quarter 2* (April to June), 2009, Pretoria.

Statistics SA (2009d) *General household survey 2008,* Statistical Release P0318 (September), Pretoria.

Statistics SA (2008a) *Income & Expenditures of Households 2005/2006,* Statistical Release P0100, Pretoria.

Statistics SA (2008b) *Income & Expenditures of Households 2005/2006: analysis of results,* Pretoria. Available at http://www.sarpn.org.za/documents/d0003023/index.php

Statistics SA (2008c) *General Household Survey 2007,* Statistical Release P0318 (September), Pretoria.

Statistics SA (2008d) *Mid-year population estimates,* Statistical Release P0302. Available at http://www.statssa.gov.za

Statistics SA (2008e) *Labour Force Survey: Historical revision March series 2001 to 2007,* Statistical Release P0210 (August), Pretoria.

Statistics SA (2006). *Mortality and causes of death in South Africa, 2003 and 2004: Findings from death notification,* Pretoria.

Statistics SA (2005a) *Labour Force Survey,* Statistical Release P0210 (September), Pretoria.

Statistics SA (2005b) *Mortality and causes of death in South Africa, 1997–2003: Findings from death notification,* Pretoria. Available at: http://www.statssa.gov.za/publications/P03093/P03093.pdf

Statistics SA (2005c) *General Household Survey,* Pretoria. Available at http://www.statssa.gov.za/publications/P0318/P0318July2004.pdf.

Statistics SA (2003) *General Household Survey 2002,* September, Pretoria.

Statistics SA (2002a) *Earning and spending in South Africa: Selected findings and comparisons from the income and expenditure surveys of October 1995 and October 2000,* Pretoria.

Statistics SA (2002b) *The South African Labour Market,* Pretoria.

Stein, H. (ed) (1995) *Asian Industrialisation and Africa: Studies in Policy Alternatives to Structural Adjustment,* St Martin's Press, London.

Stein, J. (2003) 'Sorrow makes children of us all: a literature review on the psycho-social impact of HIV/AIDS on children', Working Paper No. 47, Centre for Social Science Research, Cape Town.

Steyn, N. P. & Labadarios, D. (2005) 'Nutrition policy implementation'. In: *The National Food Consumption Survey (NFCS): Fortification Baseline, South Africa,* Department of Health, Pretoria, pp. 533–43.

Steinberg, J. (2008a) *Three-Letter Plague: One Man's Journey through a Great Epidemic,* Jonathan Ball, Johannesburg.

Steinberg, J. (2008b) *Thin Blue: The Unwritten Rules of Policing South Africa,* Jonathan Ball, Johannesburg.

Steiner-Khamsi, G. (2006) 'The economics of policy borrowing and lending: a study of late adopters', *Oxford Review of Education,* Vol. 32, No. 5, pp. 665–78.

Stiglitz, J. (1998) 'More instruments and broader goals: moving toward the Post-Washington Consensus', WIDER annual lecture (January 7), Helsinki.

Stillwagon, E. (2006) 'The ecology of poverty, nutrition, parasites and vulnerability to HIV/AIDS'. In: Gillespie, S. (ed) *AIDS, Poverty and Hunger: Challenges and Responses,* International Food Policy Research Institute, Washington.

Stockhammer, E. (2008) 'Some stylized facts on the finance-dominated accumulation regime', *Competition & Change,* Vol. 12, No. 2 (June), pp.184–202.

Stoll, S. (2008) 'Fear of fallowing: the specter of a no-growth world', *Harper's Magazine,* March.

Strebel, A. *et al* (2006) 'Social constructions of gender roles, gender-based violence and HIV/AIDS in two communities of the Western Cape, South Africa', *Journal of Social Aspects of HIV/AIDS,* Vol. 3, No. 3, pp. 516–28.

Stuckler, D. *et al* (2010) 'Mining and the risk of tuberculosis in sub-Saharan Africa', *American Journal of Public Health,* published ahead of print, June 1.

Stuckler, D. King, L. & McKee, M. (2009) 'Mass privatisation and the post-communist mortality crisis: a cross-national analysis', *Lancet,* Vol. 373, No. 9661: 399–407.

Sundararaman, T. (2007) 'Community health workers: scaling up programmes', *Lancet,* Vol. 369, No. 9579, pp. 2058–9.

Suttner, R. (2009) 'ANC crisis and the rise of COPE', *ZNet,* 14 March. Available at http://www.zcommunications.org/znet/viewArticle/20867

Suttner, R. (1992) 'Ensuring stable transition to democratic power', *African Communist,* No. 131 (Fourth Quarter), Johannesburg.

Suttner, R. & Cronin, J. (1986) *Thirty Years of the Freedom Charter,* Ravan Press, Johannesburg.

Sweezy, P. M. & Magdoff, H. (1992) 'Globalization: To What End?' *Monthly Review,* Vol. 43, No. 9 (February), New York.

Swilling, M. *et al* (2010) 'Growth, resource use and decoupling: towards a "Green New Deal" for South Africa'. In: Southall, R. *et al* (eds) *South Africa Review 2009,* forthcoming.

Swilling, M. (2006) 'Sustainability and infrastructure planning in South Africa: a Cape Town case study', *Environment and Urbanisation,* Vol. 18, No. 1, pp. 23–50.

Swilling, M. *et al* (2005) *Economic policy-making in a developmental state: Review of the South African government's poverty and development approaches, 1994–2004,* Economic Policy and Poverty Alleviation Report Series, Report 3 & 4, Centre for Civil Society, University of KwaZulu-Natal, Durban.

Swilling, M. & Russel, B. (2002) *The Size and Scope of the Non-profit Sector in South Africa,* University of the Witwatersrand & University of KwaZulu-Natal, Johannesburg & Durban.

Swilling, M. (1991) 'The case for associational socialism', *Work in Progress,* No. 76 (February), Johannesburg.

Swilling, M. & Phillips, M. (1989a) 'The emergency state: its structure, power and limits', *South African Review No. 5,* Ravan Press, Johannesburg.

Swilling, M. & Phillips, M. (1989b) 'State power in the 1980s: from "total strategy" to counter-revolutionary warfare'. In: *War and Society: The Militarization of South Africa,* David Philip, Cape Town.

Tawfik, L. & Kinoti, K. N. (2003) *The impact of HIV/AIDS on health systems in sub-Saharan Africa with special reference to the issue of human resources,* USAID Bureau for Africa, Washington DC.

Taylor, I. (2002) 'Botswana's "developmental state" and the politics of legitimacy' (paper presented at the conference, Towards a new political economy of development: Globalisation and governance), 4–6 July, University of Sheffield.

Taylor, S. & Yu, D. (2008) 'The importance of social economic status in determining educational achievement in South Africa' (paper prepared for the conference on The Regulatory Environment and its Impact on the Nature and Level of Economic Growth and Development in South Africa), May, University of Cape Town. Available at http://www.ekon.sun.ac.za/wpapers/2009/wp012009/wp-01-2009.pdf

Terreblanche, S. (2002) *A History of Inequality in South Africa, 1652–2002,* University of KwaZulu-Natal Press, Pietermaritzburg.

Therborn, G. (2009) 'The killing fields of inequality', *openDemocracy,* 6 April. Available at http://www.opendemocracy.net

Theron, J. (1999a) 'Labour standards versus job creation: the impact of the BCEA on small business', *SA Labour Bulletin,* Vol. 23, No. 5 (October), Johannesburg.

Theron, J. (1999b) 'Terms of empowerment', *SA Labour Bulletin*, Vol. 23, No. 1 (February), Johannesburg.

Tilly, C. (1985) 'Models and realities of popular action', *Social Research*, Vol. 52, No. 4, pp. 717–47.

Toussaint (1988) 'On workerism, socialism and the Communist Party', *African Communist*, No. 114 (Third Quarter).

Trevor, A. (1984) 'The question of an uprising of the people as a whole', *African Communist*, No. 97 (Second Quarter).

Tsoukalas, C. (1999) 'Globalisation and the executive committee: the contemporary capitalist state'. In: Panitch, L. & Leys, C. (eds) Socialist Register 1999: *Global Capitalism versus Democracy*, Merlin, Suffolk.

Tuchman, B. W. (1978) *A Distant Mirror: The Calamitous 14th Century*, Alfred A. Knopf, New York.

Turner, A.N. (2007) 'Men's circumcision status and women's risk of HIV acquisition in Zimbabwe and Uganda', *AIDS*, Vol. 21, pp. 1779–89.

Turner, G. (2008) 'A comparison of the Limits to Growth with 30 years of reality', *Global Environmental Change*, Vol. 18, pp. 397–411.

Turton, A. R. (2008) 'Three strategic water quality challenges that decision-makers need to know about and how the CSIR should respond' (keynote address to Science: Real and Relevant Conference), 18 November, Centre for Scientific and Industrial Research, Pretoria.

UNAIDS/WHO (2009) *AIDS Epidemic Update*, UNAIDS, Geneva.

UNAIDS (2008) *Towards Universal Access*, UNAIDS, Geneva.

UNAIDS/WHO (2007) *AIDS Epidemic Update*, UNAIDS, Geneva.

UNCTAD (1999) *World Investment Report 1999*, UNCTAD, New York.

UNCTAD (1997) *World Investment Report 1997: Transnational Corporations, Market Structure and Competition Policy*, New York.

UNDP (2008) *Human Development Report 2007/2008. Fighting climate change: human solidarity in a divided world*, UNDP, New York.

UNDP (2006) *Human Development Report 2006/2007. Beyond scarcity: power, poverty and the global water crisis*, UNDP, New York.

UNDP (2003) *South Africa Human Development Report 2003: the challenge of sustainable development in South Africa: unlocking people's creativity*, Oxford University Press, Cape Town. Available at http://hdr.undp.org/reports/global/2003

UNDP (2000) *Overcoming Human Poverty: Poverty Report 2000*, United Nations Development Programme, New York.

UNDP (1998a) *Poverty and Inequality in South Africa*, United Nations Development Programme, Pretoria.

UNDP (1998b) *Human Development Report 1998*, United Nations Development Programme, New York.

UNRISD (2007) 'Commercialization and globalization of health care: lessons from UNRISD research', *UNRISD Research and Policy Brief*, No. 7, December, UNRISD, Geneva.

UNRISD (2006) 'Transformative social policy: lessons from UNRISD research', *UNRISD Research and Policy Brief*, No. 5 (October), United Nations Research Institute for Social Development, Geneva.

UN Statistics Division (2010) 'Millennium Development Goals indicators: carbon dioxide emissions (CO_2), metric tons of CO_2 per capita data set'. Available at http://mdgs.un.org/unsd/mdg/SeriesDetail.aspx?srid=751&crid

US Agency for International Development (USAID) (2004) 'USAID/OFDA uses cash grants to alleviate chronic food insecurity in Ethiopia', USAID, Washington, DC. Available at: http://www.usaid.gov/our_work/humanitarian_assistance/disaster_assistance/publications/focus_articles/6_2004_Ethiopia.html

Vadney, T. E. (1987) *The World Since 1940*, Pelican Books, London.

Vale, P. & Maseko, S. (1998) 'South Africa and the African Renaissance', *South Africa and Africa: Reflections on the African Renaissance*, Foundation for Global Dialogue Occasional Paper No. 17, Johannesburg.

Vally, S. (2010) 'Outcomes-based education and its (dis)contents: learner-centered pedagogy, poverty and the education crisis in South Africa', *Southern African Review of Education* [forthcoming].

Vally, S. (2007a) 'From people's education to neoliberalism in South Africa', *Review of African Political Economy*, No. 111, pp. 39–56.

Vally, S. (2007b) 'Higher education in South Africa: market mill or public good?', *Journal of Higher Education in Africa*, Vol. 5, No. 1, pp. 17–28.

Van As, S., Parry, C. & Blecher, M. (2003) 'The alcohol injury fund', *South African Medical Journal*, Vol. 93, pp. 828–9.

Van den Heever, A.M. (2007) *Evaluation of the merger between Network Healthcare Holdings and Community Healthcare*, Council for Medical Schemes, Pretoria.

Van der Berg, S. *et al* (2007a) 'A Series of National Accounts-Consistent Estimates of Poverty and Inequality in South Africa', Stellenbosch Economic Working Papers, No. 09/07, Stellenbosch University.

Van der Berg, S. *et al* (2007b) 'Poverty trends since the transition: what we know', Stellenbosch Economic Working Papers, University of Stellenbosch.

Van der Berg, S. *et al* (2005) 'Trends in poverty and inequality since the political transition', Stellenbosch Economic Working Papers No. 1/2005, Stellenbosch University.

Van der Berg, S. (2002) 'Education, poverty and inequality in South Africa' (paper for the Economic Growth and Poverty in Africa Conference), March, Centre for the Study of African Economies, Oxford.

Van Parijs, P. (2003) 'A simple and powerful idea for the 21st century'. In: Wright, E. O. (ed) *Redesigning Distribution: Basic Income and Stakeholder Grants as Alternative Cornerstones for a More Egalitarian Capitalism*, Verso Books, London.

Van Parijs, P. (2000) 'A basic income for all', *Boston Review*, November. Available at http://www.bostonreview.net/BR25.5/vanparijs.html

Van Rensburg, H. C. J. (2004) 'The health professions and human resources for health'. In: Van Rensburg, H. C. J. (ed) *Health and Health Care in South Africa*, Van Schaik, Pretoria.

Van Rensburg, D. & Van Rensburg, N. (1999) 'Distribution of human resources'. In: Health Systems Trust (ed) *South African Health Review 1999*, Health Systems Trust, Durban.

Van Renterghem, H. (2009) 'AIDS and the city: intensifying the response to HIV and AIDS in urban areas in sub-Saharan Africa', Working paper, UNAIDS Regional Support Team, Johannesburg.

Various authors (1970) *African Communists Speak: Articles and documents from the The African Communist*, Nauka, Moscow.

Vass, J. (2003) 'Impact of HIV/AIDS on the labour force: exploring vulnerabilities', *CODESRIA Bulletin*, Special issue, 2, 3 & 4, CODESRIA, Dakar.

Vass, J. (2003b) 'The impact of HIV/AIDS'. In: *Human Resources Development Review 2003: education, employment and skills in South Africa.* Human Sciences Research Council. Cape Town.

Vetten, L. *et al* (2008) 'Tracking justice: the attrition of rape cases through the criminal justice system in Gauteng', Tshwaranang Legal Advocacy Centre, Johannesburg.

Victor, D. G. & Morse, R. K. (2009) 'Living with coal: climate policy's most inconvenient truth', *Boston Review*, September/October. Available at http://bostonreview.net/BR34.5/victor_morse.php

Victora, C. G., Black, R. E. & Bryce, J. (2007) 'Learning from new initiatives in maternal and child health', *Lancet*, Vol. 370, pp. 1113–14.

Vilas, C. M. (1996) 'Neoliberal social policy', *NACLA Report on the Americas*, Vol. 29, No. 6 (May/June), New York.

Vilas, C. M. (1993) 'The hour of civil society', *NACLA Report on the Americas*, Vol. 27, No. 2 (September/October), New York.

Vilas, Carlos M. (1989) 'Revolution and democracy in Latin America', *Socialist Register 1989*, Merlin, London.

Virilio, P. (1978) *Popular Defense and Ecological Struggles*, Semiotext(e), New York.

Von Holdt, K. (2010) 'The South African post-apartheid bureaucratic state: inner workings, contradictory rationales and the developmental state'. In: Edigheji, O. (ed) *Constructing a Democratic Developmental State in South Africa: Potential and Challenges*, HSRC Press, Cape Town.

Von Holdt, K. & Murphy, M. (2007) 'Public hospitals in South Africa: stressed institutions, disempowered management'. In: Buhlungu, S. *et al*, *State of the Nation: South Africa 2007*, HSRC Press, Cape Town, pp. 312–41.

Von Holdt, K. & Webster, E. (2005) 'Work restructuring and the crisis of social reproduction'. In: Webster, E. & Von Holdt, K. (eds) *Beyond the Apartheid Workplace: Studies in Transition*, University of KwaZulu-Natal Press, Pietermaritzburg.

Von Holdt, K. (2002) 'Social movement unionism: the case of South Africa', *Work Employment and Society*, Vol. 16, No. 2, pp. 283–304.

Von Holdt, K. (1997) 'The September Commission: shaping congress debates, stimulating activism', *SA Labour Bulletin*, Vol. 21, No. 6 (December), Johannesburg.

Von Holdt, K. (1996) 'David or Goliath? The future of the unions', *SA Labour Bulletin*, Vol. 20, No. 4 (August), Johannesburg.

Von Holdt, K. (1993) 'Cosatu Special Congress: the uncertain new era', *SA Labour Bulletin*, Vol. 17, No. 5 (September/October), Johannesburg.

Von Holdt, K. (1992) 'What is the future of labour?' *SA Labour Bulletin*, Vol. 16, No. 8 (November/December), Johannesburg.

Wade, R. (2008) 'Financial regime change?' *New Left Review*, No. 53 (September–October), pp. 5–22.

Wade, R. & Veneroso, F. (1998) 'The Asian crisis: the high debt model versus the Wall Street-Treasury-IMF complex', *New Left Review*, No. 228, pp. 3–23.

Wade, R. & Veneroso, F. (1998) 'The gathering world slump and the battle over capital controls', *New Left Review*, No. 231, pp. 13–42.

Wade, R. (1996) 'Japan, the World Bank and the art of paradigm maintenance: the East Asian miracle in political perspective', *New Left Review*, No. 217 (May/June), pp. 3–36.

Wadee, H. & Khan, F. (2007) 'Human resources for health', *SA Health Review 2007*, Health Systems Trust, Durban.

Walensky, R. P. *et al* (2009) 'When to start antiretroviral therapy in resource-limited settings', *Annals of International Medicine*, Vol. 151, pp. 157–66.

Walensky, R.P. (2008) 'Scaling up antiretroviral therapy in South Africa: the impact of speed on survival', *Journal of Infectious Diseases*, Vol. 197, No. 9, pp. 324–32.

Walker, R., Reid, G. & Cornell, M. (2004) *Waiting to Happen: HIV/AIDS in South Africa*, Double Storey, Cape Town.

Walker, C. (1982) *Women and Resistance in South Africa*, Onyx, London.

Wallerstein, I. (2003) *The Decline of American Power*, The New Press, New York.

Wallerstein, I. (1999) *The End of the World as We Know It: Social Science in the 21st Century*, University of Minnesota Press, Minneapolis.

Wallerstein, I. (1996) 'The ANC and South Africa: the past and future of liberation movements in the world system' (address to South African Sociological Association), Durban, 7 July, Durban.

Waterman, P. (2005) 'From "decent work" to "the liberation of time from work": reflections on work, emancipation, utopia and the global justice and solidarity movement' (discussion paper), Amsterdam. Available at http://www.struggle.ws/anarkismo/peterwork.pdf

Watkins, K. (1994) 'GATT: a victory for the north', *Review of African Political Economy*, No. 59, Sheffield.

Watts, M. (1994) 'Development 11: the privatization of everything' (workshop paper), University of California, Berkeley.

Wawer, M. J. *et al* (2009) 'Circumcision in HIV-infected men and its effect on HIV transmission to female partners in Rakai, Uganda: a randomized control trial', *Lancet*, Vol. 374, pp. 229–37.

Webster, E. *et al* (2008) 'Making visible the invisible: confronting South Africa's decent work deficit' (research report), March, Sociology of Work Unit, University of Witwatersrand, Johannesburg. Available at http://www.labour.gov.za/downloads/documents/research-documents/webster.pdf

Webster, E. & Bezuidenhout, A. (2005) 'Debating the flexible world of work in South Africa'. In: Edigheji, O. (ed) *Trajectories for South Africa: reflections on the ANC's 2nd National General Council's discussion documents,* special edition of *Policy: Issues and Actors,* Vol. 18, No. 2, Centre for Policy Studies, Johannesburg, pp. 22–6.

Webster, E. & Buhlungu, S. (2004) 'Between marginalisation and revitalisation? The state of trade unionism in South Africa', *Review of African Political Economy,* No. 100, pp. 39–56.

Webster, E. & Omar, R. (2003) 'Work restructuring in post-apartheid South Africa', *Work and Occupations,* Vol. 30, No. 2, pp. 194–213.

Webster, E. & Adler, A. (1999) 'Towards a class compromise in South Africa's "double transition": bargained liberalisation and the consolidation of democracy' (symposium paper), September, History Workshop of the University of the Witwatersrand, Johannesburg.

Weiss, L. (1997) 'Globalisation and the myth of the powerless state', *New Left Review,* No. 225, pp. 3–27.

Weiser, S. D. *et al* (2007) 'Food insufficiency is associated with high-risk sexual behavior among women in Botswana and Swaziland', *PLos Medicine,* Vol. 4, No. 10, 260e.

Wellings, K. *et al* (2006) 'Sexual behaviour in context: a global perspective', *Lancet,* No. 368, pp. 1706–28.

Wen, D. & Li, M. (2007) 'China: hyper-development and environmental crisis'. In: Panitch, L. & Leys, C. (eds) *Coming to Terms with Nature: Socialist Register 2007,* Monthly Review Press, New York.

Wesso, G. (2001) 'The dynamic of capital flows in South Africa: an empirical investigation', *South African Reserve Bank Quarterly Bulletin,* No. 220, June, pp. 59–77.

Westercamp, M. & Bailey, R. C. (2007) 'Acceptability of male circumcision for prevention of HIV/AIDS in sub-Saharan Africa: a review', *AIDS Behavior,* Vol. 11, No. 3, pp. 341–55.

White, G. (1998) 'Constructing a democratic developmental state'. In: Robinson, M. & Gordon, W. (eds) *The Democratic Developmental State: Political and Institutional Design,* Oxford University Press, Oxford.

White, S. (1996) 'Depoliticizing development: the uses and abuses of participation', *Development in Practice,* Vol. 6, No. 1, pp. 6–15.

Whiteford, A. & Van Seventer, D. (2000) 'Understanding Contemporary Household Inequality in South Africa', *Studies in Economics and Econometrics,* Vol. 24, No. 3, pp. 7–30.

Whiteford, A. & Van Seventer, D. (1999) *Winners and Losers: South Africa's Changing Income Distribution in the 1990s,* WEFA Southern Africa, Pretoria.

Whiteford, A., Van Zyl, E., Simkins, C. & Hall, E. (1999) *Labour Market Trends and Future Workforce Needs,* HSRC1, Pretoria.

Whiteside, A. (2008) *HIV/AIDS: A Very Short Introduction,* Oxford University Press, Oxford.

Whiteside, A. & O'Grady, M. (2003) 'AIDS and private sector: lessons from Southern Africa'. In: Sisask, A. (ed) *One Step Further: Responses to HIV/AIDS,* Sida & UNRISD, Stockholm & Geneva.

WHO (2008) 'Global tuberculosis control: surveillance, planning, financing', World Health Organization, Geneva. Available at http://www.who.int/tb/publications/global_report/2008/pdf/fullreport.pdf

WHO, UNAIDS, UNICEF (2008) 'Towards Universal Access: scaling up priority HIV/AIDS interventions in the health sector', *Progress Report 2008,* WHO, Geneva.

Wilkinson, R. G. (2002) 'Commentary: liberty, fraternity, equality', *International Journal of Epidemiology,* Vol. 31, pp. 53–43.

Wilkinson, R. G. (1996) *Unhealthy Societies: The Afflictions of Inequality,* Routledge, London.

Wilkinson, R. G. & Pickett, K. (2009) *The Spirit Level: Why More Equal Societies Almost Always Do Better,* Allen Lane, London.

Wilkinson, R. G., Kawachi, I. & Kennedy, B. P. (1998) 'Mortality, the social environment, crime and violence', *Sociology of Health and Illness,* Vol. 20, pp. 578–97.

Wilkinson, R. G. (1996) *Unhealthy Societies: The Afflictions of Inequality,* Routledge, London.

Williams, B. G. *et al* (2006) 'The potential impact of male circumcision on HIV in sub-Saharan Africa', *PloS Medicine,* No. 3:e262.

Williams, J. (2005) 'Community participation and democratic practice in post-apartheid South Africa: rhetoric vs reality', *Critical Dialogue,* Vol. 2, No. 1.

Williams, M. (2008) *The Roots of Participatory Democracy: Democratic Communists in South Africa and Kerala, India,* Palgrave Macmillan, London.

Williams, M. (2007) 'Generative politics: participatory development in South Africa and Kerala' (paper), University of Witwatersrand, Johannesburg.

Wilson, F. (2001) 'Mineral and migrants: how the mining industry has shaped South Africa', *Proceedings of the American Academy of Arts and Sciences*, Vol. 130, No. 1 (Winter), pp. 99–121.

Wilson, M. (1975) 'So truth be in the field', Alfred and Winifrid Hoernle Lecture, South African Institute for Race Relations, Johannesburg.

Wittenberg, M. & Collinson, M. A. (2007) 'Household transitions in rural South Africa: 1996–2003', *Scandinavian Journal of Public Health*, Suppl. No. 69, pp. 130–7.

Wolpe, H. (1988) *Race, Class and the Apartheid State*, James Currey, London.

Wolpe, H. (1984) 'Strategic issues in the struggle for national liberation in South Africa', *Socialist Review*, Vol. 8, No. 2, London.

Wolpe, H. (1980) 'Towards an analysis of the South African State', *International Journal of the Sociology of Law*, Vol. 8, No. 4, pp. 399–421.

Wolpe, H. (1972) 'Capitalism and cheap labour power', *Economy and Society*, Vol. 1, No. 4, pp. 425–56.

Wood, A. (2006) 'Correlating violence and socio-economic inequality: an empirical analysis'. In: McCarthy, T. E. (ed) *Attacking the Root Causes of Torture, Poverty, Inequality and Violence*, World Organisation Against Torture, Geneva. Available at http://omct.org/pdf/ESCR/2006/omct_desc_study_2006_cd/read_me_first.html?PHPSESSID=a8c3a9d95b6c8b2459b5a6dc0da76387

Wood, K., Lambert H. & Jewkes, R. (2008) '"Injuries are beyond love": young South Africans' understandings of limit and legitimacy in relation to physical violence in their sexual relationships', *Medical Anthropology*, Vol. 27, pp. 43–69. Available at http://omct.org/pdf/ESCR/2006/omct_desc_study_2006_cd/read_me_first.html?PHPSESSID=a8c3a9d95b6c8b2459b5a6dc0da76387

Wood, K. & Jewkes, R. (2001) '"Dangerous" love: reflections on violence among Xhosa township youth'. In: Morrell, R. (ed) *Changing Men in Southern Africa*, University of Natal Press & Zed Books, Pietermaritzburg & London, pp. 317–336.

Wood, K. & Jewkes, R. (1997) 'Violence, rape and sexual coercion: everyday love in a South African township', *Gender and Development*, Vol. 5, No. 2, pp. 41–46.

Wood, E. M. (1995) 'Editorial', *Monthly Review* (July/August), New York.

Wood, E. M. (1990) 'The uses and abuses of civil society'. In: Miliband, R. *et al* (eds) *Socialist Register 1990*, Merlin Press, Suffolk.

Woolard, I. (2003) *Impact of Government Programmes using Alternative Datasets: Social Assistance Grants, Project 6.2 of the Ten-Year Review Research Programme*, Government of South Africa, Pretoria.

Woolard, I. (2002) 'An overview of poverty and inequality in South Africa' (working paper), July, DFID, Pretoria. Available at http://www.sarpn.org.za/CountryPovertyPapers/SouthAfrica/july2002/woolard/index.php

World Bank (2008) *World Development Indicators*, Washington DC.

World Bank (2006) *World Development Indicators*, Washington DC.

World Bank (2005) *World Development Report 2004*, World Bank, Washington DC.

World Bank (1996a) *World Development Report 1996*, Washington DC.

World Bank (1996b) *Global Economic Prospects 1996*, Washington DC.

World Bank (1994) *Reducing Poverty in South Africa: Options for Equitable and Sustainable Growth*, Johannesburg.

World Bank (1993) *The East Asian Miracle: Economic Growth and Public Policy*, Oxford University Press, Oxford. Available at http://www-wds.worldbank.org/external/default/WDSContentServer/WDSP/IB/1993/09/01/000009265_3970716142516/Rendered/PDF/multi_page.pdf

World Bank (Southern Africa Department) (1993) *South Africa: Paths to Economic Growth*, Washington DC.

Worldwatch Institute (1990) *State of the World*, Worldwatch Institute, Washington DC.

Wright, E. O. (2006) 'Compass points: towards a socialist alternative', *New Left Review*, No. 41, September–October, pp. 93–124.

Wright, E.O. (2003) 'Basic income, stakeholder grants, and class analysis', In Wright, E.O. (ed) *Redesigning Distribution: Basic Income and Stakeholder Grants as Alternative Cornerstones for a More Egalitarian Capitalism*, Verso Books, London.

Wright, S. (2005) *In Absentia* (curator's notes to a collective contemporary art exhibition), Centre d'art Passerelle, Brest. Available at http://www.passerelle.infini.fr

Wuyts, M. (2001) 'Inequality and poverty as the condition of labour' (research paper for UNRISD meeting on The Need to Rethink Development Economics), 7–8 September, Cape Town.

Youde, J. (2005) 'South Africa, AIDS, and the development of a counter-epistemic community' (paper prepared for the 2005 International Studies Association Conference), 1–5 March, Honolulu.

Youde. J, (2001) 'All the voters will be dead: HIV/AIDS and democratic legitimacy and stability in Africa' (research paper), University of Iowa.

Zarenda, H. (1994) 'The inconsistencies and contradictions of the RDP' (address to the Johannesburg branch of the South African Economics Society), 4 October 1994.

Zelleke, A. (2009) 'Institutionalizing the universal caretaker through a basic income?', *Basic Income Studies*, Vol. 3, No. 3.

Zita, L. (1995) 'The RDP: towards a working class approach' (unpublished paper), Johannesburg.

Zita, L. (1994) 'The limit and possibilities of reconstruction' (unpublished paper), Johannesburg.

Zita, L. (1993a) 'Unity of the Left', *African Communist*, No. 134 (Third Quarter), Johannesburg.

Zita, L. (1993b) 'Moving beyond the social contract', *African Communist*, No. 133 (Second Quarter), Johannesburg.

Zuege, A. (1999) 'The chimera of the Third Way'. In: Panitch, L. & Leys, C. (eds) *Socialist Register 2000: Necessary and Unnecessary Utopias*, Merlin Press, Suffolk.

Zuern, E. (2006) 'Elusive boundaries: SANCO, the ANC and the post-apartheid South African state', In: Ballard, R., Habib, A. & Valodia I. (eds) *Voices of Protest: Social Movements in Post-Apartheid South Africa*, University of KwaZulu-Natal Press, Pietermaritzburg.

Zuma, J. (2009a) 'Address to SACP Congress by the President of the ANC, Comrade Jacob Zuma', 12 December, University of Limpopo, Polokwane.

Zuma, J. (2009b) 'Letter from the President: nothing to fear from rigorous debate', *ANC Today*, Vol. 9, No. 49, 30 October — 5 November.

Zuma, J. (2009c) 'State of the Nation Address by His Excellency J. G. Zuma, President of the Republic of South Africa', Joint Sitting of Parliament, 3 June, Cape Town. Available at http://www.info.gov.za/speeches/2009/09060310551001.htm

Zuma, J. (2009d) 'Address by his Excellency Mr Jacob Zuma on the occasion of his inauguration as fourth President of The Republic of South Africa', 9 May, Pretoria. Available at http://www.anc.org.za/show.php?doc=ancdocs/history/zuma/2009/jz0509.html

Zuma, K. *et al* (2003) 'Risk factors for HIV infection among women in Carletonville, South Africa: migration, demography and sexually transmitted diseases', *International Journal of STD and AIDS*, Vol. 14, pp. 814–17.

Index

F

I

Q